Kent Reisdorph

SAMS
Teach Yourself
Borland
Delphi™ 4

in 21 Days

SAMS

A Division of Macmillan Computer Publishing
201 West 103rd St., Indianapolis, Indiana, 46290 USA

Sams Teach Yourself Delphi™ 4 in 21 Days

Copyright © 1998 by Sams Publishing

International Standard Book Number: 0-672-31286-7

Library of Congress Catalog Card Number: 98-84674

Printed in the United States of America

First Printing: July, 1998

01   00   99   98   4   3   2   1

Trademarks

Warning and Disclaimer

EXECUTIVE EDITOR
Brian Gill

ACQUISITIONS EDITOR
Ron Gallagher

DEVELOPMENT EDITOR
Kezia Endsley

MANAGING EDITOR
Jodi Jensen

PROJECT EDITOR
Dana Rhodes Lesh

COPY EDITOR
Heather Urschel

INDEXERS
CJ East
Christine Nelsen

TECHNICAL EDITORS
William Fisher
Ellie Peters

SOFTWARE DEVELOPMENT SPECIALIST
Dan Scherf

PRODUCTION
Michael Henry
Linda Knose
Tim Osborn
Staci Somers
Mark Walchle

Overview

Contents

About the Author

KENT REISDORPH is a senior software engineer at TurboPower Software Co. He also has his own consulting business. Kent is a contributing editor for The Cobb Group's *C++Builder Developer's Journal* and contributes regularly to the *Delphi Developer's Journal*. He is also a member of TeamB, Borland's online volunteer support group. As a member of TeamB, Kent puts in many hours each week on the Borland newsgroups answering questions, primarily on C++Builder and Windows programming. He is the author of *Sams Teach Yourself C++Builder in 21 Days* and *Sams Teach Yourself C++Builder 3 in 21 Days*. Kent lives in Colorado Springs, Colorado, with his wife, Jennifer, and their six children, James, Mason, Mallory, Jenna, Marshall, and Joshua.

Dedication

This book is dedicated to my wife, Jennifer. I couldn't imagine dedicating it to anyone else. Thank you as always, Jen, for keeping everything going while I'm off in my own world.

Acknowledgments

This part of the book comes fairly easily for me. It's easy to remember those people who were instrumental in making a project like this come to completion. First I want to thank Brian Gill for his hard work on this project. I did my best to rattle Brian on one or more occasions, but he never wavered (not that I could see anyway!). I also want to thank Kezia Endsley for her work on this book. Kezia did a tremendous job as development editor. I'm certain that I have benefited from working with her. Other people at Macmillan Publishing I want to thank are Dana Lesh and Heather Urschel.

There are several people at INPRISE Corporation (formerly Borland International) whom I want to thank. Although I didn't have much direct contact with Nan Borreson on this project, I know she was there behind the scenes doing her usual excellent work. I want to thank my tech editors, Bill Fisher and Ellie Peters. They both did a good job keeping me straight. I can't mention Ellie without adding that I'm glad to have Ellie as a friend as well as a tech editor. Also thanks to Steve Teixeira, Steve Trefethen, and Ryder Rishel who were quick to answer specific questions I had during this project.

Last but in no way least, I want to thank my wife, Jennifer. This is the third such project I have undertaken, and Jennifer has always been way, way beyond supportive. She has grown far too accustomed to seeing me "head down and headphones on." One of these days I'll make it up to her. I promise.

Tell Us What You Think!

As the reader of this book, *you* are our most important critic and commentator. We value your opinion and want to know what we're doing right, what we could do better, what areas you'd like to see us publish in, and any other words of wisdom you're willing to pass our way.

As the executive editor for the Programming team at Macmillan Computer Publishing, I welcome your comments. You can fax, email, or write me directly to let me know what you did or didn't like about this book—as well as what we can do to make our books stronger.

Please note that I cannot help you with technical problems related to the topic of this book, and that due to the high volume of mail I receive, I might not be able to reply to every message.

When you write, please be sure to include this book's title and author as well as your name and phone or fax number. I will carefully review your comments and share them with the author and editors who worked on the book.

Fax: 317-817-7070
Email: prog@mcp.com
Mail: Executive Editor
          Programming
          Macmillan Computer Publishing
          201 West 103rd Street
          Indianapolis, IN 46290 USA

Introduction: You Are Here

Isn't it helpful when an arrow on a map points out exactly where you are? So you are here! Maybe you are here because you have used Delphi before and you want to see what is new in Delphi 4. Maybe you are here because your boss told you to be here. Or maybe you are here as a complete beginner who would like to explore the wonderful world of Windows programming.

Regardless of why you are here, welcome! I can assure you that the trip will be an interesting one. You will no doubt find it enjoyable, too. It will involve some work, but there will be some fun thrown in along the way. Believe me when I say that there's nothing quite like taking a passing thought and turning it into a working Windows program. I hope you get the fever and lose yourself in hour after hour of programming.

I encourage you to experiment as you read this book. Putting the book down and playing around for a while can prove more valuable than the best teacher. Getting through this book isn't a race. The first one to reach the end doesn't receive a prize. I'd rather you spent 21 *weeks* learning Delphi programming than to rush through this book without taking time to apply the concepts discussed here. By the way, my experience has been that the best way to learn is to have an application in mind that you want to write and then work on that application as you work through this book. Solving real-world problems is the kind of schooling that sticks.

So it doesn't really matter *why* you are here. What's important is that you *are* here. I'm glad you are here, and I hope you enjoy your Delphi experience. Relax, put your feet up, and have fun learning how to use Delphi. I know I did.

WEEK 1

At a Glance

In Week 1 you begin to learn how to write Windows programs in Delphi. You spend your first three days this week learning the basics of the Object Pascal language. As you work through the first three chapters, you will write simple test programs to solidify your understanding of particular features of the Object Pascal language. I warn you, though, that these programs are probably not the type that you purchased Delphi to write. They lack any flash or glitter. You probably won't be terribly impressed. These programs will, however, help you grasp the Object Pascal basics.

Starting on Day 4, you begin to learn some of the things that make the visual programming aspect of Delphi the great tool that it is. You will learn about the Delphi IDE and how it is used to create Windows programs. Toward the end of Day 4, you build your first real Windows program.

On Day 5, I talk about frameworks and what a framework means to you as a Windows programmer. On that day you learn about the visual component model, including properties, methods, and events, which are vital parts of programming in Delphi. On Day 6, you learn even more about the Delphi IDE so that you can become familiar with how the entire Delphi IDE works together to make your programming tasks easier. This is when things become more interesting.

On Day 7, I discuss some of the Visual Component Library (VCL) components you are likely to use when writing programs with Delphi. You find out about specific components and how to use them.

You will certainly spend some time reading this week. I hope that you also spend a lot of time experimenting. Reading this

1

2

3

4

5

6

7

book is not a race. The first one done doesn't receive a prize. It is better to be the tortoise than the hare when it comes to learning programming. Take time to experiment. Experience is the best teacher. So if you are ready to begin, turn the page and your Delphi programming excursion will be underway!

DAY 1

Getting Started with Delphi

Congratulations—you've chosen one of today's hottest programming tools! Before you get started using all that Delphi has to offer, though, you first need to learn a little about the Delphi IDE and about Object Pascal. In this chapter you will find

- A quick tour of Delphi
- An introduction to the Object Pascal language
- Facts about Pascal units, variables, and data types
- A discussion of arrays
- Information about strings in Pascal

What Is Delphi?

By now you know that Delphi is Borland's best-selling rapid application development (RAD) product for writing Windows applications. With Delphi, you can write Windows programs more quickly and more easily than was ever possible before. You can create Win32 console applications or Win32 graphical user interface (GUI) programs. When creating Win32 GUI applications with Delphi, you have all the power of a true compiled programming language (Object Pascal) wrapped up in a RAD environment. What this means is that you can create the user interface to a program (the *user interface* means the menus, dialog boxes, main window, and so on) using drag-and-drop techniques for true rapid application development. You can also drop ActiveX controls on forms to create specialized programs such as Web browsers in a matter of minutes. Delphi gives you all this, and at virtually no cost: You don't sacrifice program execution speed because Delphi generates fast compiled code.

I can hear you saying, "This is going to be so cool!" And guess what? You're right! But before you get too excited, I need to point out that you still have to go to work and learn about Pascal programming. I don't want you to think that you can buy a program like Delphi and be a master Windows programmer overnight. It takes a great deal of work to be a good Windows programmer. Delphi does a good job of hiding some of the low-level details that make up the guts of a Windows program, but it cannot write programs for you. In the end, you must still be a programmer, and that means you have to learn programming. That can be a long, uphill journey some days. The good news is that Delphi can make your trek fairly painless and even fun. Yes, you can work and have fun doing it!

So roll up your sleeves and put on your hiking shoes. Delphi *is* a great product, so have fun.

A Quick Look at the Delphi IDE

This section contains a quick look at the Delphi integrated development environment (IDE). I'll give the IDE a once-over now and examine it in more detail on Day 4, "The Delphi IDE Explored." Because you are tackling Windows programming, I'll assume you are advanced enough to have figured out how to start Delphi. When you first start the program, you are presented with both a blank form and the IDE, as shown in Figure 1.1.

FIGURE 1.1.

The Delphi IDE and the initial blank form.

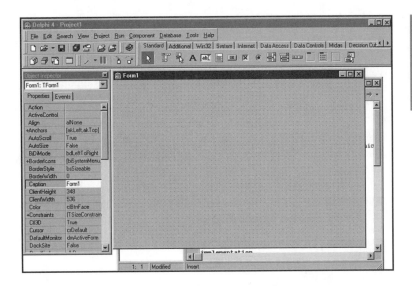

1

The Delphi IDE is divided into three parts. The top window can be considered the main window. It contains the toolbars and the Component palette. The Delphi toolbars give you one-click access to tasks such as opening, saving, and compiling projects. The Component palette contains a wide array of components that you can drop onto your forms. (Components are text labels, edit controls, list boxes, buttons, and the like.) For convenience, the components are divided into groups. Did you notice the tabs along the top of the Component palette? Go ahead and click on the tabs to explore the different components available to you. To place a component on your form, you simply click the component's button in the Component palette and then click on your form where you want the component to appear. Don't worry about the fact that you don't yet know how to use components. You'll get to that in due time. When you are done exploring, click on the tab labeled Standard, because you'll need it in a moment.

NEW TERM   A *component* is a self-contained binary piece of software that performs some specific predefined function, such as a text label, an edit control, or a list box.

The Object Inspector

Below the main window and on the left side of the screen is the Object Inspector. It is through the Object Inspector that you modify a component's properties and events. You will use the Object Inspector constantly as you work with Delphi. The Object Inspector has two tabs: the Properties tab and the Events tab. A component's *properties* control how the component operates. For example, changing the Color property of a component changes the background color of that component. The list of properties available varies from component to component, although components usually have several common elements (`Width` and `Height` properties, for instance).

 A *property* determines the operation of a component.

The Events tab contains a list of events for a component. Events occur as the user interacts with a component. For example, when a component is clicked, an event is generated that tells you that the component was clicked. You can write code that responds to these events, performing specific actions when an event occurs. As with properties, the events that you can respond to vary from component to component.

NEW TERM An *event* is something that occurs as a result of a component's interaction with the user or with Windows.

NEW TERM An *event handler* is a section of code that is invoked in your application in response to an event.

The Delphi Workspace

The main part of the Delphi IDE is the workspace. The workspace initially displays the Form Designer. It should come as no surprise that the Form Designer enables you to create forms. In Delphi, a *form* represents a window in your program. The form might be the program's main window, a dialog box, or any other type of window. You use the Form Designer to place, move, and size components as part of the form creation process.

Hiding behind the Form Designer is the Code Editor. The Code Editor is where you type code when writing your programs. The Object Inspector, Form Designer, Code Editor, and Component palette work interactively as you build applications.

Now that you've had a look at what makes up the Delphi IDE, let's actually do something.

Your First Program: `Hello World`

It's tradition. Almost all programming books start you off by having you create a program that displays `Hello World` on the screen. I'm tempted to do something else, but tradition is not a force to be reckoned with, so `Hello World` it is. You've got some work ahead of you in the next few chapters, so I thought I'd give you a taste of Delphi's goodies before putting you to work learning the seemingly less glamorous basics of the Pascal language. You'll have a little fun first. Delphi (and its cousin, C++Builder) gives you possibly the quickest route to `Hello World` of any Windows programming environment to date.

Creating the Program

Right now you should have Delphi running, and you should be looking at a blank form. By default, the form is named Form1. (The form name is significant in Delphi, but I'll address that a little later.) To the left of the form, the Object Inspector shows the properties for the form. Click on the title bar of the Object Inspector. The Caption property is highlighted, and the cursor is sitting there waiting for you to do something. (If the Caption property is not in view, you might have to scroll the Object Inspector window to locate it. Properties are listed in alphabetical order.) Type Hello World! to change the form's caption.

Note

> As you modify properties, Delphi immediately displays the results of the property change when appropriate. As you type the new caption, notice that the window caption of the form is changing to reflect the text you are typing.

Now click the Run button on the toolbar (the one with the green arrow). (You can also press F9 or choose Run|Run from the main menu.) Before you even know what has happened, Delphi has built the program. The form is displayed, and the caption shows Hello World!. In this case, the running program looks almost identical to the blank form. You might scarcely have noticed when the program was displayed because it is displayed in the exact location of the form in the Form Designer. (There is a difference in appearance, though, because the Form Designer displays an alignment grid and the running program does not.) Congratulations—you've just written your first Windows program with Delphi. Wow, that was easy!

"But what is it?" you ask. It's not a lot, I agree, but it is a true Windows program. Try it out and see. The program's main window can be moved by dragging the title bar, it can be sized, it can be minimized, it can be maximized, and it can be closed by clicking the Close button. You can even locate the program in Windows Explorer (it will probably be in your \Delphi40\Bin directory as Project1.exe) and double-click on it to run it.

Modifying the Program

Okay, so maybe displaying Hello World! in the caption was cheating a little. Let's spruce it up a bit. If you still have the Hello World program running, close it by clicking the Close button in the upper-right corner of the window. The Form Designer is displayed again, and you are ready to modify the form (and, as a result, the program).

To make the program more viable, you're going to add text to the center of the window itself. To do this, you'll add a text label to the form:

1. First, click on the Standard tab of the Component palette. The third component button on the palette has an *A* on it. If you put your mouse cursor over that button, the tooltip (a small pop-up window) will display Label.

2. Click the label button and then click anywhere on the form. A label component is placed on the form with a default caption of Label1.

3. Now turn your attention to the Object Inspector. It now displays the properties for Label1 (remember that previously it was showing the properties for Form1). Again the Caption property is highlighted.

4. Click on the title bar of the Object Inspector or on the Caption property and type Hello World!. Now the label on the form shows Hello World!.

5. As long as you're at it, you can change the size of the label's text as well. Double-click on the Font property. The property will expand to show the additional font attributes below it.

6. Locate the Size property under Font and change the font size to 24 (it is currently set to 8). As soon as you press Enter or click on the form, the label instantly changes to the new size.

Because the label is probably not centered on the form, you might want to move it. To move a component, simply click on it and drag it to the position you want it to occupy. When you have the label where you want it, you're ready to recompile and run the program. Click the Run button again and, after a split second, the program runs. Now you see Hello World! displayed in the center of the form as well as in the caption. Figure 1.2 shows the Hello World! program running.

FIGURE 1.2.

Your Hello World! *program running.*

Closing the Program

With this little taste of Delphi, you can see that writing Windows programs with Delphi is going to be a great deal more interesting than it was in the good ol' days. To prepare for what you are going to do next, you need to close the current project in the Delphi IDE. Choose File | Close All from the main menu. Click on No when prompted to save changes to Project1, or save the project if you are fond of your new creation.

Your Second Program: Hello World, Part II

Before you can move on to learning the Pascal language you need a little more information about how Delphi works. You'll need this information to test the various Pascal language features as you work through the next couple of days. This section will contain just a glimpse into the power of Delphi. On Days 4, 5, and 6, you get a more detailed look into how Delphi works.

Creating the Hello World II Program

The goal of this exercise is to have the words Hello World, Part II appear on the screen when a button is pressed. This exercise will also give you a pattern you can follow when you test various code snippets as you work through the next couple of days. Perform the following steps:

1. Choose File | New Application from the main menu to start a new application (click No if you're prompted to save the current project).
2. Click the Standard tab on the Component palette and click the icon that has an OK button on it (the Button component).
3. Place your cursor anywhere on the form and click. A button appears on the form.
4. Choose a Label component and place it near the center of the form.

At this point your form should look similar to Figure 1.3. Notice that the label component has a default caption of Label1 and the button has a default caption of Button1.

Modifying the Hello World II Program

In the first version of Hello World, you used the Object Inspector to change the Caption property of a label. That change was applied at design time and as such was seen as soon as the program ran. In this exercise, you are going to change the caption of the label through code.

FIGURE 1.3.

The new form after placing the button and label components.

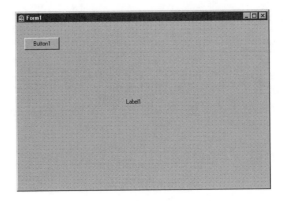

> **Note**
>
> When you change a component's properties through the Object Inspector and Form Designer, you are said to make a *design-time* change. When you modify a property through code that executes when the program runs, you are said to make a *runtime* change.

To change the Caption property at runtime, follow these steps:

1. Double-click on the button on your form. As soon as you do, Delphi generates an event handler for the button's OnClick event. The generated code looks like this:

```
procedure TForm1.Button1Click(Sender: TObject);
begin

end;
```

2. Right now you don't need to be concerned with everything you see here. You only need to understand that the OnClick event handler is a section of code that will be executed every time the button is clicked (as long as the program is running, that is). The editing cursor is placed between the begin and end statements and is waiting for you to type code. Enter this code at the cursor:

```
Label1.Caption := 'Hello World, Part II';
```

I always indent two spaces (considered by many programmers to be proper coding practice) so my completed event handler now looks like this:

```
procedure TForm1.Button1Click(Sender: TObject);
begin
  Label1.Caption := 'Hello World, Part II';
end;
```

This code is pretty simple. It simply assigns the value `Hello World, Part II` to the `Caption` property of the label (the `Caption` property is used to set the text that the label displays).

3. Now click on the Run button on the toolbar to run the program. When you run the program, notice that the label still has the caption `Label1`. Click the form's button and the label's caption changes to `Hello World, Part II`. Hey, how about that! Magic? No, just Delphi at work!

You'll be doing many such exercises in the next few days so you'll get plenty of practice placing labels, buttons, and other components on the form. I realize that I didn't fully explain what is going on behind the scenes here, but I don't want to get ahead of myself so I'll save that explanation for a later time.

Object Pascal Language Overview

Before you can learn about the RAD features of Delphi, you need to learn the basics of the Object Pascal language. This part of the book will probably not be the most exciting for you, but you need a basic understanding of Object Pascal before you move on.

It would be nice if presenting the Object Pascal language could be handled sequentially. That's not the case, though, because all the features you will learn about are intertwined. I'll take the individual puzzle pieces one at a time and start fitting them together.

By the end of Day 3, you'll have a fairly complete picture of the Object Pascal language. Don't be concerned if you don't instantly grasp every concept that is presented. Some of what is required to fully understand Object Pascal can only come with real-world experience.

During the next few days, you will see short code snippets that illustrate a particular feature of the Object Pascal language. You will also do some exercises that enable you to test your newfound knowledge. In the first few days, you will only see your Delphi applications in small sections. I don't want to get ahead of myself and go too far into the Delphi IDE or the Visual Component Library (VCL) at this early stage. You will have to settle for bits and pieces until later in the book when you start to get the complete picture. The code that you can download from the book's site contains complete programs for some of the exercises that you will perform over the next several days. (Go to `http://www.mcp.com/info` and type `0-672-31286-7`.)

In the Beginning...

Back in 1994 or so, Borland began working on a RAD tool that it code-named Delphi. When it was decided that the component model architecture was the best way to implement RAD, it was then necessary to settle on the programming language that would be the heart of the system.

At that time, Borland was the only compiler vendor mass marketing a Pascal compiler. Borland was known as the company that produced the best Pascal tools. If you were a Pascal programmer, you probably used Borland's TurboPascal in one flavor or another. Borland more or less "owned" Pascal. Although Borland didn't own the Pascal language in a legal sense, it no doubt felt that because of its position in the Pascal world, it could take considerable liberties in implementing new language features and enhancements. In addition, there was no Pascal standards committee, nor even a written standard defining the Pascal language. So Borland created Delphi using Pascal as the base language (the Borland internal code name stuck and became the official product name).

Before Delphi came into being, Borland had already modified the Pascal language in positive ways. For example, Borland had already extended Pascal by creating a new language called Object Pascal. It can be said that Object Pascal is to Pascal what C++ is to C. Object Pascal added classes to Pascal, thereby hurling Pascal into the world of object-oriented programming (OOP) languages. As Delphi was being developed, new language behavior and keywords were added to deal with the component model. Keywords such as published and property were added, as were others. This enabled Borland to fully implement the power of the component model. By modifying the Pascal language to suit the component model, Borland was able to implement RAD the right way. In essence, the Object Pascal language was modified as needed when design issues came up during the development of the then-unknown product called Delphi. The result is a language that works seamlessly with the component model.

Although modifying the Pascal language could be considered a bold step for Borland, it was not without precedent. Previously, Microsoft had taken the BASIC language and modified it to produce a new language called Visual Basic. This new language was nearly unrecognizable when compared to the original BASIC language that served as its base.

Borland took a risk in modifying Pascal. After all, it had a loyal base of customers that might not take kindly to enhancements to the language they had come to know and love. Still, Borland was in a solid position in the Pascal market and went ahead with its plans. The result was a smash hit, of course.

Make no mistake about it, Object Pascal is a powerful programming language, and I don't make that statement lightly. I have a C/C++ background and, like other C/C++ programmers, I viewed Delphi with a bit of skepticism at first. I found out quickly, though, that the Object Pascal language is very capable. In fact, in the hands of the average programmer there is almost no difference in the two languages in terms of power. Object Pascal is unique in that it is both powerful *and* relatively easy to learn. I don't in any way want to leave the impression that Object Pascal is a not a full-featured programming language. Pascal has often been knocked as a less-than-serious programming language. That has never been true, and is even less true with today's Object Pascal.

> **Note**
>
> Several different terms have been adopted by Delphi programmers to describe what they do. The base language of Delphi is, of course, Object Pascal, and some folks call it exactly that. Others might say, "I program in Pascal," or even just, "I'm a Delphi programmer." In the end it's up to you to decide what terminology you will use. I'll use the terms Object Pascal and Pascal interchangeably throughout this book and will typically reserve use of the word Delphi to refer to the Delphi IDE or its tools.

Object Pascal enables you to take advantage of object-oriented programming to its fullest. OOP is not just a buzzword. It has real benefits because it enables you to create objects that can be used in your current program and reused in future programs.

NEW TERM   An *object*, like components described earlier, is a binary piece of software that performs a specific programming task. (Components are objects, but not all objects are components. I'll explain that later.)

An object reveals to the user (the programmer using the object) only as much of itself as needed; therefore, using the object is simplified. All internal mechanisms that the user doesn't need to know about are hidden from sight. All this is included in the concept of object-oriented programming. OOP enables you to take a modular approach to programming, thus keeping you from constantly re-inventing the wheel. Delphi programs are very OOP-centric because of Delphi's heavy use of components. After a component is created (either one of your own or one of the built-in components), it can be reused in any Delphi program. A component can also be extended by inheritance to create a new component with additional features. Best of all, components hide their internal details and let the programmer concentrate on getting the most out of the component. Objects and classes are discussed in detail on Day 3, "Classes and Object-Oriented Programming."

Pascal Units

Programming is more than just typing code. Ultimately, it is the combination of concep-
tualizing a programming task and then typing code to carry out that task. The code you
type simply goes into a text file. The compiler takes that text file and compiles it into
machine code that the computer can understand. The text file that Delphi compiles into
machine code is called a unit.

NEW TERM   A *unit* is a text file that can be compiled into a module of code.

Types of Units

A Delphi GUI application will contain at least two units. The project source unit contains
the project source code. Project source code units have an extension of DPR. You can
view the project source unit by choosing Project | View Source from the main menu. It is
not normally necessary to modify the project source unit. In fact, you shouldn't modify
the project source unit unless you know exactly what you are doing. If you accidentally
modify the project source unit in undesirable ways, you might find that your application
won't compile anymore. (Certain advanced programming techniques require modification of the project source code, but that's not something you need to be concerned with
at this time.)

The second type of unit that a Delphi GUI application always has is the main form's
unit. A form unit, as its name implies, is a source code unit with an associated form. This
type of unit has a filename extension of PAS. This is the type of unit you will use most
often in your Delphi programs. A Delphi GUI application will always have one form unit
(for the main form), but it can have one or more additional form units as well. For example, an application that displays an About box will have the main form unit and a unit for
the About box.

Note

> You might have noticed that I keep saying "Delphi GUI application." This is
> because I want to distinguish a GUI application from a console mode appli-
> cation. A console mode application is a 32-bit Windows application that runs
> in a console window (DOS box). A console application has no main form and
> may or may not contain other forms. A console application does, however,
> have one or more units.

There is a third type of unit you can use in Delphi applications. This type of unit is a unit
that contains only source code. A code-only unit contains code that is called from other
units in the project. I won't go into any more detail than that right now, but you'll learn
more about this type of unit in later chapters.

1

Anatomy of a Delphi Unit

Delphi units must follow a predefined format. This shouldn't come as a surprise to you. The unit has to be in a predefined format so that the compiler can read the unit and compile the unit's code.

A Delphi project unit contains the program keyword followed by the name of the unit and a code block marked by the begin and end keywords. You can see how a basic unit looks by choosing View|Project Source from the Delphi main menu. The project source unit for a default Delphi project looks like Listing 1.1.

 Note The line numbers in Listing 1.1 are not part of the unit itself. I have put them there for reference only. Some of the listings you see in this book will have line numbers for reference and others will not. In either case, be sure to understand that the Pascal language does not use line numbers as some other languages do (most notably, BASIC).

LISTING 1.1. THE PROJECT SOURCE FOR A DEFAULT DELPHI PROJECT.

```
01: program Project1;
02:
03: uses
04:    Forms,
05:    Unit1 in 'Unit1.pas' {Form1};
06:
07: {$R *.RES}
08:
09: begin
10:    Application.Initialize;
11:    Application.CreateForm(TForm1, Form1);
12:    Application.Run;
13: end.
```

On line 1, the program keyword identifies this unit as a program's main source unit. You can see that the unit name, Project1, follows the program keyword (Delphi gives the project a default name until you save the project with a more meaningful name). Beginning on line 3, you see a section identified by the uses keyword. Any unit names following the uses keyword, up to the semicolon, are other units that this unit requires in order to compile. The uses keyword is described in more detail a little later in the section, "The uses List."

On line 7 you see a compiler directive that tells Delphi to include this project's resource file. Resource files are discussed in more detail on Day 8, "Creating Applications in Delphi."

Line 9 contains the begin keyword, and line 13 contains the end keyword. Notice that the final end keyword in the unit is followed by a period. (A unit can have many code blocks marked with begin and end, but only one final end statement.) The code on lines 10, 11, and 12 is code that initializes the application, creates the application's main form, and starts the application running. You don't need to be concerned about the details of this code to write Delphi programs.

 Note

The begin and end keywords mark a code block. A code block can contain just a few lines of code, or it can contain several hundred lines of code (or even thousands of lines). You will see the begin and end keywords used throughout the book. As you work through the book, you will get a better handle on how and when the begin and end keywords are used.

Let's take a look at another basic Pascal unit. Choose File | New from the main menu. When the New Items dialog comes up, locate the icon labeled Unit and double-click it. Delphi will create a new unit and display it in the Code Editor. Listing 1.2 shows the code generated for this unit.

LISTING 1.2. A BLANK PASCAL UNIT.

```
01: unit Unit2;
02:
03: interface
04:
05: implementation
06:
07: end.
```

There isn't much here, is there? This unit has two things in common with the unit shown in Listing 1.1. First, the unit starts with the unit keyword followed by the unit name Unit2 (again, a default name created by Delphi). I realize the code in Listing 1.1 starts with the program keyword and this code starts with the unit keyword, but there are a few common elements: A Pascal unit starts with one of these two keywords followed by the unit name, and the end keyword appears at the end of both listings. Here again, the end keyword is followed by a period to mark the end of the unit.

1

The code in Listing 1.2 differs from that of Listing 1.1 in that it has sections marked `interface` and `implementation`. A unit that is not the program's main source unit must contain an `interface` section and an `implementation` section. These two keywords will be described in more detail in the sections entitled, "The `interface` Section" and "The `implementation` Section," respectively. Listing 1.2 also differs from Listing 1.1 in that there is no `begin` statement. A program's main unit must have both `begin` and `end` statements, but a source unit only has to contain a final `end` statement.

The following sections describe keywords that are used within a Pascal unit.

The uses List

NEW TERM   The *uses list* is a list of external units that this unit references.

Refer to Listing 1.1. Notice the `uses` keyword on line 3. The `uses` keyword designates the start of a section that will contain a list of other units that this unit is dependent on. For example, line 11 of Listing 1.1 looks like this:

```
Application.CreateForm(TForm1, Form1);
```

This line of code contains information that is located in other units and cannot be found in this unit. The procedure identified by `Application.CreateForm` is located in a Delphi unit called `Forms.pas`, and the identifiers `TForm1` and `Form1` are located in the project's main form unit, which is called `Unit1.pas`. Do you see the connection? The `uses` list tells Delphi where to look for additional information that it will need to compile this unit. Here's another look at the `uses` list:

```
uses
  Forms,
  Unit1 in 'Unit1.pas' {Form1};
```

Notice that the `uses` list contains two unit names, `Forms` and `Unit1`. In some ways this is not a good example of a `uses` list because the second unit listed contains additional text not usually found in a `uses` list (`Unit1 in 'Unit1.pas' {Form1}`).

This text is used to specify a form that is contained in a unit and is only used by the project's main source unit. (The text between the curly braces is a comment used for reference and has no bearing on the rest of the code. Comments are discussed later in the section "Comments in Code.")

There are two rules you need to be aware of when constructing the `uses` list:

- First, each unit in the list must be separated from the following unit by a comma.
- Second, a semicolon must follow the last unit listed. The semicolon marks the end of the `uses` list.

Naturally the list must contain valid unit names. The uses list, then, is designated by the uses keyword and ends with a semicolon. Other than that, it doesn't matter how the uses list is organized. For example, the following two uses lists are identical as far as the compiler is concerned:

```
uses
  Windows, Messages, SysUtils, Classes, Graphics,
  Controls, Forms, Dialogs, StdCtrls;

uses
  Windows,
  Messages,
  SysUtils,
  Classes,
  Graphics,
  Controls,
  Forms,
  Dialogs,
  StdCtrls;
```

A unit can have any number of uses lists. It is not required that all units needed by this unit be in a single uses list.

Note   In some cases, Delphi will add units to your uses list for you. This is done via the File I Use Unit menu item. This feature will be discussed in more detail on Day 4.

The `interface` Section

Take another look at Listing 1.2. Notice that this listing has a section marked by the `interface` keyword. This keyword marks the start of the interface section for the unit.

The *interface section* is the section of a unit in which identifiers exported from this unit are declared. An *exported* identifier is one that can be accessed by other units in the project.

Most units will contain code that other units use. The code might be implemented as a class, a procedure, a function, or a data variable. Any objects that are available to other units from this unit must be declared in the interface section. You could say that the interface section contains a list of items in this unit that other units can use. The interface section starts with the `interface` keyword and ends at the `implementation` keyword.

The `implementation` Section

NEW TERM The *implementation section* of a unit is the section that contains the actual code for the unit.

The implementation section starts with the `implementation` keyword and ends with the next unit keyword. The next unit keyword is usually the unit's final `end` keyword, but could be the `initialization` keyword in units that have an initialization section. It's difficult to say more than that right now, because there are other aspects of Pascal that I need to discuss before tying all of this together. However, let me give you an example that will illustrate the use of the `interface` and `implementation` sections.

Let's say that you create a unit that has a procedure called `DoSomething`. Let's further say you want `DoSomething` to be available to other units in your project. In that case, you would declare the `DoSomething` procedure in the interface section and then define the procedure in the implementation section. The entire unit would look like Listing 1.3.

LISTING 1.3. A UNIT WITH A PUBLIC FUNCTION.

```
unit Unit2;

interface

  procedure DoSomething;

implementation

  procedure DoSomething;
  begin
    { Code for DoSomething goes here. }
  end;

end.
```

Notice that the `DoSomething` procedure is declared in the interface section and defined later in the implementation section. I realize I'm getting a little ahead of myself here. Functions and procedures will be discussed more tomorrow, and I'll go over declarations and definitions in detail at that time.

The `initialization` and `finalization` Sections

The `initialization` and `finalization` sections can be used to perform any startup and cleanup code that a unit requires. Any code in the `initialization` section will be executed when the unit is loaded into memory. Conversely, any code in the `finalization` section will be executed just before the unit is unloaded from memory. You can have just an `initialization` section, but you cannot have a `finalization` section without an `initialization` section. The `initialization` and `finalization` sections are optional.

Additional Keywords Used in Units

A Pascal unit can contain other, optional keywords that mark sections set aside for a particular purpose. Some of these keywords have multiple uses. The following sections describe those keywords only as they pertain to units.

The const Keyword

A unit can optionally have one or more `const` sections. The `const` section is designated with the `const` keyword. The `const` section describes a list of variables that are known as constants.

A *constant* is an identifier that cannot change. For example, let's say you have certain values that your program uses over and over. You can set up constant variables for those values. To illustrate, let's add a `const` section to the program in Listing 1.3. You'll add one `const` section for constants that are public (available to other units) and another `const` section for constants that are available only to this unit. Listing 1.4 shows the unit with the two `const` sections added.

LISTING 1.4. THE UNIT WITH const SECTIONS ADDED.

```
unit Unit2;

interface

const
  AppCaption = 'My Cool Program 1.0';

  procedure DoSomething;

implementation

const
  BaseX = 20;
  BaseY = 200;

  procedure DoSomething;
  begin
    { Code for DoSomething goes here. }
  end;

end.
```

Because the AppCaption constant is declared in the interface section, it can be used anywhere in the unit *and* in any unit that has this unit in its uses list. The BaseX and BaseY constants, however, are only available within this unit because they are declared in the implementation section.

The const keyword has other uses besides the one described here. I'll discuss one of those uses tomorrow in the section, "Value, Constant, and Variable Parameters."

The type Keyword

NEW TERM   The *type* keyword is used to declare new types that your program will use.

Declaring a new type is an esoteric programming technique that is difficult to explain at this stage of the game, so perhaps an example will help. Let's say that your application needs an *array* (a collection of values) of 20 bytes and that this type of array will be used over and over again. You can declare a new type as follows:

```
type
  TMyArray = array [0..19] of Byte;
```

Now you can use the identifier TMyArray instead of typing out array [0..19] of Byte every time you want an array of 20 bytes. I'll have to leave it at that for now, but you'll see more examples of declaring types later in the book.

The var Keyword

NEW TERM   The *var* keyword is used to declare a section of code in which variables are declared.

You use the var keyword to declare variables (variables are discussed in detail in the section entitled "Variables"). There are several places you can declare a var section. You can have a var section at the unit level, you can have a var section for a procedure or function, or both. You can even have multiple var sections in a unit. Listing 1.5 shows the sample unit with type and var sections added.

LISTING 1.5. THE UNIT WITH type AND var SECTIONS ADDED.

```
unit Unit2;

interface

type
  TMyArray = array [0..19] of Byte;

const
```

continues

LISTING 1.5. CONTINUED

```
    AppCaption = 'My Cool Program 1.0';

var
  X : Integer;
  MyArray : TMyArray;

  procedure DoSomething;

implementation

const
  BaseX = 20;
  BaseY = 200;

  procedure DoSomething;
  begin
    { Code for DoSomething goes here. }
  end;

end.
```

As with the `const` keyword, the `var` keyword has more than one use. It is also used to declare function and procedure parameters as variable parameters. Rather than go into that now, I'll save that discussion for tomorrow when you read about functions and procedures.

 Note   The sections described by the `var`, `const`, and `type` keywords begin at the keyword and end at the next keyword in the unit.

Comments in Code

Before getting into the Pascal language in detail, let me talk briefly about commenting code. *Comments* are lines of text in your source code that are there for documentation purposes. Comments can be used to describe what the code does, to supply copyright information, or simply to make a note to yourself or other programmers.

Comments can be designated in as many as three different ways. The following are all valid comments lines:

```
{ Don't forget to free this memory! }
{
```

```
ADTAPI.PAS 2.50
Copyright (c) TurboPower Software 1996-98
}
(* Mason needs to fix this section of code *)
// This is really good code!
{ This code needs to be reworked later }
```

Probably the most common type of comment used in Delphi programs uses curly braces as illustrated in the first two cases above. The opening brace is used to start a comment, and the closing brace is used to end a comment. Another type of comment uses (* to start the comment, and *) to end the comment. There is one difference between comments designated this way as opposed to using curly braces: The (*/*) comment pair can be used to block out large sections of code containing other comment lines. These two comment types can be used to comment single lines of code or multiple lines.

> **Note**
>
> Curly braces have another use in Pascal. When used in conjunction with a dollar sign, the braces signify a compiler directive. To tell the compiler not to generate compiler hints, you can put a line like this in your source code:
>
> {$HINTS OFF}
>
> When the compiler sees this line, it stops generating hints in this unit until a corresponding {$HINTS ON} directive is encountered. I'll talk about individual compiler directives at different points in the book as the need arises.

The third type of comment is designated by the double slash. This is often called the C-style comment because it is used by C and C++. This type of comment can only be used on single lines of code. You should also be aware that this type of comment is not valid in all versions of Delphi. If you are writing code that might be used in Delphi 1 as well as later versions, you should be sure not to use this style of comment.

> **Note**
>
> I use the curly brace style of comment for production code (code that others will see). I use the double slash type of comment for quickly commenting out a line or two for testing purposes, but only as a temporary measure. I rarely use the (*/*) style of comment.

Any commented text is ignored by the compiler. If you are using the default Delphi IDE settings, all comment lines will show up in italicized, blue text. This makes it easy to quickly identify comment lines.

Note

> If you work in a team programming environment, you might have to read your coworkers' code and vice versa. Concise comments in the code can save hours of time for any programmer who has to read and maintain another programmer's code. Even if you work in a single-programmer environment, commenting your code is a good idea. You'd be surprised how quickly you forget what code you wrote is supposed to do. Good code commenting can save you and your coworkers hours of time, so don't forget to comment your code!

Variables

Variables have to be declared before they can be used. You declare a variable in a special section of code designated with the var keyword, as described earlier—for example,

```
var
  X : Integer;  { variable X declared as an integer variable }
  Y : Integer;  { variable Y declared as an integer variable }
```

Earlier, I talked about the var keyword in terms of a Pascal unit. In that section, I said that variables used in the unit are declared in the unit's var section. That's true, but you can also have a var section in a function or procedure. This enables you to declare variables in functions and procedures as well as in units. Here's an example of a var section in a procedure:

```
procedure TForm1.Test;
var
  S : string;
begin
  S := 'Hello World!';
  Label1.Caption := S;
end;
```

After you declare a variable, you can then use it to manipulate data in memory. That probably doesn't make much sense to you, so let me give you a few examples. The following code snippet uses the variables called X and Y declared earlier. At the end of each line of code is a comment that describes what is happening when that line executes:

```
X := 100;      { 'X' now contains the value 100 }
X := X + 50;   { 'X' now contains the value 150 }
Y := 150;      { 'Y' now contains the value 150 }
X := X + Y;    { 'X' now contains the value 300 }
Inc(X);        { Increment. 'X' now contains the value 301 }
```

NEW TERM   A *variable* is a location set aside in computer memory to contain some value.

I want you to notice several things about this code. First, notice that the value of X changes as the variable is manipulated. (A little later I'll discuss the Object Pascal operators, functions, and procedures used to manipulate variables.) You can see that the variables are assigned values, added together, incremented, and so on.

Notice also that each statement in this code segment ends in a semicolon. The semicolon is used at the end of every statement in a Pascal program.

Note

> Very early in the process of learning the Pascal language, the budding programmer must learn the difference between an expression and a statement. The official definition of a *statement* is an expression that is followed by a semicolon. An *expression* is a unit of code that evaluates to some quantity. Confused? Consider the following statement:
>
> ```
> c := a + b;
> ```
>
> In this example, the portion to the right of the assignment operator, a + b, is an expression. The entire line is a statement. You could say that an expression is a subset of a statement. A single statement can be made up of several expressions. I know this might be a bit confusing at the moment, but it will become clearer as you go along. For now just remember that a statement is followed by a semicolon. (There are some cases in which a semicolon is not used at the end of each line, but this does not violate the rule that a semicolon is placed at the end of each statement. I'll go over those exceptions later in the book as we encounter them.)

Variable names follow the rules described for *identifiers*. In addition to variables, identifiers are used for function names, procedure names, fields in records, unit names, and more. Identifiers can mix uppercase and lowercase letters and can include numbers and the underscore (_), but they cannot contain spaces or other special characters. The identifier must start with a character or the underscore. There is no maximum allowable length for identifiers, but anything over 255 characters is ignored. In reality, anything more than about 20 characters is too long to be useful anyway. The following are examples of valid variable names:

```
aVeryLongVariableName : Integer; { a long variable name }
my_variable : Integer; { a variable with an underscore }
x : Integer; { single digit variable name }
X : Integer; { same as above }
Label2 : string;  { a variable name containing a number }
```

The Pascal language is not case sensitive. The following statements are all valid:

```
var
  XPos : Integer;

{ ...later }
XPos := 20;
XPOS := 200;
xpos := 110;
XpoS := 40;
```

If you are coming from a language where case counts (C or C++, for instance), the case-insensitive nature of Object Pascal might seem a bit odd at first, but you'll get used to it quickly enough.

Even though Pascal is case insensitive, you should strive to use consistent capitalization in your programs. Using proper capitalization makes a program easier to read and will save more than a few headaches if you ever need to port your application to other programming languages later on (porting a Delphi program to C++Builder, for example).

Object Pascal Data Types

 In Object Pascal, a *data type* defines the way the compiler stores information in memory.

In some programming languages, you can get by with assigning any type of value to a variable. For example, look at the following examples of BASIC code:

```
X = -1;
X = 1000;
X = 3.14;
```

In BASIC, the interpreter takes care of allocating enough storage to fit any size or type of number.

Declaring a Variable

In Object Pascal, you must declare a variable's type before you can use the variable:

```
var
  X1 : Integer;
  X  : Integer;
  Y  : Double;
  Z  : Byte;

{ ...later }
X1 := -1;
X  := 1000;
Y  := 3.14;
Z  := 27;
```

This enables the compiler to do type-checking and to make sure that things are kept straight when the program runs. Improper use of a data type will result in a compiler error or warning that can be analyzed and corrected so that you can head off a problem before it starts.

Some data types are signed and some are unsigned. A *signed* data type can contain both negative and positive numbers, whereas an *unsigned* data type can contain only positive numbers. Table 1.1 shows the basic data types in Object Pascal, the amount of memory each requires, and the range of values possible for each data type. This table does not include the string types. Those are discussed later in the section, "Strings."

TABLE 1.1. DATA TYPES USED IN OBJECT PASCAL (32-BIT PROGRAMS).

Data Type	Size in Bytes	Possible Range of Values
ShortInt	1	-128 to 127
Byte	1	0 to 255
Char	1	0 to 255 (same as Byte)
WideChar	2	0 to 65,535 (same as Word)
SmallInt	2	-32,768 to 32,767
Word	2	0 to 65,535
LongInt	4	-2,147,483,648 to 2,147,483,647
Int64	8	-9,223,372,036,854,775,808 to 9,223,372,036,854,775,807
Integer	4	Same as LongInt

continues

TABLE 1.1. CONTINUED

Data Type	Size in Bytes	Possible Range of Values
Cardinal	4	0 to 2,147,483,647
Single	4	1.5×10^{-45} to 3.4×10^{38}
Double	8	5.0×10^{-324} to 1.7×10^{308}
Real	8	5.0×10^{-324} to 1.7×10^{308} (same as Double)
Extended	10	3.4×10^{-4932} to 1.1×10^{4932}
Comp	8	-9,223,372,036,854,775,808 to 9,223,372,036,854,775,807
Currency	8	-922,337,203,685,477.5808 to 922,337,203,685,477.5807
Boolean	1	True or False
Variant	16	Varies

Examining Table 1.1, you might notice that an Integer is the same as a LongInt. So why does Object Pascal have two different data types that are exactly the same? Essentially, it's a holdover from days gone by. In a 16-bit programming environment, an Integer requires 2 bytes of storage and a LongInt requires 4 bytes of storage.

In a 32-bit programming environment, however, both require 4 bytes of storage and have the same range of values. Delphi 4 produces only 32-bit programs, so an Integer and a LongInt are identical. Most programmers use Integer rather than LongInt.

You might also notice that the Int64 and Comp (computational) types have an identical range of values. The difference between these two types is in the way they are treated internally by the compiler. The Int64 type is an integer type, whereas the Comp type is a real type. Probably you will have very little reason to use the Comp type in your programs.

Notice also that the Real and Double data types are identical. In previous versions of Delphi, the Real type was a 6-byte variable. Now it is an 8-byte variable. This change was made to make the Real data type compatible with today's processors. The Real type is considered obsolete and you should use Double rather than Real in your Delphi applications.

Note

New to 4 The Int64 data type is new to Delphi 4. There are many reasons for an integer type of this size. One of the most compelling is the need

1

for an integer value that can hold the huge values required by today's larger hard drives. For example, Windows contains a function called GetDiskFreeSpaceEx, which can return values much larger than 2,147,483,647 (the maximum value of an Integer). A 64-bit integer data type was needed for reasons like this.

Note

The Single, Double, Extended, and Currency data types use floating-point numbers (numbers with decimal places). The other data types deal only with integer values. You cannot assign a value containing a decimal fraction to an integer data type. For example, the following code will generate a compiler error:

```
var
  X : Integer;
{ Later... }
X := 3.75;
```

You don't really have to worry about this too much, because the compiler is very good at telling you what you can and cannot do. By the way, you'd be surprised how few times you need floating-point numbers in most Windows programs.

Converting Between Data Types

Object Pascal performs conversion between different data types when possible. Take the following code snippet for an example:

```
var
  Res : SmallInt;
  Num1 : Integer;
  Num2 : Integer;

{ Later... }
  Num1 := 200;
  Num2 := 200;
  Res  := Num1 * Num2;
```

In this case I am trying to assign the result of multiplying two Integers to a SmallInt. Even though this formula mixes two data types, Object Pascal is able to perform a conversion. Would you like to take a guess at the result of this calculation? You might be surprised to find out that the result is -25,536. What!? If you look at Table 1.1, you'll see that a SmallInt can have a maximum value of 32,767. What happens if you take a

SmallInt with a value of 32,767 and add 1 to it? You will get a value of -32,768. This is essentially the same as the odometer on a car turning over from 99,999 to 00,000 when you drive that last mile. To illustrate, perform the following steps:

1. Start with a new application and place a label and button on the form.

2. Double-click the button to create an event handler for the button's OnClick event.

3. Modify the event handler so that it looks like this:

```
procedure TForm1.Button1Click(Sender: TObject);
var
  X : SmallInt;
begin
  X := 32767;
  X := X + 1;
  Label1.Caption := IntToStr(X);
end;
```

4. Run the program and click the button.

You should see the caption of the label change to –32768 when you click the button (in case you wondering, the IntToStr function translates an integer value to a string). This exercise illustrates that 32767 plus 1 equals –32768! Okay, maybe not quite.

This example really illustrates what is known as *overflow* or *wrapping*. You should be aware of the maximum possible values your variables can contain and choose the data type that is large enough to guarantee that the variable will contain the value without overflowing. For the most part, you won't go too far wrong if you use the Integer data type as your data type of choice. You are unlikely to run into the problem of wrapping because the Integer data type gives you an approximate range of -2 billion to +2 billion.

Okay, where was I? Oh, yes, I was talking about automatic type conversion. In some cases, Object Pascal cannot perform a conversion. If that is the case, you will get a compiler error that says something along the lines of Incompatible types: 'Integer' and 'Real'. This compiler error is telling you that you are trying to assign a value that cannot be stored by this particular data type. Another compiler error you might see has to do with what is called *range checking*. Take this code, for instance:

```
var
  X : Byte;
begin
  X := 1000;
end;
```

This code will generate a compiler error that states Constant expression violates subrange bounds. The compiler is telling you that you can't assign a value of 1000 to the variable X because X is declared as a Byte and a Byte can only hold values from 0 to 255.

Tip

Learn to treat compiler hints and warnings as errors. The compiler is trying to tell you that something is not quite right in your code, and you need to respect that warning. Ultimately, you should strive for warning-free compiles. In rare cases, a warning cannot be avoided, but be sure to examine all warnings closely. Do your best to understand the reason for the warning and correct it if possible.

Object Pascal Operators

Operators are used to manipulate data. Operators perform calculations, check for equality, make assignments, manipulate variables, and perform other, more esoteric duties that most programmers never do. There are a lot of operators in Object Pascal. Rather than present them all here, I will list only the most commonly used ones. Table 1.2 contains a list of those operators.

TABLE 1.2. COMMONLY USED OBJECT PASCAL OPERATORS.

Operator	Description	Example
Mathematical Operators		
+	Addition	`x := y + z;`
-	Subtraction	`x := y - z;`
*	Multiplication	`x := y * z;`
/	Real number division	`x := y / 3.14;`
div	Integer division	`x := y div 10;`
Assignment Operators		
:=	Assignment	`x := 10;`
Logical Operators		
and	Logical AND	`if (x = 1) and (y = 2) then ...`
or	Logical OR	`if (x = 1) or (y = 2) then ...`
Equality Operators		
=	Equal to	`if (x = 10) then ...`
<>	Not equal to	`if (x <> 10) then ...`
<	Less than	`if (x < 10) then ...`
>	Greater than	`if (x > 10) then ...`

continues

TABLE 1.2. CONTINUED

Operator	Description	Example
<=	Less than or equal to	`if (x <= 10) then ...`
>=	Greater than or equal to	`if (x >= 10) then ...`
Unary Operators		
^	Pointer operator	`MyObject.Data^;`
@	Address of operator	`ptr := @MyRecord;`
and	Bitwise AND	`x := x and $02;`
or	Bitwise OR	`x := x or $FF;`
not	Bitwise NOT	`x := x and not $02;`
not	Logical NOT	`if not Valid then ...`
Miscellaneous Operators		
$	Hex value operator	`X := $FF;`
[ ]	Array subscript operator	`X := MyArray[5];`
.	Membership (dot) operator	`X := Record.Data;`

As you can see, the list of operators is a bit overwhelming. Don't worry about trying to memorize each one. As you work with Object Pascal, you will gradually learn how to use all the operators. Some operators you will rarely, if ever, use, and others you will use all the time.

You will notice that the and, or, and not keywords are used in two contexts: logical and bitwise. For example, the and keyword can be used to specify a logical AND operation or a bitwise AND operation. Take a look at this code:

```
if (Started = True) and (X > 20) then
  Z := X and Y;
```

In this example, the and keyword is being used in two completely different contexts. Without question, this can be confusing at first. Rest assured that the compiler knows how the keyword is being used and will do the right thing. I'm getting a bit too far ahead this early in the book, so don't worry if this isn't making much sense right now. Later on it will almost certainly make more sense than it does right now.

You will see many examples of these operators as you go through this book. Rather than try to memorize the function of each operator, try instead to learn through careful study of the sample programs and code snippets.

Constants

As I said earlier, a constant is an identifier assigned to a value that does not change. The terms "variable" and "constant" were not chosen at random. A variable's value can be changed by the programmer; a constant's value cannot be changed. Constants are declared using the const keyword. To declare a constant, simply list the constant's name and its value—for example,

```
const
  DefaultWidth  = 400;
  DefaultHeight = 200;
  Description   = 'Something really cool.';
```

Notice that when declaring a constant, the equal sign is used and not the assignment operator (:=). Notice also that no data type is specified. The compiler determines the data type of the constant based on the value being assigned. The constants can then be used in your code where you would normally have used a literal value.

Judicious use of constants makes the behavior of a program easy to change at a later date if change becomes necessary. To change the behavior of the program, it is only necessary to change the value of one or more constants at the top of the unit, rather than hunting through the unit for every occurrence of 100 and changing it to 120.

Arrays

You can place any of the intrinsic Object Pascal data types into an array. An *array* is simply a collection of values. For example, let's say you want to keep an array of Integers that holds five integer values. You would declare the array as follows:

```
var
  MyArray : array[0..4] of Integer;
```

In this case, the compiler allocates memory for the array, as illustrated in Figure 1.4. Because each integer requires 4 bytes of storage, the entire array will take up 20 bytes in memory.

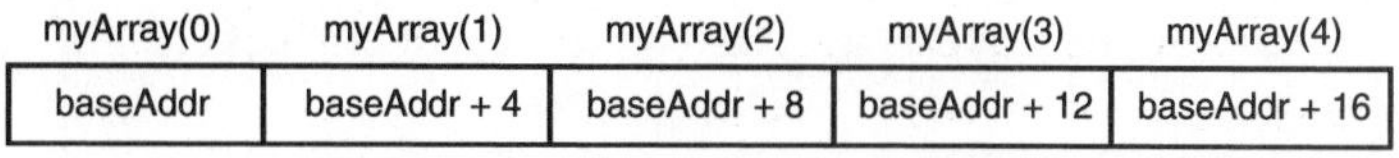

FIGURE 1.4.

Memory allocation for an array of five integers.

myArray(0)	myArray(1)	myArray(2)	myArray(3)	myArray(4)
baseAddr	baseAddr + 4	baseAddr + 8	baseAddr + 12	baseAddr + 16

Now that you have the array declared, you can fill it with values using the *subscript operator* ([]) as follows:

```
MyArray[0] := -200;
MyArray[1] := -100;
```

```
MyArray[2] := 0;
MyArray[3] := 100;
MyArray[4] := 200;
```

Later in your program, you can access the individual elements of the array, again by using the subscript operator:

```
X := MyArray[3] + MyArray[4];  { result will be 300 }
```

Multidimensional Arrays

Arrays can be multidimensional. To create a two-dimensional array of integers, you would use code like this:

```
var
  MdArray : array[0..2, 0..4] of Integer;
```

This allocates storage for 15 Integers (a total of 60 bytes, if you're keeping score). You access elements of the array like you do a simple array, with the obvious difference that you must supply two subscript operators. There are two ways of doing this. The following two lines have the same result:

```
X := MdArray[1][1] + MdArray[2][1];
X := MdArray[1, 1] + MdArray[2, 1];
```

Figure 1.5 illustrates how a two-dimensional array might look in memory.

FIGURE 1.5.

A two-dimensional array in memory.

	mdArray()(0)	mdArray()(1)	mdArray()(2)	mdArray()(3)	mdArray()(4)
MdArray(0)()	baseAddr	baseAddr + 4	baseAddr + 8	baseAddr + 12	baseAddr + 16
MdArray(1)()	baseAddr + 20	baseAddr + 24	baseAddr + 28	baseAddr + 32	baseAddr + 36
MdArray(2)()	baseAddr + 40	baseAddr + 44	baseAddr + 48	baseAddr + 52	baseAddr + 56

Note

Under normal circumstances, range checking will keep you from attempting to write beyond the end of an array. For example, the following code will result in a compiler error:

```
var
  MyArray : array[0..4] of Integer;
  X : Integer;
begin
  X := MyArray[3] + MyArray[5]; { Oops! 5 outside of range. }
end;
```

The error will state `Constant expression violates subrange bounds` because `MyArray[5]` is outside of the declared range for the array.

The array range is defined when you declare the array. For example, if you want to create an array with a lower bound of 10 and an upper bound of 20, you declare it like this:

```
var
  MyArray : array[10..20] of Integer;
```

Now the only elements of the array that can be accessed are elements 10 (the first element in the array) through 20 (the last element in the array). Array constants must be declared and initialized all at one time. The syntax looks like this:

```
const
  myArray : array[0..4] of Integer = ( -200, -100, 0, 100, 200 );
```

The Low and High Functions

The Low and High functions are used frequently when dealing with arrays. As I said earlier, an array can be declared with variable lower and upper bounds. The Low function will return the lower bound of an array, and the High function will return the upper bound of the array—for example,

```
var
  X, I, Lower, Upper : Integer;
  MyArray : array[10..20] of Integer;
begin
  { Code to initialize MyArray here. }
  Lower := Low(MyArray);  { Lower now contains 10 }
  Upper := High(MyArray); { Upper now contains 20 }
  X := 0;
  for I := Lower to Upper do
    X := X + MyArray[I];
  { Now do something with X. }
end;
```

Using the Low and High functions ensures that you don't attempt to access an array value outside of the array bounds.

Dynamic Arrays

New
to 4

Delphi 4 introduces the concept of dynamic arrays. A dynamic array is declared without an initial size, and no storage is set aside for the array at the time of declaration. Later the array can be created with a specified size using the SetLength function. Here's how it would look:

```
var
  BigArray : array of Integer; { no size }
  X : Integer;
begin
  X := GetArraySize;      { function which returns the needed size }
  SetLength(BigArray, X); { dynamically allocate array }
  { Now fill in and use BigArray }
end;
```

NEW TERM   A *dynamic array* is an array for which memory is allocated at runtime. A dynamic array can be made larger or smaller depending on the needs of the program.

The significance is that the array can be allocated based on exactly the number of elements required. To illustrate, let's say that you need an array of integers. Let's further say that in some cases you might only need to allocate enough memory for 10 integers, but in other cases you might need to allocate as many as 1,000 integers.

Your program doesn't know at compile time how many elements will be needed—that number will not be known until runtime. Before the advent of dynamic arrays, you would have been forced to declare an array with a size of 1,000 integers, wasting a lot of memory if your application really only needs 10, 20, or 30 integers. With dynamic arrays you can allocate only as much storage as is required at a given time.

You can reallocate an array using the `Copy` function. For example, let's say you initially created an array with a size of 100 elements, and you now need to reallocate the array to a size of 200 elements. In that case, the code would look like this:

```
Copy(BigArray, 200);
```

The contents of the array are retained and the array size is increased by 100 elements to a total of 200 elements.

Two-dimensional dynamic arrays are created in much the same way. To create a two-dimensional array, you use code like the following:

```
var
  BigArray : array of array of Integer;
begin
  SetLength(BigArray, 20, 20);
  BigArray[0][0] := 200;
  { More code here. }
end;
```

After a dynamic array is created, its elements are accessed just like a regular array.

Strings

Strings are used heavily in programming. Object Pascal has three distinct string types: long string, short string, and wide string. In addition to these string types, Pascal also uses null-terminated strings. I'll go over each of these types briefly, and then I'll discuss some of the string-manipulation functions.

Short String

The short string type is a fixed-length string of characters with a maximum size of 255 characters. You declare a short string in one of two ways. One way is to use the predefined type ShortString to declare a short string with a size of 255 bytes. You can also use the string keyword with the subscript operator to specify a size when you declare the string:

```
var
  S1 : ShortString; { 255 characters long }
  S2 : string[20];  { 20 characters long }
```

String manipulation using short strings is fast because the size of the memory allocated for the string doesn't change. Still, the short string is considered an obsolete type and it is recommended that long strings be used instead. Short strings are termed length-byte strings because the first element of the string contains the length of the string (the number of characters in the string). You can read the value of the first element of a short string to determine the string's length—for example,

```
var
  S   : ShortString; { 255 characters long }
  Len : Integer;
begin
  S   := 'Hello';
  Len := Ord(S[0]); { 'L' now contains the length of S, or 5 }
end;
```

This example reads the value of S[0] to determine the string's length. You can also use the Length function to determine the length of a short string. I'll discuss the Length function in just a bit.

Note   You use the Ord function to convert the value of a Char type to an integer value (and ordinal value). The Ord function is also used with enumerations.

If needed, you can write to the first element of a short string to specifically set the length of the string. This is required in certain programming situations, which I won't go into here. I should add that, in general, use of the 0 byte of a short string is an advanced programming technique and is not recommended for beginning programmers.

Long String

The long string data type is a dynamically allocated string object. The size of a long string is limited only by available memory. Object Pascal allocates and de-allocates memory for the string as needed. Long strings are very flexible but are sometimes slower than short strings when a lot of string-manipulation is being done. This is due to the overhead needed to dynamically allocate storage for the long string as the string's contents change. Still, unless execution speed is critical, you should generally stick to using long strings in your applications.

To declare a long string, simply use the string keyword without a size parameter:

```
var
  S : string;  { long string, dynamically allocated }
```

Because the string is dynamically allocated, you can modify the string in any way you want and never have to worry about what is going on behind the scenes. The long string is very easy to use because you don't have to worry about running out of space or about memory allocation for the string. It's all more or less automatic.

Long strings do not have a 0 element as short strings do. Attempting to access the 0 element of a long string will result in a compiler error. Instead, you get the length of a long string using the Length function and set the length using the SetLength procedure. I'll discuss the string manipulation functions in the section "String Functions."

Wide String

The wide string type is used when dealing with Windows API functions that require double-byte character strings (Unicode character strings). The wide string is like the long string in that the size is limited only by available memory and memory for the string is dynamically allocated. I won't go into any detail on wide string because its use is limited primarily to dealing with OLE functions.

Null-Terminated Strings: PChar and Array of Char

Unlike Object Pascal, the C and C++ languages do not have true string data types. In C and C++, strings are implemented as an array of characters terminated with a terminating null (a 0 at the end of the string). Character arrays don't have a length byte, so the terminating null is used to mark the end of the string of characters. Because Windows was written in C, many Windows functions require a character array as a parameter. The Pascal string types are not character arrays, so a way of enabling Pascal strings to work with Windows functions requiring a character array is needed. The PChar type fills this need. A PChar can be used anywhere a character array is needed. An example is the Windows MessageBox function. This function, which displays a standard Windows message dialog, has the following declaration:

```
function MessageBox(hWnd: HWND; lpText, lpCaption: PChar; uType: UINT):
Integer;
```

The second and third parameters require a pointer to a character array (the second for the message box text and the third for the message box caption). In order to call this function from a Delphi program, you have to use the PChar type as follows:

```
var
  Text    : string;
  Caption : string;
begin
  Text := 'This is a test.;
  Caption := 'Test Message';
  MessageBox(0, PChar(Text), PChar(Caption), 0);
end;
```

Here the PChar is used to cast the Pascal long string to a null-terminated string. You can also use a PChar by itself. The following illustrates:

```
var
  Text : PChar;
begin
  Text := 'This is a test.';
  MessageBox(0, Text, 'Message', 0);
end;
```

Because the strength of the Pascal string types is in string manipulation, you probably won't use a PChar like this very often. You will typically use a PChar to convert a long string to a null-terminated string as in the previous example. Note that you can pass a string literal (a string of characters within single quotes) to a Windows API function expecting a PChar.

Finally, you can use an array of the Char data type in place of a PChar. Once again, the previous code snippet is modified to illustrate:

```
var
  Text : array [0..20] of Char;
begin
  Text := 'This is a test.';
  MessageBox(0, Text, 'Message', 0);
end;
```

It really doesn't matter which of these methods you use. Just understand that you cannot use a Pascal string data type to call Windows API functions that require a null-terminated string as a parameter. In those cases, you have to use PChar or an array of Char.

String Basics

The Pascal string types have several elements in common. The following sections describe general string operations that apply to all string types.

String Concatenation Using the + Operator

A common programming task is that of concatenating (adding together) strings. Strings can be concatenated using the + operator—for example,

```
var
  S1 : string;
  S2 : string;
begin
  S1 := 'Mallory Kim';
  S2 := 'Reisdorph';
  Label1.Caption := S1 + ' ' + S2;
end;
```

This code concatenates three strings (the variable S1, a string literal containing a space, and the variable S2) and assigns the result to a label's Caption property. Any expression or function that evaluates to a string can be used in concatenation. Here's another example:

```
var
  X :   Integer;
begin
  X := 199;
  Label1.Caption := 'The result is: ' + IntToStr(X);
end;
```

In this case, the IntToStr function returns a string so that you can use the result from that function anywhere a string is required.

The Subscript Operator

Another common aspect of Pascal strings is the subscript operator ([ ]). You can extract an individual character from a string using the subscript operator, as follows:

```
var
  S1 : string;
  S2 : Char;
begin
  S1 := 'Hello World!';
  S2 := S1[1];
  Label1.Caption := S2;
end;
```

The variable S2 in this example is a Char, but it could have been a long string, a short string, or a wide string. Object Pascal makes the proper conversions behind the scenes so you don't have to deal with the different string types at the application level. The subscript operator is handy when you need to search through a string one character at a time.

Strings are one-based: the first character in the string is at S[1]. Remember that the 0 element of a short string (S[0]) contains the length of the string and not the first character in the string. You cannot access S[0] in long strings or wide strings.

Control Characters in Strings

Object Pascal enables you to embed control characters in strings. This is useful if you need to add non-printing characters to your strings. This could be as simple as starting a new line in a character string, or it could be more complex, such as embedding control characters in a string sent to a serial device.

You add control characters to a string using the # character. If, for example, you want to embed an escape character (ASCII 27) in your string, you would do so as follows:

```
S := 'This is a test. Escape follows.'#27'Finished.';
```

Notice that the embedded character, #27, is placed outside of any literal character string, and that no spaces are between the embedded character and the preceding and following strings. You must follow this structure when using embedded characters. Of course, you don't have to use literal strings, you could use string variables as well:

```
S1 := 'This is a test. Escape follows.';
S2 := 'Finished.';
S3 := S1 + #27 + S2;
```

You can easily test this theory. Place a button and a label on a form. Double-click the button and add this line to the button's OnClick event handler:

```
Label1.Caption := 'Line 1' + #10 + 'Line 2';
```

Now run the program and click the button. The label will contain two lines of text, as shown in Figure 1.6. This code simply embeds a carriage return character (ASCII 10) in the string, thereby breaking the label into two lines.

FIGURE 1.6.

A label with two lines.

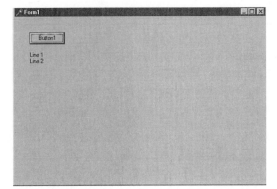

Extending Strings Across Multiple Code Lines

It is often necessary to break a literal string across two or more code lines to increase readability and maintainability of your code. A long text message, for example, might be well over 200 characters. You could put all of those characters on one line of code (the maximum line length of the Delphi Code Editor is 1,024 characters), but that would make the code almost impossible to read. Instead you can split the string across multiple lines. To do that you need to use the + operator—for example,

```
MessageBox(0, 'This is a very, very long message ' +
  'that seems to go on and on forever. In order ' +
  'to make the code more readable the message has ' +
  'been split across several lines of code.', 'Message', 0);
```

Remember earlier when I talked about semicolons at the end of each code statement? Here's an example where a statement is spread across multiple lines. It's still a single statement as far as the compiler is concerned, so the semicolon is at the end of the *statement* and not at the end of each line.

String Comparison

Strings can be compared using the comparison operators. Table 1.3 lists the usual operators and their descriptions.

TABLE 1.3. STRING COMPARISON OPERATORS.

Operator	Description
=	Equal to
<>	Not equal to
<	Less than
>	Greater than
<=	Less than or equal to
>=	Greater than or equal to

Note that these operators compare strings based on their ASCII values. Most of the time you will use just the equality operators to see whether a string is equal to a certain value or not equal to a certain value. If you are doing string sorting, you will probably use the other string comparison operators as well. The following example checks to see whether a string contains a certain value:

```
if FileName = 'TEST.TXT' then
  OpenFile(FileName)
```

```
else
  ReportError;
```

String-Manipulation Functions

Object Pascal includes many functions and procedures for string manipulation. Table 1.4 lists a few of the most commonly used string functions and procedures; this is by no means a complete list. Consult the Delphi online help for a list of all string functions and procedures.

TABLE 1.4. STRING MANIPULATION FUNCTIONS AND PROCEDURES.

Name	Description
Copy	Returns a sub-string within a string.
Delete	Deletes part of a string.
Format	Formats and returns a string based on the format string and arguments passed.
Insert	Inserts text into a string.
IntToStr	Converts an integer value to a string.
Length	Returns the length of a string.
LowerCase	Converts a string to lowercase.
Pos	Returns the position of a search string within a string.
StringOfChar	Returns a string filled with the given number of a particular character.
StrPas	Converts a null-terminated string (PChar or array of Char) to a Pascal-style string.
StrPCopy	Converts a Pascal-style string to a null-terminated string.
StrToInt	Converts a string to an integer. If the string cannot be converted, an exception is thrown.
StrToIntDef	Converts a string to an integer and supplies a default value in case the string cannot be converted. No exception is thrown if the string cannot be converted.
StrToXXX	Additional conversion functions that convert a string to a floating point, Currency, Date, or Time value.
Trim	Trims leading and trailing blank space from a string.
UpperCase	Converts a string to uppercase.
XXXToStr	Additional conversion functions that convert a floating point, Currency, Date, or Time value to a string.

Note

Object Pascal has an additional set of functions that operates on null-terminated strings. I won't list all of those here, because most of the time you will be working with Pascal strings and not null-terminated strings. Check the Delphi help for additional information on those functions. Most of the functions that operate on null-terminated strings begin with Str.

A few of the functions and procedures listed in Table 1.4 deserve special mention. The StrToInt function converts a string to an integer value. Let's say you have an edit component on a form that will be used to retrieve an integer value from the user. Because an edit component only holds text, you need to convert that text to an integer. You can do it like this:

```
Value := StrToInt(Edit1.Text);
```

The other StrToXXX functions (StrToFloat, StrToDate, and so on) work in exactly the same way. Note that these functions will throw an exception if the conversion cannot be made. If, for example, the user enters S123, an exception will be thrown because the letter *S* cannot be converted to an integer. I haven't talked about exceptions yet, so I won't go into detail on exceptions at this time.

The Format function enables you to build a string by passing a format string and additional arguments. The following is an example that adds two numbers and then uses Format to build a string to report the result:

```
var
  S : string;
  X : Integer;
begin
  X := 10 * 20;
  S := Format('The result is: %d', [X]);
  Label1.Caption := S;
end;
```

When this section of code executes, the label contains this text:

```
The result is: 200
```

In this example, the %d tells the Format function, "An integer value will go here." At the end of the format string, the variable X is inserted to tell Format what value to put at that location in the string (the contents of the variable X).

Format is a unique function in that it can take a variable number of arguments. (That is why the variable X is in square brackets; the arguments passed are in the form of an array of const.) You must supply the format string, but the number of arguments that come after the format string is variable. Here is an example of Format that uses three additional arguments:

```
var
  X : Integer;
  Y : Integer;
begin
  X := 20;
  Y := 5;
  Label1.Caption := Format('%d + %d = %d', [X, Y, X + Y]);
end;
```

When this piece of code executes, the result displayed in the label will be:

```
20 + 5 = 25
```

Notice that in this example I am assigning the return value from Format directly to the Caption property of a label. In the previous example I assigned the return value from Format to a variable, but that step was not strictly necessary.

Additional format specifiers are used to display a number as a floating point, in scientific notation, in hexadecimal, or to display characters and strings. You can specify the number of decimal places to use for floating-point numbers and the number of digits to display for integer values. See the "Format Strings" topic in the Delphi help for full details.

Summary

You've covered a lot of ground today. First, you got to tinker with the Delphi IDE by creating a Hello World! program. Following that, you got to do a little more interesting programming when you created Hello World!, Part II. After the initial playing around, you were put to work learning the basics of the Object Pascal language. There is a lot of material to absorb in this chapter. Don't feel bad if you can't remember it all. Go back and review if you are unclear about anything presented today.

Workshop

The Workshop contains quiz questions to help you solidify your understanding of the material covered and exercises to provide you with experience in using what you have learned. You can find answers to the quiz questions in Appendix A, "Answers to the Quiz Questions."

Q&A

Q **What's the difference between a Win32 GUI application and a Win32 console-mode application?**

A A GUI application is a traditional Windows program. It usually has a title bar, menu bar, and window area. A console-mode application is a 32-bit application that runs in an MS-DOS box in Windows. The console application looks like a DOS program.

Q **After I declare a constant, can I change its value in my program?**

A No. Constants are just that: constant. If you need to change values, you should use a variable not a constant.

Q **Are my units required to have an interface section?**

A Yes (all units except the project source, that is). The interface section might be empty, but it must be present.

Q **Should I use short strings or long strings in my Delphi applications?**

A For the most part you should use long strings. Long strings have virtually no size limit and all memory allocation and de-allocation is handled for you automatically. Short strings can be faster when you are doing a lot of heavy string manipulation, but most of the time the speed difference is not appreciable.

Q **Can I assign a number containing decimal places to an integer data type variable?**

A No. You cannot assign a floating point value to an integer variable.

Q **Will Object Pascal make sure I don't overwrite memory somewhere if I attempt to write past the end of an array?**

A For the most part, yes. Range checking at compile time will ensure that you don't attempt to write out of the bounds of an array.

Quiz

1. What is the filename extension of a Pascal unit?
2. What is the name of the keyword that marks the section in which variables are declared?
3. What does the `IntToStr` function do?
4. What is the purpose of the `uses` list in a Pascal unit?
5. Are the following two declarations different? Why or why not?
   ```
   var
     top : Integer;
     Top : Integer;
   ```

6. How do you concatenate Pascal strings?

7. How can you embed a control character in a string?

8. What is the maximum length of a short string?

9. Look at this line of code:

```
MyArray : array [0..10] of Byte;
```

How many bytes can this array hold?

10. What is the index number of the first element of an array, 0 or 1?

Exercises

1. Write a Windows program that displays the words Welcome to Delphi! on the window when the program runs.

2. Rewrite the program you wrote in step 1 and change the displayed text to Hello There! (Hint: You have to change only the Caption property of the Label component.)

3. Write a program that declares two variables and assign values to those variables. Multiply the two numbers together and display the result on the screen.

4. Write a program that assigns the string, "There are eggs in a dozen." to a variable and then inserts the string "12 " at the appropriate place in the string. Show the result in a label.

5. Write a program that creates the final result string in exercise 4, but formatted with the Format function.

DAY **2**

More on Pascal

You now have a pretty good start on learning Object Pascal. In this chapter, you will continue to learn about the Object Pascal language by examining more of the fundamentals of Object Pascal. Today you will learn about

- The `if`, `then`, and `else` keywords
- Loops: `for`, `while`, and `repeat`
- The `case` statement
- Scope
- Records
- Functions and procedures

if, then, else

There are some aspects of programming that are common to all programming languages. One such item that Object Pascal has in common with other programming languages is the `if` statement. The `if` statement is used to test for a condition and then execute sections of code based on whether that condition is True or False. Here's an example:

```
var
  X : Integer;
begin
  X := StrToInt(Edit1.Text);
  if X > 10 then
    Label1.Caption := 'You entered a number greater than 10.';
end;
```

This code gets the contents of an edit control and stores it in an integer variable. If the number is greater than 10, the expression x > 10 evaluates to True and the message is displayed; otherwise, nothing is displayed. Note that when the conditional expression evaluates to True, the statement immediately following the if...then expression is executed. The conditional part of an if statement is always followed by then.

New Term   The if statement is used to test for a condition and execute one or more lines of code when that condition evaluates to True.

Executing Multiple Instructions

Let's say you have multiple lines of code that should be executed when the conditional expression is True. In that case, you would need begin and end keywords to block those lines:

```
if X > 10 then begin
  Label1.Caption := 'You entered a number greater than 10.';
  DoSomethingWithNumber(X);
end;
```

When the conditional expression evaluates to False, the code block associated with the if expression is ignored and program execution continues with the first statement following the code block.

Note

Object Pascal contains a few shortcuts. One of those shortcuts involves using just a Boolean variable's name to test for True. Look at this code:

```
if FileGood then ReadData;
```

This method is shortcut for the longer form, which is illustrated with this line:

```
if FileGood = True then ReadData;
```

This shortcut only applies to Boolean variables. You can test for False by applying the not keyword to a variable name:

```
var
  FileGood : Boolean;
begin
  FileGood := OpenSomeFile;
  if not FileGood then ReportError;
end;
```

Learning the Object Pascal shortcuts helps you write code that contains a degree of elegance. Knowing the shortcuts will also help you understand Object Pascal code that you read in examples and sample listings.

2

Adding `else`

In some cases, you might want to perform an action when the conditional expression evaluates to `True` and perform some other action when the conditional expression evaluates to `False`. You accomplish this by implementing the `else` statement:

```
if X = 20 then
  DoSomething(X)
else
  DoADifferentThing(X);
```

 The `else` statement is used in conjunction with the `if` statement and identifies a section of code that is executed when the `if` statement fails (that is, evaluates to `False`).

In this example, one of the two functions will be called based on the value of X, but not both.

I want you to notice something about the preceding example. The line following the `if` statement does not end in a semicolon. This is because the entire `if...then...else` sequence is viewed as a single statement. You omit the semicolon on the first line following the `if` statement *only* if it's a single line of code (that is, you are not using `begin` and `end` following the `if` statement). Here are a couple of examples of legal `if...then...else` syntax:

```
if X = 20 then
  DoSomething(X)          { no semi-colon here because }
else                      { it's a single line of code }
  DoADifferentThing(X);

if X = 20 then begin
  DoSomething(X);         { semi-colon needed here because }
end else begin            { of the begin/end block }
```

```
    DoADifferentThing(X);
end;

if X = 20 then begin
  DoSomething(X);          { Multiple lines, use semi-colons }
  X := 200;                { at the end of each line. }
  Y := 30;
end else begin
  DoADifferentThing(X);
  X := 100;
  Y := 15;
end;
```

Note

It doesn't matter where you put the then, begin, and else keywords. The following two blocks of code are identical as far as the compiler is concerned:

```
{ One way to do it... }
if X = 20 then begin
  DoSomething(X);
  X := 200;
  Y := 30;
end else begin
  DoADifferentThing(X);
  X := 100;
  Y := 15;
end;

{ Same code, different layout... }
if X = 20
then
begin
  DoSomething(X);
  X := 200;
  Y := 30;
end
else
begin
  DoADifferentThing(X);
  X := 100;
  Y := 15;
end;
```

Ultimately it's up to you to decide on the coding style that you will use. While coding style is largely a matter of preference, be sure you settle on a style that makes your code easy to read.

> **Note**
>
> Remember that the equality operator is the equal sign (=) and that the assignment operator is colon-equal (:=). A common coding mistake is to use the assignment operator where you mean to use the equality operator. Fortunately, the compiler will issue an error when you do this.

Nested `if` Statements

2

You can nest `if` statements when needed. Nesting is nothing more than following an `if` statement with one or more additional `if` statements.

```
if X > 10 then
  if X < 20 then
    Label1.Caption := 'X is between 10 and 20';
```

Keep in mind that these are simplified examples. In the real world, you can get lost in the maze of `begin` and `end` statements that separate one code block from the next. Take a look at this code snippet, for instance:

```
if X > 100 then begin
  Y := 20;
  if X > 200 then begin
    Y := 40;
    if X > 400 then begin
      Y := 60;
      DoSomething(Y);
    end;
  end;
end else if X < -100 then begin
  Y := -20;
  if X < -200 then begin
    Y := -40;
    if X < -400 then begin
      Y := -60;
      DoSomething(Y);
    end;
  end;
end;
```

Even this is a fairly simple example, but you get the idea.

> **Tip**
>
> When a section of code contains more than two or three consecutive `if` statements testing for different values of the same variable, it might be a candidate for a `case` statement. The `case` statement is discussed later in this chapter in the section "The `case` Statement."

So far I have used only one conditional expression in the `if` examples I have given you. When you have just one conditional expression, you can use parentheses around the expression or not use parentheses as you see fit. If, however, you have more than one conditional expression, you must surround each conditional expression with parentheses. For example:

```
if (X = 20) and (Y = 50) then
  DoSomething;
```

If you forget the parentheses, the compiler will, of course, let you know by issuing a compiler error.

The `if` statement is heavily used in Object Pascal programming. It's straightforward, so you won't have any trouble with it. The main thing is keeping all the `begin` and `end` keywords straight!

The `if...then...else` Statement, Form 1

▼ SYNTAX

```
if cond_expr then
    true_statement
else
    false_statement;
```

If the conditional expression *cond_expr* is `True`, the line of code represented by *true_statement* is executed. If the optional `else` clause is specified, the line of code represented by *false_statement* is executed when the conditional expression *cond_expr* is `False`.

The `if...then...else` Statement, Form 2

```
if cond_expr_1 then begin
    true_statements;
end else begin
    false_statements;
end;
```

If the conditional expression *cond_expr_1* is `True`, the block of code represented by *true_statements* is executed. If it is `False`, the block of code represented by
▲   *false_statements* is executed.

Using Loops

The loop is a common element in all programming languages. A loop can be used to iterate through an array, to perform an action a specific number of times, to read a file from disk...the possibilities are endless. In this section, I will discuss the `for` loop, the `while` loop, and the `repeat` loop. For the most part they work in very similar ways. All loops have these common elements:

- A starting point
- A body, usually enclosed in begin and end keywords, that contains the statements to execute on each pass
- An ending point
- A test for a condition that determines when the loop should end
- Optional use of the Break and Continue procedures

NEW TERM A *loop* is an element in a programming language that is used to perform an action repeatedly until a specific condition is met.

The starting point for the loop is one of the Object Pascal loop statements (for, while, or repeat). The body contains the statements that will execute each iteration through the loop. The body can contain any valid Object Pascal code and can be a single line of code or multiple lines of code. If the body contains multiple lines of code, the code must be blocked with begin and end statements (with the exception of the repeat loop). The ending point for the loop is either the end keyword (in the case of the for loop and the while loop) or the until keyword (in the case of the repeat loop). When the body of a loop is a single line of code, the begin and end keywords are not required.

Most loops work something like this: The loop is entered and the test condition is evaluated. If the test condition evaluates to False, the body of the loop is executed. When program execution reaches the bottom of the loop, it jumps back to the top of the loop where the test condition is again evaluated. If the test condition is still False, the whole process is repeated. If the test condition is True, program execution jumps to the line of code immediately following the loop code block. The exception to this description is the repeat loop, which tests for the condition at the bottom of the loop rather than at the top.

The test condition tells the loop when to stop executing. In effect the test condition says, for example, "Keep doing this until *X* is equal to 10," or "Keep reading the file until the end-of-file is reached." After the loop starts, it continues to execute the body of the loop until the test condition evaluates to True.

Caution

It's easy to accidentally write a loop so that the test condition never evaluates to True. This will result in a program that is locked up or hung. Your only recourse at that point is to press Ctrl+Alt+Del and kill the task. The Windows Close Program box (or the Windows NT Task Manager) will come up and display the name of your program with (Not Responding) next to it. You'll have to select your program from the list and click End Task to terminate the runaway program.

Tip

In Delphi you typically run a program using the Run button on the toolbar or by pressing F9. If you need to kill a runaway program that was run from the IDE, you can choose Run I Program Reset from the main menu or press Ctrl+F2 on the keyboard. Note, however, that Windows 95 does not like you to kill tasks with Program Reset and might crash if you reset a program several times (Windows NT is much more forgiving in this area). Always run your programs to completion if possible, especially when developing on the Windows 95 platform.

Given that general overview, let's take a look at each type of loop individually.

The for Loop

The for loop is probably the most commonly used type of loop. It takes two parameters: the starting value and ending value. If the loop is to count up, the to keyword is used. If the loop is to count backward, then the downto keyword is used.

The for Loop Statement, Counting Up

▼ SYNTAX

```
for initial_value to end_value do begin
    statements;
end;
```

The for loop repeatedly executes the block of code indicated by *statements* until the ending value *end_value* is reached. The state of the loop is initialized by the statement *initial_value*. The variable indicated in *initial_value* is incremented by one each iteration through the loop. If the body of the loop is a single statement, the begin and end statements are not required.

The for Loop Statement, Counting Down

```
for initial_value downto end_value do begin
    statements;
end;
```

The for loop repeatedly executes the block of code indicated by *statements* until the ending value *end_value* is reached. The state of the loop is initialized by the statement *initial_value*. The variable indicated in *initial_value* is decremented by one each iteration through the loop. If the body of the loop is a single statement, the begin and

▲ end statements are not required.

As most syntax statements are somewhat vague, some examples will probably help. First, take a look at a typical for loop that counts up:

```
var
  I : Integer;
begin
  for I := 0 to 9 do begin
    Memo1.Lines.Add('This is iteration ' + IntToStr(I));
  end;
end;
```

This code will result in the statement inside the braces being executed 10 times. The first parameter, `I := 0`, tells the `for` loop that it is starting with an initial value of `0`. The second parameter, `9`, tells the loop to keep running until the variable `I` equals `9`. The `to` keyword specifies that the value of `I` should be incremented by one each time the loop executes.

Note

> The use of the variable name `I` has its roots in the FORTRAN language and is traditional in `for` loops. Naturally, any variable name can be used, but you will often see `I` used in `for` loops.

Let's look at a variation of this code. The following code snippet will achieve exactly the opposite effect as the first example:

```
var
  I : Integer;
begin
  for I := 9 downto 0 do begin
    Memo1.Lines.Add('This is iteration ' + IntToStr(I));
  end;
end;
```

This time I'm starting with `9` and stopping when `I` is equal to `0`. The `downto` keyword specifies that the value of `I` should be decremented each time the loop executes. This is an example of a loop that counts backward.

Note

> In the preceding examples, the `begin` and `end` keywords are not strictly required. If `begin` and `end` are not used, the statement immediately following the `for` statement is considered the body of the loop. It's up to you whether you use `begin` and `end` on single statements, although it's considered bad form to do so.

A Sample for Loop

Let's write a little program that illustrates the use of the for loop. In doing so, I will explain another Delphi component, the Memo component (used earlier in this chapter). Perform these steps:

1. Begin with a new application (File | New Application).

2. Place a button on the form.

3. Locate the Memo component on the Standard tab of the Component palette (it should be just to the left of the Button component). Click the button, and then click on the form. A memo will be placed on your form.

4. Make the memo larger by dragging the black sizing rectangle in the lower-right corner of the memo.

5. Double-click the button to create an OnClick event handler for the button. Enter code so that the event handler looks like this:

```
procedure TForm1.Button1Click(Sender: TObject);
var
  I : Integer;
begin

  Memo1.Lines.Clear;

  for I := 0 to 5 do
    Memo1.Lines.Add('This is iteration ' + IntToStr(I));

  Memo1.Lines.Add('');

  for I := 5 downto 0 do
    Memo1.Lines.Add('This is iteration ' + IntToStr(I));

end;
```

Run the program. When you click the button, lines of text are added to the memo. Figure 2.1 shows this program running.

As I said earlier, the loop variable will be incremented by one each time through the loop. Unlike other programming languages, Pascal doesn't provide a way of iterating through a for loop by a value other than one. For example, there is no way to iterate through a for loop from 0 to 100 by 10s. To accomplish this, you must make use of another variable as follows:

```
var
  I : Integer;
  X : Integer;
begin
```

```
    X := 0;
    Memo1.Lines.Clear;

    for I := 0 to 9 do begin
      Memo1.Lines.Add('Iteration value: ' + IntToStr(X));
      Inc(X, 10);
    end;
end;
```

This code will display this in the memo:

```
Iteration value: 0
Iteration value: 10
Iteration value: 20
Iteration value: 30
Iteration value: 40
Iteration value: 50
Iteration value: 60
Iteration value: 70
Iteration value: 80
Iteration value: 90
```

FIGURE 2.1.

The output from the for *loop exercise.*

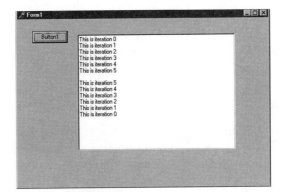

Note

Notice the use of the Inc function in the preceding snippet. This function increments the given variable (X in this example) by the specified value (10). If Inc is used without an increment parameter, the variable is incremented by one. For example:

```
Inc(X);  { X is incremented by one. Same as X := X + 1 }
```

Inc has a companion function called, predictably, Dec. Here are examples of the Dec function:

```
Dex(X);      { X is decremented by one }
Dec(X, 10);  { X is decremented by 10  }
```

Use of Inc and Dec is preferred over the long version (X := X + 1, for example).

The Pred and Succ Functions

You will often see the Pred and Succ functions used with for loops. The Pred function returns the predecessor of the passed argument. For example, Pred(10) will return the value 9, Pred(100) will return 99, and so on. Given that information, the following three for loops are identical:

```
var
  X : Integer;
begin
  X := 10;

  for I := 0 to 9 do
    DoSomething;

  for I := 0 to X - 1 do
    DoSomething;

  for I := 0 to Pred(X) do
    DoSomething;
end;
```

When you start with an initial value of 0, it's natural to make the mistake of doing one too many iterations in a loop. Using the Pred function solves this problem and is a bit more elegant than using X - 1. The Succ function, naturally, returns the successor of the argument passed. This is useful when counting backward:

```
for I := 100 downto Succ(X) do
    DoSomething;
```

Now that you've seen the for loop in action, it won't be too difficult to apply the same concepts to the while and repeat loops. Let's take a look at those now.

The while Loop

The while loop differs from the for loop in that it contains a test condition that is checked at the start of each iteration. As long as the test condition is True, the loop keeps running.

```
var
  X : Integer;
begin
  X := 0;
  while X < 1000 do begin
    X := DoSomeCalculation;
    DoSomeMoreStuff;
  end;
  { ...more code }
end;
```

In this example, I am calling a function that I assume will eventually return a value greater than or equal to 1,000. As long as the return value from this function is less than 1,000, the while loop continues to run. When the variable X contains a value greater than or equal to 1,000, the test condition yields False and program execution jumps to the first line following the body of the while loop. A common implementation of a while loop uses a Boolean test variable. The state of the test variable can be set somewhere within the body of the loop:

```
var
  Done : Boolean;
begin
  Done := False;
  while not Done do begin
    DoSomeStuff;
    Done := SomeFunctionReturningABoolean;
    DoSomeMoreStuff;
  end;
end;
```

At some point it is expected that the variable Done will be True, and the loop will terminate. Let's do another simple program that illustrates the use of the while loop. Start a new application and place a button and a memo on the form. Double-click the button and modify the event handler so that it looks like this:

```
procedure TForm1.Button1Click(Sender: TObject);
var
  I : Integer;
begin
  I := 5;
  Memo1.Lines.Clear;
  while I > -1 do begin
    Memo1.Lines.Add('Today I have ' +
      IntToStr(I) + ' problems to worry about.');
    Dec(I);
  end;
  Memo1.Lines.Add('Yeah!');
end;
```

When you run the program and click the form's button, you will see this text in the memo:

```
Today I have 5 problems to worry about.
Today I have 4 problems to worry about.
Today I have 3 problems to worry about.
Today I have 2 problems to worry about.
Today I have 1 problems to worry about.
Today I have 0 problems to worry about.
Yeah!
```

This program declares a variable, I, and initializes it to a value of 5. Next, a while loop is started. Text is added to the Memo component each time through the loop, and the variable I is decremented by one. When I is equal to -1, the loop stops and a final line is added to the memo.

The while Loop Statement

▼ SYNTAX

```
while cond_expr do begin
    statements;
end;
```

The while loop repeatedly executes the block of code indicated by *statements* as long as the conditional expression *cond_expr* is True. The state of the loop must be initialized prior to the while statement and modification of the state must be explicit in the block of code. When the conditional expression *cond_expr* evaluates to False, the loop terminates. If the body of the loop is a single statement, the begin and end statements are not

▲ required.

The repeat Loop

The repeat loop is nearly identical to the while loop. The distinction between the two is important, though. As you found out in the last exercise, the while loop checks the conditional expression at the top of the loop. In the case of the repeat loop, the conditional expression is checked at the bottom of the loop. For example, here's the previous exercise you did except that a repeat loop has been substituted for the while loop:

```
procedure TForm1.Button1Click(Sender: TObject);
var
  I : Integer;
begin
  I := 5;
  Memo1.Clear;
  repeat
    Memo1.Lines.Add('Today I have ' +
      IntToStr(I) + ' problems to worry about.');
    Dec(I);
  until I = -1;
  Memo1.Lines.Add('Yeah!');
end;
```

This code will result in the same text displayed in the memo as the previous exercise. Note that it is not necessary to use begin and end because the repeat keyword marks the beginning of the code block, and the until keyword marks the end of the code block. Whether you use a while or a repeat loop depends on what the loop itself does.

The `repeat` Loop Statement

```
repeat
    statements;
until cond_expr;
```

The `repeat` loop repeatedly executes the block of code indicated by *statements* as long as the conditional expression *cond_expr* is `False`. The state of the loop must be initialized prior to the `repeat` statement, and modification of the state must be explicit in the block of code. When the conditional expression *cond_expr* evaluates to `True`, the loop terminates.

> **Note**
>
> Due to the way the `repeat` loop works, the code in the body of the loop will be executed at least once regardless of the value of the test condition (because the condition is evaluated at the bottom of the loop). In the case of the `while` loop, the test condition is evaluated at the top of the loop, so the body of the loop might never be executed.

The `goto` Statement

I'll mention `goto` just so you know it exists. The `goto` statement enables you to jump program execution to a label that you have previously declared with the `label` keyword. The label itself is placed in the code followed by a colon. The following code snippet illustrates:

```
procedure TForm1.Button1Click(Sender: TObject);
var
  I: Integer;
label
  MyLabel;
begin
  Memo1.Clear;
  I := 0;
MyLabel:
  Inc(I);
  Memo1.Lines.Add(IntToStr(I));
  if I < 5 then
    goto MyLabel;
end;
```

It is not necessary to use `begin` and `end` here because all lines of code between the `goto` statement and the label will be executed.

> **Note**
>
> The goto statement is considered bad form in an Object Pascal program. Just about anything you can accomplish with goto you can accomplish with a while or repeat loop. Very few self-respecting Object Pascal programmers have goto in their code. If you are moving to Object Pascal from another language that uses goto statements, you will find that the basic structure of Object Pascal makes the goto statement unnecessary.

The goto Statement

```
label
    label_name;

    goto label_name
      .
      .
      .
label_name:
```

The goto statement unconditionally transfers the program execution sequence to the label represented by *label_name*.

Continue and Break Procedures

Before we leave this discussion of loops, you need to know about two procedures that help control program execution in a loop. The Continue procedure is used to force program execution to the bottom of the loop, skipping any statements that come after the call to Continue. For example, you might have part of a loop that you don't want to execute if a particular test returns True. In that case, you would use Continue to avoid execution of any code below that point in the code:

```
var
  Done  : Boolean;
  Error : Boolean;
begin
  Done := False;
  while not Done do begin
    { some code }
    Error := SomeFunction;
    if Error then Continue;  { jumps to the bottom of the loop }
    { other code that will execute only if no error occurred }
  end;
end;
```

The Break procedure is used to halt execution of a loop prior to the loop's normal test condition being met. For example, you might be searching an array of integers for a particular number. By breaking execution of your search loop when the number is found, you can obtain the array index where the number was located:

```
var
  MyArray      : array [0..99] of Integer;
  Index        : Integer;
  SearchNumber : Integer;
  I            : Integer;
begin
  FillArray; { procedure which fills the array }
  Index := -1;
  SearchNumber := 50;
  for I := 0 to High(MyArray) do begin
    if MyArray[I] = SearchNumber then begin
      Index := I;
      Break;
    end;
  end;
  if Index <> -1 then
    Label1.Caption := 'Number found at index ' + IntToStr(Index)
  else
    Label1.Caption := 'Number not found in array.';
end;
```

Continue and Break are only used within for, while, and repeat loops. If you attempt to use these procedures outside of a loop, the compiler will generate a compiler error that says BREAK or CONTINUE outside of loop.

There are many situations in which the Continue and Break procedures are useful. As with most of what I've been talking about, it will take some experience programming in Object Pascal before you discover all the possible uses for these two procedures.

The case Statement

The case statement can be considered a glorified if statement. It enables you to execute one of several code blocks based on the result of an expression. The expression might be a variable, the result of a function call, or any valid Object Pascal code that evaluates to an expression. Here is an example of a case statement:

```
case AmountOverSpeedLimit of
   0 : Fine := 0;
  10 : Fine := 20;
  15 : Fine := 50;
  20,
  25,
  30 : Fine := AmountOverSpeedLimit * 10;
  else begin
    Fine := GoToCourt;
    JailTime := GetSentence;
  end;
end;
```

There are several parts that make up a case statement. First, you can see that there is the expression, which in this example is the variable AmountOverSpeedLimit (remember, I warned you about long variable names!). Next, the case statement tests the expression for equality. If AmountOverSpeedLimit equals 0 (0 :), the value 0 is assigned to the variable Fine. If AmountOverSpeedLimit is equal to 10, a value of 20 is assigned to Fine, and so on. In each of the first three cases a value is assigned to Fine and code execution jumps out of the case statement, which means that a case matching the expression has been found and the rest of the case statement can be ignored.

Notice that cases 20 and 25 have commas following them, but no statements. If the expression AmountOverSpeedLimit evaluates to 20 or 25, those cases fall through and the next code block encountered will be executed. In this situation, values of 20, 25, or 30 will all result in the same code being executed.

Finally, you see the else statement. The code block following the else statement will be executed if no matching cases are found. Inclusion of the else statement is optional. You could write a case statement without an else:

```
case X of
  10 : DoSomething;
  20 : DoAnotherThing;
  30 : TakeABreak;
end;
```

As I said earlier, you might want to use a case statement if you find that you have several if statements back to back. The case statement is a bit clearer to others reading your program.

Note

The expression portion of a case statement must evaluate to an Object Pascal ordinal type (Integer, Word, Byte, and so on). The following, for example, is not allowed:

```
case SomeStringVariable of
  'One' : { code }
  'Two' : { code }
end;
```

String values are not allowed, nor are floating-point values.

▼ SYNTAX

The case Statement

```
case expr of
    value_1: statements_1;
    value_2: statements_2;
    .
    .
```

▼
```
        .
    value_n: statements_n;
else
    else_statements;
end;
```

The case statement offers a way to execute different blocks of code depending on various values of an expression *expr*. The block of code represented by *statements_1* is executed when *expr* is equal to *value_1*, the block of code represented by *statements_2* when *expr* is equal to *value_2*, and so on through the block of code represented by *statements_n* when *expr* is equal to *value_n*. When *expr* is not equal to any of the *value_1* through *value_n*, the block of code at *else_statements* is executed. The else
▲   statement is optional.

Scope

The term scope refers to the visibility of variables within different parts of your program. Most variables have *local scope*, which means that the variable is visible only within the code block in which it is declared. Take a look at the program in Listing 2.1. (This is the first look you've had at a complete unit as generated by Delphi. There is some code here that you haven't seen before, and I'll explain it all in due time, but for the time being you can ignore the parts you aren't familiar with.)

NEW TERM The term *scope* refers to the visibility of variables within different parts of your program.

LISTING 2.1. SCOPEU.PAS.

```
01: unit ScopeU;
02:
03: interface
04:
05: uses
06:   Windows, Messages, SysUtils, Classes, Graphics, Controls, Forms,
      ➥Dialogs,
07:   StdCtrls;
08:
09: type
10:   TForm1 = class(TForm)
11:     Button1: TButton;
12:     Memo1: TMemo;
13:     procedure Button1Click(Sender: TObject);
14:     procedure FormCreate(Sender: TObject);
```

continues

LISTING 2.1. CONTINUED

```
15:    private
16:      { Private declarations }
17:    public
18:      { Public declarations }
19:    end;
20:
21: var
22:    Form1: TForm1;
23:
24: implementation
25:
26: var
27:    X : Integer;
28
29: {$R *.DFM}
30:
31: procedure TForm1.Button1Click(Sender: TObject);
32: var
33:    X : Integer;
34:
35:    procedure Test;
36:    var
37:      X : Integer;
38:    begin
39:      X := 300;
40:      { This X variable has a value of 300. }
41:      Memo1.Lines.Add('Local Function X: ' + IntToStr(X));
42:    end;
43:
44: begin
45:    X := 100;
46:    Memo1.Lines.Clear;
47:    { Local X has a value of 100. }
48:    Memo1.Lines.Add('Local X: ' + IntToStr(X));
49:    { Unit scope X has a value of 200. }
50:    Memo1.Lines.Add('Global X: ' + IntToStr(ScopeU.X));
51:    { Call the Test procedure. }
52:    Test;
53: end;
54:
55: procedure TForm1.FormCreate(Sender: TObject);
56: begin
57:    { Initialize the unit variable X. }
58:    X := 200;
59: end;
60:
61: end.
```

The first thing you might notice (if you're still awake by this time) is that the variable X is declared three times in this program. It is declared on line 27 in the `implementation` section, it is declared on line 33 in the `Button1Click` method, and it is declared on line 37 in a Local Procedure called `Test`. If you accidentally declare a variable more than once, the compiler spits out an error that says `Identifier redeclared: 'X'`, and the compile stops. Yet this program compiles and runs just fine. Why? Because each of the X variables in Listing 2.1 has different scope.

Take a closer look at Listing 2.1. The declaration for X on line 37 is inside the local procedure `Test` and is local to that block of code. (I realize I haven't talked about local functions and procedures yet so I'm getting a bit ahead of myself again. Bear with me; I explain local functions later in the section "Local Functions and Procedures.") Effectively, the X that is declared on line 37 does not exist outside the `Test` procedure. This variable has local scope. Likewise, the declaration for X on line 33 is local to the `Button1Click` method and does not exist outside the function.

Now look at the variable X declared in the `implementation` section. This variable is visible anywhere in this unit. Think about that for a minute. Once inside the `Button1Click` procedure, there are two variables named X (the one declared in the `implementation` section and the one declared in the `Button1Click` method), and both are in scope. Which one is being used? The answer: the one in the `Button1Click` method, because it has the most immediate scope.

The variable X that is declared in the `implementation` section is said to have *unit scope*. What this means is that this variable X is available anywhere in the unit. As mentioned earlier, a local variable has precedence over a variable with unit scope. But what if you want to access the unit variable X from inside the `Button1Click` procedure and not the local variable X? You can *qualify* the variable. Line 50 of Listing 2.1 contains this line:

```
Memo1.Lines.Add('Global X: ' + IntToStr(ScopeU.X));
```

As you can see, the variable X is qualified with the unit name (`ScopeU`) followed by the dot operator. Qualifying the variable with the unit name says, "Give me the unit variable X and not the local variable X." (The dot operator is also used with records and classes, but I'll get to that when I talk about classes later.)

As I said, when the unit variable X is declared in the `implementation` section, it has unit scope. If you want a variable to be available to other units in the project, you should declare the variable in the `interface` section (the variable `Form1` in Listing 2.1 is declared in this way). A variable declared in the `interface` section can be accessed from other units in the project. A variable declared in this way is often referred to as a *global variable*. To access a variable declared in the interface section of a unit requires nothing more than adding the unit to the uses list and accessing the variable as you would any other variable. If any units in the project have variables with the same name, the variables can be qualified with the unit name as described earlier.

Note

> I just said that a variable declared in a unit's interface section is usually referred to as a global variable. That's not entirely accurate, though, because the variable cannot be automatically used by other units in the project—you have to add the unit containing the variable to the uses list of any other unit that wants to use the variable. A true global variable is a variable that can be used by any unit in the program without the need to add the unit containing the variable to the uses list. Delphi has a few global variables set up by the compiler's startup code. You cannot declare true global variables yourself.

Records

A *record* is a collection of related data rolled up into a single storage unit. For instance, let's say you want to keep a mailing list. It would be convenient to use a single data variable to hold all the fields needed in a typical mailing list. A record enables you to do that. You first declare the record and then later create an instance of that record when you want to use the record. A record is declared with the record keyword:

```
MailingListRecord = record
  FirstName : string;
  LastName : string;
  Address : string;
  City : string;
  State : string;
  Zip : Integer;
end;
```

Each of the elements in a record is called a *field*. Notice that each of the fields must be declared just as if it were a variable in a code block. This record example has five string fields and one integer field. (My apologies to my friends around the world if this looks like a U.S.-slanted mailing-list record.) A zip code/postal code field should really be a string as well, but I want to show you a record with more than one data type.

New Term
A *record* is a collection of related data identified as a single storage unit. After a record is declared, an instance of that record can be created for use. Each of the elements in a record is called a *field*.

Note

The record in this example is fine for what I am doing here, but it is not ideal for storing records in files. When you store records in files, each record should be of the exact same size in bytes. Because the record in this example uses long strings as fields, there is no way to guarantee that the records will all be the same size. When creating records that will be stored in a file, you should use short strings or even an array of Char over long strings. I'll talk about this more tomorrow when I discuss file input and output in the section "Dealing with Binary Data."

2

Now that the record is declared, it can be put to use. I first need to create an instance of the record. Here's how that looks:

```
var
  MLRecord : TMailingListRecord;
```

This statement allocates memory for the record and assigns that memory to a variable named Record. Now that I have an instance of the record set up, I can assign values to the fields:

```
MLRecord.FirstName := 'Bruce';
MLRecord.LastName  := 'Reisdorph';
MLRecord.Address   := '123 Inspiration Pt.';
MLRecord.City      := 'Merced';
MLRecord.State     := 'CA';
MLRecord.Zip       := 99999;
```

This code snippet contains some syntax you haven't seen yet (although it is very similar to earlier examples when I was discussing qualifying variables). To access the fields of a record, you need to employ the *structure member selector* operator, commonly called the dot operator. The dot operator is a period placed between the variable name and the field name. If you forget to add the record member operator, you will probably find the compiler complaining about undefined symbols. The record member operator enables you to access a particular member of the record—either to read the value of the field or to change the value of the field. Here's an example of placing the contents of a particular field in a record into an label on a form:

```
Label1.Caption := MLRecord.LastName;
```

The `record` Statement

▼ SYNTAX

```
name = record
    field_1 : data_type;
    field_2 : data_type;
        .
        .
        .
    field_n : data_type;
end;
```

▲ The `record` statement declares a grouping of fields (*field_1*, *field_2*, ..., *field_n*) and provides a name for this grouping (*name*).

The `with` Statement

As long as I am talking about records, let me introduce the `with` statement. Use of the `with` statement is not limited to records, but this is a good place to illustrate how the `with` statement is used. Earlier I gave you this example of filling in a structure:

```
MLRecord.FirstName  := 'Bruce';
MLRecord.LastName   := 'Reisdorph';
MLRecord.Address    := '123 Inspiration Pt.';
MLRecord.City       := 'Merced';
MLRecord.State      := 'CA';
MLRecord.Zip        := 99999;
```

The `with` statement can be used to help simplify this code. Here is the same code, but implementing the `with` statement:

```
with MLRecord do begin
  FirstName := 'Bruce';
  LastName  := 'Reisdorph';
  Address   := '123 Inspiration Pt.';
  City      := 'Merced';
  State     := 'CA';
  Zip       := 99999;
end;
```

The `with` statement says, "With this object (`MLRecord`) do the following...." Notice that when the `with` statement is implemented, you no longer have to qualify the field names with the record identifier and dot operator. Everything within the `begin` and `end` blocks is assumed to belong to the `MLRecord` object, so qualifying the field names is unnecessary. The `with` statement can save you a lot of typing and can also make the code more readable.

Arrays of Records

Just as you can have arrays of Integers, Chars, or Words, you can also have arrays of records. Declaring and using an array of records is not terribly complicated:

```
var
  MLRecord : array [0..9] of MailingListRecord;
begin
  MLRecord[0].FirstName := 'Bruce';
  MLRecord[0].LastName  := 'Reisdorph';
  MLRecord[0].Address   := '123 Inspiration Pt.';
  MLRecord[0].City      := 'Merced';
  MLRecord[0].State     := 'CA';
  MLRecord[0].Zip       := 99999;

  MLRecord[1].FirstName := 'Georgia';
  MLRecord[2].LastName  := 'Burleson';
  MLRecord[3].Address   := '999 Fortitude';
  MLRecord[4].City      := 'Denver';
  MLRecord[5].State     := 'CO';
  MLRecord[6].Zip       := 80888;

  Label1.Caption := MLRecord[0].LastName;
  { More code here. }
end;
```

This is only slightly more complicated than using an array of one of the integral data types. You will notice that the subscript operator and the record member operator are used together to retrieve the value of a field from a specific position in the array.

Include Files

Sometimes Pascal programmers use include files. An include file can contain any code that you don't want in your main source unit. Typically, use of include files is reserved for constants or compiler directives that are intended to be used by many other files in the project. An include file is nothing more than a text file with and extension of .INC. The INC extension is not a requirement, but it is customary. Listing 2.2 shows an example of an include file.

LISTING 2.2. TEST.INC.

```
const
  DefWidth  = 500;
  DefHeight = 300;
```

continues

LISTING 2.2. CONTINUED

```
type
  MailingListRecord = record
    FirstName : string;
    LastName : string;
    Address : string;
    City : string;
    State : string;
    Zip : Integer;
  end;
```

To create an include file, you simply start with a new text file and save it with an exten-
sion of INC. First, choose File | New from the main menu. Next, double-click on the Text
icon in the New Items dialog. A new text file will be created and opened in the Code
Editor. Enter code and then save the file by choosing File | Save As from the main menu.
Be sure to give the file an INC extension or the file will be saved with a TXT extension by
default.

To use an include file, you use the $I compiler directive in any other units that need to
use the declarations in the include file. It looks like this:

```
unit Unit2;

interface

uses
  Windows, Messages, SysUtils, Classes, Graphics, Controls, Forms,
  Dialogs,
  StdCtrls;

{$I Test.inc}

{ ... rest of unit follows }
```

The $I compiler directive tells the compiler to compile the contents of the include file
into the unit at that point. It's as if the include file were pasted into the unit at that point.
You need to be sure that any code in the include file is syntactically correct, or a compiler error will be generated. Don't be too concerned if this is a little confusing right now. It
will probably take some experience writing real programs for all this to come together
for you.

Functions, Procedures, and Methods

Functions and procedures are sections of code separate from the main program. These
code sections are executed when needed to perform specific actions in a program. For

example, you might have a function that takes two values, performs a complex mathematical calculation on those two values, and returns the result. You might need a function that takes a string, parses it, and returns a portion of the parsed string. You can call (use) these functions any time throughout your programs.

Functions and procedures can collectively be called *subroutines*. (While the term subroutine is not commonly used in Pascal, it is a convenient word to cover both functions and procedures, so I'll use it here.) Subroutines are an important part of any programming language, and Object Pascal is no exception. The simplest type of subroutine takes no parameters and returns no value. Other subroutines might take one or more parameters and might return a value. Rules for naming functions and procedures are the same as those discussed earlier for variables.

NEW TERM A *function* is a section of code separate from the main program that performs some action and returns a value.

NEW TERM A *parameter* is a value passed to a function or procedure that is used to alter its operation or indicate the extent of its operation.

Figure 2.2 shows the anatomy of a function.

FIGURE 2.2.

The anatomy of a function.

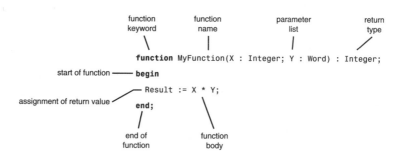

NEW TERM A *procedure* is a section of code separate from the main program that performs some action but does not return a value.

Figure 2.3 shows the anatomy of a procedure.

NEW TERM A *method* is a function or procedure that is a member of a class.

As you can see from these descriptions, the only difference between a function and a procedure is that a function returns a value and a procedure does not return a value.

FIGURE 2.3.

*The anatomy of a pro-
cedure.*

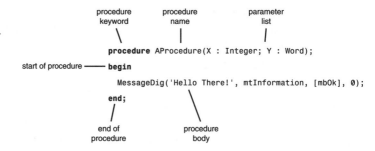

```
                    procedure      procedure      parameter
                     keyword         name            list
                        \            |              |
                     procedure APprocedure(X : Integer; Y : Word);
start of procedure ——— begin
                          MessageDlg('Hello There!', mtInformation, [mbOk], 0);
                     end;
                     /                            \
                   end of                        procedure
                  procedure                        body
```

Let's write a program that uses a function. Once again, start with a new application.
Then perform the following steps:

1. Place a button component and a label component on the form.

2. Double-click the button to create an OnClick event handler.

3. Use the up-arrow key on the keyboard to move the editing cursor above the event
   handler just created.

4. Type the following function in the Code Editor:

   ```
   function Multiply(Num1, Num2 : Integer) : Integer;
   begin
     Result := Num1 * Num2;
   end;
   ```

   Your Code Editor should now look similar to Figure 2.4.

FIGURE 2.4.

*The Code Editor
showing the Multiply
function.*

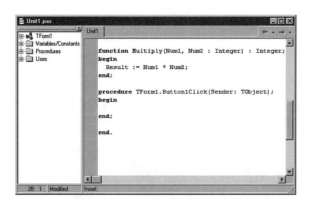

5. Move back down to the OnClick event handler and type code until the event handler looks like this:

   ```
   procedure TForm1.Button1Click(Sender: TObject);
   var
   ```

```
    X : Integer;
  begin
    X := Multiply(10, 20);
    Label1.Caption := IntToStr(X);
  end;
```

Run the program and click the button. The label will change to 200 when you click the button. Here's how it works: When you click the button, the Button1Click event handler is called. This, in turn, calls the Multiply function, passing the values of 10 and 20 as parameters. The result is stored in the variable X, which is then displayed in the label.

Note

This example illustrates the use of a standalone function in a Delphi program. I normally would have made this function part of the main form's class, but because we haven't talked about classes yet I would be getting ahead of myself by using that technique here.

You might be thinking, "Okay, but how does the product of the two numbers get back from the function?" Take another look at the Multiply function:

```
function Multiply(Num1, Num2 : Integer) : Integer;
begin
  Result := Num1 * Num2;
end;
```

Every Object Pascal function has a local variable called Result. This variable is declared invisibly by the compiler, and it is used to hold the return value from the function. To return a specific value from a function, then, is a simple matter of assigning that value to the Result variable within the function.

Note

There is another way of specifying the return value for a function. Rather than assigning the return value to the Result variable, you assign the return value to the function name. For example:

```
function Multiply(Num1, Num2 : Integer) : Integer;
begin
  Multiply := Num1 * Num2;
end;
```

You might see this method used in older Pascal programs or in programs ported to Delphi from Turbo Pascal (one of Delphi's predecessors).

The Multiply function can be called in one of several ways. You can pass variables, literal values, or even the results of other function calls. For example:

```
X := Multiply(2, 5);    { passing literal values }
X := Multiply(A, B);    { passing variables }
{ return value used as a parameter for another function }
Label1.Caption := IntToStr(Multiply(X, Y));
Multiply(X, Y);            { return value ignored }
```

Notice in the preceding example that the return value is not used. In this case, it doesn't make much sense to call the Multiply function and ignore the return value, but ignoring the return value is something that is done frequently in Object Pascal programming. There are many functions that perform a specific action and then return a value indicating the status of the function call. In some cases the return value is not relevant to your program, so you can just ignore it. If you don't do anything with the return value, it is simply discarded and no harm is done.

Now let's add a procedure to the program by following these steps:

1. Double-click the button on your form. The OnClick event handler is displayed just as you left it.

2. Move the editing cursor up a few lines so that it is between the Multiply function and the OnClick event handler. Type the following code:

```
procedure SayHello;
begin
  MessageDlg('Hello There!', mtInformation, [mbOk], 0);
end;
```

3. Move down a few lines and add one line of code to the end of the OnClick event handler so that it looks like this:

```
procedure TForm1.Button1Click(Sender: TObject);
var
  X : Integer;
begin
  X := Multiply(10, 20);
  Label1.Caption := IntToStr(X);
  SayHello;
end;
```

Now run the program again. This time when you run the program, the result of the Multiply function is shown in the label as before, and then a message box appears. The message box is shown as a result of calling the SayHello procedure. Calling the SayHello procedure is extremely simple because the procedure takes no parameters. It's important to understand that the code in a function or procedure is executed only if you specifically call the function or procedure from somewhere in your code.

Any time you find yourself repeating code more than a couple of times in your programs, think about moving that code to a subroutine. Then you can call the subroutine when you need to execute that code.

Subroutines can (and frequently do) call other subroutines. Subroutines can even call themselves. This is called *recursion* and is one way to get into trouble when programming! Recursion is best left alone until you've put in some time with the Object Pascal language.

NEW TERM *Recursion* is the process by which a procedure or function calls itself.

Declaration and Definition

Functions and procedures often have a declaration and always have a definition.

NEW TERM A *declaration* is a single statement that describes a method's name and parameters, if any. In the case of a function, the declaration also indicates the function's return type.

NEW TERM A function or procedure's *definition* is the actual body of the function or procedure in the `implementation` section of the unit.

There are three primary cases where a declaration is necessary:

- When the function or procedure will be used by other units.
- When the function or procedure definition falls below the place in the code where that function or procedure is called.
- When the function or procedure is a member of a class.

I haven't used declarations up to this point, only definitions. This is because the function definition always came before the place in the code where the function was actually used. Take the `Multiply` function, for example. If I had written a function declaration for this function, it would look like this:

```
function Multiply(Num1, Num2 : Integer) : Integer;
```

As you can see, the function declaration simply describes the function.

Function and procedure declarations are placed in the `interface` section. Placing a declaration in the `interface` section automatically makes that function or procedure available to other units (makes it public, so to speak). If you don't want the function or procedure to be visible to other units, you can't use a declaration. Instead, you will have to make sure that the function or procedure is defined near the top of the `interface` section so that it can be seen by all other methods in the unit that use the function. As I said, the examples of functions and procedures up to this point have used this method. I could have done it the other way and used both declaration and definition. Here's part of a unit that contains a declaration for the `Multiply` function, a `Button1Click` method that calls the `Multiply` function, and the definition of the `Multiply` function:

```
unit Unit1;

interface

{ some code removed... }

function Multiply(Num1, Num2 : Integer) : Integer;

implementation

procedure TForm1.Button1Click(Sender: TObject);
var
  X : Integer;
begin
  X := Multiply(10, 20);
end;

function Multiply(Num1, Num2 : Integer) : Integer;
begin
  Result := Num1 * Num2;
end;

end.
```

In this case the declaration is necessary because the `Multiply` function is defined *after* the `Button1Click` method that calls it. The declaration tells the compiler that a function can be found later in the unit. You'll learn more about function declarations tomorrow when we talk about methods in classes.

 Note   If you declare a function but neglect to define it, the compiler will issue an error that says, `Unsatisfied forward or external declaration: 'Multiply.'`

Value, Constant, and Reference Parameters

Parameters to functions or procedures can be of at least three different types (more than three, actually, but I'll only discuss three types here).

Value Parameters

First, parameters can be *value parameters*. All the parameters you have seen up to this point have been value parameters. The value parameter acts like a local variable in the function or procedure. You can modify the variable within the function and the original variable will remain unchanged. Let's create a new function that illustrates the point. This function will be called SquareAndMultiply. It will take two numbers, square them, multiply them together, and return the result. Here it is:

```
function SquareAndMultiply(Num1, Num2 : Integer) : Integer;
begin
  Num1 := Num1 * Num1;
  Num2 := Num2 * Num2;
  Result := Num1 * Num2;
end;
```

Now let's look at the code that will call this function:

```
procedure TForm1.Button1Click(Sender: TObject);
var
  X : Integer;
  Y : Integer;
  Z : Integer;
begin
  X := 2;
  Y := 3;
  Z := SquareAndMultiply(X, Y);
  Label1.Caption := IntToStr(Z);
end;
```

If you want, you can enter this code to test it out. Two values are passed to SquareAndMultiply. The two values are modified inside the SquareAndMultiply function because the numbers need to be squared before they are multiplied together. However, the original values of X and Y in the Button1Click method do not change. When a function uses a value parameter, the compiler first makes a copy of the variable passed to the function and then sends the copy to the function. The original variable is unchanged because the copy is sent to the function and not the actual variable.

Constant Parameters

Another way to send values to functions is to use *constant parameters*. A constant parameter cannot be changed inside the function body. Here's an example of a procedure that takes a constant parameter:

```
procedure SaySomething(const S : string);
begin
  S := S + 'Test';
  ShowMessage(S);
end;
```

This is one of the few code examples in this book that contains an error (I hope!). The compiler will issue an error on the first line in this procedure. The compiler error will say, Left side cannot be assigned to. The error is generated because the const keyword stipulates that the variable S cannot be modified. Any attempts to modify the constant parameter will result in a compiler error. Write procedures and functions using constant parameters when you don't want the passed variable to be modified within the function.

Reference Parameters

A third way to send values to functions is to use *reference parameters*. When you use a reference parameter, the compiler does not make a copy of the object as it does when using value parameters. Rather, the actual variable is passed. This means that any changes made to the variable in the function or procedure will modify the original variable. The following is an example of a procedure that uses a reference parameter (both the procedure and the use of the procedure are shown):

```
procedure Square(var Number : Integer);
begin
  Number := Number * Number;
end;

procedure TForm1.Button1Click(Sender: TObject);
var
  X : Integer;
begin
  X := 20;
  Square(X);
  Label1.Caption := IntToStr(X);
end;
```

First look at the Square procedure. Notice that the variable parameter is designated by using the var keyword. Because the var keyword is used to declare reference parameters, those parameters are commonly called *var parameters*. I'll use the terms interchangeably in this section.

Note

Many Object Pascal keywords do double duty. In this case, the var keyword is used to declare a reference parameter. Previously you have seen the var keyword used to declare variables in a function, procedure, or unit. The compiler knows the context in which the keyword is being used and therefore knows how to compile the code correctly.

Notice also that the body of the function modifies the variable Number by multiplying it times itself. Next, notice the code in the Button1Click method that calls Square. First the variable X is assigned a value. Next, that variable is passed to the Square procedure. After Square executes, the value of X will be 400. Because Square takes a variable parameter, the variable passed to the procedure (X in this case) will be modified. Use variable parameters when you want the procedure or function to make some change to a variable. The fact that an object can be modified by the function or procedure is the most important aspect of variable parameters.

Because Square uses a variable parameter you must pass a variable of the same type as the variable parameter. You cannot, for example, do this:

```
Square(30);
```

This code will generate a compiler error because you can't pass a literal value for a variable parameter. This won't compile either:

```
var
  X : Word;
begin
  X := 20;
  Square(X);
```

In this case, X is declared as a Word, and the variable parameter of the Square procedure is declared as an Integer. The compiler will generate an error because the types don't match. The compile error generated is Types of actual and formal var parameters must be identical.

Tip

Remember that a function can return only one value. By using variable parameters, you can achieve the effect of a function returning more than one value. The function still returns only one value, but the objects passed by reference are updated, so the function effectively returns multiple values.

Local Functions and Procedures

A local function or procedure is a subroutine that is contained within another subroutine. Here's an example:

```
procedure TForm1.Button1Click(Sender: TObject);
var
  X : Integer;

  { A local procedure. }
  procedure Test;
```

```
begin
  Memo1.Lines.Add('Local Function, X = ' + IntToStr(X));
end;

begin
  X := 100;
  Memo1.Lines.Clear;
  Memo1.Lines.Add('Main Function, X = ' + IntToStr(X));
  Test;
end;
```

Note that the procedure called `Test` is contained within the var section of the
`Button1Click` procedure. A procedure declared in this way is called a local procedure
because it is local to the function or procedure in which it is contained. A local subroutine can be called only from the containing routine; it cannot be called from anywhere
else in the program.

An important fact of local procedures and functions is that the variables of the containing
procedure are available inside the local subroutine. In this example, the variable `X` is
available in the main body of the `Button1Click` procedure *and* in the local procedure.
When this code executes, the memo component will contain this text:

```
Main Function, X = 100
Local Function, X = 100
```

This illustrates that the variable `X` is available in the local procedure as well as in the
main procedure.

Method Overloading

Starting with Delphi 4, Object Pascal enables you to work with functions that have the
same name but take different parameters.

 Method overloading is having two or more procedures or functions with the
same name but with different parameter lists.

Methods that share a common name are called *overloaded methods*.

Earlier I showed you a sample program that contained a function called `Multiply`. Not
surprisingly, this function multiplied two values together. The function took two integers,
multiplied them, and returned the result. What if you want to have the function multiply
two `Doubles` or two `Words`? Previous versions of Delphi would require you to have several functions:

```
{ declarations for a program written in Delphi 1, 2, or 3 }
function MultiplyInt(Num1, Num2 : Integer) : Integer;
function MultiplyDouble(Num1, Num2 : Double) : Double;
function MultiplyWord(Num1, Num2 : Word) : Word;
```

Wouldn't it be a lot easier if you could just have one function called `Multiply` that would be smart enough to know whether you wanted to multiply `Integers`, `Doubles`, or `Words`? That is now possible in Delphi thanks to function overloading. Here's what the declarations for an overloaded function look like:

```
{ declarations in Delphi 4 }
function Multiply(Num1, Num2 : Integer) : Integer; overload;
function Multiply(Num1, Num2 : Double) : Double; overload;
function Multiply(Num1, Num2 : Word) : Word; overload;
```

You still have to write separate functions for each of these declarations, but at least you can use the same function name. The compiler takes care of calling the correct function based on the parameters you pass to the function. For example:

```
var
  X, Y, Z : Double;
begin
  X := 1.5;
  Y := 10.5;
  Z := Multiply(X, Y);
end;
```

The compiler sees that two `Doubles` are passed to the function and calls the version of the `Multiply` function that takes two `Doubles` for parameters. Likewise, if two `Integers` are passed, the compiler calls the version of `Multiply` that takes two `Integers`.

Note

It is the parameter list that makes overloaded functions work. You can vary either the type or the number of parameters a function takes (or both), but you cannot create an overloaded function by changing just the return value. For example, the following does not constitute an overloaded function:

```
function DoSomething : Integer; overload;
function DoSomething : Word; overload;
```

If you try to compile a program containing these lines, you will get a compiler error that says `Declaration of 'DoSomething' differs from previous declaration`. The two functions need to vary by more than just the return value to qualify as overloaded functions.

Default Parameters for Functions

 NEW TERM   A procedure or function can have *default parameters* that, as the name implies, supply a default value for a parameter if no value is specified when the procedure or function is called.

A function implementing a default parameter might look like this:

```
{ Procedure declaration. }
{ Parameter 'EraseFirst' will be false by default. }
procedure Redraw(EraseFirst : Boolean = False);

{ Procedure definition. }
procedure Redraw(EraseFirst : Boolean);
begin
  if (EraseFirst) then begin
    { erase code }
  end;
  { drawing code }
end;
```

You can call this function with or without a parameter. If the parameter is supplied at the time the function is called, the function behaves as a regular function would. If the parameter is not supplied when the function is called, the default parameter is used automatically. Given this example, the following two lines of code are identical:

```
Redraw;
Redraw(False);
```

As you can see, when a parameter has a default value, it can be omitted from the function call altogether.

When declaring functions and procedures, you can mix default and nondefault parameters in the same function:

```
{ declaration }
function PlayWaveFile(Name : string;
  Loop : Boolean = False; Loops : Integer = 10) : Integer;

{ calls to PlayWaveFile }
R := PlayWaveFile('chime.wav');            { does not loop sound }
R := PlayWaveFile('ding.wav', True);       { plays sound 10 times }
R := PlayWaveFile('bell.wave', True, 5); { plays sound 5 times }
```

Default parameters are helpful for many reasons. For one thing, they make your life easier. You might have a function that you call with the same parameters 99 percent of the time. By giving it default parameters, you shorten the amount of typing required each time you make a call to the function. Whenever you want to supply parameters other than the defaults, all you have to do is plug in values for the default parameters.

Note

Any default parameters must come at the end of the function's parameter list. The following is not a valid function declaration:

```
procedure MyProcedure(X : Integer; Y : Integer = 10; Z :
Integer);
```

In order for this function declaration to compile, the default parameter
must be moved to the end of the function list:

```
procedure MyProcedure(X : Integer; Z : Integer; Y : Integer =
10);
```

If you don't put the default parameters at the end of the parameter list, the
compiler will generate an error message.

Summary

This chapter contains essential information on some of Object Pascal's basic operations.
You need to understand what is presented here in order to program in Delphi. First, you
learned about the different types of loops in Object Pascal, and then you learned about
the case statement and how to use it. I talked a little about scope and what that means to
your variables. Then you found out about records and how they can be used in your programs. You finished the day by learning about functions and procedures.

Workshop

The Workshop contains quiz questions to help you solidify your understanding of the
material covered and exercises to provide you with experience in using what you have
learned. You can find answers to the quiz questions in Appendix A, "Answers to the Quiz
Questions."

Q&A

Q How many levels deep can I nest if statements?

A There's no limit. There is, however, a practical limit. If you have too many nested
if statements, it gets very hard to keep it all straight!

Q Will loops automatically terminate if something goes wrong?

A No. If you accidentally write an endless loop, that loop will continue to run until
you do something to stop it. You can stop a program stuck in an endless loop by
bringing up the Windows Task Manager (or the Close Program box) and ending the
errant task. If you executed the program from the Delphi IDE, you can choose Run|
Program Reset from the main menu to kill the program.

Q Does a `case` statement have to include an `else` section?

A No. The `else` section is optional.

Q Can I have more than one variable with the same name?

A Yes, provided they are in different scopes. For example, you can have a global variable named `X` and a local variable with the same name.

Q Why have overloaded procedures and functions?

A Overloaded functions provide a means by which you can have several functions that perform the same basic operation and use the same function name but take different parameters. For example, you might have an overloaded function called `DrawObject`. One version might take a `Circle` class as a parameter, another might take a `Square` class as a parameter, and a third might take a class called `Polygon` as a parameter. By having three functions with the same name, you avoid the need to have three different function names.

Q Can I use a record by itself without creating an instance of the record?

A No. Before you can use a record, you have to create an instance of the record and access the record through the instance variable.

Quiz

1. What statements are executed in the event an `if` expression evaluates to `True`?
2. How many return values can a function return?
3. Besides syntax, what is the difference between a `while` loop and a `repeat` loop?
4. What do the `Break` and `Continue` procedures do?
5. What is a global variable?
6. Can a record contain a mixture of data types (`Char`, `Integer`, `Word`, and so on)?
7. How do you access the members of a record?
8. How many functions or procedures can a program have?
9. Can a function call another function or procedure?
10. Is it legal to have arrays of records?

Exercises

1. Write a procedure called `Test2` that changes the caption of a `Label` component. Put a button on a form and have the button's `OnClick` handler call the `Test2` procedure.
2. Take the program from exercise 1 and create another procedure called `Test1` that, in turn, calls the `Test2` procedure. Change the event handler of the button so that it calls `Test1` rather than `Test2`.

3. Create a program that displays I will never talk back to my mother 20 times in a Memo component.

4. Write a record containing fields representing employee information. Include first name, last name, address, hire date, and a field indicating whether the employee is in the company's insurance plan.

2

DAY **3**

Classes and Object-Oriented Programming

Today you get to the good stuff. In this chapter you will learn about classes. Classes are the heart of Object Pascal and a major part of object-oriented programming. Classes are also the heart of the Visual Component Library (VCL), which you will use when you start writing real Windows applications. (The VCL is discussed in detail on Day 5, "The Visual Component Model.") Today you will find out what a class is and how it's expected to be used. Along the way you will learn the meaning of Object Pascal buzzwords like *inheritance*, *object*, and *data abstraction*. Before you get to that, however, I want to cover a few more aspects of Object Pascal that I haven't yet covered.

Sets

Sets are used frequently throughout Delphi, so you need to know what sets are and how they work.

NEW TERM   A *set* is a collection of values of one type.

That description doesn't say too much, does it? An example that comes to mind is the Style property of a VCL font object. This property can include one or more of the following values:

- fsBold
- fsItalic
- fsUnderline
- fsStrikeout

A font can have any combination of these styles or none of them at all. A set of font styles, then, might have none of these values, it could have all of them, or it could have any combination.

So how do you use a set? Let me use the Style property to illustrate. Typically, you turn the individual Style values for the font on or off at design time. Sometimes, however, you need to set the font's Style property at runtime. For example, let's say that you want to add the bold and italic attributes to the font style. One way is to declare a variable of type TFontStyles and then add the fsBold and fsItalic styles to the set. Here's how it looks:

```
var
  Styles : TFontStyles;
begin
  Styles := Styles + [fsBold, fsItalic];
end;
```

This code adds the elements fsBold and fsItalic to the Styles set. The elements are enclosed in brackets to indicate that you are adding elements to the set. The brackets, when used in this way, are called a *set constructor*. Notice that this code doesn't actually change a font's style; it just creates a set and adds two elements to it. To change a font's style, you have to assign this newly created set to the Font.Style property of some component:

```
Memo.Font.Style = Styles;
```

Now, let's say that you want the font to be bold but not italic. In that case, you have to remove the italic style from the set:

```
Styles := Styles - [fsItalic];
```

The style now contains only the fsBold value because the fsItalic value has been removed.

Often you want to know whether a particular item is in a set. Let's say you want to know whether the font is currently set to bold. You can find out whether the `fsBold` element is in the set by using the `in` keyword:

```
if fsBold in Styles then
  DoSomething;
```

Sometimes you need to make sure you are starting with an empty set. You can clear a set of its contents by assigning an empty set to a set variable. This is done with an empty set constructor—for example,

```
{ start with an empty set }
Styles := [];
{ now add the bold and italic styles }
Styles := Styles + [fsBold, fsItalic];
```

In this example the font style is cleared of all contents, and then the bold and italic styles are added. This same thing can be accomplished in a slightly different way by just assigning directly to a set:

```
Styles := [fsBold, fsItalic];
```

You don't specifically have to create a TFontStyles variable to change a font's style. You can just work with the property directly—for example,

```
Memo.Font.Style := [];
Memo.Font.Style := Memo.Font.Style + [fsBold, fsItalic];
```

A set is declared using the `set` keyword. The TFontStyles property is declared in the VCL source file GRAPHICS.PAS like this:

```
TFontStyle = (fsBold, fsItalic, fsUnderline, fsStrikeOut);
TFontStyles = set of TFontStyle;
```

The first line here declares an enumeration type called TFontStyle. (An *enumeration* is a list of possible values.) The second line creates the TFontStyles set as a set of TFontStyle values.

Sets are used often in VCL and in Delphi programming. Many component properties are defined as sets. You'll get the hang of sets quickly as you work with Delphi.

Casting

NEW TERM *Cast* means to tell the compiler to treat one data type as if it were a different type. Another term for cast is *typecast*.

Here's an example of a Char data type typecast to an Integer:

```
procedure TForm1.Button1Click(Sender: TObject);
var
  AChar : Char;
  AnInteger : Integer;
begin
  AChar := 'A';
  AnInteger := Integer(AChar);
  Label1.Caption := IntToStr(AnInteger);
end;
```

In this example, the cast Integer(AChar) tells the compiler to convert the value of AChar to an Integer data type. The cast is necessary because you can't assign the value of a Char data type to an Integer type. If you attempt to make the assignment without the cast, the compiler will issue an error that reads Incompatible types: 'Integer' and 'Char'.

By the way, when the preceding code executes, the label will display the text 65 (65 is the integer value of the character A).

It is not always possible to cast one data type to another. Take this code, for example:

```
procedure TForm1.Button1Click(Sender: TObject);
var
  Pi : Double;
  AnInteger : Integer;
begin
  Pi := 3.14;
  AnInteger := Integer(Pi);
  Label1.Caption := IntToStr(AnInteger);
end;
```

In this case, I am trying to cast a Double to an Integer. This is not a valid cast, so the compiler will issue an error that reads Invalid typecast. To convert a floating-point value to an integer value, use the Trunc, Floor, or Ceil functions. These functions do just as their names indicate, so I don't need to explain further. See the Delphi help for more information on these functions.

Pointers can be cast from one type to another using the as operator. (Pointers are discussed in the next section.) I'll discuss the as operator later in the section "Class Keywords: is and as."

Pointers

Pointers are one of the most confusing aspects of the Object Pascal language. So what is a pointer? It's a variable that holds the address of another variable. There, that wasn't so bad, was it? I wish it were that simple! Because a pointer holds the address of another variable, it is said to "point to" the second variable. This is called *indirection* because the pointer does not have a direct association with the actual data, but rather an indirect association.

NEW TERM A *pointer* is a variable that holds the address of another variable.

Let's look at an example. Let's say you have a record, and you need to pass the address of that record to a procedure requiring a pointer. You take the address of a record instance using the @ operator. Here's how it looks:

```
var
  MLRecord : TMailingListRecord;
APtr : Pointer;
begin
  { Fill MLRecord with data. }
  APtr := @MLRecord;
  SomeFunction(APtr);
end;
```

The APtr variable (which is of type Pointer) is used to hold the memory address of the MLRecord record. This type of pointer is called an *untyped pointer* because the Pointer data type simply holds a memory address. Another type of pointer is a pointer that is declared as a pointer to a specific type of object. For example, let's say that you create a new type, a pointer to TMailingListRecord record. The declaration would look like this:

```
type
  PMailingListRecord = ^TMailingListRecord;
  TMailingListRecord = record
    FirstName : string;
    LastName : string;
    Address : string;
    City : string;
    State : string;
    Zip : Integer;
  end;
```

The type PMailingListRecord is declared as a pointer to a TMailingListRecord. You will often see records and their corresponding pointers declared in this way. You might be wondering what the point is (no pun intended). Let's go on to the next section and I'll show you one way pointers are used.

Note

I almost never use long strings in records as I have done here with the TMailingListRecord. I usually use an array of Char rather than a long string. The reason for this is that long strings are dynamically allocated and are not a fixed size. Fixed-size fields are important if you are writing records to disk. I used long strings in the case of TMailingListRecord because I didn't want to muddy the waters with a discussion on fixed-length records at this point in the book.

Local Versus Dynamic Memory Usage

Yesterday when you read about records, I showed you some examples. All of those examples used local allocation of objects. That is, the memory required for the record variable was obtained from the program's stack.

NEW TERM *Local allocation* means that the memory required for a variable or object is obtained from the program's stack.

NEW TERM The *stack* is an area of working memory set aside by the program when the program starts.

Any memory the program needs for things such as local variables, function calls, and so on is taken from the program's stack. This memory is allocated as needed and then freed when it is no longer needed; usually this happens when the program enters a function or other local code block. Memory for any local variables the function uses is allocated when the function is entered. When the function returns, all the memory allocated for the function's use is freed. It all happens for you automatically; you don't have to give any thought to how the memory is freed or whether the memory is freed at all.

Local allocation has its good points and its bad points. On the plus side, memory can be allocated from the stack very quickly. The negative side is that the stack is a fixed size and cannot be changed as the program runs. If your program runs out of stack space, weird things start to happen. Your program might crash, it might start behaving oddly, or it might seem to perform normally but crash when the program terminates. This is less of a problem in the 32-bit world than in 16-bit programming, but it's still a consideration.

For things like variables of the built-in data types and small arrays, there is no point in doing anything other than local allocation. But if you are going to be using large records, you will probably want to use dynamic allocation from the heap. The heap amounts to your computer's free physical RAM plus all your free hard disk space. In other words, you can easily have 100MB of heap memory available on a typical Windows system. The good news here is that you have virtually unlimited memory available for your programs. The bad news is that memory allocated dynamically requires some additional overhead and, as such, is just a smidgen slower than memory allocated from the stack. In most programs the extra overhead is not noticed in the least. An additional drawback of dynamic allocation is that it requires more from the programmer—not a lot more, mind you, but a little.

NEW TERM *Dynamic allocation* means that memory required for an object is allocated from the heap.

NEW TERM The *heap* in a Windows program refers to all of your computer's virtual memory.

Dynamic Allocation and Pointers

In an Object Pascal program, memory can be allocated dynamically in several different ways. Perhaps the best way is to use the `AllocMem` function. `AllocMem` allocates memory and fills the allocated memory with zeros. (Other ways to dynamically allocate memory include the `GetMem` procedure and the `New` function.) All things considered, `AllocMem` probably provides the best way of allocating memory dynamically. Let's go back to the `TMailingListRecord` record. In previous examples, I allocated memory for one of these records from the stack like this:

```
var
  MLRecord : TMailingListRecord;
begin
  { Fill MLRecord with data. }
  MLRecord.FirstName := 'Per';
  MLRecord.LastName  := 'Larsen';
  { etc. }
end;
```

Now I'll create the record dynamically rather than locally:

```
var
  APtr : PMailingListRecord;
begin
  APtr := AllocMem(SizeOf(TMailingListRecord));
APtr.FirstName := 'Per';
  APtr.LastName  := 'Larsen';
  { Do some other things. }
  FreeMem(APtr);
end;
```

Notice that this time I declare a `PMailingListRecord` (a pointer to a `TMailingListRecord`) rather than a `TMailingListRecord` itself. Also notice that I allocate memory for the structure by calling the `AllocMem` function. The parameter passed to `AllocMem` is the amount of memory to allocate. The `SizeOf` function returns the size of the record, so I use that function to determine how much memory to allocate. The call to `AllocMem` allocates memory and initializes the pointer by creating a new instance of a `TMailingListRecord` dynamically. After the memory has been allocated, you can use the pointer variable just as you do a regular variable. Finally, notice that after I am done with the object, I free the memory associated with the object by using the `FreeMem` procedure. Failure to call `FreeMem` to free dynamically allocated objects will result in a program that leaks memory (uses up memory that it never releases).

> **Note**
>
> Dynamic allocation of memory for records and arrays is optional. It is mandatory for classes. I'll discuss that in just a bit when I talk about classes.

This is the process by which you dynamically create and access records in Object Pascal. You probably won't use dynamic allocation very much, but sometimes it's necessary, so you should know how it's done.

> **Note**
>
> The `nil` keyword is used to specify a pointer that has no value. If you want to clear a pointer of its value, you use the `nil` keyword like this:
>
> ```
> SomePointer := nil;
> ```
>
> You can also use `nil` to test a pointer to see whether it has been allocated:
>
> ```
> if SomePointer = nil then
>  SomePointer := AllocMem(Size);
> ```
>
> This code checks a pointer to see whether it has been assigned a value. If it hasn't been assigned a value, then memory is allocated for the pointer.

Dereferencing a Pointer

Sometimes you need to dereference a pointer.

NEW TERM *Dereferencing* a pointer means retrieving the object that the pointer points to.

Let's say that you dynamically created a mailing list record as described earlier. Now you want to assign the contents of that mailing list record to another mailing list record variable that was allocated from the stack. Here's what you have so far:

```
var
  APtr : PMailingListRecord;
  Rec  : TMailingListRecord;
begin
  APtr := AllocMem(SizeOf(TMailingListRecord));
```

Now let's say you want to copy the contents of APtr to the Rec variable. The APtr variable is a pointer to a TMailingListRecord and the Rec variable is a TMailingListRecord. You might try this:

```
Rec := APtr;
```

That won't work, however, because APtr contains a memory address, not a TMailingListRecord. In order to make this assignment, you have to dereference the pointer by using the pointer operator (^). It looks like this:

```
Rec := APtr^;
```

When you dereference a pointer, you are telling the compiler, "Give me the object pointed to by the pointer and not the value of the pointer itself."

What's a Class?

3

A *class* is a collection of fields and methods (functions and procedures) that work together to accomplish a specific programming task. In this way a class is said to *encapsulate* the task. Classes have the following features:

- The capability to control access
- Constructors
- Destructors
- Fields
- Methods (procedures and functions)
- A hidden, special pointer called Self

Before diving into an explanation of these features, let me give you a quick example of how a class might be used. Let's use a typical Windows control as an example—a check box, for instance. A class that represents a check box would have fields for the caption of the check box and for the state (checked or unchecked). This class would also have methods that enable you to set and query both the check box caption and the check state. These methods might be named GetCheck, SetCheck, GetCaption, and SetCaption. After the class has been written, you can create an instance of the class to control a check box in Windows. (It's not quite that simple, but this is just an example after all.) If you have three check boxes, you would have three instances of the CheckBox class that could then be used to control each check box individually.

```
var
  Check1 : TMyCheckBox;
  Check2 : TMyCheckBox;
  Check3 : TMyCheckBox;
```

```
begin
  Check1 := TMyCheckBox.Create(ID_CHECK1);
  Check2 := TMyCheckBox.Create(ID_CHECK2);
  Check3 := TMyCheckBox.Create(ID_CHECK3);
  Check1.SetCaption('Thingamabob Option');
  Check1.SetCheck(True);
  Check2.SetCaption('Doohickey Options');
  Check2.SetCheck(False);
  Check3.SetCaption('Whodyacallum Options');
  Check3.SetCheck(True);
  if Check1.GetCheck then DoThingamabobTask;
  if Check2.GetCheck then DoDoohickeyTask;
  { etc. }
end;
```

In this example, each instance of the class is a separate object. Each instance has its own fields, and the objects operate independently of one another. They are all objects of the same type but are separate instances in memory. With that brief introduction, you can roll up your sleeves once more and go to work on understanding classes.

Note

The previous example might have been more clear if I had used properties rather than methods called SetCheck, GetCheck, and SetCaption. I didn't because I'm not ready to talk about properties in detail at this time. In fact, most of this chapter will talk about classes without much emphasis on properties. I'll talk about properties more on Day 5.

Anatomy of a Class

A class, like a record, has a declaration. The class declaration is always in a type section.

Class Access Levels

Classes can have four levels of access:

- Private
- Public
- Protected
- Published

Each of these access levels is defined in this section.

Class access levels control how a class is used. As a single programmer, you might be not only the class's creator but also a user of the class. In team programming environments, one programmer might be the creator of the class and other programmers the users of the class. To understand the role that levels of access play in class operation, you first need to understand how classes are used.

In any class there is the *public* part of the class, which the outside world has access to, and there is the private part of a class. The *private* part of a class is the internal implementation of the class—the inner workings, so to speak.

Part of a well-designed class includes hiding anything from public view that the user of the class doesn't need to know.

> **NEW TERM** *Data abstraction* is the hiding of internal implementations within the class from outside views.

Data abstraction prevents the user from knowing more than he or she needs to know about the class and also prevents the user from messing with things that shouldn't be messed with. For example, when you get in your car and turn the key to start it, do you want to know every detail about how the car operates? Of course not. You only want to know as much as you need to know to operate the car safely. In this analogy, the steering wheel, pedals, gear shift lever, speedometer, and so on represent the public interface between the car and the driver. The driver knows which of those components to manipulate to make the car perform the way he or she wants.

Conversely, the engine, drive train, and electrical system of the car are hidden from public view. The engine is tucked neatly away where you never have to look at it if you don't want to. It's a detail that you don't need to know about, so it is hidden from you—kept private, if you prefer. Imagine how much trouble driving would be if you had to know everything the car was doing at all times: Is the carburetor getting enough gas? Does the differential have enough grease? Is the alternator producing adequate voltage for both the ignition and the radio to operate? Are the intake valves opening properly? Who needs it! In the same way, a class keeps its internal implementation private so the user of the class doesn't have to worry about what's going on under the hood. The internal workings of the class are kept private and the user interface is public.

The *protected* access level is a little harder to explain. Protected class members, like private class members, cannot be accessed by users of the class. They can, however, be accessed by classes that are derived from this class. Continuing with the car analogy, let's say you want to extend the car (literally) by making it a stretch limousine. To do this, you need to know something about the underlying structure of the car. You need to know how to modify the drive shaft and frame of the car at the very minimum. In this case you would need to get your hands dirty and, as a limousine designer, get at the parts of the car that were previously unimportant to you (the protected parts).

The internal workings of the engine are still kept private because you don't need to know how the engine works to extend the frame of the car. Similarly, most of the public parts of the car remain the same, but you might add some new public elements such as the controls for the intercom system. I've strayed a little here and given you a peek in to what is called *inheritance*, but I won't go in to further details right now. I will talk more about protected access a little later in the section "Methods," and about inheritance in the section "Inheritance." The point here is that the protected section of a class contains the parts of a class that someone extending the class will need to know about.

The *published* access level is used when writing components. Any components declared in the published section will appear in the Object Inspector at design time. I'll talk more about the published section on Day 20, "Creating Components."

The Object Pascal language has four keywords that pertain to class access. The keywords are (not surprisingly) public, private, protected, and published. You specify a class member's access level when you declare the class. A class is declared with the class keyword. Here's an example:

```
TVehicle = class
private
CurrentGear : Integer;
  Started : Boolean;
  Speed : Integer;
  procedure StartElectricalSystem;
  procedure StartEngine;
protected
  procedure StartupProcedure;
public
  HaveKey : Boolean;
  Start : Boolean;
  procedure SetGear(Gear : Integer);
  procedure Accelerate(Acceleration : Integer);
  procedure Brake(Factor : Integer);
  procedure Turn(Direction : Integer);
  procedure ShutDown;
end;
```

Notice how you break the class organization down into the three access levels. You might not use all of the access levels in a given class. For example, I am not using the published access level in this example. You are not required to use any of the access levels if you don't want, but typically you will have a public and a private section at the least.

Constructors

Classes in Object Pascal have a special method called the constructor.

NEW TERM The *constructor* is a method that is used to create an instance of a class.

The constructor is used to initialize any class member variables, allocate memory the class will need, or do any other startup tasks. The TVehicle example you just saw does not have a constructor. If you don't provide a constructor, you can use the base class's constructor when you create the class. (If not otherwise specified, all Object Pascal classes are derived from TObject. The TObject class has a constructor called Create, so it is this constructor that will be called if you don't provide a constructor. I'll discuss base classes and inheritance later in the section "Inheritance.") Although using the base class's constructor is fine for simple classes, you will almost always provide a constructor for classes of any significance. The constructor can be named anything, but it must be declared using the constructor keyword. This is what distinguishes it as a constructor. Given that, let's add a constructor declaration to the TVehicle class:

```
TVehicle = class
private
  CurrentGear : Integer;
  Started : Boolean;
  Speed : Integer;
  procedure StartElectricalSystem;
  procedure StartEngine;
protected
  procedure StartupProcedure;
public
  HaveKey : Boolean;
  Start : Boolean;
  procedure SetGear(Gear : Integer);
  procedure Accelerate(Acceleration : Integer);
  procedure Break(Factor : Integer);
  procedure Turn(Direction : Integer);
  procedure ShutDown;
  constructor Create;   { the constructor }
end;
```

Notice that the constructor is a special type of method. It does not have a return type because a constructor cannot return a value. If you try to add a return type to the constructor declaration, you will get a compiler error.

A class can have more than one constructor. This can be accomplished in two different ways. The first way is to simply give the constructor a different name—for example,

```
TVehicle = class
  { rest of class deleted }
  constructor Create;
  constructor CreateModel(Model : string);
end;
```

This example shows two constructors, one called Create and the other called
CreateModel.

Another way to declare multiple constructors is through method overloading, which I
discussed yesterday. Here is an example that uses constructors with the same name, but
with different parameters:

```
TVehicle = class
  { rest of class deleted }
  constructor Create; overload;
  constructor Create(AOwner : TObject);  overload;
end;
```

Because method overloading is new in Delphi 4, I don't expect to see this way of declaring multiple constructors used very much in Delphi programs. The traditional method is
to declare constructors with different names, and I suspect that trend will continue for
quite some time. Still, both methods are legal and either one can be used.

Note

If you create components for the retail market, you should be sure that your
components' constructors have different parameter lists. This will ensure
that your components will work with C++Builder as well as with Delphi
(C++Builder does not have named constructors, so method overloading is
used to differentiate constructors). Even if you don't plan on selling your
components to the C++Builder market, you'd be wise to plan ahead for the
possibility.

What's the point of multiple constructors? Multiple constructors provide different ways
of creating a class. For instance, a class can have a constructor that takes no parameters
and a constructor that takes one or more parameters to initialize fields to certain values.
For example, let's say you have a class called TMyRect that encapsulates a rectangle (rectangles are frequently used in Windows programming). This class could have several
constructors. It could have a default constructor that sets all the fields to 0, and another
constructor that enables you to set the class's fields through the constructor. First, let's
take a look at how the class declaration might look:

```
TMyRect = class
private
  Left : Integer;
```

```
  Top : Integer;
  Right : Integer;
  Bottom : Integer;
public
  function GetWidth : Integer;
  function GetHeight : Integer;
  procedure SetRect(ALeft, ATop, ARight, ABottom : Integer);
  constructor Create;
  constructor CreateVal(ALeft, ATop, ARight, ABottom : Integer);
end;
```

The definitions for the constructors would look something like this:

```
constructor TMyRect.Create;
begin
  inherited Create;
  Left   := 0;
  Top    := 0;
  Right  := 0;
  Bottom := 0;
end;

constructor TMyRect.CreateVal(ALeft, ATop, ARight, ABottom : Integer);
begin
  inherited Create;
  Left   := ALeft;
  Top    := ATop;
  Right  := ARight;
  Bottom := ABottom;
end;
```

The first constructor simply initializes each field to 0. The second constructor takes the parameters passed and assigns them to the corresponding class fields. The variable names in the parameter list are local to the constructor, so each of the variable names begins with an *A* to differentiate between the local variables and the class fields (the use of the leading *A* is customary for Delphi programs). Notice the use of the `inherited` keyword in the constructors. I'll talk about the `inherited` keyword later in the section "Inheritance." I wanted to point it out here just so you would know I'm not leaving you in the dark.

> **Note**
>
> It's not strictly necessary to initialize the fields to 0 as the `Create` constructor does here. All fields are automatically initialized to 0 when an object of the class is created.

 NEW TERM   *Instantiation* is the creation of an object, called an *instance*, of a class.

So how do you use one of these constructors instead of the other? You do that when you instantiate an instance of a class. The following code snippet creates two instances of the `TMyRect` class. The first uses the `Create` constructor and the second uses the `CreateVal` constructor:

```
var
  Rect1 : TMyRect;
  Rect2 : TMyRect;
begin
  Rect1 := TMyRect.Create;
  Rect2 := TMyRect.CreateVal(0, 0, 100, 100);
end;
```

You can have as many constructors as you like as long as they all have different names or, if overloaded, as long as they follow the rules of method overloading.

There is one thing that I need to point out about the previous example: Both instances of the `TMyRect` class are allocated dynamically. Earlier I said that you allocate memory for an object dynamically by calling the `GetMem` procedure. Now I seem to be contradicting myself, but in truth I am not. The reason is that memory for Object Pascal classes is *always* allocated dynamically. Although that is not true of records, it is true of classes. That also means that the previous code snippet leaks memory because I didn't free the memory associated with the two classes. I'll talk about that next. Because all Object Pascal classes are created on the heap, all class variables are, therefore, pointers. The `Rect1` and `Rect2` variables in the preceding example are both pointers to the `TMyRect` class.

Destructors

 The *destructor* is a special method that is automatically called just before the object is destroyed.

The destructor can be considered the opposite of the constructor. It is usually used to free any memory allocated by the class or do any other cleanup chores. A class is not required to have a destructor because the base class's destructor can be used instead. Like a constructor, a destructor has no return value.

Although a class can have multiple destructors, it is not something that is typically done. If you have just one destructor, you should name it `Destroy`. This is more than just tradition. When you free an instance of a class (remove it from memory), you call the `Free` method. `Free` is a method of the `TObject` class that calls the class's `Destroy` method just before the class is removed from memory. This is the typical way to free the memory associated with a class. Here's an example:

```
Rect1 := TMyRect.Create;
{ Do some things with Rect1. }
{ ... }
{ Now delete Rect1. }
Rect1.Free;
```

The example in the "Constructors" section would actually leak memory because the two TMyRect objects were never freed.

The following shows the updated code for the TMyRect class, complete with destructor (some code removed for brevity):

```
TMyRect = class
private
  Left : Integer;
  Top : Integer;
  Right : Integer;
  Bottom : Integer;
  Text : PChar;      { new field }
public
  function GetWidth : Integer;
  function GetHeight : Integer;
  procedure SetRect(ALeft, ATop, ARight, ABottom : Integer);
  constructor Create;
  constructor CreateVal(ALeft, ATop, ARight, ABottom : Integer);
  destructor Destroy; override;
end;

constructor TMyRect.Create;
begin
  inherited Create;
  { Allocate memory for a null-terminated string. }
  Text := AllocMem(1024);
end;

destructor TMyRect.Destroy;
begin
  { Free the allocated memory. }
  FreeMem(Text);
  inherited Destroy;
end;
```

The modified version of the TMyRect class allocates storage for a null-terminated string (a PChar) named Text in its constructor and frees that storage in the destructor. (I can't think of a good reason for a class that handles rectangles to have a text field, but you never know! It's just an example, after all.)

Take a closer look at the declaration of the destructor in the TMyRect class declaration. It looks like this:

```
destructor Destroy; override;
```

Notice the override keyword at the end of the declaration. This keyword tells the compiler that you are overriding a method that is also found in the base class. I'm getting ahead of myself again, so I'll continue this discussion later in the section entitled "Inheritance." (I keep saying that, so I'll bet you expect that section to be really good!)

> **Note**
>
> Typically, you will call inherited as the first statement in your constructor and the last statement in your destructor.

Data Fields

Data fields of a class are simply variables that are declared in the class declaration; they can be considered as variables that have class scope. Fields in classes are essentially the same as fields in records except that their access can be controlled by declaring them as private, public, or protected. Regardless of a field's access, it is available for use in all methods of the class. Depending on the field's access level, it can be visible outside the class as well. Private and protected fields, for example, are private to the class and cannot be seen outside the class. Public fields, however, can be accessed from outside the class but only through an object. Take the TMyRect class declared previously, for example. It has no public fields. You could try the following, but you'll get a compiler error:

```
Rect := TMyRect.CreateVal(0, 0, 100, 100);
Rect.Left := 20; { compiler error! }
```

The compiler error will say Undeclared identifier: 'Left'. The compiler is telling you that Left is a private field, and you can't get to it. If Left were in the public section of the class declaration, this code would compile.

> **Note**
>
> The preceding discussion of private data fields holds true if the TMyRect class were declared in a separate unit, but not true if the TMyRect class is declared in the unit where it is used. Classes contained in the same unit have what are sometimes called *friend privileges*, which means that the classes can access each other's private data fields. This applies only to classes declared in the same unit.

Object Pascal uses properties to control the access to private fields. A property can be read/write, read-only, or write-only (although write-only properties are rare). A property can have a read method that is called when the property is read, and a write method when a property is written to. Neither is required, however, because a property can have direct access to the private field. These read and write methods are called any time the property is accessed. The write method is particularly important, as it can be used to validate input or to carry out other tasks when the property is assigned a value. In this way the private field is never accessed directly, but always through a property. I'm getting ahead of myself again so I'll leave it at that for now. Properties are discussed in detail on Day 5.

Note

> Some OOP extremists say that fields should never be public. They would advise you to use properties to access all fields. On the other end of the spectrum is the group that recommends making all your fields public. The truth lies somewhere in between. Some fields are noncritical and can be left public if doing so is more convenient. Other fields are critical to the way the class operates and should not be made public. If you are going to err, it is better to err on the side of making fields private.

3

When you create an instance of a class, each class has its own data. You can assign a value to the variable Left in one instance of a class and assign a different value to the Left variable in a different instance of the class—for example,

```
Rect1 := TMyRect.CreateVal(100, 100, 500, 500);
Rect2 := TMyRect.CreateVal(0, 0, 100, 100);
```

This code creates two instances of the TMyRect class. Although these two instances are identical in terms of their structure, they are completely separate in memory. Each instance has its own data. In the first case, the Left field would have a value of 100. In the second case it would have a value of 0. It's like new cars on the showroom floor: Every model of a particular car comes from the same mold, but they are all separate objects. They all vary in their color, upholstery style, features, and so on.

Methods

Methods are functions and procedures that belong to your class. They are local to the class and don't exist outside the class. Methods can be called only from within the class itself or through an instance of the class. They have access to all public, protected, and private fields of the class. Methods can be declared in the private, protected, or public sections of your class. Good class design requires that you think about which of these sections your methods should go into.

- *Public methods*, along with properties, represent the user interface to the class. It is through the public methods that users of the class access the class to gain whatever functionality it provides. For example, let's say you have a class that plays and records waveform audio. Public methods might include methods named Open, Play, Record, Save, Rewind, and so on.

- *Private methods* are methods that the class uses internally to "do its thing." These methods are not intended to be called by users of the class; they are private in order to hide them from the outside world. Frequently a class has startup chores to perform when the class is created (for example, you have already seen that the constructor is called when a class is created). In some classes the startup processing might be significant, requiring many lines of code. To remove clutter from the constructor, a class might have an Init method that is called from the constructor to perform those startup tasks. This method would never be called directly by a user of the class. In fact, more than likely bad things would happen if this method were called by a user at the wrong time, so the method is private in order to protect both the integrity of the class and the user.

- *Protected methods* are methods that cannot be accessed by the outside world but can be accessed by classes derived from this class. I haven't talked yet about classes being derived from other classes; I'll save that discussion for a little later when it will make more sense. I discuss deriving classes in the section "Inheritance."

Methods can be declared as *class methods*. A class method operates more like a regular function or procedure than a method of a class. Specifically, a class method cannot access fields or other methods of the class. (In just a bit I'll tell you why this restriction exists.) Most of the time, you will not use class methods, so I won't go into any detail on them.

About Self

 All classes have a hidden field called Self. Self is a pointer to the instance of the class in memory.

Obviously, this will require some explanation. First, let's take a look at how the TMyRect class would look if Self were not a hidden field:

```
TMyRect = class
private
  Self : TMyRect;
  Left : Integer;
  Top : Integer;
  Right : Integer;
  Bottom : Integer;
  Text : PChar;
public
  function GetWidth : Integer;
  function GetHeight : Integer;
  procedure SetRect(ALeft, ATop, ARight, ABottom : Integer);
```

```
  constructor Create;
  constructor CreateVal(ALeft, ATop, ARight, ABottom : Integer);
  destructor Destroy; override;
end;
```

This is effectively what the TMyRect class looks like to the compiler. When a class object is created, the Self pointer is automatically initialized to the address of the class in memory:

```
Rect := TMyRect.CreateVal(0, 0, 100, 100);
{ Now 'Rect' and 'Rect.Self' have the same value   }
{ because both contain the address of the object in memory. }
```

"But," you ask, "what does Self mean?" Remember that each class instance gets its own copy of the class's fields. But all class instances share the same set of methods for the class (there's no point in duplicating that code for each instance of the class). How does the compiler figure out which instance goes with which method call? All class methods have a hidden Self parameter that goes with them. To illustrate, let's say you have a function for the TMyRect class called GetWidth. It would look like this:

```
function TMyRect.GetWidth : Integer;
begin
  Result := Right - Left;
end;
```

That's how the function looks to you and me. To the compiler, though, it looks something like this:

```
function TMyRect.GetWidth : Integer;
begin
  Result := Self.Right - Self.Left;
end;
```

That's not exactly accurate from a technical perspective, but it's close enough for this discussion. In this code you can see that Self is working behind the scenes to keep everything straight for you. You don't have to worry about how that happens, but you need to know that it does happen.

Caution Never modify the Self pointer. You can use it to pass a pointer to your class to other methods or as a parameter in constructing other classes, but don't change its value. Learn to treat Self as a read-only variable.

Although Self works behind the scenes, it is still a variable that you can access from within the class. As an illustration, let's take a quick peek into VCL. Most of the time, you will create components in VCL by dropping them on the form at design time. When you do that, Delphi creates a pointer to the component and does all sorts of housekeeping chores on your behalf, saving you from concerning yourself with the technical end of things. Sometimes, however, you will create a component at runtime. VCL insists (as all good frameworks do) on keeping track of which child objects belong to which parent. For example, let's say you want to create a button on a form when another button is clicked. You need to tell VCL what the parent of the new button is. The code would look like this:

```
procedure TForm1.Button1Click(Sender: TObject);
var
  Button : TButton;
begin
  Button := TButton.Create(Self);
  Button.Parent  := Self;
  Button.Left    := 20;
  Button.Top     := 20;
  Button.Caption := 'Click Me';
end;
```

In this code, you can see that Self is used in the constructor (this sets the Owner property of the button, but I'll get into that later when I cover VCL components on Day 7, "VCL Components") and also that it is assigned to the Parent property of the newly created button. This is how you will use the Self pointer the vast majority of the time in your Delphi applications.

 Note

Earlier I said that class methods can't access class fields. The reason this is true is because class methods don't have a hidden Self parameter; regular methods do. Without Self, a method cannot access class fields.

Don't worry too much about Self right now. When you begin to use VCL, it will quickly become clear when you are required to use Self in your Delphi applications.

A Class Example

Right now it would be nice if you could see an example of a class. Listing 3.1 shows a unit that contains a class called TAirplane. This class could be used by an aircraft controller program. The class enables you to command an airplane by sending it messages. You can tell the airplane to take off, to land, or to change its course, altitude, or speed. First take a look at the unit and then I'll discuss what is going on within this class.

LISTING 3.1. AIRPLANU.PAS.

```pascal
unit AirplanU;

interface

uses
  SysUtils;

const
  { Airplane types. }
  Airliner    = 0;
  Commuter    = 1;
  PrivateCraft = 2;

  { Status constants. }
  TakingOff   = 0;
  Cruising    = 1;
  Landing     = 2;
  OnRamp      = 3;

  { Message constants. }
  MsgChange   = 0;
  MsgTakeOff  = 1;
  MsgLand     = 2;
  MsgReport   = 3;

type

  TAirplane = class
  private
    Name     : string;
    Speed    : Integer;
    Altitude : Integer;
    Heading  : Integer;
    Status   : Integer;
    Kind     : Integer;
    Ceiling  : Integer;
  protected
    procedure TakeOff(Dir : Integer); virtual;
    procedure Land; virtual;
  public
    constructor Create(AName : string; AKind : Integer = Airliner);
    function SendMessage(Msg : Integer; var Response : string;
        Spd : Integer; Dir : Integer; Alt : Integer) : Boolean;
    function GetStatus(var StatusString : string) : Integer; overload;
  virtual;
    function GetStatus : Integer; overload;
    function GetSpeed : Integer;
```

continues

LISTING 3.1. CONTINUED

```
    function GetHeading : Integer;
    function GetAltitude : Integer;
    function GetName : string;
  end;

implementation

constructor TAirplane.Create(AName : string; AKind : Integer);
begin
  inherited Create;
  Name     := AName;
  Kind     := AKind;
  Status   := OnRamp;
  case Kind of
    Airliner : Ceiling := 35000;
    Commuter : Ceiling := 20000;
    PrivateCraft : Ceiling := 8000;
  end;
end;

procedure TAirplane.TakeOff(Dir : Integer);
begin
  Heading := Dir;
  Status  := TakingOff;
end;

procedure TAirplane.Land;
begin
  Speed    := 0;
  Heading  := 0;
  Altitude := 0;
  Status   := OnRamp;
end;

function TAirplane.SendMessage(Msg : Integer; var Response : string;
    Spd : Integer; Dir : Integer; Alt : Integer) : Boolean;
begin
  Result := True;

  { Do something based on which command was sent. }
  case Msg of
    MsgTakeOff :
      { Can't take off if already in the air! }
      if status <> OnRamp then begin
        Response := Name + ': I''m already in the air!';
        Result := False;
      end else
        TakeOff(dir);
```

```
      MsgChange :
        begin
          { Check for bad commands and exit if any found. }
          if Spd > 500 then
            Response := 'Command Error: Speed cannot be more than 500.';
          if Dir > 360 then
            Response := 'Command Error: Heading cannot be over 360
➥degrees.';
          if Alt < 100 then
            Response := Name + ': I''d crash!';
          if Alt > Ceiling then
            Response := Name + ': I can''t go that high.';
          if (Spd = 0) and (Dir = 0) and (Alt = 0) then
            Response := Name + ': Huh?';
          if Response <> '' then begin
            Result := False;
            Exit;
          end;

          { Can't change status if on the ground. }
          if status = OnRamp then begin
            Response := Name + ': I''m on the ground.';
            Result := False;
          end else begin
            Speed := Spd;
            Heading := Dir;
            Altitude := Alt;
            Status := Cruising;
          end;
        end;
      MsgLand :
        { Can't land if already on the ground. }
        if status = OnRamp then begin
          Response := Name + ': I''m already on the ground.';
          Result := False;
        end else
          Land;
      MsgReport :
        begin
          GetStatus(Response);
          Exit;
        end;
    end;

  { Standard response if all went well. }
  if Result then
    Response := Name + ': Roger.';
end;
```

continues

LISTING 3.1. CONTINUED

```
function TAirplane.GetStatus(var StatusString : string) : Integer;
begin
  StatusString := Format('%s, Altitude: %d, Heading: %d, ' +
    'Speed: %d', [Name, Altitude, Heading, Speed]);
  Result := Status;
end;

function TAirplane.GetStatus : Integer;
begin
  Result := Status;
end;

function TAirplane.GetSpeed : Integer;
begin
  Result := Speed;
end;

function TAirplane.GetHeading : Integer;
begin
  Result := Heading;
end;

function TAirplane.GetAltitude : Integer;
begin
  Result := Altitude;
end;

function TAirplane.GetName : string;
begin
  Result := Name;
end;

end.
```

ANALYSIS Look first at the class declaration in the interface section. Notice that the TAirplane class has one overloaded function called GetStatus. When called with a string parameter, GetStatus will return a status string as well as the status data member (the string parameter is a variable parameter). When called without a parameter, it just returns Status. Note that the only way to access the private fields is via the public methods. For example, you can change the speed, altitude, and heading of an airplane only by sending it a message. To use an analogy, consider that an air traffic controller cannot physically change an aircraft's heading. The best he can do is send a message to the pilot and tell him to change to a new heading.

> **Note**
>
> This class would benefit greatly from properties. As I said earlier, I'm not ready to discuss properties in detail at this point in the book, so I'll have to admit that this class could be much better than it is and move on.

Now turn your attention to the definition of the TAirplane class in the interface section. The constructor performs some initialization chores. You have probably noticed that the SendMessage function does most of the work. A case statement determines which message was sent and takes the appropriate action. Notice that the TakeOff and Land procedures cannot be called directly (they are protected) but rather are called through the SendMessage function. Again, as an air traffic controller, you can't make an aircraft take off or land, you can only send it a message telling it what you want it to do.

There's something else here that I haven't discussed yet. Note the virtual keyword. This specifies that the function is a virtual method.

NEW TERM A *virtual method* is a method that is automatically called if a method of that name exists in the derived class.

I'll discuss virtual methods in the next section, but I wanted to point them out to you now.

The book's code contains a program called Airport, which enables you to play air traffic controller. (You can find the book's code at the Web site http://www.mcp.com/info. Type in the book's ISBN: 0-672-31286-7.) The program first sets up an array of TAirplane classes and then creates three instances of the TAirplane class. You can send messages to any airplane by selecting the airplane, setting up the parameters for the message, and then clicking the Execute button. Clicking the button results in a call to the selected airplane's SendMessage function. When you send a message, you get a response back from the airplane, and that response is displayed in a memo component. Run the program and play with it to get a feel for how it works. Figure 3.1 shows the Airport program running.

FIGURE 3.1.

The Airport program running.

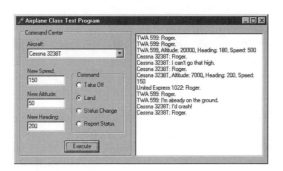

Inheritance

One of the most powerful features of classes in Object Pascal is that they can be extended through inheritance.

NEW TERM   *Inheritance* means taking an existing class and adding functionality by deriving a new class from it.

NEW TERM   The class you start with is called the *base class* or *ancestor class*, and the new class you create is called the *derived class*.

To illustrate, let's go back to the TAirplane class. The civilian and military worlds are quite different, as you know. To represent a military aircraft, I can derive a class from TAirplane and add functionality to it:

```
TMilitaryPlane = class(TAirplane)
private
  TheMission : TMission;
  constructor Create(AName : string; AType : Integer);
  function GetStatus(var StatusString : string) : Integer; override;
protected
  procedure TakeOff(Dir : Integer); override;
  procedure Land; override;
  procedure Attack; virtual;
  procedure SetMission; virtual;
end;
```

A TMilitaryPlane has everything a TAirplane has, plus a few more goodies. Note the first line of the class declaration. The class name in parentheses after the class keyword is used to tell the compiler that I am inheriting from another class. The class from which I am deriving this class is the base class and, in this case, is the TAirplane class.

Note   When you derive a class from another class, the new class gets all the functionality of the base class plus whatever new features you add. You can add fields and methods to the new class, but you cannot remove anything from what the base class offers.

You'll notice that in the private section there is a line that declares a variable of the TMission class. The TMission class is not shown here, but it could encapsulate everything that deals with the mission of a military aircraft: the target, navigation waypoints, ingress and egress altitudes and headings, and so on. This illustrates the use of a field that is an instance of another class. In fact, you'll see that a lot when programming in Delphi.

Overriding Methods

I want to take a moment here to discuss virtual methods. Note that the `TakeOff` procedure is a virtual method in the `TAirplane` class (refer to Listing 3.1). Notice that `TakeOff` is called by `SendMessage` in response to the `MsgTakeOff` message. If the `TMilitaryPlane` class did not provide its own `TakeOff` method, the base class's `TakeOff` method would be called. Because the `TMilitaryPlane` class *does* provide a `TakeOff` method, that method will be called rather than the method in the base class.

NEW TERM   Replacing a base class method in a derived class is called *overriding* the method.

In order for overriding to work, the method signature must exactly match that of the method in the base class. In other words, the return type, method name, and parameter list must all be the same as the base class method. In addition, the method in the derived class must be declared with the `override` keyword.

3

> **Note**
>
> Object Pascal also has *dynamic methods*. Dynamic methods can be treated the same as virtual methods as far as most programmers are concerned. The difference is in the way the method pointers are stored in the class's virtual method table (VMT). It's not important for you to understand the difference right now, but I wanted you to know about dynamic methods in case you encounter them looking through any of the Delphi examples or VCL source code. For the most part, you can treat dynamic methods in your programs just as you would treat virtual methods.

You can override a method with the intention of replacing the base class method, or you can override a method to enhance the base class method. Consider the `TakeOff` method, for example. If you want to completely replace what the `TakeOff` method of `TAirplane` does, you would override it and supply whatever code you want:

```
procedure TMilitaryPlane.TakeOff(Dir : Integer);
begin
  { New code here. }
end;
```

But if you want your method to take the functionality of the base class and add to it, you would first call the base class method and then add new code. Calling the base class method is done with the `inherited` keyword—for example,

```
procedure TMilitaryPlane.TakeOff(Dir : Integer);
begin
  { First call the base class TakeOff method. }
  inherited TakeOff(Dir);
  { New code here. }
end;
```

By calling the base class method, you get the original behavior of the method as written
in the base class. You can then add code before or after the base class call to enhance the
base class method. Note that the TakeOff method is declared in the protected section of
the TAirplane class. If it were in the private section, this would not work because even
a derived class cannot access the private members of its ancestor class. By making the
TakeOff method protected, it is hidden from the outside world but still accessible to
derived classes.

Note There is an exception to the rule of protected versus private access. If a
derived class is declared in the same unit as the base class, the private fields
and methods of the base class are available to the derived class. If the
derived class is declared in a separate unit, only protected fields and methods of the base class are available to the derived class.

When you derive a class from another class, you must be sure to call the base class's
constructor so that all ancestor classes are properly initialized. Calling the base class constructor is also done with the inherited keyword. Look again at the constructor for the
TAirplane class:

```
constructor TAirplane.Create(AName : string; AKind : Integer);
begin
  inherited Create;
  Name      := AName;
  Kind      := AKind;
  Status    := OnRamp;
  case Kind of
    Airliner : Ceiling := 35000;
    Commuter : Ceiling := 20000;
    PrivateCraft : Ceiling := 8000;
  end;
end;
```

Notice that the base class Create constructor is called to ensure that the class is properly
created. "Hey, wait a minute!" I can hear some of you saying. "The TAirplane class
doesn't have a base class!" Actually, it does. If no base class is specified when the class
is declared, the base class is automatically TObject. Be sure to call the base class constructor in your class constructor. Figure 3.2 illustrates the concept of inheritance.

FIGURE 3.2.

An example of inheritance.

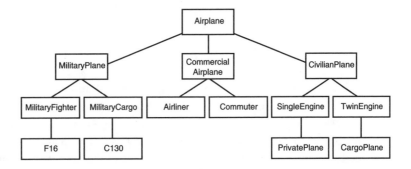

You can see in Figure 3.2 that the class called F16 is descended from the class called MilitaryFighter. Ultimately, F16 is derived from TAirplane because TAirplane is the base class for all of the airplane classes.

Class Keywords: is and as

Object Pascal has two operators that pertain specifically to classes. The is operator is used to determine whether a class is of a specific type. Let's go back to the example of the TAirplane and TMilitaryPlane classes. Let's say you have an instance of a class called Plane. The class might be an instance of the TAirplane class, it might be an instance of the TMilitaryPlane class, or it might be an instance of a different class altogether. You can use the is operator to find out. For example:

```
if Plane is TMilitaryPlane then
   Attack;
```

The is operator returns a Boolean value. If the variable is of the requested type, is returns True. If the variable is not of the requested type, is returns False. The is operator will also return True if the requested class type is an ancestor of the variable. For example, because TMilitaryPlane is derived from TAirplane, the following will be True:

```
if Plane is TAirplane then
   DoSomething;
```

Note

Because all classes are derived from TObject, the following will always be True:

```
if AnyClass is TObject then
   DoSomething;
```

The is operator is not used as much as the as operator. The as operator is used to cast a pointer to a specific class type. It looks like this:

```
with Plane as TMilitaryPlane do
  Attack;
```

The as operator is usually used in conjunction with the with operator (yes, this conversation is a bit confusing). In this code snippet the Plane variable is a pointer that could be an instance of the TAirplane class, the TMilitaryPlane class, or neither. The as operator is used to cast the pointer to a TMilitaryPlane type and then the Attack method is called. If the Plane variable is not an instance of the TMilitaryPlane class (or one of its ancestor classes), this cast will fail and the Attack method will not be called. If, however, the Plane variable is a pointer to an instance of the TMilitaryPlane class, the cast will succeed and the Attack method will be called.

Summary

Today you have learned about classes in Object Pascal. A well-designed class is easy to use and saves many programming hours. I'd even go so far as to say a well-designed class is a joy to use—especially when it's your own creation.

The lessons of these first three days are important to understand as you progress through this book. If they don't make complete sense to you yet, don't despair. As you continue through the next days, you will see these concepts repeated and put to use in programs that have more practical application than the short, incomplete examples you've been working with thus far.

 Caution

Learning Object Pascal can and will lead to brain overload! It's natural and you shouldn't worry about it. You might put down this book for the evening, turn out the lights, and think, "I'll never get it." Trust me, you will.

Sometimes it's necessary to take a couple of days off and let it all soak in. In fact, if I thought I could get by with it, I'd make Day 4 a blank chapter called "A Day of Rest." Take it a little at a time, and one of these days you'll be just like Archimedes—you'll be running around your office or your house shouting "Eureka!" because the light just came on in your head. But keep track of your clothes, will you? The neighbors could be watching.

Workshop

The Workshop contains quiz questions to help you solidify your understanding of the material covered and exercises to provide you with experience in using what you have learned. You can find the answers to quiz questions in Appendix A, "Answers to the Quiz Questions."

Q&A

Q How can I keep a method private to the outside world but enable derived classes to call it?

A Make it protected. A protected method is not accessible to users of your class but is accessible to derived classes.

Q What does *data abstraction* mean?

A Data abstraction means hiding the details of the class that the users of the class don't need to see. A class might have dozens of fields and methods but only a few that the user can see. Only make visible (public) the methods that a user needs to know about to use the class.

Q What is an object?

A Effectively, an object is any block of code that can be treated as a separate entity in your programs. An object in Object Pascal generally means a class. In Delphi that definition is expanded to include VCL components. ActiveX controls are also objects.

Q Can my class have more than one constructor?

A Yes. Your class can have as many constructors as needed.

Q Are all VCL objects pointers?

A Yes. Because all VCL objects are allocated from the heap, all VCL objects are pointers.

Q Pointers confuse me. Am I alone?

A No! Pointers are one of the most confusing aspects of Object Pascal programming. After you have used Delphi for a period of time, you will come to understand pointers.

Quiz

1. How do you clear a set of all values?
2. What is the purpose of having private fields and methods?
3. How can you keep fields private and yet enable users to read and set their values?

4. When is a class's destructor called?

5. What does it mean to override a method of the base class?

6. How can you override a base class method and still get the benefit of the operation the base class method performs?

7. What operator is used to dereference a pointer?

8. Can a class contain other class instances as fields?

9. What keyword is used to specify a pointer that has no value?

10. What is the as keyword used for?

Exercises

1. Write a class that takes a person's height in inches and returns the height in feet.

2. Derive a class from the class in exercise 1 that also returns the height in meters, centimeters, or millimeters. (Hint: There are 25.4 millimeters in an inch.)

3. Take a day off. You've earned it!

DAY 4

The Delphi IDE Explored

One of the most difficult aspects of learning how to use a new programming environment is finding your way around: getting to know the basic menu structure, what all the options do, and how the environment works as a whole. If you are new to programming or new to Object Pascal, this task is complicated by the fact that you have to learn a new program (the Delphi IDE) *and* learn a new language at the same time. It can be overwhelming at times. I'll do my best to make learning the Delphi IDE an enjoyable experience. For the most part, you will learn by example, which is more interesting (not to mention more effective).

The Delphi IDE

So, without further ado, take a look at Figure 4.1 and let's get on with it. Oh, by the way, if you have used Delphi before, you might find this chapter elementary. If that is the case, you might want to at least skim the chapter lightly to catch any tidbits that you did not previously know, particularly features that are new to Delphi 4.

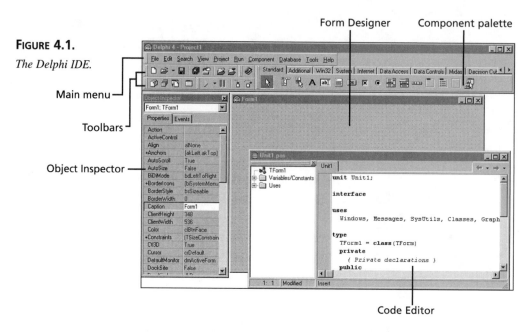

FIGURE 4.1.

The Delphi IDE.

Form Designer   Component palette

Main menu

Toolbars

Object Inspector

Code Editor

The Delphi IDE consists of these main parts:

- The main menu and toolbars
- The Component palette
- The Form Designer
- The Code Editor
- The Object Inspector
- The Code Explorer
- The Project Manager

I can't cover all these in a single chapter, so over the next several chapters I will show you around the Delphi IDE and examine each of these features in detail. I'll start today by discussing projects and how they are used in writing Delphi applications. After that you'll look at the Delphi toolbar and the Component palette. Then I'll move to discussing forms in greater detail than I have up to this point.

Along the way you'll create some sample programs to illustrate various aspects of Delphi. You'll also take a closer look at the Object Inspector. This will be a warm-up for Day 6, "Working with the Form Designer and the Menu Designer," when you learn all about the Delphi Form Designer. Later today, I will cover the IDE's dockable windows. Dockable windows make it easy to customize the IDE to suit your tastes and your work style.

For starters, let's look at the way Delphi views applications and how it has simplified the process of creating programs.

Projects in Delphi

As you know by now, a lot goes on behind the scenes as you write a Delphi application. In fact, more goes on than I have told you about up to this point. It's not vital that you know every detail about what happens behind the scenes as you write a Delphi application, but it is a good idea to have a general overview.

NEW TERM A *project* is a collection of files that work together to create a standalone executable file or dynamic link library (DLL).

NEW TERM In addition to a single project, Delphi enables you to create what is known as a project group. A *project group* is a collection of Delphi projects.

A project group is used to manage a group of Delphi projects that work together to form a complete software product. I'll talk about project groups in more detail on Day 9, "Projects, the Code Editor, and the Code Explorer." For now, you only need to understand that Delphi creates a new, unnamed project group for you each time you start Delphi (provided you haven't turned on the option to save the desktop when you close Delphi). Any new projects you create will go into that project group. You can save the project group if you like, or you can treat the default project group as temporary.

4

Files Used in Delphi Projects

Delphi manages a project through the use of several support files. To illustrate, let's create a simple application to get a look at some of what goes on when Delphi builds an executable file for your program. Perform the following steps:

1. Before you begin, create a fresh directory on your hard drive. (You can name the directory anything you like.)

2. First choose File | Close All from the main menu so that you are starting from scratch. Now choose File | New Application from the main menu. A blank form is displayed.

3. Choose File | Save All from the main menu. You will be prompted for the name of the unit file. Be sure to navigate to the empty directory you just created.

4. Type the name MyUnit for the unit filename and click the Save Button.

5. Now you are prompted for the project name. Type Test in the File Name field and click Save.

6. Choose Project I Build Test from the main menu. Delphi compiles the program. (It takes just a few seconds.)

7. Choose File I Close All from the main menu. (Yes, this exercise does have a purpose.)

8. Now run Windows Explorer and locate the directory where you saved the project. You will see a number of files.

You should see a total of about eight files. (The exact number depends on the Delphi IDE options.) First, let me tell you what happens when Delphi builds an application; then I'll explain what each of these files is for.

Note

Files with extensions that begin with a tilde (~) are backup files. Delphi might create several backup files depending on the number of source files in the project and the project options you have set. Project options are discussed on Day 9.

When you first create a project, Delphi creates a minimum of four files (assuming a typical Delphi GUI application):

- The project source file
- The main form unit
- The main form resource file
- The project resource file

The *project source file* is the file that contains the Delphi startup code. You can view the project source file by choosing Project I View Source from the main menu. The *main form unit* contains the class declaration and definition for the main form's class. Delphi will create an additional unit file for each new form you create. The *main form resource file* and *project resource file* are binary files that describe the main form and the application's icon.

When you tell Delphi to compile the project, it compiles the project source, the main form unit, and any other units in the project. Several things happen during this process. First, the Object Pascal compiler compiles the project's units into binary object files. Then, the resource compiler compiles any resources, such as the program's icon and form files, into binary resource files. Next, the linker takes over. The linker takes the binary files the compiler created, adds any library files the project needs, and binds them all together to produce the final executable file. When it's all over, you have a stand-alone program that can be run in the usual ways.

Okay, but what are all those files for? Table 4.1 lists the file extensions Delphi uses with a description of the role that each file type plays.

TABLE 4.1. TYPES OF FILES USED IN DELPHI.

Extension	Description
.pas	The Object Pascal source files. There will be one for each unit, as well as any other source files that you add to the project.
.dfm	The form file. This file is actually a binary resource file (.res) in disguise. It is a description of the form and all its components. Each form has its own .dfm file.
.dsk	The project desktop file. This file keeps track of the way the desktop appeared when you last saved (or closed) the project. All the open windows' sizes and positions are saved so that when you reopen the project it looks the same as you left it. This file is created only if you turn on the option to save your desktop (Environment Options dialog box).
.dof	The project options file. This file contains the project options as set in the Project Options dialog.
.exe	The final executable program.
.cfg	The project configuration file. This file primarily contains the current compiler and linker settings for the project.
.dcu	The compiled binary object files. These are the files that the compiler produces when it compiles your Object Pascal units.
.dpr	The project source file.
.res	The compiled binary resource file.

Note

Delphi has other associated file extensions as well. For example, the .bpg extension is used to denote a project group, the .dpk extension is used to designate a Delphi package source file, and the .bpl extension represents a compiled package. Packages are discussed in detail on Day 8, "Creating Applications in Delphi," and project groups are discussed on Day 9.

The files that Delphi produces can be divided into two categories: files Delphi relies on to build the project and files that Delphi creates when it compiles and links a project. If you were to move your source files to another computer, for example, you wouldn't have to move *all* the files, just the files Delphi needs to build the application. Conveniently, the source files happen to be the smallest files in the project. It does not take a lot of disk space to back up just the project source files.

The minimum set of files consists of the .pas, .dfm, and .dpr files. All other files are files that Delphi will re-create when you compile the program. The desktop file (.dsk) is one that you might want to hang on to because it keeps track of the state your project was in when you last worked on it.

Note

In addition to the source files I've mentioned, some applications use a resource script file (resource scripts have an .rc extension). *Resource scripts* are text files that are used to define resources such as bitmaps, icons, or cursors. If you use a resource script, be sure to keep it with the project if you move the project to another location. Resource script files are not commonly used with Delphi projects.

Figure 4.2 illustrates how Delphi compiles source files and links them to form the final executable file.

FIGURE 4.2.

The Delphi compile/link process.

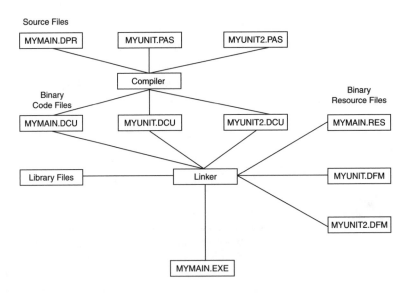

Tip

If you find yourself running low on hard disk space, you can delete some of the Delphi files from projects you are not currently working on. It is safe to delete the files with a .dcu extension. These files will be regenerated when the project is built, and there is no use in keeping them for noncurrent projects.

> **Caution**
>
> Do not delete any files from the Delphi directories other than the Examples directory. If in doubt, *don't delete!*

Source Code Units

Earlier I mentioned that most applications of any size have several source files, which are called *units*. Each time you create a new form, Delphi does the following:

- Creates a form file (.dfm)
- Derives a class from TForm
- Creates a unit (.pas file) for the class definition
- Adds the new form information to the project source

Initially Delphi assigns a default name of Form1 to the form and Unit1.pas to the form's unit. The second form created for the project would have a default name of Form2, and so on. Each time you create a new form, Delphi creates a new unit (.pas) and form file (.dfm) for that form.

4

> **Note**
>
> As soon as you create a new project, you should save it with a meaningful name. Likewise, every time you create a new form, you should save it with a descriptive name. This makes it easier to locate forms and units when you need to make modifications. Remember, you can use long filenames when naming your units.

> **Note**
>
> When writing a technical book, a difficult situation often arises. I want to use meaningful examples to reinforce the presentation of information. In order to write those examples, I have to use techniques or methods that I haven't talked about yet. But I can't talk about those methods until I've given you some good, meaningful examples. But I can't...well, you see my dilemma. So I'm going to digress a little here and talk about the main menu, toolbar, and Component palette. As you read the next section, remember that I'm off on a tangent, but for a good reason.

The Delphi Main Menu and Toolbar

The Delphi main menu has all the choices necessary to make Delphi work. Because programming in Delphi is a highly visual operation, you might not use the main menu as much as you might with other programming environments. Still, just about anything you need is available from the main menu if you prefer to work that way. I'm not going to go over every item on the main menu here because you will encounter each item as you work through the next several chapters.

The Delphi toolbars provide a convenient way of accomplishing often-repeated tasks. A button is easier to locate than a menu item, not to mention that it requires less mouse movement. The Delphi main window toolbars are illustrated in Figure 4.3. (The Component palette has been removed for clarity.)

FIGURE 4.3.

The Delphi main window toolbars.

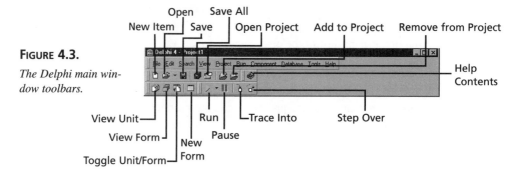

If you are like me, you often forget to use the toolbar. But I'm telling you: Don't forget to learn and use the toolbar! As the old saying goes, "Do as I say, not as I do." If you take the time to learn the toolbar, it will save you time and make you more efficient in the long run. One of the reasons you bought Delphi was to produce Windows applications quickly, so you might as well make the most of it.

The Delphi toolbar is fully customizable. You can place the toolbars anywhere you want on the main window. You can rearrange the placement of the menu, the toolbars, or the Component palette to suit the way you work.

Customizing the toolbars is remarkably easy. Delphi enables you to add buttons to the toolbar, remove buttons, and rearrange buttons however you see fit. To configure a toolbar, right-click on the toolbar to display the context menu. Choose Customize from the context menu. When you choose this menu item, the Customize dialog box is displayed.

The Customize dialog box contains three tabs:

- The first tab, Toolbars, shows you the toolbars available with a check mark next to toolbars that are currently visible. You can add or remove existing toolbars or reset the toolbars to their original default settings.

- The second tab, labeled Commands, shows all the available toolbar buttons. To add a button to the toolbar, just locate its description in the Commands list box and drag it to the place you want it to occupy on any toolbar. To remove a button from a toolbar, grab it and drag it off the toolbar. It's as simple as that. Figure 4.4 shows the act of adding a button to a toolbar. If you really make a mess of things, simply go back to the Toolbars page and click the Reset button. The toolbar will revert to its default settings.

FIGURE 4.4.

Customizing the toolbar.

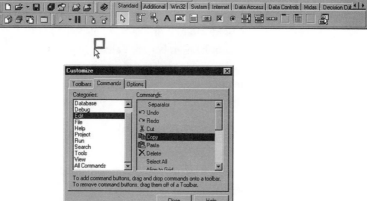

- The third tab, Options, contains options such as whether the tooltips are displayed and how they are displayed.

Feel free to customize the Delphi IDE any way you like. It's your development environment, so make it work for you.

Using the Component Palette

The Delphi Component palette is used to select a component or other control (such as an ActiveX control) in order to place that control on a form. The Component palette is a multipage window. Tabs are provided to enable you to navigate between pages. Clicking on a tab displays the available components or controls on that page.

Placing a component on a form is a two-step process. First, go to the Component palette and select the button representing the component you want to use. Then click on the form to place the component on the form. The component appears with its upper-left corner placed where you clicked with the mouse.

You have already seen the Component palette's basic operations, but it has a couple of other features that you haven't seen yet. The following sections explain these features.

Placing Multiple Copies of a Component

So far you have placed only one component at a time on a form. You can easily place multiple components of the same type without selecting the component from the Component palette each time. To place multiple components on a form, press and hold the Shift key as you select the component from the Component palette. After you select the component, you can release the Shift key.

The component's button on the Component palette will appear pressed and will be highlighted with a blue border. Click on the form to place the first component. Notice that the button stays pressed on the Component palette. You can click as many times as you like; a new component will be placed each time you click the form. To stop placing components, click the selector button on the Component palette (the arrow button). The component button pops up to indicate that you are done placing components.

Seeing is believing, so follow these steps:

1. Create a new project.

2. Press and hold the Shift key on the keyboard and click the Label component button in the Component palette.

3. Click three times on the form, moving the cursor each time to indicate where you want the new component placed. A new Label is placed on the form each time you click.

4. Click the arrow button on the Component palette to end the process and return to form design mode.

Tip

It's fastest to place all components of a particular type on your form at one time using this technique. Components can always be rearranged and resized at a later time.

Note

When placing multiple copies of a particular component, it's easy to forget to click the arrow button when you're done. If you accidentally place more components than you intend, you can simply delete any extras.

Placing and Centering a Component on the Form

Delphi provides a shortcut method of placing a component on a form. Simply double-click the component's button in the Component palette and the component will be placed on the form. The component will be centered on the form both horizontally and vertically. Components placed with this method can be moved to another location on the form just like components placed in the usual method.

Note

Each time you double-click a button on the Component palette, a component will be placed on the center of the form in the component's default size. If you repeatedly double-click the component button, multiple copies of the component will be placed on the form. Each component will be placed in the center of the form and will be stacked on top of the previous one. It will appear as if you have a single component, so you might not realize that you have several components occupying the same space. If you accidentally place multiple components, just click the extra components and delete them from the form.

The Component Palette Context Menu

When you place the mouse cursor over the Component palette and right-click, you will see a menu specific to the Component palette (see Figure 4.5).

FIGURE 4.5.

The Component palette context menu.

The Show Hints item toggles the tooltips on and off for the component buttons. Unless you really dislike tooltips, this should be left on. The Hide item on the context menu hides the Component palette. In order to show the Component palette again, you have to choose Component Palette from the toolbar context menu.

The Help item on the context menu brings up Delphi help with the Component Palette page displayed. The Properties item brings up the Palette page of the Environment Options dialog box, where you can customize the Component palette. Here you can add and remove pages of the Component palette. You can also add, remove, or rearrange the order of components on the individual pages. I'll discuss this in more detail on Day 11, "Delphi Tools and Options," when you learn about setting the environment options.

Navigating the Component Palette

When the Component palette is sized small enough so that it cannot display all its tabs, you will see scroll buttons in the upper-right corner of the Component palette. Click these scroll buttons to display tabs not currently in view. Likewise, if a particular page of the Component palette contains more buttons than will fit the width of the display window, scroll buttons will be enabled to allow you to scroll through the available buttons. Figure 4.6 shows the Component palette with both types of scroll buttons enabled.

FIGURE 4.6.

The Component palette scroll buttons.

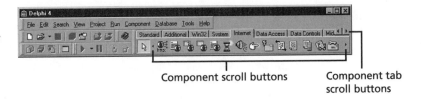

Component scroll buttons   Component tab
                            scroll buttons

The Component palette is not terribly complicated, but a basic understanding of its use is vital for programming with Delphi. Now that you've finished with this quick overview of the Delphi main window, you can return to the main topic again.

A Multiple-Form Application

To illustrate how Delphi uses units, you can create an application with multiple forms. You'll create a simple application that displays a second form when you click a button:

1. Create a new project by choosing File | New Application from the main menu.

2. Change the `Name` property to `MainForm` and the `Caption` property to `Multiple Forms Test Program`.

3. Save the project. Save the unit as `Main` and the project as `Multiple`.

4. Now place a button on the form. Make the button's `Name` property `ShowForm2` and the `Caption` property `Show Form 2`.

5. Choose File | New Form from the main menu (or click the New Form button on the toolbar) to create a new form. At this point, the new form has a name of `Form1` and is placed exactly over the main form. You want the new form to be smaller than the main form and more or less centered on the main form.

6. Size and position the new form so that it is about 50 percent of the size of the main form and centered on the main form. Use the title bar to move the new form. Size the form by dragging the lower-right corner.

7. Change the new form's `Name` property to `SecondForm` and the form's `Caption` property to `A Second Form`.

8. Choose File | Save from the main menu (or click the Save File button on the tool-bar) and save the new form with the name Second.

9. Choose a Label component and drop it on the new form. Change the label's Caption property to This is the second form. Change the label's size and color as desired. Center the label on the form. Your form should now look roughly similar to the one shown in Figure 4.7.

FIGURE 4.7.

The form up to this point.

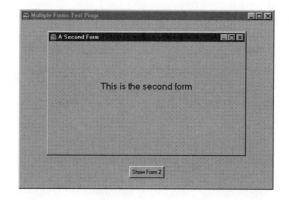

10. Click on the main form. The second form is covered by the main form. Double-click the Show Form 2 button. The Code Editor is displayed and the cursor is placed just where you need to begin typing code (double-clicking a button is a shortcut way of generating an OnClick event handler).

11. Type in code so that the function looks like this (you have to type only one line of code):

```
procedure TMainForm.ShowFrom2Click(Sender: TObject);
begin
  SecondForm.ShowModal;
end;
```

12. Run the program.

At this point you get a message box that says, Form 'MainForm' references form 'SecondForm' declared in unit 'second' which is not in your USES list. Do you wish to add it? Click Yes and Delphi will add the unit Second to the uses list of the unit Main. Click the Run button again and this time the application will run. When you click the Show Form 2 button on the main form, the second form is displayed. You can close the second form by clicking the system close box on the form's title bar.

Adding Units

Rather than having Delphi prompt you to add a unit to your uses list, you can add units
yourself. You can manually type the unit name in the uses list for the form, or you can
choose File I Use Unit from the main menu. When you choose the latter method, the Use
Unit dialog box is displayed, as shown in Figure 4.8. The Use Unit dialog box shows a
list of available units. Choose the unit you want to add and click OK. Delphi will add the
unit to the current form's uses list. Note that the Use Unit dialog box will show only
those units that exist in the project *and* have not yet been included in this unit. Units that
have already been included do not show up in the list of available units.

FIGURE 4.8.

*The Use Unit dialog
box.*

As you can see, Delphi does a good job of managing units for you. Later, when your
programming needs are more sophisticated, you'll have to do a little more source file
management, but at this stage of the game Delphi does most of the work for you.

Now let's take a moment to look at the different compiling options available to you
when writing programs in Delphi.

Compiling, Building, and Linking

Each time you click the Run button, Delphi compiles and links your program. But it
doesn't necessarily compile every unit in the project. It only compiles any units that
have changed since the last compile. This feature saves you time because you don't have
to wait for the compiler to compile files that haven't changed. Delphi keeps track of
which files have changed and which haven't, so you don't need to do anything special to
use this feature—it's automatic.

Most of the time you want to see the results of any changes you have made in action. In
those cases, click the Run button and the program is compiled, linked, and executed.
Sometimes, however, you don't want to run the program. For example, you might just
want to compile the program to see whether there are any errors.

Delphi has three menu items in addition to Run that enable you to control the
compile/link process. If you choose the Project menu item on the main menu, you see
three menu items called Compile, Build, and Syntax Check. These menu items' text
changes to reflect the name of the active project. For example, when you first start

Delphi, these menu items will say Compile Project1, Build Project1, and Syntax Check Project 1. (There are also menu items called Compile All Projects and Build All Projects, but I'll save that discussion for Day 9 when I discuss project groups.) Let's take these in order of simplest to most complex (from the compiler's perspective):

- The Syntax Check option is one I really like. This feature causes Delphi to compile the project and report any errors and warnings. This is the fastest way to check for errors in your code. Delphi only compiles the project—it does not perform a link. The purpose of the Syntax Check option is to check your code for syntax errors as quickly as possible. Because the link phase takes extra time, the Syntax Check option skips that step.

- The Compile option compiles any units that have changed since the last compile just as Syntax Check does, but it also links the entire project. Naturally, this takes slightly longer than the Syntax Check option. Use the Compile option when you want to be sure the program will compile and link but you don't want to run the program.

Tip

The keyboard shortcut for the Compile option is Ctrl+F9.

4

- The Build option takes the longest to perform. This option compiles every unit in the project regardless of whether it has changed since the last build. After compiling all units, Delphi links the entire project.

So far, you have been letting Delphi add units to your projects. Further on down the road you might have to do some hand-editing of your source files to add units or compiler directives. You might even end up editing the project source. From time to time things can get goofed up (hey, we all make mistakes). Performing a build will bring everything up-to-date so that you can better sort out any problems you might be running into. Sometimes a build resolves compiler and linker errors without the need for you to do anything further.

Tip

Any time you get unexpected (out of the ordinary) compiler or linker errors, first try a build. It could just be that something is out of sync, and a build might cure it. If performing a build doesn't fix the problem, you'll have to go to work figuring out where the problem lies.

Delphi gives you the option of displaying a compile status dialog box during compiles. You can turn on this option through the Environment Options dialog box (Preferences page). When this option is on, the compile status dialog box shows the filename of each unit as the unit is being compiled. If there are errors, the compile status dialog box will report There are errors and will list the number of errors that were detected as well as any warnings.

Figure 4.9 shows the compile status dialog box after detecting errors. Delphi compiles your projects so quickly that the compile status dialog box is not generally necessary. In fact, the compile status dialog box will increase your compile times because it takes time to display information in the compile status dialog box.

FIGURE 4.9.

The compile status dialog box reporting errors.

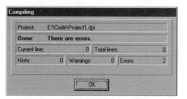

Regardless of the method chosen to compile the project, if errors are detected, the Code Editor will come to the top and the message window at the bottom of the Code Editor will show a list of errors and warnings. The Code Editor highlights the line where the first error occurred. After a successful syntax check, compile, or build, you can immediately run the program via the Run button if you choose.

Compiling and Building Other Object Pascal Programs

Delphi's strength is in its visual programming environment. That environment is tied directly to VCL and cannot be separated from it. To get the most out of Delphi, you will most likely be writing applications based on VCL. There are times, however, when you might want to write other types of applications.

 A *dynamic link library* (DLL) is an external file that contains code that can be executed from a program or from another DLL.

Probably the most obvious type of "other" program you might want to build is a DLL. DLLs might seem a bit like black magic, but they are really not very complicated: They are simply bits of compiled code that you can call from your application. After you create the DLL, calling a function contained in a DLL is no different than calling a function contained in your main program. That's a bit of an oversimplification, but it is still accurate. DLLs are discussed on Day 19, "Creating and Using DLLs."

Another type of application you might write with Delphi is a Win32 console application.

NEW TERM A Win32 *console application* is a 32-bit program that runs in a DOS box under Windows 95 or Windows NT.

Console applications are useful for small utility programs, servers such as TCP/IP servers or mail servers, and a whole host of other possibilities. Basically, any application that does not require a graphical interface is a good candidate for a console application.

More About Delphi Forms

Before I continue with the discussion about the Delphi IDE, I need to spend some time explaining forms. You have seen several forms in action as you have worked through this book, and on Day 6 you are going to learn all about the Form Designer. Before you get there, you need some more background information on forms, so I'll cover that now.

Main Window Forms

Forms are the main building block of a Delphi application. Every GUI application has at least one form that serves as the main window. The main window form might be just a blank window, it might have controls on it, or it might have a bitmap displayed on it. In a typical Windows program, your main window would have a menu. It might also have decorations such as a toolbar or a status bar. Just about anything goes when creating the main window of your application. Each application is unique, and each has different requirements.

Dialog Box Forms

Forms are also used for dialog boxes. In fact, to the user there is no difference between a Delphi form acting as a dialog box and a true dialog box. (By "true dialog box" I mean a dialog box created the traditional way with a resource editor and a resource script file. This is how dialog boxes are created in some other programming environments. Delphi doesn't use traditional dialog boxes, so you will likely never have to deal with dialog boxes on this level.) Dialog boxes usually have several traits that distinguish them from ordinary windows:

- Dialog boxes are not usually sizable. They usually perform a specific function, and sizing of the dialog box is neither useful nor desirable.

- Dialog boxes almost always have an OK button. Some dialog boxes have a button labeled Close that performs the same task. A simple dialog box such as an About dialog box typically has only the OK button.

- Dialog boxes can also have a Cancel button and a Help button.

- Dialog boxes typically have only the system close button on the title bar. They do not usually have minimize and maximize buttons.

- Some dialog boxes are *tabbed dialog boxes* that display several tabs from which the user can choose. When a tab is clicked, a different page of the dialog box is displayed.

- The Tab key can be used to move from one control to the next in most dialog boxes.

There are certainly exceptions to every rule. Most dialog boxes have the usual characteristics, but some dialog boxes perform specialty tasks and as such depart from the norm in one way or another.

Dialogs the Old-Fashioned Way

In a traditional Windows program (one written in Borland Pascal or using a framework such as OWL), a dialog box is created with a dialog box editor. In most cases, the dialog box editor is a visual tool that works somewhat like the Delphi Form Designer. When the user is done designing the dialog box, the visual representation of the dialog box is converted into a dialog box definition in a resource script file. To illustrate, take a look at the dialog box shown in Figure 4.10.

 A *resource script* is a text file that is later compiled into a binary resource file by the resource compiler.

FIGURE 4.10.

A typical About dialog box.

Figure 4.10 shows a typical About dialog box. It contains the program name, the copyright information, and the application's icon. The resource script definition for the dialog box is shown in Listing 4.1.

LISTING 4.1. A DIALOG BOX RESOURCE DEFINITION.

```
 1: IDD_ABOUT DIALOG 58, 53, 194, 119
 2: STYLE DS_MODALFRAME or WS_POPUP ¦
 3:   WS_VISIBLE or WS_CAPTION or WS_SYSMENU
 4: CAPTION 'About TMMPlayer Example Program'
 5: FONT 8, 'MS Sans Serif'
 6: {
 7:   DEFPUSHBUTTON 'OK', IDOK, 72, 96, 50, 14
 8:   CTEXT 'TMMPlayer Example Program', -1, 48, 22, 128, 8
 9:   CTEXT 'Copyright © 1996, by Kent Reisdorph', -1, 32, 47, 136, 8
10:   CTEXT 'March 15, 1996', -1, 24, 59, 146, 8
11:   CONTROL '', 99, 'button', BS_GROUPBOX ¦
12:     WS_CHILD or WS_VISIBLE or WS_GROUP, 12, 4, 176, 70
13:   CONTROL 1, 1, 'static', SS_ICON ¦
14:     SS_SUNKEN or WS_CHILD or WS_VISIBLE, 24, 17, 20, 20
15: }
```

4

The resource script contains information that Windows uses to build the dialog box at runtime. This information includes the number and type of controls on the dialog box, their size, position, text, options, and so on. Of course, the resource script also includes the same type of information for the actual dialog box.

Some Windows programmers don't use a dialog box editor at all, but prefer to write the dialog box definition from scratch with a text editor. Although I can't fault those programmers for creating dialog boxes in that manner, I can say that for most programmers to take that approach would be, er…, less than 100 percent efficient. It takes many times longer to create a dialog box in that manner as opposed to the visual approach.

Usually, all the application's dialog box definitions are contained in a single resource script file that has a filename extension of .rc. At some point in the program-creation process, the resource script is compiled into a .res file (the binary resource file), which then is linked to the .exe by the linker. At runtime the dialog box is displayed either modally or modelessly depending on the dialog box's intended purpose. When the dialog box is invoked, Windows loads the dialog box resource from the executable file, builds the dialog box, and displays it.

Dialog Boxes the Delphi Way

In Delphi, dialog boxes are simply another form. You create a dialog box just like you do a main window form or any other form. To prevent the dialog box from being sized, you can change the BorderStyle property to bsDialog or bsSingle. If you use bsDialog, your dialog box will have only the close box button on the title bar, which is traditional for dialog boxes. Other than that, you don't have to do anything special to get a form to behave like a dialog box. All Delphi forms have tabbing support built in. You can set the tab order by altering the TabOrder property of the individual controls on the dialog box.

| NEW TERM | A *modal* dialog box is one that must be dismissed before the user can continue using the application. The main window of an application is disabled while this type of dialog box is open. Most dialog boxes are modal. |

| NEW TERM | A *modeless* dialog box is one that allows the user to continue to work with the application while the dialog box is displayed. The Find dialog box in some word-processing programs is an example of a modeless dialog box. |

A Delphi dialog box (any Delphi form, actually) is modal or modeless depending on how it is displayed. To execute a modal dialog box, you call the ShowModal method of TForm. To create a modeless dialog box, you call the Show method.

Creating a Dialog Form

You can now add an About box to the multiple-forms project you created earlier. If you don't have that project open, choose File | Open Project from the main menu or click the Open Project button on the toolbar and locate the file. (You should have saved it with the project name of Multiple.)

| Tip | Delphi keeps a list of the files and projects you have used most recently. Choose File | Reopen to view the MRU (most recently used) list. The MRU list is divided into two parts. The top part shows the projects you have used most recently, and the bottom part shows the individual files that you have used most recently. Just click on one of the items to reopen that project or file. |

First you'll add a button to the form that displays the About dialog box:

1. Bring the main form into view. Choose the Button component from the Component palette and drop a button on the form.

2. Arrange the two buttons that are now on the form to balance the look of the form.

3. Change the Name property of the new button to AboutButton and the Caption property to About....

4. Double-click the AboutButton you just created on the form. The Code Editor is displayed with the cursor placed in the event-handler function. Add this line of code at the cursor:

```
AboutBox.ShowModal;
```

You haven't actually created the About box yet, but when you do you'll name it AboutBox, so you know enough to type the code that will display the About box.

Now create the dialog box itself by following these steps:

1. Create a new form (click the New Form button on the toolbar). Size the form to the size of a typical About box (roughly the same size as the form named SecondForm you created earlier).

2. Change the Name property to AboutBox and change the Caption property to About This Program.

3. Locate the BorderStyle property (it's just above Caption) and change it to bsDialog.

4. Now add three text labels to the box. Edit the labels so that the About box resembles the one shown in Figure 4.11. (You can type any text you want, of course.) You can leave the default names Delphi generates for the text labels' Name properties. You aren't actually going to do anything with the Name property, so you don't need a descriptive name.

FIGURE 4.11.

The About box with text labels added.

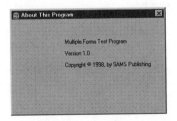

The copyright symbol (©) has an ASCII value of 169 in most typefaces. To create the copyright symbol, press and hold the Alt key and type the numbers 0169 on the numeric keypad (be sure Num Lock is on). When you let go of the Alt key, the copyright symbol appears. You can insert the ASCII value of any character this way. You must type all four numbers, though. For example, the ASCII value of a capital A is 65. To insert an A, you have to hold down Alt and type 0065 on the numeric keypad.

Next, you can add an icon to the About box:

1. Click the Additional tab on the Component palette and choose the Image component. Place the component to the left of the text on the form.

2. Locate the AutoSize property for the Image component and change it to True.

3. Locate the Picture property and double-click the Value column. The Picture Editor dialog box is displayed.

4. Click the Load button. In the File Open dialog box, navigate to the \Borland Shared Files\Images\Icons directory and choose an icon from the icon files listed. Click Open. The icon you selected is displayed in the Picture Editor window. Click OK to close the Picture Editor. The icon is displayed on the form. Note that the Image component has sized itself to the size of the icon.

5. Position the icon as desired.

At this point you need an OK button on the form. Let's branch out a little and take a look at a new component:

1. If you're not already there, click the Additional tab on the Component palette. Select the BitBtn component and place a BitBtn on the form near the bottom and center it horizontally.

2. Locate the Kind property and change it to bkOK. Notice that a green check mark has appeared on the button and the Caption property has changed to OK. That's all you have to do with the button. The BitBtn component already includes code to close the form when the OK button is clicked.

Let's add one final touch to the About box:

1. Locate the Bevel button (on the Additional tab in the Component palette) and click it.

2. Move to the form, but rather than clicking on it, drag a box around the three text labels. The Bevel component appears when you stop dragging. If you didn't get it quite right, you can resize or reposition the component.

3. Locate the Shape property and change it to bsFrame. You now have a 3D frame around the static text.

Your form should now look something like the one shown in Figure 4.12. Save the unit (File|Save) and give it the name About.

FIGURE 4.12.

The finished About box.

Are you ready to compile and run the program? Not yet. You need to add the About unit to the main form's uses list. Perform these steps:

1. Switch to the Code Editor (press F12) and select the Main.pas tab.
2. Choose File | Use Unit from the main menu.
3. Choose the About unit from the Use Unit dialog box and click OK.

Now you're ready to run the program, so click the Run button. When the program runs, click the About button, and the About dialog box is displayed. Note that the dialog box is modal (you can't go back to the main window while the dialog box is displayed) and that it cannot be sized. The About form behaves in every way like a regular Windows dialog box.

Note

The common dialog box classes (TOpenDialog, TSaveDialog, TFontDialog, and so on) do not represent dialog boxes created as Delphi forms. Windows provides these dialog boxes as a set of common dialog boxes that all Windows applications can use (the actual dialog boxes are contained in a file called COMDLG32.DLL). The VCL dialog box classes encapsulate the common dialog boxes to make using them easier. *Encapsulate* in this sense means to take a common dialog box's functionality and roll it into a VCL component. The component makes it much easier to use the dialog box than it would otherwise be.

Note

Delphi includes several prebuilt forms that you can choose from to help you build dialog boxes as quickly as possible. I'll discuss those on Day 8.

Secondary Windows Versus Dialog Boxes

A *secondary window* is a form that you display from your main window. So when is a form a secondary window and when it is a dialog box? When it really comes down to it, there is no difference between a secondary window and a dialog box in Delphi. You might have windows that resemble dialog boxes, and you might have other windows that resemble a traditional window.

In the grand scheme of things, they all are forms and it doesn't make much sense to differentiate between the terms *dialog box* and *secondary form*. It's all the same in the end. In traditional programming environments, you have to specifically create a dialog box or specifically create a secondary window in an application. Delphi frees you from that restriction and enables you to treat both dialog boxes and windows exactly the same.

The Multiple Document Interface Model

So far, you have built only single document interface (SDI) applications. An *SDI application* has a single main window and typically displays dialog boxes as needed, but does not otherwise display child windows.

NEW TERM Some programs follow the multiple document interface (MDI) model. *MDI applications* consist of a main window (the MDI parent) and child windows (the MDI children).

Examples of programs that use the MDI model are the Windows System Configuration Editor (SYSEDIT) and the Windows 3.1 Program Manager.

One of the most obvious characteristics of the MDI model is that the MDI child windows are confined to the parent. You can drag the child windows within the parent window, but you cannot drag them outside the parent. MDI applications almost always have a Window item on their main menu. This menu usually contains items named Cascade and Tile, which enable you to display the MDI child windows in either a cascaded or tiled arrangement. When an MDI child is minimized, its icon is contained within the MDI parent's frame. When a regular (non-MDI) child window is minimized, its icon is placed on the Windows desktop.

To create an MDI application in Delphi, you must set the main form's FormStyle property to fsMDIForm. Each of the MDI child windows must have the FormStyle property set to fsMDIChild. Aside from that restriction, there is very little to creating an MDI application in Delphi. You simply create the main window form and one or more forms to be used as child windows, and you're off and running.

Key Properties for Forms

The TForm class has a lot of properties. Some of these properties are obscure and rarely used; others are widely used. I'll touch on the most widely used properties here. I won't include obvious properties such as Caption, Color, Left, Top, Width, and Height unless they have a particular feature you should be aware of.

Design-Time Properties

The properties outlined in this section can be set at design time and also at runtime. Almost all these properties can be read at runtime as well.

ActiveControl   The ActiveControl property is used to set the control that will have focus when the form is activated. For example, you might want a particular edit control to have focus when a dialog box form is displayed. At design time, the Value column for the ActiveControl property contains a list of components on the form. You can choose one of the components from this list to make that component the active control when the form is first displayed.

AutoScroll, HorzScrollBar, and VertScrollBar   Together, the AutoScroll, HorzScrollBar, and VertScrollBar properties control the scrollbars for a form. If AutoScroll is set to True (the default), scrollbars automatically appear when the form is too small to display all its components. The HorzScrollBar and VertScrollBar properties each have several properties of their own that control the scrollbar operations.

BorderIcons   The BorderIcons property controls which system buttons will appear on the form at runtime. Choices include the system menu, the minimize button, the maximize button, and the help button.

BorderStyle   The BorderStyle property indicates what type of border the form will have. The default value is bsSizeable, which creates a window that can be sized. Non-sizable styles include bsDialog and bsNone.

ClientWidth and ClientHeight   You can specify the client area width and height rather than the full form's width and height by using the ClientWidth and ClientHeight properties. (The *client area* of the form is the area inside of the borders and below the title bar and menu bar.) Use these properties when you want the client area to be a specific size and the rest of the window to adjust as necessary. Setting the ClientWidth and ClientHeight properties makes automatic changes to the Width and Height properties.

New to 4 **Constraints**   The Constraints property is used to set the maximum and minimum width and height of the form. Simply set the MaxHeight, MaxWidth, MinHeight, and MinWidth values as desired and the form will conform to those constraints.

4

New to 4 **DefaultMonitor**   The DefaultMonitor property determines which monitor the form will appear on in a multimonitor environment (such as Windows 98).

DockSite   The DockSite property determines whether the form will act as a dock site for dockable components. Dock sites and dockable components are discussed on Day 13, "Beyond the Basics."

Font   The Font property specifies the font that the form uses. The important issue to understand here is that the form's font is inherited by any components placed on the form. This also means that you can change the font used by all components at one time by changing just the form's font. If an individual control's font has been manually changed, that control's font will not be changed when the main form's font changes.

FormStyle   This property is usually set to fsNormal. If you want a form to always be on top, use the fsStayOnTop style. MDI forms should use the fsMDIForm style and MDI child forms should use the fsMDIChild style. MDI forms and MDI child windows were discussed earlier in this chapter in the section "The Multiple Document Interface Model."

HelpContext and HelpFile   The HelpContext property is used to set the help context ID for a form. If context help is enabled for a form, the Windows Help system will activate when the F1 key is pressed. The context ID is used to tell the Help system which page in the help file to display. The HelpFile property is the name of the help file that will be used when F1 is pressed.

Icon   The Icon property sets the icon that is used on the title bar for the form when the form is displayed at runtime and also when the form is minimized. In some cases, setting this property has no effect. For example, when the FormStyle is set to fsDialog, the Icon property is ignored.

KeyPreview   When KeyPreview is True, the form's OnKeyPress and OnKeyDown events will be generated when a key is pressed in any component on the form. Ordinarily, forms don't receive keyboard events when a component on the form has focus.

Position   The Position property determines the size and position of the form when the form is initially displayed. The three basic choices are poDesigned, poDefault, and poScreenCenter:

- poDesigned causes the form to be displayed in the exact position it was in when it was designed.

- poDefault enables Windows to set the size and position according to the usual Windows Z-ordering algorithm. (Z-ordering is what Windows uses to decide where it displays a new window on the screen. If the new window does not have specific placement information, it will be displayed just below and to the right of the last window displayed on the screen.)
- The poScreenCenter option causes the form to be displayed in the center of the screen each time it is shown.

Visible   The Visible property controls whether the form is initially visible. This property is not particularly useful at design time, but at runtime it can be read to determine whether the form is currently visible. It can also be used to hide or display the form.

WindowState   The WindowState property can be read to determine the form's current state (maximized, minimized, or normal). It can also be used to indicate how the form should initially be displayed. Choices are wsMinimized, wsMaximized, and wsNormal.

Runtime-Only Properties

Some properties can be accessed only at runtime through code. The following are the most commonly used runtime properties.

ActiveMDIChild   When read, the ActiveMDIChild property returns a pointer to the currently active MDI child window. This property is read only. If no MDI child is currently active or if the application is not an MDI application, ActiveMDIChild returns nil.

Canvas   The form's canvas represents the drawing surface of the form. The Canvas property gives you access to the form's canvas. By using the Canvas property, you can draw bitmaps, lines, shapes, or text on the form at runtime. Most of the time you will use a Label component to draw text on a form, an Image component to display graphics, and a Shape component to draw shapes. However, there are times when you need to draw on the canvas at runtime and the Canvas property enables you to do that. The Canvas property can also be used to save an image of the form to disk. Canvases are discussed in more detail on Day 12, "Graphics and Multimedia Programming."

ClientRect   The ClientRect property contains the top, left, right, and bottom coordinates of the client area of the form. This is useful in a variety of programming situations. For example, you might need to know the client area's width and height in order to place a bitmap on the center of the form.

Handle   The Handle property returns the window handle (HWND) of the form. Use this property when you need the window handle to pass to a Windows API function.

4

ModalResult The ModalResult property is used to indicate how a modal form was closed. If you have a dialog box that has OK and Cancel buttons, you can set ModalResult to mrOK when the user clicks the OK button and to mrCancel when the user clicks the Cancel button. The calling form can then read ModalResult to see which button was clicked to close the form. Other possibilities include mrYes, mrNo, and mrAbort.

Owner The Owner property is a pointer to the owner of the form. The owner of the form is the object that is responsible for deleting the form when the form is no longer needed. The parent of a component, on the other hand, is the window (a form or another component) that acts as the container for the component. In the case of a main form, the application object is both the owner of the form and the parent of the form. In the case of components, the owner would be the form, but the parent could be another component such as a panel.

Parent The Parent property is a pointer to the parent of the form. See the previous section about Owner for an explanation of Owner versus Parent.

Form Methods

Forms are components, too. As such, forms have many methods in common with components. Common methods include Show, ShowModal, and Invalidate, to name just a few. There are some methods, however, that are specific to forms. As before, I'll discuss only the most commonly used methods.

BringToFront

The BringToFront method causes the form to be brought to the top of all other forms in the application.

Close and CloseQuery

The Close method closes a form after first calling CloseQuery to ensure that it's okay to close the form. The CloseQuery function in turn calls the OnCloseQuery event handler. If the Boolean variable passed to the OnCloseQuery handler is set to False, the form is not closed. If it is set to True, the form closes normally. You can use the OnCloseQuery event handler to prompt the user to save a file that needs saving and to control whether a form can close.

Print

The Print method prints the contents of the form. Only the client area of the form is printed, not the caption, title bar, or borders. Print is handy for quick screen dumps of a form.

ScrollInView

The ScrollInView method scrolls the form so that the specified component is visible on the form.

SetFocus

The SetFocus method activates the form and brings it to the top. If the form has components, the component specified in the ActiveControl property will receive input focus (see the ActiveControl property in the section "Design-Time Properties").

Show and ShowModal

The Show and ShowModal methods display the form. The Show method displays the form as modeless, so other forms can be activated while the form is visible. The ShowModal method executes the form modally. Recall that a modal form must be dismissed before the user can continue to use the application.

MDI Methods

Several form methods deal specifically with MDI operations. The ArrangeIcons method arranges the icons of any minimized MDI children in an MDI parent window. The Cascade method cascades all nonminimized MDI child windows. The Tile method tiles all open MDI child windows. The Next method activates (brings to the top) the next MDI child in the child list, and the Previous method activates the previous MDI child in the child list. The MDI methods apply only to MDI parent windows.

Form Events

Forms can respond to a wide variety of events. Some of the most commonly used are listed in the following sections.

OnActivate

The OnActivate event occurs when the form is initially activated. The form might be activated as a result of its initial creation or when the user switches from one form to another. The Application object also has an OnActivate event that is generated when the user switches from another application to your application.

OnClose and OnCloseQuery

When an application is closed, the OnClose event is sent. OnClose calls the OnCloseQuery event to see whether it is okay to close the form. If the OnCloseQuery event returns False, the form is not closed.

OnCreate

The OnCreate event occurs when the form is initially created. Only one OnCreate event will occur for any instance of a particular form. Use the OnCreate handler to perform any startup tasks that the form needs in order to operate.

OnDestroy

The OnDestroy event is the opposite of OnCreate. Use this event to clean up any memory a form allocates dynamically or to do other cleanup chores.

OnDragDrop

The OnDragDrop event occurs when an object is dropped on the form. Respond to this event if your form supports drag and drop.

OnMouseDown, OnMouseMove, and OnMouseUp

Respond to the OnMouseDown, OnMouseMove, and OnMouseUp events in order to respond to mouse clicks and mouse movements on a form.

OnPaint

The OnPaint event occurs whenever the form needs repainting, which could happen for a variety of reasons. Respond to this event to do any painting that your application needs to display at all times. In most cases, individual components will take care of painting themselves, but in some cases you might need to draw on the form itself.

OnResize

The OnResize event is sent every time the form is resized. You might need to respond to this event to adjust components on the form or to repaint the form.

OnShow

The OnShow event occurs just before the form becomes visible. You can use this event to perform any processing that your form needs to do just before it is shown.

Note

When a form is created, many events are generated. Likewise, when a form is destroyed, several events are generated. But in what order are these events generated? When a form is created, the following events occur in this order (the constructor and AfterConstruction virtual methods are listed in addition to the events):

> The form's constructor
>
> OnCreate event
>
> AfterConstruction method

```
        OnShow event

        OnActivate event
When a form is destroyed, the following events are generated in this order:

        OnCloseQuery event

        OnClose event

        BeforeDestruction method

        OnDestroy event

        The form's destructor
```

In most applications, keeping the order straight generally is not important. In some cases, however, it can be critical. Knowing the order in which the event handlers, the constructor, and the destructor are called can save you some frustration when you really need to know.

The Object Inspector

An integral part of the Delphi IDE is the Object Inspector. This window works with the Form Designer to aid in the creation of components. I'm going to discuss the Form Designer on Day 6, but before I do I want to talk a little about the Object Inspector.

The Object Inspector is where you set the design-time properties that affect how the component acts at runtime. The Object Inspector has three main areas:

- The Component Selector
- The Properties page
- The Events page

You have been using the Object Inspector quite a bit up to this point, so I'll review what you already know and show you a few features you probably don't know about.

The Component Selector

Normally, you select a component by clicking the component on a form. The Component Selector provides an alternative way of selecting a component to view or modify. The Component Selector is a drop-down combo box that is located at the top of the Object Inspector window.

4

Note   Usually the quickest way to select a component is by clicking the component on the form. Choosing the component from the Component Selector is convenient if the component you are looking for is hidden beneath another component or is off the visible area of the form.

The Component Selector displays the name of the component and the class from which it is derived. For example, a memo component named Memo would appear in the Component Selector as

Memo: TMemo

The class name does not show up in the drop-down list of components; it only appears in the top portion of the Component Selector. To select a component, click the drop-down button to reveal the list of components and then click the one you want to select.

 Note   The Component Selector shows only the components available on the current form and the name of the form itself. Other forms and their components will not be displayed until they are made active in the Form Designer.

After you select a component in the Component Selector, the component is selected on the form as well. The Properties and Events tabs change to display the properties and events for the selected component. (Remember that a form is a component, too.) Figure 4.13 shows the Object Inspector with the Component Selector list displayed.

FIGURE 4.13.

The Component Selector list.

The Properties Page

The Properties page of the Object Inspector displays all the design-time properties for the currently selected control. The Properties page has two columns: The Property column is on the left side of the Properties page and shows the property name; the Value column is on the right side of the Properties page and is where you type or select the value for the property.

If the selected component has more properties than will fit in the Object Inspector, a scrollbar will be provided so that you can scroll up or down to locate other properties.

> If you have multiple components selected on the form, the Object Inspector shows all the properties that those components have in common. You can use this feature to modify the properties of several components at one time. For example, to change the width of several components at one time, you can select all the components and then modify the Width property in the Object Inspector. When you press Enter or move to another property, all the components you selected will have their Width property modified.

Figure 4.14 shows the Object Inspector when a Memo component is selected.

FIGURE 4.14.

The Object Inspector showing Memo component properties.

Properties can be integer values, enumerations, sets, other objects, strings, and other types. (Properties are discussed in detail tomorrow.) The Object Inspector deals with each type of property according to the data type of the property. Delphi has several built-in property editors to handle data input for the property. For example, the Top property accepts an Integer value. Because the Integer type is a basic data type, no special handling is required, so the property editor is fairly basic. The property editor for this type of property enables you to type a value directly in the Value column for integer properties such as Top, Left, Width, and Height.

Note

> In most cases, the property editor does parameter checking for any properties in which you can enter an integer value. The Width property, for example, cannot be a negative number. If you attempt to enter a negative number for the Width of a control, Delphi will force the width to the minimum allowed for that control (usually 0). If you enter a string value for a property that expects an integer value, Delphi will display an error message. It is the job of the property editor to do parameter checking.

In many cases, the property editor for the property contains a list of items from which you can choose. Properties that have an enumeration or Boolean value as their base data type fall into this category. When you click the Value column with this type of property editor, you will see a drop-down button on the right side of the Value column. Clicking this button displays the list of possible values.

Tip

> If you double-click the Value column for this type of property, the property editor will cycle through the possible choices. To quickly change a Boolean property, for example, simply double-click its value. Because the only choices are True and False, double-clicking the value has the effect of toggling the property's value.

If you look closely at the Object Inspector, you will see that some properties have a plus sign preceding their names. Properties that are sets and properties that are classes both have the plus sign in front of their names. The plus sign indicates that the property node can be expanded to show the set or, in the case of properties that are classes, the properties of that class. To expand a node, double-click on the Property column for that property (on the property name) or choose Expand from the Object Inspector context menu. To collapse the node, double-click it again or choose Collapse from the Object Inspector context menu.

To see an example of a set property, choose a form and then double-click the BorderIcons property in the Object Inspector. The node expands and you see four members of the set. You can turn on or off any of the four members as needed.

In the case of properties that are objects (instances of a VCL class), you have two choices in editing the property. First, you can click the Value column for the property and then click the button to the right side of the value (if one exists). This button is indicated by an ellipsis (...) on its face. Clicking this button invokes the property editor for that particular control. For example, click the Font property and then click the ellipsis button. The Choose Font dialog box is displayed so that you can select the font.

The second way you can edit this type of property is by expanding the property node. The property's properties (yes, it's true) will be displayed, and you can edit them just like any other property. Again, locate the Font property and double-click it. The TFont properties will be displayed. You can now modify the font's Height, Color, Name, and other properties.

Some properties have only the ellipsis button as a means of editing the property. Earlier you used the Image component to select an icon for the Multiple program's About box. As you found out then, the Image component's Picture property can be changed only by invoking that property's property editor. In that case, the property editor is the Delphi Picture Editor.

Rest assured that each property knows what it needs to do to present you with the correct property editor. You will see different types of property editors as you are introduced to new components and new properties.

The Events Page

The Events page lists all the events that the component is designed to handle. Using the Events page is pretty basic. In order to create an event handler for an event, you simply double-click in the Value column next to the event you want to handle. When you do, Delphi creates an event-handling function for you with all the parameters needed to handle that event. The Code Editor is displayed and the cursor is placed in the event handler. All you have to do is start typing code. The name of the function is generated based on the Name property of the component and the event being handled. If, for example, you have a button named OKBtn and are handling the OnClick event, the function name generated would be OKBtnClick.

You can let Delphi generate the name of the event-handling function for you or you can provide the function name for Delphi to use. To provide the function name yourself, type the name in the Value column next to the event and press Enter. The Code Editor is displayed, and so is the event-handling function, complete with the name you supplied.

Note

> Delphi will remove any empty event handlers when you run, compile, or save a unit. For example, let's say you created an event handler for the OnCreate event but didn't type any code. The next time you run, compile, or save the unit, Delphi will remove the event handler you just created because it doesn't contain any code. This is the way Delphi is designed and it makes perfect sense, but it can be a bit puzzling if you aren't aware of what is going on. If you don't want Delphi to remove the event handler, either type code right away or type a comment line so that the event handler won't be removed.

After you create an event-handling function for a component, you can use that event handler for any component that handles the same event. Sometimes it's convenient to have several buttons use the same OnClick event, for example. To take it a step further, you might have a main menu item, a pop-up menu item, and a toolbar button all use the same OnClick handler. You will learn to appreciate this kind of code reuse as you gain experience with Delphi. Even though you are dealing with three different components, they can still share a common OnClick handler. The Value column of the Events page contains a drop-down button that can be used to display a list of all event handlers compatible with the current event. All you have to do is choose an event from the list.

Dockable IDE Windows

New to 4 A new feature in Delphi 4 is dockable windows.

NEW TERM A *dockable window* is a window that can be dragged from its current location (using the mouse) and docked to one of the IDE's dock sites.

NEW TERM A *dock site* is a specific location in the IDE where a dockable window can be docked. The IDE has several dock sites.

Just about every window in Delphi is dockable. This includes the Project Manager, the Code Explorer, the Object Inspector, the Watch List window, the Message window, and on and on. In fact, there are very few windows in Delphi that are not dockable.

Am I enamored with dockable windows just for the sake of dockable windows alone? Not in the least. I don't even bother with dockable windows in most Windows programs I own. In the Delphi IDE, however, dockable windows make me more productive and that's why I like them.

Dock Sites

You can't talk about dockable windows without talking about dock sites. Sure, you can undock a window and drag it around on the screen, dropping it wherever you want. That just makes for a bunch of scattered windows all over your screen, though. In order for dockable windows to make sense, you have to have a place to dock them. In the Delphi IDE that usually means the Code Editor window.

The Code Editor has three dock sites. One dock site is along the left side of the Code Editor window. This dock site is where the Code Explorer is docked when you first start Delphi. Another dock site is along the bottom of the Code Editor window. The default Delphi configuration places the Message window in the bottom dock site (although you don't see the Message window unless there are messages to display). The third Code

Editor dock site is along the left edge of the Code Editor window. These three dock sites are really all you need to fully customize the IDE.

There is one other type of dock site that I want to mention. If you have a tool window open (such as the Project Manager), you can dock another tool window to it. This enables two or more Delphi windows to be hosted within the same tool window. For example, the Code Explorer and Project Manager can both be docked in the same floating tool window. A floating tool window has five dock sites: right, left, top, bottom, and center.

When you dock a window to the center of a tool window, the tool window becomes a tabbed window. Each tab in the window contains the title of the window that tab represents. I realize that doesn't make a lot of sense, so in just a bit I'll show you how to dock two tool windows together.

Experimenting with Dockable Windows

Rather than trying to put the relationships between the various windows into words, I think an exercise is in order. I'll start with the most basic docking operations and move to the more complex. This exercise doesn't take long and should prove very enlightening. Here goes:

1. Create a new application and switch to the Code Editor. Notice the Code Explorer is docked to the left side of the Code Editor.

2. Click the grip at the top of the Code Explorer window and drag to the right. Notice that you are dragging a gray rectangle. This rectangle indicates where the Code Explorer will appear when you stop dragging.

3. Drag the Code Explorer to the middle of the Code Editor and let go of the mouse. The Code Explorer becomes a floating tool window.

4. Click on the title bar of the Code Explorer tool window and drag it back to the left side of the Code Editor. When your mouse pointer reaches the left edge of the Code Editor, the drag rectangle pops into place. Let go of the mouse and the Code Explorer is once again docked to the Code Editor.

5. Undock the Code Explorer again and drag it to the bottom of the Code Editor. When your mouse pointer reaches the bottom edge of the Code Editor window, the drag rectangle snaps into place and is as wide as the Code Editor. Let go of the mouse button. The Code Explorer is docked to the Code Editor's bottom dock site. Notice that the drag grip is vertical when the Code Explorer is docked to the bottom dock site.

6. Move the Code Explorer back to the dock site on the left side of the Code Editor window. The Code Editor and Code Explorer should now look like they did when you started.

4

This exercise is simple but gives you an idea of what you can do with dockable windows at the most basic level. The next exercise is a little more interesting. Perform these steps:

1. Undock the Code Explorer and move it to the right. Drop it anywhere on the right side of the Code Editor.

2. Size the Code Explorer window so that it is roughly square.

3. Choose View | Project Manager from the main menu. The Project Manager is displayed.

4. Drag the Project Manager over the Code Explorer window. When the drag rectangle snaps into place in the center of the Code Explorer window, release the mouse button. The floating tool window should now look similar to Figure 4.15. Notice that the floating tool window has become a tabbed window and has the title Tool Windows. You can click on either of the two tabs to see the Code Explorer or the Project Manager.

FIGURE 4.15.

The Code Explorer and Project Manager docked together in a tool window.

5. Drag the tool window back to the left side of the Code Editor and dock it there. Now you have both the Code Explorer and the Project Manager docked where you can get to them easily whenever you want them.

Are you starting to get the picture? You can have as many tool windows as you want in one tabbed window. Let's do one more exercise along the same lines. Often you want the debugger Watch List window in view while you are debugging (debugging is discussed on Day 10, "Debugging Your Applications"). Let me show you how you can keep the Watch List window handy at all times. Perform these steps:

1. Right-click on the Code Editor and choose Message View from the Code Editor context menu. The message window appears in the Code Editor's bottom dock site.

2. Choose View | Debug Windows | Watches from the main menu. The Watch List window is displayed as a floating tool window.

3. Drag the Watch List window over the Message window and dock it to the center of the Message window. Two tabs appear in the dock site: Messages and Watch List.

Now you can click on the Watch List tab at the bottom of the Code Editor anytime you want to view your watches. The Message window takes care of itself, as it will come and go in the tabbed window any time there are messages to display. Figure 4.16 shows the IDE after performing the last exercise.

FIGURE 4.16.

Four tool windows docked to the Code Editor.

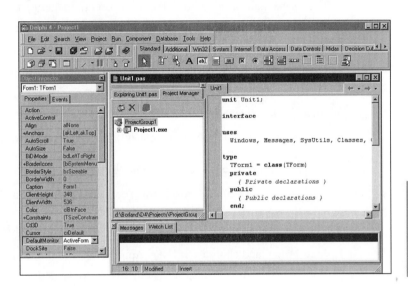

No Docking, Please

Sometimes you don't want a particular window to be dockable. As nice as dockable windows are, sometimes it's hard to find a location to place a window when you don't want it docked. It seems like anywhere you try to put the window it wants to dock to something. The good news is that you can shut off the docking capability of any tool window.

Each of the dockable tool windows has a menu item at the bottom of its context menu called Dockable. If Dockable is checked, the window is dockable. If Dockable is not checked, the window is not dockable and you can place it anywhere in the IDE.

The dockable windows in the Delphi IDE are a great feature. You can arrange the tool windows you use most often in any way you want. You no longer have to go hunting for a Project Manager, Watch List, or Object Inspector hidden under other windows. The window you are looking for is just a couple of mouse clicks away.

An MDI Sample Program

To help solidify today's discussion of projects and forms, let's create an MDI application. This application will enable you to open and save graphics files such as bitmaps, icons, and metafiles. In order to complete the task, you should have a master plan. Here's what you need to do:

1. Create the main window form (an MDI parent), including a menu.
2. Write code for the File I Open and File I Save menu selections.
3. Write code for the Cascade, Tile, and Arrange All items on the Window menu.
4. Create the MDI child forms.
5. Create an About box.
6. Stand back and admire your work.

There's no point in dawdling (time is money!), so let's get right to it.

Creating the Main Window Form

First you'll create the main window form. The main window for an MDI application must have the `FormStyle` property set to `fsMDIForm`. You also need to add a menu to the application, as well as File Open and File Save dialog boxes. Follow these steps:

1. Start Delphi and choose File I New Application from the main menu.
2. For the main form, change the `Name` property to `MainForm`.
3. Change the `Caption` property to `Picture Viewer`.
4. Change the `Height` to `450` and the `Width` to `575` (or other suitable values for your display resolution).
5. Change the `FormStyle` to `fsMDIForm`.

Okay, now you've got the main part of the form done. Next you'll add a menu to the form. Because I haven't discussed the Menu Designer yet, you will take the easy route to creating a menu. To do that, you can take advantage of a Delphi feature that enables you to import a predefined menu, as follows:

1. Click the Standard tab of the Component palette and click the MainMenu button.
2. Click on the form to place a `MainMenu` component on the form. It doesn't matter where you place the component because the icon representing the menu is just a placeholder and won't show on the form at runtime. This is how nonvisual components appear on a form.
3. Change the `Name` property to `MainMenu`.

4. Double-click the MainMenu component. The Menu Designer is displayed. (You'll read about the Menu Designer in more detail on Day 6.)

5. Place your cursor over the Menu Designer and click your right mouse button. Choose Insert from Template from the context menu. The Insert Template dialog box appears. Figure 4.17 shows the Insert Template dialog box with the Menu Designer behind it.

FIGURE 4.17.

The Menu Designer with the Insert Template dialog box open.

6. Choose MDI Frame Menu and click OK. The menu is displayed in the Menu Designer.

7. Click the system close box on the Menu Designer to close it.

Now you should be back to the main form. Notice that you have a menu on the form. You can click on the top-level items to see the full menu. Don't click on any menu subitems at this point—you'll do that in a minute. Notice that there are a lot of menu items. You won't need all them, but for now you can just leave the extra items where they are.

Now you need to prepare the File Open and File Save dialog boxes:

1. Click the Dialogs tab on the Component palette. Choose an OpenPictureDialog component and place it on the form. The OpenPictureDialog component's icon can be placed anywhere on the form.

2. Change the Name property of the Open dialog box to OpenPictureDialog.

3. Change the Title property to Open a Picture for Viewing.

4. Add a SavePictureDialog component.

5. Change the Name property of the component to SavePictureDialog and the Title property to Save a Picture.

Your form should now look like the one shown in Figure 4.18.

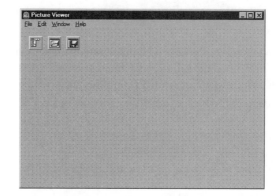

FIGURE 4.18.

The form up to this point.

Writing Code for the File I Open and File I Save As Menu Items

Now you are ready to write the code to implement the File I Open and File I Save As menu items. Delphi provides a slick way of writing menu handlers with a minimum amount of fuss. You haven't created the MDI child form yet, but you know enough about it to write the code for the menu handlers. Keep in mind that the application won't compile until you create the MDI child form. Here you go:

1. On the main form, choose File I Open from the menu. An event handler is created for that menu item and the Code Editor is displayed.

2. Type code so that the event handler looks like this:

```
procedure TMainForm.Open1Click(Sender: TObject);
var
  Child : TChild;
begin
  if OpenPictureDialog.Execute then begin
    Child := TChild.Create(Self);
    with Child.Image.Picture do begin
      LoadFromFile(OpenPictureDialog.FileName);
      Child.ClientWidth := Width;
      Child.ClientHeight := Height;
    end;
    Child.Caption := ExtractFileName(OpenPictureDialog.FileName);
    Child.Show;
  end;
end;
```

This code first executes the File Open dialog box and gets a filename. If the Cancel button on the File Open dialog box is clicked, the function returns without doing anything more. If the OK button on the File Open dialog box is clicked, a new TChild object is created (TChild will be the name of the MDI child class you'll create later). The image file is loaded into the Image component on the child form and the MDI child's client area is sized to match the size of the image. Finally, the Caption property is set to the filename selected and the child window is displayed.

> **Note**
>
> In the Open1Click method the ExtractFileName function is used to extract just the filename from the path and filename contained in the FileName property of the OpenPictureDialog component. Related functions include ExtractFilePath, ExtractFileDir, ExtractFileDrive, and ExtractFileExt.

> **Note**
>
> Remember yesterday's discussion about calling Free for all objects created dynamically? Notice that I appear to be violating that rule in the preceding code. In reality I am not, because VCL will take the responsibility of freeing the memory allocated for the MDI child windows. Notice that the single parameter in the TChild constructor is Self. That tells VCL that the Owner of the MDI child is the MDI form window. When the MDI form is destroyed (when the application closes), it will be sure to delete all its MDI child objects.

4

3. Press F12 to switch back to the form. Now choose File | Save As from the menu. The File | Save As event handler is displayed.

4. Type code so that the File | Save As event handler looks like this:

```
procedure TMainForm.SaveAs1Click(Sender: TObject);
begin
  if SavePictureDialog.Execute then
    with ActiveMDIChild as TChild do
      Image.Picture.SaveToFile(SavePictureDialog.FileName);
end;
```

The code for the File | Save As menu item is simple. The first two lines check to see whether an MDI child window is active. If so, the File Save dialog box is displayed. If the user clicks OK, the image is saved to disk using the TPicture class's SaveToFile method.

Note

In the preceding code you see the as operator in use. The ActiveMDIChild property returns a pointer to a TForm object. What you actually need in this case is a pointer to a TChild object (your MDI child class, derived from TForm) so that you can access the Image property of the MDI child form. The as operator casts the ActiveMDIChild variable to a TChild pointer. If for some reason as is unable to perform the cast, the code block following the as statement is ignored.

Before going on, it is a good idea to save the project. Choose File | Save All from the main menu. Save Unit1 (the default name Delphi assigns to a new unit) as PctViewU and the project as PictView.

Writing Code for the Window Menu

Now you can add code to the Window menu. This part is simple:

1. Switch back to the form by pressing F12. Choose Window | Tile from the form's menu.

2. You need to enter only a single line of code for the event handler. The finished event handler will look like this:

```
procedure TMainForm.Tile1Click(Sender: TObject);
begin
  Tile;
end;
```

3. Switch back to the form and repeat the process for Window | Cascade. The finished function looks like this:

```
procedure TMainForm.Cascade1Click(Sender: TObject);
begin
  Cascade;
end;
```

4. Repeat the steps for the Window | Arrange All menu item. The single line of code to add for the function body is the following:

```
ArrangeIcons;
```

Okay, now you're done with the main form. You can now move on to creating the MDI child form.

Creating the MDI Child Form

The MDI child form is surprisingly simple. In fact, you don't have to write any code at all. Just follow these steps:

1. Create a new form using the New Form button on the toolbar or by choosing File | New Form from the main menu.
2. Change the Name property to Child. The Caption property can be ignored because you will be setting the dialog box's caption at runtime.
3. Change the FormStyle property to fsMDIChild. This is necessary for the form to be treated as an MDI child window.

That's it for the form itself. Now let's put an Image component on the form. The Image component will display the graphics file selected by the user.

1. Click the Additional tab on the Component palette. Click the Image button and place an Image component anywhere on the form.
2. Change the Name property to Image.
3. Change the Stretch property to True.
4. Change the Align property to alClient. The Image component expands to fill the client area of the form.
5. Choose File | Save and save the form's unit as MDIChild.
6. Switch to the Code Editor (press F12 to toggle between the Form Designer and the Code Editor). Click the PctViewU tab. Now choose File | Use Unit from the main menu, select the MDIChild unit, and click OK. This is so the compiler is happy when you reference the TChild object.

The form is fairly unimpressive at this point, but it should look similar to Figure 4.19.

FIGURE 4.19.

The MDI child form with an Image *component.*

4

You still have to create the About box, but right now you're probably eager to try the program out. Go ahead and click the Run button. After a while, the program is displayed. You can choose File | Open and open any graphics file (any file with a `.bmp`, a `.wmf`, or an `.ico` extension, that is).

Notice that the MDI child window sizes itself to the graphic it contains. Open several files and then try out the Cascade and Tile options under the Window menu. If you want, you can save a file with a different name using the File | Save As menu item.

Creating the About Box

By now you should know enough about Delphi to create the About box on your own. Create the About box so that it looks something like the one in Figure 4.20. If you get stuck, you can jump back a few pages and review the steps you took to create the About box earlier in the chapter. Feel free to make your About box as personalized as you like.

FIGURE 4.20.

The About box for the application.

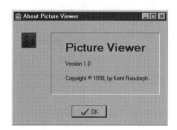

After you create the box, you can take these steps to call the box from the menu:

1. Change the Name property to AboutBox.
2. Save the unit as PVAboutU.

> **Note**
>
> Delphi has full support for long filenames. I use the 8.3 file-naming convention in this book for reasons related to electronic publishing. For applications you write, you can take advantage of long filenames.

3. Switch to the PctViewU tab in the Code Editor (press F12). Choose File | Use Unit from the main menu and include the PVAboutU unit.
4. Press F12 to switch back to the main form. Choose Help | About from the menu. You are taken to the Code Editor with the OnClick handler for the menu item displayed.

5. Add this line to the event handler:

```
AboutBox.ShowModal;
```

That should do it for now. Click the Run button and try out the About item on the Help menu. Figure 4.21 shows the Picture Viewer program running with several child windows open.

FIGURE 4.21.

The Picture Viewer program running.

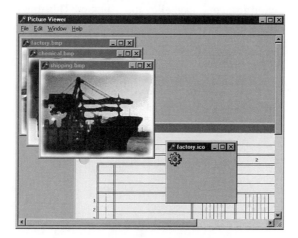

Polishing It Up

At this point the program is functional, but it isn't polished by any means. Still, for a 30-minute programming job, it's not too bad! There are a few problems with the program as it stands right now. If you try to open a file that is not a graphic, you will find that the program will throw an exception. I discuss exceptions and exception handling on Day 14, "Advanced Programming." Also, you have a lot of extra menu items that you need to get rid of. I'll show you how to do that on Day 6 as you work more with the Menu Designer.

There are two problems with this program that I think you should deal with because they are easy to fix. First, did you notice that a blank MDI child window was displayed when the application started? That's because a Delphi application automatically creates all forms when the application runs. In the case of an MDI child, that means the window is displayed when the application becomes visible. You are creating each MDI child form as needed, so you don't need to have Delphi auto-create the form for you.

4

Fortunately, removing the MDI child window form from the auto-create list is easy. Follow these steps:

1. Choose Project | Options from the main menu. The Project Options dialog box is displayed.

2. If necessary, click the Forms tab. The list of forms to auto-create is displayed.

3. Click the child form and then click the > button. This removes the child form from the auto-create list and puts it in the Available forms list. Figure 4.22 shows the Project Options dialog box after moving the child form to the Available forms list.

FIGURE 4.22.

The Project Options dialog box.

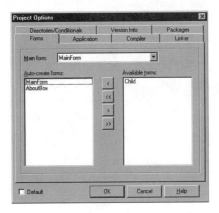

Now run the program again. This time the blank MDI child is not displayed.

If you remove a form from the auto-create list, you must be sure to specifically create the form prior to using it. If you do not create the form, the pointer to the form is uninitialized, which means that the pointer has not yet been assigned a meaningful value. (Remember that the pointer is automatically created by Delphi.) Attempting to use the pointer will result in an access violation or erratic program behavior. After you remove a form from the auto-create list, it is your responsibility to make sure the form has been created before using it.

Your application has one other problem I need to address. When you click the close button on one of the MDI windows, you will find that the window minimizes instead of closing. Believe it or not this is the standard behavior as prescribed by Microsoft.

Standard behavior or not, it's weird, so you can fix it so that clicking the close box actually closes the window (as any rational person would expect). To do so, follow these steps:

1. Bring up the child window form in the Form Designer. Be sure the form itself is selected and not the Image component on the form (choose the Child from the Component Selector at the top of the Object Inspector, if necessary).

2. Double-click the Value column next to the OnClose event in the Object Inspector. Add a line of code to the event handler so that it looks like this:

```
procedure TChild.FormClose(Sender: TObject; var Action:
TCloseAction);
begin
  Action := caFree;
end;
```

Setting the close action to caFree tells VCL to close the child window and to free the memory associated with the window. Now the child window will behave as it should when the close box is clicked.

3. Again run the program to prove that the program behaves as advertised.

Summary

The Delphi IDE can be intimidating until you become familiar with it. If you learn it a little at a time, it's not nearly so daunting. Today you learned more about the various pieces that make up the Delphi IDE. Then you learned about how projects are used to create an executable file. You also learned more about forms. You found out how Delphi deals with dialog boxes and other child windows. You found out more about the Object Inspector and how it can be used to change a component's properties. You also learned about the docking features of the Delphi IDE. Finally, you got to create a program that actually does something interesting. Tomorrow you'll find out about the visual component model.

Workshop

The Workshop contains quiz questions to help you solidify your understanding of the material covered and exercises to provide you with experience in using what you have learned. You can find the answers to the quiz questions in Appendix A, "Answers to the Quiz Questions."

Q&A

Q The Delphi toolbar doesn't have buttons for the features I use most often. Can I change the toolbar?

A Absolutely. The toolbar is fully customizable. You can add or remove buttons as you see fit.

Q I placed multiple `Label` components on a form and then attempted to select them all by dragging. Instead I just got another big `Label` component. What have I done wrong?

A You forgot to turn off the multiple placement option. After placing multiple components on the form, you need to click the arrow button on the Component palette to turn off the multiple placement option.

Q I'm trying to position one of the IDE windows off to the side of the Code Editor. Every time I try, however, the window wants to dock to the Code Editor. How do I prevent the window from docking?

A Right-click on the window and turn the Dockable option off.

Q When I accidentally type a character for my form's `Top` property, I get an error message. I realize I should type a number rather than a character, but where does the error message come from?

A The Object Inspector knows what kind of value is correct for a given property. A character is not valid for an integer property, so an error message is shown. In some cases it is the property editor that performs checks on the value input.

Q What do I need to do in order for my application to be an MDI application?

A Just be sure that the main form has a `FormStyle` of `fsMDIForm` and that any MDI child forms have a `FormStyle` of `fsMDIChild`.

Q What's the difference between a dialog box and a child window in Delphi?

A There is no real difference. A dialog box form might have certain traits such as a dialog box border rather than a sizing border; OK, Cancel, and Help buttons; and no minimize or maximize buttons. But a dialog box is just a form like any other. A form might have the appearance of a dialog box or of a child window, but a form is just a form.

Q Can I check the unit I'm working on for errors without running the program?

A Yes. Just choose Project | Syntax Check from the main menu. Delphi will compile any units that have changed since the last compile and will report any errors encountered.

Quiz

1. How do you invoke the main window's Customize dialog box?

2. When you have the Customize dialog box open, how do you add buttons to a toolbar?

3. How do you remove buttons from a toolbar?

4. What's the easiest way to place multiple components of the same type on a form?

5. What's the easiest way to place a component in the center of the form?

6. List the file types needed to build an application in Delphi.

7. What VCL method do you use to display a form modelessly?

8. What VCL method do you use to display a form modally?

9. How can you attach an event to an event handler that has been previously defined?

10. When using the Object Inspector, how can you enumerate the choices for a particular property?

Exercises

1. Remove the Pause, Step Over, and Trace Into buttons from the Delphi View toolbar. Add Compile, Build, and Syntax Check buttons to the toolbar.

2. Reset the toolbar to its default settings.

3. Spend some time looking over the components on each page of the Component palette. Place any components you are curious about on a form and experiment with them.

4. Create a new directory on your hard drive. Create a new application in Delphi. Add three new forms to the project (they can be blank if you want). Save the project to the new directory you created and run the program. Close the program. Now examine the directory where the project was saved. Compare the files you see there with the file types listed in Table 4.1.

5. Run the Picture Viewer program you created earlier. Open several graphics files. Drag the MDI child windows around in the parent window. Attempt to move a child window outside the parent. What happens?

6. Experiment with docking various IDE windows to the dock sites on the Code Editor.

7. Start a new application. Place several components on the form. Click on each component and observe the properties for each component in the Object Inspector.

8. Create a blank form. Double-click in the Value column next to the Color property to invoke the Color dialog box. Choose a color and click OK.

4

DAY **5**

The Visual Component Model

Today I am going to talk about the visual component model and Borland's Visual Component Library (VCL). Before getting into that, though, I'll talk a little about class frameworks. In this chapter you will find

- The fundamentals of frameworks
- The Visual Component Library overview
- VCL classes, including the form, application, and component classes

Frameworks Fundamentals

"In the beginning there was C. . . ." Well, not quite. As far as Windows programming is concerned, though, that statement is accurate. In the beginning, the vast majority of Windows programs were written in C. In fact, the Windows Application Programming Interface (API) is just a huge collection of C functions—hundreds of them. There are still undoubtedly thousands of programmers out there writing Windows programs in C.

Somewhere along the line, the folks at Borland decided, "There has got to be an easier way." (Actually, the framework revolution might have started on several different fronts, but Borland was certainly a leader.) It was apparent that Windows programming was very well suited to object-oriented programming. By creating classes that encapsulate common Windows programming tasks, a programmer could be much more productive. After a class was created to encapsulate a window's various duties, for instance, that class could be used over and over again. The framework revolution began.

But I haven't yet told you what a framework is.

NEW TERM   A *framework* is a collection of classes that simplifies programming in Windows by encapsulating often-used programming techniques. Frameworks are also called *class libraries*. *Encapsulation* means taking a complex programming task and making it easier by providing a simplified interface.

Popular frameworks have classes that encapsulate windows, edit controls, list boxes, graphics operations, bitmaps, scrollbars, dialog boxes, and so on.

So Why Should I Care About Frameworks?

That's a good question. The bottom line is that frameworks make Windows programming much easier than it would be in straight C, in assembler, or in the original Pascal language (the Pascal that came prior to Object Pascal). Let me give you an example. Listing 5.1 contains a portion of a Windows program written in C++. This section of code loads a bitmap file from disk and displays the bitmap in the center of the screen. None of this will make sense to you right now, but be patient.

LISTING 5.1. C++ CODE TO LOAD AND DISPLAY A BITMAP.

```
HPALETTE hPal;
BITMAPFILEHEADER bfh;
BITMAPINFOHEADER bih;
LPBITMAPINFO lpbi = 0;
HFILE hFile;
DWORD nClrUsed, nSize;
HDC hDC;
HBITMAP hBitmap;
void *bits;
do {
  if ((hFile = _lopen(data.FileName, OF_READ)) == HFILE_ERROR) break;
  if (_hread(hFile, &bfh, sizeof(bfh)) != sizeof(bfh)) break;
  if (bfh.bfType != 'BM') break;
  if (_hread(hFile, &bih, sizeof(bih)) != sizeof(bih)) break;
  nClrUsed =
    (bih.biClrUsed) ? bih.biClrUsed : 1 << bih.biBitCount;
```

```
nSize =
  sizeof(BITMAPINFOHEADER) + nClrUsed * sizeof(RGBQUAD);
lpbi = (LPBITMAPINFO) GlobalAllocPtr(GHND, nSize);
if (!lpbi) break;
MoveMemory(lpbi, &bih, sizeof(bih));
nSize = nClrUsed * sizeof(RGBQUAD);
if (_hread(hFile, &lpbi->bmiColors, nSize) != nSize) break;
if (_llseek(hFile, bfh.bfOffBits, 0) == HFILE_ERROR) break;
nSize = bfh.bfSize-bfh.bfOffBits;
if ((bits = GlobalAllocPtr(GHND, nSize)) == NULL) break;
if (_hread(hFile, bits, nSize) != nSize) break;
hDC = GetDC(hWnd);
hBitmap = CreateDIBitmap(hDC, &(lpbi->bmiHeader), CBM_INIT,
                        bits, lpbi, DIB_RGB_COLORS);
if (hBitmap) {
  LPLOGPALETTE lppal;
  DWORD nsize = sizeof(LOGPALETTE)
    + (nClrUsed-1) * sizeof(PALETTEENTRY);
  lppal = (LPLOGPALETTE) GlobalAllocPtr(GHND, nSize);
  if (lppal) {
    lppal->palVersion = 0x0300;
    lppal->palNumEntries = (WORD) nClrUsed;
    MoveMemory(lppal->palPalEntry, lpbi->bmiColors,
    nClrUsed * sizeof(PALETTEENTRY));
    hPal = CreatePalette(lppal);
    (void) GlobalFreePtr(lppal);
  }
}
}  while(FALSE);
if (hFile != HFILE_ERROR) _lclose(hFile);
HPALETTE oldPal = SelectPalette(hDC, hPal, FALSE);
RealizePalette(hDC);
HDC hMemDC = CreateCompatibleDC(hDC);
HBITMAP oldBitmap =(HBITMAP)SelectObject(hMemDC, hBitmap);
BitBlt(hDC, 0, 0, (WORD)bih.biWidth, (WORD)bih.biHeight,
  hMemDC, 0, 0, SRCCOPY);
SelectObject(hMemDC, oldBitmap);
DeleteDC(hMemDC);
SelectPalette(hDC, oldPal, FALSE);
ReleaseDC(hWnd, hDC);
if (bits) (void) GlobalFreePtr(bits);
if (lpbi) (void) GlobalFreePtr(lpbi);
```

5

That looks just a little intimidating, doesn't it? Now look at the equivalent using Borland's VCL:

```
Image.LoadFromFile('winnt.bmp');
```

So which would you rather use? You don't even have to know what these code snippets do to make that decision. It's easy to see that the VCL version is shorter (just a bit!) and more readable.

These examples sum up what frameworks are all about. Frameworks hide details from you that you don't need to know. Everything that is contained in Listing 5.1 is performed behind the scenes in the VCL code (albeit in Pascal rather than in C++). You don't need to know every detail about what goes on behind the scenes when VCL does its job, and you probably don't want to know. All you want is to take the objects that make up a framework and put them to use in your programs.

A good framework takes full advantage of OOP, and some do that better than others. Borland's Object Windows Library (which came in both C++ and Pascal versions) and Visual Component Library are excellent examples of object-oriented programming. They provide the proper abstraction needed for you to rise above the clutter and get down to the serious business of programming.

So What's the Catch?

A little skeptical, are you? Good. You're bright enough to figure out that if you have all that ease of use, you must be giving up something. Truth is, you are right. You might think that a program written with a framework would be larger and slower than its counterpart written in a low-level language. That's partially correct. Applications written with frameworks don't necessarily have to be slower than those other programs, though. There is some additional overhead inherent in an object-oriented language, certainly, but for the most part, it is not noticeable in a typical Windows program.

The primary trade-off is that Windows programs written in Delphi tend to be larger than programs written in languages such as C. For example, let's say you had a simple Windows program written in C that was 75KB. The equivalent program written with Delphi might be 250KB. That might seem like a significant difference, but this example demonstrates the worst-case scenario. The difference in final program size between a C application and a Delphi application written with a framework is most noticeable in very small programs. As your programs increase in size and sophistication, the size difference is much less noticeable.

One reason for the size difference is simply the difference between a procedural language and an object-oriented language. Object-oriented languages (C++ and Object Pascal, for example) carry additional overhead for features such as exception handling, runtime type information (RTTI), and other OOP goodies. In my opinion, the difference in code size is an acceptable trade-off for the features that Object Pascal provides.

Now, before you label me as a code-bloat proponent, let me say that I am as conscientious as the next person when it comes to code bloat. I believe that we should all write the tightest code we can given the tools we use. I am also a realist, and I understand that time-to-market is a driving force in the software industry today. I am willing to trade some code size for the power that Object Pascal and VCL give me. Let me put it another way. I'm not interested in spending a month to write a Windows program that compiles to a 100KB executable when I can accomplish the same thing in Delphi in two days and end up with a 400KB executable. The size of the resulting executables is insignificant when compared to the development time saved.

FRAMEWORKS TEACH OBJECT-ORIENTED PROGRAMMING AND DESIGN

If you end up getting serious about this crazy game called Windows programming, you will eventually end up peeking into the source code of your favorite framework. Sooner or later you'll want to know how the pros do things. The VCL source code is a great place to go for that kind of information.

Some weekend when the leaves are raked, the house trim is painted, the laundry is done, the kids are at Grandma's, and you think you have a good handle on Delphi, spend some time browsing the VCL source code. (Delphi Professional and Client/Server ship with the VCL source code.) It can be intimidating at first, but after a while you'll see what the designers were doing. Don't strain yourself. Attempt to understand the things that bump up against the limits of your knowledge regarding Object Pascal. Leave the complicated stuff for later.

But notice how the VCL designers use private, protected, and public access in classes. Notice how things that should be kept hidden from the user aren't in public view. Studying the VCL source can teach you a great deal about Object Pascal and object-oriented design.

The Visual Component Library

You have probably noticed that this book contains "Delphi 4" in its title. Obviously Delphi has been around a while. When Delphi 1 was introduced in 1995, it was an instant hit. Delphi offered rapid application development (RAD) using something called *components*. Components are objects that can be dropped on a form and manipulated via properties, methods, and events. It's visual programming, if you will.

The concept of form-based programming was first popularized by Microsoft's Visual Basic. Unlike Visual Basic, though, Delphi used a derivative of Pascal as its programming language. This new language, called Object Pascal, introduced OOP to the Pascal language. Delphi and Object Pascal represented the marriage of object-oriented programming and form-based programming. In addition, Delphi could produce standalone executables. Real programs. Programs that did not require a runtime DLL to run; programs that were compiled, not interpreted; programs that ran tens of times faster than Visual Basic programs. The programming world was impressed.

Delphi didn't just throw Object Pascal at you and let you flounder. It also introduced the Visual Component Library. As I have said, VCL is an application framework for Windows programming in Object Pascal. The most noticeable feature of VCL is that it was designed around the concept of properties, methods, and events—the visual component model. Let's look at the visual component model in more detail.

Components

As I talked about on Day 1, "Getting Started with Delphi," VCL components are objects that perform a specific programming task. VCL components are wrapped up in Object Pascal classes. From now on in this book, you will be encountering components on a daily basis. I won't spend a lot of time explaining every detail of components right now because you will see by example how they work throughout the rest of the book. I'll explain components in more detail on Day 7, "VCL Components."

Properties, Methods, and Events

On Day 1, I gave you a brief introduction to the properties, methods, and events model. These three ingredients make up the public interface of components in VCL (the part of the component the user will see). Let's take a look at these elements one at a time.

Properties

Properties are elements of a component that control how the component operates. Many components have common properties. All visual components, for example, have a Top and a Left property. These two properties control where the component will be positioned on a form both at design time and at runtime. All components have an Owner property, which VCL uses to keep track of the child components a particular parent form or component owns.

Properties and the Object Inspector   A picture is always worth a thousand words, so let's start up Delphi again and see properties in action. When you start Delphi, you are greeted with a blank form and the Object Inspector.

 Note

> If you have the Delphi options configured to save the desktop when you close Delphi, you might see the last project you were working on when you start Delphi. If that's the case, choose File | New Application from the main menu to get a blank form.

The Object Inspector will look something like Figure 5.1. (When Delphi starts, it sizes the Object Inspector based on your current screen resolution, so your Object Inspector might be taller or shorter than the one shown in Figure 5.1.) If necessary, click on the Properties tab of the Object Inspector window so that the form's properties are displayed. The component's properties are arranged in alphabetical order.

FIGURE 5.1.

The Object Inspector.

If more properties exist than can be displayed at one time, the Object Inspector displays a scrollbar so that you can view additional properties. The Object Inspector window can be moved and sized. I like my Object Inspector as tall as my screen permits so that I can see the maximum number of properties at one time. Scroll through the properties until you locate the Left property and then click on it. Change the value for the Left property (any number between 0 and 600 will do) and press Enter on the keyboard. Notice how the form moves as you change the value.

This illustrates an important aspect of properties: they are more than simple fields of a class. Each property has an underlying data field associated with it, but the property itself is not a class data field. Changing a property often leads to code executed behind the scenes.

 Properties are often tied to *access methods* that execute when the property is modified.

Changing a Property's Value Properties can be changed at *design time* (when you are designing your form) and at *runtime* (when the program is running through code you write). In either case, if the property has an access method, that access method will be called and executed when the property is modified. You already saw an example of changing a property at design time when you changed the Left property and watched the form move on the screen.

That is one of the strengths of VCL and how it is used in Delphi: You can instantly see on the screen the result of your design change. Not all properties show a visible change on the form at design time, however, so this doesn't happen in every case. Still, when possible, the results of the new property value are immediately displayed on the form.

To change a property at runtime, you simply make an assignment to the property. When you make an assignment, VCL works behind the scenes to call the access method for that property. To change the Left property at runtime, you use code like this:

```
Left := 200;
```

In the case of the Left property (as well as the Top property), VCL moves and repaints the form. (For you Windows API programmers, you can figure out that this eventually translates into calls to the Windows API functions SetWindowPos and InvalidateRect.)

NEW TERM **Property Access Specifiers**   Properties have two *access specifiers*, which are used when properties are read or modified. There is a *read specifier* and a *write specifier*.

Suffice it to say that access specifiers associate read and write methods with the property. When the property is read or written to, the methods associated with the property are automatically called. When you make an assignment as in the previous example, you are accessing the write specifier. In effect, VCL checks to see whether an access method exists for the write specifier. If it does, the access method is called. If no access method exists, VCL assigns the new value to the data field associated with the property.

When you reference a property (use the property as the right side of an equation), you are accessing the read specifier:

```
X := Left;
```

In this case, VCL calls the read specifier to read the value of the Left property. In many cases the read specifier does very little more than return a property's current value.

Property Attributes   The properties of the property (sorry, I couldn't resist) are determined by the writer of the component. A property can be read-only. A read-only property can be read—its value can be retrieved—but not written to. In other words, you can fetch the property's value, but you can't change it. In rare cases, a property can be made write-only (a property that can be written to but not read isn't very useful in most cases). This is obviously the opposite of a read-only property.

Finally, some properties can be specified runtime-only. A runtime-only property can be accessed only at runtime, not design time. Because a runtime-only property doesn't apply at design time, it is not displayed in the Object Inspector. A runtime-only property can be declared as read-only, too, which means that it can be accessed only at runtime and can only be read (not written to).

Property Types   Some properties use an instance of a VCL class as the underlying data field. To illustrate, let's put a memo component on our blank form:

1. Go to the Delphi Component palette, choose the Standard tab, and click the Memo button. (The tooltip will tell when you are over the Memo button.)

2. Now move to the form and click on it where you want the memo's top-left corner to appear. As soon as you place the memo component on the form, the Object Inspector switches to show you the properties of the component just placed on the form, in this case a TMemo.

3. Locate the Lines property and click on it. Notice that the property value contains the text (TStrings) and that there is a little button with an ellipsis (. . .) to the right of the property value.

> **Note**
>
> The ellipsis button tells you that this property can be edited by using a property editor. For an array of strings, for instance, a dialog box will be displayed in which you can type the strings. In the case of the Font property, clicking the ellipsis button will invoke the Choose Font dialog box. The exact type of the property editor is property-specific, although certain properties can share a common editor. You can bring up the property editor by clicking the ellipsis button or by double-clicking the property value.

The Lines property for a memo component is an instance of the TStrings class. When you double-click the Value column, the string editor is displayed and you can then type the strings you want displayed in the memo component when the application runs. If you don't want any strings displayed in the memo component, you need to clear the property editor of any strings.

The Font property is another example of a property that is an instance of a VCL class. A *font* includes things like the typeface, the color, the font size, and so on. Locate the Font property in the Object Inspector. (It doesn't matter whether you have selected the memo component or the form.)

Notice that there is a plus sign before the word *Font*. This tells you that there are individual properties within this property that can be set. If you double-click on the property name, you will see that the Object Inspector expands the property to reveal its individual elements. You can now individually edit the Font property's elements. In the case of the Font property, these same settings can be edited by invoking the property editor. You can use either method with the same results.

Some properties are sets (I talked about sets on Day 3, "Classes and Object-Oriented Programming"). The Style property within the Font object is a good example of a set.

5

Notice that `Style` has a plus sign in front of it. If you double-click on the `Style` property, you will see that the `Style` node expands to reveal the set's contents. In this case, the set consists of the various styles available for fonts: bold, italic, underline, and strikeout. By double-clicking a style, you can turn that style on or off. A set can be empty or can contain one or more of the allowed values.

NEW TERM Some properties can be *enumerations*, a list of possible choices.

An *enumeration* is a list of possible choices for a property. When you click on an enumeration property, a drop-down arrow button appears to the right of the value. To see the choices in the enumeration, click the drop-down button to display the list of choices. Alternatively, you can double-click the Value column for the property. As you double-click on the property's value, the Object Inspector will cycle through (or enumerate) the choices. The `Cursor` property gives a good example of an enumerated property. Locate the `Cursor` property and click the arrow button to expose the list of possible cursors to choose from.

Enumerations and sets differ in that with an enumeration property, only one of the presented choices can be selected (only one cursor can be in effect at any time). The set can contain none or any number of the choices (a font style can contain bold, underline, italic, or none of these).

As long as you have Delphi running and a blank form displayed, you might as well spend some time examining the various components and their properties. Go ahead, I'll wait.

HOUSE RULES: PROPERTIES

- Properties appear to be class fields and are accessed like class fields.
- Properties are *not* class fields. They are a special category of class member.
- Properties often invoke an access method when they are written to (assigned a value), but not always. It depends on how the particular component is written.
- Published properties usually have default values. The default value is the value that initially shows up in the Object Inspector when a component is first utilized and is the value that will be used if no specific value is assigned.
- Properties can be designed as read/write, read-only, or write-only.
- Runtime-only properties don't show up in the Object Inspector and can be modified only at runtime.

- Properties can include
    - Simple data types
    - Strings
    - Arrays
    - Sets
    - Enumerations
    - VCL class objects

Methods

I discussed methods on Day 3, "Classes and Object-Oriented Programming," so I don't need to cover them again here in any great detail. *Methods* in VCL components are functions and procedures that can be called to make the component perform certain actions. For example, all visual components have a method called Show, which displays the component, and a method called Hide, which hides the component. For example:

```
MyWindow.Show;
{ do some stuff, then later... }
MyWindow.Hide;
```

Methods in VCL can be declared as public, protected, or private. Public methods can be accessed by the component's users. In this example, both the Show and Hide methods are public. Protected methods cannot be accessed by the component users but can be accessed by classes (components) derived from a component. Of course, private methods can be accessed only within a class itself.

Some methods take parameters and return values, others don't. It depends entirely on how the method was written by the component writer. For example, the GetTextBuf method retrieves the text of a TEdit component. This method can be used to get the text from an edit control as follows:

```
var
  Buff     : array [0..255] of Char;
  NumChars : Integer;
begin
  NumChars := EditControl.GetTextBuf(Buff, SizeOf(Buff));
end;
```

As you can see, this particular method takes two parameters and returns an integer. When this method is called, the edit control contents are placed in the variable Buff and the return value is the number of characters retrieved from the edit control.

5

For now, that's all you need to know in order to use methods. I'll discuss them in more detail on Day 20, "Creating Components."

HOUSE RULES: METHODS

- Methods can be private, protected, or public.
- Methods are called using the dot operator.
- Methods can take parameters and can return values.
- Some methods take no parameters and return no values.
- Only public methods can be called by component users.

Events

NEW TERM Windows is said to be an *event-driven* environment. Event-driven means that a program is driven by events that occur within the Windows environment. Events include mouse movements, mouse clicks, and key presses.

Programmers moving from DOS or mainframe programming environments might have some difficulty with the concept of something being event-driven. A Windows program continually polls Windows for events. Events in Windows include a menu being activated, a button being clicked, a window being moved, a window needing repainting, a window being activated, and so forth.

Windows notifies a program of an event by sending a Windows message. There are over 200 possible messages that Windows can send to an application. That's a lot of messages. Fortunately, you don't have to know about each and every one of them to program in Delphi; there are only a couple dozen that are used frequently.

VCL Events   In VCL, an event is anything that occurs in the component that the user might need to know about. Each component is designed to respond to certain events. Usually this means a Windows event, but it can mean other things as well. For example, a button component is designed to respond to a mouse click, as you would expect. But a nonvisual control, such as a database component, can respond to non-Windows events, such as the user reaching the end of the table.

NEW TERM **Handling Events**   When you respond to a component event, you are said to *handle* the event.

Events are handled through methods called *event handlers*. You used event handlers extensively as you worked through the first three days of the book.

A typical Windows program spends most of its time idle, waiting for some event to occur. VCL makes it incredibly easy to handle events. The events that a component has been designed to handle are listed under the Events tab in the Object Inspector window. Event names are descriptive of the event to which they respond. For instance, the event to handle a mouse click is called OnClick.

Note

> You don't have to handle every event that a component defines. In fact, you rarely do. If you don't respond to a particular event, the event message is either discarded or handled in a default manner as described by either VCL or the component itself. You can handle any events you have an interest in and ignore the rest.

These concepts will make more sense if you put them into practice. To begin, let's start a new application. Choose File | New Application from the main menu. If you are prompted to save the current project, click No. Now you will again have a blank form. First, set up the main form:

1. Change the Name property to PMEForm (PME for properties, methods, and events).

2. Change the Caption property to PME Test Program.

Next, you need to add a memo component to the form:

1. Choose the Standard tab on the Component palette and click the Memo button.

2. Click on the form to place a memo component on the form.

3. Change the Name property to Memo. Be sure the memo component is selected so that you don't accidentally change the form's name instead of the memo component.

4. Double-click on the Lines property in the Value column. The String list editor will be displayed.

5. Delete the word Memo and type A test program using properties, methods, and events. Click OK to close the String list editor.

6. Resize the memo component so that it occupies most of the form. Leave room for a button at the bottom.

Your form will now look like the form shown in Figure 5.2.

5

FIGURE 5.2.

The form with a memo component added.

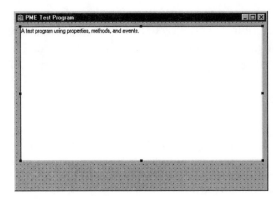

Now you can place a button on the form:

1. Choose the Standard tab on the Component palette and click the Button component.
2. Click on the form below the memo component to place the button on the form.
3. Change the Name property for the button to Button.
4. Change the Caption property to Show/Hide.
5. Center the button horizontally on the form.

Tip

> You can center components visually, but for a more exact method use the Alignment palette. Choose View | Alignment Palette from the main menu and then click the Center horizontally in window button on the Alignment palette to center a component horizontally on the form.

You will use this button to alternately show and hide the memo component. Now you need to write some code so that the button does something when it is clicked. Be sure that the button component is selected, and then click on the Events tab in the Object Inspector.

A list of the events that a button component is designed to handle is presented. The top event should be the OnClick event. Double-click on the Value column of the OnClick event. What happens next is one of the great things about visual programming. The Code Editor comes to the top and displays the OnClick procedure ready for you to type code. Figure 5.3 shows the Code Editor with the OnClick handler displayed.

FIGURE 5.3.

The Delphi Code Editor with the OnClick *handler displayed.*

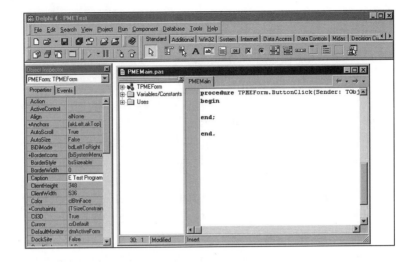

> **Note**
>
> Your Code Editor might not look exactly like Figure 5.3. I removed the Module Explorer from the Code Editor window to show more of the code. One of the great things about the Delphi IDE is that it is fully customizable. If you don't like the default layout, you can always change it.

Adding Event Handler Code   Notice that the event handler is already set up for you, all you have to do is type the code. If you take a good look at the event handler, you will see that it is a procedure, that it is called ButtonClick, that it is a member of the TPMEForm class, and that it takes a pointer to a TObject called Sender as a parameter. (I'll talk about the Sender parameter in just a bit.) All that is left to do now is type code that shows and hides the button each time the button is clicked. We'll borrow a little code from our earlier discussion of methods. Edit the ButtonClick method until it looks like this:

```
procedure TPMEForm.ButtonClick(Sender: TObject);
const
  IsVisible : Boolean = False;
begin
  IsVisible := not IsVisible;
  if IsVisible then
    Memo.Hide
  else
    Memo.Show;
end;
```

This code first declares a typed constant named IsVisible.

NEW TERM   A *typed constant*, when used in this way, is a variable that retains its value between calls to the method.

The first line of code in this method flips the `Boolean` variable between `True` and `False` by applying a logical `NOT` to the variable's present value. It works like so:

1. Initially the static variable is set to `False`. The first time the event handler is called, the variable is assigned `NOT False`, which is, of course, `True`.

2. The next time the event handler is called, the variable is assigned `NOT True`, and so on.

3. Each time the method is called, `IsVisible` contains the opposite value it had on the previous call. After that, the `if/else` pair calls either `Show` or `Hide` depending on the value of `IsVisible`.

That's all there is to it. But does it work? Let's find out. Click the Run button on the toolbar. After being compiled, the program runs and is displayed. It's the moment of truth. Click the button, and the memo component is hidden. Click the button again, and the memo component is again displayed. It works!

After playing with that for a minute, close the program (use the Close Program button in the upper-right corner of the title bar) and you are back to the Code Editor.

Before you go on, save the project. Choose File | Save All from the main menu. The first thing you are prompted for is the name of the unit (source file). Type `PMEMain` and click OK. Next, you are prompted for a filename for the project. Type `PMETest` and press Enter or click OK.

Using the `Visible` Property   All that work with a `Boolean` variable is a bit cumbersome. Think back to the discussion about properties. Wouldn't it be nice if the memo component had a property that could tell us whether the component was currently visible? Is there such a beast? Of course there is. It's called, predictably, `Visible`. Let's make use of it. Again, edit the event handler until it looks like this:

```
procedure TPMEForm.ButtonClick(Sender: TObject);
begin
  if Memo.Visible then
    Memo.Hide
  else
    Memo.Show;
end;
```

Again click the Run button. The program is displayed and, lo and behold, the button does what it's supposed to. How about that? You managed to use properties, methods, and events in the same example.

Are you getting the fever yet? Hold on, because there's much more to come. Oh, and wipe that silly grin off your face. . .your boss thinks you're working!

The Sender Parameter   As you can see, the ButtonClick method takes a pointer to a TObject called Sender (whether you know it or not, all class variables in Delphi are pointers). Every event handler will have at least a Sender parameter. Depending on the event being handled, the event handler might have one or more additional parameters. For instance, the OnMouseDown event handler looks like this:

```
procedure TPMEForm.FormMouseDown(Sender: TObject; Button: TMouseButton;
  Shift: TShiftState; X, Y: Integer);
begin
end;
```

Here you are getting information on the button that was pressed, which keyboard keys were pressed at the time the mouse was clicked, and the x, y coordinate of the cursor when the mouse button was clicked. The event handler contains all the information you need to deal with the particular event the event handler is designed to handle.

So what exactly is Sender? Sender is a pointer to the component that is sending the message to the message handler. In this example, the Sender parameter is extra baggage because you know that the Show/Hide button is the sender. Sender exists to enable you to have more than one component use the same event handler.

To illustrate, let's create a new button and make one of our buttons the Show button and the other the Hide button:

1. If the Code Editor is on top, press F12 to switch back to the Form Editor.

2. Click on the Show/Hide button to select it. Change both the Name and Caption properties to Show.

3. Add a new button to the form to the right of the Show button. Arrange the buttons if you want to give an even look to the form.

4. Change the Name property for the new button to Hide. The Caption property will also change to Hide (you'll have to press Enter before the Caption property will change).

5. Click the Show button and then click on the Events tab in the Object Inspector. Notice that the OnClick event now says ShowClick. Edit it to say ButtonClick again. (The initial event-handler name is a default name. You can change it to any name you like.)

6. Click the Hide button and find the OnClick event in the Object Inspector (it will be selected already). Next to the value is a drop-down arrow button. Click the arrow button and choose ButtonClick from the list that drops down (there will be only one name in the list at this point).

5

7. Double-click on the value `ButtonClick`. You are presented with the Code Editor with the cursor in the `ButtonClick` method. Modify the code so that it reads like this:

```
procedure TPMEForm.ButtonClick(Sender: TObject)

begin
  if Sender = Hide
    then Memo.Hide
  else
    Memo.Show;
end;
```

8. Bake at 425 degrees for one hour or until golden brown. (Just checking.)

Your form will look similar to Figure 5.4. Compile and run the program. Click each button to be sure that it functions as advertised.

FIGURE 5.4.

The form with all components added.

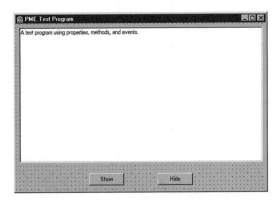

What you have done here is create a single event-handling method that handles the `OnClick` event of both buttons. You use the `Sender` parameter to determine which button sent the `OnClick` event and then either hide or show the memo component as needed. You could have created a separate `OnClick` handler for each button, but with this method the code is more compact. Besides, it's a good illustration of how `Sender` can be used.

Note that I am comparing the `Sender` variable to a component's `Name` property. Because both are pointers, a comparison is being made to see whether both variables contain the same address.

Step 6 in the previous exercise illustrates an important point: After you create an OnClick event handler for a particular component, you can attach that same handler to the OnClick event of any component on the form. This enables you to use the same event handler for multiple components. I'll discuss events in more detail as you progress through the book.

HOUSE RULES: EVENTS

- You can respond to any of a component's events as needed.

- You are not required to respond to all events a component defines.

- Events are handled by event-handling methods called event handlers.

- Several components can share a common event handler.

- Event-handler names produced by Delphi are default names and can be changed by the programmer.

- Be sure to change an event handler's name only in the Object Inspector.

- An event handler's Sender parameter can be used to determine which component generated the event.

- Double-clicking the event handler's name in the Object Inspector displays the Code Editor and takes you to the section of code containing the event handler.

- Each event handler contains the parameters needed to properly handle that event.

5

VCL Explored

The Visual Component Library is a well-designed framework. As with most good frameworks, VCL makes maximum use of inheritance. The bulk of the VCL framework is composed of classes that represent components. Other VCL classes are not related to components. These classes perform housekeeping chores, act as helper classes, and provide some utility services.

The VCL class hierarchy dealing with components is complex. Fortunately, you don't have to know every detail of VCL to begin programming in Delphi. At the top of the VCL chain, you will find TObject. Figure 5.5 shows some of the main base classes and the classes derived from them.

FIGURE 5.5.

*The VCL class
hierarchy.*

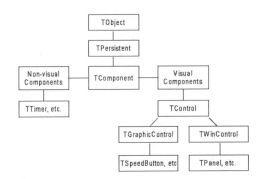

`TObject` is the granddaddy of all VCL component classes. (Remember that all classes in Object Pascal are derived from `TObject`.) Below `TObject` you see `TPersistent`. This class deals with a component's capability to save itself to files and to memory as well as other messy details you don't need to know about. I'm thankful (and you should be, too) that you don't need to know much about `TPersistent` to program most applications in Delphi.

The `TComponent` class serves as a more direct base class for components. This class provides all the functionality that a basic component requires. Nonvisual components are derived from `TComponent` itself. Visual components are derived from `TControl`, which, as you can see in Figure 5.5, is derived from `TComponent`. `TControl` provides additional functionality that visual components require. The individual components, then, are derived from either `TGraphicControl` or `TWinControl`.

When you drop a component on a form, Delphi creates a pointer to that component in the form's class declaration so that you can access the component in your code. Delphi uses the component's `Name` property for the pointer variable's name. When you created the sample application earlier, you placed a memo component on the form. At that point Delphi created a `TMemo` variable and gave it the name `Memo`.

Similarly, when you created a button on the form, Delphi created a `TButton` variable to represent the button. Before any of that took place, Delphi had already derived a new class from `TForm` and, of course, created an instance of that class to represent the form.

Some understanding of the VCL classes and components is obviously necessary before working with VCL. Although I cannot review each and every VCL class, I can hit the high points. Let's take a look at some of the classes that you will use most frequently.

Form and Application Classes

Form and application classes represent forms and the Application object in VCL. These classes are derived from TComponent and indeed are components themselves. They are listed separately to distinguish them from the controls you drop on a form.

The TApplication Class

The TApplication class encapsulates the basic operations of a Windows program. TApplication takes care of responsibilities such as managing the application's icon, providing context help, and doing basic message handling. Every Delphi application has a pointer to the TApplication object called Application. You use the TApplication class primarily to execute message boxes, manage context help, and set hint text for buttons and status bars. TApplication is a bit of an oddity in VCL in that some of its properties (Icon, HelpFile, and Title) can be set via the Application page of the Project Options dialog box.

The TForm Class

The TForm class encapsulates forms in VCL. Forms are used for main windows, dialog boxes, secondary windows, and just about any other window type you can imagine. TForm is a workhorse class in VCL. It has nearly 60 properties, 45 methods, and 20 events. I discussed forms in detail in Day 4.

Component Classes

This group of classes encompasses a wide range of classes and can be further divided into separate categories, which I've done in the following sections.

Standard Component Classes

The standard components are those that encapsulate the most common Windows controls. The standard component classes include TButton, TEdit, TListBox, TMemo, TMainMenu, TScrollBar, TPopupMenu, TCheckBox, TRadioButton, TRadioGroup, TGroupBox, TPanel, and TActionList.

Most of these classes encapsulate a Windows control, so I won't discuss all of them right now. The TMainMenu class encapsulates an application's main menu. At design time, double-clicking the MainMenu component's icon brings up the Menu Designer. TMainMenu has properties that control whether the menu item is grayed out, whether it is checked, the help context ID, the item's hint text, and others. Each menu item has a single event, OnClick, so that you can attach an event handler to a menu item being selected. I'll discuss menus and the Menu Designer in more detail tomorrow.

The TPanel Component   Another standard component of interest is TPanel.

 A *panel* represents a rectangular region on a form, usually with its own components, that can be treated as a single unit.

The Panel component is a container component. As such it can contain other components. Panels have properties that control what type of edge the panel should have;
whether the panel is raised, sunken, or flat; and the width of the border. Combinations of
these properties can be used to create a variety of 3D panels.

*New
to 4*   **The TActionList Component**   The TActionList component is new to Delphi 4. This
component can be used to easily add command enabling to a component or a group of
components. For example, an application that uses the Clipboard might have cut, copy,
and paste items on a menu, on a toolbar, and on a context menu. If there is data in the
Clipboard, the paste button and menu items should be enabled. If there is no data in the
Clipboard, the button and menu items should be disabled. All of the controls (the toolbar
button and the menu items) can be enabled or disabled at one time using the
TActionList component.

Components on the Additional Tab   Delphi has another group of components that
I'll throw in with the standard controls. These controls can be found under the Additional
tab on the Component palette. The classes representing these components include
TBitBtn, TSpeedButton, TMaskEdit, TStringGrid, TDrawGrid, TImage, TShape, TBevel,
TScrollBox, TCheckListBox, TSplitter, TStaticText, and TChart. The TBitBtn class
represents a button that has an image on it.

TSpeedButton is also a button with an image, but this component is not a true button.
Instead, it's a graphical depiction of a button. This enables you to have a large number of
speed buttons and not consume Windows resources for each button.

The TImage component enables you to place an image on a form that can then be selected from a file on disk. You can use the TBevel component to create boxes and lines that
are raised (bumps) or lowered (dips). Bevels can be used to divide a form into visual
regions and to provide an aesthetically pleasing form. The TStringGrid and TDrawGrid
classes give you a means to present information in a grid format.

Win32 Custom Control Classes

VCL has component classes that encapsulate many of the Windows 32-bit custom
controls. These classes include TListView, TTreeView, TTrackBar, TProgressBar,
TTabControl, TPageControl, TRichEdit, TImageList, TStatusBar, TAnimate,
TDateTimePicker, TToolBar, TCoolBar, and a few others. Some of these controls are, by
nature, complicated, and the VCL classes that represent them are complicated as well.

Trust me when I say that VCL does much to ease the burden of working with these common controls. You have to spend some time with these classes before you fully understand them. I cover the TToolBar, TCoolBar, TImageList, and TStatusBar components on Day 13, "Beyond the Basics."

Database Component Classes

VCL has a host of database components that include both visual and nonvisual classes. Nonvisual database components include TDataSource, TDatabase, TTable, and TQuery. These classes encapsulate behind-the-scenes database operations.

Visual database component classes are the part of the VCL database operations that users see and interact with. For instance, a TDBGrid component is used to display a database table in grid format. In this way, the TDBGrid acts as the interface between the user and the database. Through the TDBGrid, the user can view and edit the database table on disk.

The TDBNavigator component provides buttons that enable the user to move through a database table. This class includes buttons for next record, previous record, first record, last record, cancel edit, accept edit, and undo edit.

Other data-aware component classes hook standard Windows controls to database fields. These classes include TDBText, TDBEdit, TDBListBox, and TDBImage, among others.

A group of components usually associated with database programming is the QuickReport components. This group of components makes report writing easy, especially if your data source is a database. The database QuickReport components are discussed on Days 16, 17, and 18.

Common Dialog Classes

As you are no doubt aware, Windows has common dialog boxes for things like opening files, saving files, choosing fonts, and choosing colors. VCL encapsulates these common dialog boxes in classes representing each type. The classes are TOpenDialog, TSaveDialog, TOpenPictureDialog, TSavePictureDialog, TFontDialog, TColorDialog, TPrintDialog, and TPrinterSetupDialog. VCL also adds the TFindDialog and TReplaceDialog classes to this component group. All the components in this group are nonvisual in that they don't have a design-time visual interface. The dialog boxes are visible when displayed at runtime, of course.

System Component Classes

The System tab on the Component palette contains a mixture of visual and nonvisual components. The TTimer class is used to represent a Windows system timer. Its single event is OnTimer, which is called each time the timer fires. The timer interval is set through the Interval property. TTimer is a nonvisual component.

5

Tucked into this group of classes is the TMediaPlayer class. This class enables you to play media files like wave audio, AVI video, and MIDI audio. The media can be played, stopped, paused, or positioned at a particular point in the file, as well as many other operations. This class has many properties and events that greatly simplify the complex world of the Windows Media Control Interface (MCI).

The TPaintBox component gives you an empty canvas on which you can draw anything you like. This component has many potential uses. The System group includes OLE and dynamic data exchange (DDE) classes as well.

The Win 3.1 Group of Components

Don't make the mistake of automatically discarding this component group just because of the name of the tab on which it resides. This group contains some great components. (The Win 3.1 tab has its roots in Delphi 1.) In particular, I like the TTabSet and TNotebook components. This group also includes several component classes that enable you to build your own custom File Open or File Save dialog box. The classes are TFileListBox, TDirectoryListBox, TDriveComboBox, and TFilterComboBox.

Internet Components

Depending on which version of Delphi you have (Standard, Professional, or Client/Server), you might have an Internet tab. This tab contains components used in Internet programming. The components include HTML, FTP, SMTP, POP3, and HTTP components. It also contains components that are for general network programming via the Winsock API. Most of these components are native VCL components, although at least one, the THTML component, is an ActiveX control.

Sample Components

The Samples tab contains components that can be used to gain an understanding of how to write components. The source for these components is provided so that you can see how they work. The sample components include TGauge, TColorButton, TSpinButton, TSpinEdit, TDirectoryOutline, and TCalendar.

ActiveX Controls

The ActiveX tab contains ActiveX controls that you can use in your applications. These controls include Chart FX by Software FX, Inc., Visual Speller by Visual Components, Inc., Formula One Spreadsheet, Formula One VtChart, and a Graph control by Bits Per Second, Ltd.

GDI Classes

The GDI (graphics device interface) classes get a lot of work in Windows GUI applications. These classes encapsulate the use of bitmaps, fonts, device contexts (DCs), brushes, and pens. It is through these GDI objects that graphics and text are displayed on a window. The GDI classes are not associated with a specific component, but many components have instances of these classes as properties. For example, an edit control has a property called Font that is an instance of the TFont class.

The term *device context* is well known by traditional Windows programmers. In VCL, though, the term is not widely used. This is because VCL encapsulates Windows DCs in the TCanvas class. VCL uses the term *canvas* to refer to a Windows device context. A canvas provides a surface that you can draw on using methods like MoveTo, LineTo, and TextOut. Bitmaps can be displayed on the canvas using the Draw or StretchDraw methods. The concept of a canvas that you draw on makes more sense than the archaic term *device context*, don't you think? Graphics operations are discussed on Day 12, "Graphics and Multimedia Programming." The following is a list of the more common GDI classes used:

- The TCanvas class contains instances of the other GDI classes. For example, when you do a MoveTo/LineTo sequence, a line is drawn with the current pen color. The Pen property is used to determine the current pen color and is an instance of the TPen class. TPen has properties that determine what type of line to draw: the line width, the line style (solid, dashed, dotted, and so on), and the mode with which to draw the line.

- The TBrush class represents a brush used as the fill pattern for canvas operations like FillRect, Polygon, and Ellipse. TBrush properties include Color, Style, and Bitmap. The Style property enables you to set a hatch pattern for the brush. The Bitmap property enables you to specify a bitmap for the fill pattern.

- TBitmap encapsulates bitmap operations in VCL. Properties include Palette, Height, Width, and TransparentColor. Methods include LoadFromFile, LoadFromResourceID, and SaveToFile. TBitmap is used by other component classes such as TImage, TBitBtn, and TSpeedButton in addition to TCanvas. An instance of the TBitmap class can also be used as an offscreen bitmap. Offscreen bitmaps are commonly used in graphics-intensive applications to reduce flicker and improve graphics performance.

- The TFont class handles font operations. Properties include Color, Height, and Style (bold, italic, normal, and so on). The TFont class is used by all component classes that display text.

5

In addition to the GDI classes listed here, there are others that either work as helper classes or extend a base class to provide extra functionality. As you work with Delphi, you will learn more about these classes and how to use them. Figure 5.6 shows the hierarchy of the VCL classes that encapsulate GDI operations.

FIGURE 5.6.

VCL GDI class hierarchy.

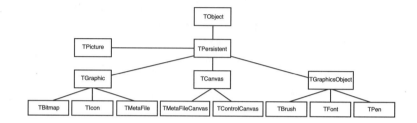

Utility Classes

VCL contains many utility classes that you can use in your applications. A *utility class* simplifies some task in Windows programming. For instance, the TIniFile class eases the use of writing and reading Windows configuration files (.INI files). Conventional wisdom has it that the use of .INI files is out and the Registry is in. To aid in Registry operations, VCL has the TRegistry and TRegkeyInfo classes.

The TStringList class enables arrays of strings. TStringList is used by many of the component classes to store strings. For instance, the TMemo class uses a TStringList object for its Lines property. TStringList has the capability to save its list of strings to file or load strings from a file using the LoadFromFile and SaveToFile methods. TStringList can also be used to read and write text files.

Another useful VCL utility class is the TList class. This class enables you to create arrays of any type of object you want. The TList class simply stores a list of pointers. The main advantage of the TList class is that it provides you with an array that will dynamically grow or shrink as new objects are added or removed.

VCL also includes a set of classes to enable reading and writing of streams (a stream is really just a block of data). The TStream, TFileStream, TMemoryStream, and TResourceStream classes all enable you to read or write data to streams. TStream is the base class for all stream classes. The TFileStream class is used when dealing with files on disk, TMemoryStream is used to manipulate data in memory, and TResourceStream is used to load binary resources from EXEs and DLLs. These classes are for more advanced uses, but they are invaluable when you need the particular functionality they provide. For more information on these classes, see the Delphi VCL Help.

And That's Not All . . .

By no means did I cover all the VCL classes here. I did, however, touch on those classes that you are most likely to use in your applications.

Flip back a few pages and take another look at Listing 5.1. I showed you how easy it was to load and display a bitmap with Delphi. Let's do an exercise that proves the point. First, begin a new application. You will be looking at a blank form. Perform the following steps:

1. Change the `Caption` property of the form to `Bitmap Test Program`.
2. Click on the Additional tab on the Component palette, choose the `Image` component, and place the component on the form.
3. Locate the `Align` property and change it to `alClient`. The picture component fills the client area of the form.
4. Locate the `Stretch` property and change it to `True`.
5. Locate the `Picture` property and double-click the `Value` column.
6. The Picture Editor dialog box is displayed. Click the Load button. The File Open dialog box is displayed.
7. Navigate to the `\Program Files\Common Files\Borland Shared Files\Images\Splash\256Color` directory and choose an image from those presented (I like `HANDSHAKE.BMP`). Click OK.
8. You are now back to the Image Editor dialog box, and the bitmap you chose is displayed in the preview window. Click OK. (If you want to choose a different bitmap, click the Load button again.) The bitmap now fills the client area of the form.
9. Click the Run button. When the application runs, you can size the window and the bitmap will always fill the client area of the window.

See how easy it is? It would have been even easier if you hadn't bothered to make the image fill the form's client area. Figure 5.7 shows the bitmap test program running.

FIGURE 5.7.

The bitmap test program running.

5

Summary

Today you learned about frameworks and how VCL fits into the framework scene. I discussed properties, methods, and events and gave you some hands-on experience in the process. You finished today with an overview of the VCL classes that you are likely to encounter when programming in Delphi. I didn't cover them all, but I gave you a brief look at the most commonly used classes.

So where is this industry going? The wave of the future appears to be components. The great thing about VCL is that if you decide (or are forced) to switch to C++, you can still use VCL. You might be surprised to learn that the very same VCL that is used in Delphi is also used in Borland C++Builder. Any time you spend learning VCL can be immediately applied to C++ if the time ever comes. It's the same VCL, so there's nothing to relearn.

Workshop

The Workshop contains quiz questions to help you solidify your understanding of the material covered and exercises to provide you with experience in using what you have learned. You can find the answers to quiz questions in Appendix A, "Answers to the Quiz Questions."

Q&A

Q What is a framework?

A A framework, also called a class library, is a set of classes that simplifies Windows programming. A good framework implements object-oriented design and object-oriented programming to apply an object-oriented approach to writing Windows applications.

Q Is VCL a framework?

A Yes, VCL is a framework. VCL is written in Object Pascal and works with both Delphi and C++Builder.

Q It seems as though the component way of doing things is the best approach. Is that true?

A For the most part, yes. VCL is a great choice for applications that use a lot of dialog boxes and for database applications. There's almost nothing that you can't do with Delphi but certainly Delphi shines in the area of RAD.

Q **Are properties just class data fields?**

A No. Properties are special creatures. Some properties simply set a data field in the class. Other properties, when modified, invoke a method that performs special operations with that property. In these cases, a property does more than just set a class field.

Q **Do I have to respond to each and every event a component defines?**

A No. You can respond to as many events as appropriate for your application or not respond to any events at all.

Q **Are the components on the Win 3.1 obsolete?**

A Not at all! These components were especially important in Delphi 1 because Delphi 1 was a 16-bit programming environment (hence the Win 3.1 tab name). That doesn't mean these components are obsolete in Delphi 4, though.

Q **There sure are a lot of VCL classes. I thought programming with Delphi was going to be easy.**

A Programming with Delphi is much easier than programming Windows with traditional tools. Windows programming, no matter how good the programming tool, requires a lot of experience and knowledge to master. You will master it if you keep at it.

Quiz

1. Are all components visible at design time?
2. Is the `OpenDialog` component a visual component or a nonvisual component?
3. What is the name of the VCL class that represents a Delphi form?
4. Do all versions of Delphi ship with the same set of components?
5. Are all VCL classes ultimately derived from `TObject`?
6. Name one nonvisual VCL component.
7. Do all components share certain common properties?
8. Name two common properties that all visual components share.
9. Can two or more components share the same event handler?
10. What is the VCL terminology for a Windows device context? What is the name of the VCL class that encapsulates device contexts?

5

Exercises

1. Write a paragraph describing how properties and class fields differ.

2. Create a Delphi application that displays a bitmap on the main form when a button is clicked.

3. Create a Delphi application that displays a message box saying `Hello, Bubba!` when the main form is clicked.

4. Place several components of your choice on a form. Click on a component and use the Object Inspector to study that component's properties. Repeat for each component on the form.

5. Switch to the Events tab and view the events of each component you placed on the form in Step 4.

DAY 6

Working with the Form Designer and the Menu Designer

As you know by now, Delphi is heavily form-based, a model that takes maximum advantage of the visual programming environment. In this chapter you will explore

- The Form Designer
- The Menu Designer

To illustrate the use of the Form Designer, you will build an application that approximates the Windows Notepad program. Along the way you will gain valuable experience working with the Form Designer. Later in the chapter, you'll explore the Menu Designer in detail.

This chapter might seem elementary if you have used Delphi extensively. Even so, be sure to take a quick look to discover things previously unknown or to rediscover things you've forgotten. I'm willing to bet there is at least one thing in this chapter that will be new to you.

Working with the Form Designer

The Delphi Form Designer is a powerful visual programming tool. It enables you to place, select, move, resize, and align components and much more. The Form Designer also enables you to size and position the form itself, add menus, and create specialized dialog boxes—everything you need to create the user interface to a typical Windows program.

I'll examine each Form Designer feature in the following sections. As you read, I encourage you to stop and experiment any time you are curious about how something works. Sometimes a few minutes playing around can teach you a technique that you will use for a long time to come.

The Form Designer's Context Menu

When you first start Delphi or when you create a new project, you are presented with a blank form in the Form Designer. The Form Designer, like most Delphi windows, has a context menu associated with it. Table 6.1 lists and describes each item on the Form Designer context menu.

TABLE 6.1. THE FORM DESIGNER'S CONTEXT MENU ITEMS.

Item	Description
Align to Grid	Aligns selected components to the Form Designer grid.
Bring to Front	Brings selected components to the front of all other components.
Send to Back	Sends selected components behind all other components.
Revert to Inherited	Causes the selected control to revert to its original state when you are working with a form that you have inherited from the Object Repository. (Inheriting forms from the Object Repository is covered on Day 8, "Creating Applications in Delphi.")
Align	Displays the Alignment dialog box.
Size	Displays the Size dialog box.
Scale	Displays the Scale dialog box.
Tab Order	Displays the Edit Tab Order dialog box.
Creation Order	Displays the Creation Order dialog box.

Item	Description
Flip Children	For non-English versions of Windows, this command changes the reading order of a component. Disabled for English versions of Windows.
Add to Repository	Adds this form to the Object Repository. Custom forms can be saved to be used later. (The Object Repository is discussed on Day 8.)
View as Text	Shows the form description as text in the Code Editor. You can edit the form's text version if you like. Choose View as Form from the Code Editor context menu to go back to the form. You can also use Alt+F12 to switch from the View as Text and View as Form options.

Note

Delphi creates a form file (DFM) for every form you create and places it in your project's directory. The form file is a binary resource file that can't be read by mere humans. When you choose the View as Text context menu item, Delphi converts the binary resource to readable form. When you switch back to the View as Form option, Delphi recompiles the form file to implement any changes you have made.

Most of the context menu options are discussed in the following sections. Others are discussed in later chapters when you examine the particular aspect of Delphi to which they pertain.

Placing Components

Placing a component on a form is simple. All you have to do is select the component you want from the Component palette and click on the form to place the component. When you click on the form, the component's upper-left corner is placed at the location you clicked. Notice that when you click a button on the Component palette, the button appears as pressed. When you click on the form to place the component, the button on the Component palette pops up again to indicate that the action is complete.

6

Tip

As you learned on Day 4, "The Delphi IDE Explored," to place a component on a form multiple times, press and hold Shift when you first select the component's button on the Component palette. Each time you click on the form, a new component will be added. Click the Arrow button on the Component palette to stop placing components.

Most components can be sized. You can place a component on a form and then size it, or you can size the component at the same time you place it on the form. To size while placing the component, click on the form where you want the top-left corner to be placed and then drag with the mouse until the component is the desired size. When you release the mouse, the component will be placed at the size you specified.

Note

Not all components can be sized in this manner. Nonvisual components, for example, are represented on the form by an icon. Although you can click and drag to place a nonvisual component, the drag size will be ignored. Another example is a single-line edit component. The edit component can be placed by dragging, but only the drag width will be used. The drag height will be ignored because the height of a single-line edit component defaults to the height of a single-line edit control.

Caution

If you change your mind while placing the control via the dragging method, you can press the Esc key on the keyboard before you release the mouse button to cancel the operation. The component's button will still be pressed on the Component palette, however, so you might need to click the Arrow button to return to component-selection mode.

Placing components is simple enough that you don't need to spend much time on the subject. You had some experience with placing components yesterday, so let's move on to other things.

The Form Designer Grid

The Form Designer has a built-in grid that aids in designing forms. By default, Delphi shows the grid. The grid size is initially set to eight pixels horizontally and eight pixels vertically. When the Form Designer is set to display the grid, a dot is placed at the intersection of each grid point. Components placed on a form will snap to the nearest grid point. By *snap to* I mean that the component's top-left corner will automatically jump to the nearest grid point. This is an advantage because you frequently want a group of controls to be aligned either on their left, right, top, or bottom edge. When the Snap to Grid option is on, you merely get close enough to the correct location and the Form Designer automatically places your component at the nearest grid point. This saves you time by sparing you from tweaking the individual component's size or position on the form.

The grid settings can be modified via the Preferences page of the Environment Options dialog box. (I'll discuss the Environment Options in detail on Day 9, "Projects, the Code Editor, and the Code Explorer.") From here you can change the grid size or turn off the Snap to Grid feature. You can also turn the grid display on or off. When the grid display is off, the grid is still active (assuming Snap to Grid is on), but the dots marking grid points are not drawn on the form.

Selecting Components

After you place a component on a form, you often have to select the component in order to modify it in some way. You might have to select a component to perform one of the following actions:

- Move the component.
- Change the component's properties.
- Align the component.
- Size the component.
- Cut or copy the component to the Clipboard.
- Order the component (bring to front or send to back).
- Delete the component.

Selecting Individual Components

To select a single component, just click on it. When you select the component, eight black sizing handles appear around the component to indicate that it is selected. (I'll discuss the sizing handles in a moment.) Figure 6.1 shows a form with a button component selected.

As soon as you select a component, the Object Inspector changes to show the properties and events for the control you selected. To deselect a control, click on the form's background or Shift+click on the control. (Shift+click is described in the next section.)

6

Tip

Each component has a default event handler associated with it. When you double-click a component on a form, the Code Editor displays the default event handler for that component, ready for you to type code. In most cases, the default event handler is the OnClick handler. Exactly what happens when the component is double-clicked depends on how the component is designed. For example, in the case of the Image component, double-clicking will display the Picture Editor dialog box.

FIGURE 6.1.

*A form with a button
component selected.*

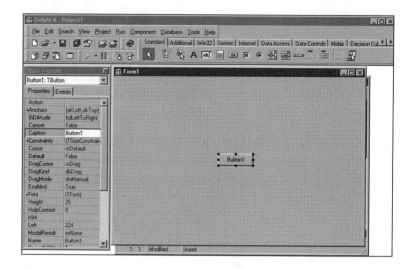

Selecting a Group of Components

You can also select multiple components so that you can act on them as a group. This is accomplished in one of three ways:

- Shift+click with the keyboard and mouse.
- Drag with the mouse.
- Choose Edit | Select All from the main menu.

To select all components on the form, choose Edit | Select All from the main menu.

Selecting Components with Shift+Click

To use the Shift+click sequence, first select one control. Then press and hold the Shift key on the keyboard and click on any other controls you want to include in the selection. Each control you click is bounded by four gray boxes to indicate that it is part of the selection.

You can remove a control from the selection by continuing to hold the Shift key and again clicking on the component. In other words, the Shift+click sequence toggles a component's inclusion in the selection. To illustrate, first start with a blank form and then perform the following steps:

1. Place three button components anywhere on the form. They will automatically be labeled Button1, Button2, and Button3.
2. Click Button1. The black sizing rectangles appear around the component.

3. Press and hold the Shift key on the keyboard. Click Button2. It is added to the selection. Gray boxes now appear at the corners of both Button1 and Button2.

4. Shift+click on Button3. Now all three buttons are part of the selection.

5. Shift+click again on Button2. Button2 is removed from the selection (the gray boxes disappear), but Button1 and Button3 are still included in the selection.

6. Shift+click on Button1. Now Button3 is the only component in the selection. The gray boxes are replaced with the black sizing rectangles.

7. Shift+click on Button1 and Button2. All three buttons are now part of the selection again.

Figure 6.2 shows the form as it will look at the end of this sequence. Keep in mind that your buttons could have been placed anywhere on the form. Keep the form handy because you'll use it again in the next exercise.

FIGURE 6.2.

A form with three buttons selected.

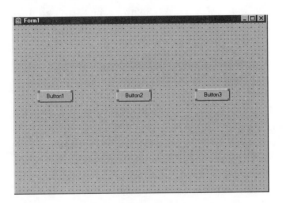

> **Note**
>
> If you click on a component that is part of a selection, nothing will happen. To select a single control that is currently part of a group selection, you need to first click on the form's background or press the Esc key to remove the group selection. Then you can click on the individual control you want to select.

6

Selecting Multiple Components by Dragging

You can select multiple controls by dragging a bounding rectangle around the controls to be selected. The *bounding rectangle* is a broken-line rectangle that changes size as you drag. In fact, you don't have to drag the bounding rectangle completely around the components. You have only to touch a component with the bounding rectangle in order for it to be included in the selection.

Be sure that you start by placing the mouse cursor over the form's background and not on a component. Hold the left mouse button down and begin dragging. You will see the bounding rectangle as you drag. Surround or touch the components you want selected and release the mouse button. Any components that were inside the bounding rectangle (or touching it) are included in the selection.

When you have selected a group of controls, you can use the Shift+click technique explained in the previous section to add other controls to the selection or to remove controls from the selection. For example, you might want to select all controls in one area of your form except for one. Surround the controls and then deselect the control you want to exclude from the selection.

Go back to the form with the three buttons you created earlier (if you've already discarded that form, create a new one and place three buttons on it). Start at the top-left corner and drag down and to the right to surround the buttons. Let go of the mouse button and the controls will be selected. Figure 6.3 shows the form and the bounding rectangle being dragged.

FIGURE 6.3.

Controls being selected by dragging.

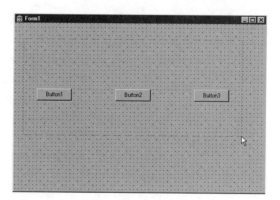

Caution

You can use Shift+drag to select non-adjacent groups of controls. If, for instance, you have two separate groups of controls in different areas on your form, you can drag around the first set and then hold the Shift key down and drag around the second set. Both groups will be selected.

Note

You don't have to drag down and to the right. You can drag in any direction to select components.

Selecting Multiple Items: Components within Components

Frequently you will have components placed within other components. The `Panel` component is often used as a container for other components. To select a group of components on a panel, you have to hold down the Ctrl key on the keyboard while you drag to select the components. (Try it without holding down the Ctrl key and see what happens!) In case you're wondering, yes, you can use a combination of Ctrl+Shift+drag. (I suppose the Borland designers could have figured out some way of working the Alt key in there, too.)

To illustrate, first start with a blank form. Then do the following:

1. Select a `Panel` component from the Component palette and place it on the form using the drag method. Drag it so that it occupies most of the form.

2. Now select a `Button` component and place six buttons on the form. Your form will look something like Figure 6.4.

FIGURE 6.4.

The form with a panel and six buttons.

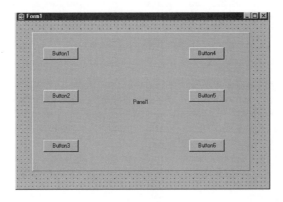

3. Drag a bounding rectangle around Button1, Button2, and Button3. Notice that you moved the panel, which is not what you expected (and not what you wanted). Move the panel back to where it was.

4. Hold down the Ctrl key and drag a rectangle around Button1, Button2, and Button3. The buttons are selected.

5. Now hold down both the Ctrl and Shift keys and drag the bounding rectangle around Button5 and Button6. Now all buttons are selected except Button4.

Using the Ctrl+drag sequence is the only way to select a group of components contained within another component if you are using the drag method. You can use the Shift+click method to select components contained within another component just as you do when selecting components on a form.

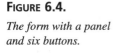

Moving Components

Moving components is a common and simple task. To move an individual component, place the mouse cursor over the component and drag. As you drag, a rectangle that represents the component moves with the mouse cursor. When you have the rectangle where you want it, let go of the mouse button and the component will be moved to that location.

Note

When you move a control via drag and drop, the control's Left and Top properties are automatically updated. If you pause for a moment while moving a component, you will notice a tooltip appear next to the mouse cursor. The tooltip shows what the new top and left position of the component will be when you stop dragging.

A similar tooltip is displayed when sizing a component by dragging. In the case of sizing a component, the tooltip shows what the new width and height of the component will be when you stop dragging. Figure 6.6 shows the tooltip you see when sizing a component (in the lower-right corner).

Note

It's easiest to move a component by drag and drop. If you need finer control, you can modify the component's Left and Top properties in the Object Inspector. You can also use various alignment options, which I'll discuss later in the chapter in the section "Aligning Components."

If you have the Snap to Grid option on, the dragging rectangle will snap to the nearest grid point as you drag.

Tip

If you change your mind while dragging, you can press the Esc key on the keyboard before you release the mouse button to cancel the drag operation. The component will return to its original position.

Dragging a group of controls works the same way. After you have a group of components selected, place the mouse cursor over any one of the controls and begin dragging. The dragging rectangle will be displayed for each control in the group. This enables you to visualize where the group will be placed when you release the mouse button.

Note

You cannot move a group of components if components in the group have different parent controls. For instance, let's say you select both a Button component on the main form and a SpeedButton on a panel. Because these two components have different parent controls, you cannot move them as a group.

Tip

When you have selected a control, you can nudge it a pixel at a time by holding down the Ctrl key while using the arrow keys on the keyboard. This technique works for both groups of controls and individual controls. The Snap to Grid feature is overridden when you use this technique.

After you have moved a component using this method, the component is no longer on a grid point—it is offset by some amount. If you now drag the component, it will maintain its offset from the grid point as you drag.

Tip

If you move a control using the Ctrl+arrow method and want to align it again to the grid, choose Edit | Align to Grid from the main menu. The control's top-left corner will snap to the nearest grid point.

A control cannot be dragged outside its parent form. If you drag a component off the form's left or top edge, you will see that the component is clipped at the form's edge. If, however, you drag the component off the right or bottom of the form and drop it, scrollbars will appear on the form so that you can scroll to see the rest of the form.

The form's Width and Height properties are not altered. If you drag the component back onto the visible part of the form, the scrollbars disappear again. This is the default behavior and will occur unless you change the form's AutoScroll property to False. Figure 6.5 shows a Memo component that has been dragged partially off the form's right edge. Notice the scrollbar that appears at the bottom of the form.

Preventing Components from Being Moved or Sized

Components can be locked into place so that they cannot be moved. Locking components is useful if you know that a form's design is final and you don't want to worry about accidentally moving controls. To lock a form's controls, choose Edit | Lock Controls from the main menu. Locked controls cannot be moved or sized. When controls

6

are locked, their sizing handles are gray with a black border. To unlock the controls, choose Edit | Lock Controls again. The controls can now be moved as before. You can lock all components on a form with this technique or none of the components. You cannot, however, lock just selected components.

FIGURE 6.5.

A form with AutoScroll *in action.*

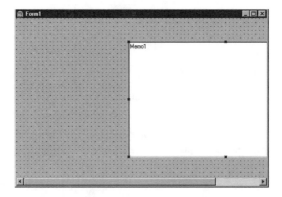

Ordering, Cutting, Copying, and Pasting Components

Sometimes you will place components on top of one another to achieve a visual effect. For example, a shadowed box can be created by placing a white box over a black box (both would be Shape components). Obviously you can't have the shadow on top of the box, so you have to order the controls to tell Delphi which controls go on top and which go on the bottom. Let's do a simple exercise that illustrates this. Along the way, you will also see how you can use Copy and Paste with components. First, start with a blank form (you know the drill by now). Now follow these steps:

1. Click on the Additional tab on the Component palette and choose the Shape component. Click on the form to place the shape. A white square appears on the form.

2. Size the shape as desired (mine ended up being 209 pixels by 129 pixels).

3. Be sure the Shape component is selected. Choose Edit | Copy from the main menu.

4. Choose Edit | Paste from the main menu. A copy of the shape is placed below and to the right of the original shape. Conveniently, this is exactly where you want it.

Note
After a paste operation, the component just pasted will be selected.

5. Double-click the Brush property in the Object Inspector and change its Color property to clBlack. The new shape is now black, but it is on top of the original shape. Can't have that!

6. Click the secondary mouse button and choose Send to Back from the context menu (you can also choose Edit | Send to Back from the main menu). The black shape is moved behind the white shape. You now have a box with a shadow. (As an alternative, you could have clicked on the white shape and used Bring to Front to move it on top of the black shape.)

This exercise illustrates two features of the Form Designer. It shows how you can change the stacking order of controls and how you can use Copy and Paste to copy components. The original component's properties are copied exactly and pasted in as part of the pasting process. Each time you paste a component, it is placed below and to the right of the previous component you pasted.

> **Note**
>
> If a component that can serve as a container is selected when you perform Paste, the component in the Clipboard will be pasted as the container component's child. For example, you might want to move a button from the main form to a panel. You can select the button and choose Edit | Cut from the main menu to remove the button from the form and place it in the Clipboard. Then you can select the panel and choose Edit | Paste from the main menu to paste the button onto the panel.

I don't need to go into much detail on the cut operation. When you cut a component, the component disappears from the form and is placed in the Clipboard. Later, you can paste the component onto the form or onto another component such as a Panel component.

> **Tip**
>
> You can also copy a component and paste it into your source code. The results will be something like this:
>
> ```
> object Edit1: TEdit
>   Left = 24
>   Top = 16
>   Width = 457
>   Height = 21
>   TabOrder = 0
>   Text = 'Edit1'
> end
> ```

6

> This is not code that will compile, but this technique will give you a component's size and position as it appears on the form. This information comes in handy when you create components on-the-fly at runtime rather than at design time. You can place a dummy component visually on the form, get its size and position using Copy and Paste, and then delete the component. Then you can write code to create the component at runtime and know that it will be properly sized and positioned.

Sizing Components

With some components, you drop them on a form and accept the default size. Buttons are a good example. A standard button has a height of 25 pixels and a width of 75 pixels. For many situations, the default button size is exactly what you want. With some components, however, the default size is rarely exactly what you need. A Memo component, for example, nearly always has to be sized to fit the specific form on which you are working.

Sizing by Dragging

When you select a control, eight black sizing handles appear around the control. When you place the mouse cursor over one of the sizing handles, the cursor changes to a double-headed arrow known as the *sizing cursor*. When you see the sizing cursor, you can begin dragging to size the control. How the component is sized depends on which sizing handle you grab.

The sizing handles centered at the top and bottom of the component size it vertically (taller or shorter). Likewise, the right and left sizing handles size the component horizontally (wider or narrower). If you grab one of the sizing handles in the component's corners, you can size both horizontally and vertically at the same time. As with moving a component, a sizing rectangle appears as you drag. When the sizing rectangle is the desired size, let go of the mouse button and the component will be resized. Figure 6.6 illustrates a memo component being sized by dragging; Figure 6.7 shows the form after the drag operation.

Note

> Sizing applies to visual components only. Nonvisual components appear on the form as an icon that cannot be sized. The sizing handles appear on nonvisual components and the handles can be dragged, but the result of the dragging operation will be ignored.

FIGURE 6.6.

A memo component being sized.

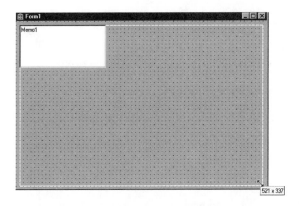

FIGURE 6.7.

The form after sizing the memo component.

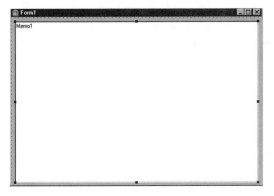

Groups of controls cannot be sized by dragging. The sizing handles (black squares) are replaced by selection indicators (gray squares) when you select more than one component.

> **Tip**
>
> To size all the components in a group at one time, modify the Width or Height property in the Object Inspector or use the Size dialog box (the Size dialog box is discussed in the next section). All components in the selection will take on the new values.

6

> **Tip**
>
> To size a control or group of controls by one pixel at a time, hold down the Shift key and press any arrow key on the keyboard. The up and down arrows size the control vertically and the right and left arrows size it horizontally. Only the component's Width and Height properties are affected. The Top and Left properties are not modified.

Sizing with the Size Dialog Box

Another sizing option is the Size dialog box. You can bring up the Size dialog box by choosing Edit | Size from the main menu. Figure 6.8 shows the Size dialog box.

FIGURE 6.8.

The Size dialog box.

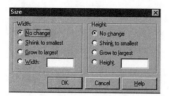

The Size dialog box is used when you want to force a group of controls to the same width or height. For instance, let's say you have six edit components on a form, all with different widths. To make the form appear more balanced, you might want to make all the edit components the same width. First, select the components and then invoke the Size dialog box. From there you can choose Shrink to smallest (in the Width column) to make all the components the width of the shortest edit component, or Grow to largest to make all the components the width of the longest component in the group. You can also enter an exact width in the Width box, in which case you would leave the Height set on No change. When you click OK, the components will all be the same width.

Tip

> The Size dialog box can also be invoked from the Form Designer context menu.

Sizing with the Scale Dialog Box

Another sizing tool is the Scale dialog box, shown in Figure 6.9. This dialog box enables you to specify a scaling percentage. To make the components twice as large, enter 200 in the Scaling factor box. To reduce the components' size by half, enter 50 in the Scaling factor box. The Scale dialog box is convenient for quickly changing the size of all the form's components. You can bring up the Scale dialog box by choosing Edit | Scale from the main menu or Scale from the Form Designer context menu.

A control can also be sized and moved by using the various Alignment options. Let's take a look at those in the next section.

FIGURE 6.9.

The Scale dialog box.

 Note

Remember, components can always be moved by modifying their Left and Top properties and sized by modifying their Width and Height properties in the Object Inspector.

Aligning Components

Regardless of whether you have the Snap to Grid option turned on, you sometimes need to align components after placing them. Aligning components could mean aligning several components along a common edge, centering components on the form, or spacing components. There are two ways to align components:

- Use the Alignment palette and Alignment dialog box.
- Modify a component's Align property.

The following sections explain these two methods.

 Note

You might have noticed the Alignment property for some components. This property pertains only to the way the component's text is aligned (centered, right-justified, or left-justified) and has nothing to do with aligning components on a form.

The Alignment Palette and the Alignment Dialog Box

It is often necessary to move or size components relative to the form or relative to one another. The Alignment palette contains several buttons that aid in that task. The Alignment dialog box performs the same operations as the Alignment palette, but in a different format. To display the Alignment palette, choose View | Alignment Palette from the main menu. Figure 6.10 shows the Alignment palette and describes each button. If you pause the mouse cursor over a button on the Alignment palette, a tooltip describing the button will appear.

6

Align Horizontal Centers ┐ ┌Center Horizontally in Window
Align Left Edges ──────┐ │ │┌Space Equally Horizontally

FIGURE 6.10.

The Alignment palette.

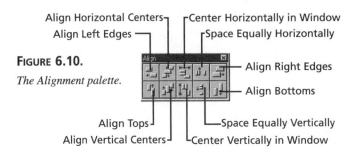

────── Align Right Edges

────── Align Bottoms

Align Tops ┘
Align Vertical Centers ┘ └Center Vertically in Window
                            └Space Equally Vertically

> **Tip**
>
> The Alignment palette can save you a lot of work. Don't spend too much time trying to get controls to line up exactly. Place the components on the form and then use the Alignment palette to position them.

The Align Left Edges button is used to line up components on their left edges. Start with a blank form and then do the following:

1. Place five button components vertically on the form without regard to their left edges.

2. Select the buttons by dragging a bounding rectangle around them. The selection indicators show that all the buttons are selected. The form will look something like the one in Figure 6.11.

FIGURE 6.11.

The form with the buttons randomly placed.

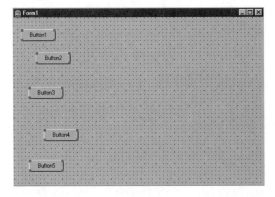

3. Choose View | Alignment Palette from the main menu. The Alignment palette is displayed. Move the Alignment palette, if necessary, so that it doesn't obscure the form.

4. Click the Align Left Edges button on the Alignment palette. The buttons are all lined up.

See how easy that is? As long as you have the buttons selected, let's look at another alignment option. The Space Equally Vertically alignment option can now be used to space the buttons evenly. The buttons should still be selected, so all you have to do is click the Space Equally Vertically button on the Alignment palette, and voilà! The buttons are perfectly spaced. The form will now look like Figure 6.12.

FIGURE 6.12.

The form with the buttons aligned and equally spaced.

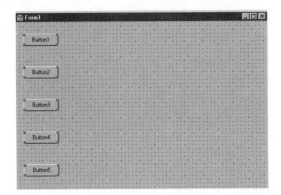

> **Note**
>
> The Space Equally Vertically alignment option spaces the components equally between the first component in the column (the top component) and the last component in the column (the bottom component). Be sure to set the first and last components where you want them before choosing the Space Equally Vertically alignment option. This is true of the Space Equally Horizontally alignment option as well.

The Center Horizontally in Window and Center Vertically in Window alignment options do exactly as their names indicate. These options are convenient for centering a single control on the form or for centering a group of controls. As long as you still have the group of buttons selected, click both the Center Horizontally in Window and Center Vertically in Window buttons on the Alignment palette. The buttons will be centered on the form both horizontally and vertically.

> **Note**
>
> When you select a group of controls and click one of the centering buttons, the controls will be treated *as a group*. If you choose each control individually and center it both horizontally and vertically on the form, all the controls will be stacked on top of one another in the middle of the form. By selecting the group and then centering, you get the entire group centered as you intended.

6

The form will now look like the one shown in Figure 6.13.

FIGURE 6.13.

The form with the buttons centered.

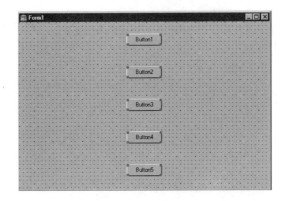

Note

The Center Horizontally in Window and Center Vertically in Window alignment options can be used to align components contained within other components, such as buttons on a panel. The components will be centered horizontally or vertically on their parent component regardless of whether the parent is a panel, a form, or some other container component.

The Align Tops, Align Bottoms, and Align Right Edges options work just like the Align Left Edges option you used earlier. There's not much point in going over all the possibilities that exist for their use.

Tip

The first component selected will be the anchor point when using any edge-alignment option. Refer to Figure 6.4. Let's say you selected Button3 first and then used Shift+click to select the remaining buttons. When you choose Align Left Edges, Button3 will remain where it is and all the other buttons will line up with Button3's left edge because Button3 is the anchor component.

The Align Horizontal Centers and Align Vertical Centers options can be used to center components relative to one another. This is best illustrated with shapes. Start with a new form (or delete the buttons from the form you have been working on). Now do the following:

1. Click on the Additional tab on the Component palette and choose the Shape component. Click somewhere on the upper left of the form to add the shape.

2. Change the Shape property to stCircle.

3. Change the Width and Height properties to 150.

4. Double-click the Brush property and change its Color property to clBlack.

5. Place another Shape component on the form.

6. Change the second shape's Shape property to stCircle as well. Now you have two circles of different sizes on the screen—a white circle and a black circle.

7. Click on the black circle. Hold the Shift key and click on the white circle. Both shapes are selected.

8. Choose View | Alignment Palette from the main menu, if necessary (it might already be displayed). Arrange the Alignment palette so you can see the two shapes on the form. Observe the shapes as you perform the last two steps.

9. Click the Align Vertical Centers button on the Alignment palette. The vertical centers are aligned.

10. Click the Align Horizontal Centers button on the Alignment palette. The horizontal centers are aligned. Congratulations—you made a tire!

Did you see the effect as you performed the last two steps? Notice that because you selected the black circle first, it did not move (it is the anchor component), but the white circle moved as you clicked the alignment buttons. You can use these alignment options to center any number of controls on one another. These two alignment options have no effect when used on a single control.

Like the Component palette, the Alignment palette has a context menu associated with it. Place the mouse cursor over the Alignment palette and click the secondary mouse button. The context menu is displayed. Table 6.2 lists the items on the Alignment palette's context menu and explains their uses.

TABLE 6.2. THE ALIGNMENT PALETTE'S CONTEXT MENU ITEMS.

Menu Item	Description
Stay on Top	Forces the Alignment palette to always be on top. This is useful if you are frequently switching back and forth between the Form Designer and the Code Editor. Because the Alignment palette is a small window, it's easy to lose it.
Show Hints	Turns the hints (tooltips) for the Alignment palette buttons on and off.

continues

6

TABLE 6.2. CONTINUED

Menu Item	Description
Hide	Hides the Alignment palette. (You can also use the close box on the Alignment palette to hide it.) To show the Alignment palette again, you have to choose View I Alignment Palette from the main menu.
Help	Brings up Delphi Help with the Alignment palette page displayed.

The Alignment dialog box performs the same actions as the Alignment palette. To bring up the Alignment dialog box, choose Edit I Align from the main menu or Align from the Form Designer's context menu. Figure 6.14 shows the Alignment dialog box.

FIGURE 6.14.

The Alignment dialog box.

In most cases, the Alignment palette is easier to use, but you can certainly use the Alignment dialog box if you prefer.

Using the `Align` Property

Another type of alignment can be set using the `Align` property. This property controls how a component is aligned with its parent. The possible values for the `Align` property and a description of each are listed in Table 6.3.

TABLE 6.3. POSSIBLE VALUES FOR THE `Align` PROPERTY.

Value	Description
alBottom	The component is aligned at the bottom of the parent window. A status bar is an example of a component aligned along the bottom of a main form.
alClient	The component expands to fill the parent window's client area. If other components occupy part of the client area, the component fills what client area remains. Examples include `Memo` components, `Image` components, and `RichEdit` components.
alLeft	The component is aligned along the parent window's left edge. A vertical toolbar is an example of a left-aligned component.

Value	Description
alNone	The component is placed as designed with no special relationship to the parent. This is the default for most components.
alRight	The component is aligned along the parent's right edge.
alTop	The component is aligned along the top of the parent's window. A toolbar is an example of this type of alignment.

An example helps explain the Align property. Start with a blank form and then perform these steps:

1. Click on the Standard tab on the Component palette and choose a Panel component. Place the panel anywhere on the form.

2. Locate the Align property in the Object Inspector (it's at the top of the list). Notice that it is set on alNone. Change the Align property to alTop. The panel is aligned at the top of the form and it expands to fill the form's width.

3. Try to move the panel back to the middle of the form. The panel will snap back to the top.

4. Try to make the panel narrower. Notice that the panel retains its width.

5. Change the panel's height. Note that the panel's height can be changed (the width cannot).

6. Change the Align to alBottom. Now the panel is glued to the bottom of the form.

7. Change the Align to alRight and then alLeft. The width is now the same as the height was before. In effect, the panel is rotated. Again, attempts to move the panel or size it vertically fail.

8. Change the Align property to alClient. The panel expands to fill the form's entire client area. The panel cannot be resized in any dimension.

9. Change the Align property to alNone. The panel can again be sized and moved.

As you see, changing Align to anything other than alNone effectively glues the panel to one edge of the form. In the case of alClient, the panel is glued to all four edges.

Setting the Tab Order

NEW TERM The *tab order* refers to the order in which components receive input focus when the user presses the Tab key on the keyboard.

Delphi forms automatically support component navigation using the Tab key. This means that you can move forward from component to component using Tab and backward using Shift+Tab.

6

Note

There are two types of visual components. *Windowed* components are components that accept keyboard focus, which means that the component can be clicked with the mouse or tabbed to with the Tab key. When a component has keyboard focus, it either displays a specialized cursor (such as the I-beam cursor in an edit control) or has a focus rectangle drawn somewhere on the component. Windowed components include the Edit, Memo, ListBox, ComboBox, and Button components, as well as many more.

Non-windowed components are components that don't accept keyboard focus. Components such as Image, SpeedButton, Label, Shape, and many others are non-windowed components.

The tab order applies only to windowed components. Non-windowed components are excluded from the tab order.

The tab order is initially set based on the order the components were placed on the form when the form was designed. You can modify the tab order by changing the TabOrder property for each control in the Object Inspector, but that method is tedious because you have to go to each control individually. The Edit Tab Order dialog box provides an easier way (see Figure 6.15).

FIGURE 6.15.

The Edit Tab Order dialog box.

The Edit Tab Order dialog box is invoked by choosing Edit | Tab Order from the main menu. This dialog box displays all windowed components currently on the form; non-windowed components are not displayed. To change the tab order, click on the name of the component you want to move in the tab order and then click the up or down buttons as needed. You can also drag the component to its new position in the tab order. After you get the tab order the way you want it, click OK to set it that way. You can confirm the new settings by viewing each control's TabOrder property.

> The tab order starts with 0. The first component in the tab order is 0, the second is 1, and so on.

Building an Example Application

To illustrate how different components work together, let's build a prototype of an application that resembles Windows Notepad, Windows standard text editor.

> Building a text editor probably doesn't sound too glamorous. To be honest, it's not. What building a text editor will do for you, however, is teach you how to conquer many of the real-world problems you will encounter when programming in Delphi. It might not be glamorous, but it will almost certainly teach you more than building Snazzy Gadgets 1.0.

A *prototype* is an application that has the appearance of a working application but lacks full functionality, usually because it's in the early stages of design.

> Delphi is perfect for quick prototyping of an application. You can have the main screens and dialog boxes designed and displayed in much less time than it would take with traditional Windows programming tools. That is not, however, to say that Delphi is just for prototyping. Delphi is fully capable of handling all your 32-bit Windows programming needs.

Step 1: Starting a New Application

1. Choose File | New Application from the main menu. If prompted to save the current project, click No.
2. The form is selected, so change the Name property to MainForm.
3. Change the Caption to ScratchPad 1.0.
4. Choose Project | Options from the main menu. Click on the Application tab and enter ScratchPad 1.0 for the application's title. Click OK to close the Project Options dialog box.

6

Step 2: Adding a Toolbar

Most Windows applications these days have a toolbar. Building a toolbar requires several steps in itself. I'm not quite ready to explain everything there is to know about toolbars in Delphi, so I'll save that for Day 13, "Beyond the Basics." You'll add a toolbar to the ScratchPad program at that time. What you can do for now, though, is add a toolbar that can be used as a placeholder for the real toolbar that you add later. Follow these steps:

1. Click on the Win32 tab on the Component palette and choose the ToolBar component (it's the third from the right).

2. Click anywhere on the form to add the toolbar. Notice that the toolbar automatically aligns itself to the top of the form.

3. Right-click on the toolbar and choose New Button. A button appears on the toolbar.

4. Repeat step 3 to add a second button.

That's all you are going to do with the toolbar for now. As I said, you'll make a real toolbar for this program on Day 13.

Step 3: Adding a Status Bar

Okay, so far, so good. Windows Notepad doesn't have a status bar (or a toolbar, for that matter), but you can put one in your application by following these steps:

1. Click on the Win32 tab on the Component palette and choose the StatusBar component.

2. Click anywhere on the form. The status bar is automatically placed at the bottom of the form. The status bar has a default Align value of alBottom.

3. Change the Name property to StatusBar.

The form will now look like Figure 6.16.

FIGURE 6.16.

The ScratchPad form up to this point.

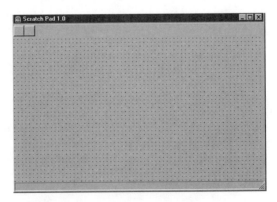

Step 4: Adding the Memo Component

You need some component in which to type text, so you can use a memo component to add this feature (believe it or not, you're almost done with your prototype):

1. Click on the Standard tab on the Component palette and choose a Memo component. Place the memo anywhere on the form's client area.

2. Change the Name property to Memo.

3. Double-click the Value column next to the Lines property. The String List Editor is displayed. Delete the word Memo and click OK.

4. Change the Scrollbar property to ssVertical. (Initially, you want only a vertical scrollbar on the memo.)

5. Change the Name property of the Font property to Fixedsys. (Because this is a Notepad copycat, you'll use the system font.)

6. Change the Align property to alClient. The memo expands to fill the client area between the toolbar and the status bar.

Stand back and admire your work. This is starting to look like a real application! If the form looks too large or too small, resize it by dragging the lower-right corner. It's your program, so make it look the way you want it to look.

> **Tip**
>
> Pressing the Esc key selects the parent of the control that currently has the selection. For example, our form's client area is covered by components, which makes it impossible to select the form itself. To make the form the active component in the Object Inspector, select the memo component and then press the Esc key on the keyboard. You can also choose the form from the Component Selector combo box on the Object Inspector.

Notice that all the controls automatically resize themselves to retain their relationship with the parent window—the form, in this case. That is one of the main advantages to the Align property. The form now looks like the one in Figure 6.17.

Running the Program

You can now click the Run button to run the program. You can type text in the window's client area and you can press the toolbar buttons (although they don't do anything at this point). Keep in mind that this is a prototype and is mostly for show right now. You add more to the program by the end of the day.

FIGURE 6.17.

The completed proto-type.

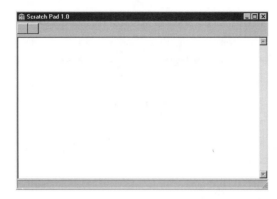

You'd better save the project because you're going to use it later in the chapter. Choose File | Save All from the main menu. Save the main form's source unit as SPMain and the project as Scratch.

May I See a Menu, Please?

Menus are a big part of most Windows applications. Some Windows programs don't have menus, but the vast majority do. Delphi makes creating menus easy with the Menu Designer. The Menu Designer has the following features:

- It can create both main menus and pop-up menus (context menus).
- It provides immediate access to the Code Editor to handle the OnClick events for menu items.
- It can insert menus from templates or from resource files.
- It can save custom menus as templates.

All the Menu Designer's commands are accessed via the Menu Designer context menu or by interacting with the Object Inspector. Figure 6.18 shows the Menu Designer's context menu.

For the most part, these menu items are self-explanatory, so I'm not going to go over each one. Rather, you can learn about them by working with them. To begin, let's add a main menu to the ScratchPad application you created earlier. After that you'll add a context menu.

FIGURE 6.18.

*The Menu Designer's
context menu.*

Creating a Main Menu

The Menu Designer enables you to quickly build any menu. The menu structure for a
main menu consists of a MainMenu component, which is represented by the VCL class
TMainMenu. Each item on the menu is a MenuItem component that is encapsulated in the
TMenuItem class. You don't need to be too concerned about the intricacies of how these
classes work together because the Menu Designer makes creating menus easy. With that
brief overview, let's add a main menu to the ScratchPad application.

Adding a Main Menu to the Form

The first thing you must do is add a MainMenu component to your form.

Note

> By now you have had some experience with Delphi. From this point on I will
> abbreviate some steps that you need to take to perform certain actions. For
> example, from here on I'll say, "Place a MainMenu component on the form"
> rather than "Click on the Standard tab on the Component palette. Click the
> MainMenu button and click on the form to place the component." Don't
> worry, I'll still give plenty of details when new operations are introduced.

1. Open the ScratchPad project you created earlier in the chapter.

2. Place a MainMenu component on the form and change its Name property to
   MainMenu. Notice that a MainMenu component has very few properties and no
   events. All the menu's work is done by the individual menu items.

3. Double-click on the MainMenu icon. The Menu Designer is displayed.

The Menu Designer looks like a blank form without grid points. The Menu Designer can
be sized in any way you want. The size is just for your convenience and has no bearing
on how the menu operates at runtime. At this point, the Menu Designer is waiting for
you to begin building the menu. After you have created your first menu, you will find
that menu creation is easy and intuitive.

6

Creating a Menu by Hand

Although there are easier ways to create a File menu, you will create your first menu by hand. The Menu Designer always has a blank menu item that acts as a placeholder for any new menu items you will create. When you first start the Menu Designer, the blank item is selected.

1. Change the Name property to FileMenu.
2. Click on the Caption property in the Object Inspector, type &File, and press Enter.

Note

> The ampersand (&) is used to create the underlined character for a menu item. The underlined character is the *accelerator* the user can type in combination with the Alt key to navigate a menu using the keyboard. You can put ampersands anywhere in the menu item's text. For instance, the customary text string for the Exit menu item would be E&xit so that the *x* is the accelerator. All you have to do is provide the ampersands before the appropriate letter, Windows will take it from there.

At this point, several things happen. First, the File menu shows up in the Menu Designer. It also appears on the main form behind the Menu Designer. The other thing that happens is that a new, blank placeholder is added below the File menu you just created (you'll have to click on the File menu in the Menu Designer to see the placeholder). In addition, a new pop-up placeholder is created to the right of the File menu. The Object Inspector is displaying a blank MenuItem component, waiting for you to enter the Caption and Name property values. Figure 6.19 shows the Menu Designer as it appears at this point.

FIGURE 6.19.

The Menu Designer and Object Inspector after creating the File menu.

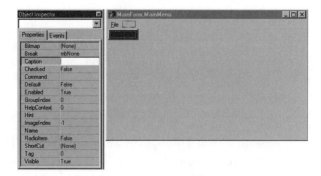

Let's continue with the creation of the menu:

1. Change the Name property for the new item to FileNew.

2. Change the Caption property to &New and press Enter. Again, a blank item is created in the Menu Designer.

3. Repeat steps 1 and 2 and create menu items for Open, Save, and Save As. If you need help on where to place the ampersand, refer to Figure 6.20. Don't worry that you might not get it exactly right. You can always go back later and fix any errors.

Tip

> Make your menus as standard as possible. Be sure that your accelerators (the underlined characters) are the same as in other Windows programs. Also, remember that an ellipsis (...) following a menu item's text is a visual cue to the user that choosing the menu item will invoke a dialog box.

At this point, you need a menu separator.

NEW TERM   A *separator* is the horizontal line on a menu that separates groups of menu items.

Adding a separator is easy with the Delphi Menu Designer. All you have to do is put in a hyphen for the Caption property. Select the blank menu item under Save As, type a hyphen for the Caption, and press Enter. A separator is placed in the menu. Continue adding menu items until your menu looks like the one in Figure 6.20. If you need to modify a menu item, just click on it and change properties in the Object Inspector as needed.

FIGURE 6.20.

The Menu Designer with the finished File menu.

6

Note

> The Menu Designer always provides a blank menu item at the bottom of each pop-up menu and on the menu bar's right side. You cannot delete these blank items, but there's no need to—they are used only in the Menu Designer and won't show on the menu when your program runs.

Now that the File menu is done, you need to create an Edit menu and a Help menu.

Inserting a Menu from a Template

This time you'll take the easy approach. First, click on the blank pop-up menu place-holder to the right of the File menu. Now click your secondary mouse button and choose Insert From Template from the context menu. The Insert Template dialog box is displayed, as shown in Figure 6.21.

FIGURE 6.21.

The Insert Template dialog box.

This dialog box shows a list of templates from which you can choose. You can use the predefined templates or create your own. In this case, you are only interested in adding an Edit menu, so choose Edit Menu and click OK. A full Edit menu is immediately inserted into the Menu Designer. In fact, it's a little too full. I'll deal with that in a moment.

As long as you're here, you can add the Help menu, too. Click on the placeholder to the right of the Edit menu. Choose Insert From Template again, and this time insert a Help menu. (Don't choose the Expanded Help menu, though.) You'll tidy up both the Edit and Help menus in the next section. Notice that the main form has been updating to show the new menu items as they are placed.

Note

> You can insert templates to create pop-up menus as easily as creating main menu items.

Yes, inserting from a template is really that easy. After using Delphi for a while, you will no doubt have your own custom templates to choose from for building menus quickly and easily. You still have to update the Name properties to meaningful names, but it's much easier than creating the whole menu from scratch.

> **Note**
>
> The Insert From Resource choice works the same as Insert From Template except that it expects a resource script file (a resource script file has the extension .RC) containing a valid menu definition. The menu resource must use the begin/end menu resource syntax and cannot use braces. For example, the following is an invalid menu resource:
>
> ```
> MENU_1 MENU
> {
>  POPUP "File"
>  {
>   MENUITEM "Open", 100
>   MENUITEM "About", 101
>  }
> }
> ```
>
> The following menu resource, however, is legal:
>
> ```
> MENU_1 MENU
> BEGIN
>  POPUP "File"
>  BEGIN
>   MENUITEM "Open", 100
>   MENUITEM "About", 101
>  END
> END
> ```
>
> This applies only to menus inserted with Insert From Resource and not to menu resources in general.

Deleting Menu Items

The process of creating a Windows application is a living, breathing thing. Rarely will you get everything exactly right the first time. Users will request new features, the boss will come up with a few changes, and some features will even be dropped. You will often need to update your application's menus as these changes occur. For example, the Edit menu inserted earlier is a little verbose for your needs; there are several items that you just don't need. No problem—you can just delete them:

1. Click on the Edit menu.
2. Click on the item called Repeat <command>.
3. Press Delete on the keyboard or choose Delete from the Menu Designer context menu to delete the item. The item disappears and the remaining items move up.
4. Delete the Paste Special menu item as well.

6

There, that was easy! You're not quite done with the Edit menu, but before going on, I want to mention a very useful feature of the Menu Designer. You are probably familiar with using Shift+click and Ctrl+click when selecting items in other Windows programs. These techniques can be used in Windows Explorer to select files, for example. The Menu Designer supports Shift+click and Ctrl+click with one qualification—you can use these to select multiple menu items but not to deselect an item. As always, an exercise can illustrate better than I can explain:

1. The Edit menu should still be displayed. If not, click on Edit to reveal the Edit menu.

2. Click on the menu item called Goto.

3. Hold down the Shift key and click on the menu item called Object. All items between those two points are selected.

4. Press Delete on the keyboard to delete all the items at one time.

5. Move to the Help menu and delete the middle two items. Only the Contents and About items remain.

As you can see, the Shift+click technique can be used to quickly delete unwanted menu items. Now you have the menus trimmed back to the way you want them to appear in the ScratchPad application.

Inserting Menu Items

Inserting menu items is pretty straightforward. Just click on the menu item above which you want to insert a new item and press the Insert key on the keyboard (or choose Insert from the Menu Designer's context menu). A blank menu item is inserted, and you can now modify the Name and Caption properties just as you did earlier. Let's insert an item into the Edit menu:

1. Click on Edit to display the Edit menu.

2. Click on the Find menu item.

3. Press the Insert key on the keyboard. A new menu item is provided, and all other menu items below the new item move down.

4. Change the Name property to EditSelectAll and change the Caption property to Select &All.

5. Click on the empty placeholder at the bottom of the Edit menu. Add a menu separator (remember, just enter a hyphen for the Caption property).

6. Click on the placeholder again and add a new item. Make the Name property EditWordWrap and the Caption property &Word Wrap.

Moving Menu Items

You can easily move menu items as needed. You can move them up or down within the pop-up menu they are already in, or you can move them across pop-ups. There are two ways to move a menu item. The first is by using Cut and Paste. Cut and Paste work as you would expect, so there's no need to go over that.

The other way to move a menu item is by dragging it to a new location and dropping it. Let's try it. You really want the Select All menu item just below the Undo item. That's easy enough to fix, you can just move it:

1. Click on Edit to display the Edit menu.
2. Click on the Select All item and drag it up until the separator under the Undo item is highlighted.
3. Let go of the mouse and the menu item is moved.

Too easy, right? Yes, but that's what Delphi is all about.

Batch Modifying Properties

Sometimes you want to modify several menu items' properties at once—that is called batch modifying. For example, you have a few menu items in the ScratchPad application that you are not ready to implement at this time. You aren't ready for printing support, for instance, nor are you ready to implement the help system. Therefore, you need to gray out (disable) those menu items:

1. Choose Help|Contents in the Menu Designer.
2. Change the Enabled property to False. The menu item is grayed out.
3. Click on the File menu.
4. Click on the Print menu item, hold the Shift key down, and click on the Print Setup menu item. Both items are selected.
5. In the Object Inspector, change the Enabled property to False. Both menu items are disabled.
6. Repeat steps 4 and 5 to disable the Find and Replace items on the Edit menu.

You can modify a group of menu items at one time with this method. Simply select the items you want to modify and then change the property you want to modify. All menu items currently selected will have the new property value.

Adding Bitmaps to Menu Items

You can easily add bitmaps to your menus. First click on a menu item for which you want to add a bitmap. Then, double-click in the Value column of the Bitmap property in

6

the Object Inspector. When the Picture Editor comes up, you can select a bitmap for the menu item. The bitmap can be a single image or a bitmap strip (an image list). If you are using an image list, you should set the ImageIndex property to the index number of the image in the image list you want to display for this menu item.

> **Note**   The menu item bitmaps don't display in the Menu Designer or on the form at design time. You will have to run the program to see the bitmaps.

Creating Submenus

There's nothing special or tricky about creating submenus. A *submenu* is a menu item that, when clicked, expands to show more menu choices. A submenu is denoted by a right-pointing arrow next to the menu item text. You can create a submenu by choosing Create Submenu from the Menu Designer context menu or by holding down the Ctrl key and pressing the right-arrow key. When you create a submenu, a blank menu item is placed to the right of the menu item. You can add menu items to the submenu just as you did when you created the main menu. You can create a submenu by inserting a menu template as well.

Adding Shortcuts

You can easily add a keyboard shortcut to a menu item by changing its ShortCut property in the Object Inspector. The Edit menu that you inserted earlier already had keyboard shortcuts built in. For example, the customary shortcut for Cut is Ctrl+X. If you look at the Edit menu, you will see Ctrl+X listed next to the Cut item (the shortcut was already assigned when you loaded the menu from a template).

Click on the Cut menu item and you will see that the ShortCut property says Ctrl+X. Click on the Value column next to the ShortCut property. On the Value column's right side you will see a drop-down button. Click on the button to display the list of available shortcuts. The list you see there contains just about any keyboard shortcut you need. To set the keyboard shortcut for a menu item, simply pick a shortcut from the list.

The standard shortcut for Select All is Ctrl+A, so let's add that as a shortcut for our Select All menu item:

1. Choose Edit | Select All from your menu in the Menu Designer.
2. Click on the ShortCut property in the Object Inspector.
3. Choose Ctrl+A from the list of available shortcuts. Now the Select All menu item shows Ctrl+A next to it.

That's all you have to do; Delphi takes care of it from there. The shortcuts function without you having to write any code.

Final Touches

Let's finish off your menu. First, you'll make the Word Wrap menu item on by default. This menu item is going to be used to turn word wrapping on or off. When word wrapping is on, the Word Wrap menu item will have a check mark next to it. When word wrapping is off, it will not have a check mark next to it. Click on the Word Wrap menu item and change the Checked property to True. A check mark shows up to indicate that the word wrap feature is on.

Another thing you need to do is to change the Name property on all of the menu items that you inserted from a template. They were given default names, and you want to change them to more meaningful names. Follow these steps:

1. Click on the Edit | Undo menu item. Change the Name property from Undo1 to EditUndo. Notice that you prepend the pop-up menu name, Edit, to the front of the menu item name and remove the 1 at the end.

2. You can use any naming convention you like, but be consistent. Repeat the process for the Cut, Copy, Paste, Find, and Replace menu items.

3. Now move to the Help menu and modify the Name property of the Contents item to HelpContents, and that of the About menu item to HelpAbout.

That about finishes your menu. Run through the menu to check it once more. If you find any errors, make the necessary changes. When you are satisfied that the menu is correct, click the close box to close the Menu Designer.

> **Note**
>
> You can access the Code Editor directly from the Menu Designer by double-clicking any menu item. When you double-click a menu item, the Code Editor displays the OnClick event for that item and you can start typing code. In this case, you are going to go back to the main form and do your code editing there.

6

Writing the Code

Okay, so you have all these menu items but no code to make them work. It's going to be a lot of work implementing all these, right? Actually, it's easy. Most of the required code is already part of the TMemo class. All you have to do is call the appropriate TMemo methods in the menu handlers. You'll have to do a few other things, but most of what you add is code you have seen before.

Adding Components to the Form

Before writing the code, you need to add the usual `OpenDialog` and `SaveDialog` components to the form:

1. Place an `OpenDialog` component on the form.

2. Change the `Name` property to `OpenDialog`.

3. Place a `SaveDialog` component on the form.

4. Change the `Name` property to `SaveDialog`.

5. Line up the `MainMenu`, `OpenDialog`, and `SaveDialog` icons on the form.

Writing the Menu Items' Code

Okay, that was easy enough. Now let's get on with writing the code for the menu items. You'll start with the File Exit menu item (hey, it's the easiest!). Be sure that the Menu Designer is closed so you don't confuse the Menu Designer with the Form Designer.

1. Choose File|Exit from the main menu. The Code Editor comes to the top and the `FileExitClick` event handler is displayed.

2. The cursor is positioned and ready to go. Type the following at the cursor (I always indent two spaces, by the way):

   ```
   Close;
   ```

> **Note**
>
> In step 2 I had you use the `Close` function to close the form. That works fine here because this is the application's main form. But if you want to terminate the application from anywhere in the program, you should use this:
>
> ```
> Application.Terminate;
> ```
>
> This code ensures that the application is terminated regardless of which form is currently open.

That's it. I told you it was the easiest. Let's do one more; then I'm going to turn you loose to finish the rest on your own.

1. Choose Edit|Cut from the main menu. The Code Editor comes to the top and the `EditCutClick` event handler is displayed.

2. Type the following at the cursor:

   ```
   Memo.CutToClipboard;
   ```

And that's all there is to that particular menu item. You might not fully realize it, but VCL does a lot for you behind the scenes. The whole idea of a framework is to take the burden of the low-level details off the programmer's back. Life is good.

Adding the Finishing Touches

One of the interesting aspects of a program like Delphi is that you rarely view your program as a whole. Delphi conveniently takes you to the section of code you need to work on to deal with a particular event, so you usually only see your program in small chunks. Listing 6.1 contains the main form unit for the ScratchPad program up to this point. The class declaration is entirely Delphi generated. Follow the examples you've just worked through to write code for each of the remaining menu items. Copy the code for each of the menu OnClick handlers from Listing 6.1. (The comment lines are there to explain to you what the code is doing. You don't have to include them when you type the code.)

Note

> The event handlers appear in the source file in the order in which they were created. Don't be concerned if the order of the event handlers in your source file doesn't exactly match Listing 6.1. The order in which the functions appear makes no difference to the compiler.

LISTING 6.1. SPMAIN.PAS.

```
unit SPMain;

interface

uses
  Windows, Messages, SysUtils, Classes, Graphics, Controls, Forms,
  ➥Dialogs,
  Menus, StdCtrls, ComCtrls, ToolWin;

type
  TMainForm = class(TForm)
    StatusBar1: TStatusBar;
    ToolBar1: TToolBar;
    ToolButton1: TToolButton;
    ToolButton2: TToolButton;
    Memo: TMemo;
    MainMenu: TMainMenu;
    FileMenu: TMenuItem;
    FileNew: TMenuItem;
    FileOpen: TMenuItem;
```

6

continues

LISTING 6.1. CONTINUED

```
        FileSave: TMenuItem;
        FileSaveAs: TMenuItem;
        N1: TMenuItem;
        FilePrint: TMenuItem;
        FilePrintSetup: TMenuItem;
        N2: TMenuItem;
        FileExit: TMenuItem;
        Edit1: TMenuItem;
        EditReplace: TMenuItem;
        EditFind: TMenuItem;
        N4: TMenuItem;
        EditPaste: TMenuItem;
        EditCopy: TMenuItem;
        EditCut: TMenuItem;
        N5: TMenuItem;
        EditUndo: TMenuItem;
        Help1: TMenuItem;
        HelpAbout: TMenuItem;
        HelpContents: TMenuItem;
        EditSelectAll: TMenuItem;
        N3: TMenuItem;
        EditWordWrap: TMenuItem;
        OpenDialog: TOpenDialog;
        SaveDialog: TSaveDialog;
        procedure FileExitClick(Sender: TObject);
        procedure EditCutClick(Sender: TObject);
        procedure EditCopyClick(Sender: TObject);
        procedure EditPasteClick(Sender: TObject);
        procedure FileNewClick(Sender: TObject);
        procedure FileSaveClick(Sender: TObject);
        procedure FileOpenClick(Sender: TObject);
        procedure FileSaveAsClick(Sender: TObject);
        procedure EditUndoClick(Sender: TObject);
        procedure EditSelectAllClick(Sender: TObject);
        procedure EditWordWrapClick(Sender: TObject);
    private
      { Private declarations }
    public
      { Public declarations }
    end;

var
  MainForm: TMainForm;

implementation

{$R *.DFM}

procedure TMainForm.FileExitClick(Sender: TObject);
```

```
begin
  { All done. Close the form. }
  Close;
end;

procedure TMainForm.EditCutClick(Sender: TObject);
begin
  { Call TMemo.CutToClipboard. }
  Memo.CutToClipboard;
end;

procedure TMainForm.EditCopyClick(Sender: TObject);
begin
  { Call TMemo.CopyToClipboard. }
  Memo.CopyToClipboard;
end;

procedure TMainForm.EditPasteClick(Sender: TObject);
begin
  { Call TMemo.PasteFromClipboard. }
  Memo.PasteFromClipboard;
end;

procedure TMainForm.FileNewClick(Sender: TObject);
var
  Res : Integer;
begin
  { Open a file. First check to see if the }
  { current file needs to be saved. }
  if Memo.Modified then begin
    { Display a message box. }
    Res := Application.MessageBox(
      'The current file has changed. Save changes?',
      'ScratchPad Message', MB_YESNOCANCEL);
    { If Yes was clicked then save the current file. }
     if Res = IDYES then
       FileSaveClick(Sender);
    { If No was clicked then do nothing. }
    if Res = IDCANCEL then
      Exit;
  end;
  { Delete the strings in the memo, if any. }
  if Memo.Lines.Count > 0 then
    Memo.Clear;
  { Set the FileName property of the Save Dialog to a }
  { blank string. This lets us know that the file has }
  { not yet been saved. }
```

6

continues

LISTING 6.1. CONTINUED

```pascal
    SaveDialog.FileName := '';
  end;

procedure TMainForm.FileOpenClick(Sender: TObject);
var
  Res : Integer;
begin
  { Open a file. First check to see if the current file needs }
  { to be saved. Same logic as in FileNewClick above. }
  if Memo.Modified then begin
    Res := Application.MessageBox(
      'The current file has changed. Save changes?',
      'ScratchPad Message', MB_YESNOCANCEL);
    if Res = IDYES then
      FileSaveClick(Sender);
    if Res = IDCANCEL then
      Exit;
  end;
  { Execute the File Open dialog. If OK was pressed then }
  { open the file using the LoadFromFile method. First    }
  { clear the FileName property. }
  OpenDialog.FileName := '';
  if OpenDialog.Execute then begin
    if Memo.Lines.Count > 0 then
      Memo.Clear;
    Memo.Lines.LoadFromFile(OpenDialog.FileName);
    SaveDialog.FileName := OpenDialog.FileName;
  end;
end;

procedure TMainForm.FileSaveClick(Sender: TObject);
begin
  { If a filename has already been provided then there is }
  { no need to bring up the File Save dialog. Just save the }
  { file using SaveToFile. }
  if SaveDialog.FileName <> '' then begin
    Memo.Lines.SaveToFile(SaveDialog.FileName);
    { Set Modified to False since we've just saved. }
    Memo.Modified := False;
  { If no filename was set then do a SaveAs. }
  end else FileSaveAsClick(Sender);

end;

procedure TMainForm.FileSaveAsClick(Sender: TObject);
begin
  { Display the File Save dialog to save the file. }
  { Set Modified to False since we just saved.     }
  SaveDialog.Title := 'Save As';
  if SaveDialog.Execute then begin
```

```
      Memo.Lines.SaveToFile(SaveDialog.FileName);
      Memo.Modified := False;
    end;
end;

procedure TMainForm.EditUndoClick(Sender: TObject);
begin
  { TMemo doesn't have an Undo method so we have to send }
  { a Windows WM_UNDO message to the memo component.     }
  SendMessage(Memo.Handle, WM_UNDO, 0, 0);
end;

procedure TMainForm.EditSelectAllClick(Sender: TObject);
begin
  { Just call TMemo.SelectAll. }
  Memo.SelectAll;
end;

procedure TMainForm.EditWordWrapClick(Sender: TObject);
begin
  { Toggle the TMemo.WordWrap property. Set the Checked }
  { property of the menu item to the same value as WordWrap. }
  Memo.WordWrap := not Memo.WordWrap;
  EditWordWrap.Checked := Memo.WordWrap;
  { If WordWrap is on then we only need the vertical scroll }
  { bar. If it's off, then we need both scroll bars.        }
  if Memo.WordWrap then
    Memo.ScrollBars := ssVertical
  else
    Memo.ScrollBars := ssBoth;
end;

end.
```

And Now, the Moment You've All Been Waiting For...

After you create the event handlers for the menu items, you are ready to run the program. Click the Run button and the program should compile and run. If you get compiler errors, carefully compare your source code with the code in Listing 6.1. Make any changes and click the Run button again. You might have to go through this process a few times before the program will compile and run. Eventually, though, it will run (I promise!).

When the program runs, you will find a program that, although not yet 100 percent feature-complete, acts a lot like Windows Notepad. Even though you have a few things

6

to add before you're finished, you have a fairly good start—especially when you consider the actual time involved up to this point. Figure 6.22 shows the ScratchPad program running.

FIGURE 6.22.

The ScratchPad *program in action.*

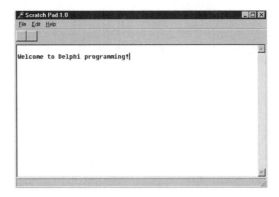

Pop-Up Menus (Context Menus)

I am not quite done with the discussion of menus. In Delphi, you can create pop-up menus as easily as you can a main menu. A nice feature of Delphi is that you can assign a particular pop-up menu to a component via the component's PopupMenu property. When the cursor is placed over the component and the secondary mouse button is clicked, that pop-up will automatically be displayed. Writing event handlers for pop-up menus is exactly the same as writing event handlers for main menus.

A common feature of text-editing programs is to place the Cut, Copy, and Paste operations on a context menu. You'll add that capability to ScratchPad. To create the pop-up, you'll cheat and copy part of the main menu. Follow these steps:

1. Choose a PopupMenu component from the Component palette and place it on the form.

2. Change the Name property to MemoPopup.

3. Double-click the PopupMenu icon to run the Menu Designer.

4. Click the secondary mouse button to bring up the Menu Designer context menu. Choose Select Menu from the context menu. A dialog box is displayed that shows the menus available for your application. Choose MainMenu and click OK.

5. Click on the Edit menu. Click on the Cut menu item, hold down the Shift key, and click on the Paste menu item. Cut, Copy, and Paste are all now highlighted.

6. To copy the selected items to the Clipboard, choose Edit | Copy from the Delphi main menu (don't choose Edit | Copy from the menu you are creating in the Menu Designer) or press Ctrl+C.

7. Again, choose Select Menu from the Menu Designer context menu. This time, choose MemoPopup and click OK. The Menu Designer shows a blank pop-up menu.

8. Choose Edit | Paste from the main menu or type Ctrl+V on the keyboard. The Cut, Copy, and Paste menu items are inserted into the pop-up.

Okay, just a few more things and you'll be done. You need to change the Name property for the new menu items:

1. For the Cut menu item, change the Name property to PopupCut.

2. For the Copy menu item, change the Name property to PopupCopy.

3. For the Paste menu item, change the Name property to PopupPaste.

The final step is to write event handlers for the pop-up menu items. Hmmm...you have already written code for the main menu's Cut, Copy, and Paste items. It would be a shame to duplicate that effort (even if it is just a single line in each case). Could you just use the same event handlers that you created earlier? Sure you can. Just follow these steps:

1. Click on the Cut popup menu item.

2. Click on the Events tab in the Object Inspector.

3. Click the drop-down arrow button in the Value column next to the OnClick event (the only event in the list). A list of event handlers created so far is displayed.

4. Choose the EditCutClick event handler from the list. Now, when the Cut pop-up menu item is clicked, the Edit | Cut handler will be called. No code duplication is required.

5. Repeat steps 1 through 4 for the Copy and Paste items on the pop-up menu. When you are done, close the Menu Designer.

6. On the main form, click on the Memo component. Change the PopupMenu property to MemoPopup (by choosing it from the list).

6

You can attach just about any event to any event handler by using this method. Now run the program again to test the new context menu. Of course it works!

Creating and Saving Menu Templates

Delphi provides you with several menu templates that you can insert into your main menus and pop-ups. You can also create and save your own templates for future use in your programs. First, start the Menu Designer and create the menu.

> **Note**
> When creating menus to use as templates, you first must have a main menu or a pop-up menu on a form in order to start the Menu Designer. You can use a temporary, blank form if you want. Start with a blank form, place a MainMenu component on it, and double-click the menu component's icon to start the Menu Designer. After you are done creating menu templates, discard the blank form without saving.

When you have created the menu, choose Save As Template from the Menu Designer's context menu. The Save Template dialog box is displayed. Give the menu a meaningful name and click the OK button, and the menu is saved as a template. To insert the menu, choose Insert From Template from the Menu Designer's context menu just as you did earlier. Any menus you have created will show up along with Delphi's prebuilt templates.

To remove a template that you previously added, choose Delete Templates from the Menu Designer's context menu. The Delete Templates dialog box is displayed, and you can choose the templates you want to delete. When you click the OK button, the selected menu templates will be deleted. Press Cancel to close the dialog box without deleting any templates.

Summary

Congratulations! You have just covered the bulk of the Delphi visual programming features. I hope it was enjoyable as well as educational. The Form Designer is a powerful tool that enables you to do as much programming as possible in a visual manner. If you haven't had to create windows and dialogs using traditional Windows programming tools, you might not fully appreciate that advantage. Trust me, it's significant. The Menu Designer is also a powerful tool, particularly because of the capability to import menus, which makes menu creation easy and actually fun with Delphi. The Menu Designer also makes updating existing menus a snap.

Workshop

The Workshop contains quiz questions to help you solidify your understanding of the material covered and exercises to provide you with experience in using what you have learned. You can find the answers to the quiz questions in Appendix A, "Answers to the Quiz Questions."

Q&A

Q I'm using the Alignment palette a lot, and every time I switch from the Code Editor back to the Form Designer, the Alignment palette gets lost somewhere. Is there anything I can do about that?

A Locate the Alignment palette (it's there somewhere!) and click your secondary mouse button to bring up the Alignment palette's context menu. Choose the Stay on Top item from the context menu. Now the Alignment palette will always be on top where you can find it.

Q I am trying to select a group of components on a panel by dragging the selection rectangle around them, but I keep moving the panel. What's wrong?

A You need to hold down the Ctrl key while dragging when you are selecting components contained on a panel.

Q I've moved my components around my form several times and now the tab order is erratic. What can I do to fix that?

A Choose Tab Order from the Form Designer's context menu. Arrange the tab order the way you want it. When you click OK, the new tab order will be implemented.

Q The menu templates provided are nice, but they have so much stuff on them that I don't need. What can I do about that?

A You can do two things. First, you can import a menu and then simply delete the items you don't want. Using the click, Shift+click method you can get rid of unwanted menu items in just a few seconds. Deleting items from a menu inserted from a template has no adverse effects. The second thing you can do is to follow the click, Shift+click method and then, when you have the menu just the way you want it, you can save it as a new template. That way you can keep the original Delphi-supplied template and have your customized template as well.

Q Can I save my own menus as templates?

A Yes. First create the menu and then choose Save As Template from the Menu Designer context menu. Give the template a name, click OK, and the template is saved. Now all you have to do to reuse the menu later is insert the menu using the Insert From Template feature.

6

Quiz

1. When do you use Ctrl+drag in selecting components?

2. What significance does the first component selected have when aligning a group of components?

3. What is the quickest method to select a group of components?

4. How can you make a group of components all have the width of the group's widest component?

5. What happens when you double-click a component on a form?

6. What does the Align property's alClient option do?

7. What does the ellipsis following a menu item mean?

8. What two ways can you move a menu item?

9. How do you add menu accelerators to menu items?

10. How do you initially disable a menu item?

Exercises

1. Place five edit components on a form and arrange them so that they are stacked vertically with their left edges aligned.

2. Turn the Snap to Grid option off (choose Tools | Environment Options from the main menu). Place five controls of your choice on a form and align their right edges.

3. Place a ListBox component on a blank form and modify it so that it always occupies the form's entire client area.

4. Add an About box to the ScratchPad program. Use the Alignment palette to quickly align the text labels.

5. Add an Undo item and a menu separator to the context menu for the ScratchPad program.

6. Start a new application. Place six edit components on a form in random fashion. Now arrange the tab order so that tabbing proceeds from top to bottom. Run the program to test the tabbing order.

7. Add the Ctrl+S keyboard shortcut to the File | Save menu item in the ScratchPad program.

8. Open the Picture Viewer project you created on Day 4. Remove all unused menu items.

DAY 7

VCL Components

As you know by now, components are much of what gives Delphi its power. Using the Form Designer, you can place a component on a form and modify its design-time properties. In some cases, that's all you have to do. If needed, you can also manipulate the component at runtime by changing its properties and calling its methods. Further, each component is designed to respond to certain events. I discussed properties, methods, and events on Day 5, "The Visual Component Model," so I'm not going to go over that again.

Today you will find out more about components. You will learn about often-used components and, as a result, learn about the Visual Component Library (VCL) classes that represent those components. As you go through this chapter, feel free to experiment. If you read something that you want to test, by all means do so. Learning by experience is as valuable as anything you can do, so don't be afraid to experiment.

A Review of Components

Let's review some of what you already know about components. Before doing that, though, I want to take a moment to explain the differences between a VCL component and a Windows control. Windows controls include components such as edit controls, list boxes, combo boxes, static controls (labels), and buttons, not to mention all the Win32 controls. Windows controls, by nature, don't have properties, methods, and events. Instead, messages are used to tell the control what to do or to get information from the control. To say that dealing with controls on this level is tedious and cumbersome would be an understatement.

A VCL component is a class that encapsulates a Windows control (not all VCL components encapsulate controls, though). A VCL component in effect adds properties, methods, and events to a Windows control to make working with the control easier. You might say that VCL takes a fresh approach to working with Windows controls. It could be said that all VCL components are controls, but not all controls are components. A VCL Edit component, for example, is a control, but a standard Windows edit control is not a VCL component. VCL components work with Windows controls to raise the job of dealing with those controls to a higher level.

Given that discussion, then, I will use the terms *control* and *component* interchangeably when referring to VCL components. (But I will never call a Windows control a component!)

Visual Components

Visual components include components such as edit controls, buttons, list boxes, labels, and so on. Most components you will use in a Delphi application are visual components. Visual components, as much as possible, show you at design time what the component will look like when the program runs.

 Some components are visual components; others are nonvisual components. A *visual component*, as its name implies, is one that can be seen by the user at design time.

Nonvisual Components

 A *nonvisual component* is one that cannot be seen by the user at design time.

Nonvisual components work behind the scenes to perform specific programming tasks. Examples include system timers, database components, and image lists. Common dialog boxes such as File Open, File Save, Font, and so on are considered nonvisual components as well. (They are nonvisual because they don't show themselves at design time. At runtime, they become visible when they are invoked.) The common dialog components are discussed later in the section "The Common Dialog Boxes."

When you place a nonvisual component on a form, Delphi displays an icon representing the component on the form. This icon is used to access the component at design time in order to change the component's properties, but the icon does not show up when the program runs. Nonvisual components have properties, methods, and events just like visual components do.

Now let's look at some of the common properties components share.

The Name Property

The Name property serves a vital role in components. On Day 5, "The Visual Component Model," in the section "VCL Explored," I discussed some of what happens when you place a component on a form. As soon as you place a component on a form, Delphi goes to work in the background while you ponder your next move. One thing Delphi does is create a pointer to the component and assign the Name property as the variable name. For example, let's say you place an Edit component on a form and change the Name property to MyEdit. At that point, Delphi places the following in the class declaration for the form (in the published section):

```
MyEdit: TEdit;
```

When the application runs, Delphi creates an instance of the TEdit class and assigns it to MyEdit. You can use this pointer to access the component at runtime. To set the text for the edit control, you would use

```
MyEdit.Text := 'Jenna Lynn';
```

Delphi also uses the Name property when creating event-handler names. Let's say that you want to respond to the OnChange event for an Edit component. Normally, you double-click the Value column in the Object Inspector next to the OnChange event to have Delphi generate an event handler for the event. Delphi creates a default function name based on the Name property of the component and the event being handled. In this case, Delphi would generate a function called MyEditChange.

You can change the Name property at any time provided that you change it *only* via the Object Inspector. When you change a component's Name property at design time, Delphi goes through all the code that it previously generated and changes the name of the pointer and all event-handling functions.

7

> **Note**
>
> Delphi will change all the code that it generated to reflect the new value of the component's Name property, but it will not modify any code you wrote. In other words, Delphi will take care of modifying the code it wrote, but it is up to you to update and maintain the code you wrote. Generally speaking, you should set the Name property when you initially place the component on the form and leave it alone after that. There's no problem with changing the name at a later time, but it might lead to more work.

Continuing with this example, if you change the Name property of the edit control from MyEdit to FirstName, Delphi will change the pointer name to FirstName and the OnChange handler name to FirstNameChange. It's all done automatically; you don't have to do anything but change the Name property and trust that Delphi will do the rest of the work.

> **Caution**
>
> Never change the Name property at runtime. Never manually change a component's name (the name that Delphi assigned to the component's pointer) or event-handler names in the Code Editor. If you perform either of these actions, Delphi loses track of components and the results are not good, to say the least. You might even lose the ability to load your form. The only safe way to change the Name property of a component is through the Object Inspector.

Delphi assigns a default value to the Name property for all components placed on a form. If you place an Edit component, for example, Delphi assigns Edit1 to the Name property. If you place a second Edit component on the form, Delphi will assign Edit2 to that component's Name property, and so on. You should give your components meaningful names as soon as possible to avoid confusion and extra work later on.

> **Note**
>
> You can leave the default names for components that will never be referenced in code. For example, if you have several label components that contain static (unchanging) text, you can leave the default names because you won't be accessing the components at runtime.

Important Common Properties

All components have certain properties in common. For example, all visual components have Left and Top properties that determine where the component is placed on the form. Properties such as Left, Top, Height, and Width are self-explanatory, so I won't go over them here. A few of the common properties, however, warrant a closer look.

The Align Property

On Day 6, "Working with the Form Designer and the Menu Designer," I discussed the Align and Alignment properties, so I won't go over those again in detail. Refer to Day 6 for complete information on Align. It should be noted here, however, that not all components expose the Align property at design time. A single-line edit control, for example, should occupy a standard height, so the features of the Align property do not make sense for that type of component. As you gain experience with Delphi (and depending on the type of applications you write), you will probably rely heavily on the Align property.

The Color Property

The Color property sets the background color for the component. (The text color is set through the Font property.) Although the Color property is simple to use, there are a few aspects of component colors that should be addressed.

The way the Color property is handled in the Object Inspector is somewhat unique. If you click the Value column, you see the drop-down arrow button indicating that you can choose from a list of color values. That is certainly the case, but there's more to it than that. If you double-click the Value column, the Color dialog box will be displayed. This dialog box enables you to choose a color from one of the predefined colors or to create your own colors by clicking the Define Custom Colors button. Figure 7.1 shows the Color dialog box after the Define Custom Colors button has been clicked.

FIGURE 7.1.

The Color dialog box.

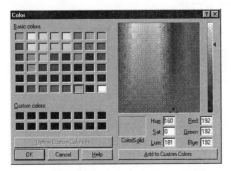

Note This is the same Color dialog box that will be displayed if you implement the `ColorDialog` component in your application.

If you choose a color from the Color dialog box, you see that the value of the `Color` property changes to a hexadecimal string. This string represents the red, green, and blue (RGB) values that make up the color. If you know the exact RGB value of a color, you can type it in (not likely!).

Most of the time you will probably choose a color from the list of color values provided. When you click the drop-down button to display the list of possible values, you will see what essentially amounts to two groups of values. The first group of colors begins with `clBlack` and ends with `clWhite`. These are the Delphi predefined colors; this list represents the most commonly used colors. To choose one of the listed colors, simply click the color in the list. If you can't find a color in the list that suits your needs, you can invoke the Color dialog box as discussed.

The second group of colors in the list begins with `clScrollBar`. This group of colors represents the Windows system colors. If you use colors from this list, your application will automatically adjust its colors when the user changes color schemes in Windows. If you want your application to follow the color scheme the user has chosen for his or her system, you should choose colors from this list rather than from the first list.

Use of color should be carefully considered. Proper use of color provides an aesthetically pleasing environment for the user. Abuse of colors makes for an obnoxious application that is annoying to use. Color is like a magnet to new programmers. It is common to want to throw lots of colors on a form because it's fun and easy, but don't get caught up in the fun at the expense of your users.

The `Cursor` Property

The `Cursor` property controls the cursor that is displayed when the user moves the mouse cursor over the component. Windows automatically changes cursors for some components. For example, Windows changes the cursor to an I-beam when the cursor is moved over an `Edit`, `Memo`, or `RichEdit` component.

To let Windows manage the cursor, leave the `Cursor` property set to `crDefault`. If you have specialized windows (components), you can specify one of the other cursors. When the mouse is moved over that component, Windows will change the cursor to the one you specified.

Frequently, you will need to change cursors at runtime. A long process, for example, should be indicated to the user by displaying the hourglass cursor. When you reset the cursor, you need to be sure to set the cursor back to whatever it was originally. The following code snippet illustrates this concept:

```
var
  OldCursor : TCursor;
begin
  OldCursor := Screen.Cursor;
  Screen.Cursor := crHourGlass;
  { do some stuff which takes a long time }
  Screen.Cursor := OldCursor;
end;
```

This ensures that the cursor that was originally set for the application is properly restored.

Another cursor property, DragCursor, is used to set the cursor that is used when the mouse cursor is over a component that supports drag-and-drop. As with colors, you should be prudent in your use of cursors. Use custom cursors when needed, but don't overdo it.

The Enabled Property

Components can be enabled or disabled through the Enabled property. When a component is disabled, it cannot accept focus (clicking on it has no effect), and usually it gives some visual cue to indicate that it is disabled. In the case of buttons, for example, the button text is grayed out as is any bitmap on the button. Enabled is a Boolean property: Set it to True to enable the component or set it to False to disable the component. Enabling and disabling windows (remember that windowed components are windows, too) is a feature of Windows itself.

Note

> Some components show their disabled state at design time, but most don't. The BitBtn component is one that does show its disabled state at design time.

The Enabled property applies mostly to windowed components, but it can apply to non-windowed components as well. The SpeedButton component is an example of a non-windowed component that can be disabled.

7

Note
> Modifying the `Enabled` property for a Panel component has additional impli-
> cations. Panels are often used as containers for other controls. Therefore, a
> panel becomes the parent of the controls that are placed on the panel. If
> you disable a panel, the components on the panel will not show as disabled,
> but they will not function because their parent (the panel) is disabled.

Although components can be disabled at design time, enabling and disabling components
is something that is usually done at runtime. Menu items, for example, should be enabled
or disabled according to whether they apply at a given time. The same is true of buttons.
There are a variety of reasons why you might want to disable other types of controls as
well.

To disable a component at runtime, just assign `False` to its `Enabled` property, and to
enable a component assign `True` to `Enabled`. The following code snippet enables or dis-
ables a menu item based on some condition:

```
if CanSave then
  FileSave.Enabled := True
else
  FileSave.Enabled := False;
```

This process is often referred to as *command enabling* and is an important part of a
professional-looking Windows program.

Tip
> The `TActionList` component can be used to enable or disable a component
> or groups of components. `TActionList` is discussed in detail on Day 13,
> "Beyond the Basics," in the section "Command Enabling."

The Font Property

The `Font` property is a major property and therefore needs to be included here, but there
is not a lot that needs to be said about it. The `Font` property is an instance of the `TFont`
class and, as such, has its own properties. You can set the `Font` properties by double-
clicking on the font name in the Object Inspector (which will expand the Font node and
show the `Font` properties) or by invoking the Font dialog box. (The Font dialog box is
discussed in more detail later in this chapter in the section "The Font Dialog Box.")
Figure 7.2 shows the Object Inspector with the `Font` property node expanded to reveal
the `TFont` properties.

FIGURE 7.2.

The Object Inspector showing the Font *property.*

The Color property sets the color of the font, and the Name property enables you to choose the typeface for the font.

The Height and Size properties of TFont deserve special mention as well:

- The Height property is used to specify the height of the font in pixels.
- The Size property is used to specify the height of the font in points.

When you change one of these properties, the other will change automatically. The Height is often specified as a negative number. Refer to the online help for TFont for an explanation of why this is the case.

The Pitch property is not particularly useful. I'll explain it in just a moment, but first a quick tutorial on fonts. A font can be either proportionally spaced or fixed space:

- Most fonts are *proportionally spaced*, which means that each letter only takes as much space as needed. For example, an uppercase M takes up much more space than a lowercase i. Take a look at the letters in this book and you will see what I mean. Examples of proportional fonts include Times New Roman, Arial, and Bookman.
- With a *fixed space* font (typically called a fixed-pitch font), on the other hand, all characters take exactly the same amount of space. This is convenient for windows such as code editors (the Delphi Code Editor, for example) or any other window where a fixed-pitch font is desired. Courier New is probably the most commonly used fixed-pitch font, although Fixedsys is the Windows fixed-pitch font of choice in some Windows applications. *Fixed space* fonts are harder to read, so they aren't normally used for long blocks of text other than code.

In theory, the Pitch property can be used to force a proportionally spaced font to fixed space and vice versa. The problem is that Windows might perform font substitutions to carry out the conversion. In other words, you really don't know what you might get. It is far better to pick exactly the font you require than to rely on the Pitch property.

7

Finally, the Style property of TFont can be used to toggle bold, italic, underline, or strikethrough. These styles are not mutually exclusive, so you can mix styles in any way you choose.

> Although you can use the Object Inspector to change font properties, the Font dialog box (invoked when you click the ellipsis button next to the Font property) has the added benefit of showing you a sample of what the font looks like as you choose different font options. To simply change the font's Style property or Size property, use the Object Inspector. But if you are looking for just the right font, the Font dialog box is a better choice.

The Hint Property

The Hint property is used to set hint text for a component. The hint text has two parts. The first part is sometimes called the *short hint*. This is the hint text that is displayed when the user places the cursor over the component and pauses. The pop-up window that displays the hint text is called a *tooltip*.

The second part of the hint text is sometimes called the *long hint*. The long hint is the optional hint text that shows in the status bar when the user moves the mouse cursor over the component. The short and long hint texts are separated by a pipe (¦). For example, to specify both the short hint text and the long hint text for a File Open speed button, you would enter the following for the Hint property:

```
File Open¦Open a file for editing
```

In order for short hints to show, you must have the Application object's ShowHint property set to True (the default) as well as the component's ShowHint property. Displaying the long hint in the status bar requires a little more work, so I'll save that discussion for tomorrow.

> You can specify the short hint text, the long hint text, or both. You can use the pipe to tell Delphi which hint text you are supplying. If you don't use the pipe, both the short hint and the long hint will use the same text.

Note

Although there are no limits on the length of either the long hint or the short hint, you should keep each hint's use in mind when you create them. Short hints should probably be limited to 30 characters or fewer. Long hints can be more descriptive, but keep in mind that long hints that are very long will be truncated when displayed in the status bar.

The `ParentColor`, `ParentCtl3D`, `ParentFont`, and `ParentShowHint` Properties

The `ParentColor`, `ParentCtl3D`, `ParentFont`, and `ParentShowHint` properties work the same way, so I'll discuss them at the same time. When these properties are set to `True`, the component takes its `Color`, `Ctl3D`, `Font`, or `ShowHint` settings from its parent. For example, for most components the `ParentFont` property is set to `True` by default. This means the component will inherit the font that its parent is currently using. To better understand this, do this exercise:

1. Create a blank form. Set the `Font` property's `Size` property to 16.

2. Place a `Label` component on the form. Notice that the label automatically uses the 16-point font.

3. Place a `Button` component on the form. It also uses the 16-point font.

You can set this property to `False`, but by the time the component is placed it is already too late and you will have to change the font manually to the font you want for the component.

The `Tag` Property

The `Tag` property is nothing more than a four-byte variable set aside for your use. You can use the `Tag` property to store any data that your component might need. The data stored might be a pointer to another class, an index value, or any number of other possibilities. Using the `Tag` property would probably be considered an advanced programming technique.

Other Common Properties

Table 7.1 lists other common properties that are frequently used. These properties don't require as much explanation, so they are listed here for your reference. Not all components have each of the properties listed.

7

TABLE 7.1. ADDITIONAL COMPONENT PROPERTIES.

Property	Description
BorderStyle	Can be bsSingle or bsNone. Use bsNone when you want the component to blend in with the background.
BoundsRect	The rectangle of the entire component (not limited to only the client area).
Caption	Sets the component's caption. Many components don't have captions, so for those components the Caption property is not exposed.
ClientHeight	Contains the height of the client area of the component.
ClientRect	Contains the rectangle for the client area of the component.
ClientWidth	Contains the width of the client area of the component.
Constraints	Sets the size constraints for the component (maximum width and height, minimum width and height). More important for forms than for other components.
Ctl3D	Indicates whether the control should be drawn with a 3D border. If BorderStyle is set to bsNone, this property has no effect.
Height	Sets the component's height.
HelpContext	The HelpContext property is used to associate an index number in a help file with a particular component.
Left	Sets the x-coordinate of the component.
Parent	A pointer to the parent of the component.
PopupMenu	Specifies the pop-up menu that will be displayed when the user clicks the secondary mouse button.
TabOrder	For windowed components. Sets this component's position in the tab order.
TabStop	For windowed components. Indicates that this component can be tabbed into. Setting this property to False removes the component from the tab order.
Top	Sets the y-coordinate of the component.
Visible	When read, indicates whether the component is currently visible. When written to, Visible either hides or shows the component.
Width	Sets the width of the component.

Primary Methods of Components

There are more than 20 methods that most components have in common. Windowed components have more than 40 common methods from which to choose. Interestingly, not many of these are widely used. Much of the functionality of components is accomplished via properties. For example, to hide a component, you can call the `Hide` method or you can set the `Visible` property to `False`. In addition, components typically have methods specific to their purpose, and it will likely be those methods that you use most when dealing with a particular component.

There are a few methods worthy of note, however, so I'll list them here (see Table 7.2). Note that some of these methods are not available to all controls. These are not the most often used methods common to every component, but rather the most commonly used methods of components in general. Also, this list concentrates on components representing controls (components placed on forms) rather than components as forms. Methods particular to forms were discussed on Day 4, "The Delphi IDE Explored."

TABLE 7.2. COMMON METHODS OF COMPONENTS.

Method	Description
Broadcast	Used to send a message to all windowed child components.
ClientToScreen	Converts client window coordinates into screen coordinates.
ContainsControl	Returns `True` if the specified component is a child of the component or form.
HandleAllocated	Returns `True` if the `Handle` property for the component has been created. Simply reading the `Handle` property automatically creates a handle if it hasn't already been created, so `HandleAllocated` can be used to check for the existence of the handle without creating it.
Hide	Hides the component. The component is still available to be shown again later.
Invalidate	Requests that the component be redrawn. The component will be redrawn at Windows's earliest convenience.
Perform	Sends a message directly to a component rather than going through the Windows messaging system.
Refresh	Requests that a component be redrawn immediately and erases the component prior to repainting.
Repaint	Requests that a component be redrawn immediately. The component's background is not erased prior to repainting.
SetBounds	Enables you to set the `Top`, `Left`, `Width`, and `Height` properties all at one time. This saves time having to set them individually.
SetFocus	Sets the focus to a component and makes it the active component. Applies only to windowed components.
Update	Forces an immediate repaint of the control. Typically, you should use `Refresh` or `Repaint` to repaint components.

7

Now let's take look at some of the events to which a component is most likely to respond.

Common Events

As with properties and methods, there are some events that will be responded to most often. Components cover a wide variety of possible Windows controls, so each component will have individual needs. Events specific to forms are not covered here because I covered that information on Day 4. The most commonly used events are listed in Table 7.3.

TABLE 7.3. COMMONLY HANDLED COMPONENT EVENTS.

Event	Description
OnChange	This event is triggered when a control changes in one way or another. Exact implementation depends on the component.
OnClick	Sent when the component is clicked with either mouse button.
OnDblClick	This event occurs when the user double-clicks the component.
OnEnter	This event occurs when a windowed component receives focus (is activated).
OnExit	This event occurs when a windowed component loses focus as the result of the user switching to a different control. It does not occur, however, when the user switches forms or switches to another application.
OnKeyDown	This event is triggered when the user presses a key while the control has focus. Keys include all alphanumeric keys as well as keys such as the arrow keys, Home, End, Ctrl, and so on.
OnKeyPress	This event is also triggered when the user presses a key, but only when alphanumeric keys or the Tab, backspace, Enter, or Esc keys are pressed.
OnKeyUp	This event occurs whenever a key is released.
OnMouseDown	This event is triggered when the mouse button is pressed while it's over the component. The parameters passed to the event handler give you information on which mouse button was clicked, special keys that were pressed (Alt, Shift, Ctrl), and the x,y coordinate of the mouse pointer when the event occurred.
OnMouseMove	This event occurs any time the mouse is moved over the control.
OnMouseUp	This event is triggered when the mouse button is released while over a control. The mouse button must first have been clicked while on the control.
OnPaint	This event is sent any time a component needs repainting. You can respond to this event to do any custom painting a component requires.

DEALING WITH MOUSE EVENTS

Mouse events have a couple of peculiarities that you should be aware of. If you are responding just to a mouse click on a component, you will want to keep it simple and only respond to the OnClick event. If you must use OnMouseDown and OnMouseUp, you should be aware that the OnClick event will be sent as well as the OnMouseDown and OnMouseUp events. For example, a single click will result in these events occurring (and in this order):

OnMouseDown
OnClick
OnMouseUp

Similarly, when the user double-clicks with the mouse, it can result in the application getting more events than you might think. When a component is double-clicked, the following events occur:

OnMouseDown
OnClick
OnDblClick
OnMouseUp

The point I am trying to make is that you need to take care when responding to both double-click and single-click events for a component. Be aware that you will get four events for a double-click event.

Multiple events will occur when a key is pressed, too. A keypress in an edit control, for example, will result in OnKeyDown, OnKeyPress, OnChange, and OnKeyUp events occurring.

The book's code (go to http://www.mcp.com/info and type 0-672-31286-7) contains a program called EventTst, which illustrates the fact that multiple events occur on mouse clicks and keypresses. Run this program and you will see how multiple events can be triggered based on certain user actions.

In just a moment you're going to look at some of the VCL components in more detail. First, however, I want to introduce you to a class that is used by certain VCL components—TStrings.

TStrings

The TStrings class is a VCL class that manages lists of strings. Several VCL components use instances of TStrings to manage their data (usually text). For example, on Day 6 you used TStrings when you built the ScratchPad application. "I don't recall using a TStrings class," you say. Well, you did, but you just weren't aware of it. Remember when you saved and loaded files? You used something like this:

```
Memo.Lines.SaveToFile(SaveDialog.FileName);
```

7

The Lines property of TMemo is an instance of the TStrings class. The SaveToFile method of TStrings takes the strings and saves them to a file on disk. You can use the same technique to load a list box from a file on disk or save the contents of a list box to disk. In the case of the TListBox class, the property that holds the list box items is called Items. For example, try this exercise:

1. Create a new application and place a ListBox component on the form. Size the list box as desired.

2. Change the Name property of the list box to ListBox.

3. Double-click the background of the form (not on the list box). The Code Editor displays the FormCreate function.

4. Modify the FormCreate function so that it looks like this:
```
procedure TForm1.FormCreate(Sender: TObject);
var
  WinDir   : array [0..255] of Char;
  FileName : string;
begin
  GetWindowsDirectory(WinDir, SizeOf(WinDir));
  FileName := WinDir + '\win.ini';
  ListBox.Items.LoadFromFile(FileName);
end;
```

5. Click the Run button to compile and run the program.

When the program runs, the list box will contain the contents of your WIN.INI file. Using this method, it's easy to load a list box from any ASCII text data file. The ComboBox component also has an Items property that works in exactly the same way.

You can add, delete, insert, and move items in a list box, combo box, or memo by calling the Add, Append, Delete, Insert, and Move methods of the TStrings class.

 Note
> How Add performs depends on the value of the Sorted property. If the Sorted property is set to True, Add will insert the string where it needs to be in the list of items. If Sorted is False, the new string will be added at the end of the list.

A component can be cleared of its contents by calling the Clear method. An individual string can be accessed by using the array subscript operator. For example, to retrieve the first string in a list of strings, you would use

```
Edit.Text := ListBox.Items[0];
```

Note

The strings in a TStrings class are actually contained in the Strings property. The Strings property is declared as the *default array property* for the TStrings class, so you don't specifically have to reference it when retrieving a specific string (although you can if you want to). Given that, then, the following two lines result in the same code being generated by the compiler:

```
Edit.Text := ListBox.Items[0];
Edit.Text := ListBox.Items.Strings[0];
```

Each string in a TStrings array contains the string itself and four bytes of extra storage. This extra storage can be accessed through the Objects property, and you can use the extra storage any way you like. Let's say, for example, that you create an owner-drawn list box that displays bitmaps. You can store the string in the usual way and store a pointer to the TBitmap object in the Objects array.

Tip

There might be times when you need to manage a list of strings unrelated to a component. The TStringList class is provided for exactly that purpose. This class works just like TStrings but can be used outside of components. TStringList is particularly convenient for reading, manipulating, and storing text files.

Note

In reality, TStrings is what is called an *abstract base class*. An abstract base class is never used directly; it serves only as a base class from which to derive other classes. The Lines property is actually an instance of the TMemoStrings class rather than an instance of the TStrings class as I said in this section. This can be confusing because the Lines property *is* declared as a TStrings pointer but is actually an instance of TMemoStrings. The declaration and creation of the Lines property looks like this:

```
var
   Lines : TStrings;
{ ...later }
   Lines := TMemoStrings.Create;
```

This is why the Lines property appears to be a TStrings but is really not. I didn't mean to lead you astray, but I thought it was best to make this distinction after the discussion on TStrings rather than confuse you with this information during that discussion.

7

An *abstract base class* is a class that cannot be used directly. A descendent class must be created using the abstract base class, and an instance of the descendent class is used instead.

Standard Windows Control Components

Back in the Jurassic age, there was something called Windows 3.0. Windows 3.0 gave you options such as edit controls (single line and multiline), list boxes, combo boxes, buttons, check boxes, radio buttons, and static controls. These controls must have been fairly well designed because they are very prevalent in Windows programs today—even considering all the new Win32 controls.

I'm not going to go over every Windows control and its corresponding VCL component. There are a few points, though, that you should know regarding the standard components, which are covered in the next sections.

> **Note**
> I will refer to components in one of two ways: by the component's name or by the name of the VCL class that defines the component. I might say, "The Label component is used for..." or I might say, "TLabel is used for...." In either case, I am talking about the same component.

Edit Controls

Delphi comes with four edit-control components. The Edit, Memo, and MaskEdit components are based on the standard Windows edit control. The RichEdit component is based on the Win32 rich edit control, which is not one of the standard Windows controls. Still, I will discuss RichEdit here because it has many features in common with the other edit controls.

The Edit Component

The Edit component encapsulates the basic single-line edit control. This component has no Align or Alignment property. It has no Alignment property because the text in a single-line edit control can only be left-justified. The Edit component has no Align property because it cannot (or more accurately, should not) be expanded to fill the client area of a window.

> **Tip**
> If you need text in an edit component to be right-justified or centered, use a Memo component but make its height the height of a standard Edit component. Then set the Alignment property as needed.

Note

> Keep your forms standard whenever possible. Although you can make an
> Edit component as tall as you like, it will confuse users if you make its
> height greater than a standard Windows edit control (it might appear to the
> user to be a multiline edit).

The MaskEdit Component

The MaskEdit component is an Edit component with an input filter, or mask, attached.
The MaskEdit does not represent a Windows control per se, but rather is just a VCL
extension of a standard edit control. A mask is used to force input to a specific range of
numbers or characters. In addition, the mask can contain special characters that are
placed in the edit control by default. For example, a date is commonly formatted as follows:

`03/21/98`

An edit mask for a date can already have the slashes in place so the user only has to
enter the numbers. The edit mask would specify that only numbers can be entered to
avoid the possibility of the user entering a nonnumeric character.

Note

> The DateTimePicker component (found on the Win32 tab) enables you to
> pick a date or a time from a specialized edit component. When the Kind
> property is set to dtkDate, the component displays a drop-down calendar
> from which the user can choose a date. When Kind is set to dtkTime, the
> DateTimePicker displays a multi-field edit control that enables the user to
> set the hours, minutes, seconds, and AM or PM. The DateTimePicker is pre-
> ferred over the MaskEdit for date and time entry.

The EditMask property controls the mask that is used. When you click the ellipsis button
in the Value column for the EditMask property, the Input Mask Editor is displayed. This
dialog box enables you to choose from one of the predefined masks or to create your
own. You can choose prebuilt masks from several countries. Figure 7.3 shows the Input
Mask Editor displaying the United States' set of predefined input masks.

7

FIGURE 7.3.

The Input Mask Editor.

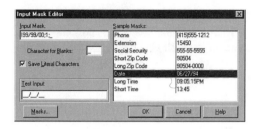

For more information on building your own masks, see the Delphi online help.

The Memo Component

The Memo component encapsulates a multiline edit control. The Lines property is the most significant property in a Memo component. As I mentioned earlier in the discussion on TStrings, the Lines property enables you to save the contents of the Memo component to disk, load the Memo with text from a file, or access the memo's lines individually.

The ScrollBars property is unique to the Memo component. This property enables you to specify whether your component has a horizontal scrollbar, a vertical scrollbar, or both. You used the ScrollBars property on Day 6 when you wrote the ScratchPad application. The Memo component is a very versatile component that you will probably find yourself using frequently.

The RichEdit Component

The RichEdit component is the biggest and the best of all the edit components; it is based on the Win32-rich edit control. The RichEdit component enables you to change fonts, use indentation, set text to bold, italic, or underlined, and much more. Basically, the RichEdit component is a mini word processor in one neat package. RichEdit has surprisingly few design-time properties over what the Memo component has.

Key runtime properties include SelAttributes and Paragraph. The RichEdit component is complex but easy to use, considering its complexities. See the Delphi online help for full details on the RichEdit component.

Common Edit Control Properties

Table 7.4 lists the properties specific to components based on edit controls.

TABLE 7.4. PROPERTIES FOR EDIT CONTROLS.

Item	Applies To	Description
Properties		
AutoSelect	Edit, MaskEdit	When set to True, text in the edit control will automatically be selected when the user tabs to the control. Default: True
AutoSize	Edit, MaskEdit	When set to True, the edit control will automatically resize itself when the font of the edit control changes. Otherwise, the edit control does not change size when the font changes. Default: True
CharCase	Edit, MaskEdit	Determines whether the edit control displays uppercase (ecUpperCase), lowercase (ecLowerCase), or mixed text (ecNormal). Default: ecNormal.
HideScrollBars	RichEdit	When set to True, the scrollbars will be shown when needed but hidden otherwise. When set to False, the scrollbars are shown as determined by the value of the ScrollBars property.
HideSelection	Edit, Memo, RichEdit	When set to True, any text selected will not show as selected when the user tabs to another control. Default: False
Lines	Memo, RichEdit	The text contained in the component. Lines is an instance of the TStrings class.
MaxLength	All	Specifies the maximum number of characters that the component will hold. When set to 0, the amount of text that can be input is unlimited (limited only by system considerations). When set to any non-zero value, limits the number of characters to that value. Default: 0
OEMConvert	Edit, Memo	Set this property to True when the text input will consist of filenames. Default: False
PasswordChar	Edit, MaskEdit	When this property is set to a value other than ASCII #0, any text entered will be echoed with the character provided. The actual text in the edit control is unaffected. Most password edits use the asterisk (*) as the password character. Default: #0

continues

7

TABLE 7.4. CONTINUED

Item	Applies To	Description
		Properties
PlainText	RichEdit	When set to True, RTF (rich text format) files will be shown as plain text without character and paragraph formatting. When set to False, RTF files are displayed with full formatting. Default: False
ReadOnly	All	When set to True, the component will display its text, but new text cannot be entered. The user can, however, highlight text and copy it to the Clipboard. Default: False
ScrollBars	Memo, RichEdit	Determines which scrollbars to display. Choices are ssNone, ssBoth, ssHorizontal, and ssVertical. Default: ssNone
Text	Edit, MaskEdit	Contains the text in the component.
WantReturns	Memo, RichEdit	When set to True, the component keeps the return character and a new line is inserted in the edit control when the user presses Enter. When set to False, return characters go to the form and are not placed in the edit control. If you have a form with a default button and WantReturns set to False, pressing Enter will cause the form to close. Default: True
WantTabs	Memo, RichEdit	When set to True, a tab character is placed in the edit control when the user presses the Tab key. When set to False, tab characters go to the form, which would enable tabbing out of the edit control. Default: False
WordWrap	Memo, RichEdit	When set to True, text entered will wrap to a new line when the right edge of the edit control is reached. When set to False, the edit control automatically scrolls as new text is entered. Default: True

Item	Applies To	Description
Runtime Properties		
Modified	All	Indicates whether the contents of the edit control have changed since the last time the Modified property was set. After saving the contents of a Memo or RichEdit component to a file, you should set Modified to False.
SelLength	All	Contains the length of the text currently selected in the edit control.
SelStart	All	Contains the starting point of the selected text in the edit control. The first character in the edit control is 0.
SelText	All	Contains the currently selected text in an edit control.

Edit controls have many common methods; they are too numerous to list here. The CutToClipboard, CopyToClipboard, PasteFromClipboard, and Clear methods deal with Clipboard operations and text manipulation. The GetSelTextBuff and GetTextBuff methods retrieve the selected text in the component and the entire text in the component, respectively. See the Delphi online help topics TEdit, TMaskEdit, TMemo, and TRichEdit for a complete list of methods associated with each edit component.

The edit component events that you are most likely to be interested in are dependent on the type of edit control you are using. In general, though, the OnEnter, OnExit, OnChange, OnKeyDown (or OnKeyPress), and OnKeyUp events will be the most widely used.

The ListBox and ComboBox Components

The ListBox and ComboBox components are also widely used. The ListBox component represents a standard Windows list box, which simply presents a list of choices that the user can choose from. If the list box contains more items than can be shown at one time, scrollbars provide access to the rest of the items in the list box.

 Some list boxes are *owner-drawn* list boxes. In an owner-drawn list box, the programmer takes the responsibility for drawing the items in the list box.

7

You can do owner-drawn list boxes if needed. Owner-drawn list boxes are fairly common, although you might not realize it. On Day 4 I talked about customizing the Delphi toolbar. As part of that discussion, you looked at the Delphi Toolbar Editor dialog box. The Toolbar Editor dialog box contains two list boxes (see Figure 7.4).

FIGURE 7.4.

The Toolbar Editor's Commands list box is owner-drawn.

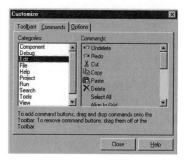

The list box on the left is a regular list box; it lists the possible button groups you can choose from. The list box on the right is an owner-drawn list box. It shows the actual button as it will appear on the toolbar, as well as a textual description of what function the button performs.

Combo boxes are specialized list boxes. Actually, a combo box is a combination of a list box and an edit control. The user can choose from the list or type in a value in the edit portion. When the user chooses an item from the list, that item is placed in the edit control. There are three different types of combo box. The combo box type is determined by the Style property. Table 7.5 lists the types of combo boxes and a description of each.

TABLE 7.5. TYPES OF COMBO BOXES.

Item	Description
Simple	The simple style of the combo box is nothing more than an edit control placed on top of a list box. The user can choose from the list or type text in the edit portion.
Drop-down	Similar to the simple style, except the list box portion is not initially displayed. A drop-down button is provided so that the user can view the list and choose an item. The user can also type text in the edit portion.
Drop-down list	This is the most restrictive type of combo box. As with the drop-down style, the list is not initially exposed. The user can click the drop-down button to expose the list and choose an item from the list, but cannot enter text in the edit portion. Use this style when you want the user to select only from a predetermined set of choices.

The book's code contains a program called ComboTst that illustrates the different types of combo boxes. Figure 7.5 shows the test program running. Run the program and try out the combo boxes to get a feel for how each works.

FIGURE 7.5.

The ComboTst
program.

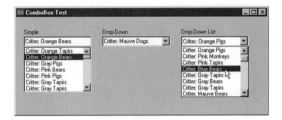

Table 7.6 lists the properties common to list boxes and combo boxes.

TABLE 7.6. PROPERTIES FOR EDIT CONTROLS.

Property	Applies To	Description
		Properties
Columns	ListBox	Contains the number of columns in the list box. You can create multiple columns by making this property greater than 1. Default: 0
ExtendedSelection	ListBox	Determines whether extended selection is allowed. *Extended selection* enables the user to select items using Shift+click and Ctrl+click. Has no effect if MultiSelect is set to False. Default: True
IntegralHeight	ListBox	When True, the list box height will be resized to be sure that no partial lines are displayed. When False, the list box might show partial lines. Default: False
ItemHeight	Both	For use with owner-drawn list boxes and combo boxes. Sets the height of the items in the control. Default: 13
Items	Both	A TStrings instance that contains the list of items in the list box. (See the section on TStrings earlier in this chapter for a description of available properties and methods.)
MaxLength	ComboBox	The maximum number of characters the user can type in the edit portion of the combo box. Same as MaxLength in edit controls. Default: 0 (no limit)
MultiSelect	ListBox	When True, the list box enables multiple items to be selected. Default: False

continues

7

TABLE 7.6. CONTINUED

Property	Applies To	Description
		Properties
Sorted	Both	When set to `True`, the list box items are sorted in ascending order. When set to `False`, the items are not sorted. Default: `False`
Style	ComboBox	The style of the combo box. Choices are `csSimple`, `csDropDown`, `csDropDownList`, `lbOwnderDrawFixed`, and `csOwnerDrawVariable`. (See Table 7.5 for a description of the three basic styles.) Default: `csDropDown`
	ListBox	Style choices for list boxes are `lbStandard`, `lbOwnderDrawFixed`, and `csOwnerDrawVariable`. Default: `lbStandard`
TabWidth	ListBox	List boxes can use tabs. This property sets the tab width in pixels. Default: `0`
Text	ComboBox	Contains the text in the edit portion of the combo box.
		Runtime Properties
ItemIndex	ListBox	Contains the index of the currently selected item, with `0` being the first item in the list. Returns `-1` if no item is selected. When written to, selects the specified index.
SelCount	ListBox	Contains the number of items selected in a multiple-selection list box.
Selected	ListBox	Returns `True` if the specified item is selected or `False` if it is not.
SelLength	ComboBox	Contains the length of the text currently selected in the edit control part of the combo box.
SelStart	ComboBox	Contains the starting point of the selected text in the edit control. The first character in the edit control is `0`.
SelText	ComboBox	Contains the currently selected text in the edit control.
TopIndex	ListBox	Returns the list box item that is at the top of the list box. Can be used to set the top item to a certain list box item.

As with the edit components you looked at earlier, there are very few `ListBox` and `ComboBox` methods. The `Clear` method clears the control of all data. The `ItemAtPos` methods return the list box item at the specified x and y coordinates. The `SelectAll` method selects the text in the edit control portion of a combo box.

Easily the most-used events when dealing with combo boxes and list boxes are the
OnChange and OnClick events. Use these events to determine when a selection has been
made in the list box.

> Clicking the edit portion of a combo box or the drop-down button does not
> result in an OnClick event being sent. Only when the list box portion of a
> combo box is clicked will the OnClick event occur.

The OnChange event can be used to detect changes to the edit portion of a combo box
just as it is used with edit controls. The OnDropDown event is used to detect when the
drop-down button on a combo box has been clicked. The OnMeasureItem and
OnDrawItem events are used with owner-drawn list boxes and owner-drawn combo
boxes.

VCL Button Types

VCL contains several types of buttons that you can use in your applications. Although
not all of them are based on the standard Windows button control, I will still address all
the button types here. Before you look at the specific button components, though, let's
cover some of the basics.

Note

> When setting a button's Caption property, use the ampersand (&) just as you
> would when setting the Caption property of menu items. The character
> after the ampersand will be underlined and will be the accelerator for the
> button.

Button Properties

The button components have only four properties of note, as follows:

- ModalResult
- Default
- Cancel
- Enabled

The ModalResult Property   The ModalResult property is used to provide built-in
form closing for forms displayed with ShowModal. By default, ModalResult is set to

7

mrNone (which is 0). Use this value for buttons that are used as regular buttons on the form and that don't close the form. If you use any non-zero value for ModalResult, pressing the button will close the form and return the ModalResult value. For example, if you place a button on a form and set the ModalResult property to mrOk, pressing the button will close the form, and the return value from ShowModal will be mrOk (1). Given that, then, you can do something like the following:

```
var
  Res : Integer;
begin
  Res := MyForm.ShowModal;
  if Res = mrOK then
    DoSomething;
  if Res = mrCancel then
    Exit;
end;
```

Table 7.7 lists the ModalResult constants that VCL defines.

TABLE 7.7. VCL ModalResult CONSTANTS.

Constant	Value
mrNone	0
mrOk	1
mrCancel	2
mrAbort	3
mrRetry	4
mrIgnore	5
mrYes	6
mrNo	7
mrAll	8
mrNoToAll	9
mrYesToAll	10

 Note

You don't have to use one of the predefined ModalResult constants for your buttons; you can use any value you like. Let's say, for example, you have a custom dialog box that could be closed by using a variety of buttons. You could assign a different ModalResult value to each button (100, 150, and 200, for example), and you would then know which button closed the dialog box. Any nonzero number is valid, up to the maximum value of an Integer.

The book's code contains a program called ButtnTst that demonstrates the use of ModalResult. The program enables you to execute a form containing several buttons. When you click a button, the ModalResult will be reported on the main form.

The Default Property   The Default property is another key property of buttons. Windows has a standard mechanism for dealing with dialog boxes. One of the features of this mechanism is as follows: If a control other than a button has keyboard focus and the user presses the Enter key on the keyboard, the dialog box will behave as if the user had clicked the *default button*.

The default button is the button that has the BS_DEFPUSHBUTTON style set (usually the OK button). This feature has been the bane of programmers and the curse of data-entry personnel for years. The Default property is used to set a button as the default button for a form. The default value for this property is False. To make a button the default button, set its Default property to True. If you don't specifically set any button's Default property to True, the form will not close when the user presses the Enter key.

> **Note**
>
> When the user closes the form by pressing the Enter key, the OnClick handler of the default button (if one exists) will be called before the form closes.

The Cancel Property

The Cancel property works with the Esc key in much the same way as the Default property works with the Enter key. When the user presses the Esc key to close a form, the return value from ShowModal will be the ModalResult value of the button whose Cancel property is set to True. If no button has its Cancel property set to True, mrCancel will be returned if the user uses the Esc key to close the form (mrCancel is equal to 2; see Table 7.7).

> **Note**
>
> Closing a form by clicking the system close box or by pressing Alt+F4 will result in mrCancel being returned from ShowModal, as you would expect. Pressing the Esc key, however, will result in a return value of the ModalResult property being set to whatever button has the Cancel property set to True. The OnClick handler for the Cancel button will be called before the form closes. No OnClick handler is called if the user uses the system close box or Alt+F4 to close the form. Be sure to anticipate the different ways users might use (or abuse) your forms.

7

> **Note**
>
> You can have more than one button with a Default property set to True. Likewise, you can have more than one button with the Cancel property set to True. However, when the user presses Enter on the keyboard, the first button in the tab order that has its Default property set to True will be invoked. Similarly, when the user presses the Esc key to close the form, the return value from ShowModal will be the ModalResult value of the first button in the tab order that has its Cancel property set to True.

The Enabled Property   Earlier I discussed the Enabled property when I discussed components in general. This property is used often with buttons to enable or disable the button depending on the current state of the program or of a particular form. When a button is disabled (its Enabled property is set to False), its text is grayed out and the button does not function. In the case of buttons with bitmaps on them (BitBtn and SpeedButton), the bitmap will also be grayed out automatically.

Button components have only one method of interest: the Click method, which simulates a mouse click. When you call Click for a button, the OnClick event of the button is executed just as if the user had clicked the button. As for events, typically only the OnClick event is used.

Now let's take a look at the different button components Delphi provides.

The Button Component

The standard Button component is sort of like actor Danny DeVito: He ain't pretty, but he sure gets a lot of work. There really isn't anything to add concerning the standard Button component. It has a default Height property value of 25 pixels and a default Width property value of 75. Typically you will place a button on a form and respond to its OnClick event, and that's about it.

The BitBtn Component

The BitBtn component is a perfect example of how a component can be extended to provide additional functionality. In this case, the standard Button component is extended to enable a bitmap to be displayed on the face of the button.

The BitBtn component has several properties in addition to what the Button component provides. All these properties work together to manage the bitmap on the button and the layout between the bitmap and the button's text. They are explained in the following sections.

The `Glyph` Property The `Glyph` property represents the bitmap on the button. The value of the `Glyph` property is a picture, or glyph.

NEW TERM A *glyph* is a picture that is usually in the form of a Windows bitmap file (BMP).

The glyph itself consists of one or more bitmaps that represent the four possible states a button can be in: up, down, disabled, and stay down. If you are creating your own buttons, you can probably get by with supplying just one glyph, which the `BitBtn` component will then modify to represent the other three possible states. The bitmap will move down and to the right when the button is clicked and will be grayed out when disabled. The glyph in the stay-down state will be the same as in the up state, although the button face will change to give a pressed look.

If you provide more than one glyph, the glyphs must all be the same height and width and must be contained in a bitmap strip. The bitmaps that ship with Delphi provide two glyphs. Figure 7.6 shows the bitmap for the print button that comes with Delphi (`print.bmp`) in both its actual size and zoomed in to show detail. Note that the two glyphs each occupy the same width in the bitmap.

FIGURE 7.6.

The PRINT.BMP *bitmap.*

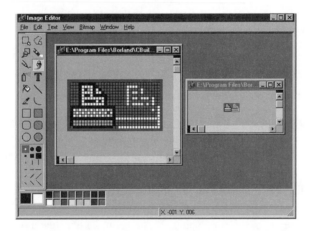

Tip

> The pixel in the lower-left corner of the bitmap is the color that will be used for the transparent color. Any pixels in the bitmap having that color will be transparent when the glyph is displayed on the button. You must keep this in mind when designing your bitmaps. If you are not using transparency, you will need the pixel in the lower-left corner to be a color not present anywhere else on the bitmap. If you don't want to use the lower-left pixel as the transparent color, you can set the `TransparentMode` property to `tmFixed` and then set the `TransparentColor` property to the transparent color of your choice.

7

To set the glyph for a BitBtn, double-click the Value column in the Object Inspector next to the Glyph property. The Picture Editor will be displayed, and you can choose the bitmap that will be used for the glyph.

> **Note**   The standard button glyphs that come with Delphi are 15×15 pixels in size. This size fits well with the standard button height of 25 pixels. Your glyphs can be any size you like, but the BitBtn component makes no effort to size the button according to the size of the bitmap. If you use larger glyphs, you will have to size the button accordingly.

The Kind Property   The Kind property is a nice feature of the BitBtn component that enables you to choose from several predefined kinds of buttons. The default value for the Kind property is bkCustom, which means that you will supply the glyph and set any other properties for the button. Choosing any of the other predefined kinds will result in these five events happening:

- The Glyph property is automatically set for the kind of button chosen.
- The Cancel or Default properties are modified according to the kind of button chosen.
- The Caption property is modified for the type of button chosen.
- The ModalResult property is set according to the kind of button chosen.
- The button on the form is updated to reflect all these settings.

For example, if you set the value of Kind to bkOK, the button will become an OK button. The glyph is set to a green check mark, the Cancel property is set to False, the Default property is set to True, the ModalResult property is set to mrOk, the Caption property is set to OK, and the results show up on the form. You can always override any of the properties modified by changing the Kind property, but it is not usually necessary to do so. Figure 7.7 shows the Button Test program from the code that comes with this book, with the BitBtn Test form displayed. The form contains each of the predefined button types available plus one custom button.

The Layout Property   The Layout property determines where the button is placed relative to the text. The default is blGlyphLeft. You can also choose to place the glyph on the face of the button to the right of the text, above the text, or below the text.

FIGURE 7.7.

The predefined BitBtn
types.

The Margin Property   The Margin property specifies the margin between the glyph
and the edge of the button (which edge this property affects is determined by the value of
the Layout property). The default is -1, which centers the glyph and the text in the button. Enter any positive value to set an absolute margin (in pixels).

The NumGlyphs Property   The NumGlyphs property specifies the number of glyphs you
have in your bitmap strip for a particular button. You can supply from one to four glyphs,
as I've mentioned. The glyphs must appear in the bitmap strip in this order: up, disabled,
down, stay down.

The Spacing Property   The Spacing property controls the distance in pixels between
the glyph and the button's text. The default value is four pixels.

The SpeedButton Component

The SpeedButton component was designed to be used with the Panel component to
build toolbars. It is different from the Button and BitBtn components in that it is not a
windowed component. This means that a speed button cannot receive input focus and
cannot be tabbed to.

On the other hand, the SpeedButton component has several features in common with the
BitBtn component. The way in which the Glyph property is handled by the SpeedButton
component is exactly the same as with the BitBtn component, so I'm not going to go
over that ground again. There are a couple of major differences, though, so let's look at
those.

7

By default, speed buttons are square and are 25×25 pixels. Your speed buttons can be any size you like and can contain text, although speed buttons don't usually contain text. There are some properties specific to speed buttons that you should be aware of, which I've broken down in the following sections.

Note

The Delphi 1.0 method of creating toolbars involved using a Panel component on which various components (SpeedButtons, primarily) were placed. Delphi 4 has the Toolbar component, which is the preferred method of creating a toolbar. The Toolbar component has some added benefits but is slightly more complicated to use.

GroupIndex   Speed buttons can be grouped to make them behave like radio buttons (radio buttons will be discussed later in this chapter in the section "Radio Buttons and Check Boxes"). When one button in the group is pressed, it stays down, and the button that was previously pressed pops up again. To group speed buttons, simply assign the same value to the GroupIndex property for all buttons in a group. (The default value of 0 indicates that the button is not part of any group.) To better understand this, try the following exercise:

1. Create a blank form and place five speed buttons on the form. (I won't bother adding glyphs to the buttons in this simple exercise, but you certainly can if you want.)

2. Select all the buttons and change the value of the GroupIndex property to 1. The GroupIndex for all buttons will be changed to 1.

3. Optional: Change the Down property of one of the buttons to True.

4. Click the Run button to compile and run the program.

When you run the program, click several of the buttons. You will notice that only one button can be in the down state at one time. As you can see when you assign a nonzero value to GroupIndex, the speed buttons change their behavior. A speed button with a GroupIndex of 0 pops back up when you click it, whereas a speed button that is part of a group stays down when clicked.

AllowAllUp   By default, one button in the group must be down at all times. You can change that behavior by setting the AllowAllUp property to True. Doing this for one button automatically changes the AllowAllUp property for all other buttons in the group to True as well. Now you can have any one button in the group selected or no buttons.

Tip

Sometimes you want a speed button to act as a toggle button. A toggle button is used to turn an option on or off and is not part of a button group. To make an individual speed button a toggle button, assign a nonzero value to its GroupIndex property and set its AllowAllUp property to True. Be sure to set the GroupIndex property to a value not used by any other components on the form. When the user clicks the button, it stays down. When the button is clicked again, it pops back up.

Down   The Down property, when read, returns True if the button is currently down and False if it is not. When written to, the Down property can be used to toggle a button as pressed or not pressed. Writing to the Down property has no effect unless the speed button is part of a group.

Radio Buttons and Check Boxes

Although radio buttons and check boxes are specialized buttons, they are, in the end, still buttons. I'm not going to spend a lot of time discussing these two components because implementing them is straightforward. Both the RadioButton and CheckBox components have a property called Checked that can be used to set the check state and can be read to retrieve the current check state.

The radio button is usually used in a group of buttons. A radio button typically signifies a group of options, only one of which can be selected at one time (like a group of speed buttons, which you just learned about). Although you can use a radio button by itself, it is not recommended because it is confusing to your users. When tempted to use a radio button by itself, use a check box instead—that's what a check box is for, after all.

Any radio buttons placed on a form will automatically be considered part of the same group. If you have more than one group of radio buttons, and those groups need to operate independent of one another, you need to use a RadioGroup component. This component enables you to quickly set up a group of radio buttons with a 3D frame around the buttons and a caption as well. To better understand this concept, try the following exercise:

1. Create a blank form or use the form you created in the previous exercise. Place a RadioGroup component on the form (you will find it on the Standard tab).

2. Locate the Items property and double-click the Value column.

3. The String list editor is displayed. Type the following lines in the String list editor:
   ```
   Redtailed Hawk
   Peregrine Falcon
   Gyrfalcon
   Northern Goshawk
   ```

7

4. Click OK to close the String list editor. The group box is populated with radio buttons containing the text you typed.

5. Change the `Caption` property of the radio group box to `Apprentice Falconers Can Legally Possess:`.

6. Click Run to compile and run the program.

When you click one of the radio buttons, the previously selected button pops up as expected. Using the `RadioGroup` component, you can put more than one group of radio buttons on a form. Like the list box and combo box components discussed earlier, the `RadioGroup` component has an `ItemIndex` property that you can read at runtime to determine which item in the group is selected. You can also set the `ItemIndex` to force a particular radio button to be selected. You might have noticed that none of the radio buttons were selected when the application ran. Change the `ItemIndex` to `0` in the Object Inspector and run the program again. This time the first radio button is selected.

Oh, by the way—if you live in the U.S., the answer to the quiz is Redtailed Hawk (American Kestrel would also have been an acceptable answer, but it was not presented in the list).

Note

> You can also use a `GroupBox` component to hold radio buttons. The `GroupBox` component is less convenient to use than the `RadioGroup` component, but it has more flexibility. You can place any type of control in a group box. After they're placed in the group box, the controls and the group box itself can be moved as a unit at design time.

The `CheckBox` component is used to enable users to turn an option on or off or to indicate to a user that an option is currently on or off. A check box can have up to three states, depending on its style: on, off, or grayed. If the check box's `AllowGrayed` property is `False`, it can only be checked or unchecked. When the `AllowGrayed` property is `True`, the check box can be any one of the three states. The grayed, or indeterminate, state is handled programmatically.

In other words, it's up to you to decide what the grayed state means for your application. If the `AllowGrayed` property is `False` (the default), you can use the `Checked` property to determine whether the check box is checked or unchecked. If the `AllowGrayed` property is `True`, you must use the `State` property to determine (or set) the check box state. `State` will return `cbChecked`, `cbUnchecked`, or `cbGrayed`.

Tip

Sometimes you might want to use a check box to indicate that some feature is on or off but not enable the user to change the state by clicking on the check box. In that case, you want the check box to be disabled but to appear normal. To make a check box read-only but not grayed out, place it on a panel and change the panel's Enabled property to False.

The Label Component

The Label component is used to display text on a form. Sometimes the label text is determined at design time and never changed. In other cases, the label is dynamic and is changed at runtime as the program dictates. Use the label's Caption property to set the label text at runtime. The Label component has no specialized methods or events beyond what is available with other components. Table 7.8 lists the properties specific to the Label component.

TABLE 7.8. PROPERTIES FOR THE Label COMPONENT.

Property	Description
AutoSize	When set to True, the label sizes itself according to the text contained in the Caption property. When set to False, text is clipped at the right edge of the label. Default: True
FocusControl	A label is a non-windowed component, so it cannot receive input focus and it cannot be tabbed to. Sometimes, however, a label serves as the text for a control such as an edit control. In those cases you could assign an accelerator key to the label (using the ampersand) and then change the FocusControl property to the name of the control you want to receive focus when the label's accelerator key is pressed.
ShowAccelChar	Set this property to True if you want an actual ampersand to show up in the label rather than the ampersand serving as the accelerator key. Default: True
Transparent	When this property is set to True, the Color property is ignored and anything beneath the label shows through. This is useful for placing labels on bitmap backgrounds, for example. Default: False
WordWrap	When set to True, text in the label will wrap around to a new line when it reaches the right edge of the label. Default: False

7

Note

> The StaticText component (found on the Additional tab) is another type of label component. This component is different from the regular Label component in that it is a windowed control (it has a window handle). The StaticText component is handy when you use a label with an Edit component and you want an accelerator key to be associated with the component.

The ScrollBar Component

The ScrollBar component represents a stand-alone scrollbar. It's standalone in the sense that it is not connected to an edit control, list box, form, or anything else. I have not found that the scrollbar is a control I use very frequently. Certain types of applications use scrollbars heavily, of course, but for day-in, day-out applications its use is fairly uncommon.

The scrollbar's performance is set by setting the Min, Max, LargeChange, and SmallChange properties. The scrollbar's position can be set or obtained via the Position property. The Kind property enables you to specify a horizontal or vertical scrollbar.

The Panel Component

The Panel component is sort of a workhorse in Delphi. There is almost no limit to what you can use panels for. Panels can be used to hold toolbar buttons, to display text labels such as a title for a form, to display graphics, and to hold regular buttons as well. One of the advantages of a panel is that components placed on the panel become children of the panel. As such, they go with the panel wherever the panel goes. This can be a great aid at runtime and at design time.

Much of the power of the Panel component lies in its Align property. For example, let's say you want a title to be displayed on the top of a form. Let's further assume that you want it centered no matter how the user sizes the window. By setting the Align property to alTop and the Alignment property to taCenter, your title will always be centered. It's as simple as that.

A panel can have many appearances. The panel's appearance can be altered by changing the BevelInner, BevelOuter, BorderStyle, and BorderWidth properties, as displayed in Figure 7.8.

FIGURE 7.8.

The Panel Styles Example showing different styles.

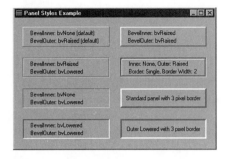

The Panel component is so versatile that it will take you a while to discover all its possible uses.

And That's Not All...

Unfortunately, there isn't sufficient space here to go over all the components Delphi provides. You saw the Image component on Day 4 when you created the Picture Viewer program. You also got a brief glimpse at the Bevel component on Day 4 when you built an About dialog box, and the Shape component on Day 6 as part of an exercise in aligning components. These represent just a sampling of the components that are waiting for you. You need to test drive each one of them to determine their usefulness for you.

There is one other group of components that I need to discuss before you move on: the Dialog group.

The Common Dialog Boxes

Windows provides a set of common dialog boxes that any Windows program can use, including the following:

- File Open
- File Save
- File Open Picture
- File Save Picture
- Font
- Color
- Print

7

- Printer Setup
- Find
- Replace

The common dialog boxes are found on the Dialogs tab of the Component palette. These components are considered nonvisual because they don't have a visual design-time interface. The following sections discuss each of these dialog boxes with one exception—I'll leave the discussion of the Print and Printer Setup dialog boxes for Day 13 when I discuss printing.

The Execute Method

One feature that all the common dialog boxes have in common is the Execute method, which is used to create and display the dialog box. The dialog box is displayed modally except for the Find and Replace dialog boxes, which are displayed modelessly. Execute returns True if the user clicked the OK button, double-clicked a file name (in the case of the file dialogs), or pressed Enter on the keyboard. Execute returns False if the user clicked the Cancel button, pressed the Esc key, or closed the dialog box with the system close box. A common dialog box is often implemented like this:

```
if OpenDialog.Execute then begin
  { user pressed OK so use the filename }
  Memo.Lines.LoadFromFile(OpenDialog.FileName);
  { do some other stuff }
end;
```

This code displays the File Open dialog box and gets a filename from the user. If the user clicked the OK button, the code inside the if block is executed and the file is loaded in to a Memo component. If OK was not pressed, the code inside the if block is ignored and no action takes place.

Note

The code used in the previous snippet is another example of Object Pascal shortcut syntax. The first line

```
if OpenDialog.Execute then begin
```

is equivalent to

```
if OpenDialog.Execute = True then begin
```

Use either method, but the first is preferred.

The File Open and File Save Dialog Boxes

The File Open and File Save dialog boxes have several properties in common. File Open is used when you want to allow the user to open a file in your application (see Figure 7.9). It is encapsulated in the OpenDialog component. The File Save dialog box is used when getting a filename from the user in order to save a file. It is also used as the Save As dialog box. The File Save dialog box is encapsulated by the SaveDialog component.

FIGURE 7.9.

A typical File Open dialog box.

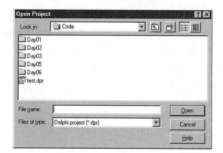

The file dialog boxes are fairly easy to use in their most basic form. They do have a few features, however, that need to be explained in order for you to get the full benefit of using them. The following sections examine the properties that are specific to the file dialog boxes.

Note

The OpenDialog and SaveDialog components merely retrieve a filename from the user. It is up to the programmer to write code that actually does something with the filename.

The DefaultExt Property

Use the DefaultExt property to set the default extension that the dialog box will use. The *default extension* is the extension that will automatically be appended to the filename if the user does not supply an extension.

The FileName Property

The FileName property is the most obvious of the file dialog box properties: It holds the text of the file that the user chose. Set this property prior to calling the dialog box if you

7

want a filename to show in the edit portion of the file dialog box when it is initially displayed. After the user clicks OK to close the dialog box, this property will contain the full path and filename of the file chosen.

The `Files` Property

`Files`, a read-only property, is a `TStrings` instance that contains the list of files selected when multiple file selection is enabled.

The `Filter` Property

The `Filter` property contains a list of the file types from which the user can choose. The file types are displayed in the File of type: combo box in the file dialog box. You can set `Filter` to reflect types of files specific to your application. For example, a simple text-editing program could have the filter set to show files of type `.TXT`, `.INI`, and `.LOG`, to name just a few.

The filter can easily be set at design time through the Filter Editor dialog box. To invoke the Filter Editor, double-click the Value column next to the `Filter` property in the Object Inspector. Figure 7.10 shows the Filter Editor for a File Open dialog box, as described previously.

FIGURE 7.10.

The Filter Editor dialog box.

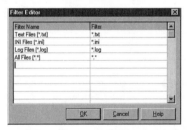

The Filter Name column contains a textual description of the file type. The Filter column is the actual file mask that will be used to display files of that type.

Although you can enter the filter string directly in the Value column of the Object Inspector, it is easiest to use the Filter Editor. If you are using only a single filter, you can type it directly into the Value column for the `Filter` property. Separate the description and filter with a pipe. For example, to have a single filter for all file types, you would enter the following:

```
All Files (*.*)¦*.*
```

The `FilterIndex` Property

The `FilterIndex` property is used to set the filter that will be used when the dialog box is initially displayed. The index is not 0-based as you might expect, however. The first filter in the list is 1, the second is 2, and so on. For example, refer to Figure 7.10. If you want the All Files filter to be the one initially displayed, you would set the `FilterIndex` property to 4.

The `InitialDir` Property

The `InitialDir` property is used to specify the directory that will be used as the initial directory when the file dialog box is displayed. If no value is supplied for the `InitialDir` property, the current directory will be used (as determined by Windows).

Tip

> A top-notch Windows program keeps track of the last directory the user used both when opening files and when saving them. Usually this information is stored in the Registry. Before displaying a File Open or File Save dialog box, set the `InitialDir` to the previous directory the user used. After the user selects a file, update the Registry to reflect the new directory if necessary.

The `Options` Property

The `Options` property controls the way the file dialog box is used. The list of options is too long to list here, but common items include whether you enable new files or directories to be created, whether the Help button is shown on the dialog box, whether long filenames are allowed, whether multiple file selection is allowed, and others. See the Delphi online help regarding the `OpenDialog` and `SaveDialog` components for complete information.

The `Title` Property

The `Title` property is used to set or read the title of the file dialog box. If no title is specified, the common dialog box defaults of Open for the `OpenDialog` component and Save for the `SaveDialog` component are used.

A Save As dialog box is nothing more than a `SaveDialog` component with the `Title` property set to `Save As`.

The file dialog boxes have no events associated with them.

You can implement a File Open dialog box (or any of the common dialog boxes) at runtime without ever placing an `OpenDialog` component on your form. To accomplish this, create an instance of the `TOpenDialog` class and then call its `Execute` method, as follows:

```
procedure TForm1.Button1Click(Sender: TObject);
var
  OpenDlg : TOpenDialog;
begin
  OpenDlg := TOpenDialog.Create(Self);
  if OpenDlg.Execute then begin
    { do something here }
  end;
  OpenDlg.Free;
end;
```

If necessary, you can set any of the `OpenDialog` component's properties prior to calling `Execute`.

The File Open Picture and File Save Picture Dialog Boxes

These two dialog boxes are nothing more than the regular File Open and File Save dialog boxes with an extra feature: They display a preview window that enables you to see the image that is currently selected. These dialog boxes also have the `Filter` property pre-set to the common Windows image formats. Otherwise, they behave just like the File Open and File Save dialog boxes. Figure 7.11 shows a File Open Picture dialog box in action.

The Color Dialog Box

The Color dialog box enables the user to choose a color. When the OK button is clicked, the `Color` property will contain the color information (refer to Figure 7.1 to see the Color dialog box). The Color dialog box, like the file dialog boxes, has no events to respond to.

FIGURE 7.11.

*The File Open Picture
dialog box.*

The Font Dialog Box

The Font dialog box enables the user to choose a font from the list of fonts available on his or her system. Through the `Device` property, you can choose whether you want screen fonts, printer fonts, or both types of fonts to be displayed. You can limit the maximum and minimum font sizes that the user can select by modifying the `MaxFontSize` and `MinFontSize` properties. As with the file dialog boxes, the `Options` property contains a wide variety of options you can use to control how the Font dialog box functions.

If the user clicks OK, the `Font` property will contain all the information you need to implement the new font. Figure 7.12 shows the Font dialog box in the default configuration.

FIGURE 7.12.

The Font dialog box.

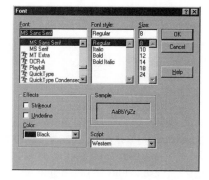

The Font dialog box has one event in addition to the usual events for dialogs. `OnApply` will occur when the user clicks the Apply button on the Find dialog box. The Apply button will not be present on the Font dialog box unless you first create a valid (not empty) event handler for the `OnApply` event.

7

The Find and Replace Dialog Boxes

The Find and Replace dialog boxes provide users the capability to enter text to search for and text to replace the found text with, and a variety of search and replace options. The Find dialog box is encapsulated in the VCL component FindDialog, and the Replace dialog box is represented by the ReplaceDialog component. The Replace dialog box, which contains everything found on the Find dialog box plus the extra replace features, is shown in Figure 7.13.

FIGURE 7.13.

The Replace dialog box.

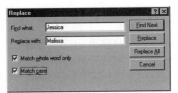

Major properties of the FindDialog and ReplaceDialog components include FindText (the text to find), ReplaceText (the text with which to replace the found text), and Options. Obviously, the FindDialog does not have a ReplaceText property. The Options property contains a wide variety of information about the various options that the user set at the time the Find Next, Replace, or Replace All button was clicked.

The Execute method for the FindDialog and ReplaceDialog components is a little different than it is with the other common Dialog components. First of all, the Find and Replace dialog boxes are modeless dialog boxes. As soon as the dialog box is displayed, the Execute method returns.

Because the dialog box is modeless, the return value from Execute is meaningless (it's always True). Instead, the Find and Replace dialog boxes use the OnFind and OnReplace events along with the Options property to determine what is happening with the dialog box. The OnFind event occurs when the Find Next button is clicked. The ReplaceDialog has an OnFind event, but it also has an OnReplace event that is fired when the Replace or Replace All button is clicked. Use these events to determine when the user has requested a find or replace action. Your programs should read the Options property to determine how the user intended the find or replace operation to be carried out.

Summary

Today you have had a look at some of the basic components that Delphi provides. You have learned about components in general, and then you learned about some of the specifics of the components that are based on Windows controls. It is important to understand the basic controls available in Windows and the Delphi components that represent those controls. Finally, you examined some of the Windows common dialog boxes.

Workshop

The Workshop contains quiz questions to help you solidify your understanding of the material covered and exercises to provide you with experience in using what you have learned. You can find answers to the quiz questions in Appendix A, "Answers to the Quiz Questions."

Q&A

Q If I change the `Name` property of a component using the Object Inspector, Delphi will automatically change all references to that component in my code, right?

A Yes and no. Delphi will change all references to that component name in Delphi-generated code, but it will not change any user-written code.

Q The `OpenDialog` component is obviously a visible component. Why is it called a nonvisual component?

A Because it is not visible at design time. It is visible only at runtime when you invoke it with the `Execute` method.

Q Why is it important to change the `Name` property only with the Object Inspector?

A As you work with the Form Designer, Delphi writes code based on the `Name` property. If you later change the `Name` property either by directly editing the source files or at runtime, all references to that form or component will be incorrect and will likely lead to your program refusing to compile or crashing at runtime.

Q I seem to be using properties more than methods when dealing with my components in code. Is that wrong?

A Not at all. In fact, that's the way VCL components are designed. A well-written component makes maximum use of properties. For this reason you cannot use a component's methods very often. Use methods when necessary, but otherwise use properties to manipulate your components at runtime.

7

Q **I'm responding to both the** OnDblClick **and the** OnClick **events for a component. Every time I double-click a component, both the** OnClick **and the** OnDblClick **event handlers get called. Why?**

A Because when you double-click a component, Windows will generate both single- and double-click messages. You can't prevent it, so you have to write code to account for that fact.

Q **I want to use the features of the** TStrings **class to keep a list of strings my program needs in order to operate. The compiler won't let me use a** TStrings **object. What do I do?**

A Use a TStringList object instead. The TStringList class is provided for this purpose.

Q **I need a single-line edit control to be right-justified, but there is no** Alignment **property for the** Edit **component. Can I right-align text in a single-line edit?**

A No. What you can do, though, is use a Memo component and make it appear to be a regular Edit component. Be sure to set the Memo component's WantReturn property to False, its Height to the height of a standard edit component (21 pixels), and its Alignment property to taRightJustify. The component will give all appearances of being a single-line edit control that is right-justified.

Q **I have a form that has several buttons on it. When the user closes the form using the Esc key I get one return value from** ShowModal, **and when the user closes the form with the system close box I get a different return value from** ShowModal. **Why?**

A You have a button on the form that has a Cancel property set to True. When the user presses the Esc key, the ModalResult value of that button is used as the return value from ShowModal. When the user closes the form with the system close box, you will always get a return value of mrCancel. You need to be prepared to take into account both ways that a form can be closed.

Quiz

1. Can you change the Name property of a component at runtime?
2. What property is used to enable and disable controls?
3. How can you tell at runtime that a button is disabled?
4. What is the difference between the long hint and the short hint?
5. Name three of the four methods that can be used to tell a control to repaint itself.
6. How many types of combo boxes are there?

7. How is the `ModalResult` property used for button components?

8. What component is often used as a container for other components?

9. What is the return value from the `Execute` method for an `OpenDialog` component if the user clicks OK to close the dialog box?

10. How do you make the `SaveDialog` component into a Save As dialog box?

Exercises

1. Create a program that contains two edit components. When the user types information in the first control, make it appear in the second edit control as it is entered.

2. Create a program with a list box. Write code to load the list box from a text file prior to the application being visible.

3. Add an edit component to the program in Exercise 2. When the user selects an item in the list box, have the item's text appear in the edit control.

4. Add a button to the program in Exercises 2 and 3. Write code so that when the button is clicked, any text in the edit control is added as a new item in the list box.

5. Create a program that has a `RadioGroup` with four items in the group. Add a label component whose text changes depend on which radio button is clicked.

6. Create a program that has a title on the form that is centered at the top of the form regardless of how the program's window is sized.

7. Modify the program in Exercise 6 so that the font of the title can be changed to any font available on the system by clicking a button.

8. Reopen the Picture Viewer program created on Day 4. Modify the program so that it uses File Open Picture and File Save Picture dialog boxes rather than the regular dialog boxes.

7

WEEK 1

In Review

You covered a lot of ground this week. In some ways this was the toughest week. Object Pascal, while not as daunting as some other programming languages, still takes some time to learn. But there is no doubt that you can learn to program in Delphi if you stay with it. Don't forget to take a break now and then. This book is titled *Sams Teach Yourself Delphi 4 in 21 Days*, but that doesn't mean that they have to be consecutive days! Sometimes it's good to take a few days off to let it all soak in.

If you are confused by some of the Object Pascal syntax, don't feel you are alone. It all can be confusing at first. Don't worry, though, because you will start to get the hang of it before long. As you work with Delphi, little by little it begins to make sense. What you probably lack at this point is real-world experience. That is where you really learn. Knowledge gained by experience is the kind that sticks. My advice is to take an idea and turn it into a working program. You can't necessarily do that at this point, but you can get a good start. The program doesn't have to be as advanced as Microsoft Word, Netscape Navigator, or a game like DOOM, mind you. It just needs to be a little something to help you tie your education in with some experience.

The first part of this week, you worked on Object Pascal language keywords and syntax. Items such as loops and if statements are fairly easy to comprehend. Don't be concerned, though, if you have to go back and look up the syntax once in a while. There is a lot to learn, and you aren't expected to memorize every keyword and its syntax. Later on you will be, but at this stage of the game, it isn't expected.

1

2

3

4

5

6

7

On Day 3, you were introduced to Object Pascal classes. Classes are a big part of Object Pascal and programming in Delphi. Sometimes it takes a while to perceive where classes can be used in your programs. For a long time, you might deal only with the classes that the Visual Component Library (VCL) provides and not write any classes of your own. Later on you will probably find situations where a class will fit perfectly with a particular task you have to accomplish. When that time comes, you will be ready to tackle writing your own class. After you've written one or two, you will be off and running.

On Day 4, you learned about the IDE: how to customize it to your liking, how the Component Palette works, what the Object Inspector is for, and so on. This part of the week you experienced the fun stuff. It's okay to use the word *fun*. I find all kinds of programming a great deal of fun. That's why I do it. I hope that you find it fun, too.

On Day 5, I gave you an introduction to class libraries, also known as *frameworks*. VCL is a framework. A framework makes your life easier by encapsulating difficult Windows programming tasks into classes that you can deal with on a more rational level. Believe me, sometimes the raw Windows API seems to be anything but rational. VCL takes care of dealing with those issues for you and provides you with a higher level of programming objects that you can easily incorporate in your applications. No, VCL is not easy, but it is much easier than dealing with the API. As part of the discussion on frameworks, you were introduced to the component model. You learned about properties, methods, and events and how you use them to build Windows programs in Delphi.

On Day 6, you learned about the Form Designer. The Form Designer is where the bulk of your Delphi applications will be designed—the graphical part of the application, anyway. Working with the Form Designer can be fun, too. Using the Form Designer, you can create great-looking forms. Remember, a form represents a window in your applications. Most applications have a main window and several dialog boxes that are displayed, based on user interaction with the program. On Day 6, you also created a simple but useful program. This program, ScratchPad, gave you a start in building an application with Delphi. ScratchPad will be used throughout the book. As you build your programming knowledge, you will add new features to ScratchPad to give you practice with the techniques presented. If you are developing an application of your own, I encourage you to add new features to your program as you learn about them.

On Day 7, you learned about some of the VCL components available to you. I didn't cover all the VCL components, but I covered the components that are most commonly used in Windows programming with Delphi. You will be introduced to other VCL components as you work through the rest of the book.

I hope this week hasn't left you too worn out. If it has, take a short break and then jump right back into the game. If you found this week exhilarating and energizing, just keep on turnin' those pages. I'm ready if you are.

WEEK 2

At a Glance

Are you ready for the fun stuff? This week you learn about
Windows programming in earnest. You start off learning
more about creating applications with Delphi. You learn
about creating applications using Delphi's wizards. These
wizards help you get a program up and running in minimum
time.

Day 9 is about Delphi projects, which are the key to managing your files when you create an application. You learn
about the Delphi Project Manager, a vital tool in project management. Day 9 also covers the Delphi Code Editor in detail.
You will spend a great deal of time with the Code Editor as
you become more proficient in Delphi programming. It's a
good idea to learn just what features the Code Editor has so
that you can be a more efficient programmer.

On Day 10, you learn about debugging your programs. Yes,
your programs will have bugs. Don't fight it. Just learn how
to find those nasty critters in your programs and squash them.
Debugging is a vital application development tool, and you
must learn how to debug your programs. Knowing how to use
the debugger will save you hours and hours of effort in the
long run.

Day 12 introduces you to graphics and multimedia programming. You learn the basics of graphics programming, such as
drawing shapes, displaying bitmaps, and working with
palettes. You also learn about simple multimedia operations
such as playing waveform audio and AVI video.

Finally, late in the week you begin to learn about more
advanced programming techniques, such as status bars,

8

9

10

11

12

13

14

toolbars, and printing. On Day 14, you learn how to use context help and how to use the Windows Registry to store information for your program. I think you'll like what you find there. By the end of the week, you will be on a steamroller that can't be stopped.

DAY 8

Creating Applications in Delphi

Delphi provides a variety of tools that aid you in creating forms, dialog boxes, and applications. Today you learn about the following:

- The Object Repository
- The Dialog Wizard
- The Application Wizard
- Adding methods and data fields to your code
- Component templates
- Using resources in your Delphi applications
- Packages

For starters, I'll spend some time discussing the Object Repository, which is where Delphi stores any prebuilt forms, applications, or other objects for you to reuse.

Following that discussion, you meet the wizards. Wizards provide a series of dialog boxes that guide you step by step through the creation process. You provide the details, and Delphi builds the form or application based on the information you provided. The wizards are a powerful tool for rapid application development. Later in the day I'll tell you how you can use resources in your Delphi applications. Finally, I'll close the day by talking about packages in Delphi.

Working with the Object Repository

The Object Repository is the means by which you can select predefined objects to use in your applications.

The Object Repository enables you to do the following:

- Choose a predefined application, form, or dialog box to implement in your application.
- Add your own forms, dialog boxes, and applications to the Object Repository.
- Add other objects to your application such as ASCII text files and additional source code units.
- Manage data modules.
- Create new components.
- Create new packages.
- Create new ActiveX controls or ActiveForms.
- Invoke wizards to help you build a dialog box or an application.

That's just a sampling of what the Object Repository provides. There are other objects you can create in addition to those listed here.

Object Repository Pages and Options

The Object Repository is displayed automatically whenever you choose File | New from the main menu. Figure 8.1 shows the Object Repository window as it initially appears when you choose File | New with no project open.

Note

Strange as it might seem, the Object Repository is titled New Items, and the Object Repository configuration dialog box is titled Object Repository. To say that this is confusing is a bit of an understatement.

FIGURE 8.1.

The Object Repository window.

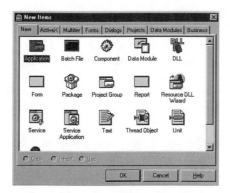

8

The Object Repository has several pages, each of which contains different objects that you can incorporate into your applications. As you can see from Figure 8.1, the New tab is what is initially selected when the Object Repository is displayed. Table 8.1 lists the Repository pages and a description of the items you find on each page.

TABLE 8.1. THE OBJECT REPOSITORY PAGES.

Page/Tab	Description
New	Enables you to create a new application, form, or unit for use in your application. Also enables you to create advanced objects such as packages, DLLs, components, NT service applications, Web server applications, and data modules.
ActiveX	Enables you to create new ActiveX controls, type libraries, COM objects, ActiveForms, and other ActiveX objects.
Multitier	Enables you to create CORBA and MTS objects and data modules (Client/Server version only).
Forms	Enables you to create standard forms from prebuilt forms such as an About box, a dual list box, tabbed pages, or QuickReports.
Dialogs	Presents choices of several basic dialog box types from which you can choose. Also contains the Dialog Wizard.
Projects	Displays full projects that you can choose from to initially set up an application. Also contains the Application Wizard.
Data Modules	Enables you to choose from data modules in your application.
Business	Includes wizards for database forms, database Web applications, reports, and charts, and a Decision Cube sample application.

> If you invoke the Object Repository when you already have a project open, you will see an additional tab in the Object Repository. The tab will have the name of your project on it. Clicking this tab will display a page that contains all the objects currently in the project. This enables you to quickly reuse a form or other object by simply selecting it from the Object Repository.

Across the bottom of each page you see three radio buttons. These buttons, labeled Copy, Inherit, and Use, determine how the selected object is implemented. Depending on the object selected, some of the radio buttons (or all) might be disabled. For example, all three radio buttons are always grayed out when the New page is displayed. This is because Copy is the only option available for objects on this page, so Delphi grays out all choices and applies the Copy option automatically.

> The Object Repository is sometimes called the Gallery.

The Copy Button

When you choose the Copy radio button, Delphi creates a copy of the selected object and places it in your application. At this point you are free to modify the object in any way you choose. The original object in the Repository is not altered when you make changes to the new object in your application.

To illustrate, let's say you have an often used form (a form in the traditional sense, not in the Delphi sense) printed on paper—a work schedule, for example. Let's say that you want to fill in that form with scheduling information. You wouldn't modify the original form because it would then be unusable for future reuse. Instead, you would put the original form in the copy machine, make a copy, and then return the original to some location for safekeeping.

You would then fill out the copy of the form as needed. Making a copy of an object in the Repository works in exactly the same way. You are free to modify the copy in any way you choose and the original remains safely tucked away. Making a copy is the safest method of object usage.

The Inherit Button

The Inherit method of usage is similar to Copy, but with one important distinction: The new object is still tied to the base object. If you modify the base object, the newly created object will be updated to reflect the changes made to the base object. The inverse is not true, however. You can modify the new object without it having any effect on the base object.

To illustrate this type of object usage, consider the following scenario: Frequently, information managers create a spreadsheet in a spreadsheet program and use the contents of that spreadsheet in a word-processing program to present a report.

They usually opt to link the data to the spreadsheet when pasting from the Clipboard or importing the spreadsheet into the word processor. That way, when changes are made to the spreadsheet, the word-processing document is automatically updated to reflect the new data. In the same way, changes made to a base form will automatically be reflected in all forms inherited from the base form. Use the Inherit option when you want to have several forms based on a common form that might change at some point. Any changes in the base form will be reflected in all inherited forms.

The Use Button

The Use option is not common. When you use an object, you are opening that object directly for editing. Select this option when you have saved an object in the Repository and you want to make permanent changes to that object. In the section about the Inherit option, I said that changes made to a base form would be reflected in all inherited forms. If you wanted to make changes to a base form, you would open it in the Object Repository with the Use option.

Using the Object Repository

Exactly what takes place when you select an object from the Object Repository depends on several factors. The factors include the type of object selected, whether a project is currently open, and the usage type you select (Copy, Inherit, or Use).

If you have an application open and you choose to create a new application from the Object Repository, you are prompted to save the current project (if necessary) before the new project is displayed.

Tip
Choosing File | New Application from the main menu is a shortcut for starting a new application. It is equivalent to choosing New from the main menu and then choosing the Application object from the Object Repository. Similarly, the New Form item on the main menu is a shortcut for its equivalent in the Object Repository.

Creating a new form from the Object Repository is treated differently based on whether a project is open at the time. If a project is open, the new form is added to the application as a form/unit pair. If no project is open, a new form and unit are created as a standalone form. A form created outside of a project must be added to a project before it can be used at runtime. Use this option when creating a new base form to add to the Object Repository.

If you choose to create a new unit or text file, the new file is simply created in the Code Editor (and, in the case of a new unit, added to the current project). You might create a new text file for several reasons. For example, let's say you want to implement a configuration file (an .ini file) in your application. You could create a new text file in the Object Repository to initially create the configuration file. Create a new unit any time you want to start a new source file for your application that is not associated with a form (an include file, for example).

Choosing a new DLL results in a new project being created with the project set up for a DLL target. Creating a new component or thread object results in a dialog box being presented that asks for more information about the object you are creating.

The Object Repository Views

The actual Object Repository window is a Win32 list view control similar to the right side of Windows Explorer (where the files are listed). As such, it has several views that you can choose from: Large Icons, Small Icons, List, and Details. By default, the view is set to Large Icons. To change the Object Repository view, right-click on the Object Repository and choose the view you want from the Object Repository context menu. Figure 8.2 shows the Object Repository with the Forms page selected and the view set to Details.

FIGURE 8.2.

The Object Repository in Details view.

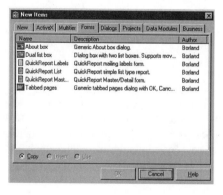

The Object Repository context menu also shows several sorting options. You can sort by object name, description, date, or author.

 Tip

When the Object Repository is in the Details view, you can click a column header (Name, Description, Date, or Author) to instantly sort by that category.

Creating New Objects from the Object Repository

Certainly the most basic use of the Object Repository is creating a new object using an object from the Repository. To illustrate, you can create a simple application with a main form, an About dialog box, and a second form. Follow these steps:

1. Ensure that no other application is open. Choose File|New from the main menu. The Object Repository is displayed.

2. Click the Application icon and click OK to create a new application. A new application is created and a blank form is displayed.

3. Place two buttons on the form. Change the Caption property of one of the buttons to About... and the Caption property of the other button to Display Form2. Change the Name properties if desired.

4. Choose File|New from the main menu. The Object Repository is displayed again.

5. Click the Forms tab in the Object Repository.

6. Choose the About box object. Ensure that the Copy radio button is selected and click OK to create a new About Box form. The About box is displayed. Change any properties as needed.

7. Modify the About box as desired. (Enter your own information, change the icon, size, position, and so on.)

8. Select File|New from the main menu again. The Object Repository is displayed for the third time.

9. Click the Forms tab and choose the Dual list box object. Click OK to close the Object Repository. A dual list box form is displayed. (I had you choose this one just so you could see it.)

10. Write event handlers for the two buttons that display the About box and the second form as required. Don't forget to add the units for the About box and the second form in the uses clause of your main form.

11. Compile, run, and test the program.

No, this program doesn't do anything, but it does illustrate how you can use the Object Repository to quickly prototype an application. As time goes on, you will add your own custom objects to the Object Repository and then you can really be effective! Let's look at that next.

Adding Objects to the Object Repository

The Object Repository wouldn't be nearly as effective if you couldn't add your own objects to it. But you can add your own objects and you should. Adding frequently used objects to the Object Repository makes you a more efficient and, therefore, a more valuable programmer. There is no point in reinventing the wheel.

After you create an application, form, or other object, save it to the Repository so that you can reuse it whenever you want. Of course, you don't want to save every form you ever create in the Object Repository, just the ones you will reuse most often.

You can set out to create an object with the express purpose of adding it to the Repository, or you can add an object to the Repository during the normal course of application development. (The term *object* is pretty broad, so I'll use a specific example in order for this to make sense.) Let's say that you create an About box form while creating an application. Suddenly it dawns on you that you'd like to save this About box to use in all your programs. After all, it has your company name, logo, and all the copyright information all laid out just the way you like it, so it'd be a shame to have to re-create the same About box for every application you write. No problem—just add it to the Repository.

To add a form to the Object Repository, first save the form (if you don't save the form, you will be prompted to save it before continuing). Next, right-click anywhere on the form and choose Add To Repository from the Form Designer context menu. When you do, the Add To Repository dialog box is displayed as shown in Figure 8.3.

FIGURE 8.3.

The Add To Repository dialog box.

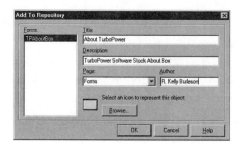

The Forms list box on the left side of this dialog box lists the current forms as well as any other objects in the application (such as data modules). First, select the form that you want to add to the Object Repository.

Note The active form in the Form Designer will already be selected in the Forms list box in the Add To Repository dialog box.

Now enter the object's title. This is the title that will appear below the icon in the Object Repository. The Description field is used to give further information about the object. This description is displayed when the Object Repository view is set to display all object details (refer to Figure 8.2). The Author field is where you type your name as the author of the object. You can enter your personal name, a company name, or any other identifying name.

Note Most of the prebuilt objects in the Object Repository that come with Delphi have "Borland" as the author name (the exceptions are the QuickReport and TeeChart objects).

The Page field is used to select the Object Repository page where the new object will be placed. You can choose from one of the existing pages or simply type the name of a new page in the Page field. If a page with the name you type doesn't exist, Delphi will create a new page with that name. Near the bottom of the dialog box is a button labeled Browse that you can use to select the icon used to represent the object.

Tip You can choose icons from the `Borland Shared Files\Images\Icons` directory or the `Delphi 4\Objrepos` directory. The icons in the `Delphi 4\Objrepos` directory are the icons used by Delphi for the items it places in the Object Repository.

After you fill in all the fields and select an icon, click OK to add the object to the Repository. The object is added to the Object Repository on the page you specified. You can now reuse that object any time you want. As you can see, adding an object to the Object Repository is nearly as easy as using an object.

Caution When you add an object to the Object Repository, Delphi makes an entry in the Object Repository file that describes the object. This information includes the pathname where the form and source file for the object are located. If you move or delete an object's form or source file, you will not be able to use the object from the Object Repository.

Adding Projects to the Object Repository

Adding projects to the Object Repository is not much different than adding individual forms. To add a project to the Object Repository, choose Project | Add to Repository from the main menu. The Add To Repository dialog box is displayed just like it is when you add objects to the Repository, except the Forms list box is not displayed. Fill in any required information (title, description, author, and so on) and click OK and the project is added to the Repository.

After you are familiar with Delphi, you should create an application shell that has the features you use most often in your applications. Each time you start a new standard application, make a copy of the shell from the Object Repository. This way you can have your menus, toolbar, About box, and other standard dialog boxes all set up and ready to go in a matter of seconds. After the new application has been created, it can then be modified as with any project. You can add new forms, delete any unwanted forms, and so on.

Object Repository Housekeeping

You can manage the pages and objects in the Object Repository by using the Object Repository configuration dialog box.

To view the Object Repository configuration dialog box, choose Tools | Repository from the main menu or, if you have the Object Repository open, choose Properties from the Object Repository context menu. The configuration dialog box is displayed as shown in Figure 8.4.

This dialog box enables you to delete objects and pages from the Object Repository, move objects from one page to another, change the order of pages in the Object Repository, and more. The list of pages in the Object Repository is displayed in the list box labeled Pages on the left side of the dialog box. When you select one of the pages in the Pages list, the list box on the right (labeled Objects) displays the objects contained on that page.

FIGURE 8.4.

The Object Repository configuration dialog box.

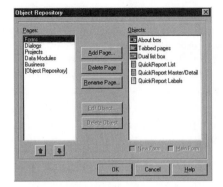

8

> **Note**
>
> The Pages list box has two important items of note. First, notice that the New page, which is always the first page displayed when the Object Repository is invoked, is not listed here. (The ActiveX and Multitier pages aren't listed in the Pages list box, either.) The New page is fixed and cannot be altered. Also notice that there is an item labeled [Object Repository]. This item is actually a list of all items on all pages of the Repository.

Managing Objects

Before you can edit, delete, or move an object, you must first select it. To select an object, click the object in the Objects list box. After you select an object, you can edit it by clicking the Edit Object button. Editing an object enables you to change the object's name, description, and author information, as well as the page on which the object is displayed.

> **Tip**
>
> To quickly edit an object, double-click it in the Objects list box.

You can delete an object by selecting it and then clicking the Delete Object button. You are prompted for confirmation before the object is removed from the page and from the Repository.

Note
When an object is deleted from the Object Repository, it is removed from the Object Repository file and no longer shows up on any page in the Object Repository. However, the actual form file and source file that describe the object are not deleted from your hard drive.

An object can be moved from one page to another by simply dragging the object from the Objects list box to the Pages list box. Drop the object on the page on which you want the object to be located, and the object is moved.

Managing Pages

The previous section deals with editing, deleting, and moving individual objects. You can also add, delete, or remove Object Repository pages through the Object Repository configuration dialog box. Before you can delete a page, you must first delete all the objects on the page. After a page is empty, you can remove the page by clicking on the page name in the Pages list box and then clicking the Delete Page button. After checking to be sure the page is empty, Delphi deletes the page from the Object Repository.

A new page can be added by clicking the Add Page button. A dialog box pops up asking for the name of the new page. Just supply a new page name and when you click OK, the new page appears in the Pages list box. Renaming a page works essentially the same way. When you select a page and click the Rename Page button, a dialog box appears prompting you for the new page name.

The order in which the pages appear in the Object Repository can be changed. To change a page's position in the page order, click the page to highlight it and then click the up or down arrow button underneath the Pages list box to move the page up or down in the list. You can also drag a page to its new location if you want.

Setting Default Forms and Projects

The Object Repository configuration dialog box enables you to set three default objects:

- The default form that is used when you choose File | New Form from the main menu.
- The default form that is used as the main form when you choose File | New Application from the main menu.
- The default project that is used when you choose File | New Application from the main menu.

You will notice that, depending on the object you select, one or two check boxes appear beneath the Objects list box. If you select a form, the New Form and Main Form check boxes appear. If you select a project, the New Project check box appears.

Making a form or project the default is easy. Let's say you create a main form that you want to be the default main form when a new application is created. Select the form from the Objects list box and click the Main Form check box at the bottom of the screen. When you click OK, that form will now be the default. Similarly, if you have a project that you want to be the default project, first locate it in the Object Repository configuration dialog box, click on it, and then check the New Project check box. From that point on, when you choose File | New Application from the main menu, the project you set as the default will appear.

Note

If you aren't careful, you can accidentally select a form as the default form for a new application. If this happens, be sure you check each form in the Object Repository configuration dialog box. One form will have the Main Form check box checked. Clear the check box and all will be back to normal. This also applies to the default project. Check the Projects page for any items that have the New Project check box checked.

Building Forms and Applications with the Wizards

Delphi has two built-in wizards designed to guide you through the application creation process. The Dialog Wizard aids you in creating dialog boxes, and the Application Wizard helps you create the basic layout of an application. These wizards are discussed in the following sections.

Using the Dialog Wizard

Truthfully, there isn't very much for a dialog box wizard to do because dialog boxes of any real value will need to be customized with the Form Designer. The Dialog Wizard is started from the Object Repository. First, choose File | New from the main menu to display the Object Repository. Next, switch to the Dialogs page and then double-click the Dialog Wizard icon. The Dialog Wizard is displayed as shown in Figure 8.5.

FIGURE 8.5.

You can choose to create a single-page dialog box or a tabbed (multipage) dialog box. The icon on the left side of the dialog box shows you what the dialog box looks like at each step. If you choose to create a single-page dialog box, when you click the Next button, you will see the next page of the Dialog Wizard (see Figure 8.6).

FIGURE 8.6.

The second page of the Dialog Wizard.

This page enables you to choose whether you want buttons on the dialog box and, if so, whether you want them on the right side or the bottom of the dialog box. This is the last page of the Dialog Wizard when creating a single-page dialog box. After choosing the button layout you want, click the Finish button to have Delphi create the dialog box for you.

The new dialog box is displayed on the Form Designer complete with the features you chose through the wizard. It also has its `BorderStyle` property set to `bsDialog`, which is customary for forms used as dialog boxes. After the Dialog Wizard has created the basic dialog box, you can go to work with the Form Designer to add functionality to the dialog box.

If you choose to create a tabbed dialog box, the second page of the dialog box looks like the one shown in Figure 8.7. (Figure 8.7 shows the dialog box after page names have been added.)

This page has a multiline edit control in which you can enter the names of the individual tabs you want to see on the dialog box. Enter the text for each tab on a separate line, as illustrated in Figure 8.7. When you click the Next button, you will see the last page of the Dialog Wizard as you saw in Figure 8.6. Choose the location of the buttons, if any, and click the Finish button to have Delphi create the tabbed dialog box.

FIGURE 8.7.

The Dialog Wizard creating a tabbed dialog box.

Note

> The Dialog Wizard is most useful when creating tabbed dialog boxes. When creating single-page dialog boxes, it is easier to choose one of the pre-defined dialog boxes from the Object Repository rather than going through the Dialog Wizard.

Creating Applications with the Application Wizard

The Application Wizard is a useful tool that can help you quickly set up the shell of an application. To create a new application using the Application Wizard, choose File | New from the main menu. When the Object Repository appears, click the Projects tab and then double-click the Application Wizard icon.

Note

> The New Application item on the main menu creates a new application based on the current default project setting. It doesn't start the Application Wizard as you might expect.

Let's walk through the Application Wizard one page at a time.

Page One: Selecting the Menus

When you start the Application Wizard, the first page is displayed as shown in Figure 8.8.

This page enables you to select the items you want on your application's main menu. You can choose to add a File menu, an Edit menu, a Window menu, and a Help menu. Place a check in the box for each menu item you want to appear on your menu bar.

Tip

> The Window menu is usually reserved for MDI applications. You probably won't put a Window menu on your SDI application's menu bar unless you have a specialty application that requires it.

FIGURE 8.8.

Page one of the
Application Wizard.

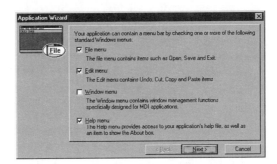

 Note

The menus added by the Application Wizard are a reasonable representation of the menu items that are most commonly used in Windows applications. Remember that the Application Wizard is intended to give you a head
start in creating your application. It is up to you to take the basic structure
and modify it to make a working application.

After you have chosen the menus you want for your application, click the Next button to
move to the next page.

Page Two: Setting the File Dialog Filters

If you chose to add a File menu to your application, the next page displayed will look
like the one shown in Figure 8.9.

FIGURE 8.9.

Setting filters for the
file dialog boxes.

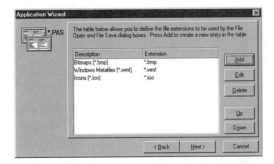

This page enables you to set the filters that your application's File Open and File Save
dialog boxes will use. (Figure 8.9 shows the dialog box after the filters have been
added.) Click the Add button to add a new filter. A dialog box is displayed asking for the
description and the filter. Enter the filters exactly as you do when setting the Filter
property for the common file dialog box components. Enter the textual description and

then the actual file mask (`*.bmp`, for example). The Edit, Delete, Up, and Down buttons can be used as necessary to change, delete, or move the filter in the list.

Pages two and three will be displayed only if you previously selected menus on page one of the Application Wizard. More specifically, page two will be displayed only if you selected a File menu on page one.

Page Three: Setting Up the Speedbar

Page three of the Application Wizard aids you in setting up a speedbar (also called a toolbar) for your application. This is possibly the most useful feature of the Application Wizard (not that the other features aren't useful). You can quickly lay out your speedbar through this page. Figure 8.10 shows the third page of the Application Wizard after a speedbar has been created.

FIGURE 8.10.

Setting up the speed-bar.

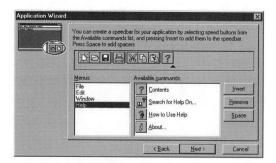

The list box on the left side of the page, labeled Menus, shows the four menus for which you can add buttons. When you choose one of the menus, the available buttons for that menu are displayed in the list box to the right of the Menus list box (labeled Available Commands). To add a speedbar button, click the button in the Available Commands list box and then click the Insert button. The button will be added to the sample speedbar at the top of the page.

The Space button can be used to add a separator to the speedbar. Adding separators visually distinguishes groups of buttons. Continue to add buttons and spaces as needed until the speedbar is complete. If you decide to remove a button, just click it in the sample speedbar and then click the Remove button.

Note

If you elected not to add a particular menu to your application, no buttons will be shown for that menu group. For example, if you did not add a Window menu, the Available Commands list box will be empty when you click on the Window item in the Menus list box.

Tip

Some specialty applications have a speedbar but don't have a menu. To create a speedbar with the Application Wizard, you must first have created a menu. To work around this, tell the Application Wizard that you want a menu and then build the speedbar. After the application has been generated, you can delete the MainMenu component from the application to remove the menu.

Page Four: Setting the Final Options

The fourth and last page of the Application Wizard enables you to set the program name, the path where the project should be stored on disk, and a few final options. Figure 8.11 shows the last page of the Application Wizard.

FIGURE 8.11.

The final Application Wizard settings.

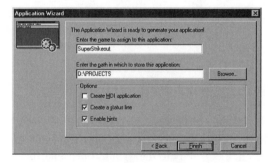

The first field on this page is where you specify the name of the application. This is not the name as it appears on the Project Options dialog box, but the filename that Delphi will use to save the project. You still need to set the application name in the Project Options dialog box. The second field is used to specify the directory in which the project should be saved. If you don't know the exact path, click the Browse button to the right of this field and choose the path from the Select Directory dialog box.

> **Tip**
>
> You can use the Select Directory dialog box to create a directory as well as to select a directory. Click the Browse button to display the Select Directory dialog box. Enter the path for the directory you want to create and then click OK or press Enter. Delphi will prompt you to create the new directory if the directory you entered doesn't exist.

The bottom half of the final page gives you three additional options. If you are creating an MDI application, click the check box marked Create MDI Application. (MDI applications were discussed on Day 4, "The Delphi IDE Explored.") The remaining two check boxes enable you to implement a status bar and hint text for your components.

When you are sure you have made all the choices for your new application, click the Next button. Delphi creates the application based on the options you specified. Delphi writes as much code as possible for the application. This doesn't amount to a lot of code, but some of the basic code is already written for you. For example, if you chose a File menu, the `FileOpenClick` handler has been written and looks like this:

```
procedure TMainForm.FileOpen(Sender: TObject);
begin
  if OpenDialog.Execute then
  begin
    { Add code to open OpenDialog.FileName }
  end;
end;
```

The code to execute the File Open dialog box is in place; you only have to write the code that actually deals with the returned filename.

> **Tip**
>
> After you create an Application Wizard project, you can choose Project | Add to Repository to save the project for later use. This will save you the trouble of going through the Application Wizard to create your basic application. You might want to add an About box before saving the project to the Repository.

Using the wizards is fast and easy. You will still need to write the program, of course, but Delphi gives you a head start by saving you from the tedium of creating the basic application elements. As RAD-friendly as Delphi is overall, the wizards simplify this process even more. The Delphi wizards are sort of like RAD on RAD!

Note Delphi provides wizards other than the Dialog Wizard and the Application Wizard. For example, the Database Form Wizard (discussed on Day 17, "Building Database Forms") is used to create database forms, and the ActiveX Control Wizard (discussed on Day 15, "COM and ActiveX") aids in the creation of ActiveX controls. These are specialized wizards, so I didn't cover them in this chapter.

Adding Methods and Data Fields to Code

As you know by now, Delphi is a great tool for quickly creating the UI (user interface) portion of a Windows application. It creates event handlers for you so that you can begin entering code to drive your application. It won't be long, however, before you find the need to start adding more complicated code to your applications.

Part of that means adding your own data fields and methods to the code that Delphi generates. For example, a simple application might contain two dozen event handlers of various types. Delphi creates all these event handlers for you; you simply fill in the blanks with working code. To make the application a viable, working application, however, you might have to write another two-dozen methods of your own.

Adding your own methods and data fields to code generated by Delphi is not a difficult task, but you need to know the rules or you can get into trouble.

How Delphi Manages Class Declarations

As you know, when you create a new form in the Form Designer, Delphi creates the unit's source file automatically. When Delphi creates the class declaration, it essentially creates two sections. The first section is the part of the class declaration that Delphi manages. The second section is the part that you manage.

On Day 6, "Working with the Form Designer and the Menu Designer," you created the ScratchPad program. If you did the exercises at the end of that chapter, you also created an About box for the program and added a few more buttons. Listing 8.1 contains the main form's class declaration as it appears after adding these enhancements.

Keep in mind that the individual component declarations appear in the order the components were placed on the form. Your class declaration should have the same components as shown in Listing 8.1, but they might not be in the same order.

LISTING 8.1. THE class DECLARATION FOR ScratchPad's MAIN FORM.

```
TMainForm = class(TForm)
    StatusBar1: TStatusBar;
    ToolBar1: TToolBar;
    ToolButton1: TToolButton;
    ToolButton2: TToolButton;
    Memo: TMemo;
    MainMenu: TMainMenu;
    FileMenu: TMenuItem;
    FileNew: TMenuItem;
    FileOpen: TMenuItem;
    FileSave: TMenuItem;
    FileSaveAs: TMenuItem;
    N1: TMenuItem;
    FilePrint: TMenuItem;
    FilePrintSetup: TMenuItem;
    N2: TMenuItem;
    FileExit: TMenuItem;
    Edit1: TMenuItem;
    EditReplace: TMenuItem;
    EditFind: TMenuItem;
    N4: TMenuItem;
    EditPaste: TMenuItem;
    EditCopy: TMenuItem;
    EditCut: TMenuItem;
    N5: TMenuItem;
    EditUndo: TMenuItem;
    Help1: TMenuItem;
    HelpAbout: TMenuItem;
    HelpContents: TMenuItem;
    EditSelectAll: TMenuItem;
    N3: TMenuItem;
    EditWordWrap: TMenuItem;
    OpenDialog: TOpenDialog;
    SaveDialog: TSaveDialog;
    MemoPopup: TPopupMenu;
    PopupCut: TMenuItem;
    PopupCopy: TMenuItem;
    PopupPaste: TMenuItem;
    procedure FileExitClick(Sender: TObject);
    procedure EditCutClick(Sender: TObject);
    procedure EditCopyClick(Sender: TObject);
    procedure EditPasteClick(Sender: TObject);
    procedure FileNewClick(Sender: TObject);
    procedure FileSaveClick(Sender: TObject);
    procedure FileOpenClick(Sender: TObject);
    procedure FileSaveAsClick(Sender: TObject);
    procedure EditUndoClick(Sender: TObject);
    procedure EditSelectAllClick(Sender: TObject);
```

continues

LISTING 8.1. CONTINUED

```
    procedure EditWordWrapClick(Sender: TObject);
    procedure HelpAboutClick(Sender: TObject);
private
  { Private declarations }
public
  { Public declarations }
end;
```

It is important to understand that the section between the first line of the class declaration and the `private` keyword should be considered off-limits. As they say, "Don't go there." Leave this section to Delphi to manage.

Caution

Placing any code in the Delphi-managed section of a form's class declaration can cause problems with your program. In some cases, you might just get compiler errors. In other cases, your program might be beyond repair (unusual but possible). Get in the habit of avoiding this section of the class declaration like the plague.

You can safely place any of your own class data fields or method declarations in either the `private` or the `public` section of the class declaration. You could add a `protected` section and place data fields or methods there too, of course.

A WORD ABOUT STATUS BARS AND HINTS

In a moment you're going to add support for hint text displayed in the status bar of the ScratchPad program. Before you do, though, you need a brief primer on how hint text is handled.

When the Application object's ShowHint property is set to True (the default) and the mouse cursor is placed over a component that also has its ShowHint property set to True, a hint event is triggered. The Application object has an event called OnHint that occurs whenever a hint event is triggered. The Application's Hint property will contain the hint text for the control that generated the hint event. An application can use the OnHint event to display the hint on a status bar.

The problem is that you can't directly access the OnHint event of the Application object. What you can do, however, is reassign the value of OnHint to point to one of your own methods. Then, when the hint event occurs, the event gets rerouted to your own OnHint handler. To do that, you have to write your own event handler for the OnHint event. Let's do that next.

Adding a Method to Your Code

To illustrate adding a method to an application, let's implement hint text for the ScratchPad program you wrote earlier. First, reopen the ScratchPad program.

8

What you do in this series of steps is assign hint text to each of the toolbar buttons and prepare the status bar to receive the hints. Remember, the toolbar buttons you placed on the toolbar on Day 6 are just for show right now, but that doesn't prevent you from adding hints to them. Do the following:

1. Ensure that the ScratchPad main form is visible. Click the first button on the main form's toolbar.

2. Locate the Hint property in the Object Inspector and type the following for the hint text:

   ```
   Open¦Open an Existing File
   ```

3. Change the ShowHint property to True.

4. Repeat steps 2 and 3 for any other buttons on the toolbar, adding whatever hint text you like for each button.

5. Click the status bar component along the bottom of the main form. Change the SimplePanel property to True. This enables the full status bar to display a text string through the SimpleText property.

Okay, now everything is ready to go, so it's time you did what you came here for. You're going to create your own OnHint handler and then name the method MyOnHint. Let's take this one step at a time. First, add the method declaration to the class declaration. Here goes:

1. Switch to the Code Editor and be sure the SPMain.pas file is visible.

2. Scroll down through the class declaration for the TScratchPad class until you locate the private section. Add this line of code after the private keyword:

   ```
   procedure MyOnHint(Sender : TObject);
   ```

   To give you perspective, the last few lines of the class declaration should now look like this:

   ```
   private
     { Private declarations }
     procedure MyOnHint(Sender : TObject);
   public
     { Public declarations }
   end;
   ```

Okay, so far, so good. Now you've added the method declaration for your new method. Two more steps and you'll be done. First, you need to add the actual method to the implementation section. After that, you need to assign your new method to the `Application` object's `OnHint` event. Follow these steps:

1. Scroll to the bottom of the implementation section.

2. Enter the following code (just above the unit's final end keyword):
   ```
   procedure TMainForm.MyOnHint(Sender: TObject);
   begin
     StatusBar.SimpleText := Application.Hint;
   end;
   ```

3. Go to the Object Inspector. Select the main form, `ScratchPad`, from the Object Selector.

4. Switch to the Events page in the Object Inspector and double-click in the Value column next to the `OnCreate` event. The Code Editor is displayed and is ready for you to type code.

5. Enter a line of code so that the `FormCreate` method looks like this:
   ```
   procedure TMainForm.FormCreate(Sender: TObject);
   begin
     Application.OnHint := MyOnHint;
   end;
   ```

6. Compile and run the program. The long hint text you entered will appear in the status bar when you place the mouse cursor over a toolbar button. The short hint text will be displayed in a tooltip when you pause over the button.

Step 2 sets the hint text (from the `Hint` property of the `Application` object) to the `SimpleText` property of the `StatusBar` component. Step 5 takes the method you created in step 2 and assigns it to the `OnHint` event of the `Application` class. Each time an `OnHint` event occurs, the `MyOnHint` method is called and the hint text is displayed in the status bar.

> **Note**
>
> *New to 4* In the preceding example of implementing status bar hints, I took you the long way around. I wanted to show you how to add a method to your form and how to assign a method to an event. There is an easier way to implement status bar text, though. Simply set the status bar's `AutoHint` property to `True`. You still have to specify each component's hint text, but the rest is automatic. The `AutoHint` property is new in Delphi 4.

Adding a Class Data Field

Adding class data fields to a class generated in Delphi works in exactly the same way. All you have to do is ensure that you add the data field to the private or public section of the class declaration as you did earlier when adding a method to the class. You can also place data field declarations in the protected section if you have created one for your class.

Deleting Delphi-Generated Code

There might be times when you need to delete code that Delphi generated in your application. For example, you might have a button on a form that, due to design changes, is no longer needed. To delete the button, of course, all you have to do is select the button in the Form Designer and press the Delete button on the keyboard. No more button. Delphi deletes the button, but the OnClick handler associated with that button is still in the code.

Delphi knows that the button associated with that OnClick handler is gone, but it still doesn't delete the event handler because it is possible that other components are using the same event handler. It's up to you to delete the event handler if you want it removed from your code.

The actual deletion of the event handler is a trivial task. Simply remove the code from the event handler and save or compile the project. Delphi will remove any empty event handlers it finds.

Note

Some might say that if you are unsure about an event handler being used by other components, just leave it in the code. That's a bad solution, in my opinion. You need to take the responsibility for knowing what is in your code and getting rid of any unused methods. Although unused code doesn't hurt anything, it leads to a larger .exe file. In some cases, unused code can lead to performance degradation. Be diligent in paring your programs of unused or inefficient code.

Creating Component Templates

NEW TERM A *component template* is a component or group of components that you modify as desired and then save for later reuse.

Component templates enable you to create, save, and reuse groups of components. In fact, a component template doesn't have to be a group of components at all—it can be a single component. A quick example would probably help you see how useful component templates can be. But first, a quick lesson on the Windows edit control.

The standard Windows single-line edit control, like all Windows controls, has certain predefined behaviors. One of those behaviors deals with the way the Enter key is handled. If the user presses the Enter key when in an edit control, Windows looks for a default button on the window. If a default button is found, Windows essentially clicks the button.

What does this mean to you? Let's say you have several edit controls on a form and a default button such as an OK button (or any button with the Default property set to True). When you press the Enter key when an edit control has focus, the form will close. If there is no default button on the form, Windows will just beep. Although this is standard Windows behavior, many users find it annoying and confusing. What many users prefer, particularly when working with a form that has several edit fields, is that the Enter key moves focus to the next control rather than closing the form.

The solution to this problem is really pretty simple. All you have to do is provide an event handler for the OnKeyPress event and add code so that it looks like this:

```
procedure TForm1.Edit1KeyPress(Sender: TObject; var Key: Char);
begin
  if Key = Char(VK_RETURN) then begin
    Key := #0;
    PostMessage(Handle, WM_NEXTDLGCTL, 0, 0);
  end;
end;
```

This code first checks to see whether the key pressed was the Enter key (a virtual key code of VK_RETURN). If so, it sets the value of Key to #0. This eliminates the beep that Windows emits when the Enter key is pressed in an edit control. The next line posts a Windows WM_NEXTDLGCTL message to the form. This message sets focus to the next control in the tab order. That's all there is to it.

After you have written the code for your new Edit component, you can save it as a component template. When you do, all the code is saved as well. Any code templates you create go into the Templates page of the Component palette. Let's create a component template so that you can see how it works. Perform these steps:

1. Place an Edit component on a blank form. Change its Name property to EnterAsTab and clear its Text property.

8

2. Switch to the Events page in the Object Inspector and create an event handler for the OnKeyPress event. Enter this code in the event handler:

```
if Key = Char(VK_RETURN) then begin
  Key := #0;
  PostMessage(Handle, WM_NEXTDLGCTL, 0, 0);
end;
```

3. Be sure the Edit component is selected and choose Component|Create Component Template from the main menu. The Component Template Information dialog box is displayed.

4. Enter TEnterAsTab in the Component Name field. The Component Template Information dialog box should now look like the one shown in Figure 8.12.

FIGURE 8.12.

The Component Template Information dialog box.

5. Click OK to save the component template.

Now your Component palette has a tab called Templates. Switch to the Templates tab (you might have to scroll the Component palette tabs to find it), select your new component, and place it on the form. You will see that the code for the OnKeyPress event handler was included when the component was placed on the form.

 Tip

If you have several of these components on a form, the code for the OnKeyPress event handler would be repeated for every EnterAsTab component on the form. Rather than duplicating code, you can just place one EnterAsTab component on the form. Any other components could be standard Edit components that have their OnKeyPress events hooked up to the OnKeyPress event handler for the EnterAsTab component.

One of the biggest advantages of component templates is that the code written for each component's event handlers is saved along with the component. Component templates enable you to have a collection of customized components at your disposal: common dialog boxes with predefined filters and titles, speed buttons with glyphs already included, list boxes or combo boxes that automatically load items from a file, or any of a number of other possibilities.

Although the concept of a component template works for a single component, it makes even more sense when dealing with multiple components. If you have a group of components that you place on your forms over and over again, you can create a component template from those components. After you have created a component template, reusing a group of components is only a click away.

 Note   There are certainly some similarities between component templates and saving forms in the Object Repository. Use component templates for groups of components that you typically use as part of a larger form. Use the Object Repository to save entire forms that you want to reuse.

Using Resource Files

 NEW TERM   Every Windows program uses resources. *Resources* are those elements of a program that support the program but are not executable code.

A typical Windows program's resources include

- Accelerators
- Bitmaps
- Cursors
- Dialog boxes
- Icons
- Menus
- Data tables
- String tables
- Version information
- User-defined specialty resources (sound and video files, for example)

 Note   Version information can be easily added to your Delphi projects through the Version Info tab of the Project Options dialog box. The Project Options dialog box is discussed in detail tomorrow.

8

Resources are generally contained in a *resource script file* (a text file with an .rc extension). The resource script file is compiled by a resource compiler and then bound to the application's .exe file during the link phase.

Resources are usually thought of as being bound to the executable file. Some resources, such as bitmaps, string tables, and wave files, can be placed in external files (.bmp, .txt, and .wav) or they can be bound to the .exe and contained within the application file. You can opt to do it either way. Placing resources in the .exe file has two main advantages:

- The resources can be accessed more quickly because it takes less time to locate a resource in the executable file than it does to load it from a disk file.
- The program file and resources can be contained in a single unit (the .exe file) without the need for a lot of supporting files.

The downside to this approach is that your .exe will be slightly larger. The program file won't be any larger than the combined external resource files plus the executable, but the extra size could result in slightly longer load times for the program.

Your exact needs will determine whether you decide to keep your resources in external files or have your resources bound to the .exe. The important point to remember is that you can do it either way (or even both ways in the same program).

Resources in Delphi

A traditional Windows program will almost always contain at least one dialog box and an icon. A Delphi application, however, is a little different. First of all, there are no true dialog boxes in a Delphi application, so there are no dialog box resources per se (Delphi forms are stored as resources, but they are RCDATA resources and not dialog box resources).

A Delphi application does have a traditional icon resource, though. Delphi takes care of creating the resource file for the icon for you when you create the application. Similarly, when you choose bitmaps for speed buttons, Image components, or BitBtn components, Delphi includes the bitmap file you chose as part of the form's resource. The form and all its resources are then bound to the program file when the application is built. It's all more or less handled for you automatically.

There are times, however, when you will want to implement resources aside from the normal Delphi processes. For example, if you want to do animation, you will have to have a series of bitmaps that can be loaded as resources for the fastest possible execution speed. In that kind of situation, you are going to need to know how to bind the resources to your Delphi program file.

The act of binding the resource file to the executable is trivial, actually. It's much more difficult to actually create the resources. Creating basic resources such as bitmaps, icons, and cursors is not difficult with a good resource editor, but creating professional quality 3D bitmaps and icons is an art in itself. How many times have you seen a fairly decent program with really awful bitmap buttons? I've seen plenty. (Sorry, I'm getting off-track here.) You can create bitmaps, icons, and cursors with the Delphi Image Editor. (The Image Editor is discussed on Day 11, "Delphi Tools and Options.")

If you are going to create string resources, user data resources, wave file resources, or other specialty resources, you will probably need a third-party resource editor.

> If you have an old copy of Borland Pascal lying around, you can use the Resource Workshop from that product to edit specialty resources. After creating the resources, you will have an .rc file that you can compile into a .res file using the Borland Resource Compiler (BRCC32.EXE). The Borland Resource Compiler comes with Delphi. Technically, you could create the .rc file with any text editor and compile it with the Resource Compiler, but in reality it is much easier to use a resource editor.

Compiling Resource Files

After you create a resource file, you need to compile it with the resource compiler. You can do this in one of two ways:

- Compile the resource file manually from the command line.
- Add a batch file target to your project group.

Either way you end up with a .res file that you link to your application (I'll discuss that in just a bit). Project groups are discussed in detail tomorrow.

Compiling from the Command Line

To compile a resource file from the command line, simply open a command prompt box in Windows and enter a line similar to this:

```
brcc32 jjres.rc
```

This assumes, of course, that your Delphi 4\Bin directory is on the system path. If not, you'll have to type the full path to BRCC32.EXE. The resource compiler is very fast, so you might not even notice that the resource script was compiled.

Using a Batch File Project

Adding a batch file project to your project group is just as simple as compiling from the command line and has the added benefit of ensuring that the resource file will always be up to date. To get an idea how a batch file project works, perform these steps:

1. Create a new application. This application is just to add perspective to the process.

2. Choose View | Project Manager to open the Delphi Project Manager.

3. Click the Add New Project button on the Project Manager toolbar. The Object Repository is displayed.

4. Double-click the Batch File icon to create a new batch file project. The batch file project is added to the Project Manager as Project2.

5. Right-click on the batch file node and choose Save. Save the file as test.bat.

6. Right-click the batch file node again and choose Edit | Options. The Batch File Options dialog box is displayed.

7. Enter the following text in the Commands memo field:

```
del myfile.res
brcc32 myfile.rc
```

Figure 8.13 shows the Batch File Options dialog box after performing this step.

FIGURE 8.13.

The Batch File Options dialog box.

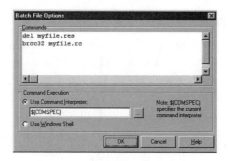

8. Click OK to close the Batch File Options dialog box.

What you did in this exercise is create a batch file that will execute when the project group is compiled. The batch file commands you entered in step 7 delete a file called myfile.res and then call the Delphi resource compiler to build myfile.rc. Compiling myfile.rc with the resource compiler will produce a file called myfile.res.

Presumably the next project in the project group would be the project that uses myfile.res. You might be wondering why I delete the myfile.res first. I delete the file so that I am certain the resource compiler will build the file. If the resource compiler fails to create the resource file, any subsequent projects that use that resource file will fail to compile and a compiler error will alert me that something has gone wrong building the resource file.

| Note | The book's code for today includes a project group that uses a batch file project in exactly this way. You can download the code from http://www.mcp.com/info. |

Linking Resource Files to Your Executable

After you compile the resource script file, you must bind the compiled resource file to the program's executable file. You do this with the $R compiler directive. For example, to bind the binary resources contained in myfile.res, you place this line near the top of your main form's unit:

```
{$R myfile.res}
```

That's all there is to it. As long as the specified file exists, Delphi will bind the compiled resources to the executable file at link time.

A Sample Program Using Resources

Listing 8.2 contains the main form unit for a program called Jumping Jack. This program shows a simple animation with sound effects. The main form contains just two buttons, an Image component and a Label component. The Jumping Jack program illustrates several aspects of using resources in a Delphi application. Specifically, it shows how to load a bitmap stored as a resource, how to load and display a string resource, and how to play wave audio contained as a resource. Listing 8.3 is a partial listing of the resource file that is used by the Jumping Jack program. Examine the listings, and then I'll discuss what the program does.

| Tip | Download this project from http://www.mcp.com/info to examine the resource file and the project group. |

LISTING 8.2. JJMain.pas.

```
unit JmpJackU;

interface

uses
  Windows, Messages, SysUtils, Classes, Graphics, Controls,
  Forms, Dialogs, StdCtrls, ExtCtrls, MMSystem;

{$R JJRES.RES}

const
  IDS_UP = 101;
  IDS_DOWN = 102;

type
  TMainForm = class(TForm)
    Image: TImage;
    Label1: TLabel;
    Start: TButton;
    Stop: TButton;
    procedure FormCreate(Sender: TObject);
    procedure StartClick(Sender: TObject);
    procedure StopClick(Sender: TObject);
  private
    { Private declarations }
    Done : Boolean;
    procedure DrawImage(var Name: string);
  public
    { Public declarations }
  end;

var
  MainForm: TMainForm;

implementation

{$R *.DFM}

procedure TMainForm.FormCreate(Sender: TObject);
begin
  Image.Picture.Bitmap.
    LoadFromResourceName(HInstance, 'ID_BITMAP1');
end;

procedure TMainForm.StartClick(Sender: TObject);
var
  S       : string;
```

continues

LISTING 8.2. CONTINUED

```
    ResName : string;
    I       : Integer;
    Buff    : array [0..9] of Char;
begin
  { When the Start button is clicked the animation }
  { loop starts. The bitmap resources are named    }
  { ID_BITMAP1 through ID_BITMAP5 so we'll start    }
  { with a string called 'ID_BITMAP' and append     }
  { the last digit when needed. }
  S := 'ID_BITMAP';

  { A flag to let us know when we're done. }
  Done := False;

  { Start the loop and keep looping until the }
  { 'Stop' button is pressed. }

  while not Done do begin
    { Loop through the five bitmaps starting with }
    { 1 and ending with 5. }
    for I := 1 to 5 do begin
      { Append the value of 'I' to the end of the string }
      { to build a string containing the resource name.  }
      ResName := S + IntToStr(I);
      { Call a method to display the bitmap. }
      DrawImage(ResName);
    end;
    { Load the 'Up' string resource using the WinAPI }
    { function LoadString, display the string, and   }
    { tell Windows to repaint the Label. }
    LoadString(HInstance, IDS_UP, Buff, SizeOf(Buff));
    Label1.Caption := Buff;
    Label1.Refresh;
    { Play the 'up' sound using the WinAPI function }
    { PlaySound. Play it asynchronously. }
    PlaySound('ID_WAVEUP',
      HInstance, SND_ASYNC or SND_RESOURCE);
    { Pause for a moment at the top of the jump. }
    Sleep(200);
    { Repeat all of the above except in reverse. }
    for I := 5 downto 1 do begin
      ResName := S + IntToStr(I);
      DrawImage(ResName);
    end;
    PlaySound('ID_WAVEDOWN',
      HInstance, SND_ASYNC or SND_RESOURCE);
```

```
    LoadString(HInstance, IDS_DOWN, Buff, SizeOf(Buff));
    Label1.Caption := Buff;
    Label1.Refresh;
    Sleep(200);
  end;
end;

procedure TMainForm.StopClick(Sender: TObject);
begin
  { Stop button pressed, so tell the loop to }
  { stop executing. }
  Done := True;
end;

procedure TMainForm.DrawImage(var Name : string);
begin
  { Load the bitmap from a resource }
  { using the name passed to us. }
  Image.Picture.Bitmap.
    LoadFromResourceName(HInstance, name);
  { Must pump the message loop so that Windows }
  { gets a chance to display the bitmap. }
  Application.ProcessMessages;
  { Take a short nap so the animation doesn't }
  { go too fast. }
  Sleep(20);
end;

end.
```

LISTING 8.3. JJRes.rc.

```
STRINGTABLE
BEGIN
 101, "Up"
 102, "Down"
END

ID_WAVEUP    WAVE "up.wav"
ID_WAVEDOWN WAVE "down.wav"

ID_BITMAP1 BITMAP LOADONCALL MOVEABLE DISCARDABLE IMPURE
BEGIN
 '42 4D 76 02 00 00 00 00 00 00 76 00 00 00 28 00'
 '00 00 20 00 00 00 20 00 00 00 01 00 04 00 00 00'
 '00 00 00 02 00 00 00 00 00 00 00 00 00 00 00 00'
 remainder of bitmap resources follow
```

ANALYSIS The main form's class declaration declares a Boolean data field called Done that is used to determine when to stop the animation. The DrawImage method is used to display the bitmap in the Image component.

In Listing 8.2, notice that two Windows API functions are used to load the string and wave file resources. In the StartClick method, the LoadString function loads a string resource into a text buffer based on the numerical identifier of the string (refer to Listing 8.3 to see how the string resources are created). The string is then assigned to the Caption property of the Label component on the form.

The PlaySound function is used to play a wave file contained as a resource. The SND_ASYNC flag used with the PlaySound function tells Windows to play the sound and immediately return control to the program (playing sounds is discussed in detail on Day 12, "Graphics and Multimedia Programming"). This enables the animation to continue while the sound is being played. The SND_RESOURCE flag tells Windows that the sound is contained as a resource and not as a file on disk. Both the LoadString and PlaySound functions use the HInstance global variable to tell Windows to look in the executable file for the resources. The bitmap resources are loaded using the VCL method LoadFromResourceName.

The first five lines of Listing 8.3 illustrate how a string table looks in a resource script file. Creating string tables is very easy with any text editor. Following that, a WAVE resource is created for each of the two wave files, which were previously recorded and reside in the project's directory. When the resource compiler sees the WAVE declaration, it reads the individual sound files and compiles them into the binary resource file.

Note

As you can see from Listing 8.3, you can create some types of resources easily with a text editor. If you have bitmaps and wave audio stored as external files, you can include them in an .RC file as illustrated in Listing 8.3 and have them compiled into the binary resource file using the resource compiler. Later, the binary resource file can be bound to your application's executable file.

Listing 8.3 is a partial listing. Bitmaps created with a traditional resource editor are often contained in the resource file as numerical data. The resource descriptions for bitmaps can get very long. The rest of the bitmap resource descriptions for the Jumping Jack bitmaps require about 200 lines of resource code, so I decided not to list them all. Figure 8.14 shows Jumping Jack in mid-stride.

FIGURE 8.14.

*Jumping Jack in
action.*

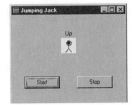

8

Creating additional resources for your programs is not rocket science, but it is not exactly trivial, either. It takes some time to realize how it all fits together. You might never need to add additional resources to your applications. If you do, though, it's good to have an idea where to begin. If this section left you a little dazed and confused, don't worry. Over time, it all starts to make sense.

Note

Bitmaps, icons, and cursors found in other programs are usually copyrighted material. Don't use resources from any copyrighted program without permission. Further, assume all programs are copyrighted unless they are specifically said to be freeware. You are free to use the bitmaps, icons, and cursors that are provided with Delphi (in the `Common Files\Borland Shared Files\Images` directory) in your applications without permission from Borland.

Using Packages

After your application is written you can deploy it in one of two ways. (*Deploying* means the act of distributing your application to your users.) You might be distributing your application to the general public or possibly to users within your company. Either way, you need to know what options are available to you. Essentially you have two choices: static linking or dynamic linking using packages. In this section, I'll discuss those options so that you can make an informed choice on how to deploy your application. I'll start with a discussion of packages and then I'll discuss deployment options.

What's a Package?

Before I discuss the options available to you, it is a good idea to define what a package is.

 A *package* is a piece of compiled code that resides in a file with an extension of BPL.

That explanation probably doesn't tell you enough, so let me explain further. When you take off the wrappings, a package is, essentially, just a DLL with an extension of .bpl rather than the traditional .dll extension. (There's a bit more to it than that, but that description is close enough for the purposes here.) There are two types of packages in Delphi: runtime packages and design packages. I'll go over each of these two types next so that you can get an understanding of how packages work.

Runtime Packages

A runtime package contains code your application needs to run. Although Delphi provides many different packages, the primary package is called VCL40.BPL. This package contains all the base VCL code in one package. If you choose to use packages in your application, your application will load a package called VCL40.BPL and call routines from that package as needed. If your application is a database application, it will also load VCLDB40.BPL and call routines from that package as needed. There are other Delphi packages in addition to the two mentioned here.

In addition to the VCL packages, your application might require other packages. This will be the case if you are using any third-party components or any components that you write yourself. You will have to check the documentation for any third-party components to find out which packages your application requires to run. I'm getting ahead of myself a little, so let me tell you about design packages and then I'll get back to deploying applications that use packages.

Design Packages

To explain design packages it might be a good idea to first give you a short tutorial on component design. Most components created for Delphi include a runtime package and a design package. The runtime package contains all the code needed for a component to operate. The design package contains the code needed for the component to operate on a form at design time, including property editors and component editors.

The design package has a Requires list that tells Delphi which packages it requires to operate. The design package almost always requires code from the runtime package and probably code from one or more VCL packages as well. It's important to understand that one package (both runtime and design) can contain the code for several components. It's not necessary to have a separate package for each component.

Because design packages contain just the code needed to display components at design time, they are usually much smaller than their runtime counterparts. Design packages are used by Delphi only at design time—they are not needed for your application to operate.

Static Linking Versus Dynamic Linking

Now that you know a little about packages, you can learn about static linking versus dynamic linking.

Static Linking

When an application uses static linking of the VCL, it doesn't use packages at all. Any code your application requires to run is linked directly into your application's executable file. Your application is a standalone program and doesn't require any supporting files (packages or DLLs).

Note

> There are exceptions to every rule. The statement that a statically linked application doesn't require any supporting DLLs makes a couple of assumptions. The first assumption is that the application is not a database application. A Delphi database application needs the Borland Database Engine (BDE) to operate. The BDE is primarily a collection of DLLs, so a database application will require DLLs to operate, even if the application is statically linked. The second assumption is that the application doesn't use any ActiveX controls. ActiveX controls are actually a form of DLL, so if your application uses ActiveX controls, it is no longer a standalone application.

Although Delphi gives you a choice of linking options, static linking is the default. Static linking has two primary advantages over dynamic linking:

- The first advantage is that you don't have to worry about shipping any additional files with your application. Your application contains all the code it needs to run and no runtime libraries are required.

- The second advantage is that an application that is statically linked is generally smaller in total size than an application that requires packages. I'll talk about this more in just a bit when I talk about the advantages and disadvantages of dynamic linking.

Static linking has one major drawback but it only shows up in applications that use many user-defined DLLs. The drawback is that the VCL and RTL code is duplicated in every module (the main application itself) and in every DLL. This means that code is duplicated unnecessarily.

For example, let's say that every module requires a minimum of 200KB of VCL base code and RTL code. Now let's say that you have a main application and 10 supporting DLLs. That means that 2200KB of code is used (11 modules × 200KB each) when only

200KB is actually required. The application and DLLs are all statically linked and can't share the VCL and RTL code among themselves.

Dynamic Linking

Dynamic linking refers to a scenario in which an application dynamically loads its library code at runtime. In the case of a Delphi application, this means that any required packages are loaded at runtime. Required packages will certainly include one or more VCL packages and might require third-party packages as well.

> **Note**
>
> The loading of packages by your application is automatic. You don't have to write code to load the packages. Delphi takes care of that for you. Choosing dynamic linking over static linking doesn't require any changes to your code. It does require changes to the way you deploy your application, which I tell you about shortly.

Dynamic linking has one primary advantage over static linking: Several modules can share code from a central location (the packages). Remember earlier when I gave an example of an application and 10 supporting DLLs? Using dynamic linking, the application and all DLLs can all share code from the VCL packages. Each module will be at least 200KB smaller because all the base code is contained in the runtime DLLs. This is an advantage when your overall product contains several applications or many DLLs.

Dynamic linking comes with a couple of problems. The first problem is that the packages and DLLs that you need to ship with your application can be quite large. The primary VCL package, VCL40.BPL, is 1.8MB alone. Your application might require other packages besides the base VCL package. This means that your application will require a minimum of 1.8MB of DLLs to run.

A second problem with dynamic linking is more subtle and more troublesome. The problem could be summed up in one word: versioning. To explain the problem, let me give you a possible scenario. Let's say you create an application using Delphi 4.02 (assuming a couple of revisions to Delphi) and that you use dynamic linking, which requires you to ship the VCL packages and RTL DLL. Your customer installs your application on his or her machine and everything works fine.

Meanwhile, I build an application using Delphi 4.0 (I'm too cheap to pay the shipping for the update) and I also use dynamic linking. Your customer buys my application and installs it. My installation program is homemade and doesn't play by the rules, so I overwrite the packages and DLLs that your application installed. Suddenly your application quits working because my packages are older than yours and the two are not compatible. Do you see the problem?

In reality, commercial software companies such as Inprise prevent this problem by naming their packages and DLLs by different names for each release of a product and by embedding version information in the packages and DLLs. (A good installation program will check the version number and only install a package if the package is newer than any existing packages on the user's system.) But packages from Borland aren't the real problem.

The real problem comes when using components from companies that are less careful about how they do business. If you buy a component package from Billy Bob's Software Company, you are trusting that Billy Bob knows what he is doing when it comes to creating packages. That might or might not be a good assumption. Let's face it, with the boom of the Internet, components are available from a wide variety of sources. You don't know what you are getting in a lot of cases, so be careful when purchasing inexpensive or freeware components.

So Which Is Better?

I can hear you thinking, "So should I use static linking or dynamic linking?" The answer to that question depends on the type of applications you write. In general, if you are writing a single small or medium-sized application, you should use static linking. If you are writing very large applications or applications with a large number of DLLs, you should probably use dynamic linking.

A simple case study might help put this in perspective. On Day 6 you created the `ScratchPad` program. That program compiles to around 365KB (give or take a few KB) when static linking is used. If you link `ScratchPad` using packages, you can get the EXE size down to around 21KB, *but* you have to ship 1.8MB of packages. As you can see, dynamic linking is not a good choice in this case.

Using Runtime Packages in Your Applications

If you choose to use dynamic linking, you need to change only one setting in the project options. Here's what you need to do:

1. Choose Project | Options from the main menu to bring up the Project Options dialog box.

2. Click the Packages tab and check the Build with runtime packages option near the bottom of the page (you can ignore the top of the page that deals with design packages).

3. Click OK to close the Project Options dialog box.

4. Rebuild the project.

That's all there is to it. Remember, using dynamic linking doesn't require any changes to your code.

Deploying Applications Using Packages

Deploying an application that uses dynamic linking requires you to know which packages your application uses. If you followed the steps in the previous section, you can be assured that you need VCL40.BPL at a minimum. You might need other VCL packages as well depending on the components your application uses.

To find out for sure, you have to run a utility such as TDUMP.EXE and examine the imports that your EXE references. TDUMP can be found in your \Delphi 4\Bin directory. To run TDUMP, just open a command-prompt box and switch to the directory where your application resides. Then type the following at the command line (assuming that \Delphi 4\Bin is on your path, you don't have to type the path to TDUMP):

```
tdump myproject.exe
```

Get ready on the Pause button because TDUMP will start spitting out information right away. Somewhere along the line you will see some lines like this:

```
Imports from Vcl40.bpl
    System::initialization() __fastcall
    System::Finalization() __fastcall
    System::RegisterModule(System::TLibModule*) __fastcall
```

This might be repeated several times. You will have to watch for any files with a .BPL extension and make note of their filenames. When you are done, you will have a list of packages that you must ship with your application.

Note   The output from TDUMP can be redirected to a text file for easier viewing. For example:

```
tdump myproject.exe > dump.txt
```

Now you can open DUMP.TXT in the Delphi Code Editor and view the contents.

Note

> You can save yourself a lot of time and trouble by getting a good installation program. InstallShield Express comes with Delphi Professional and Client/Server versions, so you might already have an installation program that you can use. I also like Wise Install from Great Lakes Business Solutions. The better installation programs figure out which packages your application requires and automatically includes them in the installation. I don't recommend writing your own installation program under any circumstances. There are just too many issues that you can fail to take into account when writing an installation program.

8

Most of the time you probably won't use runtime packages in your applications. On the other hand, sometimes packages are just what you need.

Summary

The Object Repository is a great tool for reusing previously created forms, dialog boxes, projects, and other objects. The capability to add your own objects to the Repository is a huge benefit to you.

The Dialog Wizard and Application Wizard take it a step further and guide you through the creation process. The Application Wizard, in particular, is a very useful tool. In the middle of the chapter you learned how to add data fields and methods to the classes that Delphi generates.

Toward the end of the chapter I touched on the different types of resources that you might need to incorporate into your applications and how to add them to your Delphi projects. At the end of the chapter I talked about packages. Packages give you flexibility in deciding how to deploy your applications and also make installing custom components easier.

Workshop

The Workshop contains quiz questions to help you solidify your understanding of the material covered and exercises to provide you with experience in using what you have learned. You can find the answers to the quiz questions in Appendix A, "Answers to the Quiz Questions."

Q&A

Q **When would I use the Use option of the Object Repository?**

A When you have an object stored in the Object Repository that you want to update or make other changes to.

Q **Is there a limit to the number of objects that can be stored in the Object Repository?**

A Technically, you can store as many objects as you like. Remember, though, that the purpose of the Object Repository is to help you quickly locate and reuse your forms, dialog boxes, and other objects. If you put too many seldom-used objects in the Object Repository, you will start to lose efficiency because it takes longer to find the specific object you are looking for. It also takes longer for the Object Repository to load and display all those objects.

Q **I've got a bunch of old objects in the Object Repository that I don't use any more. How can I get rid of them?**

A Choose Tools | Repository from the main menu. The Object Repository configuration dialog box is displayed. To remove an object, first select the object in the Objects list box and then click the Delete Object button. The object will be removed from the Object Repository.

Q **I had an object stored in the Object Repository. Now, when I try to use that object, I get a message box that says, `Unable to find both a form and a source file`. What's the problem?**

A You have either moved or deleted the source or form file for the object. The Object Repository keeps track of the directory where the object is stored. If you move or delete the object, the Object Repository is unable to find the object and reports an error.

Q **Can I add objects to the New page of the Object Repository?**

A No. The New page of the Object Repository is fixed. It cannot be deleted or modified. You'll have to place your objects on another page.

Q **I added a method to my main form class. Now I can't compile. What's the problem?**

A You probably added the method declaration to the Delphi-managed section of the class declaration accidentally. Be sure that the declaration for your method is in either the `public` or the `private` section of the class declaration (or the `protected` section if you have one).

Q I have a resource editor that enables me to decompile resources contained in other programs. This lets me "borrow" bitmaps and other resources from other programs. Is this okay?

A The short answer is, "No." You should assume all resources in other programs to be copyrighted material that cannot be freely copied. Consult a lawyer for a qualified opinion.

Q I have a lot of bitmaps and sound files that go with my application. Can I put all those resources in a file other than the program's executable file?

A Yes. You can store your resources in a dynamic link library (DLL).

Quiz

1. When do you use the Inherit option when selecting an object in the Object Repository?

2. What is the procedure for saving a project to the Object Repository?

3. What happens to inherited forms when you change the base form?

4. Where in the form's class declaration do you place user method declarations?

5. Where do you place the method definition (the method itself) when you add your own methods to Delphi code?

6. How can you determine who wrote a particular object in the Object Repository?

7. Where do you add and delete pages in the Object Repository?

8. Is it easier to create a basic application from scratch or by using the Application Wizard?

9. Which is better for small applications: static linking or dynamic linking using packages?

10. Can you create a resource script file containing a string table with a text editor?

Exercises

1. Create a new form. Add several components of your choosing to the form. Save the form to the Forms page of the Object Repository with the name BaseForm.

2. Start a new application. Choose File | New to view the Object Repository. Switch to the Forms page. Click the Inherit radio button. Choose the BaseForm object you created in exercise 1 and add it to the application. (Be sure you used the Inherit option.) Save the project and close it.

3. Open the `BaseForm` object you created in exercise 1. Delete all components on the form and save the form.

4. Reopen the project you created in exercise 2. Display the new form you created in that exercise. Note that the components are all gone. (Remember, you inherited this object, so all changes made to the base form were also made to the inherited form.)

5. Choose Tools | Repository from the main menu. Delete the `BaseForm` created earlier.

6. Create a project using the Application Wizard. Use all menu options and make the application an MDI application.

7. Add a multipage dialog box to the application you created in exercise 6. Use the Dialog Wizard.

8. Use the Object Repository to add an About box to the program you created in exercise 6.

9. Create a simple program and build it. Run Windows Explorer and examine the size of the `.EXE` created by Delphi. Now change the project options to use runtime packages. Rebuild the program. Check the size of the `.EXE` now. What is the difference in size?

10. Write "I will not borrow bitmaps from other programs." 100 times on the blackboard.

DAY 9

Projects, the Code Editor, and the Code Explorer

Today you learn more about the Delphi IDE and how it all works together to create real-world working programs. Specifically you learn about

- Projects and the Project Manager
- The Code Editor
- The Code Explorer

It will be a long day, but a rewarding one.

Everyone Needs a Project

On Day 4, "The Delphi IDE Explored," you were introduced to Delphi projects and found out a little about how projects work. In this section, I cover projects in detail. Projects are a fact of life with Delphi. You cannot create a program without a project. The project makes sure that everything works together to create a working application. The following sections talk about

- The Project Manager
- Project groups
- The Project Options dialog box

Using the Project Manager

At some point, every project needs some management. Maybe you must add a new source unit to the project, or maybe you must remove a source unit. You might need to add another type of file to the project, such as a binary resource file. You add and remove units and other project files through the Project Manager.

Project Groups

On Day 4, I said that a project is a collection of files that work together to create a stand-alone executable file or DLL. That's the definition of a project as far as the Delphi IDE is concerned. In the real world, you might have a different kind of project, such as a job that you have to complete.

A large project might include one or more executable files and several DLLs. Because some projects consist of more than a single executable program, Delphi enables you to group several Delphi projects together and deal with them as a single unit. This unit is called a *project group*.

Why Use Project Groups?

You might be wondering what advantage project groups provide. Project groups give you the following:

- Better control over a complete software project.
- The ability to work on a DLL and a test EXE for the DLL at the same time.
- The ability to build (compile and link) a group of projects all at one time.
- The ability to have several projects open at one time and to easily switch between open projects.
- A way to organize related projects.

A project that creates a single executable file doesn't need a project group. A single project can hardly be considered a group, right? In the case of a single project, the concept of a project group is out of place.

But imagine for a moment a program that includes an EXE and a single supporting DLL. Both the DLL and the EXE go together. Usually, if you are working on the DLL, you will want the EXE present so that you can immediately test any changes you make to the DLL. In this scenario, a project group makes perfect sense because the EXE and DLL go everywhere together.

You can create a project group that contains these two individual projects and save it. When you want to work on either the application or the DLL, you can open the project group rather than an individual project. When you open the project group, both the EXE project and the DLL project are displayed. You can work on either the DLL or the EXE in the Code Editor and switch back and forth between them any time you want. Figure 9.1 shows the Project Manager window with this type of project group open.

FIGURE 9.1.

The Project Manager window showing a project group.

Another reason to have a project group is so that you can group related projects. That probably sounds like it doesn't make much sense, so let me explain. Here at TurboPower Software we have a product called Async Professional, which is a collection of serial communications components. These components include three main categories: basic serial communications, faxing, and TAPI. We include dozens of sample programs with Async Professional covering each of these three categories.

Given that scenario, we could create a project group for all of our faxing examples, one for all of our TAPI examples, and one for all of our basic serial communications examples. Our users could then open the TAPI Examples project group and have all the TAPI examples in one neat package. The entire project group could be built at one time, thereby saving the time and aggravation of opening and building each project individually. In this case, the projects don't work together like a DLL and EXE do, but the projects are related, so the concept of a project group makes just as much sense.

The Active Project

In any project group there is always an active project. The active project is displayed in the Project Manager in bold type. In Figure 9.1, the active project is the project called TestD11. The active project is the project that will be built when you choose Make or Build from the Project menu on the Delphi main menu.

These menu items are modified each time a project is made the active project. For example, if the active project is called Project1, the menu items will be called Make Project1 and Build Project1. If a project called PictView is made the active project, these two menu items will be called Make PictView and Build PictView.

The active project also has significance when a new form or a new unit is added using the Project Manager. When you create a new form using the Project Manager, the new form will be added to the active project regardless of which node in the Project Manager is currently selected. The active project is also the project to which new forms or units are added if you add new elements via the Delphi main menu or the Delphi toolbar.

You can make a project the active project in one of several ways. One way is to select any item in the project node that you want to make the active project and click the Activate Selected Project button on the top of the Project Manager. Another way is to simply double-click the project node itself. Finally, you can choose Activate from the project node context menu to activate a particular project.

The Project Manager Window

New to 4 The Project Manager in Delphi 4 is brand-new. The Project Manager concept is not new to Delphi 4, but the current implementation is much better than the previous Project Manager. The Project Manager is the central controller for all of your projects and your program groups. It enables you to add files to a project, delete files from a project, view a unit or form, add projects to the project group, change the order of projects, and more. To display the Project Manager, choose View | Project Manager from the main menu or press Ctrl+Alt+F11.

The Project Manager window contains a tree view control that displays up to four levels. Those levels are as follows:

- The project group
- The projects within the project group
- Forms and other files within the project
- Individual form files and units under the form node

Naturally, the individual nodes can be collapsed or expanded as with any tree view control. The Project Manager nodes have icons that indicate whether the node contains a project, an individual file, a form, or a form/unit pair. Refer to Figure 9.1 to see the different icons and levels that the Project Manager displays.

In previous versions of Delphi, the Project Manager showed the path to any units as well as the unit filename. The Delphi 4 Project Manager does not show the path and filename in the same way. To see the path and filename, click on a unit in the Project Manager window and the Project Manager status bar will show the full path and filename for the unit (refer to Figure 9.1).

9

The Project Manager Context Menus

Most of the Project Manager's work is done through the Manager's context menus. There are four separate context menus for the Project Manager. The following sections describe each of the context menus.

The Project Group Context Menu

The project group context menu is the context menu you see when you right-click the project group node at the top of the Project Manager tree. Table 9.1 lists the project group context menu items that appear on this menu.

TABLE 9.1. THE PROJECT GROUP CONTEXT MENU ITEMS.

Item	Description
Add New Project	Opens the Object Repository so that you can choose a new target. Targets include applications, DLLs, forms, data modules, components, or any other object available from the Object Repository.
Add Existing Project	Opens a project file from disk and adds it to the project group.
Save Project Group	Saves the project group. Project groups have a .bpg extension.
Save Project Group As	Saves the project group with a new name.
View Project Group Source	Displays the project group source. The project group source is a special file (a makefile) that contains references to all projects within the project group.
Toolbar	Toggles the Project Manager toolbar on and off.
Status Bar	Toggles the Project Manager status bar on and off.
Dockable	Specifies whether the Project Manager is dockable.

The Toolbar, Status Bar, and Dockable menu items appear on each of the Project Manager context menus. I won't mention them again when I discuss the other Project Manager context menus.

The Project Context Menu

The project context menu is displayed when you right-click a project node in the Project Manager. Table 9.2 lists the context menu items specific to the project context menu.

TABLE 9.2. THE PROJECT CONTEXT MENU ITEMS.

Item	Description
Add	Opens the Add to Project dialog box so that you can add a file to the project. The same as choosing Project I Add to Project from the main menu or from the Delphi toolbar.
Remove File	Opens the Remove From Project dialog box so that you can remove a file from the project. The same as choosing Project I Remove from Project from the main menu or from the Delphi toolbar.
Save	Saves the project. The same as choosing File I Save from the Delphi main menu.
Options	Displays the Project Options dialog box for this project. The same as choosing Project I Options from the Delphi main menu.
Activate	Makes this project the active project.
Compile	Compiles this project. The difference between compile and build was discussed on Day 4.
Build	Builds this project.
View Source	Displays the project source file. The same as choosing Project I View Source from the Delphi main menu.
Close	Closes this project and all its files. If the project is part of a saved project group, the project node icon will be grayed out. The project is still part of the group but is not open in the IDE. If the project is part of the default project group, the project is closed and removed from the default group.
Remove Project	Removes this project from the project group. The project is not deleted from your hard drive, just removed from the project group. Same as clicking the Remove Selected Project button on the Project Manager toolbar.
Build Sooner	Moves the project up in the project tree. Projects are built from the top of the Project Manager down.
Build Later	Moves the project down in the project tree.

Note The Project Manager context menus are even more diverse than represented in this section. The project context menus contain additional items if the project is a Batch File or a Package project. The differences are not significant, so I won't go over those additional menu items.

The Unit Context Menu

The unit context menu is displayed when you right-click a unit node in the Project Manager. Table 9.3 lists the unit context menu items.

TABLE 9.3. THE UNIT CONTEXT MENU ITEMS.

Item	Description
Open	Displays the unit in the Code Editor (for standalone units) or Form Designer (if the unit has an associated form).
Remove From Project	Removes the unit from the project. The Project Manager does not prompt you to remove the unit and there is no undo for this action. You can always add the unit back to the project if you remove a unit by accident.
Save	Saves the unit. The same as choosing File | Save from the Delphi main menu.
Save As	Opens the Save As dialog box so that you can save the unit with a new name. The same as choosing File | Save As from the Delphi main menu.

The File Context Menu

The file context menu is displayed when you right-click a node other than the project group node, a project node, or a unit node (usually a .pas or .dfm file). This context menu has only one item. The Open menu item displays the selected node in either the Code Editor or the Form Designer, depending on the type of the selected node.

The Project Manager Toolbar and Keyboard Commands

In addition to the Project Manager context menus, the Project Manager has a toolbar to make working with the Project Manager easier. The Project Manager toolbar contains three buttons:

- The Add New Project button displays the Object Repository so that you can add a new project to the project group. This is the same as clicking the Add New Project menu item from the project context menu.

- The Remove Selected Project button removes the selected project from the project group. Use this button only to remove an entire project, not to remove a particular form or file from a project.
- The Activate Selected Project button makes the selected target the active project.

Keyboard commands include the Delete key and the Insert key. When you press Delete, the selected node is removed. If a project node is selected, the project is removed from the project group. If a unit node is selected, the unit is removed from the project to which the unit belongs. The Insert key behaves exactly the same as choosing Add to Project from the project context menu.

> The Project Manager toolbar buttons can be either large or small. By default, the Project Manager toolbar buttons are small. You can change the toolbar button size by dragging the bottom of the toolbar either up (to show the small buttons) or down (to show the large buttons).

Creating and Using Project Groups

Project groups are a great benefit for complex projects, but using project groups is not mandatory. You don't have to use project groups with every project. The Project Manager has a default project group called `ProjectGroup1` that is used when you don't specifically open or create a project group. Try this:

1. Choose File | Close All to close any open projects or project groups.
2. Choose File | New Application to create a new application.
3. Choose View | Project Manager to display the Project Manager. The Project Manager is displayed as shown in Figure 9.2.

FIGURE 9.2.

The Project Manager showing the default project group.

The project group called `ProjectGroup1` is a temporary project group. When you choose Save All from the File menu, you are prompted to save the project, but not the project group. If you want to save the project group, you must explicitly save it using the Save Project Group or Save Project Group As menu item from the Project Manager context menu.

Adding Units

Adding existing units to your projects is as simple as clicking the Add To Project button on the Project Manager toolbar or choosing Add To Project from the Project Manager context menu.

9

> **Note**
>
> You cannot add a unit to a project if a form with the same name already exists in the project. For example, if you have a form called MainForm and try to add a unit from another project that also has a form named MainForm, you get an error message from Delphi even if the filenames are different.

Removing Units

You use the Remove From Project option to remove files from the project. Alternatively, you can select the unit you want to remove and press the Delete key on the keyboard. Files removed from the project are not deleted from your hard drive, but are just removed from the project compile/link process.

> **Caution**
>
> Be careful when removing units from your projects. You must take care not to remove units that are referenced by other units in the project. If you remove units that are required by your project, a compiler error will result. Before removing a unit, be sure it is not used in your project. If you accidentally remove a needed unit from your project, you can add it back to the project with the Add To Project option as explained in the preceding section.

The Remove From Project dialog box enables multiple selection, so you can remove several units from a project at one time if you want.

Viewing Units or Forms

To view a unit, form, or other file, just double-click the node representing the form or unit you want to view. You can also choose Open from the Project Manager context menu. The form or unit will be displayed in either the Form Designer or Code Editor, depending on the type of node you are viewing.

Building Projects or Project Groups

To build a particular project, you can do one of the following:

- Right-click the project node in the Project Manager and choose Build from the context menu.
- Choose Project | Build *<project name>* from the Delphi main menu. The name of this menu item will change based on the name of the active project.
- Press Ctrl+F9 on the keyboard to compile the active project.

To build an entire project group, choose Project | Build All Projects from the Delphi main menu. All projects in the project group will be built starting with the first project in the group (the project at the top of the Project Manager tree) and proceeding down through the last project in the group.

Understanding Project Options

Project options are another of those features that are easy to ignore. For one, the defaults are usually good enough when you are just starting out. After all, who has time to worry about all those compiler/linker options when you are simply struggling to learn a new programming environment? At some point, though, you will start to become more interested in what all those options do, and it's good to have some reference when the time comes.

This section looks at the Project Options dialog box. You can invoke this dialog box by choosing Project | Options from the main menu. The Project Options dialog box is a tabbed dialog box with several pages:

- Forms
- Application
- Compiler
- Linker
- Directories/Conditionals
- Version Info
- Packages

I won't discuss every page of the Project Options dialog box, but you'll take a look at the most important pages so that you can understand more about what each of these pages does. I'll start you out easy by discussing the Forms and Application pages. After that I'll move on to the more complicated pages.

Note

At the bottom of each page of the Project Options dialog box is a check box labeled Default. If you want the current settings to become the default settings for all new projects created, check the Default box. When you click OK, the current settings become the new default settings.

The Forms Page

The Forms page of the Project Options dialog box is where you control how your application handles its forms. You saw this dialog box on Day 4 when you created the Picture Viewer program. Figure 9.3 shows the Forms page of the Project Options dialog box for the ScratchPad program.

FIGURE 9.3.

The Forms page of the Project Options dialog box.

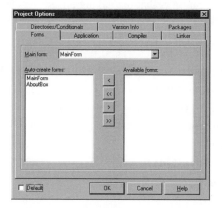

At the top of the Forms page is the Main form combo box. This is where you tell Delphi which form to display when the application starts. By default, the first form you create will be the main form. If you change your project around in such a way that a different form becomes the main form, you must change this setting so that the new form becomes the application's main form.

In the middle of the dialog box are two list boxes. The list box on the left is labeled Auto-create forms; the one on the right is labeled Available forms. Before I talk about how to use these two list boxes, let's take a moment to go over auto-creation of forms.

NEW TERM   *Auto-creation* means that Delphi will construct the form during the application startup process.

Each time you create a form, Delphi places that form in the auto-create list for the application. Forms that are auto-created display more quickly than forms that are not auto-created. The disadvantage to auto-creation of forms is that your application will use more memory than it would if your forms were not auto-created. Another disadvantage, although probably insignificant, is that your application will take slightly longer to load if you are auto-creating a lot of forms.

Note

> The first form in the Auto-create forms list box is always the main form. If you change the main form, the new form selected will move to the top of the Auto-create forms list box. Another way to set the main form is to drag and drop any of the forms in the Auto-create forms list box to the top of the list.

The nice thing about auto-creation is that displaying an auto-created form is easy. All you do is call that form's Show or ShowModal function:

```
AboutBox.ShowModal;
```

If you do not have your forms auto-created by Delphi, you must take the responsibility of creating the form before you use it:

```
procedure TForm1.Button1Click(Sender: TObject);
var
  About : TAboutBox;
begin
  About := TAboutBox.Create(Self);
  About.ShowModal;
  About.Free;
end;
```

This example does not use the Delphi-generated pointer to the About box. It creates a local pointer, displays the form, and then deletes the pointer as soon as the form is no longer needed. As is often the case in Object Pascal programming, there are several ways to perform this particular task. Because Delphi always creates a pointer to the form object, you could have written the previous code like this:

```
if not Assigned(AboutBox) then
  AboutBox := TAboutBox.Create(Self);
AboutBox.ShowModal;
```

This code checks to see whether the form has already been created. If it has not, the object is created, and then the ShowModal method is called. Deciding which method of form creation you will use is up to you, but I prefer the former because it handles everything locally.

Note

Each time you create a form in the Form Designer, Delphi creates a pointer to the form. If you enable Delphi to auto-create a form, you don't have to worry about the pointer being valid. If you choose not to have a form auto-created, the pointer to the form will be `nil` until you explicitly create the form and initialize the pointer. If you forget and use the pointer before it is initialized, Windows will generate an access-violation error.

Okay, now turn your attention back to the Project Options dialog box. The Auto-create forms list box contains a list of the forms that will be auto-created. If you do not want a form to be auto-created, drag the form from the Auto-create forms list box to the Available forms list box. To move several forms at one time, simply select the forms you want to move (both list boxes support multiple selection) and drag and drop them all at once. It's that easy.

Note

You can use the buttons between the two list boxes to move forms from one list box to the other, but it's usually easier to use drag and drop.

The Application Page

The Application page of the Project Options dialog box is very simple (see Figure 9.4).

FIGURE 9.4.

The Application page.

The Title field on this page is used to set the title of the application. The title is the text that will appear on the Windows taskbar when your application is minimized.

9

Note

The application's title and the caption of the main form are two separate items. If you want your program's name to show up when you minimize your program, you must be sure that you set the title for the application in the Project Options dialog box. If you do not provide an application title, the name of the project file is used by default.

The Help file field of the Application page is used to set the help file that your application will use. This is the help file that the program will load when you press F1 while your application is running. You can use the Browse button to locate the help file if you can't remember the name or location of the help file. If you do not supply a help file, pressing F1 in your application will have no effect.

The Icon option enables you to choose an icon for your application. This is the icon that will be displayed in the Windows taskbar when your application runs and when it is minimized. In addition, this icon will be displayed on your main form's title bar unless you have explicitly set an icon for the main form. To choose an icon, click the Load Icon button and locate the icon file (.ico) using the Application Icon dialog box.

You use the Target file extension field to specify the filename extension of the project when the project is built. For example, if you were creating a screen saver, you would change this field to scr so that your screen saver would be created with an extension of .scr rather than .exe. Control Panel applets are another example. These are special programs saved with a .cpl extension. The project filename extension is automatically set to .exe for executable projects (console applications and GUI applications) and to .dll for DLLs, so you don't have to provide a value for this field for normal projects.

The Compiler Page

The Compiler page of the Project Options dialog box is where you set the options that the compiler uses to build your project. Figure 9.5 shows this page of the Project Options dialog box.

The Compiler page is divided into five sections. I'll take each section and examine it so that you can better understand the different options on this page.

FIGURE 9.5.

The Compiler page of the Project Options dialog box.

Code Generation

The compiler can be configured to perform optimizations on your code. When optimizations are turned off (the Optimization check box is not selected), the compiler makes no attempts to optimize code in any way. If you turn the Optimization option on, the compiler will generate the fastest code possible without regard to code size. In most cases, you should leave this option on the default setting. Sometimes, however, it is better to turn optimization off while debugging your application. I'll discuss optimization and debugging in more detail on Day 10, "Debugging Your Applications."

The Aligned Record Fields option is used to control how records are aligned in memory. When this option is on, records are aligned on 4-byte boundaries. When this option is off, records are byte-aligned.

You might want to turn the Stack Frames option on when debugging. When you are finished debugging, you can turn off this option to have the compiler generate smaller and faster code, but compile times will be slightly longer with the Stack Frames option off.

The Pentium-Safe FDIV option causes the compiler to generate code that detects a faulty floating-point division instruction.

Syntax Options and Runtime Errors

These two sections affect how the compiler generates code for a project. The Delphi help for the Compiler page explains what each of these options is for, so I won't repeat that information here. To display the help page for the compiler options, click the Help button when the Compiler page is displayed or press the F1 key on the keyboard.

Debugging

The Debugging section of the Compiler page of the Project Options dialog box controls how the compiler generates code for debugging sessions. When the Debug information option is enabled, Delphi generates debug information for the project. If you do not generate debug information, you will not be able to stop on breakpoints and inspect variables during debugging. Put another way, you can't debug your program unless you tell Delphi to generate debug information.

Note If you change any of the options on the Compiler page, you should do a build immediately following the change. This will ensure that all units are rebuilt using the same compiler settings.

Messages

The Messages section determines whether you want the compiler to report hints and warnings after compiling. I always leave both the Show Hints and Show Warnings options on. Hints and warnings should not be ignored in the long term (in the short term, you can ignore warnings that you know are due to temporary conditions in your code). Usually, compiler warnings can, and should, be resolved. Learn to treat hints and warnings as errors. Quality code compiles without warnings.

The Linker Page

The Linker page of the Project Options dialog box is where you set options that specify how you want the linker to operate. Until you become very familiar with Delphi, you can leave this page alone and accept the default settings. Figure 9.6 shows the Linker page of the Project Options dialog box. The options available on this page are explained in the following sections.

FIGURE 9.6.

Project Linker options.

Map File

The Map File settings control whether a map file is generated and how much detail is included in it. A map file is an advanced debugging tool and is something that you will not likely use until you get further into Delphi. For that reason, I won't go into more detail on the Map File options.

EXE and DLL Options

The EXE and DLL Options section determines the type of executable file produced by Delphi for an application project. When the Generate Console Application check box is checked, Delphi produces a console application as opposed to a GUI application.

The Include TD32 Debug Info option causes the linker to link the debug information into the EXE or DLL. ("TD32" refers to the 32-bit version of the venerable old Turbo Debugger. TD32 is an advanced standalone debugger that used to ship with Borland C++ products and with some versions of Delphi.) Some debugging utilities use debug information in TD32 format. TurboPower's Memory Sleuth, for example, requires TD32 debug information to be present in the EXE. Turn this option on when using programs like Memory Sleuth.

The Include Remote Debug Symbols option generates the debug symbols necessary for remote debugging of Web broker applications.

Linker Output

The Linker Output section determines what type of compiled binary file the linker should produce. Normally the linker produces DCU files (the default for Delphi applications). You might, however, want to generate C or C++ object files (OBJs) rather than DCUs, thereby allowing your Pascal units to be used with a C or C++ program built with Borland C++Builder.

Memory Sizes

The Memory Sizes section can be ignored by all but the most advanced users. The default values are acceptable for all applications. In some cases, you might change the Image base address when building a DLL, but doing so is rarely necessary.

Description

The EXE Description field is used to specify a string that will be embedded in the application. This field is sometimes used to add copyright information to an EXE or DLL. Most of the time, you will use version info to store copyright information in a file rather than using the EXE Description field on this page. Version info is described later in the section "The Version Info Page."

The Directories/Conditionals Page

The Directories/Conditionals page of the Project Options dialog box is where you set the directories that your project uses to find library files. Figure 9.7 shows the Directories/Conditionals page. The fields on this page are described in the following sections.

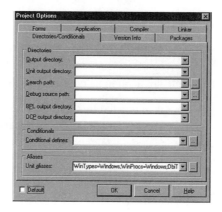

Directories

The fields in this section determine where Delphi can find various source files during compilation of the project. It also contains fields that determine where certain files created by the compiler and linker will be placed during a build of the project.

The Output Directory field is used to specify the directory where the final executable file or DLL will be placed. The Unit Output Directory determines where the DCU files will be placed for each unit compiled. The Search Path field is used to specify the directories where any additional libraries needed to build the project can be found. The Debug Source Path field is used to specify the path to any source units that you want to debug, but which are not in the current project's directory. For example, if you want to step into a DLL while debugging, you have to enter the path to the DLL's source code in this field. The BPL Output Directory and the DCP Output Directory fields specify where the BPL and DCP files should be placed when building a package.

Note that a small button with an ellipsis on it appears next to several of the fields on the Directories/Conditionals page. Clicking this button displays an editor that enables you to add, remove, or rearrange the items in a particular field. Figure 9.8 shows this dialog box while editing the Search Path field.

FIGURE 9.8.

The Directories editor dialog box.

Conditionals

You use the Conditional Defines field to specify any defines that you want to add at the project level. For example, let's say you have code in your project that will be compiled only if the symbol TRIALRUN is defined. In that case, you would add TRIALRUN to the Conditional Defines field. If you have more than one symbol to define, make sure that each symbol is separated by a semicolon.

Aliases

The Unit Aliases field is used to specify any unit aliases. For example, Delphi 1 used units called WinTypes.pas and WinProcs.pas for all Windows-specific code. Delphi 2, 3, and 4 use a unit called Windows.pas in place of WinTypes and WinProcs. The Unit Aliases field aliases WinTypes and WinProcs to the Windows unit. In this case, aliasing enables programs written in Delphi 1 to compile in Delphi 4 without modification of the uses list.

The Version Info Page

The Version Info page enables you to set the version information for your applications. Version information is stored in your program's EXE file or in a DLL or ActiveX file. It is used by installation programs to determine whether a file being installed is older or newer than the file it is replacing.

Version info has other uses as well. You can view the version information for a file from Windows Explorer. Just right-click the file and choose Properties from the Explorer context menu. When the Properties dialog box comes up, click the Version tab to view the version information for the file. Figure 9.9 shows the Properties dialog box displaying version information for the Database Desktop utility that comes with Delphi.

FIGURE 9.9.

The Properties dialog box showing version information for DBD32.EXE.

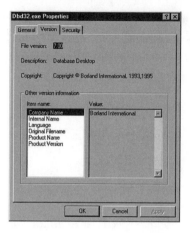

Figure 9.10 shows the Version Info page of the Project Options dialog box. At the top of the page is a check box labeled Include Version Information in Project. When this check box is checked, version information will be included in the project's executable file. When this check box is not checked, version information is not included in the project, and the rest of the page is disabled.

FIGURE 9.10.

Version information for your projects can be supplied on the Version Info page.

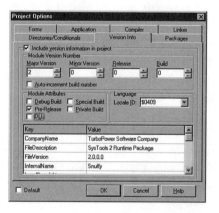

The remaining fields on the Version Info page are used to specify the various pieces of version information. The Major Version, Minor Version, Release, and Build fields work together to form the file version number. The version number of the file in Figure 9.10 is version 2.0, build 0. If you check the Auto-Increment Build Number option, the build number will automatically increment by one each time you perform a build.

The Module Attributes section can be used to determine any special attributes you want specified for the file. The Language section enables you to select a locale identifier for the file. For more information on the possible values for the Locale ID field, see the Windows API online help under the topic "Language Identifiers and Locales."

The table at the bottom of the Version Info page can be used to set a variety of information. This information includes your company name, the file description, the internal name of the file, the legal copyright or trademark information, the product name, product version, and any comments you want to add.

You can provide information for any of these fields or none at all (the `FileVersion` field is set based on the fields in the Module Version Number section). You can even add your own custom version information fields. To add a custom version info field, simply click in the version info table and scroll to the end of the table using the down-arrow key. Type the down-arrow key once more and a dialog box will be displayed asking you for the version key to add. Supply a key name and that key is added to the version info for the project. Adding version information to a project has never been so easy!

The Packages Page

The Packages page is where you determine the type of linking that your projects will use. The top part of the page enables you to add or remove design packages, but that really doesn't have anything to do with the current project. The only option that pertains to the current project is the Build with Runtime Packages check box.

When this option is selected, your application will use dynamic linking of the VCL and any third-party components. This means that your executable file will be smaller, but you will have to be sure to ship the correct packages with your application. When this check box is off, your application uses static linking. *Static linking* means that any VCL code and the code from any third-party components that your application uses is linked directly into your executable file. Packages were discussed in detail yesterday in the section "Using Packages." Figure 9.11 shows the Packages page of the Project Options dialog box.

FIGURE 9.11.

The Packages page.

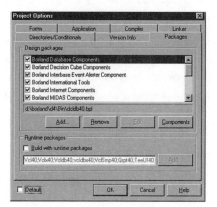

The Delphi Code Editor

There is no question that Delphi is highly visual in nature—that's one of the great benefits of programming with Delphi. Still, any program of any significance will have a great deal of code that must be written by hand. After you get the UI part of your application written with Delphi's impressive visual tools, you'll likely spend a long stretch with the Delphi Code Editor. The Code Editor has some features you'll learn to appreciate when you discover them.

In this section, you learn about the following:

- Basic editor operations
- Specialized editor features
- The Code Editor context menu
- Changing the editor options

 Note

> The Delphi Code Editor enables you to choose from four keyboard-mapping configurations: Default, IDE Classic, BRIEF, and Epsilon. The rest of this chapter assumes Default keyboard mapping. If you are already familiar with one of the other keyboard mapping configurations, you can ignore any references to specific keystrokes.

Basic Editor Operations

I'm going to assume that you know enough to be able to enter and delete text, highlight text with the mouse, cut, copy, paste, and so on. I won't spend any time going over functions at that level.

When it comes right down to it, the Delphi Code Editor is a typical code editor. It features syntax highlighting, which makes identifying keywords, strings, numeric constants, and comments at a glance easy. You'll look at setting the editor preferences a little later.

The Code Editor is a tabbed window. You can open as many editor windows as you like; each window will be represented by a tab along the top of the editor window that will display the name of the file. To switch to a source file, simply click the tab corresponding to the file you want to view. If more tabs exist than can be displayed at one time, scroll buttons will appear so that you can scroll among the tabs.

The status bar at the bottom of the Code Editor gives status information (obviously). The current line number and the cursor position on the line are reported in the left panel of the status bar. If the file has changed since it was last saved, the status bar will say Modified in the center panel of the status bar. The right panel of the status bar shows the current mode, either Insert or Overwrite. If the file has been set to read-only, this panel will say Read Only.

The editor window has a gray strip in the left margin that is called the *gutter*. The gutter is used to display icons at different stages of the development process. For example, when you set a debugger breakpoint (discussed tomorrow), a red dot is placed in the gutter. When you set a bookmark (discussed in just a bit), an icon representing the bookmark is placed in the gutter.

9

> **Note**
>
> If you accidentally click on the gutter when trying to select text or place the cursor, you will find that a breakpoint is set on that line. Click the gutter again to clear the breakpoint.

Opening and Saving Files

Nothing is very mysterious about opening and saving files in the Code Editor. It should be pointed out, though, that there is a difference between opening a project and opening a source file. When you choose File | Open Project from the main menu, you are prompted for the name of a project file to open. When you choose File | Open from the main menu, you can open an individual Delphi source file or form file. Actually, you can open any type of text file (including file types not listed in the Open dialog box's Files of Type field). This includes .pas, .rc, .txt, and even C++ source and header files (.cpp and .h). Both the Open and Open Project menu items have corresponding toolbar buttons.

> **Note**
>
> If you open a unit file (.pas) that contains a form, Delphi will open the source file in the Code Editor and will also open the form in the Form Designer.

You can also open multiple files at one time. To open multiple files, choose the files you want to open in the Open dialog box and click OK. Each file selected will be loaded, and a tab for each file will be placed at the top of the editor window.

> **Tip**
>
> You can also use drag-and-drop to open files. For example, you can choose a file (or a group of files) in Explorer, drag it onto the Code Editor, and drop it. The file will be opened in the Code Editor.

To save a file, choose File | Save or File | Save As from the main menu or type Ctrl+S on the keyboard. If the file has not been previously saved, the Save As dialog box will appear, and you can enter a filename at that time.

Highlighting Text

Although text highlighting is basic text-editor stuff, I thought it wouldn't hurt to remind you of a few basic highlighting techniques you can use in the Delphi Code Editor.

To highlight a short block of text, you can use the mouse to drag across any text you want to highlight. After you've selected the text, you can cut, copy, or paste as needed. To highlight longer blocks of code, you can use the Click+Shift+Click method. First, click at the beginning of the block you want to highlight. Next, hold the Shift key on the keyboard and then click again at the end of the block. All text between the starting point and the ending point is highlighted.

Another useful feature is the capability to quickly select an individual word. To select a keyword, function name, or variable, just double-click on the word. Now you can perform any editing operations you want with the highlighted word.

> **Tip**
>
> To select a single line of code with the mouse, click at the beginning of the line and drag straight down to the beginning of the next line. To highlight a single line of code with the keyboard, first press the Home key to move to the beginning of the line and then use Shift+down-arrow key to highlight the line.

Dozens of keyboard combinations can be used to highlight text and do other editing chores. For a complete list of all the keyboard shortcuts available, consult the Delphi online help.

> **Tip**
>
> As you program you often add, delete, or move blocks of text. Sometimes you will need to indent an entire block of code. At other times you will need to un-indent (outdent?) an entire block of code. To indent a block of code, highlight the lines that you want to indent and then press Ctrl+Shift+I on the keyboard. The entire block will be indented. To un-indent a block of code, press Ctrl+Shift+U on the keyboard.

The Code Editor also supports drag-and-drop editing. To move a section of code, first highlight it. Next, place the mouse cursor over the highlighted text and drag. Drag until the cursor reaches the location where you want the code to be placed. Release the mouse button and the code will be moved to the new location. To copy text rather than move it, repeat the preceding steps but hold down the Ctrl key before you drop the text.

Undo

The Code Editor has a virtually limitless number of undo levels (32,767 by default). Normally, you can only undo commands up to the last time you saved a file. By changing the editor options, you will be able to undo past commands even after saving the file. I'll talk about editor options and preferences later in the chapter in the section titled "Changing the Editor Options."

In general, it pays to remember this simple maxim: "Undo is your friend."

Find and Replace

Find and Replace are used fairly heavily in programming. You might use Find to find a specific piece of code or a specific variable in your code. You might use Replace to change a variable's name or to change the name of a method. The possibilities are endless.

The Delphi Find Text and Replace Text dialog boxes implement more or less standard find-and-replace operations. To bring up the Find Text dialog box, choose Search | Find from the main menu or press Ctrl+F. Enter text in the Text to find field and click OK or press Enter. If the text is found, it will be highlighted.

Note

Text highlighted by the Find Text dialog box is not the same as text highlighted with the mouse. You will notice that searched text is highlighted in black whereas text selected with the mouse is highlighted in blue (assuming you haven't changed the editor defaults). Text highlighted after a search operation is not selected for editing, it's just marked so that you can see it better.

To invoke the Replace Text dialog box, choose Search | Replace from the menu or press Ctrl+R. Figure 9.12 shows the Delphi Replace Text dialog box. With a few obvious exceptions, the Find Text dialog box contains the same options.

For the most part, the options on the Find Text and Replace Text dialog boxes do exactly what they indicate. If you choose the Case Sensitive option, you must type the search text exactly as it appears in the source file.

FIGURE 9.12.

The Replace Text dialog box.

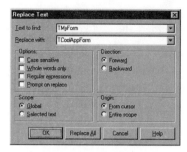

Use the Whole Words Only option when you want to be sure that text for which you are searching is not part of a longer word or variable name. For example, let's say you want to replace Form with MyForm. In this case, you would want to search for whole words only because the word Form might be used in other variable names (such as TForm).

The Regular Expressions option requires explanation as well. When this option is on, you can use special and wildcard characters when doing searches. The special characters enable you to find elements such as the beginning of a line or the end of a line in your search strings. Wildcard characters work much like they do in directory operations. For a complete description of regular expressions, see the Delphi online help under the topic "Regular Expressions."

When replacing text, it is safest to leave the Prompt on Replace option on. When you do a Replace All operation with this option on, the editor will highlight each found word and prompt you whether to replace it. It is easy to miscalculate the results of a Replace All operation, so always use Replace All with care. Even then, it still pays to remember that maxim: "Undo is your friend."

The rest of the Find and Replace options are self-explanatory and therefore don't need additional mention.

Find in Files

Find in Files is a great tool for searching for text in multiple files. I frequently use Find in Files to search the VCL source code for particular methods, variables, or classes. This tool is useful and convenient, and you should learn how to use it.

To display the Find Text dialog box, you can choose Search | Find in Files from the main menu. Perhaps an easier way is to type Ctrl+F on the keyboard to bring up the Find Text dialog box and then click the Find in Files tab. Figure 9.13 shows the Find Text dialog box with the Find in Files tab showing.

FIGURE 9.13.

The Find Text dialog box.

9

Find in Files uses some of the same search options as the regular Find operation (case-sensitive, whole word only, and regular expressions). In addition, you have the option to search all files in the project, all open files, or files in a particular directory, including subdirectories.

When you start Find in Files, a small window with a title of Searching appears in the lower-right portion of your screen. This window shows the status of the Find in Files operation. It will show you the current file being searched and the number of matches up to this point. To cancel the search, just close the Searching window.

Any matches are reported in the Code Editor's message window. The message window shows the filename of the file in which the text was found, the line number where the text was found, and the line containing the search text with the search text displayed in bold. To view the file that contains a match, just double-click a line in the message window. Delphi will open the appropriate file and display the exact line containing the text for which you are searching. Figure 9.14 shows Delphi searching a set of files.

When specifying the file mask, all the usual wildcard characters apply. For example, if you want to search all text files in a directory, you would enter the following in the File masks field:

```
c:\MyStuff\*.txt
```

Find in Files is an indispensable tool. I find myself using it all the time. Learning to use Find in Files will save you a lot of time.

FIGURE 9.14.

Delphi searching for text.

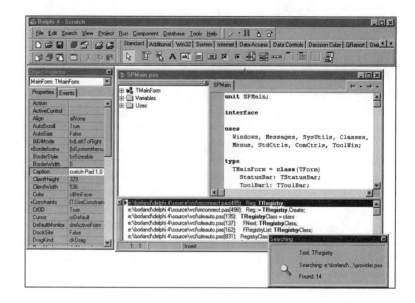

Getting Help

One of the most useful features of the Code Editor is its integration with the Delphi help system. Just place the editor cursor over an Object Pascal keyword, a VCL property or method, or any other Delphi-specific text and press F1. If a help topic for the text under the cursor exists in the Delphi help files, Windows Help will run with the appropriate page showing. If no help topic exists for the selected text, an error message will be displayed.

This feature is extremely useful when you can't remember how to use a particular aspect of Delphi, Object Pascal, or VCL. Help, as they say, is just a keystroke away.

Specialized Editor Features

The Delphi Code Editor has a few features that are extremely useful when you are writing a lot of code. They are explained in the following sections.

Code Templates

Code templates are another nice feature of the Delphi Code Editor. Code templates enable you to insert any predefined code (or any text, for that matter) in your source units. To use code templates, just type Ctrl+J on the keyboard while editing in the Code Editor. When you do, a list box will pop up giving you a list of templates from which to choose. Choose a template from the list, press Enter, and the text corresponding to that code template will be inserted into your source code. Figure 9.15 shows the code template list box as it appears when you type Ctrl+J.

FIGURE 9.15.

The Delphi code template list box.

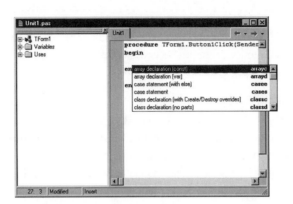

You can add new templates or edit existing templates via the Code Insight page of the Environment Options dialog box. Or, if you prefer, you can open the code template file with any text editor (such as the Delphi Code Editor) and edit the code templates there. The code template file is called DELPHI32.DCI and is located in the Delphi 4\Bin directory.

Feel free to modify the code templates in any way you see fit. For example, I have modified my code template representing the for statement to look like this:

```
for I := 0 to Pred(¦) do begin
end;
```

Notice the pipe character (¦) in the code snippet. The pipe in a code template entry is a placeholder that determines where the cursor will be placed after the text is inserted into your source code.

Tip

If you make a lot of modifications to the code template file, be sure to keep a backup of the file in a safe location. You will need a backup because the Delphi installation program will overwrite your modified DELPHI32.DCI file when you update or reinstall Delphi.

You can use code templates for more than just code. Here at TurboPower Software our source files always have a header at the top of the unit. It looks something like this:

```
{************************************************************};
{*                 Filename and version                   *};
{*         Copyright (c) TurboPower Software 1998          *};
{*                All rights reserved.                     *};
{************************************************************};
```

Because most of this text stays constant, I have a template that quickly inserts the header in any new source units I create. Use code templates for any text that you use frequently in your day-to-day programming.

Code Parameters

The code parameters feature of the Code Editor displays a tooltip that prompts you with the needed parameters of a VCL method or Windows API function. With hundreds of VCL methods and Windows API functions, there is virtually no way to remember every function's parameters. The code parameters feature saves you time by showing you the parameters of a method as you type. For example, let's say you are calling the SetBounds method. When you type the opening parentheses, a hint window pops up as shown in Figure 9.16.

FIGURE 9.16.

Code parameters in action.

As you can see in Figure 9.16, each parameter is listed in the tooltip. The parameter you need to type next is displayed in bold. As you type a parameter, the next parameter is displayed in bold. This continues until you type all the method's parameters. After you have typed all the required parameters, the code parameters tooltip disappears. The code parameters options are set on the Code Insight page of the Environment Options dialog boxes. I'll discuss that page later in the section "The Code Insight Page."

Code Completion

Code completion is another Code Editor feature that can save you development time. Type a class variable name followed by the dot operator, and the Code Editor will display a list box with all of that class's properties and methods. If, for example, you have a memo component called Memo, you will type

```
Memo.
```

and pause for a moment. A list box pops up as shown in Figure 9.17.

FIGURE 9.17.

*Code completion
displaying the
properties and
methods of* TMemo.

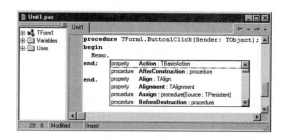

When you see the list box, you can select an item from the list in one of two ways. One way is to locate a property or method in the list box using the mouse or the keyboard and press Enter. The property or method will be inserted into your code. Alternatively, you can type the first few letters of the property or method you want to insert into your code. As you type, Delphi searches the list of properties and methods for a match and highlights the item in the list that most closely matches the text you are typing.

When you see the property or method you want, press the Enter key and the property or method will be inserted into your code. If you don't want to use the code completion list box, you can press the Esc key on the keyboard and the code completion list box will disappear.

Code completion saves you time by providing a list of properties and methods from which to choose. It has the added benefit of providing perfect spelling and capitalization of property and method names. Just choose the property or method you want, press the Enter key, and Delphi inserts the identifier in your code.

Tooltip Symbol Insight

*New
to* **4** Tooltip symbol insight pops up a tooltip when you place your mouse cursor over just about any identifier in your source code. For example, a standard new project will have this line in the interface section:

```
TForm1 = class(TForm)
```

When you place your mouse cursor over the identifier TForm, a tooltip pops up that says:

```
type Forms.TForm = class(TCustomForm) - Forms.pas (584)
```

This line shows you the `TForm` class declaration and tells you that `TForm` is declared on line 584 of the `Forms.pas` unit.

Tooltip symbol insight will tell you information about any variable in your program. This is particularly convenient when you forget the type of a variable (was `X` declared as a `Byte`, a `Word`, or an `Integer`?).

Class Completion

New to 4 Class completion is a new feature in Delphi 4. Type any properties or method declarations in the `interface` section and type Ctrl+Shift+C on the keyboard. Delphi will add the necessary code to the `implementation` section to complete the class. This is best illustrated by performing an exercise. Perform these steps:

1. Start with a blank project.
2. Switch to the Code Editor and locate the form's class declaration in the `interface` section.
3. Type the following code in the `public` section of the form's class declaration:
   ```
   procedure Test;
   function GetSomething : Integer;
   ```
4. Type Ctrl+Shift+C on the keyboard.

When you perform step 4, Delphi automatically adds the bodies of the `Test` and `GetSomething` methods to the `implementation` section and places the editing cursor in the first method. The added code looks like this:

```
function TForm1.GetSomething: Integer;
begin

end;

procedure TForm1.Test;
begin

end;
```

Keep this unit handy because you will use it again in the next section when I discuss module navigation.

Code completion works with property declarations as well as methods. Type a property declaration, type Ctrl+Shift+C, and Delphi completes the property declaration. It even adds a `write` method for your property. I don't cover writing properties until Day 20, "Creating Components," so this might not make much sense to you right now. It will be more clear when you begin writing your own components.

For me, class completion is one of the best of Delphi 4's new features. This feature alone has saved me a lot of time when writing components. I wouldn't be without it now that I have been using it for a period of time.

Module Navigation

Module navigation enables you to quickly move from a method in the `implementation` section to that method's declaration in the `interface` section, and vice versa. Again, an exercise is worth a thousand words. Do this:

9

1. Navigate to the class declaration of the form you modified in the previous exercise.

2. Click on the line containing the `Test` procedure's declaration.

3. Type Ctrl+Shift+down arrow on the keyboard. The Code Editor jumps to the `Test` procedure body in the `implementation` section.

4. Type Ctrl+Shift+up arrow. The Code Editor jumps back to the `Test` procedure's declaration in the `interface` section.

5. Move down a line to the `GetSomething` function declaration. Type Ctrl+Shift+down arrow again. The Code Editor jumps to the `GetSomething` method in the `implementation` section.

As you can see, module navigation makes it easy to quickly move between the `implementation` and `interface` sections.

> It doesn't matter whether you use the up arrow button on the keyboard or the down arrow button. Either button acts as a toggle between the `interface` and `implementation` sections.

Module Browsing

Module browsing is another module navigation tool. In the Code Editor, hold down the Ctrl key and place the mouse cursor over an identifier name. The identifier will be highlighted in blue and underlined. Click on the identifier and Delphi will take you to the place in the source where that identifier is declared.

In this regard, the module browser is like the module navigation feature. It goes beyond that, however. With the module browser, you can click on a VCL identifier as well as your own identifiers. Let me illustrate with an example. Before starting, however, I should point out that this exercise will work only if you have the Professional or Client/ Server version of Delphi. It requires the Delphi source code to work. Perform these steps:

1. Create a new application. Place a button and a memo on the form.

2. Choose Project | Options from the main menu. Click on the Directories/Conditionals tab of the Project Options dialog box. Type the following in the Search path field:

   ```
   $(DELPHI)\source\vcl;$(DELPHI)\source\rtl\win
   ```

   Click OK to close the Project Options dialog box.

3. Double-click the button and add this text in the OnClick event handler for the button:

   ```
   Memo1.Clear;
   ```

   The Clear method of TMemo clears the memo of its contents. Are you curious about what the VCL source looks like for the Clear method? Keep going. . .

4. Hold down the Ctrl key on the keyboard and click on Clear.

5. After a few moments, the VCL StdCtrls unit is displayed in the Code Editor with the cursor on the TCustomEdit.Clear method (the Clear method is defined in the TCustomEdit class, one of TMemo's ancestor classes). The method looks like this:

   ```
   procedure TCustomEdit.Clear;
   begin
     SetWindowText(Handle, '');
   end;
   ```

   Interesting. Just one line of code. But where does SetWindowText come from? Next step, please.

6. Hold down the Ctrl key again and click on SetWindowText. After a few seconds the Windows unit is opened and the cursor is on this line:

   ```
   function SetWindowText; external user32 name 'SetWindowTextA';
   ```

   This line tells you that SetWindowText is a Windows function contained in the DLL called USER32. Case closed. You're not quite done yet, though.

7. Now look at the tab in the top-right corner of the Code Editor window. See the *back* and *next* browse buttons? Click the back button (the one that points to the left). The Code Editor switches to the previous browse point (the Clear method in the StdCtrls unit).

8. Click the next button. The Code Editor displays the SetWindowText import in the Windows unit.

9. Click on the drop-down arrow next to the back button. You will see a list of source code locations in the browser history list. Click a location to switch the Code Editor cursor to that location.

The module browser is a great tool for navigating not only your own code, but also the VCL source code and the source code of any third-party component libraries you have installed. Remember, reading the VCL source code can teach you a lot, so don't be afraid to browse through the source.

Using Bookmarks

You can set bookmarks in your code to temporarily mark your place in a source file. For example, you often must temporarily leave a block of code on which you are working to review previously written code or to copy code from another location. By dropping a bookmark at that point in your code before running off to do your other work, you can return to that section of code with a simple keystroke. You can have up to 10 bookmarks set at any one time.

To set a bookmark at a particular location, press Ctrl+Shift and the number of the bookmark to set. For example, to set bookmark 0 (the first bookmark), place the editor cursor at the location you want to mark and then press Ctrl+Shift+0 (Ctrl+K+0 will work as well). When you set a bookmark, an icon is placed in the Code Editor gutter to indicate that a bookmark exists on that line. The icon shows the number of the bookmark. Figure 9.18 shows the Code Editor with a bookmark dropped on a line.

FIGURE 9.18.

The Code Editor with a bookmark set.

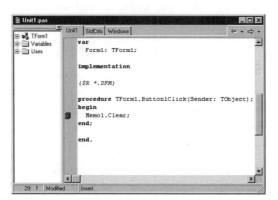

To return to the bookmark, press Ctrl plus the number of the bookmark to which you want to return. Using the same example, you would type Ctrl+0 to go back to the bookmark. (You can also set bookmarks and go to bookmarks using the Code Editor context menu.) To clear a bookmark, place the editor cursor anywhere on the line containing the bookmark and again press Ctrl+Shift+0.

Note

Bookmarks can be set for each file you have open in the Code Editor. For example, you can have bookmark #0 set in one source file and another bookmark #0 set in another source file. This means that bookmarks cannot be found across source files. If you set bookmark #0 in Unit1.pas, you cannot press Ctrl+0 in Unit2.pas and expect to be taken to the bookmark in Unit1.pas.

To illustrate the use of bookmarks, do the following:

1. Open any source file in the Code Editor.

2. Scroll almost to the bottom of the file and click on a line of code.

3. Press Ctrl+Shift+0 to set a bookmark. The bookmark icon shows in the Code Editor gutter.

4. Press Ctrl+Home to move to the top of the source file.

5. Now press Ctrl+0 to jump back to the bookmark. The Code Editor changes to show the line of code where the bookmark was set, and the cursor is placed exactly where it was when you set the bookmark.

6. Type Ctrl+Shift+0 again to clear the bookmark. The bookmark is cleared and the bookmark icon disappears from the Code Editor gutter.

Note that bookmarks are temporary. When you close the source file and reopen it, the bookmark is not preserved. Note also that to set and remove bookmarks you must type the number keys on the main keypad. The numeric keypad is ignored when setting and removing bookmarks.

Incremental Search

You can use the incremental search option to quickly find a short series of characters. To start an incremental search, choose Search | Incremental Search from the main menu or press Ctrl+E on the keyboard. To understand how the incremental search works, it is easiest to do an exercise. Do the following:

1. Create a new text file from the Object Repository. (It doesn't matter whether you currently have a project open.)

2. Type the following text:
   ```
   Learning to write Windows
   programs a bit at a time
   is not so bad. Isn't it
   time you got back to work?
   ```

3. Move the cursor back to the top of the file (Ctrl+Home).

4. Press Ctrl+E to start the incremental search. You will be searching for the word back. Note that the Code Editor status bar says Searching for:.

5. Type a b on the keyboard. The letter b in the word bit is highlighted. That's not what you are looking for.

6. Now type an a on the keyboard. The next occurrence of ba is found, this time in the word bad. That's still not what you are looking for.

7. Type a c on the keyboard. The letters bac in the word back are highlighted. Now type a k. The Code Editor status bar now says Searching for: back and the word back is highlighted. Congratulations, you found what you were looking for!

8. Press Esc (or Enter) on the keyboard to stop the incremental search. Close the text file without saving it.

That's all there is to it. The incremental search is handy when you are searching for short amounts of text.

Tip

If you make a mistake when typing the characters while doing an incremental search, you can use the Backspace key to remove from the search string the last character typed.

Finding Matching Brackets and Parentheses

The Code Editor has a feature to help you find a bracket or parenthesis that matches the bracket or parenthesis the cursor is currently on. To find a matching bracket, place the cursor before a bracket (it doesn't matter whether it's the opening or closing bracket). Now press Alt+[on the keyboard. The cursor jumps to the bracket that matches the bracket on which you started.

Press Alt+[again, and the cursor jumps back to where you started. The same keystrokes work for parentheses as well as brackets. Getting lost in the maze of parentheses and brackets is still a possibility, but at least now you know how to find your way out again.

The Code Editor Context Menu

Like most of the different windows you encounter in Delphi, the Code Editor has its own context menu. The Code Editor context menu can essentially be divided into two parts: editor items and debugger items. I will leave the debugger items of the context menu for tomorrow when I discuss debugging, but I'll go over the editor items on the context menu now. Table 9.4 contains a list of the context menu items that pertain to the editor, along with a description of each.

TABLE 9.4. THE CODE EDITOR CONTEXT MENU ITEMS.

Item	Description
Close Page	Closes the active page in the edit window. If the file on the page has been modified since it was last saved, you are prompted to save the file.
Open File At Cursor	Opens the file under the cursor. This option has an effect only when the text under the cursor represents a source code file. For example, if you have a file in your uses list called MyUnit2, you could click on the filename and choose this menu item to open the file. The file will be placed in a new editor window and focus will be set to the window.
New Edit Window	Opens a new copy of the Code Editor. This is convenient if you want to compare two source files side by side.
Browse Symbol At Cursor	Starts the browser with the current symbol as the browse target.
Topic Search	Displays the help topic for the item under the cursor (if it can be found). Same as pressing F1 on the keyboard.
Add to Interface	Adds a property, function, or procedure to an ActiveX component. This item is disabled if the project is not an ActiveX project.
Toggle Bookmarks	Toggles a bookmark (0 through 9) on or off. The bookmark is set on the source code line containing the editing cursor.
Goto Bookmarks	Moves the source code editor to a bookmark.
View As Form	If the active file in the Code Editor is displaying a form's contents as text, choosing this option will again display the form in the Form Designer.
Read Only	Toggles the currently active file between read-only and read/write mode. When set to read-only, the file cannot be modified, although text can be selected and copied to the Clipboard. The status bar displays Read Only to indicate the file is read-only. When the file is closed and reopened, it is again in read/write mode.
Message View	Displays or hides the Delphi message window. The message window automatically appears when there are compiler or linker errors or warnings, but can be specifically shown or hidden with this command.
View Explorer	Sets focus to the Code Explorer window. If the Code Explorer is not docked, this command will bring it to the top of all other windows.
Properties	Displays the Environment Options dialog box so that the editor options can be set.

Depending on the current state of the Code Editor and the particular type of file open, some of the items in Table 9.4 can be disabled at any given time.

Changing the Editor Options

The editor options occupy three pages of the Environment Options dialog box. To view this dialog box, choose Tools | Environment Options from the main menu.

Tip

You can also choose Properties from the Code Editor context menu to view the editor options. The difference with this method is that only the four pages pertaining to the editor options will be displayed. When displayed this way, the dialog box is titled Editor Properties rather than Environment Options. The figures in the following sections were taken using this method.

The four pages of the Environment Options that are specific to the Code Editor are as follows:

- Editor
- Display
- Color
- Code Insight

Let's examine these pages in the following sections.

The Editor Page

The Editor page of the Editor Properties dialog box enables you to control how the editor works for you. As you can see from Figure 9.19, a lot of options are available on this page.

FIGURE 9.19.

The Editor page of the Editor Properties dialog box.

At the top of the page is a combo box labeled Editor SpeedSetting. You can choose Default Keymapping, IDE Classic, BRIEF Emulation, or Epsilon Emulation from the combo box. If you change the setting in this combo box, the Editor Options will change to reflect the defaults for the type you chose.

Note

> If you are new to programming or if you have been using other Borland compilers using the Default keymapping, you don't have to worry about what you are missing. If you are accustomed to years of using a particular type of editor, you will be glad to know that you can still use the keyboard shortcuts and editor options that you know and love simply by changing the Editor SpeedSetting field on this page and on the Display page.

Toward the bottom of the screen, you will see the Block Indent and Tab Stops fields. You can use these two fields to change the amount by which code is indented when you block indent or when you tab to the next tab stop. Block indenting is discussed earlier in this chapter in the section "Highlighting Text."

Note

> *Real* programmers use tab stops of either two or three characters. (I use two-character tabs.)

The Undo Limit of 32,767 is probably sufficient for most needs (I hope!), so I doubt you'll feel the need to modify that setting. The Syntax Extensions field enables you to select the types of files for which syntax highlighting will be applied. For example, you probably don't want syntax highlighting applied to regular text files (.txt) that you open in the Code Editor, so that file type is not listed by default.

In the middle of the Editor page, you will find a whole gaggle of editor options from which to choose. Because so many options are available, and because determining exactly which of the available options are the most important is difficult, I'll refer you to the Delphi online help. Simply press F1 while on this page or click the Help button and you will have explanations of each of the editor options you see on this page. As with some of the other options you looked at today, you can probably feel comfortable in accepting the Delphi defaults.

One thing I will add is that I always turn on the Find Text at Cursor option (contrary to what Figure 9.19 might indicate). When this option is on, the text at the editing cursor is automatically placed in the Text to Find field of the Find Text dialog box when the dialog box is invoked. For me, searching for text is much quicker when I don't have to type the search text. This is particularly convenient when using Find in Files.

The Display Page

The Display page of the Environment Options dialog box has additional options from which you can choose. These options pertain to the actual display of the text in the Code Editor window (see Figure 9.20).

FIGURE 9.20.

The Display page.

9

In the Display and File Options section, you will find the BRIEF Cursor Shapes option. Turn on this option if you want the horizontal cursor in the editor window rather than the vertical cursor. Check the Create Backup File option if you want Delphi to create a backup file every time you save your file or your project. Backup file extensions begin with a tilde (~). For example, the backup file for a source file called MyApp.pas would be MyApp.~pa.

Note

I usually get fed up with all those backup files cluttering up my project directories and turn off file backups. Suit yourself.

The Zoom to Full Screen option controls how the Code Editor acts when maximized. If this option is on, the Code Editor will fill the entire screen when maximized. When this option is off (the default), the top of the Code Editor window will stop at the bottom of the Delphi main window when maximized. In other words, the Delphi main window will always be visible when the Code Editor is maximized if this option is off.

You can also choose whether your editor windows have a visible right margin. The right margin is not binding—you can still type text beyond it—but it gives you a visual cue that your lines might be getting too long. This section also enables you to determine whether you want a visible gutter and how wide the gutter should be (in pixels).

You can also change the Code Editor font and point size. A combo box is provided for you to choose these options. Only fixed-space screen fonts are listed; proportional and printer fonts are not. Choose the typeface and point size that best suit your needs. A preview window is provided so that you can see how the font you have chosen will look.

The Color Page

The Color page of the Environment Options dialog box enables you to fully customize the Code Editor's window and syntax highlighting options (see Figure 9.21).

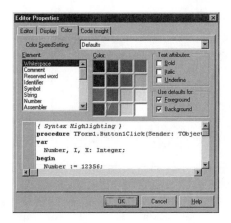

At the top of the page is the Color SpeedSetting combo box. This combo box gives you four predefined color schemes from which to choose. You can choose one of these color schemes or use one of them as a base for creating your own color scheme.

The Color page is very easy to use. At the bottom of the page is a text window that contains sample code. If you click one of the key elements of the code, that element will be selected in the Element list box, and its current settings will be displayed on the Color grid.

To change the foreground, background, and text attributes for that element, simply choose the settings you like. For example, keywords are displayed in bold text with a black foreground and a white background (assuming the default color scheme). To change the keywords to green, bold text, click the procedure keyword in the sample code window and then change the foreground color to green. The text colors in the sample window change to reflect the new color you have chosen. Continue changing colors until you have the sample window just the way you want it. When you click OK, the Code Editor will change to the new colors you have chosen.

The Code Insight Page

The Code Insight page is used to enable or disable Code Completion, Code Parameters, Tooltip Expression Evaluation (a debugging tool), and Tooltip Symbol Insight. The scroller labeled Delay is used to set the delay time before the code insight features engage. This page also enables you to add, edit, or delete code templates. Figure 9.22 shows the Code Insight page of the Environment Options dialog box.

FIGURE 9.22.

The Code Insight page of the Editor Properties dialog box.

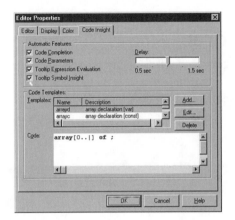

The Add button enables you to add a new code template. When you click the Add button, the Add Code Template dialog box is displayed. Type a template name and a description and click OK. Now type the code for the template in the Code memo field. You can also paste code from the Clipboard. You can add as many templates as you want. When you click the OK button on the Environment Options dialog box, the new templates are added to the template file. To abandon changes to the code template file, click the Cancel button.

> **Tip**
>
> You can edit the code template file with the Delphi Code Editor if you find the Code Insight dialog box too small. The code template file is called DELPHI32.DCI and is located in the Delphi 4\Bin directory.

To delete a code template, first select the template in the Templates table and then click the Delete button. If you delete a template by mistake, just click the Cancel button on the Environment Options dialog box and your changes to the code template file will not be saved.

The Edit button enables you to change the name and description of a code template. When you click the Edit button, the Edit Code Template dialog box is displayed. This dialog box is identical to the Add Code Template dialog box. Type in a new name or description for the template and click OK. As with adding or deleting templates, the changes you make to the templates are not saved unless you click the OK button on the Environment Options dialog box. To edit the code for a template, modify the code in the Code memo field.

The Code Explorer

New to 4 The Code Explorer is a new feature that is a much-welcomed addition to the Delphi IDE. The Code Explorer, as its name indicates, is used to quickly explore your source code units. The Code Explorer is normally docked on the left side of the Code Editor. When you first start Delphi, the Code Editor and Code Explorer appear as shown in Figure 9.23.

FIGURE 9.23.

The Code Explorer for a new project.

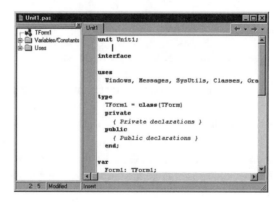

The Code Explorer shows all of a unit's classes, functions, procedures, variables, and the uses list for the unit. The class node expands to show all of the properties, variables, fields, and methods of a particular class.

The Code Explorer shows the structure of the unit in the active Code Editor window. When you switch units in the Code Editor, the Code Explorer changes to show the new unit.

The Code Explorer Context Menu

Like most Delphi windows, the Code Explorer window has a context menu. Table 9.5 lists the items on the Code Explorer context menu.

TABLE 9.5. THE CODE EXPLORER CONTEXT MENU ITEMS.

Item	Description
New	Adds a new variable, method, function, or procedure to the unit. Also used to add a unit to the uses list. You can also use the Insert key on the keyboard to insert a new item.
Rename	Renames an identifier (variable, method, function, procedure, and so on). You can also use in-place editing to change an identifier's name.
View Editor	Brings the Code Editor to the top when the Code Explorer is not docked to the Code Editor window.
Dockable	Specifies whether the Code Explorer window is dockable.

The Insert menu item is a powerful feature. Insert enables you to add a procedure, function, method of a class, or variable to either the unit or to a class in the unit. I'll talk more about that in just a bit.

Navigating a Unit

To navigate to a particular method, function, or procedure, simply double-click the identifier name in the Code Explorer. The Code Editor jumps to the location in the source where that method is located. To locate a data field in a class or a unit variable's declaration, locate that variable's identifier in the Code Explorer window and double-click the identifier. The Code Editor displays the variable's declaration.

Adding Code Using the Code Explorer

The Code Explorer can be used to add method and variable declarations to your source. To add a field variable to a class, for example, choose Insert from the Code Explorer context menu and type the declaration for the variable you want to add. For example, to add an Integer variable called X you would type the following:

```
X : Integer;
```

When you press the Enter key on the keyboard, the variable is added to the class.

You can add methods to a class just as easily. To see exactly how this works, perform the following exercise:

1. Start a new application and switch to the Code Editor window.
2. Right-click on the TForm1 node in the Code Explorer window and choose New from the context menu (or press the Insert key on the keyboard).

3. Type the following code in the edit box on the Code Explorer window and press Enter on the keyboard:

```
procedure Test;
```

Delphi adds a node called Public under the TForm1 class node. Expand the Public node. You will see the Test procedure listed there.

4. Right-click on TForm1 and choose New again. Type the following code in the edit box and press Enter:

```
function GetSomething : Byte;
```

5. Insert another item. This time type

```
AVariable : Integer;
```

You probably didn't notice, but while you were adding items, Delphi was busy making changes to the unit. Listing 9.1 shows the unit after performing this exercise.

LISTING 9.1. THE UNIT AFTER ADDING ITEMS WITH THE CODE EXPLORER.

```
unit Unit1;

interface

uses
  Windows, Messages, SysUtils, Classes,
  Graphics, Controls, Forms, Dialogs;

type
  TForm1 = class(TForm)
  private
    { Private declarations }
  public
    AVariable: Integer;
    procedure Test;
    function GetSomething: Byte;
    { Public declarations }
  end;

var
  Form1: TForm1;

implementation

{$R *.DFM}

function TForm1.GetSomething: Byte;
begin
```

```
end;

procedure TForm1.Test;
begin

end;

end.
```

Notice that not only are the declarations for the items you added present in the class declaration, but also the bodies of the methods are completed in the implementation section. The Code Explorer works together with class completion to make your job as a programmer easier. Figure 9.24 shows the Code Editor and Code Explorer after performing this exercise.

FIGURE 9.24.

The Code Explorer showing the new methods and data field.

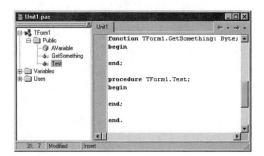

The Code Explorer is both a unit browser and a production tool. You can use it to navigate your units as you write code. I find it extremely useful for this purpose alone. You can also use the Code Explorer to add code to your units. The Code Explorer is a great productivity booster. A major bonus is that it is easy to use, too.

Code Explorer Options

The Code Explorer display options are shown on the Explorer page of the Environment Options dialog box (Tools | Environment Options from the main menu). Figure 9.25 shows the Explorer page.

The various settings on this page control how the Code Explorer acts and how much or how little information it displays. See the Delphi help for the Explorer page for complete details on these settings.

FIGURE 9.25.

The Explorer page of the Environment Options dialog box.

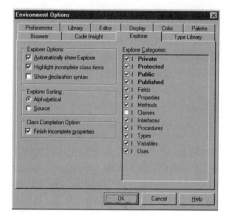

Summary

Today was one of those days when you learned a lot about the features that are often overlooked. I hope you picked up some tips that you can use as you work with Delphi projects and the Delphi Code Editor. You also got an explanation of what some of the project and editor options are for. Even if it didn't make much sense to you now, this chapter is something you can refer back to at a later date. Finally, you ended the day with a look at the Code Explorer. The Code Explorer is a tremendous tool, so be sure you spend some time learning how to use it. After you have used the Code Explorer, you won't be able to work without it.

Workshop

The Workshop contains quiz questions to help you solidify your understanding of the material covered and exercises to provide you with experience in using what you have learned. You can find answers to the quiz questions in Appendix A, "Answers to the Quiz Questions."

Q&A

Q Must I use a project group even if I have just one project?

A No. You don't need a project group for a single project. You can use the default project group instead.

Q **When I start my application, one of my dialog boxes is displayed instead of my main form. What gives?**

A You have accidentally set the main form for the application to be the dialog form. Go to the Project Options dialog box, click the Forms tab, and select your main form from the Main Form combo box on the top of the page. Run your program again, and the main form will be displayed as you would expect.

Q **All those project compiler and linker options confuse me. Do I need to know about each of those options to write programs with Delphi?**

A No. The default project options work well for almost all Delphi applications. At some point you might get further into the mysteries of the compiler and linker, and at that time you can learn more about the project options. Until then, don't worry about it.

Q **When my application is minimized, the icon and caption do not match what I set up in my application's main form. Why not?**

A Setting the icon and caption of the main form does not affect how your application is displayed when minimized. To set the caption and icon for the application, go to the Project Options dialog box, choose the Application page, and supply the application title and icon.

Q **Can I find and replace a variable name across all my source files?**

A No. You will have to open each source file and execute the Replace dialog box in each source file. You can, however, use the F3 key to repeat the last find or replace command. Remember not to change any Delphi-generated variable names.

Q **Can I open several source files at one time in the Code Editor?**

A Yes. The Open dialog box supports multiple selection of files. You can also select multiple files in Windows Explorer and drop them onto the Code Editor.

Q **I find that 32,767 undo levels is not enough for my needs. What do you suggest?**

A Don't quit your day job.

Quiz

1. How can you quickly switch between a unit's form and source code when working with Delphi?

2. If you remove a file from your project via the Project Manager, is the file removed from your hard drive?

3. How do you set the main form for an application?

4. What does it mean if you do not have Delphi Auto-create forms?

5. How do you add new items to your unit using the Code Explorer?

6. What is the significance of generating debug information for your application?

7. What is the Find in Files option used for?

8. What is the keyboard shortcut for saving a file in the Code Editor?

9. How do you set a bookmark in an editor window? How many bookmarks are available?

10. How do you set a file to read-only in the Code Editor?

Exercises

1. Create a new application. Display the Project Manager. Click the Add Unit button to add a new unit to the project. Navigate to the `\Demos\Coolstuf` directory and choose the file called `main.pas`. Click OK to add the file to the project.

2. Remove the `main.pas` unit from the project in exercise 1.

3. Open the `ScratchPad` project. Change the main form to the `AboutBox` form. Close the Project Options dialog box and run the program. The About box will be displayed when the program starts. Close the About box to end the program and change the main form back to the `ScratchPad` form.

4. Create a new application. Save the project and the project group. Now add a new project to the project group.

5. Open any source file in the Code Editor. Set four bookmarks at random locations in the source file. Jump from bookmark to bookmark and observe the effects in the Code Editor. When you are finished, clear all the bookmarks.

6. Open the `ScratchPad` project (or any other project) and switch to the Code Editor. View the project's main form source file. Choose Search | Find from the main menu. Type `Click` in the Text to find box and click OK to find the first occurrence of the word Click.

7. Press F3 several times to repeat the search until the entire file has been searched.

8. Continuing with the same project, press Ctrl+Home to go to the top of the file. Press Ctrl+R to display the Replace Text dialog box. Type `Click` in the Text to find box and `Test` in the Replace with box. Turn off the Prompt on replace option and then click the Replace All button. Scroll through the file to view the results. **IMPORTANT:** Select Edit | Undo to undo the replace operation. Close the project without saving (just to be safe).

9. Open a file in the Code Editor. Choose Properties from the Code Editor context menu. Change the syntax highlighting for strings, integers, and floats to dark gray. Click OK to view the results in the Code Editor.

10. Change the colors back to the Default color scheme.

9

WEEK 2

DAY 10

Debugging Your Applications

A major feature of the Delphi IDE is the integrated debugger. The debugger enables you to easily set breakpoints, watch variables, inspect objects, and do much more. Using the debugger, you can quickly find out what is happening (or not happening) with your program as it runs. A good debugger is vital to efficient program development.

Debugging is easy to overlook. Don't tell anyone, but when I first started Windows programming, I ignored the debugger for a long time because I had my hands full just learning how to do Windows programming. When I found out how valuable a good debugger is, I felt a little silly for cheating myself out of the use of that tool for so long. Oh well, live and learn. You have the luxury of learning from my mistakes. Today, you learn about what the debugger can do for you.

The IDE debugger provides several features and tools to help you in your debugging chores. The following are discussed today:

- Debugger menu items
- Using breakpoints
- Inspecting variables with the Watch List
- Inspecting objects with the Debug Inspector
- Other debugging tools
- Stepping through code
- Debugging techniques

Why Use the Debugger?

The quick answer is that the debugger helps you find bugs in your program. But the debugging process isn't just for finding and fixing bugs—it is a development tool as well. As important as debugging is, many programmers don't take the time to learn how to use all the features of the IDE debugger. As a result, they cost themselves time and money, not to mention the frustration caused by a bug that is difficult to find.

You begin a debugging session by starting up the program under the debugger. You automatically use the debugger when you click the Run button on the toolbar. You can also choose Run | Run from the main menu or press F9 on the keyboard.

The Debugging Menu Items

Before getting into the details of the debugger, let's review the menu items that pertain to the debugger. Some of these menu items are on the main menu under Run, and others are on the Code Editor context menu. Table 10.1 lists the Code Editor context menu items specific to the debugger along with their descriptions.

TABLE 10.1. CODE EDITOR CONTEXT MENU DEBUGGING ITEMS.

Item	Shortcut	Description
Toggle Breakpoint	F5	Toggles a breakpoint on or off for the current line in the Code Editor.
Run to Cursor	F4	Starts the program (if necessary) and runs it until the line in the editor window containing the cursor is reached.

Item	Shortcut	Description
Inspect	Alt+F5	Opens the Debug Inspect window for the object under the cursor.
Goto Address	Ctrl+Alt+G	Enables you to specify an address in the program at which program execution will resume.
Evaluate/Modify	Ctrl+F7	Enables you to view and/or modify a variable at runtime.
Add Watch at Cursor	Ctrl+F5	Adds the variable under the cursor to the Watch List.
View CPU	Ctrl+Alt+C	Displays the CPU window.

The Run item on the main menu has several selections that pertain to running programs under the debugger. The Run menu items enable you to start a program under the debugger, to terminate a program running under the debugger, and to specify command-line parameters for your program, to name just a few functions. Some items found here are duplicated on the Code Editor context menu. Table 10.2 shows the Run menu items that control debugging operations.

TABLE 10.2. THE RUN MENU'S DEBUGGING ITEMS.

Item	Shortcut	Description
Run	F9	Compiles the program (if needed) and then runs the program under the control of the IDE debugger. Same as the Run toolbar button.
Parameters	None	Enables you to enter command-line parameters for your program and to assign a host application when debugging a DLL.
Step Over	F8	Executes the source code line at the execution point and pauses at the next source code line.
Trace Into	F7	Traces into the method at the execution point.
Trace to Next Source Line	Shift+F7	Causes the execution point to move to the next line in the program's source code.

continues

10

TABLE 10.2. CONTINUED

Item	Shortcut	Description
Run to Cursor	F4	Runs the program and pauses when program execution reaches the current line in the source code.
Show Execution Point	None	Displays the program execution point in the Code Editor. Scrolls the source code window if necessary. Works only when program execution is paused.
Program Pause	None	Pauses program execution as soon as the execution point enters the program's source code.
Program Reset	Ctrl+F2	Unconditionally terminates the program and returns to the Delphi IDE.
Inspect	None	Displays the Inspect dialog box so that you can enter the name of an object to inspect.
Evaluate/Modify	Ctrl+F7	Displays the Evaluate/Modify dialog box.
Add Watch	Ctrl+F5	Displays the Watch Properties dialog box.
Add Breakpoint	None	Displays a submenu that contains items to add a source, address, data, or module load breakpoint.

You will use these menu items a lot when you are debugging your programs. You should also become familiar with the various keyboard shortcuts for the debugging operations. Now let's take a look at breakpoints and how to use them in your program.

Using Breakpoints

When you run your program from the Delphi IDE, it runs at full speed, stopping only where you have set breakpoints.

 A *breakpoint* is a marker that tells the debugger to pause program execution when it reaches that place in the program.

Setting and Clearing Breakpoints

To set a breakpoint, click in the editor window's gutter to the left of the line on which you want to pause program execution (the gutter is the gray margin along the Code Editor window's left edge). The breakpoint icon (a red circle) appears in the gutter and the entire line is highlighted in red. To clear the breakpoint, click on the breakpoint icon and the breakpoint is removed. You can also press F5 or choose Toggle Breakpoint from the Code Editor context menu to toggle a breakpoint on or off.

> **Note**
>
> A breakpoint can be set only on a line that generates actual code. Breakpoints are not valid if set on blank lines, comment lines, or declaration lines. You are not prevented from setting a breakpoint on these types of lines, but the debugger warns you if you do. Attempting to set a breakpoint on any of the following lines will produce an invalid breakpoint warning:
>
> ```
> { This is a comment followed by a blank line. }
>
> X : Integer;  { a declaration }
> ```
>
> Breakpoints *can* be set on a function or procedure's end statement.

10

If you set a breakpoint on an invalid line, the Code Editor will display the breakpoint in green (assuming the default color scheme) and the breakpoint icon in the gutter will be grayed.

When the program is run under the debugger, it behaves as it normally would—until a breakpoint is hit, that is. When a breakpoint is hit, the IDE is brought to the top and the breakpoint line is highlighted in the source code. If you are using the default colors, the line where the program has stopped is highlighted in red because red indicates a line containing a breakpoint.

NEW TERM   The *execution point* indicates the line that will be executed next in your source code.

As you step through the program, the execution point is highlighted in blue and the editor window gutter displays a green arrow glyph. Understand that the line highlighted in blue has not yet been executed but will be when program execution resumes.

Note

The current execution point is highlighted in blue unless the line containing the execution point contains a breakpoint. In that case, the line is highlighted in red. The green arrow glyph in the gutter is the most accurate indication of the execution point because it is present regardless of the line's highlighting color.

When you stop at a breakpoint, you can view variables, view the call stack, browse symbols, or step through your code. After you have inspected any variables and objects, you can resume normal program execution by clicking the Run button. Your application will again run normally until the next breakpoint is encountered.

Note

It's common to detect coding errors in your program after you have stopped at a breakpoint. If you change your source code in the middle of a debugging session and then choose Run to resume program execution, the IDE will prompt you with a message box asking whether you want to rebuild the source code. If you choose Yes, the current process will be terminated, the source code will be recompiled, and the program will be restarted.

The problem with this approach is that your program doesn't get a chance to close normally, and any resources currently in use might not be freed properly. This scenario will almost certainly result in memory leaks. Although Windows 95 and Windows NT handle resource leaks better than 16-bit Windows, it is still advisable to terminate the program normally and then recompile it.

The Breakpoint List Window

The Delphi IDE keeps track of the breakpoints you set. These breakpoints can be viewed through the Breakpoint List window. To view the breakpoint list, choose View | Debug Windows | Breakpoints from the main menu. The Breakpoint List window is displayed as shown in Figure 10.1.

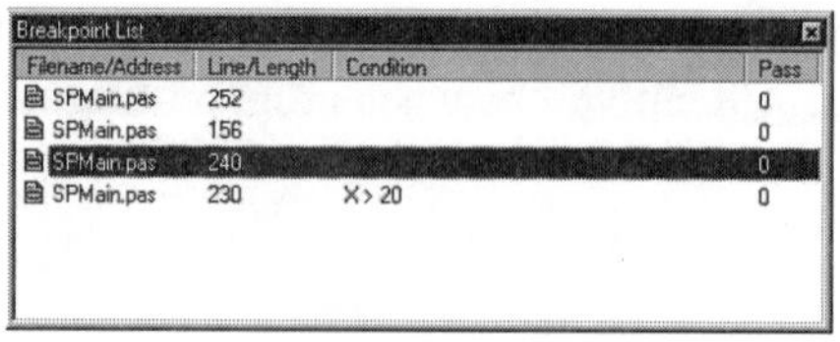

FIGURE 10.1.

The Breakpoint List window.

Filename/Address	Line/Length	Condition	Pass
SPMain.pas	252		0
SPMain.pas	156		0
SPMain.pas	240		0
SPMain.pas	230	X > 20	0

The Breakpoint List window has four columns:

- The Filename/Address column shows the filename of the source code unit in which the breakpoint is set.
- The Line/Length column shows the line number on which the breakpoint is set.
- The Condition column shows any conditions that have been set for the breakpoint.
- The Pass column shows the pass count condition that has been set for the breakpoint. (Breakpoint conditions and pass count conditions are discussed in the section "Conditional Breakpoints.")

The columns can be sized by dragging the dividing line between two columns in the column header.

Note The Pass column doesn't show the number of times the breakpoint has been hit; it only shows the pass condition that you have set for the breakpoint.

10

Breakpoint List Context Menus

The Breakpoint List window has two context menus. Table 10.3 lists the context menu items you will see when you click the right mouse button over any breakpoint. I will refer to this as the window's *primary context menu*.

TABLE 10.3. THE PRIMARY BREAKPOINT LIST CONTEXT MENU.

Item	Description
Enable	Enables or disables the breakpoint. When a breakpoint is disabled, its glyph is grayed out in the Breakpoint List window. In the source window, the breakpoint glyph is also grayed, and the breakpoint line is highlighted in green to indicate that the breakpoint is disabled.
Delete	Removes the breakpoint.
View Source	Scrolls the source file in the Code Editor to display the source line containing the breakpoint. (The Breakpoint List retains focus.)
Edit Source	Places the edit cursor on the line in the source file where the breakpoint is set and switches focus to the Code Editor.
Properties	Displays the Source Breakpoint Properties dialog box.
Dockable	Determines whether the Breakpoint List window is dockable.

Tip

To quickly edit the source code line on which a breakpoint is set, double-click on the breakpoint in the Filename column of the Breakpoint List window. This is the same as choosing Edit Source from the Breakpoint List context menu.

The secondary context menu is displayed by clicking the right mouse button while the cursor is over any part of the Breakpoint List window that doesn't contain a breakpoint. This context menu has items called Add, Delete All, Disable All, Enable All, and Dockable. These items are self-explanatory, so I won't bother to comment on them.

Note

In my opinion, the Add context menu item isn't very useful. It is much easier to set a breakpoint in the Code Editor than to add a breakpoint via the Add command in the Breakpoint List window.

Enabling and Disabling Breakpoints

Breakpoints can be enabled or disabled any time you like. You disable a breakpoint if you want to run the program normally for a while; you can enable the breakpoint later without having to re-create it. The debugger ignores breakpoints that are disabled. To enable or disable a breakpoint, right-click on the breakpoint in the Breakpoint List window and toggle the Enable item on the context menu.

Modifying Breakpoints

If you want to modify a breakpoint, choose Properties from the primary Breakpoint List context menu. When you do, the Source Breakpoint Properties dialog box is displayed (see Figure 10.2).

FIGURE 10.2.

The Source Breakpoint Properties dialog box.

The primary reason for modifying a breakpoint is to add conditions to it. (Conditional breakpoints are discussed in the section "Conditional Breakpoints.")

To remove a breakpoint, select the breakpoint in the Breakpoint List window and then press the Delete key on the keyboard. To delete all breakpoints, right-click and then choose Delete All. Now let's take a look at the two breakpoint types: simple and conditional.

Simple Breakpoints

A *simple breakpoint* causes program execution to be suspended whenever the breakpoint is hit. When you initially set a breakpoint, it is by default a simple breakpoint. Simple breakpoints don't require much explanation. When the breakpoint is encountered, program execution pauses and the debugger awaits your bidding. Most of the time you will use simple breakpoints. Conditional breakpoints are reserved for special cases in which you need more control over the debugging process.

Conditional Breakpoints

In the case of a *conditional breakpoint*, program execution is paused only when predefined conditions are met. To create a conditional breakpoint, first set the breakpoint in the Code Editor. Then choose View | Debug Windows | Breakpoints from the main menu to display the Breakpoint List window. Right-click on the breakpoint for which you want to set conditions and choose Properties. When the Source Breakpoint Properties dialog box is displayed, set the conditions for the breakpoint.

Conditional breakpoints come in two flavors. The first type is a *conditional expression breakpoint*. Enter the conditional expression in the Condition field of the Source Breakpoint Properties dialog box (refer to Figure 10.2). When the program runs, the conditional expression is evaluated each time the breakpoint is encountered. When the conditional expression evaluates to True, program execution is halted. If the condition doesn't evaluate to True, the breakpoint is ignored. For example, look back at the last breakpoint in the Breakpoint List window shown in Figure 10.1. This breakpoint has a conditional expression of X > 20. If at some point in the execution of the program X is greater than 20, the program will stop at the breakpoint. If X is never greater than 20, program execution will not stop at the breakpoint.

The other type of conditional breakpoint is the *pass count breakpoint*. With a pass count breakpoint, program execution is paused only after the breakpoint is encountered a specified number of times. To specify a pass count breakpoint, edit the breakpoint and specify a value for the Pass Count field in the Source Breakpoint Properties dialog box. If you set the pass count for a breakpoint to 3, program execution will stop at the breakpoint the third time the breakpoint is encountered.

10

Note

> The pass count is 1-based, not 0-based. As indicated in the preceding exam-
> ple, a pass count of 3 means that the breakpoint will be valid the third time
> the breakpoint is encountered by the program.

Use pass count breakpoints when you need your program to execute through a breakpoint a certain number of times before you break to inspect variables, step through code,
or perform other debugging tasks.

Note

> Conditional breakpoints slow down the normal execution of the program
> because the conditions need to be evaluated each time a conditional break-
> point is encountered. If your program is acting sluggish during debugging,
> check your breakpoint list to see whether you have conditional breakpoints
> that you have forgotten about.

Tip

> The fact that conditional breakpoints slow down program execution can
> work in your favor at times. If you have a process that you want to view in
> slow motion, set one or more conditional breakpoints in that section of
> code. Set the conditions so that they will never be met, and your program
> will slow down but not stop.

The Run to Cursor Command

There is another debugging command that deserves mention here. The Run to Cursor
command (found on the Run menu on the main menu and on the Code Editor context
menu) runs the program until the source line containing the editing cursor is reached. At
that point, the program stops as if a breakpoint were placed on that line.

Run to Cursor acts as a temporary breakpoint. You can use this command rather than set
a breakpoint on a line that you want to immediately inspect. Just place the cursor on the
line you want to break on and choose Run to Cursor (or press F4). The debugger behaves
exactly as if you had placed a breakpoint on that line. The benefit is that you don't have
to clear the breakpoint after you are done debugging that section of code.

Watching Variables

So what do you do when you stop at a breakpoint? Usually you stop at a breakpoint to inspect the value of one or more variables. You might want to ensure that a particular variable has the value you think it should, or you might not have any idea what a variable's value is and simply want to find out.

The function of the Watch List is basic: It enables you to inspect the values of variables. Programmers often overlook this simple but essential feature because they don't take the time to learn how to fully use the debugger. You can add as many variables to the Watch List as you like. Figure 10.3 shows the Watch List during a debugging session.

FIGURE 10.3.

The Watch List in action.

10

The variable name is displayed in the Watch List followed by its value. How the variable value is displayed is determined by the variable's data type and the current display settings for that watch item. I'll discuss the Watch List window in detail in just a bit, but first I want to tell you about a feature that makes inspecting variables easy.

Tooltip Expression Evaluation

The debugger and Code Editor have a nice feature that makes checking the value of a variable easy. This feature, the Tooltip expression evaluator, is on by default, so you don't have to do anything special to use it. If you want, you can turn off the Tooltip evaluator via the Code Insight page of the Environment Options dialog box (the Code Insight page was discussed yesterday).

So what is Tooltip expression evaluation (besides hard to say)? It works like this: After you stop at a breakpoint, you place the editing cursor over a variable and a tooltip window pops up showing the variable's current value. This makes it easy to quickly inspect variables. Just place your cursor over a variable and wait a half second or so.

The Tooltip evaluator has different displays for different variable types. For regular data members (Integer, Char, Byte, string, and so on), the actual value of the variable is displayed. For dynamically created objects (an instance of a class, for example), the Tooltip evaluator shows the memory location of the object. For records, the Tooltip evaluator shows all the record elements. Figure 10.4 shows the Tooltip expression evaluator inspecting a record's contents.

FIGURE 10.4.

Tooltips are a great debugger feature.

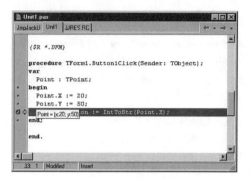

> **Note**
>
> Sometimes the Tooltip evaluator acts as if it's not working properly. If, for example, you place the editing cursor over a variable that is out of scope, no tooltip appears. The Tooltip evaluator has nothing to show for that particular variable, so it doesn't display anything.
>
> Be aware, also, that variables optimized by the compiler might not show correct values. Optimization was discussed yesterday and is also discussed later in this chapter.
>
> Another case where the Tooltip evaluator doesn't work is within a `with` block. Take this code, for example:
>
> ```
> with Point do begin
>   X := 20;
>   Y := 50;
>   Label1.Caption := IntToStr(X);
> end;
> ```
>
> If you were to place the mouse cursor over the variable X, the Tooltip evaluator would not report the value of X because X belongs to the target of the `with` statement (the `Point` variable). Instead, place the mouse cursor over the `Point` variable, and the debugger shows you the value of `Point` (including the X field).

The Tooltip expression evaluator is a great feature, so don't forget to use it.

The Watch List Context Menu

As with every other Delphi window discussed so far, the Watch List has its own context menu. (You'd be disappointed if it didn't, right?) Table 10.4 lists the Watch List context menu items and their descriptions.

TABLE 10.4. THE WATCH LIST CONTEXT MENU.

Item	Description
Edit Watch	Enables you to edit the watch item with the Watch Properties dialog box.
Add Watch	Adds a new item to the Watch List.
Enable Watch	Enables the watch item.
Disable Watch	Disables the watch item.
Delete Watch	Removes the watch item from the Watch List.
Enable All Watches	Enables all items in the Watch List.
Disable All Watches	Disables all items in the Watch List.
Delete All Watches	Deletes all items in the Watch List.
Stay on Top	Forces the Watch List to the top of all other windows in the IDE.
Break When Changed	When the variable in the watch window changes, the debugger will break. The watch variable is displayed in red to indicate that Break When Changed is in effect.
Dockable	Determines whether the Watch List window is dockable.

Both the Edit Watch and Add Watch context menu items invoke the Watch Properties dialog box, so let's look at that next.

Using the Watch Properties Dialog Box

You use the Watch Properties dialog box when you add or edit a watch. Figure 10.5 shows the Watch Properties dialog box as it looks when editing a variable called `Buff`.

FIGURE 10.5.

The Watch Properties dialog box.

The Expression field at the top of the Watch Properties dialog box is where you enter a variable name to edit or add to the watch list. This field is a combo box that can be used to select previously used watch items.

You use the Repeat count field when you are inspecting arrays. For example, let's say you have an array of 20 integers. To inspect the first 10 integers in the array, you would enter the first element of the array in the Expression field (Array[0], for example) and then enter 10 in the Repeat Count field. The first 10 elements of the array would then be displayed in the Watch List.

Note

If you add just the array name to the Watch List, all elements in the array will be displayed. Use the Repeat Count field when you want to view only a specific number of array elements.

The Digits field is used only when inspecting floating-point numbers. Enter the number of significant digits you want to see when your floating-point number is displayed in the Watch List. The displayed digits are rounded, not truncated. Another field in this dialog box, the Enabled field, determines whether the watch item is currently enabled.

The remainder of the Watch Properties dialog box is composed of various display options. Each data type has a default display type, which is used if you choose the Default viewing option. The Default viewing option is the default. (Sorry, there's just no other way to say it.) Select the other viewing options to view the data in other ways. Figure 10.6 shows the Watch List window with two variables added and with various viewing options applied. The Buff variable is a character array, and the I variable is an integer.

FIGURE 10.6.

The Watch List with various viewing options.

To modify a watch item, click the item in the Watch List and choose Edit Watch from the Watch List context menu. You can also double-click a watch item to edit it. The Watch Properties dialog box is displayed, and you can edit the watch item as needed.

Tip

The fastest way to edit a watch item is to double-click its name in the Watch List.

Enabling and Disabling Watch Items

As with breakpoints, individual items in the Watch List can be enabled or disabled. When a watch item is disabled, it is grayed and its value shows <disabled>.

To disable a watch item, click the item's name in the Watch List and choose Disable Watch from the Watch List context menu. To enable the watch item again, choose Enable Watch from the context menu.

> **Note**
>
> You might want to disable watch items that you don't currently want to watch but will need later. Having a number of enabled items in the Watch List slows down program execution during the debugging process because all the Watch List variables must be updated each time a code line executes.

Adding Variables to the Watch List

You can add variables to the Watch List in several ways. The quickest way is to click the variable name in the editor window and then select Add Watch at Cursor from the Code Editor context menu or press Ctrl+F5. The watch item will be immediately added to the Watch List. You can then edit the watch item to change the display properties, if needed.

To add a variable to the watch without first locating it in the source file, choose Run | Add Watch from the main menu. When the Watch Properties dialog box comes up, enter the name of the variable you want to add to the Watch List and click OK.

> **Note**
>
> Although you can add a class instance variable to the Watch List, the displayed value will not likely be useful. For viewing all the class data members, you should use the Debug Inspector, which I'll discuss in a minute.

Using the Watch List

When a breakpoint is hit, the Watch List displays the current value of any variables that have been added to the Watch List. If the Watch List isn't currently open, you can choose View | Debug Windows | Watches from the main menu to display it.

> **Tip**
>
> Dock the Watch List window to the bottom of the Code Editor window so that it will always be in view when stepping through code.

Under certain circumstances, a message will be displayed next to the variable instead of the variable's value. If, for example, a variable is out of scope or not found, the Watch List displays `Undeclared identifier:'X'` next to the variable name. If the program

10

isn't running or isn't stopped at a breakpoint, the Watch List displays [process not accessible] for all watch items. A disabled watch item will have <disabled> next to it. Other messages can be displayed depending on the current state of the application or the current state of a particular variable.

As I said yesterday, you might on occasion see Variable 'X' inaccessible here due to optimization in the Watch List. This is one of the minor disadvantages of having an optimizing compiler. If you need to inspect variables that are subject to optimization, you must turn optimization off. Turn off the Optimization option on the Compiler page of the Project Options dialog box. Be aware that variables that have not been initialized (assigned a value) will report random values until they are initialized.

Tip

The Watch List can be used as a quickie decimal/hexadecimal converter. To convert a hex number to decimal, choose Run | Add Watch from the main menu. Type the hexadecimal number in the Expression field and click OK. Both the hexadecimal number and the decimal equivalent are displayed in the Watch List. To convert a decimal number to hex, perform the same procedure, except click the Hexadecimal radio button to change the display type to hexadecimal. Because the Expression field will accept a mathematical expression, you can also use the Watch List as a hex calculator. You can even mix hexadecimal and decimal values in the same expression. The only drawback is that your application must be stopped at a breakpoint before this technique will work.

The Watch List is a simple but vital tool in debugging applications. To illustrate the use of the Watch List, perform this exercise:

1. Create a new application and place a button on the form. Change the button's Name property to WatchBtn and its Caption to Watch Test. Change the form's Name property to DebugMain and the Caption property to whatever you like.

2. Double-click the button to display its OnClick handler in the Code Editor. Modify the OnClick handler so that it looks like this:

```
procedure TForm1.Button1Click(Sender: TObject);
var
  S : string;
  X, Y : Integer;
begin
  X := Width;
  S := IntToStr(X);
  Y := Height;
  X := X * Y;
  S := IntToStr(X);
```

```
   X := X div Y;
   S := IntToStr(X);
   Width := X;
   Height := Y;
end;
```

3. Save the project. Name the unit DbgMain and the project DebugTst.

4. Set a breakpoint on the first line after the begin statement in the OnClick handler. Run the program.

5. Click the Watch Test button. The debugger will stop at the breakpoint. When the debugger stops at a breakpoint, the IDE and Code Editor come to the top.

6. Add watches for the variables S, X, and Y. (Initially the variables X and Y will be inaccessible due to optimization, but don't worry about that.)

7. Arrange the Watch List and Code Editor so that you can see both (dock the Watch List to the bottom of the Code Editor if you want).

8. Switch focus to the Code Editor and press F8 to execute the next line of code. That line is executed and the execution point moves to the next line. The variable X now shows a value.

9. Continue to step through the program by pressing F8. Watch the results of the variables in the Watch List.

10. When the execution point gets to the last line in the method, click the Run button on the toolbar to continue running the program.

Click the Watch Test button as many times as you want to get a feel for how the Watch List works. Experiment with different watch settings each time through.

Note

> The code in this example obtains the values for the form's Width and Height properties, performs some calculations, and then sets the Width and Height back to where they were when you started. In the end nothing changes, but there is a good reason for assigning values to the Width and Height properties at the end of the method.
>
> If you don't actually do something with the variables X and Y, you can't inspect them because the compiler will optimize them and they won't be available to watch. Essentially, the compiler can look ahead, see that the variables are never used, and just discard them. Putting the variables to use at the end of the method avoids having them optimized away by the compiler.
>
> I've brought this up several times now, but I want to make sure you have a basic understanding of how an optimizing compiler works. When you start debugging your applications, this knowledge will help avoid some frustration when you start getting those Variable 'X' inaccessible here due to optimization messages in the Watch List.

10

The Debug Inspector

 The Debug Inspector is a new feature in Delphi 4. Simply stated, the Debug Inspector enables you to view data objects such as classes and records. You can also inspect simple data types such as integers, character arrays, and so on, but those are best viewed with the Watch List. The Debug Inspector is most useful in examining classes and records.

> **Note**
>
> You can use the Debug Inspector only when program execution is paused under the debugger.

To inspect an object, click the object's name in a source file and choose Inspect from the Code Editor context menu (or press Alt+F5). You can also choose Run | Inspect from the main menu.

The Debug Inspector window contains details of the object displayed. If the object is a simple data type, the Debug Inspector window shows the current value (in both decimal and hex for numeric data types) and the status line at the bottom displays the data type. For example, if you inspect an integer variable, the value will be shown and the status bar will say Integer. At the top of the Debug Inspector is a combo box that initially contains a description of the object being inspected.

If you are inspecting a class, the Debug Inspector will look like Figure 10.7.

FIGURE 10.7.

The Debug Inspector inspecting a form class.

To better understand the Debug Inspector, follow these steps:

1. Load the DebugTst program you created earlier (if it's not already loaded).

2. Set a breakpoint somewhere in the WatchBtnClick method.

3. Run the program and click the Watch Test button. The debugger stops at the breakpoint you have set.

4. From the main menu, choose Run | Inspect. The Inspect dialog box is displayed.

5. Type Self in the Expression field and click OK.

6. The Debug Inspector is displayed and you can examine the main form's data.

 Note You can inspect Self only from within a method of a class. If you happen to set a breakpoint in a regular function or procedure and then attempt to inspect Self, you will get an error message stating that Self is an invalid symbol. In the previous example, Self refers to the application's main form.

Debug Inspector Pages

When inspecting classes, the Debug Inspector window contains three pages, as you can see. The first items listed are the data items that belong to the ancestor class. At the end of the list are the items that belong to the immediate class. You can choose whether to view the ancestor class information. To turn off the ancestor class items, right-click and select Show Inherited from the Debug Inspector context menu.

By using the arrow keys to move up and down the data members list, you can tell at a glance what each data member's type is (look at the status bar on the Debug Inspector window). To further inspect a data member, double-click the value column on the line showing the data member. A second Debug Inspector window is opened with the selected data member displayed. You can have multiple Debug Inspector windows open simultaneously.

The Methods page of the Debug Inspector displays the class's methods. In some cases the Methods tab isn't displayed (when inspecting simple data types, for example). The status bar shows the selected method's declaration.

The Properties page of the Debug Inspector shows the properties for the class being inspected. Viewing the properties of a class is of limited value (the information presented is not particularly useful). Most of the time you can accomplish what you are after by inspecting the data member associated with a particular property on the Data page.

Note The Methods page and the Properties page of the Debug Inspector are available only when you're inspecting a class. When you're inspecting simple data types, the Data page alone is displayed.

> **Tip**
>
> If you want your Debug Inspector windows always on top of the Code Editor, go to the Debugger page of the Environment Options dialog box and check the Inspectors stay on top check box.

Debug Inspector Context Menus

The Debug Inspector context menu has several items that enable you to work with the Debug Inspector and the individual variables. For example, rather than open a new Debug Inspector window for each object, you can right-click and choose Descend to replace the current object in the Debug Inspector window with the selected object. For example, if you are inspecting a form with a button called Button1, you can select Button1 in the Debug Inspector and choose Descend from the context menu. The Debug Inspector will then be inspecting Button1. This method has an added advantage: The IDE keeps a history list of the objects you inspect. To go back to an object you have already inspected, just choose the object from the combo box at the top of the Debug Inspector window. Choosing one of the objects in the history list will again show that object in the Debug Inspector window.

The Change item on the Debug Inspector context menu enables you to change a variable's value.

> **Caution**
>
> Take great care when changing variables with the Debug Inspector. Changing the wrong data member or specifying a value that is invalid for that data member might cause your program to crash.

The Inspect item on the Debug Inspector's context menu enables you to open a second Debug Inspector window with the item under the cursor displayed. The New Expression context menu item enables you to enter a new expression to inspect in the Debug Inspector.

The Show Inherited item on the Debug Inspector context menu is a toggle that determines how much information the Debug Inspector should display. When the Show Inherited option is on, the Debug Inspector shows all data members, methods, and properties of the class being inspected as well as the data members, methods, and properties of the immediate ancestor class. When the Show Inherited option is off, only the data members, methods, and properties of the class itself are shown. Turning off this option can speed up the Debug Inspector because it doesn't have as much information to display.

Tip

> If you have a class data member and you don't remember its type, you can click on it when you are stopped at a breakpoint and press Alt+F5 to display the Debug Inspector. The status bar at the bottom of the Debug Inspector window will tell you the variable's data type.

Other Debugging Tools

Delphi has some additional debugging tools to aid you in tracking down bugs. Some of these tools are, by nature, advanced debugging tools. Although the advanced debugging tools are not as commonly used as the other tools, they are very powerful in the hands of an experienced programmer.

The Evaluate/Modify Dialog Box

The Evaluate/Modify dialog box enables you to inspect a variable's current value and to modify the value if you want. Using this dialog box, you can test for different outcomes by modifying a particular variable. This enables you to play a what-if game with your program as it runs. Changing the value of a variable while debugging allows you to test the effects of different parameters of your program without recompiling each time. Figure 10.8 shows the Evaluate/Modify dialog box inspecting a variable.

10

FIGURE 10.8.

The Evaluate/Modify dialog box.

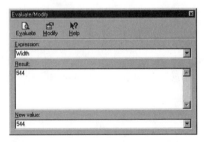

Note

> The Evaluate/Modify dialog box's toolbar can display either large toolbar buttons or small toolbar buttons. By default, it shows small toolbar buttons. The small buttons don't have captions, so you will have to pass your mouse cursor over the buttons and read the tooltip to see what each button does. To see the large toolbar buttons, drag the sizing bar immediately below the toolbar downward to resize the toolbar. The toolbar will then show the large toolbar buttons with captions underneath each button. Figure 10.8 shows the Evaluate/Modify dialog box with large toolbar buttons.

The Evaluate/Modify dialog box works similarly to the Watch List or the Debug Inspector. If you click a variable in the source code and choose Evaluate/Modify from the Code Editor context menu, the variable will be evaluated. If you want to enter a value not currently showing in the source code, you can choose Run | Evaluate/Modify from the main menu and then type a variable name to evaluate.

The Expression field is used to enter the variable name or expression you want to evaluate. When you click the Evaluate button (or press Enter), the expression will be evaluated and the result displayed in the Result field.

> **Tip**
>
> The Evaluate/Modify dialog box can be used as a quickie calculator. You can enter hex or decimal numbers (or a combination) in a mathematical formula and have the result evaluated. For example, if you type
>
> `$400 - 256`
>
> in the Evaluate field and press Enter, the result, 768, is displayed in the Result field.
>
> You can also enter logical expressions in the Evaluate field and have the result shown in the Result field. For example, if you enter
>
> `20 * 20 = 400`
>
> the Result field would show True. The program must be stopped at a breakpoint for the Evaluate/Modify dialog box to function.

If you want to change a variable's value, enter a new value for the variable in the New Value field and click the Modify button. The variable's value will be changed to the new value entered. When you click the Run button to restart the program (or continue stepping), the new value will be used.

> **Note**
>
> The Evaluate/Modify dialog box doesn't update automatically when you step through your code, as do the Watch List and Debug Inspector. If your code modifies the variable in the Evaluate/Modify dialog box, you must click the Evaluate button again to see the results. This aspect of the Evaluate/Modify dialog box has one primary benefit; stepping through code is quicker because the debugger doesn't have to evaluate the expression each time you step (as it does for the Watch List and Debug Inspector). A typical interaction with this dialog box would be to evaluate a variable or expression and then immediately close the Evaluate/Modify dialog box.

The Call Stack Window

While your program is running, you can view the call stack to inspect any functions or procedures your program called. From the main menu, choose View | Debug Windows | Call Stack to display the Call Stack window. This window displays a list of the functions and procedures called by your program and the order in which they were called. The most recently called function or procedure is at the top of the window.

Double-clicking a method name in the Call Stack window takes you to the source code line for that method if the method is in your program. In case of functions or procedures for which there is no source code (VCL methods, for example), the Call Stack window contains just an address and the name of the module where the procedure is located. Double-clicking a listed function or procedure without source code will display the CPU window (the CPU window is discussed in the next section).

Viewing the call stack is most helpful after a Windows Access Violation error. By viewing the call stack, you can see where your program was just before the error occurred. Knowing where your program was just before it crashed is often the first step in determining what went wrong.

10

Tip

If the call stack list contains seemingly nonsensical information, it could be that the call stack was corrupted. A corrupted call stack is usually an indicator of a stack overflow or a memory overwrite. A stack overflow isn't as likely to occur in a 32-bit program as in a 16-bit program, but it still can happen.

The CPU Window

New to 4 Officially speaking, the CPU window is new to Delphi 4. You could get the CPU window in previous versions of Delphi, but only if you knew the magical Registry entry. The CPU window is now officially part of Delphi and can be found on the main menu under View | Debug Windows | CPU (Ctrl+Alt+C on the keyboard).

The CPU window enables you to view your program at the assembly instruction level. Using this view, you can step into or over instructions one assembly instruction at a time. You can also run the program to a certain assembly instruction just as you can run the program to a certain source line with the regular debugger. The CPU window has five panes: the disassembly pane, the register pane, the flags pane, the raw stack pane, and the dump pane.

Each pane has a context menu associated with it. The context menus provide all the functions necessary to use that pane. To be used effectively, the CPU window requires a knowledge of assembly language. Obviously, the CPU window is an advanced debugging feature.

The Go to Address Command

The Go to Address command is also an advanced debugging tool. When your program crashes, Windows displays an error message showing the address of the violation. You can use the Go to Address command to attempt to find out where in your program the crash occurred. When you get an Access Violation error message from Windows, you see a dialog box similar to the one shown in Figure 10.9.

FIGURE 10.9.

A Windows message box reporting an access violation.

When you see this error message, write down the address at which the violation occurred and then choose Debug | Go to Address from the Code Editor context menu to display the Goto Address dialog box. Enter the address you just wrote down in the Address field of the Goto Address dialog box.

When you click OK, the debugger will attempt to find the source code line where the error occurred. If the error occurred in your code, the cursor will be placed on the line that generated the error. If the error occurred somewhere outside your code, you will get a message box saying that the address could not be found. As I said, this is an advanced debugging tool and one that you might never use.

Stepping Through Your Code

Stepping through code is one of the most basic debugging operations, yet it still needs to be mentioned here. Sometimes you fail to see the forest for the trees. (Just as sometimes authors of programming books fail to include the obvious!) Reviewing the basics from time to time can reveal something you were not previously aware of.

Debugging Gutter Symbols

Before beginning this section, I'll say a few words about the symbols that appear in the Code Editor gutter during a debugging session. In the section "Setting and Clearing Breakpoints," I told you that a red circle appears in the gutter when you set a breakpoint on a code line. I also said that a green arrow glyph indicates the execution point when you are stepping through code.

One point I didn't mention, though, is the little blue dots that appear in the gutter next to certain code lines. These dots indicate lines in your source code that actually generate assembly code. Figure 10.10 shows the Code Editor with the debugger stopped at a breakpoint. It shows the small dots that indicate generated code, the arrow glyph indicating the execution point, and the breakpoint glyph as well. The check mark on the breakpoint glyph indicates that the breakpoint was checked and was determined to be a valid breakpoint.

FIGURE 10.10.

The Code Editor showing gutter symbols.

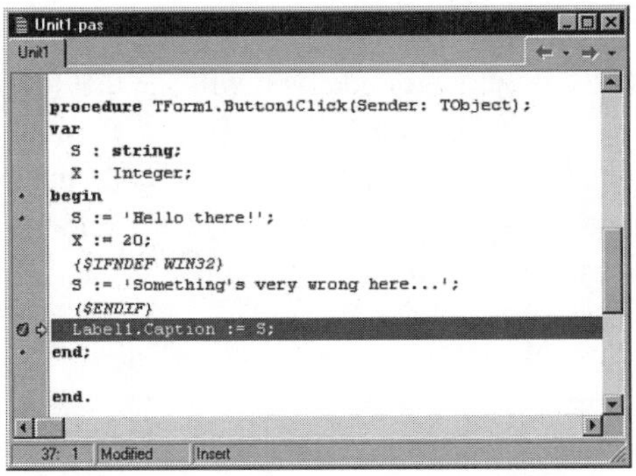

Take a closer look at Figure 10.10. Notice that the small dots only appear next to certain code lines. Lines without the dots don't generate any compiled code. Take these lines, for example:

```
var
  S : string;
  X : Integer;
```

Why don't these lines generate code? Because they are variable declarations. How about this line:

```
X := 20;
```

Why is no code generated for this line? Here's that word again: *optimization*. The compiler looks ahead and sees that the variable X is never used, so it completely ignores all references to that variable. Finally, notice these lines:

```
{$IFNDEF WIN32}
S := 'Something's very wrong here...';
{$ENDIF}
```

The compiler doesn't generate code for the line of source code between the compiler directives because the symbol WIN32 is defined in a Delphi 4 program. The compiler

$IFNDEF WIN32 directives tell the compiler, "Compile this line of code only if the target platform is not 32-bit Windows." Because Delphi 4 is a 32-bit compiler, this line of code is not compiled. This line of code *will* be compiled if this code is compiled in Delphi 1 (a 16-bit environment).

Step Over and Trace Into

Okay, back to stepping through code. When you stop at a breakpoint, you can do many things to determine what is going on with your code. You can set up variables to watch in the Watch List, inspect objects with the Debug Inspector, or view the call stack. You can also step through your code to watch what happens to your variables and objects as each code line is executed.

As you continue to step through your code, you will see that the line in your source code to be executed next is highlighted in blue. If you have the Watch List and Debug Inspector windows open, they will be updated as each code line is executed. Any changes to variables or objects will be immediately visible in the watch or inspector window. The IDE debugger has two primary stepping commands to aid in your debugging operations: Step Over and Trace Into.

Step Over

Step Over means to execute the next line in the source code and pause on the line immediately following. Step Over is sort of a misnomer. The name indicates that you can step over a source line and the line won't be executed. That isn't the case, however. Step Over means that the current line will be executed and any functions or procedures called by that source line will be run at full speed. For example, let's say you set a breakpoint at a line that calls a method in your program. When you tell the debugger to step over the method, the debugger will execute the method and stop on the next line. (Contrast this with how Trace Into works, which you'll learn about in a minute, and it will make more sense.) To use Step Over to step through your program, you can either press F8 or choose Run | Step Over from the main menu.

Note

As you step through various source code units in your program, the Code Editor will automatically load and display the needed source units if they are not already open.

Trace Into

The Trace Into command enables you to trace into any functions or procedures that are encountered as you step through your code. Rather than execute the function or procedure and return to the next line as Step Over does, Trace Into places the execution point on the first source code line in the function or procedure being called. You can then step line-by-line through that function or procedure using Step Over or Trace Into as necessary. The keyboard shortcut for Trace Into is F7.

After you have inspected variables and done whatever debugging you need to do, you can again run the program at full speed by clicking the Run button. The program will function normally until the next breakpoint is encountered.

 Tip

> If you have the Professional or Client/Server version of Delphi, you can step into the VCL source code. When you encounter a VCL method, Trace Into will take you into the VCL source code for that method. You can inspect whatever variables you need to see. You must add the path to the VCL source in to the Search path field of the Project Options (Directories/Conditionals page). To enable this option, you must do a Build after adding the VCL source directory to the Search path field. Stepping into the VCL source is of doubtful benefit to most programmers. Experienced programmers, though, will find it useful.

10

Trace To Next Source Line

Another, less frequently used debugging command is Trace To Next Source Line (Shift+F7 on the keyboard). You will not likely use this command a lot, particularly not until you get more familiar with debugging and Windows programming in general. Some Windows API functions use what is termed a *callback function*. This means that the Windows function calls one of your own functions to perform some action.

If the execution point is on a Windows API function that uses a callback, using Trace To Next Source Line will jump the execution point to the first line in the callback function. The effect is similar to Trace Into, but the specific situation in which Trace To Next Source Line is used is altogether different. If that doesn't make sense to you, don't worry about it. It's not important for what you need to learn today.

When you are stepping through a method, the execution point will eventually get to the end statement of the method. If the method you are stepping through returns control to Windows when it finishes, pressing F8 when you're on the end statement will exit the method and return control to the program being debugged. There is no obvious indication that the program is no longer paused because the IDE still has focus. This behavior can be confusing the first few times you encounter it unless you are aware of what has happened. To switch back to your program, just activate it as you would any other program (click its button on the Windows taskbar or use Alt+Tab).

As I said, stepping through your code is a basic debugging technique, but it is one that you will use constantly while debugging. Of all the keyboard shortcuts available to you in Delphi, F7 (Trace Into), F8 (Step Over), and F9 (Run) should definitely be in your arsenal.

Debugging a DLL

For the most part, debugging a DLL (dynamic link library) is the same as debugging an executable file. You place breakpoints in the DLL's code and when a breakpoint is hit, the debugger will pause just as it does when debugging an EXE. Normally you test a DLL by creating a test application and running the test application under the debugger.

Sometimes, however, you need to test a DLL for use with executable files built with other development environments. For example, let's say you are building a DLL that will be called from a Visual Basic application. You certainly can't start a VB application running under the Delphi debugger. What you can do, though, is tell the Delphi debugger to start the VB application as a host application. (Naturally, the host application has to contain code that loads the DLL.) You tell Delphi to start an external host application through the Run Parameters dialog box.

To display the Run Parameters dialog box, choose Run | Parameters from the main menu. Type an EXE name in the Host Application field, click the Load button, and the host application will run. Figure 10.11 shows the Run Parameters dialog box as it appears just before debugging a DLL.

FIGURE 10.11.

*Specifying a host
application with the
Run Parameters dialog
box.*

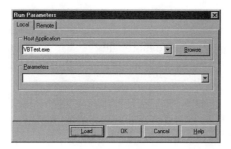

After the host application has started, you debug your DLL just as you do when using a
Delphi test application: Simply place breakpoints in the DLL and begin debugging.

 Note

> The Run Parameters dialog box has a tab called Remote. This tab enables
> you to set the parameters for debugging an application on a remote
> machine. Remote debugging is an advanced topic and won't be covered
> here.

10

The Event Log Window

The Event Log is a special Delphi file that shows diagnostic messages—messages generated by Delphi, by your own applications, and sometimes by Windows itself. For example, the Event Log contains information regarding modules that are loaded (mostly
DLLs), whether they include debug info, when your application was started, when it was
stopped, when a breakpoint was encountered, and more. You view the Event Log through
the Event Log window. To see the Event Log window, choose View | Debug Windows |
Event Log from the Delphi main menu. Figure 10.12 shows the Event Log window
while debugging an application.

FIGURE 10.12.

*The Event Log win-
dow.*

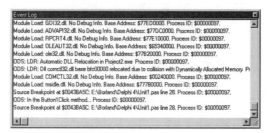

The Event Log window has a context menu that enables you to clear the Log, save it to a text file, or add comments to the Event Log. Saving the Event Log to a text file enables you to browse the messages list more thoroughly or search for specific text you want to see. The Event Log window context menu also has a Properties menu item that enables you to further customize the Event Log. When you choose this menu item, a dialog box is displayed that enables you to change Event Log options. This dialog box is the same as the Event Log page in the Debugger Options dialog box (discussed later in the section "The Event Log Page").

You can send your own messages to the Event Log using the Windows API function OutputDebugString. OutputDebugString is discussed later in the section "The OutputDebugString Function."

The Module Window

The Module window shows you the modules currently loaded, source files attached to those modules, and symbols (functions, procedures, and variables) exported from that module. You can invoke the Module window by choosing View | Debug Windows | Modules from the main menu. The Module window is primarily an advanced debugging tool, so I won't go into a detailed discussion of its features here. You should take some time to experiment with the Module window to see how it works. Figure 10.13 shows the Module window in action.

FIGURE 10.13.

The Module window.

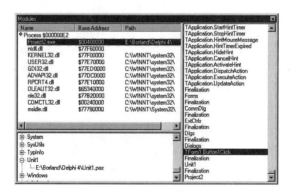

Debugging Techniques

I have already touched on a few debugging techniques as I examined the various aspects of the IDE debugger in this chapter. I now mention a few more techniques that make your debugging tasks easier.

The `OutputDebugString` Function

Sometimes it is helpful to track your program's execution as your program runs. Or maybe you want to see a variable's value without stopping program execution at a breakpoint. The `OutputDebugString` function enables you to do exactly that. This function is a convenient debugging tool that many programmers overlook, primarily because of a general lack of discussion on the subject. Look at the last entry in the Event Log shown in Figure 10.12 (earlier in the chapter). That entry was generated using this code:

```
OutputDebugString('In the Button1Click method...');
```

That's all you have to do. Because Delphi is installed as the system debugger, any strings sent using `OutputDebugString` will show up in the Event Log. You can place calls to `OutputDebugString` anywhere you want in your code.

To view the value of a variable, you must format a string and send that string to `OutputDebugString`. For example:

```
procedure TForm1.FormCreate(Sender: TObject);
var
  X : Integer;
  S : string;
begin
  { Some code here...}
  S := Format('X := %d', [X]);
  OutputDebugString(PChar(S));
end;
```

Using `OutputDebugString` you can see what is going on with your program even in time-critical sections of code.

Tracking Down Access Violations

When a program attempts to write to memory that it doesn't own, Windows issues an Access Violation error message. All Windows programmers encounter access violations while developing their applications.

Note

> The term GPF (General Protection Fault) was used in 16-bit Windows. Its use is still prevalent in the 32-bit Windows programming world even though 32-bit Windows actually generates Access Violation errors instead of General Protection Faults.

Access violations can be difficult to track down for beginning and experienced Windows programmers alike. Often, as programmers gain experience in writing Windows programs,

10

they develop a sixth sense for locating the cause of access violations. Here are some clues to look for when trying to track down the elusive access violation. These are not the only situations that cause a program to crash, but they are some of the most common.

Uninitialized Pointers

An *uninitialized pointer* is a pointer that has been declared but not set to point to anything meaningful in your program. An uninitialized pointer will contain random data. In the best case, it points to some harmless spot in memory. In the worst case, the uninitialized pointer points to a random memory location somewhere in your program. This can lead to erratic program behavior because the pointer might point to a different memory location each time the program is run. Always set a pointer to nil both before it's used for the first time and after the object it points to is deleted. If you try to access a nil pointer, your program will stop with an access violation, but the offending line in the source code will be highlighted by the debugger, and you can immediately identify the problem pointer.

Deleting Previously Deleted Pointers

Deleting a pointer that has already been deleted results in an access violation. The advice given for working with uninitialized pointers applies here as well: Set deleted pointers to nil. It is perfectly safe to delete a nil pointer. By setting your deleted pointer to nil, you ensure that no ill effects will occur if you accidentally delete the pointer a second time.

Array Overwrites

Overwriting the end of an array can cause an access violation. In some cases the overwritten memory might not be critical, and the problem might not show up right away but later the program will crash. When that happens, you will likely look for a bug at the point the program crashed, but the actual problem occurred in a completely different part of the program. In other cases the memory that is overwritten is critical, and the program will immediately stop. In extreme cases you might even crash Windows.

Array overwrites can be minimized somewhat by range checking. When you have range checking on (the default), the compiler will examine any array references to see whether you are accessing an array element outside the valid range. For example, this code will result in a compiler error:

```
procedure TForm1.Button1Click(Sender: TObject);
var
  A : array [0..20] of Char;
begin
  A[30] := 'a';
end;
```

Here I am accessing element 30 in an array that has only 21 elements. The compiler sees that the array is accessed outside its declared range and generates a compiler error. Range checking does not work with variables, however. This code, for example, will not result in a compiler error:

```
procedure TForm1.Button1Click(Sender: TObject);
var
  X : Integer;
  A : array [0..20] of Char;
begin
  X := 30;
  A[X] := 'a';
end;
```

Although the array is overwritten by nine bytes, no compiler error will result because the compiler doesn't know the value of X at compile time.

Access Violation on Program Termination

When a program halts with an access violation on normal shutdown, it usually indicates that the stack size is set too small. Although this isn't likely in a 32-bit program, it could happen under extreme circumstances. An access violation on program termination can also be caused by deleting an already deleted pointer, as already discussed.

Debug Quick Tips

In addition to the many tips offered on the preceding pages, you might want to implement these:

- Change the form's Caption property to display a variable without using breakpoints. Because placing a Label component on a form is so easy, you can use a label, too. Change the text in the label to show the variable's value or any other information you want to display.

- Enable a conditional breakpoint or a data watch breakpoint to temporarily slow down your program (possibly to view program effects in slow motion). These breakpoints slow down program execution while they check the breakpoint's condition.

- Use the Evaluate/Modify dialog box to temporarily change a variable's value at runtime. This enables you to view the effects that different values have on your program without recompiling your code each time.

- Choose Run | Inspect from the main menu and enter Self in the Expression field to inspect the class where the debugger is currently stopped.

10

- Use `MessageBeep($FFFF)` as an audible indicator that a certain point in your program has been reached. This Windows API function beeps the PC speaker when called with a parameter of `-1`.

- Choose Run | Program Reset from the main menu or press Ctrl+F2 to stop an errant debuggee.

- Use temporary variables to break down long equations or chained method calls so that you can examine the results in more manageable pieces.

- Use the `ShowMessage`, `MessageBox`, or `MessageDlg` functions to display program tracing information. (`ShowMessage` is preferred because it takes only the message string as its single parameter.)

> **Caution**
>
> If you are running Delphi on Windows 95, use the Program Reset option sparingly. In some cases, using Program Reset to kill an application can crash Windows 95. Not all Windows 95 systems behave the same way, so you might not experience this problem. Windows NT doesn't suffer from this problem nearly to the degree that Windows 95 does, so you can use Program Reset more liberally under Windows NT. Personally, I use Program Reset only when the application I am debugging locks up.

One of the best tips I can give you on debugging is to use a memory checking program such as TurboPower Software's Memory Sleuth. You might have received Memory Sleuth as part of Delphi 4 (it was included free with Delphi 4 for a limited time). Memory Sleuth checks your programs for memory leaks. This type of program can save you a lot of trouble when you put your applications in service. If your application is leaking memory, it will cause problems for your users. Problems for your users means problems for you. By taking care of those leaks early on, you save yourself and your users frustration.

If you didn't get Memory Sleuth with Delphi 4, you can check it out at TurboPower's Web site (`www.turbopower.com`). Another leak-checking program is BoundsChecker by NuMega Technologies.

Debugger Options

 Debugging options can be set on two levels: the project level and the environment level. Project debugging options were discussed yesterday in the sections "The Compiler Page" and "The Linker Page." The debugging options you set at the global level can be found in the Debugger Options dialog box. To invoke the Debugger Options dialog box, choose Tools | Debugger Options from the main menu.

At the bottom of the dialog box is a check box labeled Integrated debugging. This option controls whether the IDE debugger is used for debugging. If the Integrated debugging check box is checked, the IDE debugger is used. If this option is unchecked, the IDE debugger isn't used. This means that when you click the Run button, the program will execute but the debugger is disabled, so no breakpoints will function.

The Debugger Options dialog box has four pages: General, Event Log, Language Exceptions, and OS Exceptions. These pages are discussed in the following sections.

The General Page

The General page is where you set general debugging options. This page is shown in Figure 10.14.

10

FIGURE 10.14.

The Debugger Options dialog box General page.

The Map TD32 keystrokes on run option in this section tells the Code Editor to use the keystroke mapping used in Borland's stand-alone debugger, Turbo Debugger. This is a nice feature if you have spent a lot of time using Turbo Debugger and are familiar with that program's key mappings.

The Mark buffers read-only on run option sets the Code Editor buffers to read-only when the program is run under the debugger. After you start the program under the debugger, you cannot edit your source code until the program is terminated. I leave this option off because I frequently make changes to my source code while debugging.

The Inspectors stay on top check box controls whether the Debug Inspector windows are always on top of the Code Editor. This is a nice feature because most of the time you want the Debug Inspector windows to stay on top when stepping through your code.

The Rearrange editor local menu on run option changes the appearance of the Code Editor context menu when a program is running under the debugger. When this option is on, the Code Editor context menu items specific to debugging are moved to the top of the context menu so that they are easier to find.

The Event Log Page

The Event Log page enables you to set the options for the Event Log. You can choose a maximum number of messages that can appear in the Event Log at any one time or leave the number unlimited. You can also select the types of messages you want to see in the Event Log.

The Language Exceptions Page

The Language Exceptions page is used to control the types of VCL exceptions that are caught by the debugger (exceptions are discussed on Day 14, "Advanced Programming"). The most important item on this page is the Stop on Delphi Exceptions option. When this option is on, the debugger pauses program execution when an exception is thrown. When this option is off, the VCL exception is handled in the usual way—with a message box informing the user of what went wrong in the program.

Note

When the Stop on Delphi Exceptions option is on, the debugger breaks on exceptions *even if the exception is handled in your program*. If you don't want the debugger to break on every exception, turn this option off. This option replaces the Break on exception option found in previous versions of Delphi.

The Exception Types to Ignore option is used to specify the types of exceptions that you want the debugger to ignore. Any exception classes in this list will be ignored by the debugger and the exception will be handled in the default manner. This is effectively the same as turning off the Stop on Delphi Exceptions option for selected exception types.

To add an exception type to the list, simply click on the Add button and enter the name of an exception class. To tell the debugger to ignore divide by zero exceptions, for example, you click the Add button and enter EDivByZero in the Exception Type field. Figure 10.15 shows this process.

FIGURE 10.15.

Adding an exception type to the Exception Types to Ignore list.

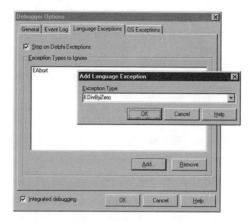

Any exception type added to the list will be persistent across all projects (including any new projects).

The OS Exceptions Page

The OS Exceptions Page controls whether operating system exceptions are handled by the debugger or by the user program. Figure 10.16 shows the OS Exceptions page of the Debugger Options dialog box.

FIGURE 10.16.

The Debugger Options OS Exceptions Page.

When the Handled By option is set to User Program, the debugger pauses program execution when an exception is thrown. When this option is set to Debugger, the VCL exception is handled in the usual way—with a message box informing the user of what went wrong in the program.

Note | When the Handled By option is set to Debugger, the debugger breaks on exceptions *even if the exception is handled in your program*. If you don't want the debugger to break on every exception, set this option to User Program. This option replaces the Break on exception option found previous versions of Delphi.

The On Resume option determines how the exception will be treated when program execution is resumed following an exception.

The Exceptions list box contains a list of possible operating system exceptions. To set the options for a particular type, click on the exception in the Exceptions list box and then set the Handled By or On Resume options as desired. Glyphs in the right margin of the Exceptions list box indicate the handling and resume settings.

Summary

Debugging is a never-ending task. Debugging means more than just tracking down a bug in your program. Savvy programmers learn to use the debugger from the outset of a new project. The debugger is a development tool as well as a bug-finding tool. After today, you should have at least a basic understanding of how to use the debugger. You will still have to spend time actually using the debugger before you are proficient at it, but you now have a place to start.

Workshop

The Workshop contains quiz questions to help you solidify your understanding of the material covered and exercises to provide you with experience in using what you have learned. You can find the answers to the quiz questions in Appendix A, "Answers to the Quiz Questions."

Q&A

Q My program used to run at regular speed when I ran it from the IDE. Now it's as slow as molasses in January. Why is that?

A More than likely you have either a large number of breakpoints that you disabled and forgot about or one or more conditional breakpoints in your code. Go to the Breakpoint List and delete any breakpoints you are not currently using. Also, be sure you don't have a lot of variables listed in the Watch List.

Q **I have a variable that I want to view in both decimal and hexadecimal format. Can I do that with the Watch List?**

A Yes. First, add the variable to the Watch List. Next double-click on the variable in the Watch List. When the Watch Properties dialog box comes up, choose the Decimal viewing option. Now add the variable to the Watch List again, but this time choose the Hexadecimal viewing option. Both items will be listed in the Watch List, one in decimal format and the other in hex format.

Q **I want to stop at a breakpoint when a variable reaches a certain value *and* after the breakpoint has been hit a certain number of times. Can I do that?**

A Sure. Enter a conditional expression in the Condition field of the Source Breakpoint Properties dialog box and a value in the Pass Count field. When the condition is met for the number of times indicated by the pass count, the program will pause at the breakpoint.

Q **I'm stepping through my code and I get to a function in my program that I want to debug. When I press F8, the execution point jumps right over the function. How do I get into that function?**

A When the execution point is on the line where the function is called, press F7 (Trace Into) instead of F8. Now you can step through the function one line at a time.

Q **When I step through my code, the debugger won't let me see the values of certain variables. Why is that?**

A In a word: optimization. The compiler optimizes out certain sections of code and won't let you view the values of variables that have been optimized. In essence, those variables don't exist at that time as far as the debugger is concerned. To avoid optimization, turn off optimizations on the Compiler page of the Project Options dialog box. Remember to turn optimizations back on before you ship your application.

Q **I step through a method line by line. Sometimes when I get to the method's end statement, I press F8 one more time and nothing happens. Why?**

A Because when that particular method returns, your program has nothing more to do, so it goes back into its idle state. Essentially, there is no more code to step through at that point, so the debugger returns control to the program being debugged.

Q **How do I use the CPU window when debugging?**

A Just choose View | Debug Windows | CPU from the main menu to display the CPU window. Knowing what to do with the CPU window, however, is another matter entirely!

10

Quiz

1. How do you set a breakpoint on a particular code line?

2. What is an invalid breakpoint?

3. How do you set a conditional breakpoint?

4. How can you change the properties of an item in the Watch List?

5. What's the quickest way to add a variable to the Watch List?

6. What tool do you use to view the data fields and methods of a class?

7. How do you trace into a method when stepping with the debugger?

8. How can you change the value of a variable at runtime?

9. How can you send your own messages to the Event Log?

10. What does the Integrated debugging option on the Debugger Options dialog box do?

Exercises

1. Load the ScratchPad program that you created on Day 6, "Working with the Form Designer and the Menu Designer." Place breakpoints in the FileOpenClick and FileSaveClick methods. Run the program. When program execution pauses, inspect the OpenDialog and SaveDialog classes, respectively.

2. Continuing with exercise 1, step through the program when you stop at a breakpoint and examine the program's operation as you step through the methods.

3. Load the DebugTst program you created earlier in this chapter. Place a breakpoint in the WatchBtnClick method. Add the S and X variables to the Watch List. Add each variable to the Watch List four times. Edit each of the watches and change the display options. Run the program and step through the method to see the effects in the Watch List.

4. Add a conditional breakpoint to the method in exercise 3. Place it on the line immediately after the line that reads X := Width. Make the condition X = 0 and run the program. What happens? (Nothing happens because the value of X never reaches 0.)

5. Continuing with exercise 4, edit the breakpoint and change the condition to X > 400. Run the program. Change the window's size and click the Watch Test button. Repeat this process several times, changing the window's size each time. What happens? (This time the debugger stops at the breakpoint when the window's width is greater than 400 pixels.)

6. Load any program and switch to the Code Editor. Place the cursor on any code line and choose the Run to Cursor item from the Code Editor context menu. Experiment with the program until the breakpoint is hit.

7. Again load the DebugTst program you created earlier. Place a breakpoint in the WatchBtnClick method and run the program. When the breakpoint is hit, use the Debug Inspector to inspect the WatchBtn.

10

DAY **11**

Delphi Tools and Options

Delphi comes with several tools to aid in your application development. Today you learn about some of Delphi's tools. Specifically, you learn about the following:

- The Image Editor
- Messages and the Windows messaging system
- WinSight
- Package Collection Editor
- Configuring the Tools menu
- Delphi Environment Options

First, you take a general look at these tools. Then you learn how to add your own tools to the Delphi Tools menu. The day ends with a look at the Delphi Environment Options dialog box.

Note

In addition to the tools listed here, Delphi also comes with a host of database tools such as Database Desktop, BDE Administrator, SQL Builder, and SQL Explorer. A discussion of those tools would be too lengthy for today's purposes.

Using the Image Editor

The Delphi Image Editor is a tool that enables you to create and edit bitmaps (.bmp), icons (.ico), and cursors (.cur). You can also create a resource project containing multiple bitmaps, icons, and cursors in a single resource file (.res). The resource file can then be added to your Delphi project, and you can use the resources as needed. Figure 11.1 shows the Image Editor editing a bitmap.

FIGURE 11.1.

The Image Editor.

Note

All Windows images are bitmaps, whether they are actual Windows bitmap files (.bmp) or icons or cursors. In this chapter, I refer to all images collectively as *bitmaps*.

Image Editor deals only with Windows bitmap files. Other file formats such as PCX, TIFF, JPEG, and GIF are not supported.

You can start the Image Editor by either double-clicking on the Image Editor icon in the Delphi folder or choosing Tools | Image Editor from the Delphi main menu. The Image Editor is a stand-alone program and doesn't have to be run from the Delphi IDE.

Foreground and Background Colors

The Image Editor enables you to create 2-color, 16-color, and, in the case of bitmap files, 256-color images. You can choose any available colors when drawing on a bitmap. In the bottom-left corner of the Image Editor are two boxes containing the current foreground and background colors. (The foreground color is represented by the far left box.)

When using a drawing tool, you can draw with either the foreground color or the background color. To draw with the foreground color, use the left mouse button. For example, if you choose the filled rectangle tool and draw a rectangle on the bitmap, the rectangle will be filled with the foreground color. To draw a filled rectangle with the background color, use the right mouse button to drag the rectangle. The same is true for most of the other drawing tools.

> **Note**
>
> The Text tool uses only the foreground color. You cannot place text with the background color. If you want to use the background color, you have to change the foreground color and then place your text.

To change the foreground color, click a color on the color palette with the left mouse button. (The color palette is located along the bottom of the Image Editor window.) When you choose a new foreground color, the square that represents the foreground color changes to show the new color selected. To change the background color, click a color in the color palette with your right mouse button.

11

> **Note**
>
> If you are editing a 256-color image, the color palette will have scroll buttons on either side so that you can scroll through the available colors.

The colors that appear in the color palette are determined by the bitmap when you are loading a bitmap that already exists. If you are starting a new 256-color image, the default 256-color palette is used.

You can also set the foreground or background colors with the Eyedropper tool. The Eyedropper enables you to set the foreground or background color by picking up a color that is already used on the image.

To set the foreground color with the Eyedropper, choose the Eyedropper tool from the Tools palette, place the tip of the Eyedropper over a portion of the image that has the color you want to use, and then click the left mouse button. The foreground color changes to the color under the Eyedropper. To set the background color, click with your right mouse button instead of the left mouse button. The Eyedropper tool is invaluable when you want to exactly match a color that was previously used on your bitmap.

 Note

> The foreground and background colors might work differently in the Image Editor than in other bitmap editors you have used. For example, in some bitmap editors, the outline of a filled rectangle is drawn with the foreground color and filled with the background color. With the Image Editor, filled objects have no discernible border. A filled rectangle is in either the foreground or the background color.

Transparent and Inverted Colors

In the case of icons and cursors, you can also choose the transparent color (the word *color* being relative here). When you use the transparent color, the background beneath the icon shows through wherever the transparent color is used. That could mean the Windows background in the case of a shortcut, or it could mean the title bar of your application.

Whether you use the transparent color depends on your personal tastes and the particular icon you are creating. In the case of cursors, you will almost always use the transparent color as the background for the icon. Rarely do you have a cursor that appears as a solid block.

Choosing the inverted color causes the background underneath the icon to be inverted (like reverse video). Use of the inverted color isn't common, but it is there if and when you need it.

Both the transparent and inverted colors are shown next to the color palette when editing icons and cursors. They are represented by color squares with a curved line running through them.

 Note

> By default, new icon and new cursor resources have the background filled with the transparent color.

Image Editor Drawing Tools

The Image Editor drawing tools are similar to most paint programs. Because these are common drawing tools, I'm not going to go over each and every one. Fifteen minutes of experimentation with the Image Editor will be more beneficial than anything I can tell you. Fire up the Image Editor and experiment with it for a while. I'll wait.

At the top of the Image Editor Tools palette, you find the Marquee and Lasso tools. These work in essentially the same way, so I'll cover them together. Both tools enable you to select a region on the current image. The Marquee tool is used to define a rectangular region. Choose the Marquee tool and then drag a bounding rectangle on the image. When you stop dragging, a marquee is drawn around the region to mark it. The Lasso tool works in much the same way but enables you to define a freehand region. A Lasso region is filled with a hatch pattern to identify it.

Tip

When using the Lasso tool, you don't have to close the region. When you release the mouse button, the Image Editor automatically closes the region by drawing a connection line between the start point and the end point.

When a region is defined, you can cut or copy the image within the region and paste it somewhere else on the image or to another image you are working on (you can have multiple bitmaps open at one time). When you choose Edit | Paste from the main menu, the image within the marquee is placed in the upper-left corner of the bitmap with a marquee around it. The pasted image can now be dragged into position.

When you place your mouse cursor within the marquee, the cursor changes to a hand. When you see the hand cursor, you can drag the bitmap within the marquee to another location and drop it. You can continue to move the bitmap until you have it positioned exactly where you want it. After you have the bitmap where you want it, click again on the image outside the marquee and the bitmap within the marquee merge into the existing image.

Tip

The Image Editor has a shortcut method of cut and paste. Create a Marquee or Lasso region, place your mouse cursor inside the region, and drag. The image within the region moves as you drag.

When you cut a region or move it by dragging, the current background color will fill the area that the image originally occupied. The background shows through the hole created by the cut operation.

You can copy portions of one bitmap to another using cut and paste. First, open both images in the Image Editor. Place a marquee around the portion of the original image you want to copy and then choose Edit | Copy from the main menu. Switch to the other image and choose Edit | Paste from the main menu. Move the pasted image as needed.

If you have a marquee selected when you paste, the pasted image will shrink or stretch to fit the size of the marquee.

The Eraser tool works just the opposite of the other tools in regard to the left and right mouse buttons. With the Eraser, the left mouse button draws with the background color and the right mouse button draws with the foreground color.

The Text tool enables you to place text on the image. The text is drawn using the current text settings. The text settings can be changed by clicking the Text item on the main menu. Here you can set the text alignment (left, right, or centered) or the font (typeface). To change the typeface, choose Text | Font from the main menu. Now you can choose a new typeface or make the font bold, italic, underlined, and so on.

The other drawing tools are self-explanatory. As I said earlier, a little time behind the wheel of the Image Editor will teach you just about everything you need to know about those tools.

When drawing rectangles, you can press and hold the Shift key to force a rectangle to a square. Likewise, you can draw a perfect circle by choosing the Ellipse or Filled Ellipse tool and holding the Shift key as you drag. Using the Shift key with the Line tool enables you to draw straight lines (vertical, horizontal, or 45-degree angles).

Zooming

The Image Editor enables you to zoom in so that you can work on your bitmaps up close and personal. You can zoom either by using the Zoom tool or via the View menu. To zoom in on a particular part of your image using the Zoom tool, first select the Zoom tool from the Tools palette and then drag a bounding rectangle around the portion of the image you want to magnify. The magnification will change depending on the size of the rectangle you created when you dragged. You can now see well enough to change fine details in your bitmap.

To zoom using the menu, choose View | Zoom In or press Ctrl+I. When you choose Zoom In from the menu, the image is magnified by a predetermined amount. To zoom out again using the menu, choose View | Zoom Out (Ctrl+U) or View | Actual Size (Ctrl+Q).

When you are creating a cursor or an icon, the Image Editor shows a split view. Figure 11.2 shows an Image Editor window while creating an icon.

FIGURE 11.2.

Editing an icon.

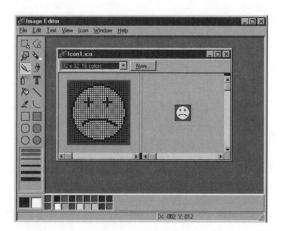

Although you can zoom either side of the split window, you will usually work with a zoomed-in copy on the left side and an actual-size image on the right, as shown in Figure 11.2.

The Line Width Palette

The Line Width palette is displayed directly below the Tools palette. Depending on the currently selected tool, the Line Width palette might show line widths or brush shapes that you can choose. To pick a line width, click one of the five widths displayed. Subsequent drawing operations will use the new line width until you change it. Similarly, to change a brush shape, just click the brush shape you want to use. If you refer to Figure 11.1, you will see the Line Width palette showing brush shapes.

Working with Bitmap Files

You can create a bitmap from scratch or load an existing bitmap and modify it. To open an existing bitmap file, choose File | Open from the main menu (bitmap files have a

BMP extension). To create a new bitmap file, choose File | New from the main menu and then choose Bitmap File from the pop-up menu. The Bitmap Properties dialog box is displayed, as shown in Figure 11.3.

FIGURE 11.3.

The Bitmap Properties
dialog box.

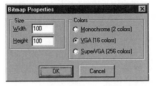

Here you can set the initial size of the bitmap (in pixels) as well as the color depth. You can create a 2-color, 16-color, or 256-color bitmap.

> The Image Editor does not support bitmaps of more than 256 colors.

Select the size and color depth you want and click OK. A blank bitmap is displayed in an editor window. Do any drawing you want on the bitmap. When you are finished editing, choose File | Save or File | Save As to save the bitmap file to disk.

Any time you are working with a bitmap file, the Image Editor main menu has a menu item called Bitmap. This menu has a single item under it called Image Properties. Choosing Bitmap | Image Properties displays the Bitmap Properties dialog box just as when you create a new bitmap file. The Bitmap Properties dialog box enables you to change the size and color depth of the bitmap. Select a new width, height, or color depth and click OK.

> There is one difference in the Bitmap Properties dialog box when it is displayed for an existing bitmap as opposed to when you're creating a new bitmap. When displayed for an existing bitmap, the Bitmap Properties dialog box has a check box labeled Stretch. This is used by the Image Editor when changing the bitmap size. If the Stretch option is off, the bitmap will not be stretched (either larger or smaller) when the bitmap size is changed. If the Stretch option is on, the bitmap will be stretched to fill the new bitmap size. Stretching a bitmap is an inexact science, so sometimes the results of stretching are less than perfect.

All in all, there isn't much to working with bitmap files. Although the Image Editor is fine for simple bitmaps, you will probably not find it adequate for sophisticated graphics. If you need high-quality bitmaps, you might consider purchasing a full-featured image-editing package or hiring a computer artist to create your bitmaps.

Tip

> Don't forget to check online sources for computer-graphic artists. These people know their craft far better than all but the most gifted programmers and are often very reasonable in their pricing. Repeat this 10 times: "I am a programmer, not an artist." (Okay, maybe some of you are doubly blessed.)

Working with Icons

Creating icons is also an art form, but icons are not quite as demanding as full-color bitmaps. Most of the time you can create your own icons, but great-looking icons still require skill. If you flip back to Figure 11.2, you will see an icon as it is displayed in the Image Editor while editing.

Tip

> Load icon files from any source you can find and zoom in on them to get tips on how the best-looking icons are created. Creating 3D icons takes practice (and is something I never get quite right).

11

An icon in 32-bit Windows is actually two icons in one. The large icon is 32×32 pixels. The large icon can be placed on a dialog box such as an About box. It is also the icon that Windows uses when creating a shortcut to your application. In addition, the large icon is used by Windows Explorer when the file list view is set to display large icons.

The small icon is 16×16 pixels and is the icon used by Windows on the title bar of your application, on the Windows taskbar, in the File Open dialog box, and in Windows Explorer when the view is set to small icons. Both the large and the small icons are stored in the same icon file (.ico).

Note

> You don't have to supply both a large icon and a small icon. If you supply only the large icon, Windows will shrink the large icon when it needs to display a small icon. Sometimes, however, the results are not quite what you expect and might not be good enough quality for your tastes. In those cases, you can also create the small icon so that you are in control of how your application looks, rather than rely on Windows to do the right thing.

Creating a New Icon Resource

To create a new icon resource, choose File | New from the main menu and then choose
Icon from the pop-up menu. When you create a new icon in the Image Editor, you see
the Icon Properties dialog box, as shown in Figure 11.4.

FIGURE **11.4.**

*The Icon Properties
dialog box.*

This dialog box enables you to choose the icon you are creating (either the large or the
small icon) and the number of colors to use for the icon. The default is to create the standard icon (the large icon) and to use 16 colors. (In reality, 2-color icons are rarely used.
When was the last time you saw one?)

Note

Even if you are creating both the large icon and the small icon, you must
choose one or the other to start with. For example, if you are creating a
new icon, you should start with the large icon. After creating the large icon,
you can then create the small icon.

When you are editing an icon, the Image Editor menu bar has an item called Icon. The
Icon menu has items called New, Delete, and Test. The New menu item enables you to
create a new large or small icon. For example, if you had already created the large icon,
you could choose Icon | New from the main menu to create the small icon.

Tip

The Icon Editor window has a button called New that also creates a new
icon and is faster than using the main menu (refer to Figure 11.2).

When you choose New to create a second icon, the Icon Properties dialog box is displayed just as before. If you have already created the large icon, the small icon will be
selected by default and all you have to do is click OK. The editor window will change to
display the new, blank icon. The Image Editor will not let you create an icon that already
exists in the icon file.

Tip

When both icons are present, you can switch between them using the combo box at the top of the Icon Editor window.

Icon Editing Options

The Delete item on the Icon menu enables you to delete either the large or the small icon from the icon resource. You cannot delete the last icon in the icon resource.

The Test item on the Icon menu displays the Icon Tester dialog box, which shows you what the icon will look like when displayed. Figure 11.5 shows the Icon Tester dialog box in action.

FIGURE 11.5.

The Icon Tester dialog box.

The Icon Tester enables you to change the background color so that you can view the effect that different backgrounds have on the appearance of your icon. If you are currently editing the large icon, the large icon appears in the Icon Tester. If you are currently editing the small icon, the Icon Tester dialog box displays the small icon.

Working with Cursors

Working with cursors is not much different than working with icons. A cursor has only two colors: white and black. (Multicolor and animated cursors are not supported by the Image Editor.) Draw the cursor as you want it to appear.

Note

A peculiarity of the Cursor Editor is that the transparent color is set to the color of your system's background color instead of the dark green color used for the Icon Editor. If you have your Windows background color set to a very light color, it can be difficult to see what is transparent and what is white. If you are having difficulty distinguishing the background color from white, set your Windows background color to a different value (such as dark green).

11

As when editing bitmap files and icons, the Image Editor menu displays a menu item called Cursor when you are editing a cursor. This menu item has two items: Set Hot Spot and Test.

The Set Hot Spot item enables you to specify the cursor's hot spot. The *hot spot* is the specific pixel of the cursor that Windows uses to report the mouse coordinates when your cursor is being used. For example, the hot spot on a crosshair cursor is the exact center of the crosshairs. For a pointer cursor, the hotspot is set to the tip of the arrow's point. To set the hot spot, choose Cursor | Set Hot Spot from the main menu. The Set Cursor Hot Spot dialog box appears, where you can enter the x and y coordinates of the hot spot.

> You must enter the exact x and y coordinates for the hot spot. To make this easier, before setting the hot spot, place the editing cursor over the point on the cursor where you want the hot spot. The Image Editor status bar will display the x and y coordinates of the point under the cursor. Make note of the x and y coordinates, and then choose Cursor | Set Hot Spot from the main menu and enter those x and y coordinates.

The Test item on the Cursor menu gives you the opportunity to try out your new cursor. Choose Cursor | Test from the main menu and the Cursor Tester dialog box will be displayed, as shown in Figure 11.6.

FIGURE 11.6.

Testing the cursor.

Hold down either mouse button to draw on the Cursor Tester window. If you haven't yet set the hot spot, you will probably notice that the hot spot is set to the upper-left corner of the cursor by default. You should always set the hot spot to a point on your cursor that will be logical to users of your application.

Image Editor Context Menus

The Image Editor has context menus for each editing mode (Bitmap, Cursor, and Icon). You might recall that the right mouse button is used for drawing, so you can't bring up the context menus by clicking the mouse button while over the image. To display the

Image Editor context menus, right-click when the cursor is within the editor window but outside the image. The context menus contain the same items found on the individual menus, as discussed in the previous sections.

Creating Resource Projects

The Image Editor also enables you to create a resource project file for storing all your bitmaps, icons, and cursors. To create a resource project, choose File | New from the main menu and then choose Resource File from the pop-up menu. A project window is displayed. The project window is a tree view control that shows the bitmaps, icons, and cursors in the project. Figure 11.7 shows the project window for a sample project.

FIGURE 11.7.

*The Image Editor
project window.*

The project window has a context menu that can be used to create new resources, edit resources, rename resources, and delete resources. The items on the context menu are also duplicated on the main menu under the Resource menu item.

When you save the resource project, the Image Editor will compile it into a binary resource file (.res). You can then add the binary resource file to your Delphi project.

Creating New Resources

To create a new resource for your project, choose New from the project window context menu or Resource | New from the main menu. You can then choose to create a new bitmap, icon, or cursor, as you did before when creating an individual resource file. A resource editor window will be displayed where you can create the resource using the drawing tools as needed.

Editing Resources

When you have a resource created, you might need to edit it to make changes to the resource. To edit a resource in a resource project, locate the resource in the project window tree and double-click the resource name. A resource editor window will appear where you can edit the resource as needed.

11

Renaming Resources

Renaming resources can be accomplished using in-place editing on the tree view. To select the item you want to rename, just click it and then click on it again to begin editing the item. You can also choose Rename from the context menu to begin the in-place editing. After you have typed a new name for the resource, press Enter or click on another item in the tree view, and the name of the resource will change.

Deleting Resources

To delete a resource from the resource project, just click the resource name in the project tree to select it and then choose Delete from the context menu. You will be prompted to make certain you want to delete the item, after which it will be deleted. There is no undo for deleting a resource, so make sure a resource is no longer needed before you delete it.

Adding Resources from Other Resource Files

Unfortunately, there is no simple way to add a resource contained in a separate file to a resource project. What you can do, however, is open your project file and then open the individual bitmap, icon, or cursor file that contains the resource you want to add to the project. Go to the individual file and choose Edit | Select All from the main menu to select the resource; then choose Edit | Copy to copy the object to the Clipboard. Create the new resource in the resource project. When the resource editor window is displayed, choose Edit | Paste from the main menu to paste the resource into the new resource.

 Note   If the object you are adding to the resource project is a bitmap, be sure you check the bitmap attributes so that you know the width, height, and color depth of the bitmap. You will need those settings when you create the new bitmap in the resource project.

The Image Editor is not a high-end image editor, but it's good enough for many image-creation tasks. It's easy to use and is more than adequate for creating most icons and cursors.

WinSight: Spying on Windows

WinSight is a utility that enables you to spy on Windows. WinSight will show you every application running and every window running under that application. (Remember: Controls are windows, too.) WinSight shows you every message generated by Windows (every message sent to a window, that is).

You can elect to view all messages or just messages sent to a specific window. To start WinSight, locate WS32.EXE from Windows Explorer and double-click the file (it's in the Delphi 4\Bin directory). WinSight, like the Image Editor, is a stand-alone program that can be run outside the Delphi IDE. Figure 11.8 shows WinSight spying on Windows Explorer.

FIGURE 11.8.

WinSight in action.

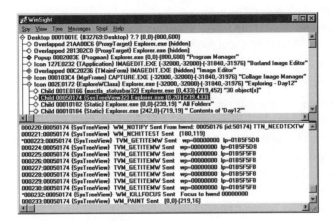

11

As you can see in Figure 11.8, the WinSight window is split into two panes. The top pane lists the active windows, and the bottom pane shows the messages being sent to a particular window or to all windows. You can adjust the size of the panes by dragging the sizing bar between the two windows. The default is for the windows to be split horizontally, but you can opt to split the windows vertically. To change the window layout, choose either Split Horizontal or Split Vertical from the View menu.

You'll examine each of the two windows in more detail in just a bit, but first let me take a moment to talk about Windows messages.

The Windows Messaging System

Spying on Windows isn't helpful if you don't know what any of it means. (The thrill of being a legal Peeping Tom wears off quickly.) The truth is, you have to spend a fair amount of time at Windows programming before you can understand all the information presented by WinSight.

Delphi is great for enabling you to write true stand-alone Windows applications in the shortest time possible. If there is a disadvantage to this kind of programming environment, it is that you do not have the opportunity to learn what really makes a Windows program run.

What makes a Windows program run is messages. Lots and lots of messages. Windows sends a window message to instruct the window to do something or to notify the window that some event has taken place. When a window is in need of repainting, for example, Windows sends it a `WM_PAINT` message. The `WM_PAINT` message instructs the window to repaint itself.

When a window is resized, Windows sends a `WM_WINDOWPOSCHANGING` message to notify the window that its size and/or position is changing. This message is followed by `WM_WINDOWPOSCHANGED` and `WM_SIZE` messages after the window has been sized. The sending of messages happens dozens or even hundreds of times each second in an average Windows environment.

There are more than 100 messages that Windows can send to an application. I talked a little about that on Day 5, "The Visual Component Model," when I discussed events in VCL. Many events that a Delphi program responds to are Windows messages. The `OnCreate` event is generated in response to a `WM_CREATE` message, the `OnSize` event is generated in response to a `WM_SIZE` message, and the `OnMouseDown` event corresponds to both the `WM_LBUTTONDOWN` and `WM_RBUTTONDOWN` messages. The list goes on and on. Delphi enables you to deal with messages at a higher level, thus freeing you to write the more important parts of your application.

Eventually you will want to learn more about what makes Windows tick. The great benefit of Delphi, though, is that you can write Windows programs immediately and gradually learn about all the low-level stuff.

> **Note**
>
> Some very good Windows programmers would argue that you should first learn to write Windows programs in C like in the good old days. The theory is that this kind of foundation is necessary for a Windows programmer to be effective in any programming environment. Although I would agree that that is the optimum scenario, I also recognize that few programmers these days have the time for that kind of learning process.

With that primer on Windows messages behind you, let's get back to WinSight and how it works.

The Window Tree

The top pane of WinSight is called the Window Tree. The Window Tree shows you all windows currently open. It also tells you some details about the window class of a specific window. The detail looks like this (except that onscreen it all appears on one line):

```
Overlapped 00000D74 {ExploreWClass}
  EXPLORER.EXE (730,14)-(935,460) 'Exploring - aTemplate'
```

The first item in this line shows the window style of the window. In this case it is an overlapped window (WS_OVERLAPPED for you old Windows hackers). Other possibilities include child and pop-up windows. (There are other window types, but overlapped, child, and pop-up are the most common.) The second column shows the window handle (HWND) of the window, which correlates to the Handle property of a VCL windowed component.

Next, you see the window class name in curly braces. This is the class name that the application used to register this particular window with Windows. Frequently, windows share a class name. The common button control, for example, has a class name of Button. Dozens of buttons might exist in different applications at any given time, but they are all of the same window class. In the case of Delphi applications, forms and components show the VCL class that represents that component. For a button component, the class name in WinSight shows TButton.

Note

> When Delphi 1 was in development, the code name for the project was Delphi. The intended name for the product, however, was AppBuilder. The name Delphi stuck and became the official product name. If you spy on the Delphi IDE with WinSight, you will discover that the Delphi main window has a class name of TAppBuilder, thereby lending credibility to this tale.

11

Following the class name is the module name of the process that created the window. Usually the module is an executable program. In this example, the module name is EXPLORER.EXE. After the module name, you see the window's size and position. Finally, you see the window text of the window. For overlapped windows, this usually means the text appearing in the title bar. For other types of windows, it means different things depending on the window type. For a button, for example, it will show the text on the button.

Note

> A common practice with commercial applications is to create hidden windows to accomplish a specific task in the application. Hidden windows just show the text (hidden) after the module name. Because the window is hidden, there is no size and position information, nor is there any window text.

The Window Tree is hierarchical. At the top of the tree is the Windows Desktop. Under that are any windows created as children of the desktop. An executable file, for example, appears under the desktop node. A given window can have other child windows under it. Lines connect the parents, their children, and any siblings.

You will notice back in Figure 11.8 that a diamond appears to the left of each item in the Tree Window. If a window has children, the diamond contains either a plus sign or a minus sign. If the diamond has a plus sign, it means the node is contracted and can be expanded to reveal the child windows. If the node has a minus sign, the plus is already expanded. You can expand or contract a node by clicking anywhere to the left of the item. Blank diamonds indicate a window without children.

> If a particular window is enabled in the Window Tree, the diamond next to the item flashes whenever the window receives a message from Windows.

The Message Trace Window

The Message Trace window shows the individual messages as they are generated by Windows. A typical Message Trace item looks like this:

```
000684:00000854 {TMemo} WM_KEYDOWN Dispatched 48h 72d VK_H Scan 23h Down
```

It doesn't pay to analyze this in detail because the exact details vary so much from message to message. In this case, a memo component received a WM_KEYDOWN message with a parameter of VK_H. In other words, the user pressed the *h* key with the cursor in a memo component. As you can see, some of the information shown in a Message Trace item also appears in the Window Tree. For example, the window handle is displayed as well as the class name.

You begin the message trace by choosing the Start! item in the main menu. The messages will begin appearing in the Message Trace window as they are received by the window or windows you have selected. To stop the message trace, choose the Stop! item in the main menu.

> The Stop! and Start! items in the main menu occupy the same place on the menu bar. If the message trace is off, the menu item reads Start! If the trace is running, the menu item reads Stop!.

Messages scroll through the Message Trace window as they are received. You can always stop the message trace and scroll back through the list to view any messages that have scrolled out of view. Another option is to send the message output to a log file. WinSight options are discussed later in the section "Message Trace Options."

Spying on a Window

WinSight enables you to view all messages sent to all windows or messages sent to a particular window. To view all messages, choose Messages | All Windows from the main menu. Although you can choose to view all messages sent to all windows, it isn't usually productive. There are so many messages flying around that it is hard to pick out the specific ones you are looking for.

A better method is to select a specific window and then watch the messages for just that window. That will keep the clutter in the Message Trace window to a manageable level. To view the messages for a specific window, locate the window in the Message Tree and click on it to select it. Now choose Messages | Selected Windows from the main menu. Choose Start!, and any messages sent to the selected window will show up in the Message Trace window.

Tip

It's best to have a specific idea of what you are looking for when you are using WinSight. Because there are so many messages sent to an individual window, the message you are looking for will probably scroll off the screen very quickly. To maximize the effectiveness of WinSight, select the window for which you want to see messages, start the message trace, manipulate the window any way you need to, and turn off the message trace again.

11

Message Trace Options

You can control the messages displayed in the Message Trace window via the Message Trace Options dialog box (see Figure 11.9). You can also change the way the message is displayed. To view the Message Trace Options dialog box, choose Messages | Options from the main menu.

FIGURE 11.9.

The Message Trace Options dialog box.

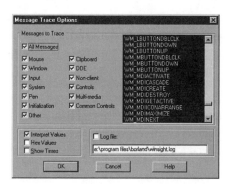

The section entitled Messages to Trace comprises the bulk of this dialog box. This section shows several message groups on the left and a list box displaying all Windows messages on the right. As you select or deselect message groups, the corresponding messages will be selected or deselected in the list box.

 Note

The list box messages that are all uppercase are the standard Windows messages. The lowercase messages are *undocumented* Windows messages. Undocumented messages are messages that are used by Windows, usually for internal use, but are not documented in the Windows API help files.

When the All Messages option is checked, WinSight will trace all Windows messages. To further specify your messages and thus to reduce clutter in the Message Trace window, you can elect to view only certain groups of messages. If, for example, you want to view only mouse messages, you can turn off the All Messages check box and turn on the Mouse check box. To further specify, you can turn off all options and then choose a specific message from the list box on the right of the dialog box. For example, if you want to see only the WM_LBUTTONDOWN message, you can turn off all options and then select just the WM_LBUTTONDOWN message from the list box. Only the WM_LBUTTONDOWN messages will be reported in the Message Trace window.

Another group of options on the Message Trace Options dialog box controls how the messages are displayed in the Message Trace window. The Interpret Values option tells WinSight to break down each message's parameters into a more readable format. For example, given a WM_KEYDOWN message, would you rather see

```
0000309:00000474 {TMemo} WM_KEYDOWN Dispatched
```

or

```
0000309:00000474 {TMemo} WM_KEYDOWN Dispatched 44h 68d VK_D Scan 20h Repeat
```

Most of the time I opt to see more detail, so I generally leave the Interpret Values option on.

The Hex Values option tells WinSight to display the values in the Message Trace window in hexadecimal format. This is useful in some situations but probably not until you've been programming for a while. The Show Times option is of limited use because it shows a system time that isn't generally meaningful.

The Log file option enables you to send the message trace output to a file on disk. When this option is on, the messages are still displayed in the Message Trace Window. This option is useful when you need a hard copy of the messages being generated.

Tip

Creating a log file has another advantage. After you create a log file and load it into a text editor, you can use the text editor's Find function to search for specific messages or message parameters you want to review.

Other WinSight Features

WinSight has other features that make finding and examining windows easier.

Viewing Window Details

The Detail feature of WinSight shows you all the pertinent details of a particular window. To view a window's details, select the window in the Window Tree and then choose Spy | Open Detail from the main menu. You can also double-click the window in the Message Tree or press Enter on the keyboard. Figure 11.10 shows the details of Windows Explorer.

FIGURE 11.10.

The WinSight Detail window.

As you can see, the Detail window shows you a great deal about the window you are examining (probably more than you want to know!).

Follow Focus

This option enables you to select a window in an application and have that window become the active window in the Window Tree. The Window Tree usually contains dozens of windows. It is often difficult to find the window you are looking for, so the Follow Focus feature really comes in handy.

To use this feature, choose Spy | Follow Focus from the main menu. Next, switch to the application that contains the window for which you want to view messages and, if needed, click the specific control within that window that you want to spy on. WinSight automatically selects the window in the Window Tree. To begin spying on the window, choose Start! from the main menu.

> **Tip**
>
> The Follow Focus option stays on until you turn it off. Unless you want to view other windows or controls in your application, you should turn off Follow Focus as soon as you locate the window you want to spy on.

Find Window

The Find Window feature of WinSight is the opposite of Follow Focus: In the Window Tree, you locate the window you're searching for and then choose Spy | Find Window from the main menu. WinSight will place a thick frame around the window and will flash the frame.

The frame stays around the window until you click the window or choose another window from the Window Tree. The thick frame is drawn on top of all windows so that you can find a window even if it's hidden under other windows. A window located with Find Window doesn't come to the top or gain input focus; it is merely identified for you.

> **Note**
>
> Find Window cannot find hidden windows or windows that are minimized.

The Find Window mode shuts off as soon as focus leaves the Window Tree. If you click on another application or anywhere else in WinSight, the Find Window mode will turn off.

Switch To

The Switch To feature enables you to switch to a particular window in an application. To switch to a window, just find the window in the Window Tree and then choose Spy | Switch To from the main menu. The window will come to the top and will have input focus. If the window is minimized, it will be restored to its previous location. Switch To has no effect on hidden windows.

It will take time working with WinSight before you understand each message and its significance. In time, though, you will pick it up.

TDUMP

TDUMP is a command-line program that outputs the structure of an .exe or .dll (and other file types as well). By default, the output from TDUMP goes to the console, but it can be redirected to a text file that you can later examine to obtain information about the program. TDUMP will tell you about the structure of the file, what DLLs the program uses, what functions in those DLLs the program calls, and other information. For example, here is part of the file dump results on a program produced by Delphi:

```
Portable Executable (PE) File

Header base: 00000200

CPU type                80386
Flags                   818E [ executable 32bit ]
DLL flags               0000 [ ]
Linker Version          2.19
Time stamp              00000000
O/S Version             1.0
User Version            0.0
Subsystem Version       4.0
Subsystem               0002 [ Windows GUI ]
Object count            00000008
Symbols offset          00000000
Symbols count           00000000
Optional header size    00E0
Magic #                 10B
Code size               0003C000
Init Data size          00009000
Uninit Data size        00001000

...(other information)...

Imports from OLEAUT32.dll
    SysAllocStringLen
    SysStringLen
    VariantChangeTypeEx
    VariantClear
    VariantCopyInd

Imports from MPR.dll
    WNetGetConnectionA

Imports from USER32.dll
    AdjustWindowRectEx
    BeginPaint
    CallNextHookEx
    CallWindowProcA
    CharLowerA

... (more DLL imports) ...
```

11

Typically you run TDUMP from the command line. Because the output from TDUMP is usually long, you are better off if you redirect the output to a text file. The following illustrates this:

```
tdump MyApp.exe > dump.txt
```

Now you have an ASCII text file that you can browse with the Delphi Code Editor or any other text editor. Although you might not use TDUMP often, it can be invaluable when you need it.

 Note   TDUMP is mostly used for obtaining a list of exported functions and procedures in a DLL.

The Package Collection Editor

The Package Collection Editor provides a way of deploying several packages that are meant to work together. To invoke the Package Collection Editor, choose Tools | Package Collection Editor from the main menu. The Package Collection Editor has a help menu that explains more about how to use it.

This tool is primarily meant for component vendors who ship several packages together. The Package Collection Editor has undergone some change in Delphi 4 and is therefore more useful than it was in Delphi 3. You'll have to experiment with this tool to see if it is something that you can use. Still, you might find that it is not robust enough to be used in heavy-duty commercial component deployment.

Configuring the Delphi Tools Menu

The Delphi Tools menu is configurable. By default, the Delphi Tools menu has items for Database Desktop and Image Editor. You can add your own tools to the Tools menu, add other Delphi tools, or add any other program you use frequently. You can also change the order of items on the Tools menu or even delete items.

Using the Configure Tools Dialog Box

Just about any application you use frequently can be added to the Tools menu. By adding items to the Tools menu, you can quickly load any program you frequently use during program development. Adding a tool to the Tools menu is a trivial task and takes only a few minutes. Adding, deleting, and moving items on the Tools menu is accomplished through the Tool Options dialog box. To display the Tool Options dialog box, choose Tools | Configure Tools from the main menu (see Figure 11.11).

FIGURE 11.11.

The Tool Options dialog box.

The list box labeled Tools shows the tools that currently appear on the Tools menu. The tools are listed in the order in which they appear on the Tools menu. To reorder the list of tools, click the tool you want to move and click either the up or down arrow button. To remove a tool from the Tools menu, select the tool from the list box and click the Delete button. The tool will be removed from the menu.

Adding Tools to the Menu

To add a tool to the Tools menu, click the Add button. The Tool Properties dialog box is displayed, and you can enter the properties for the tool you are adding. The Tool Properties dialog box is shown in Figure 11.12 with the properties for Windows Explorer displayed.

FIGURE 11.12.

The Tool Properties dialog box.

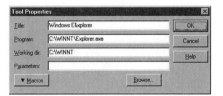

The Title field is where you type the tool's title as you want it to appear on the Tools menu. You can use an ampersand to indicate the shortcut key character. The Program field is where you enter the tool's path and filename. To ensure finding the program, you should enter the program's full path. If you don't know the exact path and filename, you can click the Browse button and go hunting for the file. The Working dir field is used to set the working directory for the tool. If you browse to find the tool, the working directory will be automatically set to the directory where the program resides.

The Parameters field requires some explanation. In its simplest form, this field is used to set the tool's command-line parameters. Type any parameters needed to run the tool. You can, however, use Delphi's predefined macros in the Parameters field. If you click the Macros button in the Tool Properties dialog box, you get a list of macros from which you can choose.

11

To use a macro, you can type it in directly or you can choose it from the list and click the Insert button. Figure 11.13 shows the Tool Properties dialog box with the list of macros displayed.

Figure 11.13.

The Tool Properties dialog box showing macros.

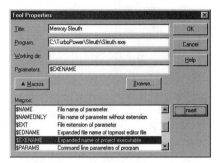

The $EXENAME macro will return the full path of the project's target executable. For example, if you have a project named MyApp in a directory called Projects, the $EXENAME parameter will pass the string c:\Projects\MyApp.exe to the program. Some macros require parameters. To use only the path from your project's target without the filename, you would specify a parameters string of $PATH($EXENAME). Continuing with this example, that combination of parameters would yield c:\Projects\. For a complete list of the macros available, see the Delphi online help.

Editing Tools on the Menu

Editing a tool on the Tools menu is as easy as clicking the Edit button on the Tool Options dialog box. The Tool Properties dialog box is displayed, and you can change any of the fields as necessary.

When you are done adding, editing, or rearranging your tools, click the Close button. The Delphi Tools menu will reflect your changes.

Setting the Environment Options

The Delphi Environment Options enable you to make changes to the Delphi IDE at the global level. (The Project Options dialog box controls settings at the project level.) To display the Environment Options dialog box, choose Tools | Environment Options from the main menu. This is a tabbed dialog box with nine pages. You learned about the Editor, Display, Color, Code Insight, and Explorer pages when you looked at the Code Editor and Code Explorer on Day 9. You'll look at the Preferences, Library, and Palette pages now.

Note

The Environment Options dialog box also contains a page for the Browser settings. This requires more explanation than I can provide in this chapter, so I won't attempt to cover the Browser or the Browser options.

The Preferences Page

The Preferences page of the Environment Options dialog box is where you set general Delphi preferences: how the Delphi IDE controls compiling, autosaving, and the appearance of the Form Designer. You can also set the Form Designer preferences on this page (see Figure 11.14).

FIGURE 11.14.

The Preferences page of the Environment Options dialog box.

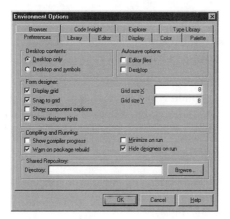

The Desktop contents section determines how much of the desktop layout Delphi will save when the project is saved.

The Autosave options section enables you to specify that either the Editor files or the Desktop be saved automatically every time the program is run. Personally, I do not like to have my editor files saved automatically; I want the ability to abandon current edits if necessary. Still, I know others who really like this feature and wouldn't program without it.

For one, if your application misbehaves and crashes the Delphi IDE or Windows, you know that your last edits have been saved. The Desktop option saves the current size and position of the Code Editor, all forms, the Alignment palette, the Object Inspector, and so on.

For the most part, the Form Designer section is self-explanatory. The Display grid option turns the visible grid in the Form Designer on and off. This affects only the grid's visible display, not whether objects snap to the grid. The Snap to grid option determines whether components placed and moved will snap to the grid points. The X and Y grid size fields enable you to set the size of the grid. By default, it is set at eight pixels. The Show component captions option pertains to nonvisual components placed on your forms. When this option is on, the Form Designer displays the Name property of nonvisual components below the icon representing the component.

The Compiling and Running section has four options as follows:

- The Show compiler progress option controls whether Delphi displays the compiler progress dialog box when compiling projects. Most of the time you will leave this option off because Delphi compiles your programs so quickly you really don't need to watch the progress.

- The Warn on package rebuild option warns you before you rebuild a package that is currently loaded in the Component Palette.

- The Hide designers on run option hides the Form Designer, Object Inspector, and other Form Designer support windows when the program is run. The Delphi main window and Code Editor are still visible, however.

- The Minimize on run option is similar to Hide designers on run. When this option is on, the entire Delphi IDE minimizes whenever the target program is run from the IDE.

 Note

When the Minimize on run option is on, any action in the program that requires the debugger (exceptions, breakpoints, and so on) results in the Delphi IDE being displayed again.

The Shared Repository section enables you to specify where the Object Repository information is saved by specifying the appropriate path in the Directory edit box. This can be very helpful in the case of repository items being used by a group of people working on the same project. You can set the Shared Repository's Directory to point to a place on the network, and all the items that you add to the Object Repository will be saved to the location on the network and can be inherited from by the other group members.

The Library Page

The Library page of the Environment Options dialog box has just three fields. The Library Path field is used to specify the path to the library files that Delphi uses for the Component Palette. Normally you don't have to change this path. The BPL output directory and DCP output directory fields are used to specify directories in which package output files will be placed. For example, you might opt to have your packages (.bpl

files) created in your `Windows\System` or `Winnt\System32` directory (package files need
to be on the system path).

The Palette Page

The Palette page of the Environment Options dialog box enables you to customize the
Component Palette (see Figure 11.15).

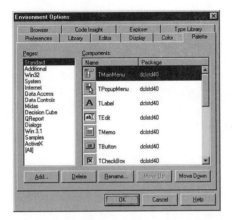

This page enables you to change the order in which the pages appear in the Component
Palette. The Pages list box on the left side of the dialog box shows all the pages currently
in the Component Palette. Note that depending on the version of Delphi you own, the
palette pages you see listed might differ from those shown in Figure 11.15. (The Midas
tab, for example, is only available for the Client/Server version of Delphi.) At the bottom
of the list you will see an item labeled [All]. This item shows all the installed components in all pages of the Component Palette. The Components list box shows the components appearing in the page that is selected in the Pages list box.

To reorder the pages, drag a page within the Pages list box to the position you want it to
occupy in the Component Palette. If you want the Samples page to appear first on the
Component Palette, you can drag it to the top of the list in the Pages list box and drop it.
You can also click on a page and use the Move Up or Move Down buttons to move the
page to a new location.

Pages can be added, deleted, or renamed, and those operations work exactly as you
would expect. To add a page, click the Add button. You will be prompted for a name for
the page. After you supply the page name, the new page is created. You might add a
page, for example, if you have created your own components and want them on their
own page in the Component Palette. You can also take any of the VCL components that
you use a lot and move them to a new page so that you can get to them quickly.

11

Tip

You can move components from page to page, but you cannot copy components from one page to another. You can, however, add any installed component to any page on the Component Palette. First select [All] in the Pages list box. Then drag a component from the Components list box to any of the pages in the Pages list box.

Deleting and renaming pages is straightforward. As with the Object Repository, you delete a page only after it has been emptied of its components.

Components on a page can be rearranged just as pages can. To move a component, drag it to its new position in the Components list box or use the Move Up or Move Down buttons. To move a component to a new page, drag and drop it on the name of the page in the Pages list box where you want it to appear. To delete a component, first select the component and then click the Delete button.

Summary

So now you know more about the tools included as part of the Delphi suite. Some of these tools are easy to miss, so it helps to have an overview of what is available to you. Some tools you might not use right away, but in the future you can take another look at what's available to you. I ended the day by going over the Environment Options dialog box. For the most part, you can leave these settings on their defaults. When you begin customizing the IDE, you will have a better understanding of what the individual options do.

Workshop

The Workshop contains quiz questions to help you solidify your understanding of the material covered and exercises to provide you with experience in using what you have learned. You can find answers to the quiz questions in Appendix A, "Answers to the Quiz Questions."

Q&A

Q **I'm creating an icon and trying to get an ellipse with a black border and a yellow fill. I set the foreground color to black and the background color to yellow, but all I get is a black circle. What do I have to do to get what I want?**

A The Image Editor works differently than some bitmap editors in this regard. To accomplish what you're after, you have to first draw a black, hollow ellipse and then fill it with yellow.

Q **How can I draw perfect circles or straight lines in the Image Editor?**

A Hold down the Shift key as you draw the circle or line. The same is true for drawing perfect squares.

Q **I created my own arrow cursor, but when I click with it, I can't seem to click with the point of the arrow. What's wrong?**

A You need to set the hot spot for the cursor. By default, the hot spot is in the upper-left corner. Edit the cursor in the Image Editor and change the hot spot to the pixel at the tip of the arrow.

Q **Am I required to create both a large version and a small version when I create an icon?**

A Not necessarily. If you supply only a large icon, Windows will shrink it when needed. If, however, you don't like the way your icon looks when Windows reduces it, you can design a small icon as well as the large one. When a small icon exists, Windows uses it.

Q **How can I copy part of one of my bitmaps to a new bitmap?**

A In the Image Editor, open the original bitmap in one editor window and a new bitmap in another editor window. Drag a marquee around the section of the original bitmap and choose Edit | Copy from the Image Editor menu. Switch to the new bitmap and choose Edit | Paste. The bitmap in the Clipboard is pasted into the new bitmap you are creating.

Q **I want some components on the Component Palette to appear not only in their original location but also in a new page that I create. Can I do that?**

A Yes. Go to the Palette page of the Environment Options dialog box. Click the [All] item in the Pages list box. Now drag a component from the Components list box to any page in the Pages list box.

Quiz

1. How is the transparent color used for icons and cursors?

2. How do you choose a color in the Image Editor?

3. How do you select an area on a bitmap to cut or copy?

4. What is the maximum number of colors allowed in an Image Editor bitmap?

5. What is a cursor's hot spot?

6. Can WinSight spy on hidden windows?

7. What's the fastest way to locate a window in the WinSight Window Tree?

8. How can you have your editor files automatically saved each time your program runs through the debugger?

9. Where do you go to rearrange the contents of the Component Palette?

Exercises

1. Using the Image Editor, create a bitmap that can be used as a splash screen for your company or for a specific application of yours.

2. Using the Image Editor, create an icon that has a transparent background and uses both the large and small icons.

3. Create a cursor resource in the Image Editor. Make certain you set its hot spot and test the cursor with the Cursor Tester.

4. Create a new resource file. Create two bitmaps and a cursor. Save the file.

5. Using the resource file you created in exercise 4, create a new icon resource and copy the icon created in exercise 2 to the new icon.

6. Open the Environment Options dialog box. Go to the Palette page. Create a new page in the Component Palette. Name it MyStuff. Copy the Label, Image, and OpenDialog components to the new page. Close the Environment Options dialog box. Examine the new layout of the Component Palette. Delete the MyStuff page when you are done with it.

7. Load a program in Delphi. Open the Environment Options dialog box. On the Preferences page, turn on the Minimize on Run option. Click Run to run the program. Notice the behavior of the Delphi IDE.

DAY **12**

Graphics and Multimedia Programming

Graphics and multimedia programming represent the fun part of programming. In this chapter, you are introduced to graphics and multimedia programming with Delphi. In the case of graphics programming, most of that introduction comes in the form of an examination of the TCanvas and TBitmap classes.

I start with a look at the easiest ways to display graphics in Delphi. After that, you learn about the Windows Graphics Device Interface and the components that make up that interface. Along the way, you learn about the various line and shape drawing routines and the different ways to display bitmaps. Later in the day, you learn about offscreen bitmaps and how they can benefit you. The multimedia programming sections deal with how to play sound files with the Windows API. You also learn how to play wave audio, MIDI, and AVI video files using the TMediaPlayer class. So let's get started!

Graphics the Easy Way

Graphics programming does not have to be difficult. Sometimes all you need to do is display a picture or a simple shape on a form. VCL provides ready-made components for those times. I'll take a brief look at some of these components before moving on to real graphics programming.

The Shape component (found on the Additional tab of the Component palette) can be used to add simple shapes to your forms. Using the Shape component is easy. Just drop one on a form and change the Brush, Pen, and Shape properties as desired. You can draw circles, ellipses, squares, rectangles, and rectangles with rounded edges. Change the Brush property to modify the background color of the shape. Change the Pen property to change the color or thickness of the border surrounding the shape.

An Image component can be used to display a bitmap on a form. This component is great for many graphics operations, including a bitmap background for a form. The Picture property of TImage is an instance of the TPicture class. You can select the picture at design time through the Object Inspector, or you can load a picture at runtime. For example, here's how you change the image in the component at runtime:

```
Image1.Picture.Bitmap.LoadFromFile('bkgnd.bmp');
```

The Stretch property determines whether the image will be enlarged or compressed to fit the size of the component. The Center property determines whether the bitmap is centered in the component. The AutoSize property can be used to force the component to size itself according to the size of the image.

I'll also mention the PaintBox component here. If you want drawing confined to a certain area of a form, this component provides a canvas on which you can draw. The only significant property of the PaintBox component is the Canvas property. This property is an instance of the TCanvas class. It is with this class that most drawing is done in a Delphi application. Let's look at the TCanvas class now.

Device Contexts and TCanvas

Windows uses the term *device context* to describe a canvas on which you can draw. A device context can be used to draw on many surfaces:

- To a window's client area or frame
- To the desktop
- To memory
- To a printer or other output device

These are just a few examples. There are other, more obscure device contexts (menus, for example), but those listed above are the device contexts that you will be most interested in.

Dealing with device contexts at the API level can be a bit complex. First, you have to obtain a handle to a device context from Windows. Then you have to select various objects into the device context (pens, brushes, or fonts). After that, you can draw on the device context. When you are done drawing, you have to be sure that the objects you select into the device context are removed before deleting the device context. If you forget to remove objects selected into the device context, your application will leak memory (use up memory that is never released back to the system). It's a tedious process to say the least.

The good news is that VCL provides the TCanvas class to make dealing with device contexts easier. Let me give you a quick example. The following code uses the Windows API to draw a circle on the screen with a blue outline and red interior:

```
procedure TForm1.Button1Click(Sender: TObject);
var
  DC : HDC;
  Brush, OldBrush : HBrush;
  Pen, OldPen : HPen;
begin
  DC := GetDC(Handle);
  Brush := CreateSolidBrush(RGB(255, 0, 0));
  Pen := CreatePen(PS_SOLID, 1, RGB(0, 0, 255));
  OldBrush := SelectObject(DC, Brush);
  OldPen := SelectObject(DC, Pen);
  Ellipse(DC, 20, 20, 120, 120);
  SelectObject(DC, OldBrush);
  SelectObject(DC, OldPen);
  ReleaseDC(Handle, DC);
end;
```

12

This code isn't so terribly bad, but it's easy to forget to restore objects when you are done with them. When that happens, your application will leak resources. Now look at the equivalent VCL code:

```
Canvas.Brush.Color := clRed;
Canvas.Pen.Color := clBlue;
Canvas.Ellipse(20, 20, 120, 120);
```

Not only is this code shorter and more readable, it is also much more robust. The TCanvas class takes care of freeing resources as needed, so you don't have to worry about it. TCanvas is a simpler *and* more effective approach than using the API.

The TCanvas class has many properties and methods. I'll look at some of these properties and methods while working through today's material. Table 12.1 lists the primary properties of TCanvas and Table 12.2 lists the primary methods.

TABLE 12.1. PRIMARY TCanvas PROPERTIES.

Property	Description
Brush	The brush color or pattern used for filling shapes.
ClipRect	The current clipping rectangle for the canvas. Any drawing is confined to this rectangle. This property is read-only.
CopyMode	Determines how drawing will be performed (normal, inverse, xor, and so on).
Font	The font the canvas uses for drawing text.
Handle	The handle (HDC) of the canvas. Used when calling the Windows API directly.
Pen	Determines the style and color of lines drawn on the canvas.
PenPos	The current drawing position in x and y coordinates.
Pixels	An array of the canvas' pixels.

TABLE 12.2. PRIMARY TCanvas METHODS.

Method	Description
Arc	Draws an arc on the canvas using the current pen.
BrushCopy	Displays a bitmap with a transparent background.
CopyRect	Copies part of an image to the canvas.
Draw	Copies an image from memory to the canvas.
Ellipse	Using the current pen, draws an ellipse that is filled with the current brush on the canvas.
FloodFill	Fills an area of the canvas with the current brush.
LineTo	Draws a line from the current drawing position to the location specified in the x and y parameters.
MoveTo	Sets the current drawing position.
Pie	Draws a pie shape on the canvas.
Polygon	Draws a polygon on the canvas from an array of points and fills it with the current brush.
Polyline	Using the current pen, draws a line on the canvas from an array of points. The points are not automatically closed.
Rectangle	Draws a rectangle on the canvas outlined by the current pen and filled with the current brush.
RoundRect	Draws a filled rectangle with rounded corners.

Method	Description
StretchDraw	Copies a bitmap from memory to the canvas. The bitmap is stretched or reduced according to the size of the destination rectangle.
TextExtent	Returns the width and height in pixels of the string passed in the Text parameter. The width is calculated using the current font of the canvas.
TextHeight	Returns the height in pixels of the string passed in the Text parameter. The width is calculated using the current font of the canvas.
TextOut	Using the current font, draws text on the canvas at a specified location.
TextRect	Draws text within a clipping rectangle.

Believe it or not, these properties and methods represent just a small part of the functionality of a Windows device context. The good news is that these properties and methods cover 80 percent of the tasks you will need to perform when working with graphics. However, before I can talk more about the TCanvas class in detail, I need to talk about graphics objects used in Windows programming.

GDI Objects

The Windows Graphics Device Interface (GDI) has many types of objects that define how a device context functions. The most commonly used GDI objects are pens, brushes, and fonts. Other GDI objects include palettes, bitmaps, and regions. Let's take a look at pens, brushes, and fonts first and then move on to more complex objects.

Pens, Brushes, and Fonts

Pens, brushes, and fonts are straightforward. Let's take a brief look at each of these GDI objects and how the TCanvas class uses them.

Pens

A pen defines the object that is being used to draw lines. A line might be a single line from one point to the next, or it might be the border drawn around rectangles, ellipses, and polygons. The pen is accessed through the Pen property of the TCanvas class and is an instance of the TPen class. Table 12.3 lists the properties of TPen. There are no methods or events of TPen that are worthy of note.

12

TABLE 12.3. TPen PROPERTIES.

Property	Description
Color	Sets the color of the line.
Handle	The handle to the pen (HPEN). Used when calling the GDI directly.
Mode	Determines how lines will be drawn (normal, inverse, xor, and so on).
Style	The pen's style. Styles can be solid, dotted, dashed, dash-dot, clear, and more.
Width	The width of the pen in pixels.

For the most part, these properties are used exactly as you would expect. The following example draws a red, dashed line:

```
Canvas.Pen.Color := clRed;
Canvas.Pen.Style := psDash;
Canvas.MoveTo(20, 20);
Canvas.LineTo(120, 20);
```

To test this code, drop a button on a form and type the code in the OnClick handler for the button. When you click the button, the line will be drawn on the form.

Note

The simple examples in this chapter can all be tested in this manner. However, if you cover the application and bring it to the top, the drawing will be gone. This is because the drawing is temporary. If you want the drawing to be persistent, place the drawing code in the OnPaint event handler for the form. Any time a window needs to be repainted, its OnPaint event is generated and your drawing code will be executed.

The dashed and dotted pen styles can be used only with a pen width of 1. The psClear pen style can be used to eliminate the line that the Windows GDI draws around the outside of objects such as rectangles, ellipses, and filled polygons.

Tip

You can experiment with the various properties of TPen by dropping a Shape component on a form and modifying the shape's Pen property. This is especially useful for seeing the effects of the Mode property of the TPen class.

Brushes

A brush represents the filled area of a graphical shape. When you draw an ellipse, rectangle, or polygon, the shape will be filled with the current brush. When you think of a brush you probably think of a solid color. Many times this is the case, but a brush is more than just a color. A brush can also include a pattern or a bitmap. The TCanvas class has a property called Brush, which you can use to control the appearance of the brush. The Brush property is an instance of the TBrush class. As with TPen, the TBrush class doesn't have any methods or events of note. The TBrush properties are listed in Table 12.4.

TABLE 12.4. TBrush PROPERTIES.

Property	Description
Bitmap	The bitmap to be used as the brush's background. For Windows 95 the bitmap must be no larger than 8×8.
Color	Sets the color of the brush.
Handle	The handle to the brush (HBRUSH). Used when calling the GDI directly.
Style	The brush's style. Styles include solid, clear, or one of several patterns.

By default, the Style property is set to bsSolid. If you want a pattern fill, you should set the Style property to one of the pattern styles (bsHorizontal, bsVertical, bsFDiagonal, bsBDiagonal, bsCross, or bsDiagCross). The following example draws a circle on the form using a 45 degree hatched pattern. Figure 12.1 shows the form when this code executes.

```
Canvas.Brush.Color := clBlue;
Canvas.Brush.Style := bsDiagCross;
Canvas.Ellipse(20, 20, 220, 220);
```

12

FIGURE 12.1.

A circle filled with a hatched brush.

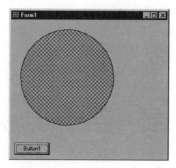

When using a pattern brush, the brush's Color property defines the color of the lines that make up the pattern. For some reason, VCL automatically forces the background mode to transparent when using a pattern fill. This means that the background color of the brush will be the same as the background color of the window on which the shape is drawn.

Take another look at Figure 12.1 and you will see that the background color of the circle is the same color as the form (I know it's not easy to see in grayscale). If you want to specify a background color, you need to circumvent VCL and go to the API. Here's how the code would look if you want to use a blue hatch on a white background:

```
Canvas.Brush.Color := clBlue;
Canvas.Brush.Style := bsDiagCross;
SetBkMode(Canvas.Handle, OPAQUE);
SetBkColor(Canvas.Handle, clWhite);
Canvas.Ellipse(20, 20, 220, 220);
```

Now the background color of the brush will be white. Figure 12.2 shows the circle with the new code applied.

FIGURE 12.2.

The hatched brush with a white background.

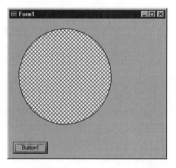

Another interesting feature of brushes is the bitmap background option. First look at the code and then I'll tell you more about bitmap brushes. Here it is:

```
Canvas.Brush.Bitmap := TBitmap.Create;
Canvas.Brush.Bitmap.LoadFromFile('bkgnd.bmp');
Canvas.Ellipse(20, 20, 220, 220);
Canvas.Brush.Bitmap.Free;
```

The first line in this code snippet creates a TBitmap object and assigns it to the Bitmap property of the brush. The Bitmap property is not assigned by default, so you have to specifically create a TBitmap object and assign it to the Bitmap property. The second line loads a bitmap from a file. The bitmap must be no larger than 8 pixels by 8 pixels. You can use a larger bitmap, but it will be cropped to 8×8. The third line in this example draws the ellipse. After the ellipse has been drawn, the Brush property is deleted. It is necessary to delete the Brush property because VCL won't do it for you in this case. If you fail to delete the Brush property, your program will leak memory. Figure 12.3 shows the ellipse drawn with a bitmap brush.

FIGURE 12.3.

An ellipse with a bitmap brush.

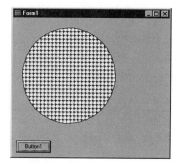

Sometimes you need a hollow brush. A hollow (or clear) brush enables the background to show through. To create a hollow brush, just set the brush's Style property to bsClear. Let's take the previous example and add a second circle inside the first using a hollow brush. Figure 12.4 shows the results. Here's the code:

```
Canvas.Pen.Width := 1;
Canvas.Brush.Bitmap := TBitmap.Create;
Canvas.Brush.Bitmap.LoadFromFile('bkgnd.bmp');
Canvas.Ellipse(20, 20, 220, 220);
Canvas.Brush.Style := bsClear;
Canvas.Pen.Width := 5;
Canvas.Ellipse(70, 70, 170, 170);
Canvas.Brush.Bitmap.Free;
```

FIGURE 12.4.

A circle with a hollow brush.

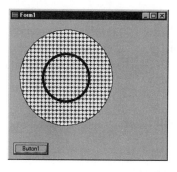

12

You can do other things with brushes if you go directly to the API. Most of the time, though, the VCL TBrush class does the job.

Fonts

Fonts aren't anything new to you; you have been using them throughout the book. Fonts used with the TCanvas class are no different than those used with forms or other components. The Font property of TCanvas is the same as the Font property of any other component. To change the font for the canvas, just do this:

```
Canvas.Font.Name := 'Courier New';
Canvas.Font.Size := 14;
Canvas.Font.Style := Canvas.Font.Style + [fsBold];
Canvas.TextOut(20, 20, 'Testing');
```

That's all there is to it. I'll talk more about what to do with fonts a little later in the section "Drawing Text."

Bitmaps and Palettes

Bitmaps and palettes go together most of the time. The TBitmap class encapsulates a bitmap object in Delphi. Loading and displaying bitmaps is easy when using this class. You already saw TBitmap in action in the Jumping Jack program on Day 8, "Creating Applications in Delphi." The TBitmap class is used in a wide variety of situations. I'll look at some of those situations later today when talking about drawing bitmaps and about memory bitmaps. The TBitmap class is complex, so I won't go over every property and method here.

Palettes are one of the most confusing aspects of Windows programming. Most of the time the palette is maintained by the TBitmap object, so you really don't have to worry about it. Rather than trying to explain the importance of palettes, let me show you an example.

Start a new application and type the following code in the OnPaint event handler, or use a button click event. Be sure to enter the correct path to the HANDSHAK.BMP file. (You should find it in the Borland Shared Files/Images/Splash/256Color directory.) Here's the code:

```
var
  Bitmap : TBitmap;
begin
  Bitmap := TBitmap.Create;
  { Bitmap.IgnorePalette := True; }
  Bitmap.LoadFromFile('handshak.bmp');
  Canvas.Draw(0, 0, Bitmap);
  Bitmap.Free;
end;
```

Notice that one line is commented out with curly braces. Run the program and you will see a nice bitmap on the form. Now uncomment the line that is commented out. This line tells the VCL to ignore the palette information when displaying the bitmap. Run the program again. This time you should notice that the bitmap's colors are all wrong (you might not notice this effect if your video adapter is set to display more than 256 colors). This is because the palette is not being applied. The palette makes sure that the correct colors for the bitmap are mapped to the system palette.

Bitmap and palette objects play an important role in graphics operations. It takes some time to understand everything that they entail, so don't feel bad if you don't catch onto it right away.

Clipping Regions

Regions are areas of the screen that can be used to control the parts of the canvas that can be drawn on. The TCanvas class has a ClipRect property, but it is read-only. To change the clipping region, you have to use the Windows API. Let's take the previous example and modify it slightly to illustrate how clipping regions work. Here's the code:

```
var
  Bitmap : TBitmap;
  Rgn : HRGN;
begin
  Bitmap := TBitmap.Create;
  Bitmap.LoadFromFile('handshak.bmp');
  Rgn := CreateRectRgn(50, 50, 250, 250);
  SelectClipRgn(Canvas.Handle, Rgn);
  Canvas.Draw(0, 0, Bitmap);
  Bitmap.Free;
end;
```

Now when you run the program you will see that only a portion of the bitmap is displayed. The SelectClipRgn function sets the canvas' clipping region to the rectangle identified by the coordinates 50, 50, 250, and 250. The bitmap is still being drawn in the same location it was before, yet now only a portion of the bitmap (defined by the clipping region) can be seen. Everything outside the clipping region is ignored.

Regions don't have to be rectangular. Let's take the previous example and make it more interesting. Remove the line that creates the rectangular region and replace it with this line:

```
Rgn := CreateEllipticRgn(30, 30, 170, 170);
```

Now run the program again. This time, the bitmap is limited to a circular region. Figure 12.5 shows the program with the elliptical region in place.

12

FIGURE 12.5.

An elliptical clipping region.

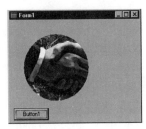

Let's try another type of region. Again, remove the line that defines the region and replace it with these lines:

```
const
  Points : array[0..3] of TPoint =
    ((X:80;Y:0), (X:0;Y:80), (X:80;Y:160), (X:160;Y:80));
var
  Bitmap : TBitmap;
  Rgn : HRGN;
begin
  Bitmap := TBitmap.Create;
  Bitmap.LoadFromFile('handshak.bmp');
  Rgn := CreatePolygonRgn(Points, 4, ALTERNATE);
  SelectClipRgn(Canvas.Handle, Rgn);
  Canvas.Draw(0, 0, Bitmap);
  Bitmap.Free;
end;
```

This time you are using a polygon region. The points array defines the points that create the region. The CreatePolygonRgn function creates a region from a series of points. You can use as many points as you want. You don't even have to specify the closing point because the region is automatically closed between the first point and the last point. Run the program again and see what you get. Figure 12.6 shows the results of this exercise.

FIGURE 12.6.

A polygon clipping region.

Note

This code snippet also shows how to initialize a const array of records. Here's the code I'm referring to:

```
const
  Points : array[0..3] of TPoint =
    ((X:80;Y:0), (X:0;Y:80), (X:80;Y:160), (X:160;Y:80));
```

This code declares an array of TPoint records and initializes it with data. TPoint has two fields: X and Y. Notice that the field name is listed, followed by a colon and the value to be assigned to that field (X:80, for example). Notice also that both the X and Y fields are assigned values and those values are paired with parentheses. This is done four times because the array has four elements. This is the only way to declare and initialize a const array of records.

Regions can be very useful when you are doing certain kinds of drawing operations. You might not need to use clipping regions often, but when you need them, they are invaluable.

Basic Drawing Operations

You have already encountered some of the basic graphics routines as you have worked through the book. By now you know that the Rectangle method is used to draw squares and rectangles, the Ellipse method is used to draw circles and ovals, and that the MoveTo and LineTo methods are used to draw lines.

There is also the Arc method for drawing arcs and the Pie method for drawing pie-shaped objects. All in all, it's fairly basic. There's not much point in going into a lot of detail on the methods of TCanvas. Instead, let's move on to the more interesting (and troublesome) graphics operations you are likely to encounter when writing Delphi applications.

12

Drawing Text

Drawing text doesn't sound like it should be too difficult, does it? The truth is that there are several little pitfalls that, if you aren't aware of them, can make drawing text a difficult experience. In addition, there are several nice text drawing features that you should know about.

The TextOut and TextRect Methods

The TextOut method is the most basic way to draw text on a canvas. There really isn't too much to say about TextOut. You just pass it the X position, the Y position, and the text to display—for example,

```
Canvas.TextOut(20, 20, 'Joshua Reisdorph');
```

This code displays the given string at position 20, 20 on the form. The X and Y coordinates specify the top left corner of the text to be drawn, not the baseline. To illustrate what I mean, test this code:

```
Canvas.TextOut(20, 20, 'This is a test.');
Canvas.MoveTo(20, 20);
Canvas.LineTo(100, 20);
```

This code displays some text at position 20, 20 and then draws a line from that same position to position 100, 20. Figure 12.7 shows the results of this code. Notice that the line is drawn across the top of the text.

FIGURE 12.7.

Text drawn with TextOut.

Use TextOut whenever you have text to display that doesn't need a lot of fine positioning.

The TextRect method enables you to specify a clipping rectangle in addition to the text to be displayed. Use this method when the text needs to be constrained within certain boundaries. Any of the text that falls outside the boundary will be clipped. The following code snippet ensures that no more than 100 pixels of the text will be displayed:

```
Canvas.TextRect(Rect(20, 50, 120, 70), 20, 50,
  'This is a very long line that might get clipped.');
```

Both TextOut and TextRect can only draw single lines of text. No wrapping of the text is performed.

Tip

To draw text with tab stops, see the Windows API function TabbedTextOut.

Text Backgrounds

Refer to Figure 12.7. Notice that the text has a white background—not very appealing on a gray form. The text background is obtained from the current brush (white by default). To remedy the unsightly results of Figure 12.7, you need to take one of two actions: Either change the color of the canvas brush, or make the text's background transparent.

Changing the background color of the text is fairly easy. The question is, do you know what color to make the text's background? In this case, the text's background can be the same color as the form, so you can do this:

```
Canvas.Brush.Color := Color;
```

This code will work for most situations, but in some cases you need more control. It would be easier if you could just make the background of the text transparent. The good news is, you can. Here's how the code would look:

```
var
  OldStyle : TBrushStyle;
begin
  OldStyle := Canvas.Brush.Style;
  Canvas.Brush.Style := bsClear;
  Canvas.TextOut(20, 20, 'This is a test.');
  Canvas.Brush.Style := OldStyle;
end;
```

First, save the current brush style. Next, set the brush style to transparent (bsClear). After you display the text, set the brush style back to what it was before. You should get into the habit of saving the previous style and resetting it when you are done drawing the text. It is unlikely that you'll want to leave the brush style set to transparent, so resetting the previous style is always a good idea.

Using a transparent background has other advantages as well. Let's say you want to display some text over a bitmap background. In that case you can't use a solid background. Here's a code snippet that illustrates the point (the FACTORY.BMP file can be found in your Borland Shared Files\56Color directory):

```
var
  OldStyle : TBrushStyle;
  Bitmap   : TBitmap;
begin
  Bitmap := TBitmap.Create;
  Bitmap.LoadFromFile('factory.bmp');
  Canvas.Draw(0, 0, Bitmap);
  Canvas.Font.Name := 'Arial Bold';
  Canvas.Font.Size := 13;
  OldStyle := Canvas.Brush.Style;
  Canvas.Brush.Style := bsClear;
  Canvas.TextOut(20, 5, 'Transparent Background');
  Canvas.Brush.Style := OldStyle;
  Canvas.TextOut(20, 30, 'Solid Background');
  Bitmap.Free;
end;
```

This code draws a bitmap on the form. Next, text is drawn on the form (over the bitmap) with a transparent background. After that, more text is drawn with the regular

12

background. Figure 12.8 shows the results of this code. As you can see, making the background transparent creates a much more appealing image.

Another reason for using transparent backgrounds for text is illustrated on Day 13 in the section, "Owner-Drawn Status Panels." There you give the status bar text a 3D look by drawing the text once in white and drawing it again, slightly offset, in black. The only way that code works is by using a transparent background. As you can see, sometimes a transparent background is the only option for achieving the effect you are looking for.

The DrawText Function

The Windows API DrawText function gives you much greater control over text that is drawn on the canvas than does TextOut. For some reason, the TCanvas class does not have a DrawText method. To use DrawText, then, means using the API directly. First, let's look at a basic DrawText example and then I'll tell you more about the power of this function:

```
var
  R : TRect;
begin
  R := Rect(20, 20, 220, 80);
  Canvas.Rectangle(20,20, 220, 80);
  DrawText(Canvas.Handle, 'An example of DrawText.',
    -1, R, DT_SINGLELINE or DT_VCENTER or DT_CENTER);
end;
```

Figure 12.9 shows the results of this code as well as results from the following examples.

FIGURE **12.9.**

Examples of the DrawText *function.*

First, a TRect record is initialized using the Windows API Rect function. After that, a regular rectangle is drawn on the canvas. (The rectangle is drawn on the canvas so that you can visualize the size of the rectangle that you are about to draw on.) Finally, the DrawText function is called to draw the text.

Let's take a minute to discuss the various parameters of this function, as follows:

- The first parameter is used to specify the device context on which to draw. The Handle parameter of TCanvas is the HDC (handle to a device context) of the canvas, so you pass that for the first parameter.
- The second parameter is the string that will be displayed.
- The third parameter is used to specify the number of characters to draw. When this parameter is set to -1, all of the characters in the string will be drawn.
- The fourth parameter of DrawText takes a var TRect. This parameter is a var parameter because some DrawText operations modify the rectangle passed in.
- The key to how DrawText behaves is in the final parameter. This parameter is used to specify the flags that are used when drawing the text. In this example, you use the DT_SINGLELINE, DT_VCENTER, and DT_CENTER flags. These flags tell Windows that the text is a single line, and to draw the text centered both vertically and horizontally. All in all, there are almost 20 flags that you can specify for DrawText. I'm not going to go over every flag, so for a complete list see the Win32 API online help.

The previous example illustrates one of the DrawText function's most common uses: to center text either horizontally, vertically, or both. This is a great feature when doing owner-drawing of components. In particular, owner-drawn list boxes, combo boxes, and menus often need to center text. You might not realize the benefit of this function right now, but you will if you start doing owner-drawn components, or if you start writing your own graphical components.

Another interesting flag of DrawText is the DT_END_ELLPSIS flag. If the text is too long to fit in the specified rectangle, Windows truncates the string and adds an ellipsis to the end, indicating the string was truncated. Take this code, for example:

```
var
  R : TRect;
begin
  R := Rect(20, 100, 120, 150);
  DrawText(Canvas.Handle, 'This text is too long to fit.',
    -1, R, DT_END_ELLIPSIS);
end;
```

12

When this code is executed, it will result in this text being displayed:

```
This text is too long...
```

You can use this flag any time you anticipate text that could be too long for the rectangle in which the text is drawn.

DT_CALCRECT is another flag that is invaluable. It calculates the height of the rectangle needed to hold the specified text. When you use this flag, Windows calculates the needed height and returns that height but doesn't draw the text. You tell Windows how wide the rectangle should be, and Windows will tell you how high the rectangle needs to be to contain the text. In fact, Windows also modifies the bottom and left members of the rectangle passed in so that it contains the needed values. This is particularly important when drawing multiple lines of text.

The following example asks Windows how high the rectangle needs to be to contain all of the text. After that, a rectangle is drawn onscreen. Finally, the text is drawn in the rectangle. Here's the code:

```
var
  R : TRect;
  S : string;
begin
  R := Rect(20, 150, 150, 200);
  S := 'This is a very long string which will ' +
    'run into multiple lines of text.';
  DrawText(Canvas.Handle, PChar(S),
    -1, R, DT_CALCRECT or DT_WORDBREAK);
  Canvas.Brush.Style := bsSolid;
  Canvas.Rectangle(R.left, R.top, R.right, R.bottom);
  Canvas.Brush.Style := bsClear;
  DrawText(Canvas.Handle, PChar(S), -1, R, DT_WORDBREAK);
end;
```

Notice that you have to cast S to a PChar for the second parameter of DrawText. This is necessary because DrawText wants a pointer to a character array for the text parameter and not a string type.

> **Note**
>
> If you are writing components that can be used with all versions of Delphi, you cannot use the cast from string to PChar. This cast won't compile under Delphi 1. Instead, you have to use the StrPCopy function as follows:
>
> ```
> var
>   Temp : array [0..50] of Char;
>   R : TRect;
>   S : string;
> ```

```
begin
  DrawText(Canvas.Handle, StrPCopy(Temp, S),
    -1, R, DT_CALCRECT or DT_WORDBREAK);
{ etc. }
```

If you don't have to worry about supporting Delphi 1, you can cast the string to a PChar as shown previously.

Place this code in the OnPaint event handler for a form. Run the program several times and modify the length of the text string that is displayed. Notice that no matter how much text you add to the string, the rectangle will always be drawn precisely around the text. Refer to Figure 12.9 for the results of this exercise as well as the results of the previous exercises on DrawText.

Tip

If you need even more text drawing options, you can use the DrawTextEx function. See the Win32 API online help for full details.

Note

Drawing text with DrawText is slightly slower than using TextOut. If your drawing operations are speed-sensitive, you should use TextOut rather than DrawText. You'll have to do more work on your own, but the execution speed will likely be better. For most drawing, though, you won't notice any difference between TextOut and DrawText.

12

DrawText is a very useful and powerful function. When you start writing your own components, you will no doubt use this function a great deal.

Drawing Bitmaps

Drawing bitmaps sounds like it should be difficult, yet as you have seen several times up to this point, drawing bitmaps is very easy. The TCanvas class has several methods for drawing bitmaps. The most often-used method is the Draw method. This method simply draws a bitmap (represented by a descendant of the TGraphic class) onto the canvas at the specified location. You've seen several examples up to this point, but here's another short example:

```
var
  Bitmap : TBitmap;
begin
  Bitmap := TBitmap.Create;
  Bitmap.LoadFromFile('c:\winnt\winnt256.bmp');
  Canvas.Draw(0, 0, Bitmap);
  Bitmap.Free;
end;
```

This code creates a TBitmap object, loads the file called WINNT256.BMP, and displays it in the upper-left corner of the form. Use Draw when you want to display bitmaps without modification.

The StretchDraw method is used when you want to alter a bitmap's size. You specify a rectangle for the location of the bitmap and an image to draw. If the supplied rectangle is larger than the original size of the bitmap, the bitmap will be stretched. If the rectangle is smaller than the bitmap's original size, the bitmap will be reduced to fit. Here's an example:

```
var
  Bitmap : TBitmap;
  R : TRect;
begin
  Bitmap := TBitmap.Create;
  Bitmap.LoadFromFile('c:.bmp');
  R := Rect(0, 0, 100, 100);
  Canvas.StretchDraw(R, Bitmap);
  Bitmap.Free;
end;
```

Note   No attempt is made by StretchDraw to maintain the bitmap's original aspect ratio. It's up to you to be sure that the bitmap retains its original width-to-height ratio.

Another bitmap drawing method is CopyRect. This method enables you to specify both a source rectangle and a destination rectangle. This enables you to split a bitmap into sections when displaying it. Take this code, for example:

```
var
  Bitmap : TBitmap;
  Src : TRect;
  Dst : TRect;
  I, X, Y : Integer;
```

```
    Strips : Integer;
    Stripsize : Integer;
    OldPal : HPalette;
begin
  Bitmap := TBitmap.Create;
  Bitmap.LoadFromFile('factory.bmp');
  Strips := 6;
  Stripsize := (Bitmap.Height div Strips);
  OldPal := SelectPalette(Canvas.Handle, Bitmap.Palette, True);
  for I := 0 to Pred(Strips) do begin
    Src := Rect(0, i * Stripsize,
      Bitmap.Width, (i * Stripsize) + Stripsize);
    X := Random(Width - Bitmap.Width);
    Y := Random(Height - Stripsize);
    Dst := Rect(X, Y, X + Bitmap.Width, Y + Stripsize);
    Canvas.CopyRect(Dst, Bitmap.Canvas, Src);
  end;
  SelectPalette(Canvas.Handle, oldPal, True);
  Bitmap.Free;
end;
```

This code loads a bitmap, dissects it into strips, and then displays the strips in random locations on the form. Figure 12.10 shows a sample run of this code. Enter this code in the OnPaint handler of your main form and run the program. Cover up the main form and then bring it to the top again. The images will be redrawn each time the form is repainted.

FIGURE 12.10.

Sections of a bitmap written randomly to the screen with CopyRect.

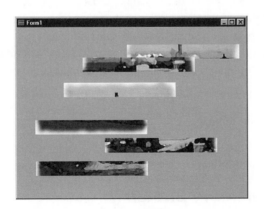

12

Copying sections of a bitmap like FACTORY.BMP might not appear to make a lot of sense at first glance. A common graphics programming technique, however, is to create one large bitmap made up of several smaller images and copy just the image you want to the screen. In that type of situation, CopyRect is the way to go.

Note

> In the previous code example I used the `SelectPalette` function to set the form's palette to the `Palette` property of the bitmap. For some strange reason, the `TCanvas` class doesn't have a `Palette` property, so you have to go to the API to set the palette for the form. If I didn't set the palette for the form, the colors would be wrong when the bitmap strips are displayed on the form. The `CopyRect` method uses a different mechanism for displaying a bitmap on the canvas, so taking this extra step is necessary when using this method.

There is one other bitmap drawing method I want to mention. The `BrushCopy` method enables you to specify a source rectangle, a destination rectangle, an image, and a transparent color. The online help for `BrushCopy` says to use the `ImageList` component rather than using this method. That's a bit extreme, in my opinion. There are times when `BrushCopy` works nicely, and it's a whole lot easier to use than the `ImageList` component. Don't overlook `BrushCopy` if you are using bitmaps with transparent backgrounds.

Offscreen Bitmaps

Offscreen bitmaps, also called memory bitmaps, are used commonly in Windows programming. Offscreen bitmaps enable you to draw an image in memory and then display the image onscreen by using the `Draw` method. Offscreen bitmaps help avoid the flicker that you see when you try to draw too much directly to the screen in a short period of time. Offscreen bitmaps are also good for complex drawing programs. You can prepare the image in memory and then display it when ready. Offscreen bitmaps are used in animation, and the most popular new technology for animation is Microsoft's DirectX SDK.

The principle behind offscreen bitmaps is a simple three step process:

1. Create a memory bitmap.
2. Draw on the memory bitmap.
3. Copy the memory bitmap to the screen.

Creating a Memory Bitmap

Creating a memory bitmap is easy. In fact, you've already done it several times in this chapter. Surprised? Each time you created a `TBitmap` object you were creating a memory bitmap. In those cases, you were loading a file into the memory bitmap. In other cases you will create a memory bitmap, set the its size, and then draw on it—for example,

```
var
  Bitmap : TBitmap;
  I, X, Y, W, H : Integer;
  Red, Green, Blue : Integer;
begin
  Bitmap := TBitmap.Create;
  Bitmap.Width := 500;
  Bitmap.Height := 500;
  for I := 0 to 19 do begin
    X := Random(400);
    Y := Random(400);
    W := Random(100) + 50;
    H := Random(100) + 50;
    Red := Random(255);
    Green := Random(255);
    Blue := Random(255);
    Bitmap.Canvas.Brush.Color := RGB(Red, Green, Blue);
    Bitmap.Canvas.Rectangle(X, Y, W, H);
  end;
  Canvas.Draw(0, 0, Bitmap);
  Bitmap.Free;
end;
```

To try out this code, place a button on a form and type the code in the event handler for the button's OnClick event. Each time you click the button, a new random set of rectangles is drawn onscreen. This code simply draws on the memory bitmap and then copies the bitmap to the form's canvas. If you are using a 256-color video adapter, the colors will be dithered because you are not implementing a palette for this exercise.

Note

When you create a memory bitmap, the bitmap will have the same color depth as the current video display settings. In other words, if you have your video display set for 256 colors, the memory bitmap will be a 256-color bitmap. If you have your video display set for 24- or 32-bit video, your memory bitmap will contain 32K, 64K, or 16 million colors.

12

Saving a Memory Bitmap

Saving a memory bitmap to a file is ridiculously easy. Here's all it takes:

```
Bitmap.SaveToFile('test.bmp');
```

Yes, that's it. In fact, you can easily create your own screen capture program. All you have to do is copy the appropriate part of the desktop to a memory bitmap and then save it to file. It looks something like Listing 12.1.

LISTING 12.1. SCREEN CAPTURE ROUTINE.

```
procedure MainForm.CaptureButtonClick(Sender: TObject);
var
  DtCanvas  : TCanvas;
  Bitmap    : TBitmap;
  NumColors : Integer;
  LogPal    : PLogPalette;
  Src, Dst  : TRect;
begin
  { Create a TCanvas object for the desktop DC. }
  DtCanvas := TCanvas.Create;
  DtCanvas.Handle := GetDC(0);

  { Create a new TBitmap object and set its }
  { size to the size of the form.          }
  Bitmap := TBitmap.Create;
  Bitmap.Width := Width;
  Bitmap.Height := Height;

  { Create a palette from the form's Canvas  }
  { and assign that palette to the Bitmap's  }
  { Palette property.                        }
  NumColors := GetDeviceCaps(Canvas.Handle, SizePalette);
  GetMem(LogPal, SizeOf(TLogPalette) +
    (NumColors - 1) * SizeOf(TPaletteEntry));
  LogPal.palVersion   := $300;
  LogPal.palNumEntries := NumColors;
  GetSystemPaletteEntries(
    Canvas.Handle, 0, NumColors, LogPal.palPalEntry);
  Bitmap.Palette := CreatePalette(LogPal^);
  FreeMem(LogPal);

  { Copy a section of the screen from the   }
  { desktop canvas to the Bitmap.           }
  Src := BoundsRect;
  Dst := Rect(0, 0, Width, Height);
  Bitmap.Canvas.CopyRect(Dst, DtCanvas, Src);

  { Save it to disk. }
  Bitmap.SaveToFile('form.bmp');
  { Clean up and go home. }
  Bitmap.Free;
  DtCanvas.Free;
end;
```

Note This code goes the extra mile and implements a palette for the form in case the form is displaying graphics. This code was translated from the code that was originally part of an article I wrote for The Cobb Group's *C++Builder Developer's Journal*. Although you probably aren't interested in the C++Builder journal, you might be interested in the *Delphi Developer's Journal*. You can sign up for a free copy of the *Delphi Developer's Journal* on The Cobb Group's Web site at http://www.cobb.com/ddj.

Sample Memory Bitmap Program

Listing 12.2 contains a program called MemBmp that illustrates the use of memory bitmaps. This program scrolls a marquee across the screen when you click one of two buttons. The first button scrolls the text across the screen without using a memory bitmap (writing directly to the form's canvas). The second button uses a memory bitmap for smoother scrolling. A third button is used to stop the marquee. Figure 12.11 shows the MemBmp program running.

FIGURE 12.11.

The MemBmp program running.

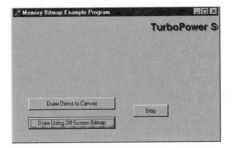

LISTING 12.2. MemBmpU.pas.

```
unit MemBmpU;

interface

uses
  Windows, Messages, SysUtils, Classes, Graphics,
  Controls, Forms, Dialogs, StdCtrls;

const
  DisplayText = 'TurboPower Software Co.';
```

continues

12

LISTING 12.2. CONTINUED

```
type
  TForm1 = class(TForm)
    Button1: TButton;
    Button2: TButton;
    Button3: TButton;
    procedure Button1Click(Sender: TObject);
    procedure Button2Click(Sender: TObject);
    procedure Button3Click(Sender: TObject);
  private
    { Private declarations }
    Done : Boolean;
  public
    { Public declarations }
  end;

var
  Form1: TForm1;

implementation

{$R *.DFM}

procedure TForm1.Button1Click(Sender: TObject);
var
  I : Integer;
begin
  Canvas.Font.Name := 'Arial Bold';
  Canvas.Font.Size := 16;
  Canvas.Brush.Color := clSilver;
  Done := false;
  while not Done do begin
    for I := -Canvas.TextWidth(DisplayText)
      to Pred(Width) do begin
      Sleep(1);
      Application.ProcessMessages;
      if Done then
        Break;
      Canvas.Font.Color := clGray;
      Canvas.Brush.Style := bsClear;
      Canvas.TextOut(i + 2, 12, DisplayText);
      Canvas.Font.Color := clBlack;
      Canvas.Brush.Style := bsClear;
      Canvas.TextOut(i, 10, DisplayText);
      Canvas.Font.Color := clSilver;
      Canvas.TextOut(i + 2, 12, DisplayText);
      Canvas.TextOut(i, 10, DisplayText);
    end;
  end;
end;
```

```
procedure TForm1.Button2Click(Sender: TObject);
var
  Bitmap : TBitmap;
  I : Integer;
begin
  Bitmap := TBitmap.Create;
  Bitmap.Width := Width;
  Bitmap.Height := 40;
  Bitmap.Canvas.Font.Name := 'Arial Bold';
  Bitmap.Canvas.Font.Size := 16;
  Bitmap.Canvas.Brush.Color := clSilver;
  Bitmap.Canvas.FillRect(Rect(0, 0, Width, 40));
  Done := False;
  while not Done do begin
    for I := -Bitmap.Canvas.TextWidth(DisplayText)
      to Pred(Width) do begin
      Application.ProcessMessages;
      if (Done) then
        Break;
      Sleep(1);
      Bitmap.Canvas.Font.Color := clGray;
      Bitmap.Canvas.Brush.Style := bsClear;
      Bitmap.Canvas.TextOut(2, 12, DisplayText);
      Bitmap.Canvas.Font.Color := clBlack;
      Bitmap.Canvas.Brush.Style := bsClear;
      Bitmap.Canvas.TextOut(0, 10, DisplayText);
      Canvas.Draw(I, 0, Bitmap);
    end;
  end;
  Bitmap.Free;
end;

procedure TForm1.Button3Click(Sender: TObject);
begin
  Done := True;
end;

end.
```

The MemBmp program is included with the book's code, along with other example programs (called BrushTst, Capture, Gradient, and Rotate) that illustrate the concepts discussed today.

Multimedia Programming

Multimedia programming is a deceivingly innocent phrase. The reason for this is that multimedia programming encompasses a wide range of possibilities. Multimedia typically includes wave audio, MIDI audio, AVI video clips, and animation. I don't want to confuse multimedia programming with game programming.

Game programming certainly involves multimedia, but it is much more involved than adding sound or video to an application. I'm going to lightly cover multimedia in this section and show you what you can do given the tools that Delphi provides right out of the box. I'm not going to talk about graphics or multimedia APIs such as OpenGL or Direct Draw. For more information on graphics programming using those libraries, get a good book that specializes in graphics programming. *Delphi 4 Unleashed* (ISBN: 0-672-312-859) would be a good choice.

Wave Audio with the Windows API

Normally I wouldn't talk a lot about Windows API functions because most of the time VCL offers you a better way of performing a task than does the API. In the case of playing a wave file, however, there is nothing more simple than the Win32 API `PlaySound` function. Playing a wave file by using this function is very easy. The first thing you need to do is add `MmSystem` to your unit's uses list. Then call `PlaySound` with the proper parameters:

```
PlaySound('test.wav', 0, SND_FILENAME);
```

That's pretty simple, isn't it? As you can see, the first parameter to `PlaySound` is used to specify a sound file to play. The last parameter is used to specify flags that determine how the sound should be played. When playing a wave audio file on disk, you specify `SND_FILENAME` as the last parameter (you can specify other flags as well, but I'll get to that in just a bit).

The `PlaySound` function can also play system sounds as well as files on disk. To play a system sound, specify the sound alias in the first parameter passed to `PlaySound`, and `SND_ALIAS` in the flags parameter—for example,

```
PlaySound('SystemAsterisk', 0, SND_ALIAS);
```

This code plays the system sound associated with the Asterisk event (assuming one has been set up on your system). To see a list of system sound events, look at the Sound applet in the Control Panel. To determine the sound alias for the event, you can look in the Windows Registration Database (the Registry). The aliases are listed under the `HKEY_CURRENT_USER` key.

If the requested sound cannot be found, Windows will play the default sound (the *ding* if you have the default sound scheme). You can prevent Windows from playing the default sound by specifying the `SND_NODEFAULT` flag. For example, if you want to play a system sound but don't want the default sound to play if the system sound cannot be found, you could use this code:

```
PlaySound('MailBeep', 0, SND_ALIAS or SND_NODEFAULT);
```

Notice that the SND_ALIAS and SND_NODEFAULT flags are or'd together.

 Note The Win32 API MessageBeep function can also be used to play system sounds by their index number. See MessageBeep in the Win32 online help for more information.

There are two other flags that are important when dealing with the PlaySound function:

- The SND_ASYNC flag stipulates that the sound should be played asynchronously. When this flag is used, the sound starts playing and immediately returns control to the calling application. This means that the sound can play while your application goes on its way.

- The SND_SYNC flag stipulates that control should not return to the calling application until after the sound is finished playing. SND_SYNC is the default for PlaySound, so you shouldn't have to specifically set this flag.

There are many other flags that can be used to control how sounds are played with PlaySound. For complete information, see the PlaySound topic in the Win32 online help.

The TMediaPlayer Component

VCL provides the MediaPlayer component for simple multimedia operations. This component, located on the System tab of the Component palette, can play wave files, MIDI files, AVI videos, and more. TMediaPlayer is easy to use, too. For just playing wave files I usually use the PlaySound function as described in the previous section. For anything more complex, though, you can use the MediaPlayer component.

The most obvious way of using TMediaPlayer is to simply drop one on a form. When you do, the media player controller is displayed. This controller has buttons for play, pause, stop, next, previous, step, back, record, and eject. Figure 12.12 shows a form with a MediaPlayer.

12

FIGURE 12.12.

A form with a
MediaPlayer
component.

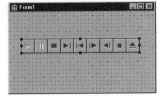

Using the media player in its most basic form is extremely simple. All you have to do is set the FileName property to the name of a valid multimedia file and click the Play button on the MediaPlayer. You can select any .WAV, .MID, or .AVI file. The MediaPlayer knows what to do with the file automatically and no additional intervention is required. Most of the time, you want to do something a little more interesting with the MediaPlayer, and for those times you'll have to dig a little deeper.

Although the visual control bar of the MediaPlayer is nice in some situations, you will probably use the MediaPlayer without the control bar at times. You can manipulate the MediaPlayer through code to play, start, stop, or rewind the media. If you don't want to see the MediaPlayer control bar at runtime, you'll have to set the Visible property to False.

MediaPlayer Properties, Methods, and Events

TMediaPlayer has a lot of properties. Most of them are pretty easy to understand, but some are a bit more complicated. Table 12.5 lists the primary properties of TMediaPlayer.

TABLE 12.5. PRIMARY TMediaPlayer PROPERTIES.

Property	Description
AutoOpen	Specifies whether the device should be opened as soon as the media player is created. Default: False
AutoRewind	When True, the media position pointer will be reset to the beginning of the media after the media has played. Default: True
DeviceType	The type of the multimedia device. Set to dtAutoSelect to have the device type automatically selected based on the filename extension. Default: dtAutoSelect
Display	Used to set the display window to a specific component (for video devices).
DisplayRect	Used to set the size and position of the playback window for video devices. The video is resized to fit this rectangle.
EnabledButtons	The buttons on the MediaPlayer that should be enabled. Default: All Buttons
EndPos	The media ending position. The media is played from StartPos to EndPos. If EndPos is not specified, the media plays to the end. The value you assign to EndPos depends on the type of media being played.
Error	The error code of the last operation.

Property	Description
ErrorMessage	A textual description of the last error.
Frames	The number of frames to move when the Back or Next methods are called, or when the Back or Next buttons on the MediaPlayer control bar are clicked.
Length	The length of the media. The value of Length depends on the type of media being played and the current value of TimeFormat.
Mode	The state of the device. Can be mpNotReady, mpStopped, mpPlaying, mpRecording, mpSeeking, mpPaused, or mpOpen.
Notify	When True, the OnNotify event is generated when the MediaPlayer finishes an operation.
NotifyValue	The results of the last notification operation. Can be nvSuccessful, nvSuperseded, nvAborted, or nvFailure.
Position	The current position in the media.
StartPos	The media starting position. The media is played from StartPos to EndPos. If StartPos is not specified, the media is played from the beginning. The value you assign to StartPos depends on the type of media being played.
TimeFormat	The time format to use for this device. The time format can be specified in milliseconds, frames, bytes, samples, tracks/minutes/seconds, hours/minutes/seconds, and more.
Tracks	The number of tracks the media contains (for CD audio devices).
VisibleButtons	Specifies the buttons that should be displayed on the MediaPlayer control bar. Default: All Buttons
Wait	Specifies whether control should be returned to the calling application immediately or only after the media has finished playing.

12

The MediaPlayer component also has a lot of methods. Many of these methods perform the same function as the control bar buttons. Table 12.6 lists the primary methods of TMediaPlayer.

TABLE 12.6. PRIMARY TMediaPlayer METHODS.

Method	Description
Back	Backs up the media the number of steps specified by the Frames property.
Close	Closes the device.

continues

TABLE 12.6. CONTINUED

Method	Description
Eject	Ejects the media, if applicable (ejects an audio CD, for example).
Next	Advances the start of the next track for devices that support tracks.
Open	Opens the device. (Used when AutoOpen is set to False.)
Pause	Pauses playback or recording.
Play	Starts playback of the device.
Previous	Moves to the beginning of the previous track.
Resume	Resumes the action (playing or recording) suspended with Pause.
Rewind	Resets the media position to the beginning of the media.
Save	Saves the media to a file specified by the FileName property.
StartRecord	Starts recording of data.
Step	Moves forward the number of frames specified in the Frames property.
Stop	Stops the current action (playing or recording).

The MediaPlayer component has only one important event. The OnNotify event is called whenever a command has completed, but only if the Notify property is set to True. You can examine the Error and NotifyValue properties to see whether the operation was successfully carried out.

Wave Audio

Playing wave audio is one of the most basic multimedia operations. It is probably also the most common. Playing a wave file synchronously would look like this:

```
Player.Wait := True;
Player.FileName := 'test.wav';
Player.Open;
Player.Play;
```

Notice that the Wait property is set to True to force the wave file to play synchronously. This is necessary if you want to play wave files back to back—for example,

```
Player.FileName := 'Sound1.wav';
Player.Open;
Player.Wait := True;
Player.Play;
Player.FileName := 'Sound2.wav';
Player.Wait := True;
Player.Play;
```

Notice that I set Wait to True before playing each file. The Wait property gets reset after an operation, so you must reset it each time you want to force the program execution to wait until the operation finishes.

If you don't set Wait to True, the first sound will start playing and will be immediately superseded by the second sound when it starts a few milliseconds later. If you want a sound to play in the background, set Wait to False.

To play a portion of a wave file, you can set the StartPos and EndPos before playing the file. The following example opens a wave file and plays two seconds of audio, starting at one second and ending at three seconds:

```
Player.FileName := 'test.wav';
Player.Open;
Player.StartPos := 1000;
Player.EndPos   := 3000;
Player.Play;
```

The StartPos and EndPos values are specified in milliseconds, the default for wave audio devices.

Note

> If you set either StartPos or EndPos to invalid values, the wave file won't play. Invalid values include a StartPos greater than the EndPos or an EndPos value larger than the media length.

Setting the Output Volume

Setting the volume of the wave output device is relatively simple, but you have to go to the Windows API to do it. The waveOutGetVolume and waveOutSetVolume functions can be used to get the volume and set the volume, respectively.

The volume is stored as an integer. The high word specifies the right channel volume setting, and the low word specifies the left channel volume setting. If the device doesn't have the capability of setting the right and left channel volumes independently, the low word is used to set the volume and the high word is ignored.

A value of 0 is no volume, and a value of $FFFF hexadecimal specifies full volume. Given that, the following code sets the volume of both channels to 50%:

```
waveOutSetVolume(0, $80008000);
```

This example sets the volume to full volume:

```
waveOutSetVolume(0, $FFFFFFFF);
```

12

Notice that I am using 0 as the first parameter to waveOutSetVolume. This is cheating a little, because I am assuming that the wave device is device 0. That's almost always the case, so you can generally get by with this trick.

Setting the volume is as easy as that. Note that waveOutSetVolume sets only the volume for the wave output device and not the master volume. The master volume can be set only through the multimedia mixer control, a subject beyond the scope of this book. I realize that this discussion about setting the volume is a bit advanced. If you didn't understand it all, don't fret. You can always come back and review this section later if you need to.

Recording Wave Audio

Recording wave audio is not quite as straightforward as it should be. You would think that all you have to do is call StartRecording. It's not quite that simple, however, because of some problems with TMediaPlayer.

To record a wave file, you first have to open an existing wave file that has the same recording parameters as you want your new file to have. You can then record the new wave data, change the FileName property to the name of the new file, and then save the file. It's a bit cumbersome, but it does work.

For example, let's say you have a file called DUMMY.WAV that was recorded with a wave format of 22050 kHz, 8 bits per sample, and one channel (you can easily create this kind of file using Windows Sound Recorder). In this case, you could start recording wave audio on a button click like this:

```
procedure TForm1.StartBtnClick(Sender: TObject);
begin
  with MediaPlayer do begin
    { Set FileName to the dummy.wav file to }
    { get the recording parameters. }
    FileName := 'dummy.wav';
    { Open the device. }
    Open;
    { Start recording. }
    Wait := False;
    StartRecording;
  end;
end;
```

At this point the recording has started and control has returned to your application. You now need to stop recording, which can be done in response to a second button click—for example,

```
procedure TForm1.StopBtnClick(Sender: TObject);
begin
  with MediaPlayer do begin
    { Stop recording. }
    Stop;
    { Change the filename to the new file we want to write. }
    FileName := 'new.wav';
    { Save and close the file. }
    Save;
    Close;
  end;
end;
```

Note

At the time of this writing, these steps are necessary to perform wave audio recording because of a bug in TMediaPlayer. It's possible that this bug will be fixed by the time Delphi 4 is released. To find out, place a MediaPlayer on a form and call the Record method. If Delphi doesn't raise an exception, the bug was fixed.

The factors that control how wave audio is recorded include the sample rate, the number of channels (mono or stereo), and the number of bits per sample (usually 8 or 16). Common waveform sampling rates are 8,000 kHz, 11,025 kHz, 22,050 kHz, and 44,100 kHz. The higher the sampling rate, the higher the quality of the recorded audio. For the most part, you probably will not use stereo recording unless you are doing game programming. Even then, you should only use stereo when needed. The number of bits per sample also affects the quality of the recorded sound. The number of bits per sample can be set at either 8 bits or 16 bits.

12

Note

The higher the quality of the sound, the more disk space a recorded waveform audio file will consume. A wave file recorded in stereo will, naturally, be twice the size of a file recorded in one channel. Likewise, using 16 bits per sample will double the size of the wave file over 8 bits per sample. A file recorded at 22,050 kHz, mono, and 8 bits per sample might be 200K, whereas its equivalent recorded at 22,050, stereo, and 16-bits per sample would be 800K. For the most part, stereo and 16 bits per sample don't provide enough benefit to warrant the additional disk space. A wave format of 22,050 kHz, mono, and 8 bits per sample offers a good compromise between sound quality and file size.

MIDI Audio

Not much needs to be said regarding MIDI audio. All you have to do is set the `FileName` property of the `MediaPlayer` to a MIDI file and call the `Play` method. MIDI files have either `.mid` or `.rmi` extensions.

 Note

> If you intend to go beyond simple playing of MIDI files, you will have to study the low-level `midiInXXX` and `midiOutXXX` functions. These functions are documented in the `MMEDIA.HLP` file. This file might be in your Delphi `Help` directory (it might be called `MM.HLP`). If not, you can probably obtain the file from Microsoft.

Most sound cards do not enable two wave files to be played at one time. Likewise, most do not enable more than one MIDI file to be played at one time. Most do, however, enable a wave file and a MIDI file to be played simultaneously. You have probably noticed this effect in games where you have a music track and sound effects being played at the same time. To play a wave file and a MIDI file at the same time, you can use two `MediaPlayer` components. Alternatively, you could use a `MediaPlayer` for the MIDI file and use `PlaySound` for any wave files you need to play.

A MIDI file is often used as background music for games. If you use a MIDI file in this way, you will want to restart the music when it reaches the end. `TMediaPlayer` doesn't have a built-in way to play a sound continuously. You can, however, make use of `MediaPlayer`'s `OnNotify` event to achieve a looping effect. First you need to tell the `MediaPlayer` to notify you when something happens. That part is easy:

```
MediaPlayer.Notify := True;
```

After that, you need to provide an `OnNotify` event handler. In the event handler, you need code that restarts the MIDI file after it successfully completes. The `OnNotify` event would look something like this:

```
procedure TForm1.MediaPlayerNotify(Sender: TObject);
begin
  with MediaPlayer do
    if NotifyValue = nvSuccessful then begin
      Position := 0;
      Play;
    end;
end;
```

First I check to see whether the `NotifyValue` property contains a value of `nvSuccessful`. If so, I reset the file position to `0` and call the `Play` method to start the file playing again. That's pretty simple, but there are a couple of issues you should be aware of.

First, notice that I am setting the `Position` property to `0`. This effectively rewinds the file to the beginning. This is not necessary if the `AutoRewind` property is set to `True`. The second issue that you should be aware of is that there are several `MediaPlayer` actions that could cause the `OnNotify` event to be called with a `NotifyValue` of `nvSuccessful`.

For example, a simple `Stop` command will result in a value of `nvSuccessful`, providing the command completed without incident. You might need to set up a state machine so that you know that the `OnNotify` event is being called in response to the file reaching the end, and not as a result of some other media player operation.

CD Audio

Playing CD audio is relatively simple with `TMediaPlayer`. To play an audio CD, you simply change the `DeviceType` property to `dtCDAudio` and click the Play button (or call the `Play` method).

The most difficult aspect to grasp in programming CD audio devices is the different time formats used in CD audio. You will use the TMSF (time, minutes, seconds, frames) time format to gather information about a particular track or to set the current position to a particular track. Any minute, second, or frame values will be set relative to the track number. For example, the following code formats a string to report the playing position within the current track:

```
var
  Time    : Integer;
  Track   : Integer;
  Minutes : Integer;
  Seconds : Integer;
  TimeStr : string;
begin
  MediaPlayer.TimeFormat := tfTMSF;
  Time    := MediaPlayer.Position;
  Track   := mci_TMSF_Track(Time);
  Minutes := mci_TMSF_Minute(Time);
  Seconds := mci_TMSF_Second(Time);
  TimeStr := Format('Track Time: %2.2d:%2.2d', [Minutes, Seconds]);
  Label1.Caption := 'Track: ' + IntToStr(Track);
  Label2.Caption := TimeStr;
end;
```

First, the `TimeFormat` is set to `tfTMSF` to ensure the proper time format. Next, the current position is stored in a variable called `Time`. Following that, the different time values (track, minutes, and seconds) are extracted using Windows' time conversion macros, `mci_TMSF_Track`, `mci_TMSF_Minute`, and `mci_TMSF_Second`. These macros are contained in the `MMSystem` unit. You will have to add that unit to your uses list if you use these

12

macros. After the individual time values have been extracted, a time string is built to display the track time. Then the track number and track time are displayed in Label components.

You will use the MSF (minutes, seconds, frames) time format to gather information about the CD at the global level. For example, you would use the MSF time format to retrieve the current position of the CD in relation to the start of the CD. Likewise you would use the MSF time format if you want to set the current position of the CD to the 30 minute mark on the CD, regardless of the track. This code shows how to retrieve and display the current position on the CD in minutes and seconds:

```
var
  Time    : Integer;
  Minutes : Integer;
  Seconds : Integer;
  TimeStr : string;
begin
  MediaPlayer.TimeFormat := tfMSF;
  Time    := MediaPlayer.Position;
  Minutes := mci_MSF_Minute(Time);
  Seconds := mci_MSF_Second(Time);
  TimeStr := Format('Total Time: %2.2d:%2.2d', [Minutes, Seconds]);
  Label3.Caption := TimeStr;
end;
```

The book's code contains a program called CDPlayer that illustrates how TMediaPlayer can be used to create an audio CD player.

AVI Video

To play an AVI video with TMediaPlayer, select an AVI file and call the Play method (or click the Play button). If you use the default MediaPlayer settings, a separate window will pop up and the AVI will play in that window. As an alternative, you can set the Display property to any windowed component, and the video will play in that component's client area.

For example, let's say you have a panel on your form called AVIPanel and that you want to play an AVI video in the panel. In this case, you would set the Display property like this:

```
MediaPlayer.Display := AVIPanel;
```

When the AVI plays, it will play in the panel. If the video is larger than the panel's rectangle, the video will be clipped to the size of the panel.

You can stretch or shrink a video by setting the `DisplayRect` property. This code will shrink or stretch a video to the size of the display panel:

```
MediaPlayer.DisplayRect := AVIPanel.ClientRect;
```

There are many types of AVI video formats, and not all AVIs will play on all systems. In order to play a particular video, you have to be sure that your users have the drivers installed for that type of video. If you want to play it safe, stick with the standard Microsoft AVI video types. Your users will almost certainly have the drivers for Microsoft AVIs installed because they are installed as part of the normal Windows installation.

> **Note**
>
> The TAnimate component (found on the Win32 tab of the Component palette) is used for playing small videos such as those you see used by Windows. Examples of these animations are those you see when Explorer is copying files and the animation that Explorer displays in the Find dialog when it is searching for files. The AVIs that can be played by TAnimate must be either uncompressed or run length encoded (RLE) compressed only. No other forms of compression are allowed. Also, the AVI cannot contain audio.

> **Note**
>
> The MediaPlayer component can play many types of videos and animations, provided the correct drivers are installed. For example, Autodesk Animator (AA) animations have a filename extension of either .fli or .flc. To play an AA animation, all you have to do is set the DeviceType property to dtAutoSelect and select an Animator file. As long as the AA drivers are installed, MediaPlayer will play the animation.

12

Summary

Graphics programming can be very interesting and very rewarding. It can also be very frustrating. VCL takes much of the frustration out of graphics programming by providing the TCanvas and TBitmap classes, along with their supporting classes such as TPen, TBrush, and TFont. These classes enable you to get on with the business of the visual aspects of graphics programming rather than worry about how to load or save bitmap files. Multimedia programming can be a lot of fun. It's rewarding to write a few lines of code and then see or hear the results a few seconds later. Multimedia can certainly add excitement to your programs, but be careful not to overdo it.

Although I can't claim that this chapter is an in-depth look at either graphics or multimedia programming in Delphi, it's a good start and introduces you to some concepts that you can carry with you for a long time.

Workshop

The Workshop contains quiz questions to help you solidify your understanding of the material covered and exercises to provide you with experience in using what you have learned. You can find answers to the quiz questions in Appendix A, "Answers to the Quiz Questions."

Q&A

Q Can the graphics concepts discussed in this chapter be used when printing as well as drawing on the screen?

A Yes. As far as Windows is concerned, a device context is a device context. It doesn't matter whether that device context is for the display screen, a memory bitmap, or a printer.

Q I see the `Ellipse` method, but I don't see a method for drawing perfect circles. How do I draw circles?

A Use the `Ellipse` method. Just be sure that the rectangle used to draw the ellipse is perfectly square and you will get a perfect circle (if that makes any sense).

Q How do I change the color of the text that `DrawText` produces?

A Change the `Color` property of the canvas font.

Q Why should I bother with a memory bitmap?

A You might not need to. However, if you ever see noticeable flicker in your drawing routines, you should think about using a memory bitmap.

Q What is the default time format for wave audio devices?

A Wave audio devices use milliseconds by default (one second is 1000 milliseconds).

Q Can I play more than one wave file at a time?

A Not with the `MediaPlayer` component. Microsoft's DirectX API has sound mixing capabilities that make it sound as if two or more sounds are playing at one time. If you need sound mixing, check out DirectX (free from Microsoft).

Q How can I play an AVI video directly on my form?

A Set the `Display` property of `TMediaPlayer` to the name of the form.

Quiz

1. What component can you use to draw graphics on a form?

2. Which TCanvas property controls the fill color of the canvas?

3. What does a clipping region do?

4. What function do you use to draw multiple lines of text on a canvas?

5. What TCanvas method can be used to draw a bitmap with a transparent background?

6. Which TCanvas method do you use to copy an entire bitmap to a canvas?

7. How do you save a memory bitmap to a file?

8. What component do you use to play a wave file?

9. What is the TimeFormat property of TMediaPlayer used for?

10. Can you record wave audio with the MediaPlayer component?

Exercises

1. Write a program that displays a circle on the screen when a button is clicked.

2. Write a program that draws random lines on the screen each time the form is shown (including when the form is restored after being hidden).

3. Write a program that creates a memory bitmap, draws text and shapes on the bitmap, and then displays the bitmap on the form's canvas.

4. Modify the program you wrote in exercise 3 to save the memory bitmap to disk.

5. Write a program that displays an AVI video on the application's main form.

6. Write a program that plays a wave file when the program starts.

12

e Basics

n a good Windows application into a great
fically, I discuss the following:

toolbars and status bars

lications

norrow as you look at implementing advanced
res in your Delphi applications.

v Decorations

tty lights around the front window of your house.
features such as toolbars and status bars. These
ow decorations. This section deals with these types
plement them in your application.

Toolbars

A toolbar (also called a control bar or a speedbar) is almost standard equipment for Windows programs today. Users expect certain amenities, and a toolbar is one of them. A top quality toolbar should have the following features and capabilities:

- Buttons representing tasks that are also available on the application's menus.
- Enabling and disabling of buttons when appropriate.
- Tooltips describing a button's function.
- Additional hint text that is displayed in the application's status bar.
- Docking capability.
- Other controls such as combo boxes or drop-down menu buttons.

Some of the features in this list are optional features that not every toolbar needs to have. With Delphi, implementing these toolbar features is easy to accomplish. A little later in the chapter I talk about command enabling in the section "Adding Functionality with Command Enabling." I'll save discussion of command enabling for toolbar buttons for that time.

Note It is considered good practice to place on the toolbar only buttons that have corresponding menu items. The toolbar is an alternative to using the menu. It should not contain items found nowhere else in the program.

On Day 8, "Creating Applications in Delphi," I said that the easiest way to construct a toolbar is to use the Application Wizard. Even if you already have a partially written application, you can still use the Application Wizard to create a toolbar. Just generate an application with the Application Wizard, copy the panel with the toolbar to the Clipboard, reopen your original application (don't bother saving the Application Wizard application), and paste the toolbar into your application from the Clipboard. Slick and easy.

However, the Application Wizard doesn't give you everything you could possibly need in a toolbar. Most notably, the Application Wizard uses the old method of creating a toolbar—with a panel and speed buttons. The preferred way of creating a toolbar is to use the ToolBar and CoolBar components (found on the Win32 tab of the Component palette). Let's take a look at those components next.

Note

> The CoolBar and ToolBar components require version 4.72.2106.4 or later of COMCTL32.DLL, which should have been installed as part of the Delphi installation. If you don't have the latest version of this DLL, you can find it at Microsoft's Web site (http://www.microsoft.com). When you deploy your applications using these components, you should install COMCTL32.DLL version 4.70 or later. Be sure you are using a good installation program so that you don't overwrite a new version of this DLL when you install your application.

The CoolBar Component

The CoolBar component is an encapsulation of the Win32 *cool bar* (sometimes called a rebar). This component is a specialized container control. Most of the time the CoolBar is used as a container for toolbars, but its use isn't limited strictly to toolbars.

Cool Bar Bands

A cool bar has bands that can be moved and resized at runtime. The bands show a sizing grip on the left side, giving the user a visual cue that the band can be moved or sized. Cool bar bands are represented by the TCoolBand class. A cool bar band can contain only one component. Usually that component is a toolbar, but it can be a combo box or any other component. Let's do an exercise to better understand how the CoolBar component works:

1. Start with a new application and drop a CoolBar component on the form.

2. Drop a ComboBox component on the cool bar. Delphi creates a new band to hold the combo box. Notice that the combo box fills the width of the cool bar.

3. Drop another ComboBox component on the cool bar. Another band is created and is placed below the first band.

4. Place your mouse cursor between the sizing grip and the combo box on the second band. The cursor will change to a pointing hand, indicating that you can move the band. (You can also use the sizing grip to drag the band.) Drag the band up into the band above it. As you do, the first band will shrink to make room for the band you are dragging. Drop the band near the middle of the cool bar. You can now use the sizing grips to resize either band.

5. Place a Panel component on the cool bar. A new band is created to hold the panel.

6. Select the cool bar and change its AutoSize property to True.

7. Place a Memo component on the form below the cool bar. Set its Align property to alClient.

13

Now your form looks like Figure 13.1.

FIGURE 13.1.

The form with a cool bar and three bands.

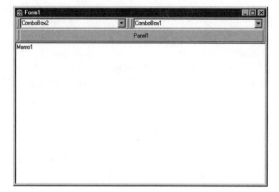

Now run the program. Experiment with the cool bar bands. Drag them up or down or resize them. Notice that as you drag the bands up or down, the cool bar resizes as needed and the memo always fills the remaining client area.

Cool bar bands are accessed through the Bands property. This property is a TCoolBands, which is a list of TCoolBand components. If you want to hide the second band, you can do this:

```
CoolBar.Bands[1].Visible := False;
```

You can add bands in two ways. As you have already seen, you can create a band by dropping any component on the cool bar, but you can also use the Bands Editor. To invoke the Bands Editor, double-click the cool bar or click the ellipsis button next to the Bands property in the Object Inspector. You add bands by clicking the Add button; you delete bands by clicking the Delete button. The Move Up and Move Down buttons enable you to change the order of the bands.

 Note If the AutoSize property is set to True, you will have to turn it off temporarily if you want to add new bands by dropping components on the cool bar. Set the AutoSize property to False, make the cool bar higher, drop a component on the cool bar, and set the AutoSize property to True again.

When you select a band in the Bands Editor, the Object Inspector displays the band's properties. Figure 13.2 shows the Bands Editor and the Object Inspector when a band is selected.

FIGURE 13.2.

The cool bar Bands Editor.

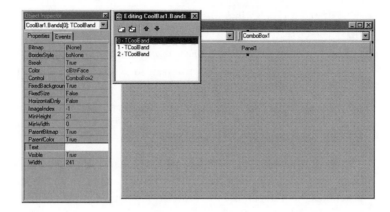

The `Bitmap` property enables you to set a background bitmap for a band. To select an image that will appear to the left of the band, you use `ImageIndex`. `ImageIndex` requires the `ImageList` property of the cool bar to be set to a valid `TImageList`. You can set a band's minimum height and width through the `MinHeight` and `MinWidth` properties. To make a band immovable, set the `FixedSize` property to `True`.

Other `CoolBar` Properties

A cool bar can be either vertical or horizontal. By default the `Align` property is set to `alTop`. To make a vertical cool bar, change the `Align` property to `alRight` or `alLeft`. Some components, when placed on a cool bar, automatically orient themselves based on whether the cool bar is vertical or horizontal. Another way to change the orientation of the cool bar is by setting the `Vertical` property.

The `Bitmap` property enables you to set a background bitmap for the cool bar. The bitmap you choose will be tiled to fill the cool bar's background. Note that this sets the background bitmap for the cool bar itself, not for any individual bands on the cool bar (as discussed in the previous section). You use the `ImageList` property to set the image list that the bands will use to display an image to the left of any band that has its `ImageIndex` property set.

13

The `AutoSize` property determines whether the cool bar will resize itself when bands are moved. You saw the effect of the `AutoSize` property in the preceding exercise.

> **Note**
>
> ***New*** Check out the `TControlBar` component on the Additional tab of the
> ***to 4*** Component palette. `TControlBar` is a native VCL component that
> works very much like a cool bar. This component does not rely on `COM-`
> `CTL32.DLL` as does `TCoolBar`, so it is less susceptible to the whims of
> Microsoft.

The `ToolBar` Component

The `ToolBar` component encapsulates the Win32 toolbar control. The toolbar will auto-matically arrange and size the controls placed on the toolbar so that they all have a con-sistent height. You can use the `ToolBar` component with or without a cool bar. If you have only a single toolbar, use the toolbar without a cool bar. If you have multiple tool-bars that you want to enable the user to move, place two or more toolbars on a cool bar.

Creating a toolbar and adding buttons to it is very easy. If your toolbar buttons will have glyphs (and most do), you have to use an `ImageList` component for the glyphs. To illus-trate how to build a toolbar with the `ToolBar` component, let's again go back to the `ScratchPad` program. You'll tear it apart and put it back together.

Removing the Old Toolbar

If you recall, the toolbar you created for `ScratchPad` originally was just a placeholder. The first thing you need to do is get rid of the old toolbar by performing these steps:

1. Click the `Memo` component and change its `Align` property to `alNone`. Drag down the top of the `Memo` to make room for the new toolbar.

2. Click the toolbar component and delete it.

Adding a New Toolbar

Now you can start adding components back again. The first thing to do is add a cool bar and a toolbar. You don't really need a cool bar at this stage because you have only one toolbar, but you might want to add another toolbar later, so it's best to plan ahead. Perform these steps:

1. Drop a `CoolBar` component on the form. It automatically aligns itself to the top of the form. Change its `Name` property to `CoolBar`.

2. Drop a `ToolBar` component on the cool bar. Change its `Name` property to `MainToolBar`.

3. Double-click the `EdgeBorders` property in the Object Inspector to show all the edge border items. Change the `ebTop` style to `False` (all `EdgeBorders` styles should now be `False`).

4. Change the `Flat` property to `True`. This gives the toolbar buttons a flat appearance until the cursor passes over them.

5. Click the cool bar and change the `AutoSize` property to `True`. The cool bar sizes itself to the size of the toolbar.

6. Click the `Memo` component and change its `Align` property back to `alClient`.

Adding Buttons to the Toolbar

Now you begin adding buttons to the toolbar; you will add several buttons and a few spacers. At first the buttons won't have glyphs on them, but you'll take care of that later. For now, follow these steps:

1. Right-click the toolbar and choose New Button. A button is placed on the toolbar. Change the button's `Name` property to `FileNewBtn`. Set the `Hint` property to `New¦Create A New File` and the `ShowHint` property to `True`. (Remember when you wrote the hint code on Day 8? That code is still in the program, so the new hints will work immediately.)

2. Right-click on the toolbar and again choose New Button. A second button is placed on the toolbar to the right of the first button. Change its `Name` property to `FileOpenBtn`. Set the `Hint` property to `Open¦Open An Existing File` and the `ShowHint` property to `True`.

3. Add another button. Change this button's `Name` property to `FileSaveBtn`. Set the `Hint` property to `Save¦Save A File` and the `ShowHint` property to `True`.

Tip

Buttons and spacers added to the toolbar always appear to the right of the toolbar's last control. You can't insert a button at a specific location in the toolbar, but after a button or spacer is added, you can drag it to a different location on the toolbar. The existing buttons will make room for the new button.

13

That finishes the first set of buttons (except for the glyphs). You are about to add a second set of buttons, but before you do, there needs to be a little separation between the first set of buttons and the second. Back to work:

1. Right-click on the toolbar again, but this time choose New Separator. A separator is added to the toolbar.

2. Add another button. This time change the `Name` property to `EditCutBtn` and the `Hint` property to `Cut¦Cut To Clipboard`.

3. Add buttons for Copy and Paste. Change their Name and Hint properties as appropriate.

4. Add another separator.

5. Add a button called HelpAboutBtn. Change its Hint property to About¦About ScratchPad.

6. Select the Cut, Copy, Paste, and Help buttons (use Shift+-Click to select each button). Change the ShowHint property to True. It will be changed for all buttons selected.

Your form now looks like the one shown in Figure 13.3.

FIGURE 13.3.

The ScratchPad *main form after adding a toolbar.*

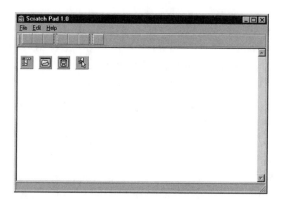

Making the Toolbar Buttons Functional

You now have a good start on the toolbar, but the toolbar buttons don't do anything because you haven't assigned any event handlers to their OnClick events. Let's do that next.

1. Click the FileNewBtn (the first button) and select the Events page in the Object Inspector. Click the drop-down arrow next to the OnClick event and choose FileNewClick. The button is now hooked up to the FileNewClick event handler.

2. Repeat step 1 for each remaining button, being careful to select the appropriate OnClick handler for each button (FileOpenClick, FileSaveClick, EditCutClick, and so on).

3. If you haven't yet created an About Box for ScratchPad, create one. When you are done, create an event handler for the Help I About menu item. Hook the OnClick event of the HelpAboutBtn to the event handler for the Help I About menu item.

Adding Bitmaps to the Toolbar Buttons

Obviously this toolbar is missing something. You need to add glyphs to the toolbar buttons. To do so, you must add an `ImageList` component to the form by following these steps:

1. Place an `ImageList` component on the form. (You find it on the Win32 tab of the Component palette.) Change the `Name` property to `ImageList`.

2. Right-click the `ImageList` component's icon on your form and choose ImageList Editor. The ImageList Editor is displayed. (You can also double-click the ImageList icon on your form to display the ImageList Editor.)

3. Click the Add button. Navigate to the `Common Files\Borland Shared\Images\ Buttons` directory. Select the `FILENEW.BMP` file and click Open.

   A message box appears and asks whether you want to separate the bitmap into two images. What is happening here is that the image list's `Width` and `Height` properties are both set to 16. The bitmap you have selected is wider than 16 pixels, so it has to be split into two images or shrunk to fit. If you recall, the button bitmaps that come with Delphi are a single bitmap with two images. The first image is the normal button bitmap, and the second image is for the disabled button. You will have the ImageList Editor split the bitmap into two images, and then you will delete the second part of the image.

4. Click Yes to have the ImageList Editor split the bitmap into two images. The ImageList Editor now shows two images. You need only the first of these images, so click on the second image (the disabled button image) and click the Delete button.

5. Click the Add button again. This time choose the `FILEOPEN.BMP` file. Click Yes again when prompted to split the bitmap into two images. Click on the disabled image for this bitmap and delete it. Figure 13.4 shows the image editor as it looks just before deleting the second image.

FIGURE 13.4.

The ImageList Editor after adding three images.

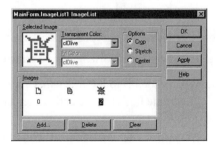

13

6. Repeat step 5 for each remaining button (File Save, Cut, Copy, Paste, and About). Use any bitmaps you like, but make certain you delete the extra bitmap each time you add an image to the list. Also make sure that the images in the ImageList editor follow the order of the buttons on the toolbar. When you are done, you will have seven images in the image list, numbering from 0 to 6.

7. Click OK to close the ImageList Editor.

You can select multiple images in the ImageList Editor's Add Images dialog box and add them all to the image list at one time.

Now you are ready to hook the image list to the toolbar. Click on the toolbar. Locate the Images property in the Object Inspector and choose ImageList from the drop-down list. If you did everything right, your buttons now have glyphs. You probably didn't notice, but each time you added a toolbar button, Delphi automatically incremented the ImageIndex property for the button. Because you created the buttons and images in the same order, the glyphs on the buttons should be correct. If a button is wrong, you can either change the button's ImageIndex property or go back to the ImageList Editor and change the order of the images in the image list.

To rearrange the images in an image list, drag them to a new position in the ImageList Editor.

Disabled Button Glyphs

Right now you have glyphs only for the buttons in the enabled state. You also need glyphs that will be displayed when the buttons are disabled. You aren't disabling the toolbar buttons yet, but you will be before the day is done. There are two ways to implement the disabled button glyphs:

- Let the toolbar create the disabled state glyphs automatically.
- Create a second image list that contains disabled state bitmaps for the buttons.

Certainly the easier of these two methods is to let the toolbar create the disabled state buttons automatically. Most of the time this is sufficient. Sometimes, however, the algorithm for creating the disabled buttons glyphs doesn't work well. (The glyphs end up losing definition and don't look quite right.) This happens with buttons that don't have enough contrasting colors. In that case, you can create a second image list that contains the disabled button glyphs. Set the `DisabledImages` property of the toolbar to the image list containing the disabled glyphs, and the rest is automatic. For `ScratchPad` you're going to go with the automatic disabling of toolbar buttons, so nothing further is required.

Poor old `ScratchPad` is back together again. This is a good time to save the project. After saving the project, click the Run button and give the program a workout. Click the buttons and see whether they do what they are supposed to do. If all went well, you have a working program again. If your program won't compile, review the steps and try to fix the problem. If all else fails, you can refer to the `ScratchPad` project of the book's code, available at http://www.mcp.com/info (Day 13).

Toolbar Tips and Hints

I covered nearly everything there is to be said about tooltips and hints in the discussion of components on Day 7, "VCL Components"; again on Day 8, "Creating Applications in Delphi," when adding hint text support for the `ScratchPad` program; and again today when rebuilding the toolbar.

There is one issue I didn't talk about, and that is changing the tooltip properties. The `TApplication` class has four properties that control how the tooltips behave. Table 13.1 lists these properties and their descriptions.

TABLE 13.1. `TApplication` PROPERTIES PERTAINING TO TOOLTIPS.

Property	Description
HintColor	Sets the background color of the tooltip window. Default: clInfoBk
HintHidePause	Controls how long to wait (in milliseconds) before hiding the tooltip if the mouse cursor remains stationary over the component. Default: 2500 milliseconds
HintPause	Controls the interval between the time the mouse cursor is paused over a component and the time the tooltip appears (in milliseconds). Default: 500 milliseconds
HintShortPause	Controls how long to wait before showing tooltips after they have already been shown—for example, when the user is roaming over a group of toolbar buttons. Default: 50 milliseconds

13

The default values for these properties are sufficient for most applications. Still, if you need to change any hint properties, you have that option.

HOUSE RULES: TOOLBARS AND HINTS

- Don't use tooltips on controls where they will be in the way when the user wants to read the text in the control. In particular, don't use tooltips for edit controls and combo boxes. At a minimum, give the user the option to turn off tooltips for those types of controls.
- Keep your tooltip hint (the short hint) brief and to the point.
- Make your status bar hint (the long hint) more descriptive and meaningful.
- Consider giving your users the option of turning off hints altogether.

Adding Other Controls to Toolbars

Because the ToolBar component is so versatile, nothing special needs to be done to add other types of controls to your toolbar. The most common type of control to add to a toolbar is a combo box. You can use a toolbar combo box to select a font, a configuration option, a zoom setting. . . the possibilities are endless.

To add a component to the toolbar, select the component from the Component palette and drop it on the toolbar. The toolbar will take care of aligning the component. Add spacers as necessary to separate components visually. When the component is on the toolbar, you deal with it just as you would a component on a form. I could try to complicate this for you, but the truth is, it's just that simple. If you've never tried to implement a combo box on a toolbar using the Windows API, you cannot appreciate how much work Delphi saves you. Take my word for it—it's significant.

Toolbars come in many shapes and sizes, and Delphi makes creating and implementing toolbars very easy. With Delphi, you no longer have the excuse, "That's too hard!" In fact, you might even enjoy creating toolbars with Delphi.

Dockable Toolbars

New to 4 Dockable toolbars are common in many Windows programs. Dockable toolbars are a paradox of sorts. On the one hand, they are a cool feature and most power users expect a good application to have dockable toolbars. On the other hand, I doubt anyone actually *uses* the docking capability of most dockable toolbars. Still, dockable toolbars are easy enough to implement in Delphi, so you might as well provide them.

> **Note**
>
> The docking features discussed in this section apply to any windowed control, not just to toolbars.

Creating a Dockable Toolbar

Making a toolbar dockable requires two steps:

- Set the DragKind property to dkDock.
- Set the DragMode property to dmAutomatic.

After you set these two properties, you can drag your toolbar around the screen. Dragging the toolbar around the screen doesn't get you very much, though. In order for dockable toolbars to make sense, you have to have a target for the drop part of the drag-and-drop equation.

Dock Sites

A dockable toolbar needs to have a place to dock. As Roger Waters said, "Any fool knows a dog needs a home." Home for a dockable toolbar is a *dock site*. A dock site is any windowed component that has its DockSite property set to True. Components that are typically used as dock sites are TCoolBar, TControlBar, TPageScroller, TPanel, and TPageControl. There are other controls that have a DockSite property, but those controls are less likely to be used as dock sites.

An exercise helps illustrate the use of dock sites. Follow these steps:

1. Drop a CoolBar component on a blank form. Set its DockSite property to True.

2. Drop a ToolBar on the CoolBar. Set the toolbar's DragKind property to dkDock and its DragMode property to dmAutomatic. Create a few buttons on the toolbar so that you can better see the toolbar.

3. Place a second CoolBar on the form. Change its Align property to alBottom and its DockSite property to True.

4. Place a third CoolBar on the form. Change its Align property to alLeft and its DockSite property to True. Size the CoolBar so that its width is 40 pixels or so.

Now run the program. Drag the toolbar from dock site to dock site. Notice how the toolbar changes its orientation when you drag it to the cool bar on the left side of the form.

Let's experiment some more. Set each of the CoolBar components' AutoSize properties to True. This will cause each CoolBar to change its size based on the controls it contains. Now run the program again and move the toolbar to the individual dock sites. Notice that

13

each cool bar is nearly invisible until the toolbar is docked to the site. Then the cool bar expands to contain the toolbar.

Floating Toolbars

A toolbar can be made into a floating toolbox by simply dragging the toolbar off its dock site and dropping it anywhere (anywhere other than another dock site, that is). The toolbar becomes a floating window. You can specify the type of window that should host the floating dock site by setting the `FloatingDockSiteClass` property to the name of the class you want to act as the parent to the floating toolbar. For example, suppose that you design a form that has all the characteristics you want for a custom floating toolbox, and that the form is called `MyToolBox`. In that case, you could cause this form to be the host for a floating toolbar with this code:

```
ToolBar.FloatingDockSiteClass := TMyToolBox;
```

When the toolbar is undocked and the mouse button released, Delphi will automatically create an instance of the `TMyToolBox` class and place the toolbar in the form for that class. To dock the floating toolbox again, simply drop it on any dock site. To make a dock site accept a floating toolbox, you must respond to the `OnDockOver` and `OnDockDrop` events for the dock site. In the `OnDockDrop` event handler, call the `ManualDock` method of the toolbar to cause the toolbar to dock.

Status Bars

A status bar is another feature that makes an application more marketable. Not all applications benefit from a status bar, but many can. The VCL `StatusBar` component, which encapsulates the Win32 status bar control, makes creating status bars a breeze. First, take a quick look at the major properties of the `StatusBar` component, listed in Table 13.2.

TABLE 13.2. StatusBar PROPERTIES.

Property	Description
AutoHint	Automatically displays hints in the status bar when the mouse cursor passes over any component whose Hint property has been set.
Panels	For status bars with multiple panels. This property defines the individual panels.
SimplePanel	Determines whether the status bar shows a simple panel or multiple panels.
SimpleText	The text for the status bar's simple panel.

Property	Description
SizeGrip	Determines whether the status bar displays the sizing grip in the lower-right corner. The sizing grip provides an area that the user can drag to size the window. The absence of the sizing grip doesn't prevent the window from being sized, but the presence of the size grip makes sizing a window easier.
UseSystemFont	Always uses the current system font, overriding the settings of the Font property. This is particularly useful for users who use Plus pack themes.

As you can see from this table, a status bar can be a simple status bar or have multiple panels. Let's discuss this choice next.

Simple or Complex?

A status bar can be either a simple status bar or a complex status bar. A *simple status bar* has a single panel that occupies the entire status bar. If you want a simple status bar, set the SimplePanel property to True. The SimplePanel property acts as a toggle. You can switch between a simple and a complex status bar at runtime by setting SimplePanel to True or False, accordingly.

A *complex status bar* is one with multiple panels. If you elect to use a complex status bar, you can use the StatusBar Panels Editor to set up the panels you want to see on your status bar. To invoke the StatusBar Panels Editor, double-click on the Value column of the Panels property. To add a panel, click the Add New button on the StatusBar Panels Editor. To delete a panel, click the Delete Selected button. To edit a panel, select the panel and then make changes to the panel's properties in the Object Inspector. Figure 13.5 shows the StatusBar Panels Editor and Object Inspector when editing panels.

FIGURE 13.5.

The StatusBar Panels Editor.

13

Note

The individual panels in a complex status bar are instances of the TStatusPanel class.

Most of the properties are self-explanatory, but a couple require further note. The Text property contains the text that will be displayed in the panel. You can also use the Text property at runtime to change the text in the panel. Setting the status bar text is discussed a little later; you don't need to supply text for the panel at design time if you are going to change the text at runtime.

You can set the Style property to either psText or psOwnerDraw. If the Style is set to psText (the default), the panel behaves as you would expect. The text is aligned in the panel according to the value of the Alignment property. If the Style is set to psOwnerDraw, it is up to you to draw any text or image that is displayed in the panel. Owner drawing of panel items is discussed later in the section "Owner-Drawn Status Bar Panels."

The Width, Bevel, and Alignment properties for the panel are straightforward. Experiment with these properties to see how they affect your status bar's appearance.

> In the Form Designer you immediately see the results of changes made to the status bar via the StatusBar Panels Editor. Position the StatusBar Panels Editor so that you can view the status bar as you work with the StatusBar Panels Editor. Each time you make a change, it will be reflected in the Form Designer.

When you are done adding panels to the status bar, close the StatusBar Panels Editor and return to the Form Designer.

> When you modify the Panels property of a StatusBar component, the Form Designer automatically sets the SimplePanel property to False. The assumption is that if you are using multiple panels, you don't want to have a simple status bar.

Changing Text in the Status Bar

There are two ways to change text in a status bar:

- Manually modify the SimpleText property of the status bar (for simple status bars) or the Text property of an individual panel (for complex status bars).

- Let VCL automatically supply the status bar text by setting the AutoHint property to True.

Manually changing the text in the status bar is simple, particularly if you have a simple status bar. When the `SimplePanel` property is `True`, you can set the `SimpleText` property to the text you want displayed in the status bar:

```
StatusBar.SimpleText := 'This shows up in the status bar.';
```

In the case of complex status bars, changing the text is only slightly more complicated. If you want to change the text for the first panel of a complex status bar, you would use something like this:

```
StatusBar.Panels[0].Text := 'Status Bar Text';
```

The `Panels` property of the `StatusBar` component has a property called `Items` that is an array of panels in the status bar. Setting the `Text` property for an element in the `Items` array changes the text for that panel (because `Items` is the default array property for the `Panels` object, you don't have to specifically reference `Items`). As you can see, the array is 0-based. The first panel in the status bar is array element 0.

Automatic status bar hint text doesn't require much in the way of explanation. All you have to do is set the `AutoHint` property to `True`. The rest is, as the property name implies, automatic.

Note

> You can still modify the status bar's text manually even when using `AutoHint`. There's nothing to stop you from changing the text manually, but remember that the text will be replaced the next time the mouse passes over a component with hint text.

Owner-Drawn Status Bar Panels

Earlier I said that a panel's `Style` property can be either `psText` or `psOwnerDraw`. When you set a panel's style to `psOwnerDraw`, you must take the responsibility of drawing anything in the panel that needs to be displayed there. It is unlikely that you are going to go to the trouble of using an owner-drawn panel just to display text. Usually it means you are going to display some sort of icon or bitmap in the status bar. Regardless of what is being drawn on the panel, the steps are the same:

13

1. Set the panel's `Style` property to `psOwnerDraw` (usually via the StatusBar Panels Editor).

2. Respond to the `OnDrawPanel` event.

Obviously, the real work here is going to take place in the event handler for the
OnDrawPanel event. The declaration for the OnDrawPanel event handler looks like this:

```
procedure TForm1.StatusBar1DrawPanel(StatusBar: TStatusBar;
  Panel: TStatusPanel; const Rect: TRect);
```

The StatusBar parameter is a pointer to the status bar. Usually you have a pointer to the
status bar anyway (the Name property of the StatusBar component), so this parameter is
not all that useful unless you are using multiple owner-drawn status bars. The Panel
property is a pointer to the particular panel that currently needs drawing. You can use
this parameter to determine which panel needs drawing if you have more than one
owner-drawn panel in your status bar. The Rect parameter contains the panel's size and
position. The Rect parameter is important because it tells you the exact dimensions of
the drawing area.

The OnDrawPanel event handler is called once for each panel that has its Style property
set to psOwnerDraw. If you have only one panel to draw, you don't have to worry about
much except the Rect parameter. If you have multiple panels to draw, you must first
determine which panel to draw and then do your drawing. An illustration might help to
explain this. The book's code includes a program called StatBar that illustrates some of
the things you can do with status bars. Run the program and examine its source for tips
on implementing status bars in your applications. Figure 13.6 shows the StatBar program running.

FIGURE 13.6.

The StatBar *program
with owner-drawn
status bar panels.*

As you can see, the status bar in this program has multiple panels. The middle three panels are owner-drawn. The panels marked OVR and EXT simulate the status bar on a word
processing program or code editor. In those types of programs, the Overtype or Extended
Selection modes might be on or off. If the mode is on, the text in the status bar panel
shows in black. If the mode is off, the text has a 3D disabled-text appearance. The third
owner-drawn panel displays a stock Windows icon to illustrate the use of a graphic on a
status bar. Run the program and experiment with it to learn how it works.

Listing 13.1 shows the OnDrawPanel event handler from the StatBar program. Examine
it and read the comments to understand what is going on in the code.

LISTING 13.1. THE StatusBarDrawPanel METHOD OF THE StatBar PROGRAM.

```
procedure TMainForm.StatusBarDrawPanel(StatusBar: TStatusBar;
  Panel: TStatusPanel; const Rect: TRect);
var
  R : TRect;
  Icon : HIcon;
begin
  with StatusBar.Canvas do begin
    { Create a temporary TRect object. The Rect parameter
    { is const so we can't change it. }
    R := Rect;
    { Check to see if panel 3 is the panel which needs
    { to be drawn. If so, draw an icon in the panel. }
    if Panel.Index = 3 then begin
        { Load one of the stock Windows icons. This time
        { using the API is easier than using VCL. }
        Icon := LoadIcon(0, IDI_HAND);
        { Draw the icon and shrink it down to 15 x 15 pixels. }
        { Center it in the panel, too. }
        DrawIconEx(Handle, Rect.Left + 6, 3,
          Icon, 15, 15, 0, 0, DI_NORMAL);
        { Nothing more to do. }
        Exit;
    end;
    { This rather lengthy if statement checks to see if
    { either the Overtype Mode or Extended Selection
    { check boxes are checked. If so, then what we need
    { to do is to draw the text twice. First, we draw it
    { in white. Then we draw it again, offset by 1 pixel,
    { in gray. The effect is a 3D disabled-text look. }
    if ((Panel.Index = 1) and (OvrMode.Checked = False)) or
      ((Panel.Index = 2) and (ExtendedSel.Checked = False))
        then begin
      { Move over and down one pixel for the offset. }
      Inc(R.Left);
      Inc(R.Top, 2);
      { Change the text color to white. }
      Font.Color := clWhite;
      { Set the backround mode to transparent so the
      { text appears hollow and so that the white
      { text can be seen under the gray. }
      Brush.Style := bsClear;
      { Draw the text using the API function DrawText. }
      { I use DrawText because it allows me to center
      { the text both horizontally and vertically within
      { the given rectangle. }
```

13

continues

LISTING 13.1. CONTINUED

```
      DrawText(Handle, PChar(Panel.Text), -1,
        R, DT_CENTER or DT_VCENTER or DT_SINGLELINE);
      { Set the color to gray because we're going to
      { draw the text in gray in a moment. }
      Font.Color := clGray;
      { Set the rect back to the original size. }
      Dec(R.Left);
      Dec(R.Top, 2);
    end;
    { Display the text. If the item is not disabled then
    { the default color (black) is used to draw the text. }
    { If the item is disabled, then the text color has
    { been set to gray by the code above. }
    DrawText(Handle, PChar(Panel.Text), -1,
      R, DT_CENTER or DT_VCENTER or DT_SINGLELINE);
  end;
end;
```

This code might seem intimidating, but most of it is comment lines. The code itself is relatively simple. The comment lines explain what is happening at each step: The 3D appearance for the disabled text is accomplished by drawing the text once in white and then drawing it again in gray with a slight offset. The result is that the text looks recessed. The icon is displayed using the Windows API functions LoadIcon and DrawIconEx.

Owner drawing of status bar panels is daunting at first, but you'll soon find out that it's not all that bad. You might write Windows applications for a long time and never need owner-drawn panels in your status bar. If you ever need them, however, you'll know that's not impossible to accomplish.

Adding Functionality with Command Enabling

Command enabling is the process of enabling or disabling buttons depending on current conditions. For example, there's not much point of having the Cut or Copy button or menu item enabled for a text editor when no text is currently selected. Likewise, if there is no text in the Clipboard, the Paste button should be disabled.

New to 4 Command enabling isn't difficult, especially with Delphi's new `TActionList` component. Still, it takes time to get right. It takes time because you have to pay attention to detail. (Sometimes it is attention to detail that separates the great applications from the mediocre applications.)

Command Enabling with `TActionList` and `TAction`

The `TAction` class provides a convenient way of performing command enabling. `TActionList`, the nonvisual component that manages actions, is found on the Additional tab of the Component palette. `TActionList`, as its name implies, contains a list of `TAction` objects. You create an action and then assign that action to any controls that need to be enabled or disabled based on that action. By controls I mean menu items, toolbar buttons, context menu items, and so on.

Let's take the Edit | Cut menu item, for example. You could have at least three objects associated with this particular task:

- A main menu item
- A toolbar button
- A pop-up menu item

You create actions with the ActionList Editor. Given the Edit | Cut example, you would create an action for Cut called, say, `CutAction`. Then, using the Object Inspector, you assign `CutAction` to the `Action` property of each of the objects that correspond to the cut operation (toolbar buttons and menus, for example). At runtime, when you need to enable the Cut option, you can do so with just one line of code:

```
CutAction.Enabled := True;
```

This will enable all components with their `Action` properties set to `CutAction`. Disabling the Cut items is as simple as assigning `False` to the `Enabled` property of the action. The `OnUpdate` event of `TAction` and `TActionList` provides a convenient place to put your command-enabling code.

Command enabling with `TAction` is something that you have to experience to fully appreciate. You add command enabling to `ScratchPad` in the next section.

Implementing Command Enabling

In this section you implement command enabling for the `ScratchPad` program. First you set up the `ActionList` component, and then you hook up the various components to the action list.

13

Creating an `ActionList`

It all starts with the `ActionList` component, which is the heart of the command-enabling system in VCL. First you add the actions for the Edit menu items. After that, you add an action for the File menu's Save and Save As menu items. The following steps will take you through the `ActionList` setup process.

Creating the Edit Menu Actions

The following steps show you how to create actions for the Edit menu's Cut, Copy, and Paste items. Perform these steps:

1. Place an `ActionList` component on the form and change the `Name` property to `ActionList`.

2. Double-click the `ActionList` icon to invoke the ActionList Editor.

3. Right-click on the ActionList Editor and choose New Standard Action from the context menu. Choose the `TEditCopy` action and click OK. Notice that the Object Inspector changes to show the properties of the `TEditCopy` action class.

   I want to pause for a moment here and explain more about how actions work. Examine the Object Inspector at this point. Notice that the `TEditCopy` action has several familiar properties and that those properties all have values. In particular, notice that the `Caption`, `Hint`, `ImageIndex`, and `ShortCut` properties already have values that correspond to an Edit menu's Copy item. These properties will be transferred to any control that you assign this action to, which means that you must set any properties of the action to the values that you want the corresponding components to acquire. That won't make much sense until you attach the action to components in the next section, but it will be clear at that time. Let's continue with the action creation process.

4. Change the new action's `Name` property to `CopyAction`, the `Hint` property to Copy ¦ Copy to Clipboard, and the `ImageIndex` property to 3.

5. Create another standard action, this time a `TEditCut` action. Change the `Name` to `CutAction`, the `Hint` property to Cut ¦ Cut to Clipboard, and the `ImageIndex` property to 4.

6. Create a third action, a `TEditPaste` action. Change the `Name` property to `PasteAction`, the `Hint` property to Paste ¦ Paste from Clipboard, and the `ImageIndex` property to 5.

You have now created the actions for the primary Edit menu items.

Creating the File Menu Actions

Next you need to create the actions for the File menu's Save and Save As menu items. Perform these steps:

1. Right-click on the ActionList Editor and this time choose New Action. A new TAction is created and is shown in the Object Inspector.

2. Change the Name property to SaveAction, the Caption property to &Save..., the Category property to File, the Hint property to Save ¦ Save a File, the ImageIndex property to 2, and the ShortCut property to Ctrl+S.

3. Create another new action. Change the Name property to SaveAsAction, the Caption property to Save &As..., and the Category property to File. You don't need to set the Hint or ImageIndex properties because this action doesn't have an associated button on the toolbar. Figure 13.7 shows the ActionList Editor at this point.

FIGURE 13.7.

The ActionList Editor after creating the action items.

4. Close the ActionList Editor.

> **Note**
>
> You can create categories of actions if you have several dozen actions to keep track of. To create an action category, simply set the Category property of one or more actions to any text you want. For example, to create a category for the edit actions created earlier, set each action's Category property to Edit. Action categories are simply for organization and don't have any bearing on the way actions operate.

Attaching Actions to Components

The next step is to attach the actions you just created to the various menu items and toolbar buttons to which those actions correspond. Perform these steps:

1. Double-click on the MainMenu component to start the Menu Editor.

2. Select the File | Save menu item and change its Action property to SaveAction.

3. Select the File | Save As menu item and change its `Action` property to `SaveAsAction`.

4. Move to the Edit menu and select the Cut menu item. Change the `Action` property to `CutAction`.

5. Repeat step 4 for the Copy and Paste items on the Edit menu using `CopyAction` and `PasteAction` for the `Action` property, respectively. Close the Menu Editor.

6. In the Form Designer, click on the File Save button on the toolbar. Change the `Action` property of the button to `FileSaveAction`.

7. Repeat step 6 for the Cut, Copy, and Paste buttons on the toolbar, setting the `Action` property to `CutAction`, `CopyAction`, and `PasteAction`, respectively.

8. Change the `Action` property of the `MemoPopup` menu items as needed.

You probably didn't notice, but when you assigned `SaveAction` to the `Action` property of a component, that component's `Caption`, `Checked`, `Enabled`, `HelpContext`, `Hint`, `ImageIndex`, `ShortCut`, and `Visible` properties all changed to the values of those properties in the `SaveAction` object. It is important to understand that the action's properties will overwrite the properties of any component that the action is assigned to. You must set up the action with that in mind. That is why I had you change the `Hint` and `ItemIndex` properties when you created the actions. Had you not done that, the hint text and toolbar button glyphs would not be correct.

Now each of the components just listed is hooked to an action. When a particular action changes, any components hooked to that action will change as well. Take the following code, for example:

```
SaveAction.Enabled := False;
```

When this code executes, any components with their `Action` property set to `SaveAction` will be disabled (the main menu Save item and the Save button on the toolbar). To enable all items associated with this action, use this code:

```
SaveAction.Enabled := True;
```

It's as simple as that. Because the main menu and toolbar Save components have their `Action` property set to `SaveAction`, the following two code snippets are equivalent:

```
{ One-shot using the Action. }
SaveAction.Enabled := False;

{ The hard way. }
FileSave.Enabled := False;
FileSaveBtn.Enabled := False;
```

Granted you save only one line of code in this example, but if you have several components that need to be enabled or disabled, actions can save you a lot of time. After you create an action and associate that action with one or more components, command enabling is as simple as one line of code. The beauty of this system is that it doesn't matter how many components you need to enable or disable. It's still just one line of code.

Run the ScratchPad program. Notice that the Cut and Copy buttons are disabled. Type some text in the memo and highlight it. The Cut and Copy buttons on the toolbar are magically enabled. Click anywhere in the memo to deselect the selected text. The Cut and Copy buttons are disabled again. Is the Paste button enabled? If so, type Alt+Print Screen on the keyboard. (This copies the current window to the Clipboard as a bitmap.) When you press Alt+Print Screen, the Paste button should become disabled because you can't paste a bitmap into a memo. Select some text and click either the Cut or the Copy button. The Paste button is now enabled because the Clipboard contains text you can paste into a memo.

How does it work? The TEditCopy, TEditCut, and TEditPaste standard actions automatically know how to enable and disable their associated components when any type of edit control has input focus. It's not magic, but it's the next best thing to it! You only have to create the standard actions and the rest is automatic. You didn't have to write any code to get the Edit menu command enablers working. You can't beat that!

Command Enabling for the Save and Save As Items

The Edit menu items were easy because you didn't have to write any code. The File menu items, Save and Save As, will take a little more work because there are no standard actions for these menu items. Not to worry, though—adding command enabling for those menu items doesn't take much time. To implement command enabling for these menu items, you will make use of the OnUpdate event. But first you need a little background information to put the OnUpdate event in perspective.

The OnUpdate event provides a convenient place to put your command-enabling code. When your application runs out of messages to process, Windows sends it a WM_ENTERIDLE message. Windows, in effect, tells your program, "I don't have anything for you to do right now, so relax and take it easy for a while." When a Delphi application receives a WM_ENTERIDLE message, it triggers a TAction's OnUpdate event. All you have to do is create an event handler for the OnUpdate event and do your command enabling there. You can use the event handler to check the state of the memo component and enable the Save and Save As items accordingly.

13

The only step remaining, then, is to create an event handler for the action's OnUpdate event. Perform these steps:

1. Double-click the ActionList component to start the ActionList Editor.

2. Select the SaveAction action from the list of available actions. Click on the File action category or (All Actions) if you don't see the action in the action list.

3. In the Object Inspector, double-click the Value column next to the OnUpdate event. The Code Editor displays the OnUpdate event handler. You add code to the event handler in just a bit.

4. Locate the ActionList Editor (use View | Window List if you can't find the ActionList Editor window). Select SaveAsAction from the list of actions.

5. In the Object Inspector, click the drop-down arrow next to the OnUpdate event. Choose SaveActionUpdate from the list. This enables the Save and Save As items to use the same OnUpdate event handler.

6. Close the ActionList Editor.

Creating the event handler is the simple part, of course. The more difficult aspect is writing the code that goes between the begin and end statements. Listing 13.2 shows the completed OnUpdate event handler. Switch to the Code Editor and enter the code shown in Listing 13.2 into your OnUpdate event handler.

LISTING **13.2.** THE ScratchPad OnUpdate EVENT HANDLER.

```
procedure TMainForm.SaveActionUpdate(Sender: TObject);
begin
  { Command enabler for Save and Save As. }
  SaveAction.Enabled :=
    Memo.Modified and (Length(Memo.Lines.Text) > 0);
  SaveAsAction.Enabled := SaveAction.Enabled;

  { The following two command enablers don't use actions. }
  { Instead the Enabled property of the two menu items    }
  { is accessed directly. }
  { Command enabler for Select All. }
  EditSelectAll.Enabled := Memo.Lines.Count > 0;
  { Command enabler for Undo. }
  EditUndo.Enabled := Memo.Modified;
end;
```

The SaveAction's Enabled property is set based on whether or not the memo has been modified and whether or not the memo contains text. In a nutshell, the Save action is enabled if the memo has been modified since it was loaded and if it contains text. The same value is assigned to the Enabled property of the SaveAsAction. This enables both Save and Save As at the same time using the same criteria.

Notice that I slipped a couple of extra commands into the OnUpdate event handler. The command enablers for the Select All and Undo items of the Edit menu do not use actions. Instead, the Enabled property of the menu items is set directly. Using actions for these two items is overkill because there is only one line of code in each case. As long as you have an OnUpdate event handler, you can use it for any type of command enabling you want. Put another way, this OnUpdate event handler is not exclusively for the File menu items Save and Save As. Any command enabling can be done in the OnUpdate event.

Note The OnUpdate event handler might be called thousands of times per second. For that reason, you must keep code in this method as short as possible.

Note Debugging code in the OnUpdate event handler is tricky. The problem is that any breakpoints in the OnUpdate event handler will be hit as soon as you run the program. You will have to use debugging methods other than straight breakpoints when debugging code in the OnUpdate event handler. Two such methods are conditional breakpoints and using OutputDebugString to send messages to the Event Log.

A TCommandList Bonus

There's an added benefit to command lists that I haven't mentioned yet. To see this hidden (up to now) benefit, perform these steps:

1. Select the MainMenu icon on ScratchPad's main form.
2. Change the Images property to ImageList.
3. Do the same for the PopupMenu.

Now run the program and look at the File and Edit menus. Wow! Instant menu bitmaps! The menu items inherit the ImageIndex property of their associated action. All you have to do to enable the bitmaps is assign the same image list use for the actions to the menu's Images property. The rest is automatic.

13

Printing in Delphi Applications

Printing is an everyday necessity for most Windows users. Whereas plenty of programs do not have printing capability, the majority of Windows applications have some form of printing support. I'll cover the basics of printing in this section.

Providing printing capabilities in a DOS application used to be a real chore. A DOS program had to provide and install printer drivers for every type of printer that the program supported. That put a huge burden on software developers, especially on small companies or shareware developers. Windows changed all that. For the most part, Windows takes on the burden of dealing with different printers, printer drivers, and so on. All you have to do is send output to the printer just as you would send output to a window. I'll get to that soon.

Printing in Delphi applications comes in several flavors. You'll probably be relieved to learn that, in many cases, printing is built into VCL and comes nearly automatically. In other cases, though, you have to do some specialized printing. Before you learn how to go about that, let's look at the common dialog boxes that pertain to printing. After that I'll discuss the different ways you can print from a Delphi application.

The Common Printing Dialog Boxes

Windows provides the common Print and Print Setup dialog boxes for use in your applications. You use the Print dialog box just before printing begins and the Print Setup dialog box to configure the printer. First, though, you must add the components to your form.

The Print Dialog Box

As I've mentioned, the Print dialog box is displayed just before printing begins, usually when the user chooses File | Print from the main menu. If the user clicks OK, printing begins; if the user clicks Cancel, printing is aborted. Figure 13.8 shows the Windows Print dialog box in its most basic form.

FIGURE 13.8.

The Windows Print dialog box.

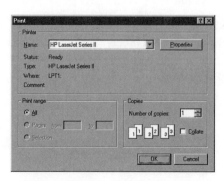

No doubt this is not the first time you have seen this particular dialog box. The combo box at the top of the dialog box enables you to choose the particular printer to which you want to print. The Properties button brings up a dialog box specific to the printer currently selected that enables you to set the orientation, resolution, and other properties specific to that printer. The Print Range section enables the user to print all pages, a page range, or any objects or text currently selected in the application. The Copies section enables the user to specify the number of copies to print as well as whether to collate the copies.

The Print dialog box is encapsulated in VCL in the `PrintDialog` component. As with the other common dialog boxes, you display the Print dialog box by calling its `Execute` method. It shouldn't disappoint you to learn that Windows carries out much of what the Print dialog box does. The printer selection, number of copies, and collating options are all handled by Windows, so you don't have to worry about them. Depending on your application, you might need to enable the user to print a specified range of pages or to print the current selection in the application. If you are providing that kind of support, you need to examine some of the `PrintDialog` properties before printing begins.

The `PrintDialog` component has the `Execute` method only and no events. All the functionality of the `PrintDialog` component takes place through its properties, as listed in Table 13.3.

TABLE 13.3. THE `PrintDialog` PROPERTIES.

Property	Description
Collate	Specifies collated copies. If this is set to `True`, Windows will print so that the copies are collated.
Copies	Specifies the number of copies to print. You can set this property before calling the Print dialog box if one of your application's options is the number of copies to print. Windows takes care of printing the correct number of copies.
FromPage	Specifies the starting page when the option of printing a range of pages is enabled. Applications that support page-range printing should read this property to determine which pages to print.
MaxPage	Specifies the maximum page number that can be specified in the `To` field when printing a range of pages. The Print dialog box takes care of validating entry in the `From` and `To` fields.
MinPage	Specifies the minimum page number that can be specified in the `From` field when printing a range of pages.

13

continues

TABLE 13.3. CONTINUED

Property	Description
Options	Contains a set of options that control which features of the Print dialog box are enabled. You can elect to have a Help button, to display the Print to File option, or to enable the page-range or print selection options.
PrintRange	Controls which of the Print Range radio buttons is selected when the Print dialog box is initially displayed.
PrintToFile	Indicates whether the user has chosen the Print to File option. It is up to the application to write the output to a file.
ToPage	Specifies the ending page number when printing a range of pages. Applications that support page-range printing should read this property to determine which pages to print.

The application doesn't have much to do in response to the Print dialog box closing unless the Print Range and Print to File options are enabled. For example, if your application enables printing a range of pages, you need to read the FromPage and ToPage properties to determine which pages to print. Other than that, you begin printing if the user clicks OK.

The Print Setup Dialog Box

The Print Setup dialog box, shown in Figure 13.9, is used when the user wants to change printers, page size, paper source, or orientation.

FIGURE 13.9.

The Print Setup dialog box.

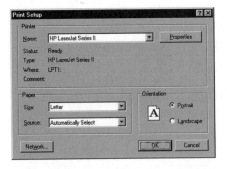

The Print Setup dialog box isn't necessary in most applications because the user can always press the Properties button on the Print dialog box to change the setup options (refer to Figure 13.8). On the other hand, implementing the Print Setup dialog box is so easy that you might as well include it in your applications. How easy is it? Well, the

`PrinterSetup` component has no properties, methods, or events specific to it. As with the `PrintDialog` component, the `Execute` method is the only method in which you are interested. To further simplify things, Windows handles everything that the Print Setup dialog box does. In fact, the `Execute` method doesn't even return a value. This is because Windows handles everything for you. If the user clicks Cancel, Windows does nothing. If the user clicks OK, Windows makes the appropriate changes in preparation for printing. All you have to do is display the Print Setup dialog box and forget about it. A typical event handler for the File | Printer Setup menu item would look like this:

```
procedure TMainForm.FilePrintSetupClick(Sender: TObject);
begin
  PrinterSetupDialog.Execute;
end;
```

That's all there is to it. As I said, implementing the Print Setup dialog box is so simple you might as well add it to your application.

Printing the Easy Way

Printing is an application-specific task. That might not sound profound, but it's true. Depending on what kind of application you develop, printing can be as simple as one line or it can entail hundreds of lines of code. Let me first discuss the easiest forms of printing, and then I'll progress to the more difficult printing operations.

The `Print` Method for Forms

The `TForm` class has a method called `Print` that can be used to print the contents of a form. Only the client area of the form is printed; the form's frame and menu bar are not. Although this method works well for a simple screen dump, it is limited in its implementation. You can choose from three print options, which are controlled through the `PrintScale` property. Table 13.4 lists the print scaling choices and their descriptions.

TABLE 13.4. THE `PrintScale` PROPERTY OPTIONS.

Option	Description
poNone	No special scaling is applied. The printed output of the form varies from printer to printer.
PoProportional	This option attempts to print the form in roughly the same size as it appears on the screen.
poPrintToFit	This increases or reduces the size of the image to fit the current printer settings.

13

You can set the `PrintScaled` property at runtime or at design time. The `Print` method's use is limited to simple screen dumps and isn't likely to be used for any serious printing.

The `Print` Method for the `RichEdit` Component

The `RichEdit` component is powerful primarily due to the amount of work done by the underlying Windows memo control. Printing in the `RichEdit` component is accomplished via a call to the `Print` method. This method takes a single parameter called `Caption` that is used by the Print Manager when it displays the print job. Printing the contents of a `RichEdit` component is as simple as this:

```
RichEdit.Print('MyApp.exe - readme.txt');
```

Everything is taken care of for you. Word wrapping and pagination are automatically implemented. If you are using a multiline edit control that requires printing, the `RichEdit` component is the way to go.

> **Tip**
>
> You can use the Windows API function `ShellExecute` to print a text file. `ShellExecute` is used, among other things, to run a program based on a filename extension. For example, by default Windows registers the `.txt` extension as belonging to Windows Notepad. If you double-click on a file with a `.txt` extension in Explorer, Windows will look up the `.txt` extension in the Registry, see that `Notepad.exe` is registered to handle `.txt` files, and will run Notepad. The file you double-clicked will be loaded automatically.
>
> You can use this behavior to your advantage. Take this line of code, for example:
>
> ```
> ShellExecute(Handle, 'print', 'readme.txt', nil, nil, SW_HIDE);
> ```
>
> This code loads Notepad, prints the file called `Readme.txt`, and then exits Notepad. In fact, you never see the Notepad program's main window because the `SW_HIDE` style is specified for the `Show` parameter. Using this technique assumes that the user has not modified the default registration of the `.txt` extension and has not deleted Notepad from his or her system. If you use `ShellExecute`, you have to add `ShellApi` to your unit's uses list.

Printing via `QuickReport`

Database programs can use `QuickReport` to print reports. I mention `QuickReport` here because it obviously pertains to printing, but because `QuickReport` is one of the database components, I will postpone a detailed discussion about its actual implementation until Day 18, "Building Database Applications."

Printing the Hard Way

Don't let the title of this section put you off. Printing isn't all that difficult; it just takes some time and organization. First, let's look at some steps you need to know in order to implement printing in your applications. After that you delve into the actual code.

What's a Device Context?

I talked about device contexts and TCanvas in detail yesterday, but a recap can't hurt. A device context (DC) is like a slate that Windows programs can draw on. A better word would be *canvas*. On this canvas you can draw text, lines, bitmaps, rectangles, ellipses, and so on. The type of line used when drawing on a device context depends on the current pen selected into the DC. The current fill color and fill pattern are taken from the brush that is currently selected into the device context. Device contexts must be carefully managed. There are a limited number of DCs available to Windows, and you have to be careful to release the device context as soon as you are finished with it. Also, if you don't properly delete the objects you select into the device context, your program will leak memory and perhaps even leave Windows itself in a precarious state. As you can imagine, working with DCs can be complicated.

The good news is that VCL shields you from having to know every detail of device contexts. VCL encapsulates Windows DCs in the TCanvas class. The Canvas property frees you from worrying about all the little details that can drive you nuts when dealing with Windows device contexts. VCL takes care of obtaining the DC, selecting the appropriate objects into the DC, and releasing the DC when it is no longer needed. All you have to do is draw on the canvas and let VCL worry about the rest.

So what does this have to do with printing? (Inquiring minds want to know.) Well, it's like this: Windows enables you to obtain a *printer device context* on which you can draw text, graphics, lines, and so on. In other words, you draw on a printer canvas just as you draw on a screen canvas. This concept represents quite a switch from the way printing was approached back in the good old days of DOS. In this case, it is Windows that comes to your rescue by enabling the use of a printer DC. VCL further aids you by encapsulating device contexts in the Canvas property. The bottom line is that printing is easier than it's ever been.

The TPrinter Class and the Printer Function

VCL aids in printing operations by providing the TPrinter class. This class encapsulates the whole of printing in Windows. TPrinter has a Canvas property that you can use to output lines, text, graphics, and other drawing objects to the printer. I don't want to make

13

it sound too easy, but all you have to do to print in your Delphi programs is add
Printers to your uses list and then do something like the following:

```
Printer.BeginDoc;
Printer.Canvas.TextOut(20, 20, 'Hello There!');
Printer.EndDoc;
```

In this code, Printer is a VCL function. This function enables you access to a TPrinter
object that is set up and ready to go. All you have to do is put it to work.

Now let's take a quick look at TPrinter's properties and methods. Table 13.5 lists the
primary TPrinter properties, and Table 13.6 shows the primary TPrinter methods.

TABLE 13.5. TPrinter PROPERTIES.

Property	Description
Aborted	This property is True if printing was started and then aborted before it was finished.
Canvas	The mechanism through which you can draw on the printer (the printer device context).
Capabilities	The current settings of a printer device driver.
Copies	The number of copies printed.
Fonts	A list of fonts supported by the current printer.
Handle	The handle to the printer device context (HDC). Use this property when you have to call a Windows API function that requires a handle to a device context.
Orientation	The printer orientation (poPortrait or poLandsacpe). This is automatically set when the user chooses a printer or modifies the printer setup, but you can also set it manually.
PageHeight	The height of the current printer page in pixels. This value varies from printer to printer. In addition, this property can contain a different value based on the orientation of the printer. Some printers can use more than one resolution, which also causes this value to vary.
PageNumber	The page number of the page currently printing. This property is incremented each time you call NewPage to begin printing a new page.
PageWidth	The width of the page in pixels. As with the PageHeight property, this value varies depending on the printer resolution, paper orientation, and paper size.

Property	Description
PrinterIndex	The index value of the currently selected printer in the list of available printers. Specify -1 to select the default printer.
Printers	A list of available printers on the system.
Printing	This property is True if the printer is currently printing.
Title	The text that identifies this printing job in the print manager window.

TABLE 13.6. TPrinter METHODS.

Method	Description
Abort	Used to abort the printing before normal completion.
BeginDoc	Begins the printing process. Sets up the printer with Windows in preparation for printing.
EndDoc	Ends the printing process. Forces the current page to be printed and performs printing cleanup with Windows.
GetPrinter	Retrieves the current printer. Use the Printers property instead of this method. (The Printers property is the preferred method for accessing printers because you can use it for both retrieving and setting the current printer.)
NewPage	Used to force printing of the current page and start a new page. Increments the PageNumber property.
SetPrinter	Sets the current printer. Use the Printers property instead of this method.

The TPrinter class has no design-time interface. Everything is accomplished at runtime.

Putting It to Work

It's time to put your newly acquired knowledge to work. Once again it's time to dust off the ScratchPad program and spruce it up a bit. After all, what good is a text editor that doesn't print?

First, you need to modify the main form slightly. You already have menu items set up for the Print and Print Setup menu items, but you need to enable them and add the Print and Printer Setup dialog boxes to the form. Here goes:

1. Double-click the MainMenu component to bring up the Menu Designer.
2. Choose File | Print from the ScratchPad menu in the Menu Designer. Change the Enabled property to True.

13

3. Do the same for the File | Print Setup menu item. Close the Menu Designer.

4. Place a `PrintDialog` component on the form and change its `Name` property to `PrintDialog`.

5. Place a `PrinterSetupDialog` on the form and change its `Name` property to `PrinterSetupDialog`.

Okay, now that you've completed the form, it's time to go to work modifying the code. To start, you have to add a couple items to the main form's declaration. Perform the following steps:

1. Switch to the Code Editor and add the `Printers` unit to the `uses` list of the main form's unit.

2. Locate the `TMainForm` class declaration in the `interface` section. Add this line to the `private` section of the class declaration:

   ```
   procedure PrintFooter(var R : TRect; LineHeight : Integer);
   ```

   This is the declaration for a method that prints the footer at the bottom of each page.

3. Type Ctrl+Shift+C to have Delphi's Class Completion feature create the `PrintFooter` procedure in the `implementation` section. You fill in the code later.

4. Switch to the Form Designer and choose File | Print from the form's main menu. The `FilePrintClick` method is displayed. For now, leave the method empty.

5. Choose File | Print Setup from the main menu. Enter one line at the cursor so that the entire `FilePrintSetupClick` method looks like this:

   ```
   procedure TMainForm.FilePrintSetupClick(Sender: TObject);
   begin
     PrinterSetupDialog.Execute;
   end;
   ```

Okay, now you're ready to fill in the `FilePrintClick` and `PrintFooter` methods. Listing 13.3 shows the `FilePrintClick` method. You can enter the code in this method by hand, or you can load the `ScratchPad` project that comes with the book's code and examine it in the Delphi IDE. Listing 13.4 shows the `PrintFooter` method. Enter the code in these methods in your `SPMain.pas` file. You don't have to type the comment lines, of course.

LISTING 13.3. THE `FilePrintClick` METHOD.

```
procedure TMainForm.FilePrintClick(Sender: TObject);
var
  I            : Integer;
  LineHeight   : Integer;
```

```
    LinesPerPage : Integer;
    LineCount    : Integer;
    R            : TRect;
    S            : string;
begin
  { Display the Print dialog. }
  if PrintDialog.Execute then begin

    { Set the title for the printer object. }
    Printer.Title := 'ScratchPad - ' + OpenDialog.FileName;

    { Set the printer font to the same font as the memo. }
    Printer.Canvas.Font := Memo.Font;

    { Determine the line height. Take the Size of the
    { font and and use the MulDiv function to calculate
    { the line height taking into account the current
    { printer resolution. Use the Abs function to get
    { the absolute value because the result could be a
    { negative number. After that add 40% for leading. }
    LineHeight := Abs(
      MulDiv(Printer.Canvas.Font.Size,
      GetDeviceCaps(Printer.Handle, LOGPIXELSY), 72));
    Inc(LineHeight, (LineHeight * 4) div 10);

    { Determine how many lines will fit on a page. Trim
    { it back by three lines to leave some bottom margin. }
    LinesPerPage := (Printer.PageHeight div lineHeight) - 4;

    { Start printing on line 4 rather than line 0 to leave
    { room for the header and to allow for some top margin. }
    LineCount := 4;

    { Tell Windows we're starting and print the header. }
    Printer.BeginDoc;
    R.Top    := LineHeight;
    R.Left   := 20;
    R.Right  := Printer.PageWidth;
    R.Bottom := LineHeight * 2;
    DrawText(Printer.Handle,
      PChar(OpenDialog.FileName), -1, R, DT_CENTER);

    { Loop through all of the lines and print each one. }
    for I := 0 to Pred(Memo.Lines.Count) do begin
```

continues

LISTING 13.3. CONTINUED

```
        { When we get to the bottom of the page reset the
        { line counter, eject the page, and start a new page. }
        Inc(LineCount);
        if LineCount = LinesPerPage then begin
          PrintFooter(R, LineHeight);
          LineCount := 4;
          Printer.NewPage;
        end;

        { Get the next string and print it using TextOut }
        S := Memo.Lines.Strings[I];
        Printer.Canvas.TextOut(0, LineCount * LineHeight, S);
      end;

    { All done. }
    PrintFooter(R, LineHeight);
    Printer.EndDoc;
  end;
end;
```

LISTING 13.4. THE PrintFooter METHOD.

```
procedure TMainForm.PrintFooter(var R: TRect; LineHeight: Integer);
var
  S : String;
begin
  with Printer do begin

    { Build a string to display the page number. }
    S := Format('Page %d', [PageNumber]);

    { Set up the rectangle where the footer will be drawn. }
    { Find the bottom of the page and come up a couple of
    { lines. }
    R.Top := PageHeight - (lineHeight * 2);
    R.Bottom := R.Top + lineHeight;

    { Display the text using DrawText so we can center the
    { text with no fuss. }
    DrawText(Handle, PChar(S), -1, R, DT_CENTER);

    { Draw a line across the page just above the 'Page X' text. }
    Canvas.MoveTo(0, R.Top - 2);
    Canvas.LineTo(R.Right, R.Top - 2);
  end;
end;
```

This code illustrates how you can print directly through Windows rather than rely on the built-in printing that VCL provides. Although I always opt to do something the easy way when possible, there are times when the easy way isn't flexible enough. In those times, it's good to have the knowledge to do the job without trouble.

Printing a Bitmap

Printing a bitmap is simple. All you need to do is create an instance of the TBitmap class, load a bitmap into the bitmap object, and send it to the printer using the Draw method of TCanvas. Here's the entire code:

```
procedure TForm1.Button1Click(Sender: TObject);
var
  Bitmap : TBitmap;
begin
  Bitmap := TBitmap.Create;
  Bitmap.LoadFromFile('test.bmp');
  Printer.BeginDoc;
  Printer.Canvas.Draw(20, 20, Bitmap);
  Printer.EndDoc;
  Bitmap.Free;
end;
```

When you print a bitmap, be aware that the bitmap might turn out very small depending on the resolution of your printer. The bitmap might have to be stretched to look right. If you need to stretch the bitmap, use the StretchDraw method instead of Draw.

Using Cursors

The use of cursors is not difficult, but I'll describe it here to give you a basic understanding of how it works. This section deals with cursors that you change at runtime. (To change a cursor at design time, select a new value for the component's Cursor property.) After a look at cursor basics, I will discuss how to load stock cursors and custom cursors.

Cursor Basics

First, you can change the cursor for a particular component or form or for the entire client area of your application. If you want to change the cursor for the entire application, you need to change the Cursor property of the Screen object. The Screen object represents your application's screen. By changing the Cursor property of the Screen object, you ensure that the cursor is the same regardless of which component the cursor is over. Let's say, for example, that you want to change the cursor to the hourglass cursor. If you change the Cursor property for the form only, the cursor will be an hourglass

13

when it's over the form itself but will revert back to the default cursor when it's over any other components on the form. Changing the Cursor for the Screen object gives you the same cursor throughout.

Cursor management is the responsibility of the Screen object. All the cursors available for your use are contained in the Cursors property of the Screen object. Note that the name of this property is Cursors and is not the same as the Cursor property discussed in the previous paragraph. The Cursors property is an array that contains a list of available cursors for the application, and the Cursor property is the property that is used to display a particular cursor. Although this is confusing at first, you'll catch on quickly. All it takes is a little experience working with cursors.

Windows provides several built-in cursors for use in your applications. In addition to these built-in cursors, VCL adds a few cursors of its own. Together, these cursors are called the *stock cursors*. Each stock cursor has a named constant associated with it. For example, the arrow cursor is named crArrow, the hourglass cursor is named crHourGlass, and the drag cursor is named crDrag. All these cursors are held in the Cursors array and occupy positions -17 through 0 in the array; the default cursor is at array index 0 (crDefault), no cursor is -1 (crNone), the arrow cursor is -2 (crArrow), and so on. The online help for the Cursors property lists all the cursors and their constant names, so check Delphi help for a complete list of the available cursors.

To use one of the cursors in the Cursors array, assign the name of the cursor you want to use to the Cursor property of the Screen object:

```
Screen.Cursor := crHourGlass;
```

At this point the VCL magic kicks in and the correct cursor is loaded and displayed. The use of the Cursors property is transparent to you because you don't directly access the Cursors property when you use a cursor. Instead, you make an assignment to the Cursor property, and VCL takes care of looking up the proper cursor in the Cursors array and displaying it. The Cursor property of a component and the Cursors property of the Screen object work together to display different cursors in your application.

You can change cursors in your applications for any number of reasons—to display the wait cursor (the hourglass), if you have a drawing program that uses special cursors, or to implement a help cursor in your application.

Loading and Using Stock Cursors

Windows provides several built-in cursors for use in your applications. In addition to those, VCL adds a few more cursors from which you can choose. You can use these stock cursors anytime you like.

One of the most obvious times to change the cursor is when you have a lengthy process your application must perform. It is considered bad practice to tie up the program without giving the user some indication that the program is busy. Windows provides the hourglass cursor (Windows calls it the wait cursor) for exactly this purpose. Let's say, for example, that you have a processing loop in your application that might take a long time. You would do something like this:

```
procedure TMainForm.DoItClick(Sender: TObject);
var
  I, Iterations : Integer;
  OldCursor     : TCursor;
begin
  Iterations := StrToInt(Time.Text);
  OldCursor := Screen.Cursor;
  Screen.Cursor := crHourGlass;
  for I := 0 to Iterations do begin
    Application.ProcessMessages;
    Time.Text := IntToStr(I);
  end;
  Screen.Cursor := OldCursor;
end;
```

Because you don't always know which cursor your application is using at any given time, it is a good idea to save the current cursor before changing the Cursor property. After you have finished with a particular cursor, you can restore the old cursor.

Note

Sometimes you will change the Cursor property before a lengthy processing loop and nothing seems to happen. The reason is that Windows didn't get a chance to change your cursor before your program entered the loop. When in the loop, your application can't process any messages—including the message to change the cursor. The fix is to pump the Windows message loop for waiting messages while you are in your loop:

```
Application.ProcessMessages;
```

Now your application enables messages to flow and the cursor changes when your loop starts.

13

You can, of course, change the cursor for an individual component. For example, a drawing program might change the client area cursor depending on the current drawing tool. You don't want to change the cursor for the Screen object in that case because you want the arrow cursor to appear when the cursor is moved over the toolbar, status bar, menu, or any other components that might be on the form. In that case, you set the cursor only for the component that represents the client window of your application:

```
PaintBox.Cursor := crCross;
```

Now the cursor is changed for just this one component and all other components use their own predefined cursor.

Loading and Using Custom Cursors

Loading custom cursors requires a little more work. As I mentioned earlier, the Cursors property of the TScreen class contains the list of cursors available to your application. To use a custom cursor requires several steps:

1. Create a cursor in the Image Editor or other resource editor and save it as a .res file.
2. Link the resource file to your program with the $R compiler directive.
3. Load the cursor into the Cursors array using the LoadCursor function.
4. Implement the cursor by assigning the index number to the Cursor property for the form, the Cursor property for the Screen object, or the Cursor property for any other component.

The first two steps were covered on Day 11 when I talked about the Image Editor and on Day 8 when I discussed resources. After you have the cursor bound to the .exe, you can load it with the LoadCursor function. Loading a cursor into the Cursors array is easy:

```
Screen.Cursors[1] := LoadCursor(HInstance, 'MYCURSOR');
```

This code assumes that you have a cursor with a name of MYCURSOR and that you are assigning the cursor to position 1 in the cursors list (remember, positions -17 through 0 are used for the stock cursors). Loading the cursor has to be done only once, so you will probably do it in your main form's OnCreate event handler.

Note   All cursors are loaded into the Screen object's Cursors property regardless of whether you use the cursor with the Screen object, with a form, or with a component. There is only one Cursors array, and it belongs to the Screen object.

To use the cursor, then, just assign it to the Cursor property of the Screen object or of any component:

```
PaintBox.Cursor := 1;
```

If you have several cursors, you might want to create constants for each cursor so that you have meaningful names to use instead of integer values that are easy to mix up. Using that method, the preceding code would look like this:

```
const
  MyCursor = 1;

{ later... }
Screen.Cursors[MyCursor] := LoadCursor(HInstance, 'MYCURSOR');

{ later still... }
PaintBox.Cursor := MyCursor;
```

As you can see, loading and implementing custom cursors isn't difficult when you know how to do it. The book's code for today includes a sample program called CursTest that demonstrates the theories discussed in this section.

Summary

Today you learned about some features that make up a top-quality Windows application and how to implement them in your own programs. I should warn you that it's tempting to overdo it with features such as control bars, status bars, and cursors. Implement whatever decorations your application needs, but don't overuse them. You also learned about printing today. In some cases, printing support is built into a particular component, and in those cases printing is incredibly easy. In other cases you have to roll up your sleeves and go to work with the TPrinter class. Even at those times, though, printing is nothing to fear.

Workshop

The Workshop contains quiz questions to help you solidify your understanding of the material covered and exercises to provide you with experience in using what you have learned. You can find the answers to the quiz questions in Appendix A, "Answers to the Quiz Questions."

13

Q&A

Q Can I disable all the components on my toolbar at one time?

A Yes. Set the toolbar's Enabled property to False.

Q I noticed that `TCoolBar` and `TControlBar` do about the same thing. Which one should I use?

A My advice would be to use `TControlBar`. There are many versions of Microsoft's common control library, `COMCTL32.DLL`. `TCoolBar` is a wrapper around Microsoft's cool bar common control and, as such, is affected by the version of `COMCTL32.DLL` the user has installed on his or her machine. `TControlBar` isn't dependent on `COMCTL32.DLL`, so its behavior won't change from system to system.

Q How do I put a bitmap on my status bar?

A Create a multipanel status bar. Change the style of the panel that will contain the bitmap to `psOwnerDraw`. Then, in your `OnDrawPanel` event handler, use the `Draw` method of `TCanvas` to draw your bitmap on the panel.

Q Why should I bother with command enabling for my menu items and toolbar buttons?

A Because users expect a consistent interface. When certain choices are not available (whether on menus or toolbars), they should be grayed out. This gives the user a visual cue that these commands are sometimes available but not currently applicable.

Q I'm a longtime Delphi user. I've got a system for command enabling in place. Why should I switch to actions and action lists?

A Actions give you a central location from which you can do all your command enabling. Rather than having your command enabling code spread throughout your code base, you can now have it in one location.

Q I just want basic output of a large, multiline edit control in my application. What's the easiest way?

A The easiest way is to use a `RichEdit` component and use its `Print` method to print the contents of the component.

Q I see that there is a `Handle` property for the `Printer` object and also a `Handle` property for the `Canvas` property of the `Printer` object. What's the difference?

A In this case there is no difference. If you are calling a Windows API function that requires the printer device context handle, you can use either `Printer.Handle` or `Printer.Canvas.Handle`.

Q When I change the cursor for my main form, the cursor is correct when it's over the form but reverts back to the arrow cursor when it's over any of my buttons. Why?

A You need to change the cursor for the `Screen` object, not for the form. Changing the cursor for the `Screen` object ensures that the new cursor will be used whenever the cursor is over any part of your application.

Quiz

1. How do you attach an event handler to a toolbar button's `OnClick` event?

2. Can you put controls other than buttons on toolbars?

3. What is the name of the `TActionList` event you respond to when doing command enabling?

4. What does the `SimplePanel` property of the `StatusBar` component do?

5. How do you change the status bar text manually?

6. How do you enable and disable menu items and buttons?

7. How do you access the printer in a Delphi application?

8. What method do you call to begin printing with the `TPrinter` class?

9. What method of `TPrinter` do you call when you want to start a new page when printing?

10. How do you change the cursor for a component at runtime?

Exercises

1. Write a program from scratch. Add a toolbar and place five buttons on it. Now add a status bar. Enable hints so that the toolbar buttons have both tooltips and hint text in the status bar.

2. Change the status bar for the `ScratchPad` program and add a second panel. In this panel, display either `Saved` or `Modified` based on the value of `Memo.Modified`.

3. Change the About box of the `ScratchPad` program to read `Version 1.05`. Also, change the `Title` property in the Project Options dialog box and the `Caption` of the main form. After all, you added features, so you must let the users know!

4. Create a custom cursor with the Image Editor. Write a program that displays the cursor when a button on the main form is pressed.

5. **Extra Credit:** Modify the `ScratchPad` program from exercise 3 to display different bitmaps on the status bar depending on whether the current file is saved. (Hint: Look at the `led1on.bmp` and `led1off.bmp` bitmaps in the `Borland Shared Files\Images\Buttons` directory.)

6. **Extra Credit:** Modify the `ScratchPad` program so that the user can specify a top margin, bottom margin, right margin, and left margin for printed output.

13

DAY 14

Advanced Programming

Today you get into some of the more advanced aspects of Windows programming with Delphi. Specifically, you learn about

- Implementing context-sensitive help
- Exception handling
- Using the Windows Registry
- Specialized message handling

You have a lot to do today, so let's get right to it.

Implementing Context-Sensitive Help

Not too long ago, you might have been able to get by with not providing context-sensitive help in your applications. In fact, for small applications you might have been able to get by without providing a help file at all. I wouldn't recommend that in today's market, though. Users are increasingly demanding when it comes to features. A help file is a no longer an option but a required component of a full-featured application.

Context-sensitive help means that when the user presses the F1 key, a particular page of the application's help file is displayed depending on the program's current context. Take the Delphi IDE, for example. Let's say you have the Project Options dialog box open and have the Application page displayed. When you press F1 (or press the Help button on the dialog box), WinHelp runs and displays the help topic for the Application page of the Project Options dialog box.

Likewise, if you press F1 when the Object Repository Options dialog box is on the screen, you get help for that particular dialog box. Context-sensitive help works with menu items as well. If you highlight a menu item and press F1, you are taken to the help file page regarding that menu item.

To implement context-sensitive help in your application, you must perform the following steps:

1. Create a help file for your application.
2. Assign the name of your help file to the `HelpFile` property of the `Application` object.
3. Set the `HelpContext` property of any forms or components for which context-sensitive help is supported.
4. Create menu items for the Help menu so that your users can invoke help from the menu.

Let's examine these steps one at a time.

Writing the Help File

Writing help files is a chore. I don't exactly hate it, mind you, but it's not one of the tasks I look forward to. If you are fortunate, you have a documentation department that writes the help files for you.

 Note

> Even some limited-budget programmers have documentation departments that write help files for them. Frequently they refer to the doc writers as "Honey" or "Dear." For example, a programmer might say to her documentation writer, "Honey, when you get done with that help page would you put the kids to bed?"

Regardless of who writes the help file, there must be some coordination between the help-file writer and the programmer. The context identifiers in the help file must match those specified for the components in the program itself. Although this is not exactly a difficult task, coordination is still required so that everyone is on the same page (pun intended).

A Windows help file might be constructed from several individual files. The source for a Windows help file is called the *topic file*. The topic file is a rich text format (.rtf) file with lots of special codes that the help compiler understands. If your help file includes graphics, you might have one or more *graphics files*. Graphics files used in creating a help file include bitmap (.bmp), Windows metafile (.wmf), and some other specialized graphics files.

Finally, you have the help *project file* (.hpj). The project file contains a description of how the help compiler should go about merging the topic file, the graphics files, and any other specialized files the target help file needs. It also includes a [MAP] section that maps context ID numbers to particular help topics. After the project file is created, it is compiled with a help compiler such as the Microsoft Help Workshop (you can find it in the \Delphi 4\Help\Tools directory). The Help Workshop takes the help project file and compiles it to produce the final help file (.hlp).

Tip

Although you can write help files with any word processor that supports .rtf files, I strongly recommend buying a help-authoring program. A good help-authoring package can take much of the frustration out of writing help files. Commercial help authoring tools include ForeHelp by Fore Front, Inc. (http://www.ff.com) and RoboHelp by Blue Sky Software (http://www.blue-sky.com). I have used ForeHelp and, for the most part, I like the way it works. There are also some good shareware help authoring tools out there. One such shareware help authoring program is HelpScribble. You can check out HelpScribble at http://www.ping.be/jg/.

Context Identifiers and the `HelpContext` Property

Regardless of what method you use to create the help file, you need to have a context number associated with each major topic in the help file. The *context number* is used by the Windows help system, WinHelp32.exe, to display a particular page in the help file.

For example, let's say you have an Options dialog box in your application. When the user presses F1 with the Options dialog box open, your program will pass the context ID for that dialog box to WinHelp. WinHelp will run and display the page in the help file that explains the application's Options dialog box. You don't need a context ID for every page in the help file, but you should have a help context ID for your main topic pages, dialog boxes, and other major components of your application.

14

Most components (forms, menu items, and controls) have a property called
HelpContext. This property contains the context ID that will be passed to WinHelp if the
user presses the F1 key when that component has focus. By default, the HelpContext
property is set to 0. If the HelpContext property is 0 for a component, the component
will inherit the HelpContext value of its parent window. This enables you to set the
HelpContext for a form and then, no matter which component on the form has input
focus, the help context for the form will be used when F1 is pressed.

 Note   You might have noticed that the SpeedButton and ToolButton components
do not have a HelpContext property. Because these components are non-
windowed controls, they can never gain input focus. Therefore, the F1 key
cannot be used with speed buttons and toolbar buttons.

At a minimum, you should provide context-sensitive help for each form in your application (a form being a dialog box or secondary window). Ultimately, it is up to you to
decide which items to provide context-sensitive help for. If you are going to err, you
should probably err on the side of providing too much context-sensitive help (if there is
such a thing) rather than not enough.

Implementing Context-Sensitive Help

Implementing context-sensitive help in your Delphi applications is relatively easy. As I
said earlier, the real work in adding context-sensitive help to your Delphi applications is
in the writing of the help file. The rest is easy in comparison.

Setting the Help File

Regardless of how you implement context-sensitive help, you first have to tell Windows
the name of the help file for your application. To do that, you assign the help filename to
the HelpFile property of the Application class. You can do this in one of two ways.
The easier way is at design time via the Project Options dialog box.

On Day 9, "Projects, the Code Editor, and the Code Explorer," you learned about the
project options. I discussed the fact that the Application page of the Project Options dialog box has a field called Help File that is used to specify the name of the help file for
the application. Simply type the name of your help file in this field. VCL will assign the
help file name to the HelpFile property, and then the application will use that filename
each time help is requested.

You can also set the name of the help file at runtime. This might be necessary if you
enable your users to place the help file in a directory of their own choosing. You could

store the location of the help file in the Windows Registry (the Registry is discussed later, in the section titled "Using the Registry") and then assign the help file's path and filename to the `Application` object's `HelpFile` property. For example, part of your `OnCreate` event handler might look like this:

```
var
  Filename : string;
begin
  Filename := GetHelpFileName; { user-defined function }
  Application.HelpFile := Filename;
```

Although it's not very common, you can change the `HelpFile` property at different points in your program if you want. You might do this to switch between different help files, for example. After you have the help filename set up, you can go on to the actual implementation of the help system.

Adding F1 Key Support

To add F1 support for forms and components, all you have to do is set the `HelpContext` property to the matching context ID in the help file; VCL takes it from there. Be sure that you have assigned a help filename to the `HelpFile` property of the `Application` class and that the help file contains valid context identifiers.

Adding Menu Support for the Help File

In addition to F1 key support, most applications have one or two menu items under the Help menu (where else?) that can be used to start WinHelp. There will usually be a menu item called Contents. Choosing this item will display the contents page for the help file. In addition to a Contents menu item, some applications have a Help menu item called Help Topics. Choosing this menu item displays the index for the help file. (The index is created as part of the help file creation process.)

To implement these and other Help items, you have to do some programming. (It's only one line of code in each case.) VCL provides a method called `HelpCommand` that can be used to display WinHelp in one of several modes. If you were to implement the Help | Contents menu item, the code would look like this:

```
procedure TForm1.Contents1Click(Sender: TObject);
begin
  Application.HelpCommand(HELP_FINDER, 0);
end;
```

The `HelpCommand` method calls WinHelp with the specified command. (See the Windows API help under `WinHelp` for a complete list of available commands.) In this case, WinHelp is invoked with a command of `HELP_FINDER`. This command tells WinHelp to display the contents page, as shown in Figure 14.1. The final parameter of the

14

`HelpCommand` method is used to pass additional data to WinHelp. This parameter is not used with the `HELP_FINDER` command, so it is set to `0`.

FIGURE **14.1.**

*The ScratchPad Help
Contents page.*

> **Note**
>
> In order for WinHelp to show the Contents page, you must have a contents file for your help file. The contents file has an extension of `.cnt` and is a text file that describes how the contents page should be displayed. You can read more about the contents file in the Microsoft Help Workshop help. You can find the Help Workshop and its help file in the `\Delphi 4\Help\Tools` directory.

> **Note**
>
> A good index for your help file is invaluable. The quality of the help file—and the quality of the help file's index—are directly proportional to the amount of technical support you will have to provide. Don't overlook this fact.

Context-Sensitive Help on Demand

Most of the time the two help implementations I just told you about are all you need for your application. At other times, however, you need to call WinHelp directly and with a specific context ID. For these times, VCL provides the `HelpContext` method. This method takes, as its single parameter, the context ID of the page you want to see when WinHelp runs. For example, let's say you have a help page with a context ID of `99`. To run WinHelp and display that specific page, you would do the following:

```
Application.HelpContext(99);
```

By supplying a specific context ID, you can cause WinHelp to display any page of your help file on demand. This is what VCL does for you when you specify the `HelpContext` property for a particular component.

Using Help Include Files

Most of the time, setting the `HelpContext` properties for the forms or components for which you want to implement context-sensitive help is all you need to do. If, however, you need to call specific help pages in your application, you might consider defining constants for your help identifiers. Using named constants is much easier than trying to remember an integer value for a particular help context ID.

In the last section, I talked about using the `HelpContext` method to call WinHelp with a particular context ID. I used the example of a help context ID of 99. Rather than using the numerical value of the context identifier, you can use a constant like this:

```
Application.HelpContext(IDH_FILEOPEN);
```

Obviously, the string is easier to remember than its integer value equivalent. The context-sensitive help symbols can be kept in a separate include file that is added to your application where needed (using the {$I} compiler directive). Listing 14.1 shows a typical include file containing context-sensitive help identifiers.

LISTING 14.1. HELP.INC.

```
const
  IDH_FILENEW        = 1;
  IDH_FILEOPEN       = 2;
  IDH_FILESAVE       = 3;
  IDH_FILESAVEAS     = 4;
  IDH_FILEPRINT      = 5;
  IDH_FILEPRINTSETUP = 6;
  IDH_FILEEXIT       = 7;
  IDH_EDITUNDO       = 8;
  IDH_EDITCOPY       = 9;
  IDH_EDITCUT        = 10;
  IDH_EDITPASTE      = 11;
  IDH_EDITSELECTALL  = 12;
  IDH_EDITWORDWRAP   = 13;
  IDH_HELPABOUT      = 14;
```

Somewhere in your source file you can add a line that includes the help file header:

```
{$I HELP.INC}
```

Now you can use the name of the context ID rather than the actual integer value.

14

How the help include file is created depends on the tools you are using to write your help files. Most help-authoring software includes an option to generate an include file of some kind that contains the named constants. The specific implementation depends on whether the help file is being written by you or by a coworker and what help-authoring software you are using. If you are not using help-authoring software, you can simply type the symbols in.

Putting It to Work

It's time to put your newly acquired knowledge into practice. In this section, you add context-sensitive help to the ScratchPad program. (You knew we'd come back to old ScratchPad, didn't you?)

The book's code contains a simple help file for the ScratchPad program. Copy the help file, Scratch.hlp, to your working directory so that Delphi can find it when you build the ScratchPad application.

Context-sensitive help should take about 10 minutes to implement. Here you go:

1. Load the ScratchPad project. Go to the Application page of the Project Options dialog box and type Scratch.hlp in the Help File field. Click OK to close the dialog box. (Be sure you have moved the Scratch.hlp file into the project's directory.)

2. Display the ScratchPad main form in the Form Designer. Double-click the MainMenu icon to invoke the Menu Designer.

3. In the Menu Designer, select the File | New menu item. Locate the HelpContext property in the Object Inspector and change its value to 1.

4. Repeat with the remaining menu items. Use the values from Listing 14.1 to set the HelpContext properties of each menu item.

5. Choose Help | Contents. Set its Enabled property to True. Close the Menu Designer.

6. In the Form Designer, choose Help | Contents from the ScratchPad main menu. The Code Editor displays the HelpContentsClick function. Type this line at the cursor:

```
Application.HelpCommand(HELP_FINDER, 0);
```

7. Change the HelpContext property of the main form to 1000 (the context ID of the contents page).

Run the program and experiment with it. If you press F1 when the cursor is in the memo window, the Contents page of the help file will be displayed. If you highlight a menu item and press F1, help for that menu item is displayed. Also check out the Contents item on the main menu to see whether it works as expected.

> **Tip**
>
> If you compile and run the ScratchPad program for Day 14 that comes with the book's code, you will see that it has a feature not discussed here. The program has a Help Mode that can be used to get help on a specific speed-bar button or menu item. To start the Help Mode, press the Help button on the speedbar. The cursor changes to the help cursor. Now select any menu item or speedbar button. The help topic for the item selected is displayed. The Help Mode turns off automatically after you choose an item. Browse the source code to see how the Help Mode is implemented. This feature also makes use of special message handling as discussed later in the chapter.

Context-sensitive help is no longer a luxury. Whether your users are members of the general public or your coworkers, they are still your users. They demand certain features and context-sensitive help is one of them. As easy as context-sensitive help is to implement in a Delphi application, there is no reason for it to be missing from your applications.

Checking Errors with Exception Handling

Even in the most well-designed program, events that are beyond the control of the programmer can go wrong. Users make mistakes. For example, a user might input a bad value into a data field or open a file of the wrong type for your application. Whatever the scenario, you should be prepared to handle these types of errors wherever and whenever possible. You can't anticipate your users' every move, but you can anticipate some of the more common blunders and handle them gracefully.

Exception handling is essentially a sophisticated form of error checking. Although any program can implement and use them, exceptions are of primary benefit to users of components and other Object Pascal classes. For example, if you are using a component and something nasty happens within the component, you need to know about it. A well-written component will raise an exception when something goes wrong. You can catch that exception and handle it however you want—maybe by terminating the program or by allowing your user to correct the problem and try again.

You might not write a lot of exception handling into your day-to-day code. Your primary use of exceptions will be in handling exceptions that VCL raises when things go wrong within a component. If you write components, you will almost certainly use exception handling more frequently.

14

> **Note**
>
> The use of exceptions in your programs should be reserved for extreme error conditions. You should raise an exception when the error condition is serious enough to make continued use of the program difficult. Most runtime errors can be handled with parameter checking, validation of user input, and other more traditional error-checking techniques.

A full discussion of exception handling could easily take an entire chapter, so I limit this discussion to how you can handle exceptions raised by VCL components.

Exception-Handling Keywords: `try`, `except`, `finally`, and `raise`

Exception-handling syntax is not terribly complicated. The four exception-handling keywords are `try`, `except`, `finally`, and `raise`. The `try`, `except`, and `finally` keywords are used when handling exceptions, and the `raise` keyword is used to initiate an exception. Let's look at these in more detail.

try with except

SYNTAX ▼

```
try
  TryStatements
except
  on TypeToCatch do begin
    ExceptStatements
  end;
end;
```

The `try` keyword marks the beginning of the `try` block. The statements in `TryStatements` are executed. If any exceptions are raised during the execution of `TryStatements`, `ExceptStatements` are executed. If no exception is raised, `ExceptStatements` are ignored and program execution proceeds to the statement following the end statement. `TypeToCatch` is of the VCL exception handling classes. If the optional `TypeToCatch` is

▲ not specified, all exceptions are caught regardless of the type of exception raised.

try with finally

SYNTAX ▼

```
try
  TryStatements
finally
  FinallyStatements
end;
```

The `try` keyword marks the beginning of the `try` block. The statements in `TryStatements` are executed. `FinallyStatements` will always be executed regardless of

▲ whether an exception occurs in `TryStatements`.

Before I attempt to explain the try and except keywords, let's look at a simple example. Listing 14.2 contains the File | Open event handler from the Picture Viewer program you created on Day 4, "The Delphi IDE Explored." The event handler has been modified to use exception handling. If you recall, this code attempts to load a picture file (.bmp, .wmf, or .ico). If the file chosen by the user is not a picture file, VCL raises an exception. If that happens, you need to catch the exception and display a message box telling the user that the file is not a picture file.

LISTING 14.2. AN EXCEPTION-HANDLING EXAMPLE.

```
01: procedure TMainForm.Open1Click(Sender: TObject);
02: var
03:    Child : TChild;
04: begin
05:    if OpenPictureDialog.Execute then begin
06:       Child := TChild.Create(Self);
07:       with Child.Image.Picture do begin
08:          try
09:             LoadFromFile(OpenPictureDialog.FileName);
10:             Child.ClientWidth := Width;
11:             Child.ClientHeight := Height;
12:          except
13:             Child.Close;
14:             Application.MessageBox(
15:                'This file is not a Windows image file.',
16:                'Picture Viewer Error', MB_ICONHAND or MB_OK);
17:             Exit;
18:          end;
19:       end;
20:       Child.Caption :=
21:          ExtractFileName(OpenPictureDialog.FileName);
22:       Child.Show;
23:    end;
24: end;
```

In this code, you see a try block (line 8) and an except block (line 12). The try block is used to define the code for which an exception might be raised. The try statement tells the compiler, "Try this and see if it works." If the code works, the except block is ignored and program execution continues. If any of the statements inside the try block raise an exception, the code within the except block is executed. The except block must immediately follow the try block.

It is important to realize that as soon as an exception is raised, program execution jumps immediately to the except block. In this example, the call to LoadFromFile on line 9

14

could raise an exception. If an exception is raised, program execution jumps to the first statement following the except keyword. In that case, lines 10 and 11 will never be executed.

Raising Exceptions

As you can see, the except statement catches an exception that was raised somewhere in the program. Most of the time, this means an exception was raised in VCL somewhere (or in a third-party component library if you have other component libraries installed). An exception is raised by using the raise keyword. The code that raises the exception does so for a particular class. For example, a typical raise statement might look like this:

```
if BadParameter then
  raise EInvalidArgument.Create('A bad parameter was passed');
```

The raise statement raises an instance of an exception-handling class, EInvalidArgument in this case. When you write your own code, you can raise exceptions of the exception classes created by VCL or you can create your own exception classes. Let's say you have an error code 111 for a particular type of error and that you have an exception class named EMyException. In that case, you can write the raise statement like this:

```
raise EMyException.Create('Error 111');
```

The compiler makes a copy of the object being raised and passes it on to the except statement immediately following the try block (I'll get back to that in a moment).

More on except

As I said, for starters your involvement with exceptions will likely be in catching VCL exceptions. If something goes wrong in a VCL component, VCL is going to raise an exception. If you do not handle the exception, VCL will handle it in the default manner. Usually this means that a message box will be displayed that describes the error that occurred. By catching these exceptions in your code, you can decide how they should be handled rather than accepting the default behavior.

Take a look at Listing 14.2 again. Starting at line 12, you see this code:

```
except
  Child.Close;
  Application.MessageBox(
    'This file is not a Windows image file.',
    'Picture Viewer Error', MB_ICONHAND or MB_OK);
  Exit;
end;
```

The except keyword tells the compiler that you want to catch all exceptions of any type. Because no case statement follows the except statement, the code in the except block will be executed regardless of the type of exception raised. This is convenient if you don't know what type of exception a particular piece of code will raise or if you want to catch any and all exceptions regardless of the type. In the real world, though, you will probably need to be more specific in what exceptions you catch.

Let's go back to Listing 14.2 again. The code on line 9 might raise an exception if the file the user is trying to open is not a graphics file. If that happens, VCL will raise an EInvalidGraphic exception. You can catch that type of exception only and let all others be handled in the default manner. The code looks like this:

```
except
  on EInvalidGraphic do begin
    Child.Close;
    Application.MessageBox(
      'This file is not a Windows image file.',
      'Picture Viewer Error', MB_ICONHAND or MB_OK);
    Exit;
  end;
end;
```

Notice that this code is catching an EInvalidGraphic exception only. This is the preferred method of catching exceptions. Now any exceptions of this type will be caught by the except block and all other exception types will be handled in the default manner.

It is important to understand that when you catch an exception, code execution continues after executing the except block. One of the advantages to catching exceptions is that you can recover from the exception and continue program execution. Notice the Exit statement in the preceding code snippet. In this case, you don't want to continue code execution following the exception, so you exit the procedure after handling the exception.

 Note

> VCL will handle many types of exceptions automatically, but it cannot account for every possibility. An exception that is not handled is called an *unhandled exception*. If an unhandled exception occurs, Windows generates an error message and your application is terminated. Try to anticipate what exceptions might occur in your application and do your best to handle them.

Multiple Exception Types

14

You can catch multiple exception types in your except block. For example, say you have written code that calls some VCL methods and also calls some functions in your program that might raise an exception. If a VCL EInvalidGraphic exception occurs, you want to handle it. In addition, your own code might raise an exception of type `EMyOwnException` (a class you have written for handling exceptions). You want to handle that exception in a different manner. Given that scenario, you write the code like this:

```
try
  OneOfMyFunctions;
  Image.Picture.LoadFromFile('test.bmp');
  AnotherOfMyFunctions;
except
  on EInvalidGraphic do begin
    { do some stuff }
  end;
  on EMyOwnException do begin
    { do some stuff }
  end;
end;
```

In this case you are preparing to catch either a VCL `EInvalidGraphic` exception or your `EMyOwnException`. You want to handle each type of exception in a specific manner, so you catch each type of exception independently.

> **Note**
>
> Creating your own exception handling class can be as simple as one line of code:
>
> ```
> type
>   EMyOwnException = class(Exception);
> ```
>
> Often you create you own exception classes simply to distinguish the type of exception. No additional code is required.

Note that in the preceding examples you are catching a VCL exception class, but you aren't actually doing anything with the class instance passed to the `except` block. In this case you don't really care what information the `EInvalidGraphic` class contains because it is enough to simply know that the exception occurred.

To use the specific instance of the exception class passed to the `except` block, declare a variable for the exception class in the do statement—for example,

```
try
  Image.Picture.LoadFromFile('test.bmp');
except
  on E : EInvalidGraphic do begin
    { do something with E }
  end;
end;
```

Here the variable E is declared as a pointer to the EInvalidGraphic class passed to the except block. You can then use E to access properties or methods of the EInvalidGraphic class. Note that the variable E is valid only within the block where it is declared. You should check the online help for the specific type of VCL exception-handling class you are interested in for more information about what properties and methods are available for that class.

Tip

The VCL exception classes all have a Message property that contains a textual description of the exception that occurred. You can use this property to display a message to the user:

```
except
  on E : EInvalidGraphic do begin
    { do some stuff }
    MessageDlg(E.Message, mtError, [mbOk], 0);
  end;
end;
```

Sometimes the VCL messages might not be descriptive enough for your liking. In those cases you can create your own error message, but often the Message property is sufficient.

Using finally

The finally keyword defines a section of code that is called regardless of whether an exception occurs. In other words, the code in the finally section will be called if an exception is raised and will be called if no exception is raised. If you use a finally block, you cannot use except.

The primary reason to use finally is to ensure that all dynamically allocated memory is properly disposed of in the event an exception is raised—for example,

```
procedure TForm1.FormCreate(Sender: TObject);
var
  Buffer : Pointer;
begin
  Buffer := AllocMem(1024);
  try
    { Code here that might raise an exception. }
  finally
    FreeMem(Buffer);
  end;
end;
```

14

Here, the memory allocated for Buffer will always be freed properly regardless of whether an exception is raised in the try block.

Catching Unhandled Exceptions at the Application Level

Your application can also handle exceptions at the application level. TApplication has an event called OnException that will occur any time an unhandled exception is raised in your application. By responding to this event, you can catch any exceptions raised by your applications.

 Note

> This event occurs when an unhandled exception is raised. Any exceptions you catch with try and except are handled; therefore, the OnException event will not occur for those exceptions.

You hook the OnException event just like you do when hooking the OnHint event like you did earlier:

1. Add a method declaration to the main form's class declaration:

   ```
   procedure MyOnException(Sender : TObject; E : Exception);
   ```

2. Add the method body to the main form's implementation section:

   ```
   procedure TForm1.MyOnException(Sender : TObject; E : Exception);
   begin
     { Do whatever necessary to handle the exception here. }
   end;
   ```

3. Assign your MyOnException method to the OnException event of the Application object:

   ```
   Application.OnException := MyOnException;
   ```

Now your MyOnException method will be called when an unhandled exception occurs.

 Caution

> If you do not handle an exception properly, you can lock up your program and possibly even crash Windows. It is usually best to let VCL and Windows handle exceptions unless you know exactly how to handle them.

The ShowException function can be used to display a message box that describes the error that occurred. This function is usually called by the default OnException handler, but you can use it in your applications as well. One of the parameters of the OnException event handler is a pointer to an Exception object (Exception is VCL's base exception-

handling class). To display the error message box, pass the `Exception` object to the
`ShowException` function:

```
procedure TForm1.MyOnException(Sender : TObject; E : Exception);
begin
  { Do whatever necessary to handle the exception here
  { then display the error message. }
  Application.ShowException(E);
end;
```

Now the error message box is displayed just as it would be if VCL were dealing with the
unhandled exception.

As you can see, handling exceptions at the application level is an advanced exception-
handling technique and is not something you should attempt unless you know exactly
what you're doing.

Debugging and Exception Handling

Simply put, debugging when using exception handling can be a bit of a pain. Each time
an exception is raised, the debugger pauses program execution at the `except` block just
as if a breakpoint were set on that line. If the `except` block is in your code, the execution
point is displayed as it would be if you had stopped at a breakpoint. You can restart the
program again by clicking the Run button, or you can step through your code.

Note

> You might not be able to continue execution of your program after an
> exception is raised. Whether you can continue debugging depends on what
> went wrong in your program.

Sometimes the `except` block is in the VCL code. This will be the case for VCL exceptions that you don't handle in your code. In this circumstance, the CPU view will show
the execution point.

Another aspect of debugging with exceptions is that the VCL exception message box is
displayed even when you are handling the exception yourself. This can be confusing and
somewhat annoying if you haven't encountered it before. To prevent the VCL message
box from being displayed and the debugger from breaking on exceptions, go to the
Language Exceptions page of the Debugger Options dialog box and uncheck the Stop on
Delphi Exceptions check box at the top of the page. When Stop on Delphi Exceptions is
off, the debugger will not pause program execution when a VCL exception is raised.

As with many other aspects of Delphi and VCL, learning exception handling takes
some time. Remember to use exception handling where necessary, but use traditional
error-handling techniques for the minor errors.

14

The book's code contains a program called EHTest. This program demonstrates raising and catching several kinds of exceptions. For this program to function properly, be sure that the Stop on Delphi Exceptions option is off as described earlier. You can download the book's code at http://www.mcp.com/info. Figure 14.2 shows the EHTest program running.

FIGURE 14.2.

The EHTest *program running.*

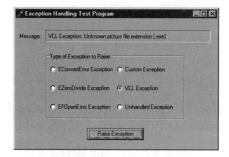

Using the Registry

Once upon a time, Windows programs used configuration files (.ini files) to store application-specific information. The master configuration file is, as you probably know, called WIN.INI. Applications could store system-wide information in WIN.INI or application-specific configuration data in a private .ini file. This approach has several advantages, but also some disadvantages.

Somewhere along the line someone smarter (presumably) than I decided that the new way to do things would be to use the Registry to store application-specific configuration information. Throughout the land, knaves everywhere bowed to the king and said, "The Registry is good." Whether good or bad, conventional wisdom has it that the use of .ini files is out and the use of the Registry is in.

The term *Registry* is short for the Windows Registration Database. The Registry contains a wide variety of information about your Windows configuration. Just about every option and every setting in your Windows setup is stored in the Registry. In addition to the system information stored in the Registry, you will find data specific to installed applications. The type of information stored for each application depends entirely on the application but can include information such as the last size and position of the window, a list of most recently used documents for the application, the last directory used when opening a file, and on and on. The possibilities are endless.

Windows 95 and NT come with a program called the Registry Editor (REGEDIT.EXE) that can be used to browse the Registry and to make changes to the entries in it.

Caution Be very careful about making changes to the Registry! Registry changes can affect how individual programs operate and even how Windows itself operates.

Figure 14.3 shows the Registry Editor as it displays the Delphi Code Insight options.

FIGURE 14.3.

The Windows Registry Editor.

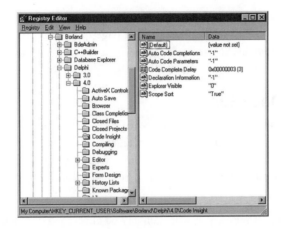

As you can see from Figure 14.3, the Registry is hierarchical. You can approach the Registry exactly as you approach files and directories on a hard drive.

Registry Keys

Each item in the Registry is called a *key*. A key can be likened to a directory on your hard drive. To access a particular key, you first have to open the key. After the key is open, you can write to or read from it. Take a look at Figure 14.3. The key that is being displayed is

```
My Computer\HKEY_CURRENT_USER\Software\Borland\Delphi\4.0\Code Insight
```

You can't see every branch of the Registry tree, but if you look at the status bar of the Registry Editor you can see the current key displayed. Also notice that the Delphi\4.0 key has several *subkeys*. You can create as many keys and subkeys as you want for your application.

An individual key can store data in its *data items*. Every key has a data item called (Default). The default value is not normally used because you will almost always create

14

your own data items for a particular key. By looking at Figure 14.3, you can see that the Code Insight key has the following data items:

```
Auto Code Completions
Auto Code Parameters
Code Complete Delay
Declaration Information
Explorer Visible
Scope Sort
```

If you've been paying attention, you will recognize that these data items correspond to the Code Insight options on the Code Insight page of the Environment Options dialog box. Each data item has an associated value. You can write to the Registry to change the data item or you can read the data item.

Registry Data Types

The Registry has the capability to store several different types of data in the data items. The primary types of data are the binary data, string, and integer data types. The *binary data type* can be used to store any kind of binary data. You can, for example, store an array of integers in a binary data item. You probably won't directly use the binary data type very often, if ever.

For most of your purposes, you will probably be concerned only with reading and writing strings or integer values. As you can see in Figure 14.3, even numerical data can be stored as strings. It's really up to you to decide how to store data in the Registry.

Up to this point, I have discussed what you can do with the Registry but not *how* you do it. Let's look at that next.

The TRegistry Class

The Windows API provides several functions for Registry manipulation. These functions include RegCreateKey, RegOpenKey, RegQueryValue, RegSetValue, RegDeleteKey, and many more. Dealing with the Registry at the API level is a bit tedious. I am thankful (and you should be, too) that the folks at Borland thought to provide a VCL class called TRegistry that encapsulates Registry operations. This class provides everything you need to write to and read from the Registry. Before I get into how to use the TRegistry class, let's go over the properties and methods of this class.

TRegistry Properties

TRegistry has just four properties. The CurrentKey property contains the value of the current key, which is an integer value that identifies the key. When you call a TRegistry method, that method acts on the current key. The CurrentKey property is set for you when you open a key. This property can be read, but reading it is of dubious value.

The RootKey and CurrentPath properties work together to build a text string to the current key. The CurrentPath property contains a text description of the current key's path excluding the RootKey value. Take this key, for example:

`\HKEY_CURRENT_USER\Software\Borland\Delphi\4.0\Code Insight`

In this case the root key, `\HKEY_CURRENT_USER`, comes from the RootKey property, and the value, `Software\Borland\Delphi\4.0\Code Insight`, comes from the CurrentPath property.

Note

> By default, the RootKey has a value of `\HKEY_CURRENT_USER`. This is where you should store application-specific data, so it is not normally necessary to change the root key. If you need to change the root key, you can assign a new value to the RootKey property. Note that the root key types are not string values, but are special Windows-defined values. Other root key values include `HKEY_CLASSES_ROOT`, `HKEY_LOCAL_MACHINE`, `HKEY_USERS`, `HKEY_CURRENT_CONFIG`, and `HKEY_DYN_DATA`.

The LazyWrite property determines how the application writes the data to the specific key. If LazyWrite is True, control is immediately returned to the application when you close the key. In other words, the writing of the key begins and then your application goes on its way. If LazyWrite is False, control will not return to the application until the writing of the key is completed. By default, LazyWrite is True, and you should leave it set to True unless you have some critical data that needs to be written before your application resumes operation.

TRegistry Methods

The TRegistry class has several methods that you use to read from and write to the Registry. Table 14.1 lists the primary methods and their descriptions.

TABLE 14.1. PRIMARY METHODS OF TRegistry.

Method	Description
CloseKey	Closes the key and writes the data to the key. You should close a key as soon as you are done with it, but you don't have to specifically call CloseKey because the TRegistry destructor will close the key for you.
CreateKey	Creates a key but does not open it for use. Use the OpenKey method rather than CreateKey if you are going to create the key and begin writing data to it.

continues

14

TABLE 14.1. CONTINUED

Method	Description
DeleteKey	Deletes the specified key. You can specify any key to delete. To delete the current key, pass an empty string to DeleteKey.
GetKeyNames	Returns all of the subkeys for the current key in a TStrings object. You can use this method if you need to iterate all the subkeys for a given key.
GetValueNames	Returns the names of all of the data items for the current key. Use this method if you need to iterate the data items of a given key.
KeyExists	Returns True if the key exists or False if it does not exist. You can use this method to check for the existence of a key before attempting to read the key.
LoadKey	Loads a key previously stored on disk. See the Delphi online help for specific details.
OpenKey	Opens the specified key. If the key does not exist, the value of the CanCreate parameter determines whether the key will be automatically created. Use this method rather than CreateKey if you are going to create the key and begin writing data to it because OpenKey creates the key and then opens it, whereas CreateKey just creates the key but does not open it.
ReadBinaryData	Reads binary data from the specified data item.
ReadBool	Reads a Boolean value from the specified data item.
ReadDateTime	Reads a date and time value from the specified data item. The returned value is an instance of the TDateTime class. To retrieve just a date value, use ReadDate; to retrieve just a time value, use ReadTime.
ReadFloat	Reads a floating-point value from the specified data item.
ReadInteger	Reads an integer value from the specified data item.
ReadString	Reads a string value from the specified data item.
SaveKey	Saves a key to disk so that it can be loaded later with LoadKey. Generally speaking, you shouldn't store more than 2KB (2048 bytes) of data by using this method.
ValueExists	Returns True if the specified data item exists.
WriteBinaryData	Writes a binary data item to the specified key. Use this item to store arrays or other types of binary data.
WriteBool	Writes a Boolean value to the specified data item. The value is converted to an integer and then stored in the data item.

Method	Description
WriteDateTime	Writes a TDateTime object to the specified data item. To store just a date object, use WriteDate. To store just a time object, use WriteTime. The TDateTime object is converted to a binary data type before being stored.
WriteFloat	Writes a floating-point value to the specified data item after converting it to binary data.
WriteInteger	Writes an integer value to the specified data item.
WriteString	Writes a string to the specified data item.

Although there are a lot of methods listed in Table 14.1, many of them perform the same operations—they just use different data types. When you know how to use one of these methods, you pretty much know how to use them all. Notice that several of these methods convert the value passed to binary data and then store it in the Registry.

Using TRegistry

Using TRegistry is fairly easy. Most of your interaction with the Registry will require just these four steps:

1. Create an instance of the TRegistry class.
2. Create, if necessary, and open a key by using the OpenKey method.
3. Read or write data using one or more of the Read or Write functions.
4. Free the instance of the TRegistry class.

> **Note**
>
> Before you can use TRegistry, you must add the Registry unit to your form's uses list.

The following code illustrates these steps:

```
procedure TForm1.FormCreate(Sender: TObject);
var
  Reg        : TRegistry;
  KeyGood    : Boolean;
  Top        : Integer;
  Left       : Integer;
  Width      : Integer;
  Height     : Integer;
```

14

```
begin
  Reg := TRegistry.Create;
  try
    KeyGood := Reg.OpenKey(
      'Software\SAMS\Delphi 4 in 21 Days', False);
    if not KeyGood then begin
      Top := Reg.ReadInteger('Top');
      Left := Reg.ReadInteger('Left');
      Width := Reg.ReadInteger('Width');
      Height := Reg.ReadInteger('Height');
      SetBounds(Left, Top, Width, Height);
    end;
  finally
    Reg.Free;
  end;
end;
```

This code opens a key and reads values for the top and left coordinates and the width and height of a form. It then calls the SetBounds function to move or size the window. Notice that the result of the OpenKey method is assigned to a Boolean variable. OpenKey returns True if the key was successfully opened and False if it was not. If the key was successfully opened, the individual data items are read. You should always check the return value of OpenKey if there is any doubt that opening the key might fail. Notice also that this code uses a try...finally block to ensure that the Reg variable is properly freed before the function returns.

Note
VCL will raise exceptions if reading data from or writing data to a key fails. If you attempt to read data from an unopened key, you will get an exception. Either be prepared to handle the exception or be sure to check the return value from OpenKey before reading or writing data items.

Finally, notice that the key is not specifically closed in the preceding code. If you neglect to close the key, the TRegistry destructor will close the key for you. In that case, the destructor will be called (and the key closed) as soon as the Reg object is deleted, so an explicit call to CloseKey is not necessary.

Note
The OpenKey function automatically prepends the value of the RootKey property (HKEY_CURRENT_USER by default) to the front of the string passed to OpenKey, so you don't have to include the root when opening a key.

Writing to the Registry

I have the cart just slightly before the horse here because I am talking about reading from the Registry when you haven't yet written to it. No matter—writing to the Registry is just as simple:

```
procedure TForm1.FormDestroy(Sender: TObject);
var
  Reg        : TRegistry;
begin
  Reg := TRegistry.Create;
  try
    Reg.OpenKey(
      'Software\SAMS\Delphi 4 in 21 Days', True);
    Reg.WriteInteger('Top', Top);
    Reg.WriteInteger('Left', Left);
    Reg.WriteInteger('Width', Width);
    Reg.WriteInteger('Height', Height);
  finally
    Reg.Free;
  end;
end;
```

This code simply opens a key and writes the form's Top, Left, Width, and Height properties to the key using the WriteInteger method. Notice that the last parameter of the OpenKey method is True. This specifies that the key should be created if it does not yet exist. If you use this construct, you should never need to call the CreateKey method at all.

That's basically all there is to reading values from and writing values to the Registry. The other data reading and writing methods are just variations on the previous code snippet.

Using the Registry to Store Data

Listing 14.3 shows the main unit of a program called RegTest that uses the Registry to store application-specific data. This program stores several items in the Registry: the last size and position of the window; the window state (normal, minimized, or maximized); the last directory, last file, and last filter index used when opening a file with the File Open dialog box; and the date and time the program was last run. To clear out the Registry key created by the RegTest program, you can click the Delete Key button on the main form (see Figure 14.4, later in the chapter). This program is also included with the book's code.

14

LISTING 14.3. RegTestU.pas.

```pascal
unit RegTestU;

interface

uses
  Windows, Messages, SysUtils, Classes, Graphics, Controls,
  Forms, Dialogs,  Menus, StdCtrls, ExtCtrls, Registry;

type
  TForm1 = class(TForm)
    Panel1: TPanel;
    Label1: TLabel;
    DeleteKey: TButton;
    Panel2: TPanel;
    Label2: TLabel;
    Label3: TLabel;
    TimeLabel: TLabel;
    DateLabel: TLabel;
    MainMenu: TMainMenu;
    File1: TMenuItem;
    FileOpen: TMenuItem;
    FileExit: TMenuItem;
    OpenDialog: TopenDialog;
    procedure FormCreate(Sender: TObject);
    procedure FileOpenClick(Sender: TObject);
    procedure FormDestroy(Sender: TObject);
    procedure FileExitClick(Sender: TObject);
    procedure DeleteKeyClick(Sender: TObject);
  private
    { Private declarations }
    KeyDeleted : Boolean;
  public
    { Public declarations }
  end;

var
  Form1: TForm1;

implementation

{$R *.DFM}

procedure TForm1.FormCreate(Sender: TObject);
var
  Reg       : TRegistry;
  KeyGood   : Boolean;
  DT        : TDateTime;
  Top       : Integer;
```

```
    Left      : Integer;
    Width     : Integer;
    Height    : Integer;
begin
  { Initialize the KeyDeleted variable to False. This
  { variable is used if the user deletes the key from
  { the program. See the MainFormClose function. }
  KeyDeleted := False;

  { Create a TRegistry object to access the registry. }
  Reg := TRegistry.Create;

  try
    { Open the key. }
    KeyGood := Reg.OpenKey(
      'Software\SAMS\Delphi 4 in 21 Days', False);

    { See if the key is open. If not, then this is the first
    { time the program has been run so there's nothing to do. }
    { If the key is good then read all of the data items
    { pertinent to application startup. }
    if KeyGood then begin
      Top := Reg.ReadInteger('Top');
      Left := Reg.ReadInteger('Left');
      Width := Reg.ReadInteger('Width');
      Height := Reg.ReadInteger('Height');
      SetBounds(Left, Top, Width, Height);
      WindowState :=
        TWindowState(Reg.ReadInteger('WindowState'));

      { The TDateTime class is a handy item to have around
      { if you are doing date and time operations. }
      DT := Reg.ReadDate('Date and Time');
      DateLabel.Caption := DateToStr(DT);
      TimeLabel.Caption := TimeToStr(DT);
    end;
  finally
    Reg.Free;
  end;
end;

procedure TForm1.FileOpenClick(Sender: TObject);
var
  Reg     : TRegistry;
begin
  { This function displays the File Open dialog but
  { doesn't actually open a file. The last path, filter,
  { and filename are written to the registry when the
  { user presses OK. }
```

14

continues

LISTING 14.3. CONTINUED

```delphi
  { Create a TRegistry object to access the registry. }
  Reg := TRegistry.Create;

  try
    { Open the key. }
    Reg.OpenKey('Software\SAMS\Delphi 4 in 21 Days', True);

    { Read the values. Check if the value exists first. }
    if Reg.ValueExists('LastDir') then
      OpenDialog.InitialDir := Reg.ReadString('LastDir');
    if Reg.ValueExists('LastFile') then
      OpenDialog.FileName := Reg.ReadString('LastFile');
    if Reg.ValueExists('FilterIndex') then
      OpenDialog.FilterIndex := Reg.ReadInteger('FilterIndex');

    { Display the File Open dialog. If the user presses OK then }
    { save the path, filename, and filter to the registry. }
    if OpenDialog.Execute then begin
      Reg.WriteString('LastDir',
        ExtractFilePath(OpenDialog.FileName));
      Reg.WriteString('LastFile',
        ExtractFileName(OpenDialog.FileName));
      Reg.WriteInteger
        ('FilterIndex', OpenDialog.FilterIndex);
    end;
  finally
    Reg.Free;
  end;
end;

procedure TForm1.FormDestroy(Sender: TObject);
var
  Reg       : TRegistry;
begin
  { If the user pressed the button to the key then }
  { we don't want to write out the information. }
  if KeyDeleted then
    Exit;

  { Create a TRegistry object to access the registry. }
  Reg := TRegistry.Create;

  try
    { Open the key. }
    Reg.OpenKey(
      'Software\SAMS\Delphi 4 in 21 Days', True);
```

```
    { Write out the values. }
    Reg.WriteInteger('WindowState', Ord(WindowState));
    if WindowState <> wsMaximized then begin
      Reg.WriteInteger('Top', Top);
      Reg.WriteInteger('Left', Left);
      Reg.WriteInteger('Width', Width);
      Reg.WriteInteger('Height', Height);
    end;
    Reg.WriteDate('Date and Time', Now);
  finally
    Reg.Free;
  end;
end;

procedure TForm1.FileExitClick(Sender: TObject);
begin
  Close;
end;

procedure TForm1.DeleteKeyClick(Sender: TObject);
var
  Reg        : TRegistry;
begin
  { The user pressed the Key button so delete the key. }
  { Set a flag so that we don't re-create the key when
  { the program closes. }
  Reg := TRegistry.Create;
  try
    Reg.DeleteKey('Software\SAMS');
    KeyDeleted := True;
  finally
    Reg.Free;
  end;
end;

end.
```

By examining this listing and running the RegTest program, you can learn a lot about using the Registry in your applications. Figure 14.4 shows the RegTest program running; Figure 14.5 shows the Registry key that is created by the program.

14

Figure 14.4.

The RegTest *program running.*

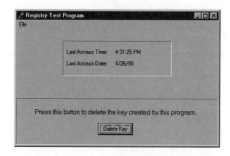

Figure 14.5.

The Registry Editor showing the key created by the RegTest *program.*

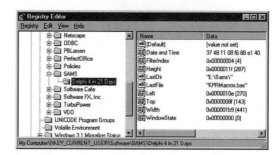

Note

The TRegIniFile class is a specialized Registry-manipulation class that can be used for applications that are moving from storing data in .ini files to storing data in the Registry. See the online help for TRegIniFile for complete information.

Note

Although conventional wisdom has it that the Registry is the place to store application-specific data, you still can use .ini files if you like. One advantage to using .ini files is that less-sophisticated users can edit them with a text editor when necessary (which is also a disadvantage in some cases). To make using .ini files easier, VCL includes the TIniFile class. Be sure to check out this class if you intend to use .ini files in your application.

Implementing Specialized Message Handling

On Day 11, "Delphi Tools and Options," I talked about Windows messages as part of the discussion of the WinSight program. For the most part, Delphi makes message handling easy through its use of events. As I have said, an event is usually generated in response to a Windows message being sent to an application. There are times, however, when you might want to handle messages yourself. There are two primary scenarios that require you to handle messages outside of the normal Delphi messaging system:

- Windows messages that VCL does not handle
- User-defined messages

Handling messages on your own requires a few extra programming techniques; you learn about those techniques in this section.

More on Windows Messages

How do Windows messages get sent? Some messages are sent by Windows itself to instruct the window to do something or to notify the window that something has happened. At other times, messages are sent by the programmer or, in the case of VCL, by the framework the programmer is using. Regardless of who is sending the messages, you can be guaranteed that a lot of messages are flying around at any given millisecond.

Message Types

Basically, messages fall into two categories:

- Command messages—Cause something to occur either in Windows or within a particular control.
- Notification messages—Sent by Windows to notify you that something has happened.

To illustrate the difference between these two types of messages, let's take a look at the standard edit control. The standard Windows edit control has almost 80 command messages and nearly 20 notification messages. Surprised? It's true, and don't forget that the edit control is just one control out of dozens of Windows controls.

Note

> I lied to you back on Day 5, "The Visual Component Model," when I talked about events (well, not exactly). At that time I said that there are over 200 messages that Windows could send to an application, and that is essentially true. But when you consider messages specific to controls as well as messages that can be sent to main windows, the count goes to something like 700 messages. Wow! And that only includes command messages, not notification messages. You should have a new appreciation for VCL after reading this section.

14

A programmer writing a Windows program in C has to send a lot of messages to accomplish tasks. For example, to get the length of the currently selected text in an edit control requires the following code:

```
int start;
int end;
long result = SendMessage(hWndEdit, EM_GETSEL, 0, 0);
start = LOWORD(result);
end = HIWORD(result);
int length = end - start;
```

This is how C programmers spend their days. Contrast that with the VCL way of doing things:

```
Length := Edit.SelLength;
```

Which do you prefer? Regardless of who is sending the message, command messages are used heavily both by programmers and by Windows itself.

Notification messages, however, are sent only by Windows itself. Notification messages tell Windows that something has happened within a control. For example, the EN_CHANGE message is sent when the contents of an edit control have changed. VCL has an event for the Edit, MaskEdit, and Memo components called OnChange that is triggered in response to the EN_CHANGE notification message (as well as some others). Programmers using traditional Windows programming tools have to intercept these messages and deal with them as needed—which brings you to the next subject: message parameters.

WPARAM, LPARAM, and Message Cracking

Every Windows message has two parameters: the WPARAM (short for word parameter) and the LPARAM (short for long parameter).

Note

In 32-bit Windows, WPARAM and LPARAM are both 32-bit values. In 16-bit Windows, the WPARAM is a 16-bit value (a Word), and the LPARAM is a 32-bit value (a LongInt). That ends your history lesson on the names WPARAM and LPARAM. And now back to your program. . .

These two parameters could be likened to the parameters sent to a function. When a Windows message is received, the parameters are examined to obtain information specific to the message being sent. For example, the WM_LBUTTONDOWN message is a notification message that is sent when the left mouse button is clicked on a window. For a WM_LBUTTONDOWN message, the WPARAM contains a special code that tells which of the other mouse buttons were pressed and also what keys on the keyboard were pressed when the event occurred. The LPARAM contains the coordinates of the mouse cursor when the mouse button was clicked: the X position is contained in the low-order word and the Y position is contained in the high-order word.

To get at this information, the message must be *cracked* to reveal what's inside. The code for cracking a WM_LBUTTONDOWN message can look like this:

```
procedure MessageCracker(wParam, lParam : Integer);
var
  Shift, X, Y : Integer;
begin
  Shift := wParam;
  X := LOWORD(lParam);
  Y := HIWORD(lParam);
  { Code that does something with Shift, X, and Y. }
end;
```

This is a fairly simple example, but it's indicative of what goes on each time a message is handled in a Windows application.

Note

Because the X and Y coordinates in the preceding example are contained in a single value (the lParam variable), they must be individually extracted. HIWORD and LOWORD are used for that purpose. In the C/C++ programming world, HIWORD and LOWORD are Windows macros. In Object Pascal, LOWORD is simply a type that is identical to a Word. HIWORD is a function that extracts the left-most 16 bits from a 32-bit variable. LOWORD, when used as you see in the preceding code snippet, extracts the right-most 16 bits.

You'll be relieved to know that VCL performs message cracking for you for all VCL events. For example, if you set up a message handler for the OnMouseDown event, Delphi generates a function in your code that looks like this:

```
procedure TForm1.FormMouseDown(Sender: TObject; Button: TMouseButton;
  Shift: TShiftState; X, Y: Integer);
begin
  if Button = mbLeft then begin
    { Put your code here. }
  end;
end;
```

As you can see, the event handler generated by Delphi contains all the information you need. VCL will crack the WPARAM and LPARAM for you and hand them to you in sensible pieces that you can deal with more easily. This same thing happens for every message for which VCL creates an event.

14

> **Note**
>
> VCL takes messaging and message cracking one step further in the case of the mouse button messages. Windows actually generates up to three different mouse down messages: one for the left button being pressed, one for the middle button (if one exists), and yet another when the right button is pressed. VCL handles all of these messages in a single event. The TMouseButton parameter of the OnMouseDown event tells you which of the three buttons was pressed.

With that primer on Windows messages under your belt, let's take a brief look at exactly how to send messages.

Sending Versus Posting

The Windows API provides two functions for sending messages: PostMessage and SendMessage. The PostMessage function posts the message to the Windows message queue and immediately returns. This function simply hands the message to Windows and goes on its way. PostMessage returns 1 if the function call succeeded or 0 if it did not. (About the only reason for PostMessage to fail is if the message is sent to an invalid window.)

The SendMessage function, however, sends the message to Windows and waits until the message is carried out before returning. The return value from SendMessage depends on the message being sent. Sometimes the biggest reason to use SendMessage over PostMessage is because you need the return value from a particular message.

> **Note**
>
> The differences between situations when you use PostMessage versus SendMessage are subtle. For example, due to timing issues within Windows, there are times when sending a message will fail to have the effect you expected. In those cases you'll have to use PostMessage. The reverse is also true: Sometimes PostMessage is wrong for a given set of circumstances and you'll have to use SendMessage. Although this is not something you really need to be concerned with right now, it is something to file away for future reference.

You can use both PostMessage and SendMessage in your Delphi applications. For example, to post yourself a message you would do something like this:

```
PostMessage(Handle, WM_QUIT, 0, 0);
```

The first parameter of both `PostMessage` and `SendMessage` is the window handle of the window to which you want to send the message. In this case you are sending the message to the main form (assuming this code was written in the main form's source code unit).

In addition to the Windows API functions, VCL provides a method called `Perform` that you can use to send messages to any VCL window. `Perform` bypasses the Windows messaging system and sends the message directly to the message-handling mechanism for a given window. The `Perform` equivalent of the preceding example is as follows:

```
Perform(WM_QUIT, 0, 0);
```

You can use any of these three functions to send messages to your application and to other windows within your application.

Handling Events

You've already learned about handling VCL events, but a short review can't hurt. When a particular component receives a Windows message, it looks up the message and checks to see whether there is an event handler assigned for that particular message. If an event handler has been assigned for that event, VCL calls the event handler. If no event handler is assigned, the message is handled in the default manner. You can handle any messages you like and ignore the rest.

What happens in your event handlers depends on a variety of factors: the particular message being handled, what your program does in response to the message, and whether you are modifying the incoming message or just using the event handler as notification that the event occurred. As you get further into Windows programming, you will see that there are literally hundreds of things you might do in response to events.

Most of the time, you will be using the event handler for notification that a particular event occurred. Take the `OnMouseDown` event, for example. If you handle the `OnMouseDown` event, you are simply asking to be notified when the user clicks the component with the mouse (remember that forms are components, too). You probably are not going to modify the message parameters in any way; you just want to know that the event occurred. A great number of your event handlers will be used for notification purposes.

Sometimes, however, you want to change one or more of the message parameters before sending the message on its way. Let's say, for example, that you want to force the text in a particular edit control to uppercase. (You could set the `CharCase` property of the `Edit` component to `ecUpperCase`, of course, but let's stick with this example for now.) To

14

change all keystrokes to uppercase, you could do something like this in your `OnKeyPress` event handler:

```
procedure TForm1.Edit1KeyPress(Sender: TObject; var Key: Char);
begin
  if Key >= 'a' then
    Dec(Key, 32);
end;
```

In this way you are actually modifying some aspect of the message before it gets sent to VCL for processing. The parameters sent in the event handler are often passed by reference for exactly this reason.

Note
> Delphi protects you a bit by passing message parameters that you should not change by value rather than by reference (by `var` parameter). This is also true of message parameters for which changing the value has no effect. Take the `OnMouseDown` event discussed earlier. This event is for notification only. There is no point in modifying the `Button`, `Shift`, `X`, or `Y` parameters, so all are passed by value.

Whether you change one or more of the parameters sent depends entirely on the message and what you intend to do with the message. Over time, you will likely run into situations where modification of a particular message is required to cause Windows to behave in a particular way. At other times, you will not modify the parameters at all, but will inspect them to determine what is happening with your application. Because the possibilities are so numerous, I'll have to leave further exploration of message parameters as an exercise for the reader.

Handling Other Windows Messages

There will undoubtedly be some point when you need to respond to a Windows message for which VCL provides no event. When that time comes, you are going to want to know how to handle those messages, and that is what this section is about.

VCL provides events for the most commonly used Windows messages. Obviously, with over 700 Windows messages, VCL does not provide events for them all. The 80/20 theory says, among other things, that 20 percent of the people do 80 percent of the work. The same is probably true of Windows messages. VCL may only provide events for 20 percent of Windows messages, but they are the messages you will use 80 percent of the time. Still, there are plenty of Windows messages that VCL does not provide events for, and you need to know how to handle those messages when the time comes.

You'll be glad to know that you can handle just about any Windows message when you know how. After you have the basics down, each message is just a variation on the same theme. The mechanism that Delphi uses to handle messages not covered by VCL events is the message keyword. This keyword is used to associate a certain Windows message with a method in your code. When your window receives that message, the method is called. Hmmm. . . sounds like events, doesn't it? There are certainly some similarities.

Implementing Message Handling

Implementing message handling at this level is as easy as the following:

1. Add the method declaration for the message handler to the class declaration.

2. Add the definition of the message handler to your form's implementation section.

Here's an example of a method declaration for a method that handles the WM_ERASEBKGND message:

```
procedure WmEraseBkgnd(var Msg : TWMEraseBkgnd); message WM_ERASEBKGND;
```

Notice the message keyword at the end of the method declaration. The message keyword is followed by the Windows message that this method is designed to handle. Notice also that the method's parameter is a var TWMEraseBknd record. VCL has a message-cracking record for most Windows messages. The record name is the Windows message name preceded by T and minus the underscore.

As you can see, the Windows message WM_ERASEBKGND gets translated into the record named TWMEraseBkgnd. You sort of have to guess at the capitalization, but for the most part it makes perfect sense. This record gets passed along to the message handler (more on that in the next section). The method itself can be named anything you like, but the form you see here is traditional.

Note

> The message-cracking records are defined in the VCL unit called Messages.pas. Browse the Messages unit if you need information on a particular message-cracking record.

To put this in perspective, you need to see the entire class declaration for a class that implements custom message handling. Listing 14.4 shows a typical main form class declaration for a class that uses custom message handling.

14

LISTING 14.4. Message.h.

```
TMainForm = class(TForm)
    ShowTBoix: TButton;
    GroupBox1: TGroupBox;
    Hatched: TCheckBox;
    LetVCLHandle: TCheckBox;
    Instructions: TButton;
    procedure InstructionsClick(Sender: TObject);
    procedure ShowTBoixClick(Sender: TObject);
    procedure HatchedClick(Sender: TObject);
  private
    { Private declarations }
    procedure WmNCHitTest(var Msg : TWMNCHitTest);
      message WM_NCHITTEST;
    procedure WmEraseBkgnd(var Msg : TWMEraseBkgnd);
      message WM_ERASEBKGND;
    procedure WmGetMinMaxInfo(var Msg : TWMGetMinMaxInfo);
      message WM_GETMINMAXINFO;
    procedure MyMessage(var Msg : TMessage);
      message My_Message;
  public
    { Public declarations }
  end;
```

Notice in particular the method declarations in the private section. I put the message keyword on the line following the method declaration in order to keep the line length down. Normally you would put the message keyword immediately following the method declaration. In the end, it doesn't matter to the compiler how you write the declarations, so suit yourself. Don't let the declaration for the WmMyMessage method throw you. This is the message handler for a user-defined message. I'll talk about user-defined messages a little later.

The Message-Handling Method

The message-handling method (or just *message handler*) is the method that is called whenever the message you are responding to is received by your application. The message handler has a single parameter: the message-cracker record I discussed earlier. The message handler for the WM_ERASEBKGND message would look like this:

```
procedure TMainForm.WmEraseBkgnd(var Msg: TWMEraseBkgnd);
begin
  { Your message handling code here. }
end;
```

As I said, the message-cracker record will contain all the parameters necessary to handle the message. The message-cracker record for the WM_ERASEBKGND message is as follows:

```
TWMEraseBkgnd = record
  Msg: Cardinal;
  DC: HDC;
  Unused: Longint;
  Result: Longint;
end;
```

All message-cracking records have two data members in common: Msg and Result. The Msg member contains the message that is being sent. This parameter is used by VCL and is not something you will be concerned with.

The Result data member, however, is important. This is used to set the return value for the message you are handling. The return value varies from message to message. For example, the return value from your message handler for WM_ERASEBKGND should return True (non-zero) if you erase the background prior to drawing, or False (zero) if you do not erase the background. (Check the Win32 API online help for the individual message you are processing to determine what to set the Result data member to.) Set the Result data member of the message-cracker record as needed:

```
procedure TMainForm.WmEraseBkgnd(var Msg: TWMEraseBkgnd);
begin
  { Do some stuff. }
  Message.Result := 0;
end;
```

Any other data members of the message-cracking record will vary from message to message.

Sometimes you will need to call the default message handler for a particular message in addition to performing your own handling. In that case, you can call DefaultHandler. For example, you might want to paint on the background of your window in some circumstances but not in others. If you don't paint the background, you want VCL to paint the background in the default way. So, you would do this:

```
procedure TMainForm.WmEraseBkgnd(var Msg: TWMEraseBkgnd);
begin
  if LetVCLHandle.Checked then begin
    DefaultHandler(Msg);
    Exit;
  end;
  { Do some other drawing. }
  Msg.Result := 1;
end;
```

14

In other cases you will use DefaultHandler to perform some default processing for you. Whether you call DefaultHandler before you do your processing or afterward depends, again, on what you are trying to accomplish.

User-Defined Messages

Besides the normal Windows messages, Windows enables you to create what is called a user-defined message.

 A *user-defined message* is nothing more than a private message that you can send to yourself or to one of the other windows in your application.

Implementing and catching a user-defined message is nearly identical to handling a regular Windows message. The one exception is that you need to first define the message. You define a user-defined message like this:

```
const
  My_Message = WM_USER + 1;
```

This code declares user-defined message called My_Message.

> **Note**
>
> The symbol WM_USER is a special symbol that marks the beginning of the range of numbers that can be used for user-defined messages. You can use anything up to WM_USER + 31,743 for user-defined messages. I usually just pick something in the WM_USER + 100 range. The exact number you use is not important; just be sure that you do not accidentally use the same value for two messages.

If you look back to Listing 14.4, you will notice the declaration for the user-defined message. After you define the message, you can declare the message handler as follows:

```
procedure MyMessage(var Msg : TMessage); message My_Message;
```

Notice that the message-cracker record passed is of the TMessage type. This is the generic message-cracker record. It is defined as follows:

```
TMessage = record
  Msg: Cardinal;
  WParam: Longint;
  LParam: Longint;
  Result: Longint);
end;
```

| Note | The actual declaration of TMessage looks slightly different, but the record shown here is the result. |

When you send a user-defined message, you pass any parameters you want in the WParam and LParam members. For example, let's say you are sending a user-defined message indicating that error code 124 occurred on iteration 1019 of a processing loop. The call to Perform would look like this:

```
Res := MainForm.Perform(MyMessage, 124, 1019);
```

You could use either PostMessage or SendMessage to send the message, too, of course. For user-defined messages, you can probably use Perform for most of your messaging.

Okay, so the message is defined and sent. Now you need to write code to handle it. The message handler for the MYMESSAGE message might look like this:

```
procedure TMainForm.WmMyMessage(var Msg: TMessage);
var
  S : string;
begin
  S := Format('Error #%d occurred on iteration number %d.',
    [Msg.WParam, Msg.LParam]);
  MessageDlg('Error Message', mtError, [mbOk], 0);
  Msg.Result := 1;
end;
```

The return value from Perform will be the value of the Result member of the TMessage record. It's up to you whether you send parameters and whether your message handler returns a result.

The book's code contains a program called MsgTest that illustrates the use of handling Windows messages not covered by VCL events. It also illustrates the use of a user-defined message. This program illustrates the implementation of a Windows programming trick: The window can be dragged by clicking and dragging anywhere on the client area of the form.

Summary

You have covered a lot of ground today. You started with a look at context-sensitive help and how to put it to use. Remember, context-sensitive help is not necessarily easy, but it is something you should implement. After that, you looked at exception handling and how you can use it to trap VCL exceptions. You have also gotten some insights into the

14

Windows Registry. The Registry is something that can and should be used to store application-specific data. Knowing how to use the Registry can help you to implement those little features that make users smile. Finally, we ended with a discussion on how to handle messages other than through the use of events. All in all, it was a long day, but a rewarding one.

Workshop

The Workshop contains quiz questions to help you solidify your understanding of the material covered and exercises to provide you with experience in using what you have learned. You can find the answers to the quiz questions in Appendix A, "Answers to the Quiz Questions."

Q&A

Q Writing help files with a word processor is kind of tedious. What do you suggest?

A Get a commercial or shareware help-authoring program. These programs take care of all the little stuff that drives you crazy when trying to write help files "the hard way." Writing help files is not much fun for most people, but using a good help-authoring program can really ease the pain. Also, be aware that more and more vendors are using HTML help systems. It's possible that HTML help will replace the traditional Windows help file in years to come.

Q Do I have to put context identifiers in my help file?

A Not necessarily. You can just have your users invoke help from the main menu. You won't be able to support context-sensitive help without help context IDs in the help file, though.

Q Why should I bother with exception handling?

A By using exception handling, you can more closely control what happens when errors occur in your program.

Q I've caught a VCL exception. How can I reproduce the error message box that VCL creates when it raises an exception?

A Call `Application.ShowException`, and VCL will display the error message.

Q Do I have to use the Registry to store my program's preferences and settings?

A No. You can use `.ini` files or any other type of configuration file. However, the Registry is the preferred location for application-specific data. The `TRegistry` class makes it easy to use the Registry, so you might as well put it to work for you.

Q I get exceptions every time I try to create a key and then use `WriteString` to write a data item to the key. What could be wrong?

A You are probably using `CreateKey` to create the key. `CreateKey` creates the key but does not open it. Use `OpenKey` to create and open your keys rather than `CreateKey`.

Q What is a user-defined message?

A A user-defined message is a message defined by you, the user, for private use in your application. This is in contrast to Windows messages that are defined and used by Windows on a global level.

Q What should I do to get the default message-handling behavior for a particular Windows message?

A Call the `DefaultHandler` method:

```
DefaultHandler(Msg);
```

Quiz

1. How do you set the help file that your application will use?
2. How do you implement F1 key support for a particular form or dialog box?
3. What method do you call to display the index for your help file?
4. What types of objects can an exception raise?
5. Is it legal to have more than one `except` statement following a `try` statement?
6. How do you raise an exception?
7. What is the default value of the `TRegistry` class `RootKey` property?
8. Must you call `CloseKey` when you are done with a key?
9. What is the difference between `SendMessage` and `PostMessage`?
10. What is the name of the VCL method that is used to send a message directly to a component?

Exercises

1. Research the availability of help-file authoring tools. Although this might seem like a strange exercise, it might be the most beneficial exercise you can do in regard to help files.
2. Create a new project. Add some components to the main form. Give each a different `HelpContext` number.
3. Attach a help file to the project (any help file will do). If you have help-authoring software, create a simple help file for the program to use. Run the program and press F1 when a component has focus.

14

4. Modify the ScratchPad program to use the Windows Registry. Save the filename and path of the last file opened.

5. Modify the ScratchPad program to use the filename and path retrieved from the Registry when the File Open and File Save dialog boxes are displayed.

6. Write a program that sends itself a user-defined message when a button is clicked. Display a message box when the message is received.

7. Add a message handler for the Windows WM_MOVE message to the program in exercise 6. When the window is moved, beep the speaker and display the new coordinates on the form.

8. **Extra Credit:** Modify the PictureViewer program from Day 4, "The Delphi IDE Explored," to catch an exception if the user attempts to open a file other than a graphics file.

WEEK 2

In Review

Wow, that was intense, wasn't it? But did you enjoy yourself? Are you starting to get the fever? By now I'll bet the wheels in your head are really turning. It's likely that you have already envisioned an application or two of your own. Maybe you have even begun work on an application. I hope you have because, as I have said many times, that is how you really learn. If you haven't yet developed an idea for an application, don't worry about it. It will come to you in good time.

This week includes a mixture of material. Early in the week, you found out the basics of building a Delphi application. You can drop components on a form all you want, but someday you have to write code. It can be daunting to branch out on your own. Delphi has lead you by the hand up to this point. But now it's time to leave the nest. You found out how to add your own functions and data members to your code. You also learned how to add resources such as bitmaps and sounds to your programs. This is good stuff. Before long you'll be doing all these things on your own like a pro.

This week's less-than-exciting material deals with more on Delphi projects and how to use the debugger. These chapters might not be flashy, but they still contain vital information that you need when developing applications. It's all about maximizing your time. Learning how to use the debugger takes a few hours or even a few days, but it will save you weeks of work in the long run. Trust me. If you know how to use the debugger, you can really get in there and find out what is going wrong when you encounter a bug in your program. If you don't have a good handle on the debugger, I urge you to go back and review Day 10. As I said, the

8

9

10

11

12

13

14

debugger is not the most thrilling Delphi feature you learn about in this book, but it certainly is one of the most valuable. Learning how to effectively use your projects falls into this same category. Proper project management will save you time in the long run, too.

You learned a bit about graphics and multimedia programming this week. Graphics and sound can really add glitz to your programs. Don't overdo it, though, or your programs might turn your readers off. It's easy to get carried away with graphics and multimedia, so be careful to use these features only where needed.

Toward the end of the week, you learned about some features that can take an average program and turn it into a great program. Let's face it, window decorations such as status bars and toolbars cannot take a weak programming idea and transform it into a great program. No amount of gadgetry can do that. But if you have a good program to start with, adding bells and whistles can make your program stand out from the competition. There's nothing stopping you from adding these kinds of goodies to your applications because Delphi makes it easy.

You also learned about printing from a Delphi programming. Printing is, by nature, nonvisual. Delphi's great visual programming tools can't help you here. Still, Visual Component Library (VCL) makes printing much less frustrating than it would be with the straight API. When you begin printing, you will find that it is not all that difficult. Once again, experiment as much as you can. Playing around can be the best teacher. Don't worry about the boss—tell him or her that I said it was okay to play around. (That's *play around* not *play a round*. Don't blame me if you're caught playing golf on company time!)

Finally, you ended the week with some more in-depth programming techniques. Implementing context-sensitive help is something you will have to do in today's competitive market. The good news is that Delphi makes it easy. The bad news is that there is no shortcut to writing good help files. Take my advice and get a good help authoring program. Such a program can take the frustration out of creating help files. If you write help files the hard way, you will probably get bogged down in the tedium and start skimping on the details. Using a good help authoring program helps you avoid that situation. Remember that the help file is as important as the program itself. After all, what good is a Maserati if you can't figure out how to get it out of first gear?

Using the Registry can put a real shine on your program, too. Oh, it won't make your program appear any different, but when you give the users options, you increase the value of your program. Storing these options in the Registry makes your job easier, too. There's no excuse for omitting features that users have come to expect. Sure, it takes a little time and you have to pay attention to detail, but there's no substitute for quality.

You ended the week with a discussion on message handling. This is a lower level of programming than you have encountered thus far. Handling messages is not something that you might have to do often, but when you must handle messages, knowing how will be more than half the battle. The section on message handling will benefit you down the road if not immediately.

WEEK 3

At a Glance

15

This week you change gears a little. The week starts with a discussion of COM and ActiveX. You learn how to create an ActiveX component and special kind of ActiveX control called an *ActiveForm*. ActiveX components are similar to Visual Component Library (VCL) components but have a completely different architecture.

After a discussion on COM and ActiveX, you begin database programming. You learn about database architecture and how Delphi and VCL implement database operations. You begin with the basics and work toward more advanced database programming techniques.

After the discussion of database programming, I tackle the subject of dynamic link libraries (DLLs). DLLs are there for the taking. You can use them if you want, or not use them. But it is important that you make an informed decision on DLLs. To do that, you have to learn what DLLs are and how you can use them in your applications. Day 19 tells you all about them. After Day 19, you can decide whether DLLs are for you. No doubt you will find that you can use DLLs at some point in your programming journeys.

On Day 20, you take on a more advanced topic—writing components. Creating a component requires a deeper understanding of properties, methods, and events than you presently have. Writing components is not for the faint of heart. It is real programming. You might love it or you might not. If you decide you don't like writing components, that's no problem. There are plenty of shareware, freeware, and commercial components available that will do almost anything you want.

20

Finally, you learn how Delphi and C++Builder are similar and how they are different. One of the great things about Delphi forms is that you can use the same forms in both Delphi and C++Builder. Delphi and C++Builder aren't competing products but rather complementary products.

So, one more week to go. Are you up for it? All right, then, let's go!

COM and ActiveX

OLE, ActiveX, COM, DCOM, VCL, CORBA, MTS. . . the industry certainly doesn't lack for acronyms when it comes to the subject of component architecture! In this chapter, I explain some of these acronyms and at least mention the others in passing. I'll explain what these terms mean and try to shed some light on the often-confusing world of COM and ActiveX. Specifically, I cover

- What COM is
- Creating COM objects
- The Delphi Type Library Editor
- Creating ActiveX controls
- Creating ActiveForms
- Deploying ActiveX controls

I'd be lying if I said that COM, ActiveX, and OLE are easy to understand. They are not. It can be very confusing at first. I can't do justice to this subject in one chapter. My goal for this chapter is to give you enough of a background on these architectures so that you can better understand the acronyms you see bandied about these days. You will also get some good hands-on training in creating COM and ActiveX controls. Fortunately, Delphi takes a great deal of the pain out of dealing with these APIs.

Understanding COM

You can't talk about OLE and ActiveX without talking about COM, which stands for Component Object Model.

NEW TERM *COM (Component Object Model)* is a Microsoft specification for creating and implementing reusable components.

"Components? I thought Delphi used VCL components." Certainly VCL components are the most effective use of components in Delphi. They aren't the only possibility, though. As you work through this hour, you will get a clearer picture of how COM and ActiveX work with Delphi.

COM is the basis for both OLE and ActiveX. An analogy might be the TObject class in VCL. All classes in VCL are ultimately inherited from TObject. Derived classes automatically get the properties and methods of TObject. They then add their own properties and methods to provide additional functionality. Similarly, OLE and ActiveX are built on top of COM. COM is the foundation for all OLE and ActiveX objects.

As a component architecture, COM has two primary benefits:

- COM object creation is language independent. (COM objects can be written in many different programming languages.)
- A COM object can be used in virtually any Windows programming environment including Delphi, C++Builder, Visual C++, Visual Basic, PowerBuilder, Visual dBASE, and many more.

Note

One major drawback to COM is that it is heavily tied to the WinTel (Windows/Intel) platform. So although you can use a COM object in many different Windows programming environments, you can't necessarily use that COM object in a UNIX programming environment. Recently Microsoft has tried to move COM to non-Windows platforms, but it remains to be seen whether this attempt will ultimately succeed. This chapter deals only with COM and ActiveX as they exist in the Win32 programming environment.

You can use a number of different languages and environments to write COM objects. You can create COM objects with Delphi, C++Builder, Visual C++, Visual Basic, and probably a few other development environments. When created, a COM object can be used in an even wider variety of development environments. A COM object created in Delphi can be used by a VB programmer, a C++Builder programmer, or even a Visual dBASE or PowerBuilder programmer.

A COM object is typically contained in a DLL. The DLL might have an extension of `.DLL` or it might have an extension of `.OCX`. A single library file (DLL or OCX) can contain an individual COM object or can contain several COM objects.

COM Terminology

COM is full of confusing terminology. The following sections explain some of the terms used in COM and how the many pieces of COM fit together. All of these pieces are interrelated, so you'll have to read the entire section to get the big picture.

COM Objects

NEW TERM   A *COM object* is a piece of binary code that performs a particular function.

A COM object exposes certain methods to enable applications to access the functionality of the COM object. These methods are made available via COM interfaces. A COM object might contain just one interface, or it might contain several interfaces. To a programmer, COM objects work a lot like Object Pascal classes.

COM Interfaces

Access to a COM object is through the COM object's interface.

NEW TERM   A COM *interface* is the means by which the user of a COM object accesses that object's functionality.

A COM interface is used to access a COM object; to *use* the object, if you will. The interface in effect advertises what the COM object has to offer. A COM object might have just one interface, or it might have several. In addition, one COM interface might implement one or more additional COM interfaces.

COM interfaces typically start with the letter I. The Windows shell, for example, implements interfaces called `IShellLink`, `IShellFolder`, and `IShellExtInit`. Although you can use any naming convention you like, the leading I universally and immediately identifies the class as a COM interface to other programmers.

COM interfaces are managed internally by Windows according to their interface identifiers (IIDs). An IID is a numerical value contained in a data structure (a record). The IID uniquely identifies an interface.

COM Classes

NEW TERM   A COM *class* (also known as a *coclass*) is a class that contains one or more COM interfaces.

You can't use a COM interface directly. Instead, you access the interface through a coclass. A coclass includes a class factory that creates the requested interface and returns a pointer to the interface. COM classes are identified by class identifiers (CLSIDs). A CLSID, like an IID, is a numerical value that uniquely identifies a COM class.

GUIDs

COM objects must be registered with Windows. This is where CLSIDs and IIDs come into play. CLSIDs and IIDs are really just different names for the same base data structure: the Globally Unique Identifier (GUID).

NEW TERM   A *GUID* is a unique 128-bit (16-byte) value.

GUIDs are created by a special COM library function called `CoCreateGUID`. This function generates a GUID that is virtually guaranteed to be unique. `CoCreateGUID` uses a combination of your machine information, random number generation, and a time stamp to create GUIDs. Although it is possible that `CoCreateGUID` might generate two GUIDs that are identical, it is highly unlikely (more like a statistical impossibility).

Thankfully, Delphi programmers don't have to worry about creating GUIDs. Delphi automatically generates a GUID when you create a new automation object, COM object, ActiveX control, or ActiveForm control. GUIDs in Delphi are defined by the `TGUID` record. `TGUID` is declared in `System.pas` as follows:

```
TGUID = record
  D1: Integer;
  D2: Word;
  D3: Word;
  D4: array[0..7] of Byte;
end;
```

When you create a new COM object, Delphi automatically creates the GUID for you. For example, here's the GUID for a test COM object I created:

```
Class_Test: TGUID = '{F34107A1-ECCF-11D1-B47A-0040052A81F8}';
```

Because GUIDs are handled for you by Delphi, you won't typically have to worry very much about GUIDs. You will, however, see GUIDs a lot as you create and use COM objects (including ActiveX controls).

 Tip

> If you need to generate a GUID manually, you can type Ctrl+Shift+G in the Code Editor. Delphi will generate a GUID for you and insert it at the cursor point.

Type Libraries

COM objects often use a type library.

 A *type library* is a special file that contains information about a COM object. This information includes a list of the properties, methods, interfaces, structures, and other elements that the control contains. The type library also provides information about the data types of each property and the return type and parameters of the object's methods.

This information includes the data types in the object, the methods and properties of the object, the version information, interfaces in the object, and so on. Type libraries can be contained in the COM object as resources or as a standalone file. Type library files have a .TLB extension. A type library is necessary if other developers are going to use your COM objects as development tools. A COM object's type library contains more information about the object than is available by simply querying the object for its interfaces. The Delphi IDE, for example, uses the information found in type libraries to display an ActiveX control on the Component palette. Users of a COM object can examine the type library to see exactly what methods and interfaces the object contains.

DCOM

Distributed COM (DCOM) is a subset of COM that provides the capability to use COM objects across networks or across the Internet. DCOM extends COM to provide the mechanism for using COM in a networking environment. A detailed discussion of DCOM is beyond the scope of this book, but note that DCOM is definitely prevalent in certain types of network programming.

Note

> CORBA (Common Object Request Broker Architecture) is a competing technology to DCOM. CORBA is platform-independent, which makes it more desirable than DCOM in many ways. In addition, CORBA is an open architecture supported by a consortium of software companies (unlike DCOM, which is a Microsoft-specific solution). Fortunately, Delphi gives you the option of creating both DCOM and CORBA objects.

Reference Counting

Every COM object has a reference count. The *reference count*, naturally, contains the number of processes that are currently using the COM object. A *process* is any application or DLL that uses a COM object. Because a COM object can be used by any number of processes at one time, reference counting is used to determine when the COM object is no longer needed in memory.

When a COM object is created, its reference count is initialized to 1. The reference count is incremented by one each time a process attaches to the COM object. When a process detaches from the COM object, the reference count is decremented by one. When the reference count gets to 0, the COM object is freed from memory.

The IUnknown Interface

All COM interfaces descend from a base interface called IUnknown. Table 15.1 lists the methods of IUnknown.

TABLE 15.1. IUnknown METHODS.

Method	Description
QueryInterface	Queries the interface to obtain a list of supported interfaces.
AddRef	Increments the interface's reference count.
Release	Decrements the interface's reference count. When the reference count reaches 0, the object is freed from memory.

I mention IUnknown primarily for historical reasons. Delphi programmers don't really have to worry much about IUnknown as other programmers do. Delphi takes care of handling reference counting and freeing the memory for the COM object. Delphi also elevates dealing with COM objects to a level that makes an intimate knowledge of IUnknown all but obsolete.

Creating a COM Object

To help bring this into perspective, let's create a COM object. This COM object will be ridiculously simple but should illustrate how to use and build COM objects in Delphi. The COM object you create will have these characteristics:

Type	Name	Description
property	X	The first number to multiply.
property	Y	The second number to multiply.
method	DoIt	A method that multiplies the two numbers and returns the result.

The following sections explain the process of creating the COM object.

Creating an ActiveX Library

The first step in creating a COM object is to create a DLL project that will contain the COM object's code. Delphi uses the term "ActiveX Library" to refer to all COM library projects. This description isn't entirely accurate, but it's close enough. Perform these steps to create an ActiveX Library:

1. Close all projects. Choose File | New from the main menu to display the Object Repository.

2. Click on the ActiveX tab to show the ActiveX page (see Figure 15.1). Double-click the ActiveX Library icon.

FIGURE 15.1.

The Object Repository's ActiveX page.

3. Choose File | Save and save the project as ComTest.

That's all there is to this particular step. Delphi creates a DLL project for you and is waiting for your next move.

Creating the Actual Object

The next step is to create the COM object itself. This step is also relatively simple. Perform these steps to do so:

1. Choose File | New from the Delphi main menu. The Object Repository is displayed. Click on the ActiveX page.

2. Double-click on the COM Object icon. Delphi displays the COM Object Wizard, as shown in Figure 15.2.

FIGURE 15.2.

The COM Object Wizard.

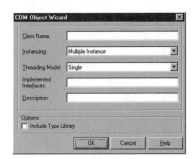

THE COM OBJECT WIZARD

Let me take a moment to talk about the COM Object Wizard. The Class Name field is used to specify the class name for your COM object. Type the class name here, but don't prepend the class name with either a T as you would for a Delphi class, nor an I as is customary for interfaces. Delphi will take care of creating the class and interface names automatically.

The Instancing field is used to control how multiple instances of the COM object are handled. Choices include Internal, Single Instance, or Multiple Instance. See the "COM object wizard" topic in the Delphi help for descriptions of these instancing options (you can click the Help button on the COM Object Wizard to display the correct help topic).

The Threading Model field is used to specify how client applications can call your COM object. Choices include Single, Apartment, Free, or Both. Again, see the Delphi help for descriptions of the threading models.

The Implemented Interfaces field is where you add the names of any interfaces that your COM object will implement. If you have an interface called IMyFileIO and you want to use that interface in your new COM object, you would type IMyFileIO in this field.

The Description field is used to supply a description for the COM object. The description is optional, but it's a good idea to provide one.

When the Include Type Library check box is checked, Delphi will create a type library for the COM object. Creating a type library enables your COM object to be used by client applications.

Okay, let's get back to work:

3. Enter Multiply in the Class Name field.

4. Enter Test COM Object in the Description field.

5. Check the Include Type Library check box. The other fields on the dialog box can be left at their default values.

6. Click OK to close the dialog box.

When you click the OK button, Delphi creates a unit for the COM object's class and displays the Type Library Editor, as shown in Figure 15.3. Before continuing, I need to take a moment to talk about the Type Library Editor.

FIGURE 15.3.

The Type Library Editor.

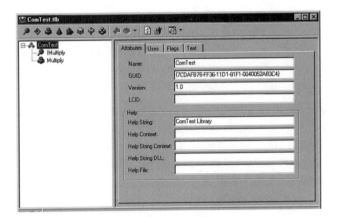

15

Using the Type Library Editor

The Type Library Editor is used to manipulate a type library. The Type Library Editor enables you to add or remove interfaces, add properties and methods to interfaces, remove elements from interfaces, and create host of other COM elements such as enumerations, records, or coclasses. The Type Library Editor makes it easy to add elements to a type library. You'll learn about adding elements in the next section when you add properties and a method to the COM object.

On the left side of the Type Library Editor is the Object pane. The Object pane contains a tree view control. At the top of the tree view hierarchy is the type library itself. Below the type library are elements contained in the type library. In Figure 15.3, you see two elements: the IMultiply interface and the Multiply coclass.

On the right side of the Type Library Editor is the Information pane. This pane provides information about the object currently selected in the Object pane. The information presented in the information pane varies with the type of object selected. The Attributes page shows the type library name, its GUID, version, help string, help file, and so on.

Note

Remember earlier when I said that Delphi programmers don't need to worry much about GUIDs? The COM object you just created already has a GUID, as does the type library itself. Delphi creates these GUIDs for you automatically. As I said before, you'll see GUIDs a lot as you work with COM objects, but you don't have to worry about creating them.

When the type library node is selected, the Information pane shows a tab labeled Uses. When you click on this tab you will see a list of type libraries that this type library relies on. In almost all cases, this list will include the OLE Automation library, but it can contain others as well. The exact libraries a particular type library relies on depends on the type and complexity of the COM object the type library describes.

The Text page shows the type library definitions in IDL syntax. IDL is sort of a scripting language used to create binary type library files. You shouldn't change any of the text on this tab unless you know exactly what you are doing. You might, however, refer to the Text page for reference. This is probably of more value to experienced programmers than to beginners.

Other pages might be displayed in the Information pane depending on the type of object selected. For complete details, be sure to read the "Type Library Editor" help topic in the Delphi help.

You will learn more about the Type Library Editor as you work through the rest of the chapter. Now let's get back to creating the COM object.

Adding Properties and Methods to the COM Object

Before going further, you should save the project again. You didn't realize it, but Delphi created a new unit when you created the COM object in the previous step. Choose File | Save All from the main menu and save the unit as MultiplyU.

Now you are ready to make the COM object do something. Remember, this COM object is incredibly simplistic, so it won't do much, but it will at least do *something*.

Adding Properties

First you will add properties to the COM object. Here are the steps:

1. Click on the IMultiply node in the Type Library Editor's Object pane. Notice that the Information pane shows the interface's name, GUID, and version. Notice also that the Parent Interface field shows the ancestor of IMultiply as IUnknown. If you recall, I said earlier that IUnknown is the base (or parent) interface from which all other interfaces are derived. Delphi automatically assumes a base interface of IUnknown. You can change the base interface to some other interface if you want by choosing an interface from the list of available interfaces. Other interfaces in the list are themselves derived from IUnknown or one of its descendants.

2. Right-click and choose New | Property from the context menu. The Type Library Editor adds two new nodes to the Objects pane under the IMulitply interface. The cursor is in editing mode so that you can type the name of the new property.

3. Type X for the property name and then press the Enter key. Both of the new nodes change to X. There are two nodes to each property because, by default, a property is assumed to be a read/write property. COM requires a Get method to read a property and a Put method to write to a property, hence the two entries. Click on either of the two nodes labeled X. Notice the Invoke Kind field in the Information pane as you select first one X node and then the other. Notice that the field changes from Property Set to Property Get.

4. Notice in the Information pane that the Type field says Integer. That's the data type you want for this property, so you don't need to change the type.

5. Create another new property but this time use a different approach. Locate the New Property button on the Type Library Editor toolbar. Click the drop-down arrow next to the New Property button. Choose Read | Write from the list of property types. The Type Library Editor creates the new property. Name this property Y. You can accept the default data type of Integer for this property as well. Behind the scenes Delphi is adding code to the project's units as you add elements.

Adding a Method

Next, you add a method. Perform these steps:

1. Select the IMultiply object in the Object pane and click the New Method button on the Type Library Editor toolbar.

2. Name the method DoIt. Notice that the Invoke Kind field says Function (as opposed to Property Get and Property Set).

   Next you must set the method's parameters. The method will have this syntax:

   ```
   function DoIt : Integer;
   ```

3. Click on the Parameters tab in the Information pane. Change the Return Type field to Integer (choose Integer from the combo box). This method doesn't have any parameters, so you can leave the Parameters list empty. After you have set the return type, click the Attributes tab to display the Attributes page. This step isn't strictly necessary, but does serve the purpose of taking you back to where you started.

4. Click the Refresh Implementation button on the Type Library Editor toolbar.

Now that you have added the two properties and methods, it's time to see what Delphi has been doing behind the scenes. Listing 15.1 shows the class's unit as it appears after performing the steps up to this point. (Don't worry if your unit doesn't look exactly like Listing 15.1. My version of Delphi might have added code in a slightly different order than yours.)

LISTING 15.1. MultiplyU AFTER ADDING PROPERTIES AND A METHOD.

```
unit MultiplyU;

interface

uses
  Windows, ActiveX, ComObj, ComTest_TLB;

type
  TMultiply = class(TTypedComObject, IMultiply)
  protected
    function DoIt: Integer; stdcall;
    function Get_X: Integer; stdcall;
    function Get_Y: Integer; stdcall;
    procedure Set_X(Value: Integer); stdcall;
    procedure Set_Y(Value: Integer); stdcall;
    {Declare IMultiply methods here}
  end;

implementation

uses ComServ;

function TMultiply.DoIt: Integer;
begin

end;

function TMultiply.Get_X: Integer;
begin

end;

function TMultiply.Get_Y: Integer;
begin

end;

procedure TMultiply.Set_X(Value: Integer);
begin

end;

procedure TMultiply.Set_Y(Value: Integer);
begin

end;
```

```
initialization
  TTypedComObjectFactory.Create(ComServer, TMultiply, Class_Multiply,
    ciMultiInstance, tmSingle);
end.
```

This is the shell of the COM object. Notice that the TMultiply class is derived from both TTypedComObject and IMultiply. (To C++ programmers, this might look like multiple inheritance. It's not exactly multiple inheritance, but it is similar in some ways.) You haven't seen the IMultiply class yet, but you will a bit later. You must fill out this shell in order to make the COM object do something. You will do that next.

Adding Code

You will now add code to the TMultiply class to make the COM object functional. Perform these steps (refer to Listing 15.2 if necessary):

1. Display the MuliplyU.pas unit in the Code Editor. Add these lines to the TMultiply class declaration, just above the protected keyword:

   ```
   private
     FX : Integer;
     FY : Integer;
   ```

   These are the declarations for the data fields that will hold the X and Y property values.

2. Scroll down into the implementation section and locate the Get_X method (use the Code Explorer if you like). Type this line of code in the method:

   ```
   Result := FX;
   ```

3. Locate the Get_Y method and add this line:

   ```
   Result := FY;
   ```

4. Locate the DoIt method and add this line of code:

   ```
   Result := FX * FY;
   ```

   This line of code multiplies the value of FX and FY and returns the result.

5. Scroll down further until you see the Set_X method. Type this line of code in the Set_X method:

   ```
   FX := Value;
   ```

6. Locate the Set_Y method and add this line:

   ```
   FY := Value;
   ```

That's all you need to do. Your code should now look like Listing 15.2.

LISTING 15.2. THE COMPLETED MultiplyU UNIT.

```
unit MultiplyU;

interface

uses
  Windows, ActiveX, ComObj, ComTest_TLB;

type
  TMultiply = class(TTypedComObject, IMultiply)
  private
    FX : Integer;
    FY : Integer;
  protected
    function DoIt: Integer; stdcall;
    function Get_X: Integer; stdcall;
    function Get_Y: Integer; stdcall;
    procedure Set_X(Value: Integer); stdcall;
    procedure Set_Y(Value: Integer); stdcall;
    {Declare IMultiply methods here}
  end;

implementation

uses ComServ;

function TMultiply.DoIt: Integer;
begin
  Result := FX * FY;
end;

function TMultiply.Get_X: Integer;
begin
  Result := FX;
end;

function TMultiply.Get_Y: Integer;
begin
  Result := FY;
end;

procedure TMultiply.Set_X(Value: Integer);
begin
  FX := Value;
end;
```

```
procedure TMultiply.Set_Y(Value: Integer);
begin
  FY := Value;
end;

initialization
  TTypedComObjectFactory.Create(ComServer, TMultiply, Class_Multiply,
    ciMultiInstance, tmSingle);
end.
```

Although you were working on the MulitplyU unit, Delphi was busy building the type library and a unit to contain the type library code. The unit has the same name as the project with a trailing _TLB. This project is named ComTest. The full unit name for the type library unit, then, is ComTest_TLB.pas. Listing 15.3 shows this unit as it exists at this point. Remember, your unit might not look exactly like Listing 15.3.

LISTING 15.3. THE ComTest_TLB.pas UNIT.

```
unit ComTest_TLB;

// ****************************************************************** //
// WARNING                                                          //
// -------                                                          //
// The types declared in this file were generated from data read from a //
// Type Library. If this type library is explicitly or indirectly (via //
// another type library referring to this type library) reimported, or //
// the 'Refresh' command of the Type Library Editor activated while //
// editing the Type Library, the contents of this file will be      //
// regenerated and all manual modifications will be lost.           //
// ****************************************************************** //
// PASTLWTR : $Revision:   1.11.1.55  $
// File generated on 6/8/98 7:16:51 PM from Type Library described below.

// ****************************************************************** //
// Type Lib: D:\Borland\D4\Bin\ComTest.tlb
// IID\LCID: {7CDAFB76-FF36-11D1-81F1-0040052A83C4}\0
// Helpfile:
// HelpString: ComTest Library
// Version:    1.0
// ****************************************************************** //

interface

uses Windows, ActiveX, Classes, Graphics, OleCtrls, StdVCL;
```

continues

LISTING 15.3. CONTINUED

```
// ************************************************************************//
// GUIDS declared in the TypeLibrary. Following prefixes are used:      //
//    Type Libraries      : LIBID_xxxx                                  //
//    CoClasses           : CLASS_xxxx                                  //
//    DISPInterfaces      : DIID_xxxx                                   //
//    Non-DISP interfaces: IID_xxxx                                     //
// ************************************************************************//
const
  LIBID_ComTest: TGUID = '{7CDAFB76-FF36-11D1-81F1-0040052A83C4}';
  IID_IMultiply: TGUID = '{7CDAFB77-FF36-11D1-81F1-0040052A83C4}';
  CLASS_Multiply: TGUID = '{7CDAFB79-FF36-11D1-81F1-0040052A83C4}';
type

// ************************************************************************//
// Forward declaration of interfaces defined in Type Library            //
// ************************************************************************//
  IMultiply = interface;

// ************************************************************************//
// Declaration of CoClasses defined in Type Library                     //
// (NOTE: Here we map each CoClass to its Default Interface)             //
// ************************************************************************//
  Multiply = IMultiply;

// ************************************************************************//
// Interface: IMultiply
// Flags:      (0)
// GUID:       {7CDAFB77-FF36-11D1-81F1-0040052A83C4}
// ************************************************************************//
  IMultiply = interface(IUnknown)
    ['{7CDAFB77-FF36-11D1-81F1-0040052A83C4}']
    function Get_X: Integer; stdcall;
    procedure Set_X(Value: Integer); stdcall;
    function Get_Y: Integer; stdcall;
    procedure Set_Y(Value: Integer); stdcall;
    function DoIt: Integer; stdcall;
  end;

  CoMultiply = class
    class function Create: IMultiply;
    class function CreateRemote(const MachineName: string): IMultiply;
  end;

implementation

uses ComObj;
```

15

```
class function CoMultiply.Create: IMultiply;
begin
  Result := CreateComObject(CLASS_Multiply) as IMultiply;
end;

class function CoMultiply.CreateRemote(const MachineName: string):
➥IMultiply;
begin
  Result := CreateRemoteComObject(MachineName, CLASS_Multiply) as
➥IMultiply;
end;

end.
```

Notice that this unit contains the declaration for the IMultiply interface. As you can see, IMultiply is derived from IUnknown. Notice also that this unit contains the coclass Multiply.

It is important to understand that this unit is regenerated each time you compile an ActiveX library project. It is generated from the type library file. Note the warning at the top of the unit. The comments are telling you that any changes you make to this file will be lost the next time the COM object is rebuilt. It really doesn't do any good to modify the type library source file, because it will be regenerated automatically.

Building and Registering the COM Object

Now you are ready to compile the ActiveX library project. This step compiles the COM object and builds the DLL in which the COM object resides. After building the COM object, you can register it. Here are the steps:

1. Choose Project | Build ComTest from the main menu. Delphi will build the DLL containing the COM object.

2. Choose Run | Register ActiveX Server from the main menu. This step registers the COM object with Windows. If you fail to perform this step, you will get an exception that says, "Class not registered" when you attempt to access the COM object.

Delphi registers the COM object DLL with Windows. After the DLL has been registered, Delphi displays a message box, as shown in Figure 15.4.

FIGURE 15.4.

Delphi reporting the COM object success- fully registered.

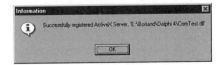

When Windows registers the COM object, it adds information about the object to the Registry. Figure 15.5 shows the Registry entry created when the COM object was registered with Windows.

FIGURE 15.5.

The Registry key created when the COM object was registered.

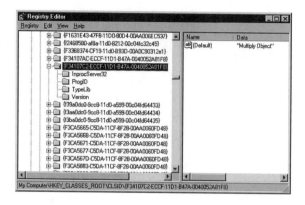

> **Note**
>
> Delphi ships with a utility called TREGSVR.EXE that can be used to register an ActiveX control from the command line. To register a control called MYSTUFF.OCX, you would run TREGSVR from a command prompt like this:
>
> tregsvr mystuff.ocx
>
> To unregister an ActiveX, use the -u switch as follows:
>
> tregsvr -u mystuff.ocx
>
> Sometimes this is more convenient than loading an ActiveX project in Delphi and registering or unregistering the control from the IDE.

> **Note**
>
> In this exercise I had you create a COM object. You could also have used an automation object. An automation object derives from IDispatch rather than IUnknown. IDispatch provides the additional functionality required for a COM object to act as an automation server (an object that can control one application from another).

Your COM object is now ready to use.

Building an Application That Uses the COM Object

A COM object doesn't do you much good if you can't use it. In this step, you create an application that uses the COM object you just created. Follow these steps:

1. Create a new application. Place a `Button` component and a `Label` component on the form. Save the project as `ComApp` and the main form's unit as `ComAppU`.

2. Switch to the Code Editor and locate the `uses` list for the main unit. Add these units to the `uses` list:

```
ComObj
ComTest_TLB
```

   This ensures that the code that references the COM object will compile.

3. Double-click the form's button to create an `OnClick` event handler. Modify the `OnClick` handler so that it looks like this:

```
procedure TForm1.Button1Click(Sender: TObject);
var
  Mult : IMultiply;
  Res  : Integer;
begin
  Mult := CreateComObject(CLASS_Multiply) as IMultiply;
  if Assigned(Mult) then begin
    Mult.Set_X (20);
    Mult.Set_Y (60);
    Res := Mult.DoIt;
    Label1.Caption := IntToStr(Res);
  end;
end;
```

This code first declares a pointer to the `IMultiply` interface called `Mult` and an Integer variable to hold the result. Next, the `CreateComObject` function is called with a parameter of `CLASS_Multiply`. `CLASS_Multiply` is a constant that contains the GUID for the COM object class (refer to Listing 15.3).

The return value from `CreateComObject` is assigned to the `Mult` pointer. Notice that I use the as operator to cast the return value to an `IMultiply` pointer. `CreateComObject` returns an `IUnknown` pointer, so the as operator is used to cast the `IUnknown` pointer to an `IMultiply` pointer.

After the COM object is created, I assign values to the `X` and `Y` properties. After that I call the `DoIt` method of the COM object and display the result in the `Label` component.

Note

In the real world, I would have written the preceding procedure differently. For example:

```
procedure TForm1.Button1Click(Sender: TObject);
begin
  with CreateComObject(CLASS_Multiply) as IMultiply do begin
```

```
    Set_X(20);
    Set_Y(60);
    Label1.Caption := IntToStr(DoIt);
  end;
end;
```

I wrote the procedure the way I did to illustrate each step.

Run the program. When you click the form's button, the label should change to say "1200" (the product of 20 * 60). That's it! Your COM object works. This COM object can be used from Visual Basic, Visual C++, C++Builder, or any other development environment that supports COM.

Understanding ActiveX

ActiveX is a relatively new term for a technology that has been around for awhile. Originally ActiveX controls were called *OCX controls*. The term *OCX* is still widely used in some circles. An ActiveX control typically has a filename extension of either DLL or OCX.

An ActiveX control is essentially a COM object in disguise. The primary difference between an ActiveX control and a COM object is that an ActiveX control has a design-time interface. An ActiveX control also has code that enables it to be deployed on a Web page or over a network. ActiveX is a subset of COM, so everything you learned about COM objects in the first part of the chapter applies to ActiveX controls as well.

Using Third-Party ActiveX Controls

There isn't a lot to know about installing and using third-party ActiveX controls. All you have to do is import the ActiveX into the IDE and begin using the control. To see how this works, let's do a quick exercise. This exercise requires that you have Microsoft Internet Explorer installed on your system. If you don't have Internet Explorer installed, skip this exercise. (You won't be missing anything because I show you how to install an ActiveX control you have built in the section "Build, Register, and Install the Control.") Perform these steps:

1. Choose Component | Import ActiveX Control from the main menu. The Import ActiveX dialog box is displayed.

2. Scroll down through the list of installed components until you find Microsoft Internet Controls (the exact text of the item will depend on the version of Internet Explorer you have installed on your system). Select the item. Figure 15.6 shows the Import ActiveX dialog box after this step.

FIGURE 15.6.

The Import ActiveX dialog box.

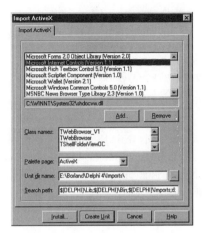

Notice the Class names list box in the middle of the page. This list box contains a list of ActiveX controls in the selected file (SHDOCVW.DLL in this case).

3. The Palette page field shows ActiveX. This is a the palette page where the new controls will be installed. Click on this field and type ActiveXTest.

4. Leave the Unit dir name and Search path fields on their default settings and click the Install button. The Install dialog box comes up and asks what package you want the controls installed into. (All controls, whether they are VCL or ActiveX, must be in a package.)

5. Click on the Into new package tab. Enter MSIE in the File name field and Internet Explorer Package in the Description field.

6. Click the OK button. Delphi creates a new package called MSIE.dpk and prompts you to build and install the package. Click Yes to install the package. After the package is built, Delphi displays a message box telling you which controls were added to the Component palette. Click Yes to dismiss the message box.

7. Scroll the Component palette to find the ActiveXText tab. You should see two or three controls on that page of the Component palette (again, depending on the version of Internet Explorer you have installed). The components are ready for use.

Experiment with the new controls and see how they work. You probably won't get very far without documentation, but at least you get a sense for how installing an ActiveX works. (For a more complete explanation of using Internet Explorer as an ActiveX, see the section, "Using Internet Explorer as an ActiveX Control" on the Bonus Day, "Building Internet Applications.")

> You must have a design-time license in order to use an installed ActiveX con-
> trol. A design-time license is a file with an `.LIC` extension. In some cases you
> can import ActiveX controls to the Delphi Component palette without a
> design-time license, but you will get an error message when you attempt to
> place the control on your form.

To remove the Internet Explorer controls from the Component palette, choose
Component | Install Packages from the main menu. Locate the Internet Explorer Package
in the Design packages list box and click the Remove button. The ActiveXTest tab is
removed from the Component palette.

> Deploying an application that uses ActiveX controls requires special atten-
> tion. Deploying applications using ActiveX controls is covered in detail on
> the Bonus Day in the section "Deploying Internet Applications."

Creating New ActiveX Controls

There are two ways to create an ActiveX control in Delphi:

- From an existing VCL component
- From scratch using an ActiveForm

In this section, you create an ActiveX control using both of these methods.

Creating an ActiveX Control from an Existing VCL Component

Creating an ActiveX control from an existing VCL component is downright simple. After
you create a component, you can turn it into an ActiveX control in no time at all. I haven't
talked about creating components yet, so I don't want to go into a lot of detail on creating
components now (covered on Day 20, "Creating Components"). What you will do, then,
is create an ActiveX control from one of the VCL components provided by Borland.

Generate the ActiveX Project with the ActiveX Control Wizard

The first step is to generate the ActiveX project. As always, Delphi does most of the
work for you. All you have to do is supply a few fields in the ActiveX Control Wizard.
Here are the steps:

1. Choose File | Close All to close all projects and then choose File | New from the
   main menu. The Object Repository is displayed.

2. Click the ActiveX page and then double-click the ActiveX Control icon. The ActiveX Control Wizard is displayed (see Figure 15.7).

FIGURE 15.7.

The ActiveX Control Wizard.

3. Select TButton from the list of classes in the VCL Class Name combo box. The next four fields are automatically filled in with default values. Because this is just a test, you can leave those fields on their default values. The fields are self-explanatory, so I don't need to go over each one.

4. The Threading Model is set to Apartment. Leave this setting as it is. Other threading models include Single, Free, and Both. See the Delphi help for more information on threading models.

5. Check the Include Design-Time License check box. When this option is checked, Delphi will create a design-time license for the control. The design-time license will prevent other programmers from using the control unless they have the license.

6. Check the Include Version Information check box. This will enable you to add version info to the control via the Project Options dialog box.

7. Check the Include About Box check box as well. When this box is checked, Delphi will automatically create an About dialog box for the control. Click OK to close the ActiveX Control Wizard.

Delphi will create a project file (ButtonXControl1.bpr) and three units for the project. The first unit is the TButtonX class unit (ButtonXImp1.pas). The second unit is the type library file for the control, named ButtonXControl1_TLB.pas. This file contains the information Delphi needs to create the type library for the control. The third file, About1.pas, is the unit for the About box. If you want to customize the About box, you can do that at this time. The About box is just another Delphi form, so feel free to customize it in any way you like.

> **Note**
>
> Version info is required in order for your ActiveX controls to work in Visual Basic.

Build, Register, and Install the Control

Because you aren't making any modifications to the control itself, you can jump right to building the control and registering it. This is the same process you went through when you registered the COM object you created earlier. An extra step is required when implementing ActiveX controls, though, because ActiveX controls have a design-time interface. Try this:

1. Choose Project I Build ButtonXControl1 from the main menu. Delphi builds the ActiveX project.

2. Choose Run I Register ActiveX Server from the main menu. The ActiveX control is registered and Delphi displays a message box telling you that the OCX is registered (ActiveX projects have a default extension of .OCX). Click OK to dismiss the message box.

3. Choose Component I Import ActiveX Control from the main menu. Choose ButtonXControl1 Library (Version 1.0) from the list of installed controls (had you not performed step 2, this entry would not have been present in the list of installed controls). The class name of the button, TButtonX, shows in the Class names list box.

4. Set the Palette page field to ActiveX. Click Install to continue.

5. The Install dialog box is displayed. You are going to install the control into the default Delphi user package DCLUSR40.BPL. The File name field should already contain this package. If it doesn't, choose it from the combo box. The Description field now says Delphi User's Components. Click the OK button to install the control.

6. Click Yes to the message box regarding building and installing DCLUSR40.BPL. Click OK when the message box confirming the installation is displayed. The control is now installed.

Test the ActiveX Control

Now you can test your new ActiveX control. First, create a new project.

> **Note**
>
> When you create a new project, Delphi will prompt you to save the package file (DCLUSR40.DPK) and the ActiveX control project. Whether you save these

> files is up to you. My intention was to have you create a quick ActiveX.
> There's really no need to save the files. If, however, you think you might
> want to save the files to examine them later, save the files.

Now follow these steps:

1. Locate the ActiveX tab on the Component palette.

2. The last control in the list is the ButtonX control. Select it.

3. Place a ButtonX control on your form. Notice that the button doesn't have a default caption as a regular VCL button does.

4. Change the Caption property to Test. The button's caption changes just as a VCL button's caption would change.

   Notice the list of properties in the Object Inspector. They are mostly the same properties you would see on a VCL button (the ActiveX was created from a VCL TButton after all), but you might have noticed that the Value column looks slightly different. Remember, this is an ActiveX control and is intended to be used in any environment that hosts ActiveX controls. For that reason, some of the property values are expressed in a more generic way.

5. Double-click the button and you will find that nothing happens. An ActiveX control doesn't have the capability to automatically create an event handler when you double-click the button like a VCL component does. Instead, switch to the Events page and double-click the Value column next to the OnClick event. An event handler is generated. Type this line of code:

   ```
   MessageDlg('Hey, it works!', mtInformation, [mbOK], 0);
   ```

6. Run the program and test the button to ensure that it works. When you have verified that the button works, close the program.

7. Bring up the form and right-click on the button. Choose About from the context menu. The control's About box is displayed. The About box is not customized in any way, but you can go back and do that later if you want (provided you saved the file earlier).

Note

> The idea behind one-step ActiveX is to take a working VCL component and create an ActiveX control from that component. Most of the time, you won't have to modify the ActiveX code in any way. However, you certainly can modify the ActiveX code after it has been generated by Delphi if you so desire. Be aware, though, that if you regenerate the ActiveX code from your original VCL component, all changes made to the ActiveX source will be lost.

Note
You can create ActiveX controls only from windowed VCL controls (controls derived from TWinControl or one of its descendents). The list of VCL controls from which you can build an ActiveX control contains all installed components that specifically meet this criteria.

Unregister the ActiveX Control

After experimenting with your new ActiveX control, you should unregister it so that it doesn't occupy space in the Registry. To unregister the ActiveX control, do this:

1. Choose Component | Import ActiveX Control from the main menu.
2. Select the ActiveX in the list of installed ActiveX controls and click the Remove button.
3. Click Yes on the confirmation dialog box to have Delphi unregister the ActiveX.

Alternatively, you can load the ActiveX project (if you previously saved it) and choose Run | Unregister ActiveX Server from the main menu.

 Note
If all else fails, you can always locate the ActiveX control in the Registry and delete the key for that control. Use the Registry Editor's find function to find the key (search for the control's name or its GUID). Naturally, you want to be careful when editing the Registry manually.

Creating ActiveForms

Creating an ActiveForm is almost as easy as creating an ActiveX from an existing VCL component. Naturally, you can create a complex ActiveX containing many components on a single form. Contrary to what its name implies, however, an ActiveForm can be used to create a simple ActiveX control from scratch (a colored button, for example). In other words, ActiveForms are not only for creating fancy forms with dozens of gadgets. They are for creating single-use ActiveX controls as well.

In this section, you will create an ActiveForm. The ActiveForm will have two edit controls, a label and a button. The button will take the contents of the two edit controls, multiply them together, and display the result in the label. Yes, I know it doesn't require a lot of imagination to stick with the "multiply two numbers" idea, but my goal is to show you how to create an ActiveForm with the minimum amount of code. Keeping the code to a minimum allows you to focus on the ActiveForm creation process without getting bogged down in code.

Create the ActiveForm

Creating an ActiveForm is so easy it's amazing. Follow these steps:

1. Close all projects and then choose File | New from the main menu. The Object Repository is displayed.

2. Double-click the ActiveForm icon. The ActiveForm Wizard is displayed. This dialog box is identical to the ActiveX Control Wizard except for the fact that the VCL Class Name field is grayed (it doesn't apply here).

3. Enter MyFormX in the New ActiveX Name field.

4. Change the Implementation Unit field to read MyFormImpl.pas.

5. Change the Project Name field to MyFormProj.dpr.

6. Leave the Thread Model set to Apartment. Check the Include Version Information check box.

7. Click the OK button to continue.

Delphi creates the required units and displays a form.

Create the Form

An ActiveForm form is just a regular form at this stage. You can add controls to the form, add code, and respond to events just like you do for a form that belongs to an application. The one difference is that the title bar on an ActiveForm does not appear on the control itself. It's just there at design time.

In this step, you will add components and code to make the ActiveForm functional. As you work through the steps, it might help to refer to Figure 15.8 later in the chapter, which shows the completed form. I'm going to give you the primary components in the following steps and let you finish the rest on your own. Perform these steps:

1. Size the form to approximately 175 (width) by 275 (height).

2. Add an Edit component near the top-center of the form (see Figure 15.8). Change its Name property to Num1Edit, its Text property to 0, and its Width to 50 or so (the exact width is not important). Change the AxBorderStyle property to afbRaised.

3. Click on the Edit component and copy it to the Clipboard; paste a new component from the Clipboard. Place the new component below the first. Change its Name property to Num2Edit.

4. Place a Label component below the two edit controls. This label will display the results. Change the label's Name property to ResultLbl and its Caption property to 0.

5. Place a Button component on the form to the right of the Edit components. Change its Name to GoButton and its Caption to Go!.

6. Double-click the button and make the OnClick event handler look like this:

```
procedure TMyFormX.GoButtonClick(Sender: TObject);
begin
  try
    ResultLbl.Caption := IntToStr(
      StrToInt(Num1Edit.Text) * StrToInt(Num2Edit.Text));
  except
    on EConvertError do
      MessageDlg('Oops! You entered an invalid value.',
        mtError, [mbOK], 0);
  end;
end;
```

This code simply extracts the values of the two edit controls, multiplies them together, and displays the result in the ResultLbl label. The exception handling code displays a message box if the user enters invalid values. An EConverError exception will be raised if the conversion from text to integer fails (if one of the edit controls contains text, for example).

7. Add additional labels to match Figure 15.8.

8. Choose View | Type Library from the main menu. In the Information page, change the Help String field to My Test ActiveForm Library. This is the text that will be displayed in the Import ActiveX dialog box when you install the ActiveForm.

9. Save the project. Accept the default filenames. (You specified them in the ActiveForm Wizard.) Figure 15.8 shows the completed form.

FIGURE 15.8.

The finished ActiveForm.

Build, Register, and Import the ActiveForm

Now you can build, register, and import the ActiveForm. When built, the ActiveForm is like any other ActiveX control. Because you've done this several times now, I'm not going to go over every step. Follow these steps:

1. Choose Project | Build MyFormProj from the main menu.

2. When the project is built, choose Run | Register ActiveX Server from the main menu.

3. Choose Component | Import ActiveX Control from the main menu. Install `My Test ActiveForm Library (Version 1)` into the `DCLUSR40` package. Install to the ActiveX page or any other page you choose.

The ActiveForm is now installed as an ActiveX control.

Try the ActiveForm

Now it's time to take the ActiveForm for a test drive. This will be fairly simple:

1. Create a new application.
2. Click the ActiveX tab on the Component palette and choose `MyFormX` button (the one with the default Delphi icon).
3. Place a `MyFormX` control on your form.
4. Run the program and test out the ActiveX.

That's all there is to it. With Delphi, great-looking ActiveX controls are a breeze to create! There simply is no better development environment for creating ActiveX controls than Delphi, bar none.

Changing the ActiveX Palette Bitmap

Ultimately you will want to change the bitmap of the ActiveX from the default that Delphi provides to one of your own design. Changing the bitmap requires following these steps:

1. Create a binary resource file (`.RES`) with Image Editor.
2. Create a 24×24 bitmap. Give the bitmap a numeric name (2 for example).
3. Link the resource file to the ActiveX project with the `$R` compiler directive. (Linking resources was discussed on Day 8, "Creating Applications in Delphi" and is discussed further on Day 20, "Creating Components.")
4. Modify the ActiveX class factory creation routine in the implementation unit (the ActiveForm's `.PAS` file). A typical class factory creation routine looks like this (it's in the `initialization` section at the bottom of the unit):

```
TActiveFormFactory.Create(
    ComServer,
    TActiveFormControl,
    TMyFormX,
    Class_MyFormX,
    1,                        { Change this number. }
    '',
    OLEMISC_SIMPLEFRAME or OLEMISC_ACTSLIKELABEL,
    tmApartment);
```

Notice the line I have marked with a comment. This parameter of
`TActiveFormFactory.Create` is the resource number of the bitmap you
want displayed on the Component palette. If you saved the new bitmap with
a name of 2, you would replace the 1 in this code snippet with a 2.

5. Rebuild, reregister, import, and install the ActiveForm again. The new bitmap
should now show up in the Component palette.

Alternatively, you can modify the ActiveForm project's .RES file and change the bitmap
named 1 to look like you want.

Web Deploying ActiveX Controls and ActiveForms

One of the great features of ActiveForms is that you can use them on a Web page. In
order to use an ActiveForm on a Web page, you must use the Web Deploy option. Using
Web Deploy requires a Web server, so I can't effectively walk you through the Web
deployment process. I can, however, give you a little insight into the process. When you
choose Web Deploy, Delphi performs two tasks:

- Builds the ActiveX control and copies the file to the Web Deploy target directory
- Creates an HTML file that contains the code needed to load the ActiveX control

The locations of these files is determined by the Web deployment options. Let's look at
that next.

Web Deployment Options

Before you can use Web Deploy, you must set the Web deployment options. To set the
Web deployment options, choose Project | Web Deployment Options from the main
menu. The Web Deployment Options dialog box is displayed, as shown in Figure 15.9.

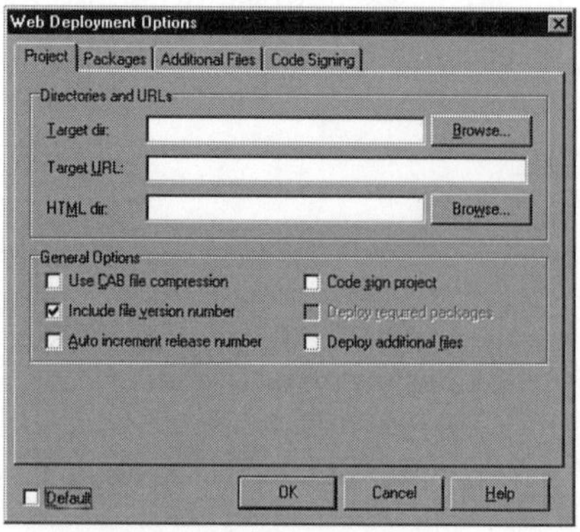

FIGURE 15.9.

The Web Deployment
Options dialog box.

At the bottom of the Web Deployment Options dialog box is a check box labeled Default. Check this box if you want the settings you have specified to be the new defaults for future projects. Most of the time, you will deploy to the same Web site, so you will probably want to set the defaults after you have everything set up just the way you want it.

Project Page: Directories and URLs Section

The Directories and URLs section is where you specify the target location for your ActiveX. The Target dir field is used to specify the directory where Delphi will copy the ActiveX after it is built. This field must be a directory—it cannot be an URL location.

If you are like me, you might not have direct access to the directory where your Web site is located. (TurboPower's Webster Royland keeps access pretty tightly controlled.) If that is the case, you will have to specify a local directory in this field and then later use your Web publishing software to publish the files to your Web site.

The Target URL field is used to specify the page where the ActiveX will reside on the server. This page is used by Delphi when it creates the HTML page that shows the control. For example, the HTML file that Delphi created for me is shown in Listing 15.4. (I had to break a couple of lines because they were too long for the page.)

LISTING 15.4. THE HTML CODE GENERATED BY DELPHI FOR THE ACTIVEX FILE.

```
<HTML>
<H1> Delphi 4 ActiveX Test Page </H1><p>
You should see your Delphi 4 forms or controls
embedded in the form below.
<HR><center><P>
<OBJECT
  classid="clsid:52FB5B97-EDA3-11D1-B47B-0040052A81F8"
  codebase="http://www.home.turbopower.com/~kentr/test/MyFormProj.cab
    #version=1,0,0,0"
  width=275
  height=175
  align=center
  hspace=0
  vspace=0
>
</OBJECT>
</HTML>
```

Notice the URL in the codebase statement. This is the path I typed in the Target URL field of the Web Deployment Options dialog box. By the way, you can copy the entire OBJECT tag from the Delphi-generated HTML code directly to your Web page's HTML source when you get ready to officially deploy your ActiveX code.

The name of the HTML file created by Delphi is the project name with an extension of .htm.

The HTML dir field of the Web Deployment Options dialog box is used to specify the location where Delphi will place the HTML code it generates (refer to Listing 15.4). As with the Target dir field, if you don't have direct access to your Web site's directories, you will have to specify a local directory and then publish the HTML file to your Web site.

Project Page: General Options Section

This section is where you specify the global Web deployment options. The Use CAB file compression field determines whether the ActiveX is compressed. Compressing the ActiveX reduces the size of your ActiveX, making downloading the control that much faster. I used CAB compression on the ActiveForm created earlier in the project and the ActiveX size went from 312KB in OCX form to 204KB in CAB form. Windows takes care of automatically decompressing and registering the ActiveX, so there's no real disadvantage to using CAB compression.

The Include file version number indicates whether Delphi should include the version number in the codebase statement (again refer to Listing 15.4). The version tag is optional, so you don't specifically need it. Note, however, that some browsers won't load the ActiveX if the version tag is present (Netscape Navigator with an ActiveX plug-in, for example).

The Auto increment release number will automatically increment the version number in the ActiveX's version info each time the ActiveX is deployed.

The Code sign project option plays an important role in ActiveX deployment. When this option is on, Delphi will code sign the ActiveX. *Code signing* is the process of attaching a binary signature to a file. This binary signature identifies the company that created the ActiveX, among other information.

Code signing is important because Internet Explorer expects ActiveX controls to be code signed. If Internet Explorer's security level is set to High or Medium, any ActiveX controls that are not code signed will not load. Simply put, if you are going to deploy your ActiveX controls so that the public can use them, they must be code signed.

The Code Signing page of the Web Deployment Options dialog box contains the information needed to code sign the ActiveX. Delphi does not provide the credentials file or the private key needed to code sign files. To obtain a credentials file and private key, you will need to contact Microsoft. For more information, search the Microsoft Web site for the terms "Digital Signing" and "Certificate Authority."

The Deploy required packages and Deploy additional files options are used if you have built your ActiveX with runtime packages or if there are additional files that must ship with your control. If you choose either of these options, you must specify the packages or additional files on the Packages and Additional Files pages of the Web Deployment Options dialog box.

> **Note**
>
> When in doubt, click the Help button in the Web Deployment Options dialog box. Delphi help explains each of the pages of this dialog box.

Web Deploy

After you set the deployment options, you are ready to deploy your ActiveX. To deploy the ActiveX, simply load the ActiveX project and choose Project | Web Deploy from the Delphi main menu. Delphi will build the ActiveX and deploy it based on the settings in the Web Deployment Options dialog box. If you elected to use CAB compression, Delphi will compress the ActiveX into a CAB file as well. Remember, if you don't have direct access to your Web site's directories, you will have to publish the ActiveX and HTML file to your Web site before you can test the ActiveX.

The act of deploying the ActiveX is trivial—setting the Web deployment options is the hard part. Figure 15.10 shows the example ActiveForm created earlier running on a Web page.

FIGURE 15.10.

The test ActiveForm running on a Web page.

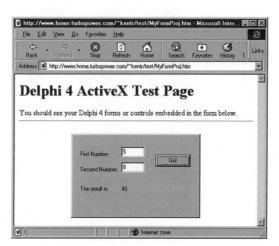

Note

> ActiveX controls have virtually no security restrictions. Be careful when downloading ActiveX controls from unknown (or unverified) sources. When downloaded, an ActiveX control has access to your entire system. Be equally careful when writing your own ActiveX controls. Make absolutely sure that your ActiveX control won't do anything to negatively impact other users' machines.

Summary

I won't lie to you—there's a lot more to COM and ActiveX than what is presented here. For example, I didn't talk about OLE. OLE, like ActiveX, is a subset of COM. OLE adds a layer to COM to enable applications to link and embed OLE automation servers in a container application. Still, you learned a great deal about COM and ActiveX today. Most importantly, you found out how to create COM objects, ActiveX controls, and ActiveForms. You also learned a bit about Web Deploy and how to use it to deploy your ActiveX controls on a Web page.

Workshop

The Workshop contains quiz questions to help you solidify your understanding of the material covered and exercises to provide you with experience in using what you have learned. You can find the answers to the quiz questions in Appendix A, "Answers to the Quiz Questions."

Q&A

Q Do I have to understand the inner workings of COM to write ActiveX controls in Delphi?

A Although some understanding of COM is certainly helpful, it is not vital to creating ActiveX controls with Delphi. Delphi makes it easy to create ActiveX controls without an in-depth understanding of COM.

Q What is a type library?

A A type library is a binary file that describes the interfaces, data types, methods, and classes in a COM library (including ActiveX).

Q Are OLE and COM the same thing?

A No. COM is the base upon which OLE is built. OLE is much more complex and convoluted than COM. Certainly OLE has more functionality, but OLE is a bloated beast that is best avoided if possible.

Q **I noticed some nifty-looking ActiveX controls registered on my system, so I installed them on the Delphi Component palette. They show up on the Component palette but when I try to use one of the controls, I get an error message about a design-time license. Why is that?**

A In short, you are not authorized to use those controls in a design environment (Delphi, for example). ActiveX users must deploy and register their ActiveX controls on every system that uses those controls. To prevent anyone from freely using those controls, the control vendors require a design-time license before the control can be used at design time. When you purchase an ActiveX control from a vendor, you get the design-time license.

Q **I created an ActiveX control and placed it on my form. The program used to work fine, but now when I try to run the program I get an exception that says, `Class not registered`. Why is that?**

A Every ActiveX control must be registered on the system on which it is being used. You might have inadvertently unregistered the ActiveX control on your system some time after you originally installed the control. To reregister the control, load the ActiveX project in Delphi and choose Run | Register ActiveX Server. Alternatively, you can register the OCX file with the `TREGSVR.EXE` utility.

Q **I created and installed an ActiveForm and everything went fine. Later I wanted to change the ActiveForm. I couldn't compile the ActiveForm project, though, because I kept getting an error, `Could not create output file MyProj.OCX`. What's wrong?**

A You need to remove the ActiveForm control from the Delphi Component palette before you can rebuild the control. When the control is installed in Delphi, its OCX file is loaded by the Delphi IDE and cannot be overwritten.

Q **Web Deploy confuses me. There are so many options. Am I the only one who doesn't understand this stuff?**

A Certainly not. After you have worked through the Web Deploy process a few times, it's not nearly so daunting as it might appear the first time you try it.

Q **I'm having problems getting my ActiveX to work on a Web page. I keep getting an error from Internet Explorer when I try to load the page. The error says, `Your current settings prohibit ActiveX controls`. What's wrong?**

A Your ActiveX control is not code signed. An ActiveX control must be code signed before Internet Explorer will download the control when the user's security settings are set to either medium or high.

15

Quiz

1. What is the base (or parent) interface for all COM interfaces?

2. What is a GUID?

3. What happens when a COM object's reference count reaches 0?

4. What is the name of the Delphi utility used when working with type libraries?

5. How do you create GUIDs when writing COM objects in Delphi?

6. What do you choose from the Object Repository when creating an ActiveX from a VCL component?

7. Can you use Delphi-created ActiveX controls in Visual Basic?

8. After your ActiveX control is built and registered, how do you install it to the Delphi Component palette?

9. How do you unregister an ActiveX that you have created?

10. Can you use the ActiveX controls created in Delphi on a Web page?

Exercises

1. Create a simple COM object from scratch. It isn't important what the COM object does, just that you go through the steps of creating it.

2. Write a Delphi application that uses the COM object created in exercise 1 (don't forget to register the COM object).

3. Create an ActiveX control from a VCL TEdit component. Install the control to the Delphi Component palette and use it on a form.

4. If you have access to Visual Basic, take the ActiveX created in exercise 3 and use it in a VB application.

5. Create an ActiveForm control of your own design.

6. If you have a Web site, deploy the ActiveForm created in step 5 and display it on a Web site page.

7. **Extra Credit:** Modify the ActiveForm control created in step 5 so that it uses a custom bitmap on the Delphi Component palette rather than the default bitmap.

DAY 16

Delphi Database Architecture

Today you begin to learn about database programming in Delphi. If you are new to database programming, at first glance it might appear overwhelming. Today I'll try to eliminate any confusion by presenting a clear picture of the labyrinth known as database programming. First, I'll give you an overview of the Delphi database architecture. After that I'll go over some of the data access components.

Make no mistake: Database programming is complicated. I'll give you a high-level view of database programming in Delphi, but I won't attempt to cover every detail.

Note

Not all the concepts and components discussed in this chapter pertain to every version of Delphi. The Professional version of Delphi has more database capabilities than the Standard version. The Client/Server version of Delphi has many more database capabilities than either the Standard or Professional version.

Database Basics

Database programming comes with a whole gaggle of buzzwords: *BDE, client, server, ODBC, alias, SQL, query, stored procedure,* and so on. The good news is that it isn't all that bad after you learn some basics. First, let's take a moment to talk about databases. When you hear the word *database,* you probably imagine data stored in table format. The table probably contains fields such as `FirstName`, `LastName`, and `PhoneNumber`. These fields are filled with data to create individual records in a database file.

If that's what you envision when you think of a database, you're not too far off, but you aren't exactly correct, either. The term *database* is used to describe an all-encompassing data creation and maintenance system. It is true that a database can be as simple as one table. On the other hand, a real-world database can include dozens or even hundreds of tables with thousands or millions of records. These tables can contain one or more index-es. A complete client/server SQL database solution can also contain numerous queries and stored procedures. (Don't worry; I'll explain some of these terms later in the chapter.) So as you can see, a database is more than just a table with data.

Speaking of tables, let's quickly cover some table basics. A table consists of at least two parts: fields and records. *Fields* are the individual categories of data in a table. For example, a table containing an address book would have a field called `FirstName`, a field called `LastName`, one called `Address`, `PhoneNumber`, and so on. Fields are also referred to as *columns*. A record, then, is one person's complete address: first name, last name, address, and so on. Records are also called *rows*.

A database is just a collection of data, of course, but database tables are often displayed in spreadsheet format. The column headers across the top indicate the field names. Each row in the table contains a complete record. Figure 16.1 shows just such a database table displayed in grid (or table) format.

FIGURE 16.1.

A typical database table.

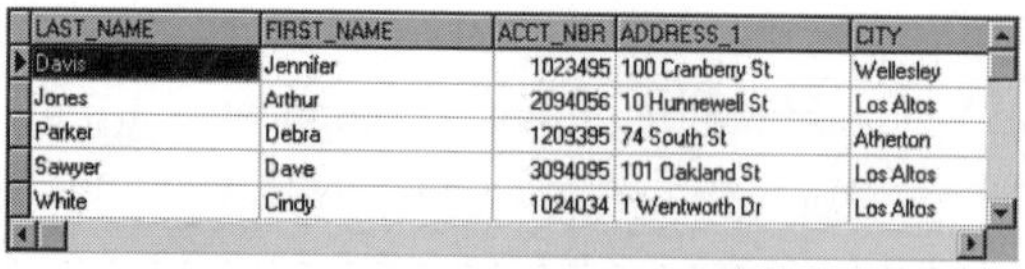

LAST_NAME	FIRST_NAME	ACCT_NBR	ADDRESS_1	CITY
Davis	Jennifer	1023495	100 Cranberry St.	Wellesley
Jones	Arthur	2094056	10 Hunnewell St	Los Altos
Parker	Debra	1209395	74 South St	Atherton
Sawyer	Dave	3094095	101 Oakland St	Los Altos
White	Cindy	1024034	1 Wentworth Dr	Los Altos

NEW TERM The pointer to the current record within a database is called the *cursor.*

The cursor points to the record that will be read if data is requested and the record that will be updated if any edits are made. The cursor is moved when a user browses the database, inserts records, deletes records, and so on.

Note When I say the cursor is a pointer, I don't mean it's a pointer in the Object Pascal sense. I merely mean it is an indicator of the current record's position.

NEW TERM A collection of data returned by a database is called a *dataset*.

A dataset can be more than just the data contained in a table. A dataset can be the results of a query containing data acquired from many tables. For example, let's say you have a database containing names and addresses of your customers, their orders, and the details of each order. This data might be contained in tables named Clients, Orders, and Order Details. Now let's say you request the details of the last 10 orders placed by Company X. You might receive a dataset containing information from the Clients table, the Orders table, and the Order Details table. Although the data comes from several different sources, it is presented to you as a single dataset.

Local Databases

The simplest type of database is the local database. A *local database* is a database that resides on a single machine. Imagine that you have a program that needs to store a list of names and addresses. You could create a local database to store the data. This database would probably consist of a single table. The table is accessed only by your program; no one else has access to it. Any edits made to the database are written directly to the database. Paradox, dBASE, and Access databases are usually local databases.

Client/Server Databases

Another way a database can be implemented is as a *client/server database*. The database itself is stored and maintained on a file server (the *server* part of the equation). One or more users (the *clients*) have access to the database. The users of this type of database are likely to be spread across a network. Because the users are oblivious to one another, more than one might attempt to access the database at the same time. This isn't a problem with client/server databases because the server knows how to handle all the problems of simultaneous database access.

The users of a client/server database almost never work with the database directly. Instead, they access the database through applications on their local computer. These applications, called *client applications*, ensure that the users are following the rules and not doing things to the database that they shouldn't be. It's up to the client application to prevent the user from doing something that would damage the database.

16

> **DATABASE SERVERS**
>
> As long as I am talking about client/server databases, let's take a moment to talk about database servers. Database servers come in several flavors. Some of the most popular include offerings from InterBase (a Borland-owned company), Oracle, Sybase, Informix, and Microsoft. When a company purchases one of these database servers, it also purchases a license that enables a maximum number of users to access the database server. These licensed users are often referred to as *seats*. Let's say a company buys InterBase and purchases licenses for 50 seats. If that company grows to the point that 75 users require access to the database, that company will have to buy an additional 25 seats to be in compliance with the license. Another way that client/server databases are sold is on a *per connection* basis. A company can buy a license for 50 simultaneous connections. That company can have 1,000 users of the database, but only 50 can be connected to the database at any one time. The database server market is big business, no question about it.

Single-Tier, Two-Tier, and Multitier Database Architecture

Local databases are often called single-tier databases. A *single-tier database* is a database in which any changes—such as editing the data, inserting records, or deleting records—happen immediately. The program has a more direct connection to the database.

In a *two-tier database*, the client application talks to the database server through database drivers. The database server takes the responsibility for managing connections, and the client application is largely responsible for ensuring that the correct information is being written to the database. A fair amount of burden is put on the client application to make sure the database's integrity is maintained.

In a *multitier client/server architecture*, the client application talks to one or more application servers that, in turn, talk to the database server. These middle-level programs are called *application servers* because they service the needs of the client applications. One application server might act as a data broker, responding to and handling data requests from the client and passing them on to the database. Another application server might only handle security issues.

Client applications run on local machines; the application server is typically on a server, and the database itself might be on another server. The idea behind the multitier architecture is that client applications can be very small because the application servers do most of the work. This enables you to write what are called *thin-client* applications.

Another reason to use a multitier architecture is management of programming resources. The client applications can be written by less experienced programmers because the client applications interact with the application server that controls access to the database itself. The application server can be written by more experienced programmers who know the rules by which the database must operate. Put another way, the application server is written by programmers whose job is to protect the data from possible corruption by errant client applications.

Although there are always exceptions, most local databases make use of the single-tier architecture. Client/server databases use either a two-tier or a multitier architecture.

So how does this affect you? Most applications you write with Delphi for use with a client/server database will be client applications. Although you might be one of the few programmers given the task of writing server-side or middle-tier applications, it's a good bet that you will write primarily client applications. As an application developer, you can't talk directly to these database servers. Let's look next at how a Delphi application talks to a database.

The Borland Database Engine

To enable access to local databases and to client/server databases, Delphi provides the Borland Database Engine (BDE). The BDE is a collection of DLLs and utilities that enables access to a variety of databases.

To talk to client/server databases, you must have the Client/Server version of Delphi. This version ships with SQL Links drivers used by the BDE to talk to client/server databases. Figure 16.2 shows the relationship between your application, the BDE, and the database.

FIGURE 16.2.

Your application, the BDE, and the database.

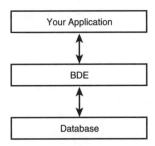

16

BDE Drivers

Naturally, database formats and APIs vary widely. For this reason the BDE comes with a set of drivers that enables your application to talk to several different types of databases. These drivers translate high-level database commands (such as open or post) into commands specific to a particular database type. This permits your application to connect to a database without needing to know the specifics of how that database works.

The drivers that are on your system depend on the version of Delphi you own. All versions of Delphi come with a driver to enable you to connect to Paradox and dBASE databases. This driver, called STANDARD, provides everything you need to work with these local databases.

The Client/Server version of Delphi includes drivers to connect to databases by Sybase, Oracle, Informix, InterBase, and others.

BDE Aliases

The BDE uses an alias to access a particular database. This is one of those terms that might confuse you at first. The terms *alias* and *database* are often used interchangeably when talking about the BDE.

NEW TERM   A *BDE alias* is a set of parameters that describes a database connection.

When it comes right down to it, there isn't much to an alias. In its simplest form, an alias tells the BDE which type of driver to use and the location of the database files on disk. This is the case with aliases you will set up for a local database. In other cases, such as aliases for client/server databases, the alias contains other information as well, such as the maximum size of BLOB data, the maximum number of rows, the open mode, or the user's username. After you create an alias for your database, you can use that alias to select the database in your Delphi programs. Later today, in the section "Creating a BDE Alias," I'll tell you how to go about creating a BDE alias for your own databases.

Delphi's Built-in Databases

As long as I am on the subject of aliases, let's take a quick look at the aliases already set up on your system. To view existing aliases, perform these steps:

1. Start Delphi or create a new application if Delphi is already running.
2. Switch to the Data Access tab of the Component palette, select a Table component, and place it on the form.
3. Click on the DatabaseName property in the Object Inspector and then click the drop-down arrow button to display a list of aliases.

After performing these steps, you'll see a list of available databases. At least one of these should be the DBDEMOS alias. This database alias is set up when Delphi is installed. Select the DBDEMOS database from the list.

Note

> The list of databases you see depends on several factors. First, it depends on whether you have the Standard, Professional, or Client/Server version of Delphi. It also depends on whether you elected to install Local InterBase. Finally, if you happen to have C++Builder or another Borland product installed (such as Visual dBASE or IntraBuilder), you might see additional databases.

As long as you are here, move to the TableName property and take a look at the available tables. The tables you see are those available for this database (this alias). Select another alias for the DatabaseName property. Now look at the table names again. You will see a different list of tables.

SQL Links

The Client/Server version of Delphi comes with SQL Links in addition to the BDE. SQL Links is a collection of additional drivers for the BDE. These drivers enable Delphi applications to connect to client/server databases such as those provided by Oracle, InterBase, Informix, Sybase, and Microsoft. Details regarding deployment of SQL Links drivers are also available in DEPLOY.TXT.

LOCAL INTERBASE

The Standard and Professional versions of Delphi come with a single-user copy of Local InterBase. Local InterBase is just what its name implies: a version of InterBase that operates on local databases. The Client/Server version of InterBase, on the other hand, is a full-featured client/server database. The main reason that Delphi ships with Local InterBase is so that you can write an application that operates on local databases and then later change to a client/server database with no programming changes. This gives you an opportunity to hone your client/server programming skills without spending the money for a client/server database.

If you attempt to access a Local InterBase table at either design time or runtime, you will be prompted for a username and password. The Local InterBase administrator is set up with a username of SYSDBA and a password of masterkey. You can use these for login, or you can go to the InterBase Server Manager utility and add yourself as a new user to the InterBase system.

Delphi Database Components

Okay, so the preceding section isn't exactly the type of reading that keeps you up all night turning pages. Still, it's important to understand how all the database pieces fit together. With that background, you can now turn your attention to the database components provided by VCL and how those components work together to create a database application. First, I'll give you a quick overview of the VCL database components, and then you'll look at individual classes and components in more detail.

The VCL database components fall into two categories: nonvisual data access components and visual data-aware components. Simply put, the nonvisual data access components provide the mechanism that enables you to get at the data, and the visual data-aware components enable you to view and edit the data. The data access components are derived from the TDataSet class and include TTable, TQuery, and TStoredProc. The visual data-aware components include TDBEdit, TDBListBox, TDBGrid, TDBNavigator, and more. These components work much like the standard edit, list box, and grid components except that they are tied to a particular table or field in a table. By editing one of the data-aware components, you are actually editing the underlying database as well.

 Note   All the VCL database components can be termed data components. I use the term *data access components* for the nonvisual database components on the Data Access tab of the Component palette and the term *data-aware components* for the visual database components from the Data Controls tab.

Interestingly, these two component groups cannot talk directly to each other. Instead, the TDataSource component acts as an intermediary between the TDataSet components and the visual data-aware components. This relationship is illustrated in Figure 16.3.

FIGURE 16.3.

The architecture of the VCL database components.

| TDBEdit | TDBMemo | TDBText | TDBImage | TDBGrid |

TDataSource

Datasets (TTable, TQuery, TStoredProc)

Database

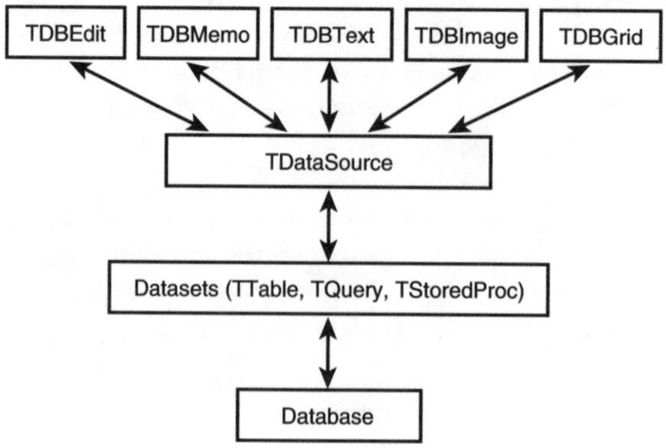

You'll look at these components in more detail, but first I'll walk you through a quick exercise to illustrate the relationship described in this section. Start Delphi or create a new application if Delphi is already running. Now do the following:

1. Place a Table component on the form.

2. Locate the DatabaseName property in the Object Inspector and choose the DBDEMOS database.

3. Locate the TableName property and choose the ANIMALS.DBF table.

4. Drop a DataSource component on the form and set its DataSet property to Table1 (choose Table1 from the drop-down list). The data source is now linked to the dataset (the Table).

5. Drop a DBGrid component on the form and change its DataSource property to DataSource1. This connects the grid to the data source and, indirectly, to the dataset.

6. Now click the Table component on your form to select it. Change its Active property to True. You now have data in the table.

That was easy, but you're not done yet. Notice, by the way, that you can use the scroll-bars on the grid even at design time. Okay, just a couple more steps:

1. Place a DBImage component on the form and change its DataSource property to DataSource1 and its DataField property to BMP (BMP is a field name in the ANIMALS.DBF table that contains a picture of the animal). Hey, a fish! Size the DBImage as desired to fit the size of the image that is showing in the component.

2. Place a DBNavigator component on the form and change its DataSource property to DataSource1.

Now run the program. Click any of the DBNavigator buttons. When you click on the Next Record button, the record pointer changes in the DBTable and the picture changes in the DBImage component. All that without writing a line of code!

The data access components are used to connect to a database and to a particular table in a database. The Table component is used to access a database table. This is the simplest way of accessing the data in a table.

The Query component is a way of accessing a database table using Structured Query Language (SQL) statements. SQL is a more powerful way of accessing tables, but it is also more complex. You will use either a Table or Query component to access a database, but not both. Another component is the StoredProc component that enables you access to a database via stored procedures. A *stored procedure* is a collection of database statements that performs one or more actions on a database. Stored procedures are usually used for a series of database commands that is repeated often.

The TDataSet Class

TDataSet is the ancestor class for TTable, TQuery, and TStoredProc. As such, most properties, methods, and events that these classes use are actually defined by TDataSet. Because so many characteristics of the derived classes come from TDataSet, I'll list the primary properties, methods, and events of TDataSet here, and later I'll list the properties, methods, and events particular to each derived class.

Table 16.1 lists the most commonly used properties of the TDataSet class, Table 16.2 lists the primary methods, and Table 16.3 lists the primary events.

TABLE 16.1. PRIMARY TDataSet PROPERTIES.

Property	Description
Active	Opens the dataset when set to True and closes it when set to False.
AutoCalcFields	Determines when calculated fields are calculated.
Bof	Returns True if the cursor is on the first record in the dataset and False if it isn't.
CachedUpdates	When True, updates are held in a cache on the client machine until an entire transaction is complete. When False, all changes to the database are made on a record-by-record basis.
CanModify	Determines whether the user can edit the data in the dataset.
DataSource	The DataSource component associated with this dataset.
DatabaseName	The name of the database that is currently being used.
Eof	Returns True if the cursor is at the end of the file and False if it isn't.
FieldCount	The number of fields in the dataset. Because a dataset might be dynamic (the results of a query, for example), the number of fields can vary from one dataset request to the next.
Fields	An array of TFields objects that contains information about the fields in the dataset.
FieldValues	Returns the value of the specified field for the current record. The value is represented as a Variant.
Filter	An expression that determines which records a dataset contains.
Filtered	When True, the dataset is filtered based on either the Filter property or the OnFilterRecord event. When False, the entire dataset is returned.

Property	Description
FilterOptions	Determines how filters are applied.
Found	Indicates whether a find operation is successful.
Handle	A BDE cursor handle to the dataset. This is used only when making direct calls to the BDE.
Modified	Indicates whether the current record has been modified.
RecNo	The current record number in the dataset.
RecordCount	Returns the number of records in the dataset.
State	Returns the current state of the dataset (dsEdit, dsBrowse, dsInsert, and so on).
UpdateObject	Specifies the TUpdateObject component to use for cached updates.
UpdatesPending	When True, the cached update buffer contains edits not yet applied to the dataset.

TABLE 16.2. PRIMARY TDataSet METHODS.

Method	Description
Append	Creates an empty record and adds it to the end of the dataset.
AppendRecord	Appends a record to the end of the dataset with the given field data and posts the edit.
ApplyUpdates	Instructs the database to apply any pending cached updates. Updates are not actually written until the CommitUpdates method is called.
Cancel	Cancels any edits to the current record if the edits have not yet been posted.
CancelUpdates	Cancels any pending cached updates.
ClearFields	Clears the contents of all fields in the current record.
CommitUpdates	Instructs the database to apply updates and clear the cached updates buffer.
Close	Closes the dataset.
Delete	Deletes the current record.
DisableControls	Disables input for all data controls associated with the dataset.
Edit	Enables editing of the current record.
EnableControls	Enables input for all data controls associated with the dataset.

continues

TABLE 16.2. CONTINUED

Method	Description
FetchAll	Gets all records from the cursor to the end of the dataset and stores them locally.
FieldByName	Returns the TField pointer for a field name.
FindFirst	Finds the first record that matches the current filter criteria.
FindNext	Finds the next record that matches the current filter criteria.
FindLast	Finds the last record that matches the current filter criteria.
FindPrior	Finds the previous record that matches the current filter criteria.
First	Moves the cursor to the first record in the dataset.
FreeBookmark	Erases a bookmark set previously with GetBookmark and frees the memory allocated for the bookmark.
GetBookmark	Sets a bookmark at the current record.
GetFieldNames	Retrieves a list of the field names in the dataset.
GotoBookmark	Places the cursor at the record indicated by the specified bookmark.
Insert	Inserts a record and puts the dataset in edit mode.
InsertRecord	Inserts a record in the dataset with the given field data and posts the edit.
Last	Positions the cursor on the last record in the dataset.
Locate	Searches the dataset for a particular record.
Lookup	Locates a record by the fastest possible means and returns the data contained in the record.
MoveBy	Moves the cursor by the specified number of rows.
Next	Moves the cursor to the next record.
Open	Opens the dataset.
Post	Writes the edited record data to the database or to the cached update buffer.
Prior	Moves the cursor to the previous record.
Refresh	Updates the data in the dataset from the database.
RevertRecord	When cached updates are used, this method discards changes previously made to the record but not yet written to the database.
SetFields	Sets the values for all fields in a record.
UpdateStatus	Returns the current update status when cached updates are enabled.

TABLE 16.3. PRIMARY TDataSet EVENTS.

Event	Description
AfterCancel	Generated after edits to a record are canceled.
AfterClose	Generated when a dataset is closed.
AfterDelete	Generated after a record is deleted from the dataset.
AfterEdit	Generated after a record is edited.
AfterInsert	Generated after a record is inserted.
AfterOpen	Generated after the dataset is opened.
AfterPost	Generated after the changes to a record are posted.
BeforeCancel	Generated before edits are canceled.
BeforeClose	Generated before a dataset is closed.
BeforeDelete	Generated before a record is deleted.
BeforeEdit	Generated before the dataset goes into edit mode.
BeforeInsert	Generated before a record is inserted.
BeforeOpen	Generated just before a dataset is opened (between the time Active is set to True and the time the dataset is actually opened).
BeforePost	Generated before edits are posted to the database (or the update cache).
OnCalcFields	Generated when calculations are performed on calculated fields.
OnDeleteError	Generated if an error occurs in deleting a record.
OnEditError	Generated if an error occurs while editing a record.
OnFilterRecord	Generated whenever a new row is accessed and Filter is set to True.
OnNewRecord	Generated when a new record is added to the dataset.
OnPostError	Generated when an error occurs while posting the edits to a record.
OnUpdateError	Generated when an error occurs while cached updates are being written to the database.
OnUpdateRecord	Generated when cached updates are applied to a record.

The Fields Editor

Any TDataSet descendant (TTable, TQuery, or TStoredProc) gives access to the Fields Editor at design time. The Fields Editor enables you to select the fields that you want to include in the dataset.

To invoke the Fields Editor, right-click on a Table, Query, or StoredProc component on your form and choose Fields Editor from the context menu. The Fields Editor is

16

displayed. At first the Fields Editor is blank, enabling all fields to be included in the dataset. You can add as many fields as you want to the dataset by selecting Add fields from the Fields Editor context menu. You can also create new fields for the table by choosing New field from the context menu. Figure 16.4 shows the Fields Editor as it appears after adding fields.

FIGURE 16.4.

The Fields Editor.

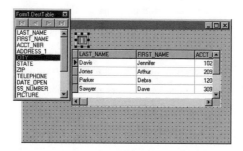

After you add fields to the dataset, you can click on any field and modify its properties. The properties show up in the Object Inspector, enabling you to change the display format, constraints, display label, or other field characteristics.

Cached Updates

Cached updates enable you to control when edits are applied to a database, and they are controlled by the CachedUpdates property. When cached updates are allowed, changes to records aren't written directly to the database. Instead, the changes are written to an update cache on the local machine. Records are held in the cache until you call the ApplyUpdates method. To abandon any changes in the update cache, you call the CancelUpdates method. You cancel the edits made to the current record by calling the RevertRecord method.

When cached edits are disabled (CachedUpdates is False), any changes made to a record are written to the database when the cursor leaves the record. This is fine for local databases, but it is not a good solution for client/server databases for a variety of reasons. Most often you hear people talk about network traffic being the primary reason for using cached updates. Although it is certainly true that cached updates help reduce network traffic, the value of cached updates goes far beyond the issue of network traffic. Let me explain further.

Many client/server databases return a read-only result set as the result of a query. One advantage of cached updates is that the client can work with a local copy of a dataset, modify it as needed, and then write the edits to the database all at one time. This is possible because the database server handles updates, insertions, and deletions of records from a read-only dataset. A local database has to lock records when they are being actively edited. When a record is locked, other database users cannot access the record. Using cached updates reduces the time a record is locked to a very short period of time.

Another advantage to cached updates is that a user can make several changes to a dataset and then either *commit* (apply) all changes or *rollback* (cancel) all changes. This a two-edged sword, however, because if something happens to go wrong on the server when changes are being written to the database, all changes are lost.

One drawback of cached updates is that several users might be working with the same record at the same time. It then becomes a race to see who gets the record updated first. In reality, this problem is reduced somewhat by implementing techniques in the client application that check whether multiple edits have taken place on a record. For example, if Joe tries to post an update to a record, the database and/or client application will notify Joe that Mary has changed the record since Joe initially retrieved it from the database. Joe will have to refresh his copy of the dataset to see whether he still needs to modify the record.

The Table Component

The Table component, represented by the TTable class, provides the quickest and simplest access to a table. Tables are more than adequate for most single-tier database applications. Usually, you will use the Table component when dealing with local databases and the Query component when dealing with SQL database servers.

The TTable class has many properties and methods in addition to those in its ancestor class, TDataSet. Table 16.4 lists the primary properties of the TTable component and Table 16.5 lists the primary methods. Remember, these are properties and methods specific to TTable and do not include those of TTable's ancestor, TDataSet.

For the most part, the properties and methods are very intuitive. By that I mean that you can usually figure out what a property or method does by just looking at its name. It doesn't take a lot to figure out that the LockTable method locks a table for an application's specific use and that the UnlockTable method unlocks the table again. Likewise, you don't have to have an IQ of 150 to guess what the CreateTable, DeleteTable, and RenameTable methods do. With that in mind, I'm not going to cover every aspect of every property and method listed here. Instead, let's get on to some of the more interesting aspects of the Table component.

TABLE 16.4. PRIMARY `TTable` PROPERTIES.

Property	Description
Exclusive	Locks a local table so that only this application can use it.
IndexDefs	Contains information about the table's indexes.
IndexFieldCount	The number of fields that make up the current key.
IndexFieldNames	Used to set the current key by specifying the names of the fields to use for the index.
IndexFields	Used to retrieve information about a specific field in an index.
IndexName	Used to specify a secondary index for a table.
KeyFieldCount	The number of fields to use when searching on partial keys.
MasterFields	The field or fields that should join the master and detail tables.
MasterSource	The table to be used as a master table when this table is used as a detail table.
ReadOnly	Specifies whether this table is read-only.
TableName	The name of the database table.
TableType	The table's type (Paradox, dBASE, or ASCII).

TABLE 16.5. PRIMARY `TTable` METHODS.

Method	Description
AddIndex	Creates a new index for the table.
ApplyRange	Applies a range to the dataset. Only records within that the range (determined by `SetRangeStart` and `SetRangeEnd`) are available for viewing or editing.
BatchMove	Moves records from a dataset into the table.
CancelRange	Removes any ranges currently in effect for the table.
CreateTable	Re-creates the table using new information.
DeleteIndex	Deletes a secondary index.
DeleteTable	Deletes a table.
EmptyTable	Deletes all records from the table.
GetIndexNames	Retrieves a list of all indexes for the table.
GotoKey	Moves the cursor to the record indicated by the current key.
GotoNearest	Moves the cursor to the record that most closely matches the current key.
LockTable	Locks a table so that other applications cannot access it.

Method	Description
RenameTable	Renames the table.
SetKey	Enables you to set keys for the dataset.
SetRange	Sets the start and end range for a dataset and applies the range. This method performs the same action as calling the SetRangeStart, SetRangeEnd, and ApplyRange methods.
SetRangeEnd	Sets the end of the range.
SetRangeStart	Sets the beginning of the range.
UnlockTable	Unlocks a table that was previously locked with LockTable.

16

> **Note**
>
> As you have already seen, the DatabaseName property is used to select a BDE alias. For local databases, rather than select an alias from the list, you can enter a directory where database files are located. The TableName property will then contain a list of database tables in that directory.

Filters

A common need of a database application is to filter a table. Before I discuss filters in detail, I want to point out that filters are primarily used on local databases. Filters are rarely used with client/server databases; instead, a SQL query is used to achieve the same effect that filters have on local databases.

So why filter? Consider that you might have a table with thousands of records, but you are interested in displaying or working on only a small subset of the table. Let's say you have a database that contains names and addresses of computer users all over the world. Your company sells these names and addresses to other companies that want to do bulk mailings.

I call and want to order a mailing list from your company, but I want the list to contain only those computer users who live in Colorado. You could filter your table by postal code and generate a list of names with only Colorado addresses. Or, maybe Borland calls you and wants a list of computer users in Great Britain who are programmers by occupation. In that case, you could filter by occupation and country, thereby giving only the names and addresses the customer is interested in.

Using Filters in the Table Component   Filters in the Table component are handled in one of two ways: through the Filter property or the OnFilterRecord event. Before I discuss these, let me talk about the Filtered property. This property determines whether the table is filtered. If Filtered is True, the table will apply the filter currently in force (either the contents of the Filter property or the results of the OnFilterRecord event). If Filtered is False, the contents of the Filter property are ignored and the OnFilterRecord event is never generated.

For the Filter property, you implement a field name, a logical operator, and a value. A filter might look like this:

```
FirstName = 'Bob'
```

This statement, in effect, says, "Show me all records in which the first name is Bob." Filters can also use the keywords AND, OR, or NOT:

```
CustNo = 1384 AND ShipDate < '1/1/94'
```

Note

> The field name and the logical operators (AND, OR, or NOT) are not case sensitive. The following two filter statements are identical:
>
> ```
> CustName = 'TurboPower' and ShipDate < '1/1/94'
> CUSTNAME = 'TurboPower' AND SHIPDATE < '1/1/94'
> ```
>
> In the case of searching for text, the FilterOptions property determines whether the search string is interpreted as case sensitive.

The following operators can be used in filter statements:

Operator	Use
<	Less than
>	Greater than
=	Equal to
<>	Not equal to
>=	Greater than or equal to
<=	Less than or equal to
( )	Used to specify the evaluation order of compound expressions
[ ]	Used around field names containing spaces
AND, OR, NOT	Logical operators

Filtering with the `Filter` Property   Earlier I said there are two ways of filtering a table. One way is by using the `Filter` property. To use this, all you have to do is type the filter statement directly into the `Filter` property in the Object Inspector at design time or assign a string value to this property at runtime. Naturally, you have to set the `Filtered` property to `True` as well.

To see what I mean, perform the following exercise. First, set up the core components:

1. Place a `Table` component, a `DataSource` component, and a `DBGrid` component on a form.

2. Click on the `Table` component and change its `Database` property to `DBDEMOS`, its `TableName` property to `ORDERS.DB`, and its `Active` property to `True`.

3. Click on the `DataSource` component and change its `DataSet` property to `Table1`.

4. Click on the `DBGrid` component and change its `DataSource` property to `DataSource1`. Size the `DBGrid` as desired.

   At this point you should have a grid with data in it. Now you can get on with the business of filtering the table.

5. Enter the following in the Value column next to the `Filter` property:

   `CustNo = 1384`

6. Set the `Filtered` property to `True`.

Now the table should be showing only the orders for customer 1384. Spend some time experimenting with the filter statement and observe the changes to the table each time a different statement is used. Try the following:

```
CustNo = 1510
CustNo = 1384 and ShipDate < '1/1/94'
CustNo = 1384 and ShipDate > '1/1/94'
OrderNo > 1100 and OrderNo < 1125
```

Here you are making changes to the filter at design time, but it's more likely that you will change the filter dynamically at runtime. In that case, it's as simple as

```
Table1.Filter := 'CustNo = 1510';
```

Note   If `Filtered` is set to `True` but the `Filter` property is blank, the entire dataset is returned just as if the table were not filtered.

Filtering with the `OnFilterRecord` **Event**   The other way you can filter a table is
with the `OnFilterRecord` event. To generate an event handler for this event, double-click
in the Value column next to the `OnFilterRecord` event in the Object Inspector. Delphi
will create an event handler. You can then write code to filter the table. Let's take the
first filter example from earlier (`CustNo = 1384`) and filter using the `OnFilterRecord`
event instead of the `Filter` property:

```
procedure TForm1.Table1FilterRecord(DataSet: TDataSet;
  var Accept: Boolean);
var
  Value : Integer;
begin
  Value := Table1.FieldByName('CustNo').Value;
  Accept := (Value = 1384);
end;
```

I've broken the actual code into two lines to make it more readable. The key element
here is the `Accept` parameter. The `OnFilterRecord` event is called once for every row in
the table. Set the `Accept` parameter to `True` for any rows that you want to show. The preceding code sets `Accept` to `True` for any rows in which the `CustNo` field contains a value
of `1384`. Earlier I gave you four sample filters to try. The first two filters would look like
this if you were to use the `OnFilterRecord` event instead of the `Filter` property:

```
Accept := Table1.FieldByName('CustNo').Value = 1510;
Accept := (Table1.FieldByName('CustNo').Value = 1384) and
  (Table1.FieldByName('ShipDate').AsDateTime < StrToDate('1/1/94'));
```

I'm sure you are thinking, "That's sort of messy." You're right. Using `OnFilterRecord`
means more work, but it's also much more powerful than filtering with just the `Filter`
property.

Using the `FilterOptions` **Property**   The `FilterOptions` property determines
how the filter will be applied. This property is a set that can contain either or both
`foCaseInsensitive` or `foNoPartialCompare`. By default this property is an empty set,
which means that filters will be case sensitive and will enable partial comparisons. When
partial comparisons are enabled, specifying a filter such as `LastName := 'M*'` results in
a dataset containing all records in which the `LastName` field begins with the letter *M*.

Finding Records

You can search a table for certain records by several different methods. In fact, this section applies to all `TDataSet` descendants, not just `TTable`.

> **Note**
>
> As with filters, finding records in a client/server database is almost always carried out via SQL queries. Finding records using the TTable methods is primarily a local database operation.

To search a filtered dataset, you can use the FindFirst, FindNext, FindPrior, and FindLast methods. These methods are the best way to search a filtered dataset because the filter is reapplied each time one of these methods is called. Therefore, if records that previously did not match the filter have been modified so that they now match the filter, they will be included in the dataset before the search is performed.

Another way to search a table is using the FindKey and GotoKey methods. These methods require an index. The FindKey method searches the primary key field or fields for a particular value. If a secondary key is in place, the secondary key field is used to perform the search. The following example sets a secondary key and then searches for a customer number of 1384:

```
Table1.IndexName := 'CustNo';
if not Table1.FindKey([1384]) then
  MessageBox(Handle, 'Record Not Found', 'Message', MB_OK);
```

A third way of searching a table includes using the Locate and Lookup methods. One advantage to these methods is that they don't require the table to be indexed. These methods differ in two ways. First, Locate will use the fastest method available to search the table; if a table is indexed, Locate will use the index.

The second way these two methods differ is that the Lookup method will also return the values of the fields you have specified in the ResultFields parameter before calling Lookup. Both of these methods enable you to specify a field or fields to search and the search value. The following example illustrates the use of the Locate method:

```
var
  Options : TLocateOptions;
begin
  Options := [loPartialKey];
  if not Table1.Locate('CustNo', '1384', Options) then
    MessageBox(Handle, 'Record Not Found', 'Message', MB_OK);
end;
```

If the record is found, Locate returns True, and the cursor is updated to reflect the record where the match was found.

16

Master/Detail Tables

Setting up a master/detail relationship with the Delphi Table component is easy. Let me explain a master/detail relationship and then I'll show you how to set up one. Let's say you have a table called CUSTOMER that contains information on your customers. That table will likely be indexed on a field called CustNo.

Let's further assume that you have a table called ORDERS that contains a list of all orders placed by your customers. Naturally, this table would also have a CustNo field. Now let's say you want to browse the table containing all your customers. Wouldn't it be nice if you could see each customer's orders while you browse? A master/detail table enables you to do that. Perform the following steps to get a good understanding of master/detail tables:

1. Start with a new application. Place a Table component on the form. Set its properties as follows:

Name	Master
DatabaseName	DBDEMOS
TableName	customer.db

2. Place a DataSource component on the form and set its DataSet property to Master.

3. Now place a second Table component on the form and change its Name property to Details. You'll set the rest of this table's properties in just a minute.

4. Place a second DataSource component on the form. Change its DataSource property to Details.

5. Click on the Details Table component. Change its properties as follows:

DatabaseName	DBDEMOS
TableName	orders.db
MasterSource	DataSource1

6. Click on the ellipsis button next to the MasterFields property. The Field Link Designer dialog box is displayed.

7. At the top of the Field Link Designer dialog box is a combo box labeled Available Indexes. Select the CustNo index from this combo box.

8. Now both the Detail Fields list box and the Master Fields list box have a CustNo entry. Select CustNo in each of these list boxes and click the Add button to create the relationship. The Joined Fields list box shows that the two tables are joined by their CustNo fields.

9. Click OK to close the Field Link Designer dialog boxes.

10. Drop two DBGrid components on the form and link one to DataSource1 and the other to DataSource2.

11. Change the Active property of both tables to True. The Master table will show all customers, and the Details table will show the orders for each customer.

What you just did was create a relationship between the master table and the detail table. This relationship joined these two tables through a common field: CustNo. To fully understand what this means, run the program and move from record to record in the master table. As you select a customer name in the master table, you will see only that customer's orders in the detail table.

16

The Query Component

The Query component is the preferred method of accessing data in client/server databases. The following sections describe the primary properties and methods of the TQuery class.

Tip

> The Query component doesn't have a TableName property as the Table does. This means that at design time, you can't immediately see a list of tables for the current database. To see a list of tables, you can perform one of two tasks. First, you can temporarily drop a Table component on the form, set the DatabaseName property, and then view the list of tables in the TableName property. You also can select the Query component on the form, right-click on it, and then choose Explore from the context menu. This will take you to either the SQL Explorer (Client/Server version) or the BDE Administrator (Standard and Professional versions). You can use either tool to view the tables in a database.

The SQL Property

The SQL property is a TStringList that contains the SQL statements to execute. You can set the SQL property's value via the Object Inspector at design time or through code at runtime.

To set the value at design time, click the ellipsis button next to the SQL property in the Object Inspector. The String List Editor dialog box is displayed, and you can type in one or more lines of SQL statements.

> **Tip**
> Remember that the String List Editor dialog box has a feature that enables you to edit string lists in the Delphi Code Editor.

When adding lines to the SQL property at runtime, make sure that you clear the previous contents—for example,

```
Query1.SQL.Clear;
Query1.SQL.Add('select * from country');
```

It's easy to think of the SQL property as a string instead of a string list. If you don't clear the SQL property before adding a string, previous SQL statements will still be in the string list. Errors will almost certainly occur when you try to execute the SQL statement.

Executing SQL Statements

The statements in the SQL property will be executed when either the Open method or the ExecSQL method is called. If you are using SQL statements that include SELECT, use the Open method to execute the SQL query. If you are using INSERT, UPDATE, or DELETE statements, you need to use the ExecSQL method to execute the query. The following example sets the SQL property and then calls the Open method:

```
Query1.SQL.Clear;
Query1.SQL.Add('select * from country');
Query1.Open;
```

The SQL SELECT statement retrieves certain columns from a database. The asterisk tells the database server to return all the columns in a table. The preceding example, then, returns the entire table called country from the current database. To return specific columns, use code such as the following:

```
Query1.SQL.Clear;
Query1.SQL.Add('select Name, Capital from country');
Query1.Open;
```

> **Note**
> Setting the Active property to True is the same as calling the Open method.

The SQL DELETE statement deletes records from a dataset. To delete a record from a dataset, you can use code like this:

```
Query1.SQL.Clear;
Query1.SQL.Add('delete from country where name = 'Royland');
Query1.ExecSQL;
```

Notice that the ExecSQL method is used instead of the Open method. As I said earlier, you need to use the ExecSQL method to execute a query containing INSERT, UPDATE, or DELETE statements.

The INSERT command inserts a record into a dataset:

```
Query1.SQL.Add('insert into country');
Query1.SQL.Add('(Name, Capital)');
Query1.SQL.Add('values ("Royland", "Royville")');
Query1.ExecSQL;
```

16

Note

Notice the use of double quotes in the preceding example. SQL syntax should not be confused with Object Pascal syntax. SQL enables the use of either double quotes or single quotes around value names. You can use either, but if you use single quotes within a string, you need to be sure to double them. Either of the following is valid:

```
Query1.SQL.Add('values ("Royland", "Royville")');
Query1.SQL.Add('values (''Royland'', ''Royville'')');
```

Updating a dataset using the UPDATE command looks like this:

```
Query1.SQL.Clear;
Query1.SQL.Add('update country');
Query1.SQL.Add('set Capital = ''Royburg''');
Query1.SQL.Add('where Name = "Royland"');
Query1.ExecSQL;
```

Although it isn't my intention to teach SQL, I thought a few examples would help get you started.

Using Parameters in SQL Statements

SQL statements use parameters to add flexibility. A parameter in a SQL statement is much like an Object Pascal variable. A parameter in a SQL statement is preceded by a colon. Take the following SQL statement, for example:

```
select * from country where name = :Param1
```

The parameter in the preceding statement is named Param1. When this SQL statement is executed, the value of Param1 in the Params property is substituted for the parameter name:

```
Query1.SQL.Add('select * from country where Name = :Param1');
Query1.ParamByName('Param1').AsString := 'Brazil';
Query1.Open;
```

You can set the parameter values of the Params property at design time via the Parameters dialog box, but most of the time you will be changing the parameters at runtime (which is the point of using parameters, of course). Notice in the preceding code that the ParamByName method is used to set the value of Param1. This is probably the easiest way to set a parameter's value. There is another way, however:

```
Query1.Params[0].AsString := 'Brazil';
```

Here the Items property of the TParam class is used to set the value of the parameter. Accessing a parameter by index is more error-prone than accessing the parameter by name because you have to remember the orders of your parameters. Most of the time you will just use ParamByName.

Note

> Not all aspects of a SQL statement can be parameterized. For example, most SQL servers don't allow a parameter for the table name. Take the following SQL statement:
>
> ```
> select * from :TableName
> ```
>
> This statement results in a SQL error because you can't use a parameter for the table name.

The StoredProc Component

The StoredProc component represents a stored procedure on a database server. A stored procedure is a set of SQL statements that executes as a single program. Stored procedures are individual programs that run against a database and can encapsulate often-performed database tasks. This makes it easier for programmers to do their work because they don't have to write line after line of code each time they want to perform a certain action. All they have to do is call the stored procedure on the server.

This also results in smaller client applications because they don't have to contain unnecessary code. Another purpose of stored procedures is to maintain data integrity. A stored procedure can validate data and either allow or disallow changes to the database based on whether the data validation passes.

As with SQL queries, some stored procedures make use of parameters and some do not. For stored procedures that don't take parameters, all you have to do is set the procedure name and execute the procedure:

```
StoredProc1.StoredProcName := 'DO_IT';
StoredProc1.Prepare;
StoredProc1.ExecProc;
```

Notice that the Prepare method is called first to prepare the stored procedure. After that, the ExecProc method is called to execute the stored procedure.

For stored procedures that take parameters, you have to set the parameters before executing the stored procedure:

```
StoredProc1.StoredProcName := 'ADD_EMP_PROJ';
StoredProc1.ParamByName('EMP_NO').Value := 12;
StoredProc1.ParamByName('PROJ_ID').Value := 'VBASE';
StoredProc1.Prepare;
StoredProc1.ExecProc;
```

By the way, if you have Delphi Professional or Client/Server, you can test the preceding code yourself by following these steps:

1. Drop a StoredProc component on a form and set its DatabaseName property to IBLOCAL.

2. Place a button on the form and double-click it to create an OnClick event handler.

3. Type the code from the preceding code snippet.

4. Place a Table component on the form and set its DatabaseName to IBLOCAL and its TableName to EMPLOYEE_PROJECT. Place DBGrid and DataSource components on the form and hook them up to the table. Set the table's Active property to True. This enables you to see changes made to the table.

5. Add one line to the end of the code in step 3:

   ```
   Table1.Refresh;
   ```

Now run the program. When you click the button, a new record is added to the table with an employee ID number of 12 and a project ID of VBASE. Close the program. Now change the code so that the employee ID number is 10 and rerun the program. This time you will get an error message from the stored procedure stating that the employee number is invalid. You will get the error because the ADD_EMP_PROJ stored procedure validates input, and a value of 10 is invalid for this database.

16

> You can view a stored procedure using the Explore feature found on the context menu. The stored procedure called ADD_EMP_PROJ looks like this:
>
> ```
> CREATE PROCEDURE ADD_EMP_PROJ (
>   EMP_NO SMALLINT,
>   PROJ_ID CHAR(5)
> ) AS
> BEGIN
>  BEGIN
>  INSERT INTO employee_project (emp_no, proj_id) VALUES (:emp_no,
> :proj_id);
>  WHEN SQLCODE -530 DO
>   EXCEPTION unknown_emp_id;
>  END
>  SUSPEND;
> END
> ```
>
> Naturally, you shouldn't change a stored procedure unless you know what you are doing.

The UpdateSQL Component

The UpdateSQL component provides a way of applying edits to a read-only dataset when cached updates are enabled. Ordinarily, a read-only dataset is just that—read only. When cached updates are enabled, however, a read-only database can be modified and the results of those modifications written to the database.

Most client/server databases have default actions that they perform when the changes in the update cache are applied. The UpdateSQL component enables you to provide your own SQL statements when a record in a read-only dataset needs to be updated, inserted, or deleted. For example, you can specify default values for certain fields in a dataset by using an UpdateSQL component.

The DeleteSQL property enables you to define a SQL query that will be executed when cached updates are applied and the update cache contains deleted records. Likewise, InsertSQL enables you to define a SQL query that will be executed when records have been inserted in a dataset and cached updates are applied. The ModifySQL property is used to define a SQL query that will be called when a record has been modified and cached updates are applied.

The DataSource Component

The DataSource component provides a mechanism to hook dataset components (Table, Query, or StoredProc) to the visual components that display the data (DBGrid, DBEdit,

DBListBox, and so on). The primary purpose of DataSource is to enable making changes to your applications easier. All the data components on a form are hooked up to the DataSource, which is then hooked up to the dataset.

Because the data components are not hooked directly to the dataset, you can easily change datasets and not have to hook up each and every data component on the form each time you change the dataset. To change your dataset from a Table to a Query, for example, all you have to do is change the DataSet property of the DataSource component. There's no need to change anything in each of the data components.

16

TDataSource has very few properties. As you have already seen, the DataSet property is used to hook the DataSource to an underlying dataset. The Enabled property determines whether the data components hooked up to this data source display data. When Enabled is True, data is displayed. When Enabled is False, the data components are blank.

The methods of TDataSource are mostly insignificant, and I won't go over them here. The OnDataChange event is generated when the current record has been edited and the cursor moves to a different record. The OnStateChange event occurs when the state of the dataset changes (when the user moves from edit mode to browse mode, for example).

The Session Component

The Session component manages a database session. Each time you start a database application, the BDE sets up a global TSession object called Session. You can use Session to access the current database session. You don't have to create your own TSession objects unless you are writing a multithreaded application. Most of the time this isn't the case, so the default TSession object is usually all you need.

TSession has a couple methods of particular interest. The AddAlias and AddStandardAlias methods can be used to create a BDE alias at runtime. You will probably need to create aliases at runtime when you deploy your applications. Creating a BDE alias is discussed in the section titled "Creating a BDE Alias."

The GetAliasNames and GetDatabaseNames methods can be used to get a list of databases. This is handy when you want to enable your users to choose a database from a list. You could put the database names in a combo box, for example:

```
Session.GetDatabaseNames(DBNamesComboBox.Items);
```

In this case, the Items property of a combo box called DBNamesComboBox is filled with the list of database names. The GetTableNames and GetStoredProcNames methods can be used in the same way.

The `Database` Component

The `Database` component gives you access to specific database operations. You don't need a `Database` component for some applications. There are certain operations, though, that require a `Database` component. These operations are discussed in the following sections.

Retaining Database Connections

The `KeepConnections` property is used to control how database connections are handled when a dataset is closed. If `KeepConnections` is `False`, the database connection will be dropped when the last dataset is closed. This requires a login the next time a dataset is opened. It's not so much that logins are an annoyance (which they are), but more importantly that logins take time. I don't mean that they take time in the sense that you have to type a username and password in a login dialog box. I mean that they take a lot of processing and network time to open a database connection and log in, even if that login process is automated. If you don't want to worry about logging in every time a dataset is opened, set `KeepConnections` to `True`.

Login Control

One reason to use a `Database` component is to control login operations. There are two ways you can control a login. One is by setting the `LoginPrompt` property to `False` and explicitly setting the login parameters. You can do this before opening a dataset:

```
Database1.Params.Values['user name'] := 'SYSDBA';
Database1.Params.Values['password'] := 'masterkey';
```

The preceding code sets the username and password for a Local InterBase database connection.

 Note　You should be very careful about hard-coding password information in your applications for security reasons. Login prompts are used for a reason. Don't bypass login requirements unless you have a very good reason to do so.

Taking this example a little further, let's assume that you have a form with a `Database` component and a `Table` component. Let's say you want to create a database connection and open a table without any login prompt. Here's the code:

```
Database1.AliasName := 'IBLOCAL';
Database1.DatabaseName := 'MyDatabase';
Database1.Params.Values['user name'] := 'SYSDBA';
Database1.Params.Values['password'] := 'masterkey';
```

```
Table1.DatabaseName := Database1.DatabaseName;
Table1.TableName := 'CUSTOMER';
Table1.Open;
```

This code first sets the `Database` component's `Alias` property to `IBLOCAL` to connect to Local InterBase. Then the `DatabaseName` property is set to an arbitrary name. You can use any name you like for the database name. Next, the database connection parameters (username and password) are set. After that, the `Table` component's `DatabaseName` property is set to the value of the `Database`'s `DatabaseName` property, which hooks the table to the database. Finally, the `TableName` property is set for the table and the table is opened.

The other way to perform a login is with the `OnLogin` event. This is generated whenever login information is required. In order to generate this event, you need to make sure that you have the `LoginPrompt` property set to `True`. After that, you can provide an event handler for the `OnLogin` event. It will look like this:

```
procedure TForm1.Database1Login(Database: TDatabase;
  LoginParams: TStrings);
begin
  LoginParams.Values['user name'] := 'SYSDBA';
  LoginParams.Values['password'] := 'masterkey';
end;
```

Does this code look familiar? It's essentially the same code used earlier when directly setting the connection parameters of the database. Usually you would not hard-code the username and password (or, at least, not the password) but would probably pull that information from an outside source, such as an edit component, a configuration file, or the Windows Registry.

Transaction Control

Another reason to use a `Database` component is for transaction control. Normally, the BDE handles transaction control for you. There might be times, however, when you require complete control over transaction processing. In that case you can use the `Database` component's transaction control methods.

A *transaction* is a collection of updates to a dataset. Updates can include changes made to records, deleting records, inserting records, and more. You begin a transaction by calling the `StartTransaction` method. Any changes made to the dataset are held until you call the `Commit` method. When you call `Commit`, all updates in the transaction are written to the database. If you want to abandon changes to all updates in the current transaction, you call the `Rollback` method. The transaction isolation level is controlled by the `TransIsolation` property's value. (See the `TransIsolation` topic in the Delphi help for more information on transaction isolation levels.)

16

> All transaction updates are treated as a single unit, which means that when you call `Commit`, all updates are committed. When you call `Rollback`, all updates are canceled. It also means that if something goes wrong during a transaction commit, none of the updates in the current transaction are written to the database.

The `BatchMove` Component

The `BatchMove` component is used to copy records from one dataset to another. The `Source` property specifies the source dataset, and the `Destination` property specifies the destination dataset for the batch move operation.

The `Mapping` property is required if your source and destination datasets don't have identical columns. `Mapping` is a `TStringList` property. To specify mappings, edit the string list and add mappings like this:

```
FirstName = FName
LastName = LName
Notes = Comments
```

> The mapping strings use the equal sign and not the Pascal assignment operator (`:=`).

The column name on the left side of the equal sign is the destination column; the column name on the right side of the equal sign is the source column. Setting the mappings like this tells `TBatchMove`, "These two datasets don't match, so copy the data from the `FName` column in the source dataset to the `FirstName` column in the destination dataset." If your source and destination datasets are not identical and you fail to set column mappings, the batch move will fail.

The `Execute` method performs the batch move. To use `TBatchMove`, all you have to do is set the `Source`, `Destination`, and `Mode` properties and call the `Execute` method. You can set the `Source` and `Destination` properties at design time or at runtime. The following code creates a copy of a table:

```
DestTable.TableName := 'copy.db';
BatchMove1.Destination := DestTable;
BatchMove1.Source := SourceTable;
BatchMove1.Mode := batCopy;
BatchMove1.Execute;
```

The Mode property specifies how records are applied to the destination dataset. Table 16.6 lists the possible values of the Mode property and their meanings.

TABLE 16.6. Mode PROPERTY VALUES.

Value	Description
batAppend	Appends records from the source dataset to the end of the destination dataset.
batAppendUpdate	Combination of batAppend and batUpdate. If a matching record already exists, it is updated. If no matching record exists, a new record is added.
batCopy	Creates a new table and copies all records from the source table to the new table.
batDelete	Deletes records in the destination dataset that match the source dataset. The destination dataset must have an index.
batUpdate	Replaces records in the destination dataset with records from the source dataset that have the same key values.

16

Caution

Be careful with the batCopy mode. Calling Execute in this mode will overwrite any existing tables and replace the contents with the contents of the source table.

The TField Component

The TField class represents a field (column) in a database. Through the TField class, you can set a field's attributes. These attributes include the data type (string, integer, float, and so on), the size of the field, the index, whether the field is a calculated field, whether it is required, and so on. You can also access or set a field's value through properties such as AsString, AsVariant, and AsInteger.

TField is a base class for more specific field classes. The descendants of TField include TStringField, TIntegerField, TSmallIntField, TWordField, TFloatField, TCurrencyField, TBCDField, TBooleanField, TDateTimeField, TDateField, TTimeField, TBlobField, TBytesField, TVarBytesField, TMemoField, and TGraphicField.

These derived classes extend the base class in small ways to add functionality. For example, numerical field classes have a DisplayFormat property that determines how the number is displayed and an EditFormat property that determines how the value appears while being edited. Each TField descendant corresponds to a specific database field type. The TIntegerField class is used when the field type is an integer, the TTimeField class is used when the field type is a date or time (or date/time), the TBlobField class is used when the field type is binary large object, and so on.

You can access the properties of TField at design time through the Fields Editor. After you add fields, you can click on a field in the Fields Editor and the properties for that field will be displayed in the Object Inspector. Figure 16.5 shows the Fields Editor and Object Inspector while editing fields.

FIGURE 16.5.

The Fields Editor and Object Inspector.

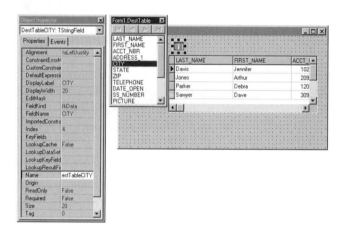

The TField properties and methods are so numerous that I'm not going to list them all here. Instead, I'll walk you through some ways you are most likely to use TField and its descendant classes.

Accessing Fields

Before you can get or set the field value, you need some way of locating a field. There are at least three ways to do this:

- By its pointer name
- By the Fields property of TDataSet
- By the FieldByName method of TDataSet

Accessing a field by its pointer name is probably the least used method. It works only if you have previously added fields to your project using the Fields Editor. When you add fields via the Fields Editor, Delphi creates a pointer for each field by combining the table name with the field name. If you have a table called Table1 and a string field called

FirstName, Delphi would create a TStringField pointer called Table1FirstName. You could use this pointer to access a field:

```
Table1FirstName.Value := 'Per';
```

The problem with this approach is that you don't always need to add fields using the Fields Editor.

The Fields property offers another way of accessing a field—by position. If you know that the LastName field is the first field in the table, you can use something like this:

```
Edit1.Text := Table1.Fields[0].Value;
```

The problem with this approach, of course, is that you have to know the exact order of fields.

Of the three ways of accessing fields, the most commonly used and reliable is the FieldByName method. Using FieldByName, you have to know only the name of the field to access the field:

```
Table1.FieldByName('LastName').AsString := Edit1.Text;
```

FieldByName returns a TField pointer. To make it more understandable, let me break down the preceding line of code:

```
var
  Field : TField;
begin
  Field := Table1.FieldByName('LastName');
  Field.AsString := Edit1.Text;
end;
```

In most cases, FieldByName is the way to go. Oh, you might be wondering which record is modified when you execute the preceding code. All these techniques retrieve the field from the current record.

Retrieving and Setting Field Values

After you obtain a pointer to a particular field, you can change its value by using the Value property or any of the As properties (by As properties I mean AsString, AsInteger, AsDateTime, AsBoolean, and so on). These properties perform conversions from one data type to another. Naturally, you can't always be assured that a conversion can be made. For example, if you try to convert a string field containing Smith to an integer, an exception will be thrown.

Setting a field's value is simple when you know the secret of FieldByName:

```
Table1.Edit;
Table1.FieldByName('LastName').AsString := Edit1.Text;
Table1.Post;
```

First, the Edit method is called to put the table in edit mode. If you fail to call Edit, you will get an exception when you try to modify a field's value. After the table is put in edit mode, the field's value is set. In this case I used AsString instead of the Value property. For a string field, it's the same thing in either case. Finally, the Post method is called to post the edit to the database (or the update cache if CachedUpdates is on). That's all there is to it. Retrieving a field's value is just as easy:

```
var
  AcctNo : Integer;
begin
  AcctNo := Table1.FieldByName('ACCT_NBR').Value;
  { More code here. }
end;
```

TField Events

The TField events of note are OnChange and OnValidate. The OnChange event is generated each time a field's value changes. This occurs after the data has been posted. You can use this event if you need to be notified of changes to a field.

The OnValidate event, on the other hand, occurs just before data is posted. If you have a data control on a form associated with a field, that control can usually do validation of data. If, however, you are setting a field's value through code, you might want to do your own validation in the OnValidate event handler. This event is somewhat strange in that it doesn't pass you a parameter that you can use to reject an edit. Instead, you should throw an exception if the validation fails:

```
procedure TForm1.Table1ACCT_NBRValidate(Sender: TField);
begin
  if Sender.AsInteger < 3000 then
    raise EDBEditError.Create('Bad Account Number.');
end;
```

When you throw an exception, the act of posting the data to the database is aborted.

To create an event handler at design time, you have to use the Fields Editor to add fields to the dataset. After you have done that, you can select a field in the Fields Editor and then double-click next to the event name in the Object Inspector, as you would for any other event.

Client/Server Database Components

The Client/Server version of Delphi comes with three additional data access components that enable the creation of multitiered database systems. (To recap, a multitiered database system is one in which client applications talk to one or more application servers [the middle tier] that in turn talk to the database server.) The multitier database components are `TRemoteServer`, `TProvider`, and `TClientDataSet`.

The `TRemoteServer` component is used in a client application to establish a connection to one or more application servers. The `TProvider` component, used in a middle-tier application server, acts as a conduit between the database server and the client application. The `TClientDataSet` component is used in a client application to gain access to the provider on an application server. A detailed account of the use of these components is beyond the scope of this book.

Creating a BDE Alias

You can go only so far in database programming without eventually creating a BDE alias. The sample databases are fine, but sooner or later you will need to create an alias for your own databases. When you deploy your Delphi database application, you will also need to create one or more aliases on your users' machines as well. There are many ways to create an alias:

- Through the BDE Administrator utility from the Delphi program group
- Through the Database Desktop program
- Through the SQL Explorer (Client/Server version only)
- Through code at runtime

To create an alias, either you must have your users run the BDE Administrator, or you must create any needed aliases through code. Obviously, creating the alias yourself through code is preferable (never underestimate the ability of your users to botch even the most simple tasks). First I'll show you how to use the BDE Administrator to create an alias. Then I'll show you how to create an alias through code.

Creating an Alias with the BDE Administrator

While you are developing your applications, you need to create one or more BDE aliases. This is most easily done using one of the BDE utility programs provided with Delphi. The steps for creating an alias using the BDE Administrator and the SQL Explorer are identical, so for simplicity's sake I'll show you how to create an alias with the BDE Administrator.

Let's assume for a minute that you are going to create a mailing list application. The first step you need to take is to create an alias for your database. You can create an alias in several ways, but the easiest is probably with the BDE Administrator utility. Perform these steps:

1. Start the BDE Administrator (locate the Delphi group from the Windows Start menu and choose the BDE Administrator icon). The BDE Administrator will start and show a list of database aliases currently installed.

2. Choose Object | New from the BDE Administrator menu (make sure the Databases tab is selected). The New Database Alias dialog box comes up and asks which driver to use for the new alias.

3. You will be creating a database using the Standard driver, and because STANDARD is already selected, you can simply click OK. Now the BDE Administrator looks like Figure 16.6.

FIGURE 16.6.

The BDE Administrator creating a new database alias.

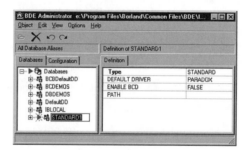

4. The BDE Administrator is waiting for you to type a name for your alias, so type MyDatabase and press Enter.

At this point, you need to provide a few items of information in the Definition window. The Type is already set to STANDARD, so there's nothing to be done there. The DEFAULT DRIVER field is set to PARADOX, which is the type you want, so there's nothing to be done there, either (other choices include dBASE, FOXPRO, and ASCIIDRV). You can also leave the default value for the ENABLE BCD field. The only information you need to supply is the path on disk where the database files will be stored:

1. Click on the PATH field and either type a path or use the ellipsis button to browse to a path.

2. Close the BDE Administrator and say Yes when asked whether you want to save your edits. That's it. You have created a BDE alias.

Switch back to Delphi and drop a Table component on a form. Check the DatabaseName property in the Object Inspector to see whether your database alias shows up. If you did everything right, you will see it listed there with the other database names. Your database doesn't have any tables yet, but that's okay. You can take care of that later.

Creating an Alias Through Code

To avoid confusion with your users, you will probably want to create any aliases your program needs the first time your program runs. Thankfully, creating an alias at runtime is simple. Here's the code to create a local Paradox alias called WayCool:

```
CreateDirectory('C:', nil);
Session.AddStandardAlias('WayCool', 'C:', '');
```

That's it? Yes, that's all there is to it. Naturally, you should perform some checks to ensure that the directory and alias were properly created, but that's about all there is to it.

16

 Note

This example uses the AddStandardAlias method to create a STANDARD type alias. To create aliases for database servers of other types, use the AddAlias method.

Summary

That's a lot to absorb. The best way to solidify the material presented in this chapter is to spend a lot of time experimenting. Take some sample databases and perform filters on the tables, try out some SQL statements, and browse the databases with the BDE Administrator or the SQL Explorer. At this point you don't have to worry about writing complete database programs. Just spend some time with the various components and get a feel for how the BDE and the VCL database components work together.

Workshop

The Workshop contains quiz questions to help you solidify your understanding of the material covered and exercises to provide you with experience in using what you have learned. You can find answers to the quiz questions in Appendix A, "Answers to the Quiz Questions."

Q&A

Q When I ship my Delphi database application, can I simply copy the appropriate BDE files to my users' machines?

A No. You must follow the guidelines outlined by Borland in the DEPLOY.TXT file. Generally speaking, this requires using an installation program certified by Borland to install any applications that use the BDE.

Q Why is it necessary to use a `DataSource` component? Why can't the data components and the data access components communicate directly?

A Using a `DataSource` as an intermediary makes your job easier if you have to change datasets later on. Rather than change the `DataSet` property of numerous data components, you only have to change the `DataSet` property of the `DataSource`. For example, let's say you change your dataset from a `TTable` to a `TQuery` (a major change). The change would be nearly transparent to your data components because the `DataSource` does all the work.

Q When do I use a `TTable` and when do I use a `TQuery`?

A Most of the time you will use a `TTable` when working with a local database (Paradox or dBASE) and a `TQuery` when working with a client/server database. In the end it is up to you to decide which to use.

Q What's the point of Local InterBase?

A Local InterBase enables you to develop a local database application that can easily be converted to a client/server application later.

Q Do I need to create a `TSession` for my application?

A Not normally. A default `TSession` is automatically created for every database application. You can use this object, called `Session`, any time you need access to the properties and methods of the `TSession` class. The only time you need to create your own `TSession` objects is when you are writing a multithreaded database application.

Q I am using a local database in my application. Do I need to worry about cached updates?

A Generally speaking, no. Cached updates are much more important for client/server databases.

Quiz

1. What is a local database?

2. What is the purpose of the BDE?

3. Are a dataset and a table the same thing? If not, explain the difference.

4. Name one advantage of cached updates.

5. What is a stored procedure?

6. What is the purpose of the `SQL` property of the `TQuery` component?

7. Name one reason you might want to use your own `TDatabase` object instead of the default.

8. Why would you want to keep a connection to a remote database open even when you are not currently using the connection?

9. What does the TBatchMove component do?

10. What is a BDE alias?

Exercises

1. Describe how your application, the BDE, and a database work together.

2. Place a DataSource, a Table, and a DBGrid on a form. Hook up the components. Select a database and a table name for the Table component. Set the Table's Active property to True. View the table contents in the grid.

3. Change the Table's TableName property several times to view different tables. (Hint: You must set the Active property to False before changing the TableName property.)

4. Place a second Table component on the form created in exercise 2. Select a database name and a table name. Set the Active property to True. Now change the DataSet property of the DataSource component to Table2 (the second table). What happens to the DBGrid?

5. Create a new BDE alias on your system.

6. **Extra Credit:** Create a table under the BDE alias created in exercise 5 and populate it with data.

16

DAY 17

Building Database Forms

After a relatively unexciting look at Delphi database architecture, you can move on to the more interesting task of building a database application. The first step in that task is to learn how to create database forms, so that's today's subject.

You'll learn how to create database forms using the Delphi Database Form Wizard. You'll also learn how to build database forms from scratch. Toward the end of the day, you will learn about the data components of Delphi. These are the components that display the data from a database and enable you to edit that data—you can find them on the Data Controls tab of the Component palette. They are often referred to as *data-aware* components. I'll just call them data components in this chapter. Let's get to it.

The Database Form Wizard

The Delphi Database Form Wizard provides a way of creating database forms quickly and easily. Using this wizard, you can create a database form from start to finish. You don't have to place any database components on the form. You just start the wizard and let the wizard take it from there.

Note

No automated process is good enough to be all things to all people. I won't pretend that the forms created by the Database Form Wizard will be everything you want or that the Database Form Wizard will do all your work for you. What the Database Form Wizard can do, though, is the initial work of setting up a database form. After the initial work is done, you can go to work customizing the form to make it look the way you want.

The Database Form Wizard enables you to create both simple forms and master/detail forms. It enables you to choose whether your dataset will be a TTable or a TQuery. The wizard enables you to select a database table and to select the fields from that table that you want displayed on the form. It gives you a choice of layout options as well. After you supply the Database Form Wizard with all the information it needs, it creates the new form for you.

To start the Database Form Wizard, choose Database | Form Wizard... from the Delphi main menu. Alternatively, you can start the Database Form Wizard from the Business page of the Object Repository.

First I'll show you how to create a simple form, and then I'll talk about master/detail forms.

Creating a Simple Form Using the Database Form Wizard

When the Database Form Wizard starts, it displays the page shown in Figure 17.1.

FIGURE 17.1.

Page one of the Database Form Wizard.

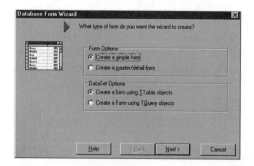

This page of the Database Form Wizard asks you to choose the type of database you want to create and the dataset type you would like to use. The Form Options section gives you the choice of creating a simple form (with a single dataset) or a master/detail form.

I talked briefly about master/detail tables yesterday in the section "Master/Detail Tables." I'll talk more about master/detail forms later today in the section "Creating a Master/Detail Form." The first page of the Database Form Wizard also enables you to select from either a TTable-based dataset or a TQuery-based dataset. For this exercise, the default settings for creating a simple form using a TTable dataset are what you want, so you can click the Next button to move on to the next page.

Tip

> In some cases, you might want to implement data from more than one table on a single form but not use a master/detail relationship. The Database Form Wizard enables you to choose only from one table. What you can do, though, is run the Database Form Wizard and select the first table. Your form will be created. Change the names of the Table and DataSource components to something meaningful. Now run the Database Form Wizard again and choose the second table. When the form is displayed, select all the database components on the form and copy them to the Clipboard. Switch back to the first form, make some room on the form for the new components, and paste them from the Clipboard onto the form. Now remove the second form from the project, and you're all set.

The next page asks you to choose a table from which to obtain the data. The Drive or Alias name combo box enables you to choose a database name just as you do when setting the DatabaseName property for a dataset component at design time. It also enables you to choose a directory from which to select a table. For this example, choose the DBDEMOS alias. The tables available in the database will show up in the Table Name list box. Select the ANIMALS.DBF table. The Database Form Wizard now looks like the one in Figure 17.2. Click the Next button to go to the next page.

FIGURE 17.2.

Selecting a table with the Database Form Wizard.

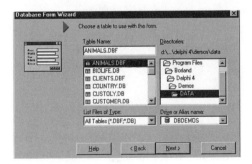

The third page of the Database Form Wizard asks you to choose the fields from the table that you want to include on the form. The Available Fields list box on the left shows the fields that are in the table you have selected. The Ordered Selected Fields list box on the right contains the fields that you want on your new form. Between the two list boxes are four buttons for adding or removing fields from the Ordered Selected Fields list box.

To add a field, click the field name in the Available Fields list box and click the > button. Add any fields you want with this method. You can select multiple fields and click the > button to add the selected fields. To add all fields in the table at one time, click the >> button.

> **Tip**
>
> You can double-click a field name to add that field to the Ordered Selected Fields list box or double-click it again to remove it from the list box.

After the fields have been added to the Ordered Selected Fields list box, you can change the order of the fields by drag and drop or by clicking the up and down arrow buttons below the list box. Figure 17.3 shows this page of the wizard. For now, add all the fields to the Ordered Selected Fields list box and click the Next button to move to the next page.

FIGURE 17.3.

Page three of the Database Form Wizard, adding fields.

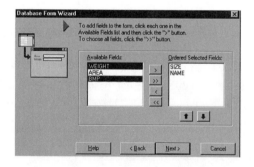

The next page of the Database Form Wizard dialog asks you how you want the components for each field arranged on the form. You have three layout choices:

- Horizontally
- Vertically
- In a grid

Click each of the three radio buttons and watch the image to the left of the wizard as you select different options. The image changes to show you the layout for each choice. Select the radio button labeled Vertically and click the Next button to continue. Figure 17.4 shows this page of the wizard.

FIGURE 17.4.

Selecting a layout style with the Database Form Wizard.

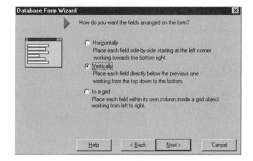

> **Note**
>
> When Delphi creates the database form, it chooses the component type that most closely matches the data type of the field that component represents. For example, a regular text field is represented by a DBEdit component, a memo field by a DBMemo component, and a BLOB image field by a DBImage component. Delphi makes a best guess as to the component type to place on the form for a given data type. You might have to edit the form to get exactly the component you want for a given field.

17

The next page asks where you want to place the labels for the fields relative to each data component. You can put the labels on top of the components or to the left. Notice that here, too, the image on the Database Form Wizard changes depending on which of the two options is currently selected. For now, choose the second option in order to place the labels on top of the components. Figure 17.5 shows this page of the Database Form Wizard.

FIGURE 17.5.

This page enables you to place the labels.

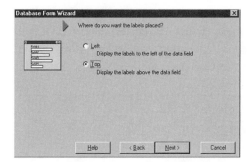

> **Note**   The page shown in Figure 17.5 appears only if you select the option for vertical component layout on the previous page of the Database Form Wizard.

The final page of the Database Form Wizard asks you to make two choices:

- The first choice, to create the new database form as the main form of the application, is in the form of a check box near the top of the page. Check this option if this form is going to be the main form of the application. If this form isn't the main form, clear the check box.

> **Note**   If you choose to have Delphi create the new database form as the main form of the application, be aware that the existing main form will still be part of the application's project. You need to remove the old main form from the project if you don't want it anymore. To remove the old main form, click the Remove from Project button and remove the main form's unit (Unit1.pas for a default project).

- The second choice asks you whether to create just the form or the form and a data module. If you choose the first option (Form Only), the form will contain all the data components, the DataSet component (Table or Query), and the DataSource component. If you choose the second option (Form and DataModule), the DataSet component and the DataSource component will be removed from the form and placed in a separate data module.

I'll talk more about data modules tomorrow in the section "Working with Data Modules." For now, make certain that the Generate a Main Form check box is checked and that the Form Generation option is set to Form Only. Figure 17.6 shows the last page of the Database Form Wizard.

FIGURE 17.6.

The last page of the Database Form Wizard.

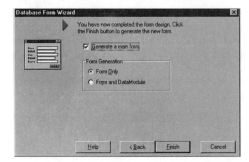

Click the Finish button and the form will be created. The finished form looks like the one shown in Figure 17.7.

FIGURE 17.7.

The finished form.

Notice in Figure 17.7 that the form contains a data component for each field that was selected and a label for each component. The label is capitalized because that's the way the field names are stored in this particular table. Notice that the top of the form contains a DBNavigator component so that you can browse the records of the table.

The New Form in Action

Now you are ready to click the Run button and see how the form works. When the application starts, the first record in the dataset is displayed. Use the buttons of the DBNavigator to move through the dataset. Keep in mind that you are working with live data at this point. You can edit a record by changing a value in one of the edit components. To save the changes to the database, click the Post button on the DBNavigator (the check mark). To cancel any changes to the record, click the Cancel button on the DBNavigator (the X button). When you post a record or move to another record, the changes are saved to the database.

Close the application and return to the Delphi IDE. Spend some time examining the components on the form and the components' properties. Later I am going to go over some of the data components, but for now just experiment a little.

Tip

> If you find yourself re-creating a database form over and over again, consider adding the form to the Object Repository. Forms in the Object Repository can be reused with just a few mouse clicks.

17

Creating a Master/Detail Form

Next, you create a master/detail form using the Database Form Wizard. When creating a master/detail form, the first few pages of the wizard are nearly the same as when creating a simple form. Only the labels that describe your options are different. First, perform the following steps. After that, I explain the specifics of the Database Form Wizard that pertain to master/detail forms. Here goes:

1. Start the Database Form Wizard. On the first page, choose the option to create a master/detail form and the option to use TTable for the dataset components. Click the Next button.

2. The next step is to choose the table that will serve as the master. Select the DBDEMOS alias and then select the CUSTOMER.DB table. Click the Next button.

3. Select just the CustNo and Company fields and add them to the Ordered Selected Fields list box. Click the Next button.

4. Click on the Horizontally option to lay out the components horizontally. Click the Next button.

5. Now choose the table that will provide the details. Select the ORDERS.DB table and then click the Next button.

6. Select the CustNo, OrderNo, SaleDate, and AmountPaid fields and add them to the Ordered Selected Fields list box. Click the Next button.

7. Choose the option to arrange the components in a grid and click the Next button.

Now you are presented with a page you haven't seen before in the Database Form Wizard. This page asks you to select the fields that will join the two tables:

1. Click on the Available Indexes combo box at the top of the page and choose the CustNo field. The CustNo field is designated as a secondary index, so you'll use that field to join the two tables.

2. Select CustNo in both the Detail Fields list box and in the Master Fields list box. After you select CustNo in both list boxes, the Add button between the two list boxes is enabled.

3. Click the Add button to add the join to the Joined Fields list box at the bottom of the page.

Note

If you are paying attention, you might notice that this page of the Database Form Wizard looks almost identical to the Field Link Designer you saw on Day 16, "Delphi Database Architecture," when you set up a master/detail form by hand. Both perform the same task.

Figure 17.8 shows the Database Form Wizard after joining the two tables.

FIGURE 17.8.

The two tables joined on the CustNo *field.*

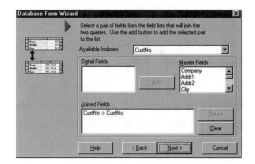

 Note

The page illustrated in Figure 17.8 is slightly different if you are using TQuery—instead of TTable—components for the datasets. Specifically, the Available Indexes combo box isn't present when using TQuery components. The reason this combo box isn't displayed when using TQuery components is that the join is created using SQL statements, and indexes are not used in the same way they are with TTable components.

17

4. Click the Next button to move to the next page of the Database Form Wizard. Because this page already has the settings you need, just click the Finish button.

Now Delphi creates the form, and you are ready to try your new creation. Click the Run button to run the program. Use the DBNavigator to move from record to record. You will notice that the customer name is displayed in the top part of the form and that all the orders for that customer are displayed in the table in the bottom part of the form. Figure 17.9 shows the master/detail application running.

FIGURE 17.9.

Your new master/detail form in action.

> **Tip**
>
> If you want to see the SQL statements for a master/detail relationship, run the Database Form Wizard again, but this time choose TQuery components for the datasets. After the form has been created, click on each Query component and examine its SQL property.

Creating Database Forms by Hand

The Database Form Wizard is a good tool for quickly laying out a form; it is particularly convenient for quick test programs. It will not be long, though, before you will need to custom-design your database forms. After you gain experience creating database forms, you might actually prefer to create your forms by hand rather than use the Database Form Wizard.

There isn't a lot to know about creating database forms by hand. You drop one or more datasets (Tables or Queries) on the form and a DataSource component for each dataset, and then place a component on the form for each field in the dataset that you want to view. Sounds easy enough, and it is.

Let's build a new form that approximates the form you created earlier in the section "Creating a Simple Form Using the Database Form Wizard." First, you lay the groundwork and start adding the data components. Perform these steps:

1. Start a new application. Place a Panel component on the form and set its Align property to alTop. Remove the caption.

2. Place a ScrollBox component on the form below the panel (you can find it on the Additional tab on the Component palette). Set the Align property to alClient.

3. Place a Table component on the form. You can place it anywhere you like, but the right side of the panel is probably the best place. Change the DatabaseName property to DBDEMOS and the TableName property to ANIMALS.DBF.

4. Place a DataSource component on the form next to the Table component. Change the DataSet property to Table1.

5. Place a DBNavigator on the panel at the top of the form. Change its DataSource property to DataSource1.

> **Tip**
>
> You can set the DataSource property quickly by double-clicking the value column next to the property in the Object Inspector. Delphi will cycle through the available DataSource components each time you double-click.

Your form now looks like Figure 17.10.

FIGURE 17.10.

The form in the initial stages.

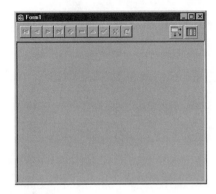

Now you need to add some data components to display the table's data. As you work through this exercise, you might want to refer to Figure 17.7 to see the result. Do the following:

1. Place a DBEdit component on the main part of the form along the left side. Change the Name property to NameEdit; change the DataSource property to DataSource1; change the DataField property to NAME (choose NAME from the drop-down list).

2. Place a Label component above the DBEdit you created in step 1 (use a regular Label component from the Standard page of the Component palette, not a DBText component). Change its Caption property to Name.

3. Repeat steps 1 and 2 and add DBEdits and Labels for the SIZE, WEIGHT, and AREA fields of the table. Make certain that you change the Name property and DataField property with respect to each field's name.

   In the next two steps, you depart from Figure 17.7 and place the component for the BMP field to the right of the components you just placed. It makes more sense for it to be there rather than below the existing components.

4. Place a DBImage component on the form to the right of the edit components. Change the Name property to BMPImage, and change the DataSource property to DataSource1 and the DataField property to BMP.

5. Place a Label component above the DBImage and change its Caption property to Picture (the field name is BMP, but the word Picture is more descriptive).

Now your form looks like the one shown in Figure 17.11.

FIGURE 17.11.

The form with the data components in place.

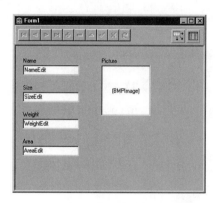

Now you need to set the size of the DBImage component. Although you can't always be sure that each image will be the same size in every database, you can be certain in this case. You might guess at the size of the bitmap, but a better solution would be to set the size with a live image in the component. That's easy enough to fix. Click on the Table component and set its Active property to True. The image for the first record in the table is displayed. Now you can size the DBImage as needed to match the bitmap size.

You have nearly completed the form, but there's one more thing you should do. To imitate the form that the Database Form Wizard created, you need to open the table when the form is created:

1. First, set the Active property of the Table to False (you just set it to True a minute ago).

2. Now select the form itself in the Object Inspector. (Remember that to select the form, you click on the panel and then press the Esc key on your keyboard. You can also select the form from the Component Selector at the top of the Object Inspector.)

3. Switch to the Events page and create an event handler for the OnCreate event. Type this line of code in the event handler:

   ```
   Table1.Open;
   ```

That's it. Your new form is finished. Click the Run button to test your new creation. It will behave exactly like the first form you created with the Database Form Wizard.

A Closer Look at the Data Components

At this point, a quick look at the data components is in order. I'll give a brief overview of each component and highlight each one's key properties and methods. Most of the data components are derived from a standard component and have many of the properties associated with that type of component. I will discuss only the properties that are specific to the data version of each component.

Properties Common to Data Components

All the data components have properties in common. For example, all the components have a `DataSource` property. This property is used to link a data component with a data source, which is itself linked to a dataset. You have been using the `DataSource` property a lot in the past couple of days, so you should have a good idea of how it works.

Most data components also have a `DataField` property. You use this property to hook the data component to a particular field in the dataset. You saw how the `DataField` property is used when you built a database form from scratch. When you hook a data component to a field in the dataset, the contents of that field are directly displayed in the data component. In the case of `Tables` (and `Queries` if the `RequestLive` property is `True`), this means that editing the data in the data control will result in changes to the data in the database.

Most data components also have a `Field` property. You use the `Field` property to gain access to a component's contents programmatically. For example, to change the contents of a `DBEdit` component, you can do the following:

```
NameEdit.Field.AsString := 'Clown Fish';
```

You can also change the field's display characteristics or other `TField` properties through the `Field` property.

You can use the `ReadOnly` property to prevent the user from editing the data in a data component that enables editing (`DBGrid` and `DBEdit`, for example).

The `DBGrid` Component

The `DBGrid` component displays a dataset in tabular, or spreadsheet, format. One of the most important properties of the `DBGrid` is the `Columns` property. This property enables you to change the number and order of the columns that appear in the grid. You can add, remove, and order columns using the Columns Editor.

To invoke the Columns Editor, right-click on the grid and choose Columns Editor from the context menu. You can also click the ellipsis button next to the `Columns` property in the Object Inspector. Using the Columns Editor, you can add columns, remove columns, and arrange the order of columns. For example, a dataset might contain a dozen fields, but you might want to view only half those fields in the `DBGrid`. Using the Columns Editor, you can hide the fields that you don't want to see.

17

> **Note**
>
> Don't confuse the DBGrid Columns property (modified with the Columns Editor) with the Table component's FieldDefs property (modified with the Fields Editor). The FieldDefs property of the Table component controls which columns are actually contained in the dataset. The Columns property only affects which fields are *visible* in the grid.

The DefaultDrawing property indicates whether VCL draws the cells in the grid or the grid cells are owner-drawn. If DefaultDrawing is False, you must respond to the OnDrawColumnCell and OnDrawDataCell events to provide drawing for the cells.

The Options property enables you to set the display and behavior options for the grid. Using this property, you can turn off column titles, allow or disallow column sizing, turn row and column lines on or off, and so on.

The TitleFont property enables you to set the font for the column titles. You use the Font property to set the font for the grid cells.

The DBGrid has only two public methods. When using an owner-drawn grid, you can call the DefaultDrawColumnCell and DefaultDrawDataCell methods to ask VCL to draw the cell for you. This is useful if you are owner-drawing particular columns but you want default drawing behavior for the rest of the columns.

The DBGrid component has several events, most of which pertain to cell editing and data navigation. I won't list the events here because it is obvious from their names what functions they perform.

The DBNavigator Component

The DBNavigator component enables the user to browse a dataset record by record. The navigator provides buttons for first record, next record, previous record, last record, insert record, delete record, edit record, cancel edits, post edits, and refresh. This component is nearly automatic in that most of the time all you have to do is drop it on the form, hook it to a DataSource, and forget about it.

The ConfirmDelete property, when set to True, causes a dialog box to be displayed whenever the user clicks the Delete button. You set the Hints property to True to enable fly-over hints for each button on the navigator. The VisibleButtons property is a set that enables you to control which buttons show up on the navigator. You can add or remove buttons at design time or runtime.

The DBNavigator has only one method of interest and one event. You can use the BtnClick method to simulate a button click on the navigator. You can use the OnClick event to detect a click on the navigator. You rarely have to use OnClick, however, because the navigator already knows what to do when its buttons are clicked.

The DBText Component

The DBText component is the data-aware version of the standard Label component. It provides a way of displaying data from a field without enabling the user to modify the data. This component provides no database-specific properties, methods, or events other than those common to all data components.

The DBEdit Component

The DBEdit component provides an edit control that is linked to a field in a dataset. You used a DBEdit earlier today when you created a database form from scratch. The DBEdit component, like the DBText component, doesn't have any database-specific properties, methods, or events other than those common to all data components.

17

The DBMemo Component

The DBMemo is the data version of the standard Memo component. You can use this component to display data contained in database fields that contain large amounts of text. The AutoDisplay property controls whether the data in the dataset field is automatically displayed when the cursor changes to a new record.

When AutoDisplay is True, the data is automatically displayed. When AutoDisplay is False, the user must double-click the DBMemo to display the data (or press Enter when the control has focus). To force the memo to display its contents through code, you use a related method called LoadMemo. This method is appropriate only when AutoDisplay is False.

The DBImage Component

The DBImage component is used to display binary large object (BLOB) data that is stored in image format. DBImage isn't necessarily a read-only component. You can change an image by pasting an image from the Clipboard or by using the Picture property to load a file from disk. The following code will change the image at runtime:

```
DBImage1.Picture.LoadFromFile('peregrine.bmp');
```

The main DBImage properties control how the image is displayed. They are described as follows:

- The `AutoDisplay` property works exactly as described for the `DBMemo` component.
- The `LoadPicture` method can be used to display the image when the `AutoDisplay` property is `False`.
- The `Picture` property enables access to the image itself and works the same as it does for components such as the standard `Image` component.
- The `Center` property determines whether the image is centered in the `DBImage` window.
- The `Stretch` property determines whether the image will be stretched to fit the current size of the `DBImage` window or whether it will be displayed in its original size. If `Stretch` is `False`, part of the image will be clipped if the image is too large for the `DBImage` window.
- The `QuickDraw` property determines whether to apply a palette to the image when it is displayed. When `QuickDraw` is `True`, no palette is used. When `QuickDraw` is `False`, a palette is used to display the image, which results in higher quality but slightly poorer performance when displaying images.

Methods of the `DBImage` component include `CutToClipboard`, `CopyToClipboard`, and `PasteFromClipboard`. These methods do exactly what their names indicate.

The `DBListBox` and `DBComboBox` Components

The `DBListBox` component is, for the most part, a standard list box. What distinguishes it is that when the user selects an item in the list box, the selected item is written to the corresponding field in the dataset (set by the `DataField` property). To provide the strings the user can select from, you add strings to the `Items` property just as you do for a regular `ListBox` component. It is important to realize that the strings for the list box don't come from the database (that's what the `DBLookupListBox` is for).

The `DBComboBox` works in exactly the same way as the `DBListBox` except for the obvious differences between a list box and a combo box.

The `DBCheckBox` Component

You use the `DBCheckBox` primarily to display the contents of a database field containing logical data (True/False, Yes/No, On/Off). Set the `ValueChecked` property to a string that should be used to check for a match against the contents of the field. For example:

```
DBCheckBox1.ValueChecked := 'On';
```

In this case, if the associated field contains the value `On`, the `DBCheckBox` will be checked. If the field contains a value other than the one specified, the check box will not be checked. You can supply more than one value to check in the `ValueChecked` property. For example:

```
DBCheckBox1.ValueChecked := 'On;Yes;True';
```

If the value of the associated field contains any one of these values, the check box will be checked. The `ValueUnchecked` property works in exactly the same way except that any values matching the contents of `ValueUnchecked` will cause the check box to be cleared (unchecked). When specifying values for both `ValueChecked` and `ValueUnchecked`, the check box state will be indeterminate (grayed check mark) for field values that don't match.

The `DBRadioGroup` Component

The `DBRadioGroup` component works much like the `DBListBox` and `DBComboBox` components. You supply the items for the radio group and when an item is selected, the value (text) associated with that radio button is written to the associated field in the database.

The `Values` property holds the current value of the field in the database. You can use the `Values` property to substitute the display string in the radio group box with a different string. For example, you might have a radio group box with radio buttons labeled Yearly, Quarterly, and Monthly. Your database, however, might store codes such as `Y`, `Q`, and `M` instead of the full names. Given that scenario, you could set the `Values` property (a string list) like so:

```
Y
Q
M
```

Now, when a radio button is selected, the one-letter code will be written to the database field instead of the display string of the selected radio button. If the `Values` property is empty, the display string of the radio button will be written to the database when a radio button is clicked.

The `DBLookupListBox` and `DBLookupComboBox` Components

The `DBLookupListBox` component enables you to display a list of field values from a lookup field. Unlike the `DBComboBox` component, the list isn't provided by you; it is provided by a separate dataset. Set the `DataSource` and `DataField` properties to the dataset and field where the selection will be written. Set the `ListSource` and `ListField` properties to the lookup field from which the list should be populated.

17

The DBLookupComboBox works just like the DBLookupListBox. In addition, the DropDownAlign, DropDownRows, and DropDownWidth properties control how the dropdown list appears.

The DBRichEdit Component

The DBRichEdit component enables you to display and edit a rich text memo field in a dataset. The AutoDisplay property and LoadMemo methods of this component work exactly as they do for the DBMemo component.

The DBCtrlGrid Component

DBCtrlGrid is a component that enables you to create custom scrollable grid components. You can place any data components you want on the first cell of the DBCtrlGrid (or any other components for that matter), and Delphi will duplicate those components for each record in the dataset.

An illustration helps this explanation make more sense. Figure 17.12 shows a form containing a DBCtrlGrid component that has been aligned so that it fills the form's client area. The DBCtrlGrid contains a DBEdit, a DBMemo, and a DBImage. All the data components are placed on the first cell of the grid. The second cell contains a hatch pattern to tell you that you can't place components on that cell. Figure 17.13 shows the same form when the application is running.

FIGURE 17.12.

A form at design time containing a DBCtrlGrid *component.*

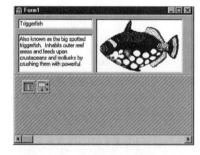

FIGURE 17.13.

The same form at run-time.

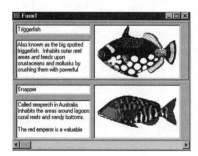

The DBCtrlGrid has a few properties worth mentioning. You use the Orientation property to determine where the scrollbar is to be placed and how the component acts when the scrollbar is clicked (the DBCtrlGrid in Figures 17.12 and 17.13 has the Orientation set to goHorizontal). You use the PanelWidth and PanelHeight properties to set the width and height of a cell in the grid. The RowCount property determines how many records to show at one time.

The DBCtrlGrid component has one event, OnPaintPanel. This event is fired each time a grid cell needs painting. You can respond to this event in order to draw on the background of the panel. This pertains only to the panel's background. Any controls on the grid will be painted automatically, so you don't have to worry about them.

Other Data Components

DBChart is a charting component included with the Professional and Client/Server versions of Delphi. This component is not only powerful, but also complex. I can't begin to explain everything the DBChart component does, so you'll have to experiment with it to discover all that it is capable of.

The Client/Server version of Delphi includes a tab named Decision Cube that contains six additional components. These components enable you to do complex data analysis such as cross tabulation of tables and graphs, drill down, pivot, and aggregation. A discussion of these components wouldn't be productive here, but I want you to be aware that these components exist in the Client/Server version of Delphi.

17

Summary

Well, that about sums up the art of building database forms. (Actually, I'm being facetious because I've just scratched the surface of database form creation and design.) Use the Database Form Wizard for quick and easy database forms. Create database forms from scratch for more flexibility. Either way you go, building good database forms takes time and experience to master. It isn't something that you can be great at overnight. On the other hand, it isn't terribly difficult, either. Keep working at it and you'll be a database whiz in no time. The important thing is knowing the data components available to you as you build your forms.

Workshop

The Workshop contains quiz questions to help you solidify your understanding of the material covered and exercises to provide you with experience using what you have learned. You can find the answers to the quiz questions in Appendix A, "Answers to the Quiz Questions."

Q&A

Q **I like the way the Database Form Wizard saves me time, but I don't like the way the components are arranged on the form. What do you suggest?**

A Run the Database Form Wizard to create components for any fields you want on your form. Then manually rearrange the components to make the form look the way you want. The Database Form Wizard just gives you a head start. You can do anything you want with the form after the Database Form Wizard has done its job.

Q **When using the Database Form Wizard, does it matter whether I create a form using TTable or TQuery objects?**

A It all depends on the type of database you are talking to. If you are dealing with a local database such as Paradox or dBASE, you will probably use a TTable. If you are dealing with a client/server database, you will likely use a TQuery.

Q **Is there any limit to the number of DataSource, Table, and Query components I can have on my form?**

A There's no absolute limit, although there are practical limits to how many datasets you can work with at one time.

Q **I noticed the DBEdit component doesn't have a Text property like the regular Edit component has. Why is that?**

A The DBEdit component doesn't have a Text property because the component contents are obtained from a dataset. To access the contents of a DBEdit component, use the dataset's GetFieldByName method and the Value property of TField.

Q **Do I have to use a DBNavigator to enable my users to browse the database?**

A No, you could provide your own buttons and then write code to move the database cursor when the buttons are clicked. Using a DBNavigator is much easier, though.

Q **My database contains a number of large images in BLOB fields, and it seems to take a long time to display the images. Is there something I can do to make the images draw faster?**

A Make certain that you have the QuickDraw property set to True. Your images will draw faster, but they might not look as good.

Quiz

1. What's the fastest and easiest way to create a database form?

2. How do you control the order and number of columns that appear in a DBGrid component?

3. What component enables you to display a dataset in table format?

4. How can you add or remove buttons from a `DBNavigator`?

5. What component do you use to display BLOB image data?

6. What property is common to all data-aware components?

7. What property is used to select the field that a data component is linked to?

8. Can you rearrange the columns in a `DBGrid` component?

9. Which component is used to edit and display text fields in a database?

10. What does BLOB stand for?

Exercises

1. Create a new application that shows the contents of the `VENDORS.DB` table (`DBDEMOS` database).

2. Modify the application in step 1 so that only the `VendorName`, `City`, `State`, and `Phone` fields are displayed.

3. Delphi Professional and Client/Server owners: Create a master/detail form from the `IBLOCAL` database (install Local InterBase from the Delphi CD if necessary). Use the `EMPLOYEE` table as the master and the `EMPLOYEE_PROJECT` table as the detail table. (Hint: Use the `EMP_NO` field to link the tables.)

4. Create a database form that uses a `DBCtrlGrid` component to browse a table. Use any table and include any fields you like.

5. Create a database form by hand (not using the Database Form Wizard) using any table and any fields you like. Add a `DBNavigator` component to browse the table.

6. Remove all buttons from the `DBNavigator` used in step 5 except the First, Next, Prior, and Last buttons.

17

DAY **18**

Building Database Applications

This chapter is about building database applications. The truth is, I cannot tell you everything there is to know about writing database applications in one short chapter. What I can do is point out some issues you are likely to encounter when writing database applications.

Because you already know how to create database forms, you will spend most of this day dealing with lower level aspects of database programming. You'll start with creating and populating a database entirely through code, and then you'll move on to data modules. Toward the end of the day you'll look at creating database reports with the QuickReport components. Finally, the day ends with a discussion on deploying database applications.

Nonvisual Database Programming

Up to this point, you have examined almost exclusively the visual aspects of database programming with Delphi. That side of database programming is fun and easy, but sooner or later you have to do some real database programming.

The kinds of programs you have written so far have dealt primarily with simple viewing and editing of data. In this section, you learn how to perform certain database operations through code.

Tip

> I will mention only database operations that pertain to the TTable class. You could also use SQL to perform database operations in code, but I won't present that aspect of databases today.

Reading from a Database

This section is short because reading from an existing database isn't difficult. As an example exercise, you will take the CUSTOMER.DB table and create a comma-delimited text file from the data. You won't write every field in the table to the file, but you'll write most of them.

The first step is to create a TTable object. Next, attach it to a database and to a particular table within the database. Here's how the code looks:

```
var
  Table : TTable;
begin
  Table := TTable.Create(Self);
  Table.DatabaseName := 'DBDEMOS';
  Table.TableName := 'Customer.db';
end;
```

This code emulates what Delphi does when you set the DatabaseName and TableName properties at design time. The next step is to read each record of the database and write it to a text file. First, I'll show you the basic structure without the actual code to write the fields to the text file. After that, I'll be more specific. The basic structure looks like this:

```
Table.Active := True;
while not Table.Eof do begin

  { Code here to read some fields from the }
  { current record and write them to a text file. }

  Table.Next;
end;
Table.Free;
```

This code is straightforward. First, the table is opened by setting the Active property to True (you could also have called the Open method). Next, a while loop reads each record of the table. When a record is written to the text file, the Next method is called to advance the database cursor to the next record. The while loop's condition statement checks the Eof property for the end of the table's data and stops the loop when the end of the table is reached. Finally, the TTable object is freed after the records have been written to the text file.

> **Note**
>
> You don't specifically have to delete the TTable object. When you create a TTable object in code, you usually pass the form's Self pointer as the owner of the object—for example,
>
> ```
> Table := TTable.Create(Self);
> ```
>
> This sets the form as the table's owner. When the form is deleted, VCL will automatically delete the TTable object. For a main form this happens when the application is closed. Although you are not required to delete the TTable object, it's always a good idea to delete the object when you are done with it.

Naturally, you need to extract the information out of each field in order to write it to the text file. To do that, you use the FieldByName method and the AsString property of TField. I addressed this briefly on Day 16, "Delphi Database Architecture," in the section "Accessing Fields." In the CUSTOMER.DB table, the first field you want is the CustNo field. Extracting the value of this field would look like this:

```
var
  S : string;
begin
  S := Table.FieldByName('CustNo').AsString + ',';
```

Notice that a comma is appended to the end of the string obtained so that this field's data is separated from the next. You will repeat this code for any fields for which you want to obtain data. The entire sequence is shown in Listings 18.1 and 18.2. These listings contain a program called MakeText, which can be found with the book's code. This short program takes the CUSTOMER.DB table and creates a comma-delimited text file called CUSOMTER.TXT. Listing 18.1 shows the main form's unit (MakeTxtU.pas). The form contains just a button and a memo. Look over these listings, and then I'll discuss how the program works.

18

LISTING 18.1. MakeTxtU.pas.

```pascal
unit MakeTxtU;

interface

uses
  Windows, Messages, SysUtils, Classes, Graphics, Controls, Forms,
➥Dialogs,
  StdCtrls, DbTables;

type
  TForm1 = class(TForm)
    CreateBtn: TButton;
    Memo: TMemo;
    procedure CreateBtnClick(Sender: TObject);
  private
    { Private declarations }
  public
    { Public declarations }
  end;

var
  Form1: TForm1;

implementation

{$R *.DFM}

procedure TForm1.CreateBtnClick(Sender: TObject);
var
  Table : TTable;
  S     : string;
begin
  { Create the Table and assign a database and Table name. }
  Table := TTable.Create(Self);
  Table.DatabaseName := 'DBDEMOS';
  Table.TableName := 'Customer.db';

  { Change to the busy cursor. }
  Screen.Cursor := crHourGlass;

  { We can use a Memo to show the progress as well as to    }
  { save the file to disk. First clear the memo of any text.}
  Memo.Lines.Clear;

  { Open the Table. }
  Table.Active := True;
  CreateBtn.Enabled := False;
```

```
{ Loop through the records, writing each one to the memo. }
while not Table.Eof do begin

  { Get the first field and add it to the string S, }
  { followed by the delimiter.                       }
  S := Table.FieldByName('CustNo').AsString + ',';

  { Repeat for all the fields we want. }
  S := S + Table.FieldByName('Company').AsString + ',';
  S := S + Table.FieldByName('Addr1').AsString + ',';
  S := S + Table.FieldByName('Addr2').AsString + ',';
  S := S + Table.FieldByName('City').AsString + ',';
  S := S + Table.FieldByName('State').AsString + ',';
  S := S + Table.FieldByName('Zip').AsString + ',';
  S := S + Table.FieldByName('Phone').AsString + ',';
  S := S + Table.FieldByName('FAX').AsString;

  { Add the string to the Memo. }
  Memo.Lines.Add(S);

  { Move to the next record. }
  Table.Next;
end;

{ Write the file to disk. }
Memo.Lines.SaveToFile('customer.txt');

{ Turn the button back on and reset the cursor. }
CreateBtn.Enabled := True;
Screen.Cursor := crDefault;
Table.Free;
end;

end.
```

18

All the action takes place in the CreateBtnClick method. When you click the Create File button, the program extracts data from the database table and puts it into the Memo component. First, the value of the CustNo field is read and put into a string, followed by a comma. After that, each subsequent field's value is appended to the end of the string, again followed by a comma. After all the data has been extracted from a record, the string is added to the memo, using the Add method. When the end of the table is reached, the memo contents are saved to disk.

I used a Memo component in this example for two reasons. First, by displaying the results in a memo, you can see what the program produces. Second, the memo component's Lines property (a TStrings) provides an easy way of saving a text file to disk. Figure 18.1 shows the MakeText program after the file has been written.

Figure 18.1.

The MakeText *program running.*

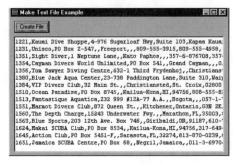

Creating a Database in Code

Most of what you read on database operations in Delphi tells you how to create a database with utilities such as Database Desktop. That's fine if your application has pre-built tables. But if your application has to dynamically create tables, that approach doesn't work. You must have a way of creating tables through code. For example, if your application enables users to specify the fields of a table, you won't know what the fields are until the user has supplied them.

Creating a table in code requires these steps:

1. Create a BDE alias for the database.
2. Create a TTable object.
3. Add field definitions to the FieldDefs property.
4. Add index definitions to the IndexDefs property if your table contains indexes.
5. Create the actual table with the CreateTable method.

Let's go over these steps individually so that you know what each step involves.

Creating a BDE Alias and a TTable Object

You already performed steps 1 and 2 on Day 16 when I talked about creating a BDE alias, and you created a TTable object in the preceding section. Here's a recap of those two steps:

```
var
  Table : TTable;
begin
  { Create the alias. }
  CreateDirectory('c:', nil);
  Session.AddStandardAlias('MyDatabase', 'c:', 'PARADOX');
  Session.SaveConfigFile;
```

```
  { Create the table. }
  Table := TTable.Create(Self);
  Table.DatabaseName := 'MyDatabase';
  Table.TableName := 'MyTable.db';
end;
```

This code first creates a BDE alias for a database called `MyDatabase` in the `C:` directory. After that, a `TTable` object is created, and the `DatabaseName` property is set to the alias created in the first part of the code. Finally, the `TableName` property is set to the name of the new table you are going to create. At this point the `TTable` object has been created, but the table itself doesn't exist on disk.

Creating the Field Definitions

The next step is to create the field definitions for the table's fields. As you might guess, the field definitions describe each field. A field definition contains the field name, its type, its size (if applicable), and whether the field is a required field. The field's type can be one of the `TFieldType` values. Table 18.1 lists the `TFieldType` values.

TABLE 18.1. DATABASE TABLE FIELD TYPES.

Field type	Description
ftUnkown	Unknown or undetermined
ftString	Character or string field
ftSmallint	16-bit integer field
ftInteger	32-bit integer field
ftWord	16-bit unsigned integer field
ftBoolean	Boolean field
ftFloat	Floating-point numeric field
ftCurrency	Money field
ftBCD	Binary-Coded Decimal field
ftDate	Date field
ftTime	Time field
ftDateTime	Date and time field
ftBytes	Fixed number of bytes (binary storage)
ftVarBytes	Variable number of bytes (binary storage)
ftAutoInc	Auto-incrementing 32-bit integer counter field
ftBlob	Binary large object field

18

continues

TABLE 18.1. CONTINUED

Field type	Description
ftMemo	Text memo field
ftGraphic	Bitmap field
ftFmtMemo	Formatted text memo field
ftParadoxOle	Paradox OLE field
ftDBaseOle	dBASE OLE field
ftTypedBinary	Typed binary field

You create a field definition by using the Add method of the TFieldDefs class. The FieldDefs property of TTable is a TFieldDefs object. Putting all this together, then, adding a new string field to a database would look like this:

```
Table.FieldDefs.Add('Customer', ftString, 30, False);
```

This code line adds a string field called Customer with a size of 30 characters. The field is not a required field because the last parameter of the Add method is False. Add as many field definitions as you need, setting the appropriate data type and size for each field.

Creating the Index Definitions

If your table will be indexed, you also need to add one or more index definitions. Adding index definitions is much the same as adding field definitions. The IndexDefs property of TTable contains the index definitions. To add a new index definition, call the Add method of TIndexDefs:

```
Table.IndexDefs.Add('', 'CustNo', [ixPrimary]);
```

The first parameter of the Add method is used to specify the index name. If you are creating a primary index (as in this example), you don't need to specify an index name. The second field is used to specify the field or fields on which to index. If you have more than one field in the index, you separate each field with a semicolon—for example,

```
Table.IndexDefs.Add('', 'Room;Time', [ixPrimary]);
```

The last parameter of the Add method is used to specify the index type. This parameter takes a TIndexOptions set. Different index options can be specified in combination. For example, an index might be a primary index that is sorted in descending order. In that case, the call to Add might look like this:

```
Table.IndexDefs.Add('', 'CustNo', [ixPrimary, ixDescending]);
```

Creating the Table

After you add all the field and index definitions to the table, you create the table. So far you have been setting up the table's layout but haven't actually created the table. Creating the table is the easiest step of all:

```
Table.CreateTable;
```

The CreateTable method performs the actual creation of the table on disk. CreateTable takes the contents of the FieldDefs and IndexDefs properties and creates the table structure, based on those contents.

Now that the table is created, you can fill it with data by using any method required for your application. You can fill the table programmatically or allow your users to add or edit the data from a form.

The book's code contains a program called MakeTabl. This program first creates a table and then fills it with data. The program fills the table with data from the CUSTOMER.TXT file created with the MakeText program earlier in the chapter. Listing 18.2 contains the unit for the main form (MakeTblU.pas). Note that the uses list for this program includes the DBGrids, DBTables, and DB units.

18

LISTING 18.2. MakeTblU.pas.

```
unit MakeTblU;

interface

uses
  Windows, Messages, SysUtils, Classes, Graphics, Controls,
  Forms, Dialogs, StdCtrls, Grids, DBGrids, DbTables, Db;

type
  TForm2 = class(TForm)
    DBGrid: TDBGrid;
    CreateBtn: TButton;
    FillBtn: TButton;
    procedure CreateBtnClick(Sender: TObject);
    procedure FillBtnClick(Sender: TObject);
  private
    { Private declarations }
  public
    { Public declarations }
  end;
```

continues

LISTING **18.2.** CONTINUED

```
var
  Form2: TForm2;

implementation

{$R *.DFM}

procedure TForm2.CreateBtnClick(Sender: TObject);
const
  Dir : PChar = 'c:';
var
  Table : TTable;
begin
{ Create a BDE alias, but only if it doesn't already exist. }
  if not Session.IsAlias('MyDatabase') then begin
    CreateDirectory(Dir, nil);
    try
      Session.AddStandardAlias('MyDatabase', Dir, 'PARADOX');
      Session.SaveConfigFile;
    except
      MessageDlg('Error Creating Alias', mtError, [mbOk], 0);
      Exit;
    end;
  end;

  { Now create the Table. }
  Screen.Cursor := crHourGlass;
  Table := TTable.Create(Self);
  try
    Table.DatabaseName := 'MyDatabase';
    Table.TableName := 'MyTable.db';

    { Add the field definitions for each field. }
    Table.FieldDefs.Add('CustNo', ftFloat, 0, True);
    Table.FieldDefs.Add('Customer', ftString, 30, False);
    Table.FieldDefs.Add('Addr1', ftString, 30, False);
    Table.FieldDefs.Add('Addr2', ftString, 30, False);
    Table.FieldDefs.Add('City', ftString, 15, False);
    Table.FieldDefs.Add('State', ftString, 20, False);
    Table.FieldDefs.Add('Zip', ftString, 10, False);
    Table.FieldDefs.Add('Phone', ftString, 15, False);
    Table.FieldDefs.Add('Fax', ftString, 15, False);

    { Add an index definition for the primary key. }
    Table.IndexDefs.Add('', 'CustNo', [ixPrimary]);
```

```
    { Everything is set up, so create the Table. }
    Table.CreateTable;
  except
    MessageDlg('Error Creating Table', mtError, [mbOk], 0);
    Screen.Cursor := crDefault;
    Table.Free;
    Exit;
  end;

  { All done, so let the user know. }
  Table.Free;
  Screen.Cursor := crDefault;
  CreateBtn.Enabled := False;
  FillBtn.Enabled := True;
  MessageDlg(
    'Table Created Successfully', mtInformation, [mbOk], 0);
end;

procedure TForm2.FillBtnClick(Sender: TObject);
var
  Table      : TTable;
  Datasource : TDataSource;
  Lines      : TStringList;
  S, S2      : string;
  I, P       : Integer;
begin
  { Create a TTable. }
  Table := TTable.Create(Self);
  Table.DatabaseName := 'MyDatabase';
  Table.TableName := 'MyTable.db';

  { Create a data source and hook it up to the Table. }
  { Then hook the DBGrid to the datasource. }
  Datasource := TDataSource.Create(Self);
  Datasource.DataSet := Table;
  DBGrid.Datasource := Datasource;

  { Open the Table and the text file. }
  Table.Active := True;
  Lines := TStringList.Create;
  Lines.LoadFromFile('customer.txt');

  { Put the Table in edit mode. }
  Table.Edit;

  { Process the Lines. }
  for I := 0 to Pred(Lines.Count) do begin
```

continues

LISTING 18.2. CONTINUED

```
{ Append a record to the end of the file. }
Table.Append;

{ Parse the string and get the first value. }
S := Lines[I];
P := Pos(',', S);
S2 := Copy(S, 1, P - 1);
Delete(S, 1, P);

{ Write the value to the CustNo field. }
Table.FieldByName('CustNo').Value := StrToInt(S2);

{ Continue for each of the fields. }
P := Pos(',', S);
S2 := Copy(S, 1, P - 1);
Delete(S, 1, P);
Table.FieldByName('Customer').Value := S2;

P := Pos(',', S);
S2 := Copy(S, 1, P - 1);
Delete(S, 1, P);
Table.FieldByName('Addr1').Value := S2;

P := Pos(',', S);
S2 := Copy(S, 1, P - 1);
Delete(S, 1, P);
Table.FieldByName('Addr2').Value := S2;

P := Pos(',', S);
S2 := Copy(S, 1, P - 1);
Delete(S, 1, P);
Table.FieldByName('City').Value := S2;

P := Pos(',', S);
S2 := Copy(S, 1, P - 1);
Delete(S, 1, P);
Table.FieldByName('State').Value := S2;

P := Pos(',', S);
S2 := Copy(S, 1, P - 1);
Delete(S, 1, P);
Table.FieldByName('Zip').Value := S2;

P := Pos(',', S);
S2 := Copy(S, 1, P - 1);
Delete(S, 1, P);
Table.FieldByName('Phone').Value := S2;
```

```
    P := Pos(',', S);
    S2 := Copy(S, 1, P - 1);
    Delete(S, 1, P);
    Table.FieldByName('FAX').Value := S2;

    { We might get a key violation exception if we try to add a }
    { record with a duplicate customer number. If that happens, }
    { we need to inform the user, cancel the edits, put the     }
    { put the Table back in edit mode, and continue processing. }
    try
      Table.Post;
    except
      on EDBEngineError do begin
        MessageBox(Handle,
          'Duplicate Customer Number', 'Key Violation', 0);
        Table.Cancel;
        Table.Edit;
        Continue;
      end;
    end;
  end;

  { All done with the TStringList so it. }
  Lines.Free;

  { We won't the Table so that the Table's data shows }
  { in the DBGrid. VCL will the Table and Datasource  }
  { for us. }
  {Table.Free; }
  {Datasource.Free; }
end;

end.
```

Using Data Modules

As you know by now, setting up database components is easy in Delphi. Still, there is some time involved, even for the simple examples you have been writing.

You have to place a Table or Query component on the form and choose the database name. Then you have to set the table name (for a Table) or SQL property (for a Query). You might have to set other properties, depending on how you are using the database. You might also have several events to handle. Next, you have to place a DataSource component on the form and attach it to the table or query. If your application makes use of a Database component, you have to set that component's properties and events as well. None of this is hard, but it would be nice if you could do it all just once for all your programs. Data modules enable you to do exactly that.

At the base level, data modules are really just specialized forms. To create a data module, open the Object Repository and double-click the Data Module icon. Delphi creates the data module and a corresponding source unit just as it does when you create a new form. You can set the Name property of the data module and save it to disk, again, just like a form.

After you create the data module, you place data access components on it. Then you set all the properties for the data access components as needed. You can even create event handlers for any components on the data module. When you have set everything just the way you want it, save the data module. Every form in your application can then access the data module.

Setting Up a Sample Data Module

A simple exercise will help you understand data modules better. First, you'll set up the data module, and then you'll put it to work:

1. Create a new application. Change the main form's Name property to MainForm. Save the project. Save the main form as DSExMain.pas and the project as DSExampl.dpr.

2. Choose File | New. When the Object Repository appears, double-click the Data Module icon to create a new data module. The Form Designer displays the data module. Change the Name property to DBDemos.

3. Click on the Data Access tab on the Component palette. Place a Table component on the data module. Change the DatabaseName property to DBDEMOS and the TableName to ANIMALS.DBF. Change the Name property to AnimalsTable.

4. Place a second Table component on the data module. Set the DatabaseName property to DBDEMOS and the TableName property to BIOLIFE.DB. Change the Name property to BiolifeTable.

5. Place a DataSource component on the data module. Change its Name property to Animals and its DataSet property to AnimalsTable.

6. Place another DataSource component on the data module. Change this data source's Name to Biolife and its DataSet property to BiolifeTable. Your data module now looks like Figure 18.2.

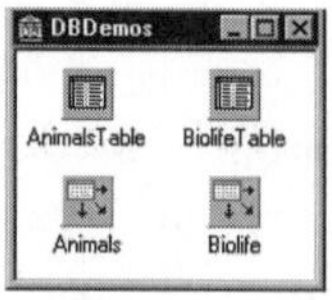

FIGURE 18.2.

The finished data module.

7. Double-click on the background of the data module. An OnCreate event handler will be created for the data module. Type this code in the event handler:

```
AnimalsTable.Open;
BiolifeTable.Open;
```

8. Save the project. When prompted, save the data module as DataMod.pas.

Adding to Your Data Module

Now let's put the new data module to use. You are going to create two buttons for the application's main form. One button will display a form that shows the Animals table, and the other will display the Biolife table. Here goes:

1. Create a new form. Change the form's Caption property to Animals Form and the Name property to AnimalsForm.

2. Choose File | Use Unit. Choose the DataMod unit from the Use Unit dialog and click OK. The data module is now accessible from the main form.

3. Place a DBGrid component and a DBNavigator component on the form. Select both the DBGrid and DBNavigator components. Locate the DataSource property in the Object Inspector and click the drop-down arrow next to the property. You will see the following displayed in the list of available data sources:

```
DBDemos.Animals
DBDemos.Biolife
```

Choose the DBDemos.Animals data source.

4. Save the unit as DSExU2.pas (or a more meaningful name if you like).

5. Again, create a new form for the project. Repeat steps 1 through 3, but this time choose DBDEMOS.Biolife for the data source and change the Caption to BioLife Form. Change the Name property to BiolifeForm. Save the form as DSExU3.pas. Figure 18.3 shows the Delphi IDE after completing this step.

Running the Data Module

These steps demonstrate that after you create a data module, you can use the components on that data module from anywhere in your program. All you have to do is use the unit for the data module, and then all data-aware components will be capable of detecting the data module. Let's finish this application so that you can try it out:

1. Place a button on the main form. Change its Caption property to Show Animals.

2. Double-click the button to generate an OnClick handler for the button. Type this code in the event handler:

```
AnimalsForm.Show;
```

18

3. Drop another button on the form. Change its `Caption` property to `Show Biolife`.

4. Create an `OnClick` event handler for this button and type the following code in the event handler:

```
BiolifeForm.Show;
```

5. Choose File | Use Unit. Choose the `DSExU2` unit and click OK.

6. Repeat step 5 to include the `DSExU3` unit.

Now you can run the program. When you click a button, the appropriate form will appear. Figure 18.4 shows the program running.

FIGURE 18.3.

The second form completed.

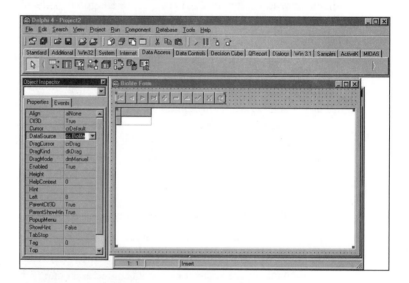

FIGURE 18.4.

The program running with both forms displayed.

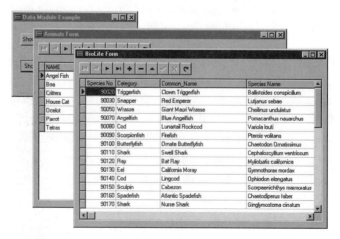

Data modules make it easy to set up your database components once and then reuse those components over and over. After you create a data module, you can save it to the Object Repository, where it is always available for your use.

Creating Reports

A database program is not complete without some way of viewing and printing data, and that is where reports enter the picture. Up to this point, you have been looking at ways to view individual records or multiple records with the DBGrid component. These methods might be perfect for some applications, but sooner or later you will need more control over the viewing of records.

Besides viewing the data onscreen, you will almost certainly need to print the data. A database application that can't print is not very useful. Delphi's QuickReport components enable you to view and print your data with ease.

QuickReport Overview

Before you can create a report, you need an overview of how the QuickReport components work.

The QuickRep Component

The base QuickReport component is the QuickRep component. This component acts as a canvas on which you place the elements that your report will display (I'll discuss the report elements soon).

The QuickRep component has properties that affect the way the report will appear when printed. For example, the Page property is a class containing properties called TopMargin, BottomMargin, LeftMargin, RightMargin, Columns, Orientation, PaperSize, and so on.

The PrinterSettings property is also a class. This property has its own properties, called Copies, Duplex, FirstPage, LastPage, and OutputBin. The ReportTitle property is used to display the print job description in the Windows Print Manager and in the title bar of the QuickReport preview window. The Units property controls whether margins are displayed in millimeters, inches, picas, or other choices. The DataSet property is used to set the dataset from which the report's data will be obtained.

18

Note

The DataSet property must be set and the associated dataset must be active before anything will show up in the report.

Primary QuickRep methods include Preview and Print. The Print method, as its name implies, prints the report. The Preview method displays a modal preview window. The preview window includes buttons for viewing options, first page, last page, previous page, next page, print, print setup, save report, open report, and close preview. Figure 18.5 shows the QuickReport preview window at runtime.

FIGURE 18.5.

The QuickReport preview window.

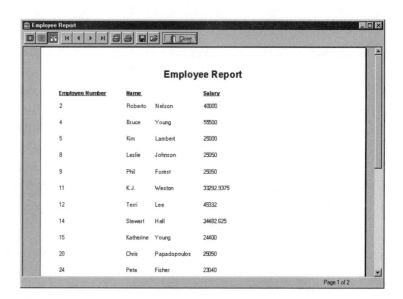

QuickRep events of note include OnPreview and OnNeedData. You can use the OnPreview event, instead of the default preview window, to provide a custom preview window. When using a data source other than a VCL database, you use the OnNeedData event. For example, you can create a report from a string list, an array, or a text file.

Report Bands

A QuickReport is composed of bands. *Bands* come in many different types. A basic report has at least three types: a title band, a column header band, and a detail band. The title band contains the report title, which is displayed only on the first page of the report. The column header band is used to display the column headers for the fields in the dataset; the column header appears at the top of every page. Some reports, such as a report used to generate mailing labels, do not have a column headers band.

The detail band is the band that does all the work. On the detail band you place any data that you want in the report. You define the contents of the detail band, and QuickReport repeats the detail band for every record in the dataset. In a minute you'll do an exercise that illustrates how the different bands work.

Other commonly used band types include page header, page footer, group header, group footer, and summary bands. The QRBand component defines a QuickReport band. The BandType property is used to specify the band type (title, detail, header, footer, and so on).

The bands automatically arrange themselves on the QuickRep component, based on the band's type. For example, if you place a QRBand on the report and change its BandType to rbPageFooter, the band will be moved below all other bands. Likewise, a page header band will be placed above all other bands.

QuickReport Design Elements

QuickReport design elements come in three forms. The first form includes components for text labels, images, shapes, headers, footers, and so on. These components are primarily used to display static design elements. For example, the report title is usually set once and then doesn't change. Another example is a graphic used to display a company's logo on the report. The components in this group are very similar to the standard VCL components. The QRLabel component resembles a standard Label component, a QRImage is similar to the VCL Image component, the QRShape component is similar to the regular Shape component, and so on. Use these components to design the static portions of your reports.

The second category of elements contains QuickReport versions of the standard VCL data-aware components. These components are placed on the detail band of a report. Components in this group include the QRDBText, QRDBRichEdit, and QRDBImage components. Data is pulled from the dataset and placed into these components to fill the body of the report.

The third group of QuickReport components includes the QRSysData component and the QRExpr component. The QRSysData component is used to display page numbers, the report date, the report time, the report title, and so on. The QRExpr component is used to display calculated results. The Expression property defines the expression for the calculation. The Expression property has a property editor called the Expression builder that is used to define simple expressions. An expression might be simple, such as multiplying two fields, or complete with formulas such as AVERAGE, COUNT, or SUM.

Creating Reports by Hand

Certainly the best way to write truly custom reports is by hand. That might sound difficult, but fortunately the QuickReport components make it easy. The best way for me to
explain how to create reports by hand is to take you through an exercise. This exercise
creates a simple application that displays and prints a report in list form. I won't tell you
to perform every single step in this exercise. For example, I won't tell you to save the
project or give you filenames to use—you can figure those out for yourself. Also, you
don't have to worry about making the report real pretty at this point. You can go back
later and tidy up.

The first step is to create the main form of the application. After that's done, you create
the basic outline of the report. Here goes:

1. Create a new application. Place two buttons on the main form. Change the caption
   of the first button to `Preview Report` and the caption of the second button to
   `Print Report`.

2. Choose File | New. Double-click the Report icon in the Object Repository. Delphi
   creates a new QuickReport form.

3. Place a `Table` component on the QuickReport form. Change the `DatabaseName`
   property to `DBDEMOS` and the `TableName` property to `EMPLOYEE.DB`. Set the `Active`
   property to `True`.

4. Select the QuickReport form. Change the `DataSet` property to `Table1` and change
   the `ReportTitle` property to `Employee Report`.

5. Switch back to the main form. Double-click the button labeled `Preview Report`.
   Type this code in the `OnClick` event handler:

   ```
   QuickReport2.Preview;
   ```

6. Double-click the `Print Report` button and type the following in the `OnClick` event
   handler:

   ```
   QuickReport2.Print;
   ```

7. Choose File | Use Unit and include the QuickReport form.

Now you have a blank report. What you need to do next is add a title band, a column
header band, and a detail band. For the next few steps you might want to look ahead to
Figure 18.6 to see the final result. Follow these steps:

1. Select a `QRBand` component from the QReport tab of the Component palette and
   place it on the report. The band is a title band by default.

2. Select a QRLabel component and place it on the title band. Change the Caption property to Employee Report and change the Font property to your preference (I used Arial, 18 point, bold). Align the component so that it is centered on the band.

3. Place another band on the report. Change the BandType property to rbColumnHeader and change the Font to bold and underlined.

4. Place a QRLabel on the left side of the column header band and change the Caption property to Employee Number. Place a second QRLabel on the band to the right of the first and change the Caption property to Name. Place a third QRLabel on the band to the right of the last label and change the Caption to Salary.

5. Place another band on the report and change the BandType property to rbDetail. Notice that the band moves below the other bands after you change the band type.

6. Place a QRDBText component on the left edge of the detail band (align it with the Employee Number label on the column header band). Change the DataSet property to Table1 and the DataField property to EmpNo.

7. Place another QRDBText on the detail band and align it with the Name component on the column header band. Change the DataSet property to Table1 and the DataField property to FirstName. Place another QRDBText just to the right of the last one (see Figure 18.6). Attach it to the LastName field of the database table.

8. Add a final QRDBText component on the detail band. Place it below the Salary component on the column header band and attach it to the Salary field in the table. Your form now looks like Figure 18.6.

18

FIGURE 18.6.

Your QuickReport form.

You are probably wondering what the report will look like on paper. Guess what? You don't have to wait to find out. Just right-click on the QuickReport form and choose Preview from the context menu. The QuickReport preview window is displayed, and you can preview the report.

To print the report, click the Print button. When you are done with the report preview, click the Close button. You can now run the program and try out the `Preview Report` and `Print Report` buttons.

> **Note**
>
> The report you just created is double-spaced. To change the spacing, reduce the height of the detail band.

Before leaving this discussion of reports, let me show you one other nice feature of QuickReport. Right-click on the QuickReport form and choose Report settings from the context menu. The Report Settings dialog will be displayed, as shown in Figure 18.7. This dialog enables you to set the primary properties of the `QuickRep` component visually rather than use the Object Inspector.

FIGURE 18.7.

The QuickReport Report Settings dialog.

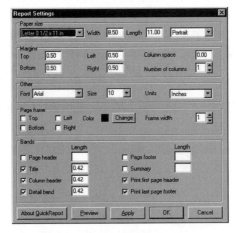

Creating Reports the Easy Way

Delphi comes with three built-in QuickReport forms, which can be found on the Forms tab of the Object Repository. The forms are called Quick Report Labels, Quick Report List, and Quick Report Master/Detail. These forms give you a head start on creating reports. You can generate one of the forms from the Object Repository and then modify the form as needed.

Deploying a Delphi Database Application

As I said on Day 16, the Borland Database Engine (BDE) is a collection of DLLs and drivers that enable your Delphi application to talk to various types of databases. When you ship an application that uses the BDE, you need to make sure that you ship the proper BDE files and that they are properly registered on your users' machines.

The most sensible way to do this is with a Borland-approved installation program. Here at TurboPower Software, we use the Wise Install System from Great Lakes Business Solutions (http://www.glbs.com). Others include InstallShield and its little brother, InstallShield Express. Conveniently, InstallShield Express comes with Delphi Professional and Client/Server, so if you have one of those versions of Delphi, you don't have to rush right out and buy an installation program.

You might be wondering why Borland is involved in dictating how the BDE must be deployed. The reason is simple when you think about it: There are many BDE versions in use. Some folks might be writing and deploying applications that use the BDE from Delphi 1. Others might be using the BDE from C++Builder 1. Still others could be using the BDE that comes with Delphi 4 in their applications.

The important point to realize is that the BDE is backward compatible. Newer BDE versions are guaranteed to work with applications written for older BDE versions. This system will only work, however, as long as everyone plays by the rules. Part of the rules say, "Thou shalt not arbitrarily overwrite existing BDE files." Certified installation programs check the version number of any BDE files they find. If the file being installed is older than the existing file, the installation program leaves the existing file in place.

This ensures that the user will always have the latest BDE files on his or her system. Another service that these certified installation programs provide is to determine exactly which files you need to deploy for your application. You should read DEPLOY.TXT in the Delphi root directory for more details on deploying applications that use the BDE.

Summary

There's no question that creating database applications requires a lot of work. The good news is that Delphi makes the job much easier than other development environments. Today you found out something about the nonvisual aspects of database programming. You also found out about data modules and how to use them. You ended the day with a look at QuickReport. QuickReport makes creating reports for your database applications easy. I also explained what is required to deploy a database application.

Workshop

The Workshop contains quiz questions to help you solidify your understanding of the material covered and exercises to provide you with experience in using what you have learned. You can find answers to the quiz questions in Appendix A, "Answers to the Quiz Questions."

Q&A

Q I am trying to create a database at runtime. I have created a BDE alias and set all the field definitions, but the table is never created on my hard disk. What have I done wrong?

A You have probably failed to call the `CreateTable` method. You must call this method to physically create the table.

Q When designing a report, can I set all my report's properties at one time?

A Yes. Just right-click the `QuickRep` component and choose Report settings from the context menu. The Report Settings dialog is displayed, and you can set most of the report properties visually.

Q Can a data module include code as well as components?

A Yes. A data module can contain any code necessary to carry out operation of the data module. The data module can contain event handlers or methods that you create. The methods you create can be public or private (for the data module's use only).

Q When I preview my report, it is blank. What is wrong?

A More than likely you have not set the `Active` property of the dataset to `True`. The dataset must be open before the report will function.

Q Can I use more than one detail band on a report?

A No. You can place more than one detail band on a report, but only the first one will be used when the report is generated.

Q Why do I need a Borland-approved installation program to install my database application?

A The BDE is complicated to install, and an approved installation program is guaranteed to do the installation correctly.

Quiz

1. What method do you call to create a database table at runtime?
2. What does the `Edit` method of `TTable` do?

3. What method do you call when you want to apply the changes made to a record?

4. How do you create a new data module?

5. Is a data module a regular form?

6. What method do you call to print a QuickReport?

7. What type of QuickReport band displays the dataset's data?

8. What component is used to display the page number on a report?

9. How can you preview a report at design time?

10. What is the QRExpr component used for?

Exercises

1. Create a database (a BDE alias) and a table for the database, either through code or by using the Delphi database tools.

2. Create a data module containing the database table from exercise 1.

3. Generate a report that creates mailing labels. (Hint: Start with a QuickReport Labels object from the Forms page of the Object Repository.)

4. Modify the QuickReport you created in this chapter so that the employee's first and last names are displayed by a QRExpr component.

5. Read the DEPLOY.TXT file in your Delphi directory to understand what is involved in deploying a Delphi database application.

18

DAY **19**

Creating and Using DLLs

If you use Windows, you can't escape dynamic link libraries (DLLs). Just take a look in your \Windows and \Windows\System directories. I run Windows NT 4, and I count more than 650 DLLs in the \Winnt directories on my system. So, let's not debate the facts. DLLs are part of everyday life in Windows.

The question, then, is whether *you* need to create and use DLLs. That's what you find out today. Specifically, you will look at the following:

- What DLLs are and why you use them
- Writing DLLs
- Calling function and procedures in DLLs
- Using forms in DLLs
- Using resource DLLs

By the end of today you will have a good idea of whether DLLs are for you. I suspect that DLLs will fit into your development plan somewhere down the road.

DLL Overview

Simply put, DLLs are very useful. Today I discuss the benefits of DLLs and how this translates for you, the Delphi programmer. First, let's explore exactly what a DLL is.

What Is a DLL?

 A *DLL* (dynamic link library) is one or more pieces of code stored in a file with a `.dll` extension.

The DLL code can be called from executable programs, but the DLL itself isn't a stand-alone program. You can consider the DLL a helper file for a main program. Applications that use code in DLLs are called *calling applications* because they call functions or procedures in the DLL.

There are two types of DLLs: code DLLs and resource DLLs. This is not an exclusive arrangement. You can have both code and resources in the same DLL, and there's no problem with that whatsoever. In some cases, though, it's convenient to store your code in one DLL and your resources in another. I'll talk about why you might want to do that in the section "Using Resources in DLLs."

Code contained in a DLL can be of two primary forms. The first form is a standalone function that you call from your main application. You have already done that several times in this book. Remember the code from Day 14, "Advanced Programming," as follows:

```
Screen.Cursors[myCursor] := LoadCursor(HInstance, 'MYCURSOR');
```

or this, also from Day 14:

```
DrawText(Canvas.Handle, Panel.Text,
  -1, Temp, DT_CENTER or DT_VCENTER or DT_SINGLELINE);
```

Both `LoadCursor` and `DrawText` are Windows API functions. You probably knew that. But did you know that these functions are called from DLLs? When you think about it, these functions have to be stored somewhere. But where? In this case, both `LoadCursor` and `DrawText` are contained in the Windows DLL called `User32.dll`.

And what about all those common dialog boxes you've been using, such as the File Open dialog box, the Print dialog box, and the Printer Setup dialog box? They have to come from somewhere. In this case, these dialog boxes are stored as resources in the file called `Comctl32.dll`. So, without knowing it, you have been using DLLs all along.

The second form of code contained in a DLL consists of procedures and functions used internally by the DLL. These functions and procedures perform some task in the DLL and are not visible to the outside world (applications using the DLL).

Using DLLs is one thing, but using and creating your own DLLs is an entirely different matter, right? Not really. After you create a DLL, you can call functions and procedures in the DLL just as you do when calling Windows API functions. Creating DLLs is not difficult, so there's nothing to stop you from putting DLLs to work for you.

Why Should You Use a DLL?

That's a good question. After all, what does a DLL give you? DLLs offer these benefits:

- Effective code reuse
- Capability to easily share code among many applications
- Capability to compartmentalize code
- Internationalization of your application
- Effective use of Windows resources

Let's take a look at these points individually and see whether I can convince you what a good thing DLLs are.

Effective Code Reuse

Code reuse is a big part of object-oriented programming. After all, why reinvent the wheel? DLLs aid in code reuse in a big way. Let's say you have a large amount of code you wrote to handle a specific task in Windows. You've worked hard to write that section of code, so it would be nice if you could reuse it in any of your applications that need it. DLLs enable you to do exactly that.

What you do is compile all of your code into a DLL. Then all you have to do in order to use the code in any of your programs is basically load the DLL from an application and begin using the code. What could be easier? (Actually, there are a couple other steps required, but they are simple and I don't want to get ahead of myself by explaining them now.)

19

Now you have this code at your fingertips any time you need it. Better yet, you can give the DLL to your programming pals, and they can use the code, too. Hey, this is starting to sound good. Better yet, you can sell the DLL to other programmers. You put all that work into it, so you might as well get out of it what you can!

Note

> You can easily create DLLs that can be called from applications written in C++Builder, Visual Basic, Visual C++, or other programming environments. Of course, this depends on the code contained in the DLL and how that code is called, but it can be done.

So, do you see where this is heading? After writing a DLL, you can use it with ease whenever and wherever you want. Getting at all the goodies contained in your DLL is just a few mouse clicks away.

Sharing Code Among Applications

Sharing code ties in with code reuse but takes it a step farther. Let's say that you are a programmer for a large corporation. You might have hundreds of users, each with his or her own system. (I'll ignore networking considerations for this example.) Let's say that you've written five applications for those users. Further, let's assume that each of those five applications uses a common set of code that compiles to 100KB (a modest figure). If you don't use a DLL, you will have 100KB of code repeated five times (once for each of the five applications) for a total of 500KB of code. That's code waste, folks.

A better approach is to put the classes in a DLL. Each of the five programs can use the same DLL for the common code. That's part of the beauty of DLLs: After the DLL is written, all your applications can share it. Each user will get an additional 100KB DLL on his or her machine, but each of the five applications will be reduced in size by 100KB. The bottom line is that each user saves 400KB of disk space. Saving 400KB might not sound like a lot, but if you multiply it by hundreds of users, it starts to add up from a corporate perspective (bean counters tend to look at those types of issues). This is just a simple example. In a real-world situation, you could easily save several megabytes per user by using DLLs.

What if three of the five programs are running simultaneously? No problem. Each program pulls code from the DLL as needed, and there are no conflicts. Windows keeps track of who's calling whom and makes sure that it all works together. All you do is write the DLL and start using it. (If this discussion sounds familiar, it is probably because I used roughly this same argument when discussing runtime packages on Day 8, "Creating Applications in Delphi.")

Compartmentalizing Code

By keeping your code compartmentalized, you can deal with it more easily when it comes time to update your code. I am not advocating a separate DLL for each aspect of your program, but when and where it is sensible to break up your program into related chunks of code, you should do so. There isn't much benefit in breaking an application into DLLs just for the sake of compartmentalizing the code. If you have libraries of common code that you have written, though, it does make sense to keep those libraries in separate DLLs. Again, this is most obvious when creating libraries that can be used by any of your programs.

One advantage to this approach is that your applications can be more easily upgraded if necessary. Let's face it. Even the best of programs go to market with bugs. It's more a question of how many or how severe than a question of whether there are bugs at all. If you discover bugs in your DLL, you can fix the bug and ship a new DLL to your users rather than recompile and ship an entire executable file.

At first this might not appear to benefit the types of applications you have written so far. However, you might eventually write programs several megabytes in size with dozens of source modules. In that case, compartmentalizing makes much more sense.

Internationalization

A few years ago, you could write a program and not worry about the international market. You would write the program and create menu items, dialog boxes, hint text, error messages, and so forth in your native language, and that was that. You put the program on the market and didn't think about it again.

The world, however, is becoming smaller. With the explosion of the Internet and the World Wide Web, things are completely different than they were just a couple of years ago. You can create a demo of your program or maybe a shareware version, and put it on the Internet. Within hours, minutes even, people all around the world have access to your program. It's exciting and frightening at the same time. This phenomenon means that you must plan ahead and prepare for translating your program into other languages.

One way you can do this is to create resource DLLs that contain string resources in various languages. You can have a separate DLL for each language, or as an alternative, you can have all the string resources in a single DLL and load the correct language version of each string at runtime. At runtime, you can use the Windows API function LoadString to load the strings and assign them to various components, as needed.

19

Note

One disadvantage to the Delphi programming model is that it doesn't use traditional resources as other programming environments do. Resources such as menus are not loaded as resources but rather are contained within the form's resource. This makes internationalization more difficult and is one of the few times that this model works against you.

Again, planning ahead can save you a lot of work later. If you plan your application with internationalization in mind, it is much easier to translate your application into other languages when necessary.

Effective Use of Windows Resources

Today's systems are faster, have more RAM, and have more hard disk space than ever before. It's easy to fall into the mode of "Hey, I'm only using 2MB of system RAM, so what's the big deal?" The truth is, you should always be conscious of how much of your users' system resources you are consuming. Here again, DLLs can help. This is really a continuation of the discussion on sharing code among different applications.

Let's go back to the example I used earlier. (Remember, you have five applications using some common code.) If you don't use DLLs, when several of your programs are running at the same time, they will all load some of the same code into memory. You are wasting system resources because each program loads its own copy of the exact same code. Rather than have each program load the same code, you use a DLL and load the code once. All your applications can use the same code in memory and reduce the drain on the system.

Anatomy of a DLL Unit

As with any other Pascal unit, a DLL unit follows a particular format. Listing 19.1 shows a minimal DLL unit.

LISTING **19.1.** A BASIC DLL UNIT.

```
library TestDLL;

uses
  SysUtils,
  Classes,
  Forms,
  Windows;

procedure SayHello(AForm : TForm);
begin
  MessageBox(AForm.Handle, 'Hello From a DLL!',
    'DLL Message Box', MB_OK or MB_ICONEXCLAMATION);
end;

exports
  SayHello;

begin
end.
```

First notice the library keyword at the top of the unit. The library keyword identifies this unit as a DLL unit. This DLL has a single procedure called SayHello. The SayHello procedure is no different than any other Object Pascal procedure.

Now turn your attention to the exports keyword near the bottom of the unit. Any procedure or function identifiers in the exports section are exported from the DLL. In this case the SayHello procedure is exported. Exporting functions and procedures is discussed in detail in the section "The exports Keyword."

Finally, at the end of the DLL unit you see begin and end keywords. This code block is the DLL's main code block and is where you put any code that your DLL needs to execute when the DLL initially loads. In many cases (as in this example), you don't need any initialization code at all, so this code block is empty.

The Basics of DLL Writing

Writing a DLL is not difficult. There are a couple of points to be aware of, but most of it is straight Object Pascal programming. Let's start with a discussion on the basics of writing DLLs. After that, you can build your first DLL.

Functions and Procedures in DLLs

Functions and procedures in a DLL fall into two basic categories:

- Functions and procedures local to the DLL
- Functions and procedures exported from the DLL

A DLL might also contain classes that could, of course, have methods. I'm not going to talk about methods of a class contained in a DLL at this time, but I'll discuss the other two types of functions and procedures next.

Functions and Procedures Local to the DLL

Functions and procedures called within a DLL require no special handling. You declare this type of function or procedure just as you do any function or procedure. The function or procedure can be called by other functions within the DLL, but it can't be called from outside the DLL. In other words, a calling application will not have access to these functions and procedures. They can be considered private to the DLL, much as private methods of a class are private to the class in which they reside. In effect, a calling application won't be able to "see" the functions and procedures to even know they exist.

19

Note

In addition to functions and procedures, a DLL can contain global data that all procedures in the DLL can access. In 16-bit Windows, global data in a DLL is shared among all instances of the DLL. In other words, if one program changed the global variable x to 100, x would have the value 100 for all other applications using the DLL as well. In 32-bit Windows, this is not the case. In 32-bit Windows, a separate copy of a DLL's global data is created for each process that attaches to the DLL.

Functions and Procedures Exported from the DLL

Another category of functions and procedures comprises those that can be called from outside the DLL. These are functions and procedures that are made public by *exporting* them from the DLL. They can be called by other functions and procedures in the DLL or by applications outside the DLL.

 Note

Functions and procedures in a DLL can be called by executable applications and also by other DLLs. In other words, one DLL can call functions and procedures in another DLL.

After a function or procedure has been exported, you call it from your application.

The exports Keyword

To export a function or procedure, you use the exports keyword in the DLL. Refer to Listing 19.1 for an example of a DLL that exports a procedure called SayHello. Because the SayHello procedure is exported, it can be called from any Delphi application.

Exporting by Name

The most common way of exporting functions and procedures is by name—for example,

```
exports
  SayHello,
  DoSomething,
  DoSomethingReallyCool;
```

These procedures are exported by their identifier name. You might have noticed that the exports section has the same syntax as a uses list. Each identifier to be exported is listed, separated by a comma. A semicolon follows the last identifier in the list.

Exporting by Ordinal Value

You can also export procedures and functions by ordinal value. Procedures and functions are exported by ordinal value by implementing the `index` keyword like this:

```
exports
  SayHello index 1,
  DoSomething index 2,
  DoSomethingReallyCool index 3;
```

When you import the function in the calling application, you specify the ordinal number (I'll discuss importing functions and procedures later in the section, "Calling Using Static Loading"). Most of the time you will export functions and procedures by name and won't bother with exporting by ordinal.

Note

> Delphi automatically assigns an ordinal value to every exported function and procedure regardless of whether you specify an index number. Specifying an index number lets you control the ordinal value of the exported function or procedure.

Exporting a function or procedure is only half the story. When you build the application that calls the function or procedure, you must *import* the functions and procedures you want to call from the DLL. I'll talk about importing functions and procedures later in the section "Calling Functions and Procedures in DLLs."

Note

> The global variable `HInstance`, when used in a DLL, will contain the instance handle of the DLL.

19

Tip

> To find out whether your code is executing in a DLL or in an application, check the value of the global variable `IsLibrary`. `IsLibrary` is `True` when called from a DLL and `False` when called from an application.

Tip

> If you are having trouble exporting functions or procedures, run the TDUMP utility on the DLL. TDUMP produces information containing a section on

> symbols exported from the DLL. Examining that section will give you a better idea of where the problem lies. To see just the exported symbols, run TDUMP with the --ee switch—for example,
>
> ```
> tdump --ee mydll.dll
> ```
>
> Remember, you can redirect the output of a command-line application to a text file with the > symbol:
>
> ```
> tdump --ee mydll.dll > dump.txt
> ```

Using a DLLProc

As I mentioned earlier, any initialization code that the DLL needs to execute can be done in the DLL's main code block. That's easy enough, but what about finalization code? DLLs don't have initialization and finalization sections as other units do. You might dynamically allocate memory in the DLL's main code block, but where do you free it? The answer is a DLLProc. A DLLProc is a procedure that is called at certain times during the life of a DLL. I'll explain how to use a DLLProc in just a bit, but first let me tell you why DLLProc exists.

A DLL receives messages from Windows when it is loaded into memory and just before it is unloaded from memory. It also receives messages when a process attaches to or detaches from an already-loaded DLL (as in the case of several applications all using the same DLL). To get these messages, you create a procedure with a specific signature and assign the address of that procedure to the global variable DLLProc. A typical DLLProc procedure might look like this:

```
procedure MyDLLProc(Reason: Integer);
begin
  if Reason = DLL_PROCESS_DETACH then
    { DLL is unloading. Cleanup code here. }
end;
```

Just declaring a DLLProc procedure is not enough to ensure that the DLLProc will be used. You must also assign the address of the procedure to the DLLProc global variable. You do that in the DLL's main code block. For example:

```
begin
  DLLProc := @MyDLLProc;
  { More initialization code. }
end.
```

This code will be executed as soon as the DLL loads. The DLLProc is now installed and will be called automatically as processes attach and detach from the DLL or when the DLL unloads. Listing 19.2 shows the source code for a DLL that implements a DLLProc.

LISTING 19.2. A DLL UNIT THAT USES A DLLProc.

```
library TestDLL;

uses
  SysUtils,
  Classes,
  Forms,
  Windows;

var
  SomeBuffer : Pointer;

procedure MyDLLProc(Reason: Integer);
begin
  if Reason = DLL_PROCESS_DETACH then
    { DLL is unloading. Cleanup code here. }
    FreeMem(SomeBuffer);
end;

procedure SayHello(AForm : TForm);
begin
  MessageBox(AForm.Handle, 'Hello From a DLL!',
    'DLL Message Box', MB_OK or MB_ICONEXCLAMATION);
end;

{ More DLL code here that uses SomeBuffer. }

exports
  SayHello;

begin
  { Assign our DLLProc to the DLLProc global variable. }
  DLLProc := @MyDLLProc;
  SomeBuffer := AllocMem(1024);
end.
```

19

As you might have surmised from Listing 19.2, the Reason parameter of the DLLProc procedure contains a value representing the reason that the DLLProc is being called. Table 19.1 lists the possible values of the Reason parameter.

TABLE 19.1. DLLProc Reason VALUES.

Value	Description
DLL_PROCESS_DETACH	The DLL is about to unload from memory.
DLL_THREAD_ATTACH	A process is attaching to the DLL.
DLL_THREAD_DETACH	A process is detaching from the DLL.

Note

> Earlier in this section I said that a DLL will receive a message from Windows when the DLL is initially loaded into memory. It is reasonable to expect that when a DLL loads, the DLLProc is called with a Reason parameter equal to DLL_PROCESS_ATTACH. That doesn't happen, however. Windows defines a DLL_PROCESS_ATTACH message, but Object Pascal does not pass it on to the DLLProc. Instead, Object Pascal calls the DLL's main code block when the DLL_PROCESS_ATTACH message is received. Because the main block is called when DLL_PROCESS_ATTACH is received, it is not necessary for Object Pascal to pass that message on to the DLLProc.

The DLL_PROCESS_DETACH message is received only once, just before the DLL unloads from memory. (The DLL_THREAD_ATTACH and DLL_THREAD_DETACH messages might be received many times if a DLL is used by several processes. Processes can include applications, multiple threads in a single application, or other DLLs.) You can use a DLLProc, then, to perform any cleanup code required for the DLL.

Loading DLLs

Before you use a function or procedure in a DLL, you first have to load the DLL into memory. Loading DLLs at runtime can be accomplished in two ways, as follows:

- Static loading
- Dynamic loading

Both methods have their advantages and disadvantages. I'll explain the differences between static loading and dynamic loading next.

Static Loading

Static loading means that your DLL is automatically loaded when the application that calls the DLL is executed. To use static loading, you declare a function or procedure that resides in the DLL with the external keyword (more on that in the section "Calling Using Static Loading"). The DLL is automatically loaded when the application loads, and you call any functions or procedures exported from the DLL just as you would any other function or procedure. This is by far the easiest way to use code contained in a DLL. The disadvantage to this approach is that if a DLL that the program references is missing, the program will refuse to load.

Dynamic Loading

Dynamic loading means that you specifically load the DLL when needed and unload it when you are done with it. This type of DLL loading has its advantages and disadvantages, too. One advantage is that the DLL is in memory only as long as you need it, so you are making more efficient use of memory. Another advantage is that your application will load more quickly when using dynamic loading because not all the code needed to run the program is loaded when the application initially loads.

The primary disadvantage to using the dynamic loading approach is that it is a bit more work for you. First, you need to load the DLL with the Windows API function LoadLibrary. Then, when you are done with the DLL, you unload it with FreeLibrary. Further (and this is where the work comes in), you need to use the GetProcAddress function to obtain a pointer to the function or procedure you want to call. To say that this approach can be a tad confusing would be an understatement. The following section describes how to call procedures and functions in DLLs using both static and dynamic loading.

Calling Functions and Procedures Located in DLLs

19

The method you use to call a function or procedure in a DLL depends on whether the DLL was statically or dynamically loaded.

Calling Using Static Loading

Calling functions and procedures from DLLs that are statically loaded is simple. First the calling application must contain a declaration for the function or procedure. After that, you call the function or procedure as you do a regular function or procedure. To import a function or procedure contained in a DLL, use the external modifier in the function or procedure declaration. For example, given the SayHello procedure shown earlier, the declaration in the calling application would look like this:

```
procedure SayHello(AForm : TForm); external 'testdll.dll';
```

The external keyword tells the compiler that the procedure can be found in a DLL (TESTDLL.DLL in this case). The actual procedure call looks no different than any other:

```
SayHello(Self);
```

After you have properly imported the function or procedure, you call it like any other function or procedure. This step presumes, of course, that the procedure has been exported from the DLL as described earlier.

> **Caution**
>
> When you declare functions and procedures contained in a DLL, be sure you get spelling *and* capitalization right. This is one place in Object Pascal programming where capitalization counts! If you misspell or improperly capitalize a function or procedure name, you will get an exception at runtime and the application will refuse to load.

USING THE external KEYWORD

The external keyword has three flavors. Using external you can import a procedure or function in one of three ways:

- By actual name
- By ordinal value
- By renaming

The first way of importing, by actual name, is the method you have seen used up to this point. You simply declare the name of the function or procedure exactly as it appears in the DLL—for example,

```
procedure SayHello(AForm : TForm); external 'testdll.dll';
```

The second way of importing, by ordinal value, requires you to specify the ordinal value of the function or procedure as exported from the DLL:

```
procedure SomeOrdinalProcedure;  external 'testdll.dll' index 99;
```

In this case, I am importing the procedure that is exported from the DLL as index 99. I can name the procedure anything I want in the calling application as long as the signature matches that of the procedure in the DLL. I can name the procedure anything I want because the procedure is exported by ordinal value and not by the procedure name.

The third method, by renaming, enables me to import the procedure by it original name, but give the procedure a new name in the calling application. It looks like this:

```
procedure CoolProcedure;
  external 'testdll.dll' name 'DoSomethingReallyCool';
```

Here I am importing a procedure called DoSomethingReallyCool and renaming it to CoolProcedure.

Of these three methods, the first, importing by name, is the most commonly used.

The trick in writing and using DLLs, then, is in getting the imports and exports right. Otherwise, there's nothing to it. Unless you need the flexibility that dynamic loading provides, you should almost always opt for static loading.

Calling Functions and Procedures Using Dynamic Loading

Calling functions and procedures in DLLs that are dynamically loaded isn't a lot of fun. It requires that you declare a pointer to the function or procedure in the DLL, and pointers to functions can be confusing. To illustrate, let's say you have a procedure in a DLL called SayHello (the SayHello procedure gets a workout in this chapter). It would look like this in the DLL's source code:

```
procedure SayHello(AForm : TForm);
begin
  MessageBox(AForm.Handle, 'Hello From a DLL!',
    'DLL Message Box', MB_OK or MB_ICONEXCLAMATION);
end;
```

To call this procedure from your program, you first have to declare a type that describes the procedure:

```
type
  TSayHello = procedure(AForm : TForm);
```

Now that you've done that, you must load the DLL, use GetProcAddress to get a pointer to the procedure, call the procedure, and, finally, unload the DLL. Here's how the whole operation looks:

```
var
  DLLInstance : THandle;
  SayHello : TSayHello;
begin
  { Load the DLL. }
  DLLInstance := LoadLibrary('testdll.dll');
  { Get the address of the procedure. }
  @SayHello := GetProcAddress(DLLInstance, 'SayHello');
  { Call the procedure. }
  SayHello(Self);
  { Unload the DLL. }
  FreeLibrary(DLLInstance);
end;
```

As I said, loading a DLL dynamically is a bit more work. Still, when you need to load a DLL at runtime, that's the way you have to do it. Note that this code is pared down a bit for clarity. You will almost always add some error-checking code to ensure that the DLL

19

loads correctly and that `GetProcAddress` returns a good address. Here's how the code looks with error checking code in place:

```
procedure TForm1.DynamicLoadBtnClick(Sender: TObject);
type
  TSayHello = procedure(AForm : TForm);
var
  DLLInstance : THandle;
  SayHello : TSayHello;
begin
  DLLInstance := LoadLibrary('testdll.dll');
  if DLLInstance = 0 then begin
    MessageDlg('Unable to load DLL.', mtError, [mbOK], 0);
    Exit;
  end;
  @SayHello := GetProcAddress(DLLInstance, 'SayHello');
  if @SayHello <> nil then
    SayHello(Self)
  else
    MessageDlg('Unable to locate procedure.', mtError, [mbOK], 0);
  FreeLibrary(DLLInstance);
end;
```

As you can see, you probably won't use dynamic loading of DLLs unless you absolutely have to.

Creating a DLL Project with the Object Repository

Creating a DLL in Delphi is accomplished through the Object Repository. (The Object Repository is covered on Day 8, "Creating Applications in Delphi.".) To create a DLL project, follow these steps:

1. Choose File | New to display the Object Repository.
2. Double-click the DLL icon.

Were you expecting it to be more complicated than that? Delphi creates the DLL project and displays the Code Editor. The file in the edit window looks like this:

```
library Project2;

{ Important note about DLL memory management: ShareMem must be the
  first unit in your library's USES clause AND your project's (select
  View-Project Source) USES clause if your DLL exports any procedures or
  functions that pass strings as parameters or function results. This
  applies to all strings passed to and from your DLL--even those that
  are nested in records and classes. ShareMem is the interface unit to
```

the DELPHIMM.DLL shared memory manager, which must be deployed along with your DLL. To avoid using DELPHIMM.DLL, pass string information using PChar or ShortString parameters. }

```
uses
  SysUtils,
  Classes;

begin
end.
```

Now you can begin adding code to the DLL. Be sure to add any exported procedure or function names to the exports section. Write any standalone functions or procedures that you need in your DLL. When you are finished adding code, you can choose Compile or Build from the Project menu to build the DLL.

COMMENTING THE DLL UNIT

I want to take a moment to explain the large comment block at the top of a DLL unit. This message is telling you that if your DLL has exported functions and procedures that take a long string type as a parameter or if your exported functions return a long string, you must do the following:

- Put ShareMem at the beginning of the uses list in both the DLL source and the calling application's main unit. Be sure that ShareMem comes before other units in the uses list.

- Ship the Borlndmm.dll file with your DLL. Notice that I said Borlndmm.dll and not Delphimm.dll, as the comments in the DLL code indicate. Borland changed the name of the memory manager DLL but neglected to change the comments generated when you create a new DLL unit. The comments are not completely misleading, however, because both Delphimm.dll and Borlndmm.dll are included with Delphi 4.

To avoid this requirement, just be sure that your DLL functions and procedures don't take any long string parameters and that your DLL functions don't return a long string. Instead of using a long string, you can use a PChar or a short string. For example, rather than use

```
procedure MyProcedure(var S : string);
begin
  { Procedure code here. }
end;
```

use this:

```
procedure MyFunction(S : PChar);
begin
  { Procedure code here. }
end;
```

19

> This situation is easy enough to work around, so you should never have the need for
> Borlndmm.dll. You just need to be aware of the restrictions placed on using the long
> string in DLL functions and procedures. Note that you can use long strings in functions
> and procedures used within the DLL itself without the need for Borlndmm.dll. This
> applies only to exported functions and procedures.

Note

I always remove the comments about Borlndmm.dll when I create a new DLL. You can certainly leave them in the DLLs source code if you want. After you understand what the comments are saying, you won't need them anymore, so you might as well remove them.

The next three listings contain code that illustrates the concepts discussed thus far. Listing 19.3 contains a DLL that will be called statically from a calling application. Listing 19.4 contains a DLL that is called dynamically from the calling application and implements a DLLProc. Finally, Listing 19.5 contains a program that calls the two DLLs. The program has a form with four buttons that call various procedures in the two DLLs. The book's code (available at http://www.mcp.com/info) contains the sample programs for the projects in these three listings.

LISTING 19.3. TestDll.dpr.

```
library TestDLL;

uses
  SysUtils,
  Classes,
  Forms,
  Windows;

procedure SayHello(AForm : TForm);
begin
  MessageBox(AForm.Handle, 'Hello From a DLL!',
    'DLL Message Box', MB_OK or MB_ICONEXCLAMATION);
end;

procedure DoSomething;
begin
  MessageBox(0, 'This procedure was exported by ordinal.',
    'DLL Message Box', MB_OK or MB_ICONEXCLAMATION);
end;
```

```
procedure DoSomethingReallyCool;
begin
  MessageBox(0, 'Something really cool.',
    'DLL Message Box', MB_OK or MB_ICONEXCLAMATION);
end;

exports
  SayHello,
  DoSomething index 99,
  DoSomethingReallyCool;

begin
end.
```

LISTING 19.4. DynLoad.dpr.

```
library TestDLL;

uses
  SysUtils,
  Classes,
  Forms,
  Windows;

procedure MyDLLProc(Reason: Integer);
begin
  if Reason = DLL_PROCESS_DETACH then
    { DLL is unloading. Cleanup code here. }
  MessageBox(0, 'DLL is unloading!',
    'DLL Message', MB_OK or MB_ICONEXCLAMATION);
end;

procedure SayHelloDyn(AForm : TForm);
begin
  MessageBox(AForm.Handle, 'Hello From a DLL!' + #13 +
    'This DLL was loaded dynamically',
    'DLL Message', MB_OK or MB_ICONEXCLAMATION);
end;

exports
  SayHelloDyn;

begin
  DLLProc := @MyDLLProc;
end.
```

19

LISTING 19.5. CallDllU.pas.

```pascal
unit CallDLLU;

interface

uses
  Windows, Messages, SysUtils, Classes, Graphics,
  Controls, Forms, Dialogs, StdCtrls;

type
  TForm1 = class(TForm)
    HelloBtn: TButton;
    OrdBtn: TButton;
    DynamicLoadBtn: TButton;
    NamedBtn: TButton;
    procedure HelloBtnClick(Sender: TObject);
    procedure OrdBtnClick(Sender: TObject);
    procedure DynamicLoadBtnClick(Sender: TObject);
    procedure NamedBtnClick(Sender: TObject);
  private
    { Private declarations }
  public
    { Public declarations }
  end;

var
  Form1: TForm1;

{ A procedure imported by name. }
procedure SayHello(AForm : TForm);
  external 'testdll.dll';

{ A procedure imported by ordinal. }
procedure OrdinalProcedure;
  external 'testdll.dll' index 99;

{ A procedure imported and renamed. }
procedure CoolProcedure;
  external 'testdll.dll' name 'DoSomethingReallyCool';

implementation

{$R *.DFM}

procedure TForm1.HelloBtnClick(Sender: TObject);
begin
  SayHello(Self);
end;
```

```
procedure TForm1.OrdBtnClick(Sender: TObject);
begin
  OrdinalProcedure;
end;

procedure TForm1.NamedBtnClick(Sender: TObject);
begin
  CoolProcedure;
end;

procedure TForm1.DynamicLoadBtnClick(Sender: TObject);
type
  TSayHello = procedure(AForm : TForm);
var
  DLLInstance : THandle;
  SayHello    : TSayHello;
begin
  { Load the DLL. }
  DLLInstance := LoadLibrary('DynLoad.dll');
  { If loading fails then bail out. }
  if DLLInstance = 0 then begin
    MessageDlg('Unable to load DLL.', mtError, [mbOK], 0);
    Exit;
  end;
  { Assign the procedure pointer. }
  @SayHello := GetProcAddress(DLLInstance, 'SayHelloDyn');
  { If the procedure was found then call it. }
  if @SayHello <> nil then
    SayHello(Self)
  else
    MessageDlg('Unable to locate procedure.', mtError, [mbOK], 0);
  { Unload the DLL. }
  FreeLibrary(DLLInstance);
end;

end.
```

19

Using Forms in DLLs

Your DLLs can contain forms as well as code. There isn't much difference in the way the form is created compared to the way a form in an application is created. First, I'll explain how to write a DLL containing a form. After that, I'll talk about the special case of using an MDI form in a DLL.

Writing a DLL Containing a Form

Writing a DLL that contains forms is not much more difficult than writing a DLL that contains code only. I believe in learning by example, so in this section, you build a DLL containing a form. Perform these steps:

1. Create a new DLL project (remove the comments at the top of the DLL, if desired). Save the DLL as MyForms.dpr.

2. Choose File | New Form to create a new form for the DLL project. Add any components you want to the form.

3. Change the Name property of the new form to DLLForm. Save the form as DLLFormU.pas.

4. Switch back to the DLL source unit. Add a function called ShowForm that creates and shows the form. Use this code:

```
function ShowForm : Integer; stdcall;
var
  Form : TDLLForm;
begin
  Form := TDLLForm.Create(Application);
  Result := Form.ShowModal;
  Form.Free;
end;
```

5. Add an exports section to the DLL and export the ShowForm function. Here's how the exports section should look:

```
exports
  ShowForm;
```

6. Choose Project | Build MyForms to build the DLL. Save the DLL.

That's all there is to creating the DLL. Notice that the ShowForm function is declared with the stdcall keyword. This keyword tells the compiler to export the function using the standard call calling convention. Exporting the function as stdcall enables this DLL to be used by development environments other than Delphi.

NEW TERM *Calling conventions* specify how the compiler should pass arguments when calling functions and procedures. The five primary calling conventions are stdcall, cdecl, pascal, register, and safecall. See the "Calling Conventions" topic in the Delphi help file for more information on calling conventions.

Notice also that the return value of the DLL's ShowForm function is the value returned from the ShowModal function. This enables you to return some status information to the calling application. Listing 19.6 shows the code for the DLL.

LISTING 19.6. THE FINISHED DLL.

```
library MyForms;

uses
  SysUtils,
  Classes,
  Forms,
  DLLFormU in 'DLLFormU.pas' {DLLForm};

function ShowForm : Integer; stdcall;
var
  Form : TDLLForm;
begin
  Form := TDLLForm.Create(Application);
  Result := Form.ShowModal;
  Form.Free;
end;

exports
  ShowForm;

begin
end.
```

Now the calling application can declare the ShowForm function and call the function. Listing 19.7 shows a Delphi application that calls the MyForms DLL.

LISTING 19.7. AN APPLICATION TO CALL THE MyForms DLL.

```
unit TestAppU;

interface

uses
  Windows, Messages, SysUtils, Classes, Graphics,
  Controls, Forms, Dialogs, StdCtrls;

type
  TForm1 = class(TForm)
    Button1: TButton;
    procedure Button1Click(Sender: TObject);
  private
    { Private declarations }
  public
    { Public declarations }
  end;
```

19

continues

LISTING 19.7. CONTINUED

```
var
  Form1: TForm1;

function ShowForm : Integer; stdcall;
  external 'myforms.dll';

implementation

{$R *.DFM}

procedure TForm1.Button1Click(Sender: TObject);
begin
  ShowForm;
end;

end.
```

Notice that I used the stdcall keyword again when I declared the function in the calling application. Because the function was exported from the DLL with stdcall, it must also be imported with stdcall. You must always import a function or procedure with the same calling convention that you used to export it.

Note

> If your Delphi DLLs are going to be used only by Delphi applications, you don't need to worry about using stdcall when exporting your functions and procedures. If, however, there is a chance that your DLL will be called from a wide range of applications, you should export your functions and procedures with stdcall.

Calling an MDI Form in a DLL

Having an MDI child form in a DLL is a special case. (MDI forms are discussed on Day 4, "The Delphi IDE Explored.") Let's say you have a Delphi application and the main form is an MDI form. If you try to use an MDI child form contained in a DLL, you will get an exception from VCL that says No MDI forms are currently active. "What? But I have an MDI form in my application!" Not according to VCL, you don't. Here's what happens.

When you attempt to show your MDI child form, VCL checks whether the Application object's MainForm property is valid. If the MainForm property is not valid, an exception is thrown. So what's the problem? The MainForm is valid, right? The problem is that the

DLL also contains an Application object, and it is the DLL Application object's MainForm that is checked, not the application's MainForm. Because a DLL doesn't have a main form, this check will always fail.

The fix for this problem is to assign the DLL's Application object to the Application object of the calling application. Naturally, this will work only if the calling application is a VCL application. That's not the whole story, though. Before the DLL unloads, you must also set the DLL's Application object back to its original state. This enables the VCL memory manager to clean up any memory allocated for the DLL. It means that you have to store the DLL's Application object pointer in a global variable in the DLL so that it can be restored before the DLL unloads.

Let's back up for a moment and review the steps required to show an MDI child form in a DLL:

1. Create a global TApplication pointer in the DLL.
2. Save the DLL's Application object in the global TApplication pointer.
3. Assign the calling application's Application object to the DLL's Application object.
4. Create and show the MDI child form.
5. Reset the DLL's Application object before the DLL unloads.

The first step is easy. Just place the following code near the top of your DLL's source unit:

```
var
  DllApp : TApplication;
```

Be sure that you place the var keyword below the uses list in the DLL source unit.

Next, create a procedure that will do the TApplication switch and create the child form. The procedure will look like this:

```
procedure ShowMDIChild(MainApp : TApplication);
var
  Child : TMDIChild;
begin
  if not Assigned(DllApp) then begin
    DllApp := Application;
    Application := MainApp;
  end;
  Child := TMDIChild.Create(Application.MainForm);
  Child.Show;
end;
```

19

Examine this code for a moment. When you call this procedure, you will pass the
`Application` object of the calling application. If the `DllApp` pointer has not yet been
assigned, you assign the DLL's `Application` object to the temporary pointer. Then you
assign the `Application` object of the calling application to the DLL's `Application`
object. This check ensures that the `Application` object is set only once. After that, the
MDI child form is created, passing the calling application's `MainForm` as the owner.
Finally, the form is shown.

All that remains is to reset the DLL's `Application` pointer before unloading the DLL.
You can use a `DLLProc` to restore the DLL's application pointer:

```
procedure MyDLLProc(Reason: Integer);
begin
  if Reason = DLL_PROCESS_DETACH then
    { DLL is unloading. Restore the Application pointer. }
    if Assigned(DllApp) then
      Application := DllApp;
end;
```

Remember, you saved the DLL's `Application` pointer earlier, so now you just restore it.

As you can see, placing an MDI child form in a DLL requires extra work, but it is certainly possible. The code for the book has an application project called `MDIApp` and a
DLL project called `MyForms`. These two projects illustrate using an MDI form in a DLL.

Showing a DLL Form from a Non-Delphi Application

Calling a form from a non-VCL application requires a slightly different approach. What
you have to do is create a standalone function in the DLL that is called by the calling
application. This function can be called from any program provided you declare the
function with `stdcall`. Within the function body, you then create and execute the form.
The function looks like this:

```
function ShowForm : Integer; stdcall;
var
  Form : TMyForm;
begin
  Form := TMyForm.Create(Application);
  Result := Form.ShowModal;
  Form.Free;
end;
```

Notice that `Application` is passed for the form's parent. This is the DLL's `Application`
object and serves as the owner of the form. Although I explicitly free the `TMyForm` object,
it isn't strictly necessary because the DLL's `Application` object will delete the form if I
neglect to.

Using Resources in DLLs

Sometimes it's convenient to have resources contained in a DLL. I've already mentioned internationalization and how a DLL can be used to make your program more easily portable to languages other than the one for which it was designed. Let's say you have an instructions screen for your application and that those instructions are contained in five strings in a DLL. The strings might be named IDS_INSTRUCTION1, IDS_INSTRUCTION2, and so on. You could load and display the strings like this:

```
LoadString(DllInstance, IDS_INSTRUCTION1, Buff, SizeOf(Buff));
InstructionLabel1.Caption := Buff;
```

The first parameter of the LoadString function contains the instance handle of the module where the strings can be found. The second parameter contains the ID number of the resource to load. You could create DLLs that contain string resources in several different languages and simply load the appropriate DLL based on a user selection. The code might look like the following:

```
var
  DLLName : String;
begin
  case Language of
    laFrench : DllName := 'french.dll';
    laGerman : DllName := 'german.dll';;
    laSpanish : DllName := 'spanish.dll';
    laEnglish : DllName := 'english.dll';
  end;
  DllInstance := LoadLibrary(PChar(dllName));
end;
```

You only have to load the correct DLL; the rest of the code remains the same (assuming the strings have the same identifiers in each of the DLLs, of course). This is just one example of using resources contained in a DLL. You will find many uses for this technique.

19

Creating a Resource DLL

You can create a DLL that contains only resources, or you can mix code and resources in the same DLL. Placing resources in a DLL is much the same as adding resources to an application. To create a resource DLL, start a new DLL project and then add a line in the DLL to link the resources:

```
{$R RESOURC.RES}
```

That's all there is to creating a resource DLL. I discussed creating resource files on Day 8, so I won't go over that ground again here.

Putting the Resource DLL to Work

You must have the DLL's instance handle before you can access resources contained in the DLL. If your DLL contains resources only, you will load the DLL dynamically. If your DLL contains resources and code, you might choose to load the DLL statically. If you load the DLL statically, you will still have to call LoadLibrary to get the instance handle:

```
DllInstance := LoadLibrary('resource.dll');
```

Now you can use the instance handle wherever required. The following code loads a bitmap resource contained in a DLL into an Image component:

```
procedure TMainForm.FormCreate(Sender: TObject);
begin
  DLLInstance := LoadLibrary('resource.dll');
  if DLLInstance <> 0 then begin
    Image.Picture.Bitmap.
      LoadFromResourceName(DLLInstance, 'ID_BITMAP1');
    FreeLibrary(DLLInstance);
  end else
    MessageDlg('Error loading resource DLL.',
      mtError, [mbOk], 0);
end;
```

Actually, there's not much left to say. To review, though, you know that you can load resource DLLs either statically or dynamically. Either way you have to use LoadLibrary to get the instance handle of the DLL. Don't forget to call FreeLibrary when you are done with the DLL or before your application closes.

 Note
> Using dynamic loading has the added advantage of allowing your application to load faster. In many cases you load the resource DLL only when it's needed and unload it when it's no longer needed. This results in your application using less memory than when the resources are contained in the executable file. The downside to static loading is that your users might see a slight pause when the resource DLL loads. Try to anticipate as much as possible and load the resource DLL when it is least likely to be noticed.

Remember JumpingJack from Day 8? The book's code has a version of JumpingJack that loads the bitmap, sound, and string resources from a DLL. Check out that program for an example of using resources in a DLL.

Summary

Using dynamic link libraries isn't as difficult as it might first appear. DLLs are a great way to reuse code. After you create a DLL, you can call it from any application that needs the functionality the code in that DLL provides. Placing VCL forms in a DLL and then calling those forms from a non-Delphi application is a powerful feature. This means that you can create forms that others can call from just about any type of Windows application, whether it is an application written in OWL, MFC, straight C, Visual Basic, and so on. Using resources in DLLs is effective if you have a lot of resources in your application and you want to control when and where those resources are loaded.

Workshop

The Workshop contains quiz questions to help you solidify your understanding of the material covered and exercises to provide you with experience in using what you have learned. You can find the answers to the quiz questions in Appendix A, "Answers to the Quiz Questions."

Q&A

Q I have a relatively small program, and I don't see the need to use DLLs. Should I reevaluate my structure?

A Probably not. For small applications, DLLs are often not necessary. Any time you have classes that can be reused, you might as well use a DLL, but don't go out of your way to use DLLs in a small application.

Q I'm trying to use a function in a DLL, but I keep getting an error on the function declaration. The error says, `Unsatisfied forward or external declaration`. What am I doing wrong?

A You have forgotten the `external` keyword in your function declaration.

Q That `GetProcAddress` thing is a little weird. Do I have to use it to call functions and procedures in my DLL?

A No. Just use static loading and you won't have to worry about the `LoadLibrary`, `GetProcAddress`, and `FreeLibrary` functions.

Q My program compiles correctly, but at runtime I get an error that says `The procedure entry point XXX cannot be found in the dynamic link library XXX.DLL`. What's wrong?

19

A There are two possibilities that can lead to that error. First, you might have accidentally misspelled or improperly capitalized a function name when you declared the function in the calling application. Second, you might have forgotten to place the function name in the exports section of the DLL.

Q **I have a form contained in a DLL, and my calling application is a Delphi program. The size of the DLL is pretty large. Is there any way I can reduce that?**

A Unfortunately, no. This is where the power of programming in Delphi works against you a little. Both the calling application and the DLL contain some of the same VCL code. In other words, the code is being duplicated in both the .exe and the .dll. You just have to live with the larger overall program size if you are using forms in DLLs. You can eliminate this problem by using runtime packages. When you use runtime packages, both the calling application and the DLL can use code in the runtime packages.

Q **I have a lot of wave files for my application. Right now they are contained in separate files, but I would like to place them all in one file. Is a resource DLL a good idea here?**

A Absolutely. The only disadvantage is that if you need just one wave file, you must load the entire DLL. Still, by using dynamic loading, you can load and unload the DLL as required. The PlaySound function makes it easy to play sounds from a DLL.

Q **I live in a French-speaking country. Why should I bother with internationalization of my program?**

A It depends entirely on your target audience. If you know that your application will be distributed only in countries where French is the native language, you don't have to worry about internationalization. But if there is even the slightest possibility that your program could be marketed in other countries, you should plan from the beginning on international support. It's much easier to do it right the first time than to go back and fix it later.

Quiz

1. How do you load a DLL using static loading?
2. How do you load a DLL using dynamic loading?
3. How do you call a function or procedure from a DLL that has been loaded statically?
4. What steps do you have to take to ensure that a function or procedure in your DLL can be called from outside the DLL?
5. In the case of a DLL that has been dynamically loaded, can you unload the DLL at any time or only when the program closes?

6. What must you do to display a Delphi form contained in a DLL from a non-Delphi program?

7. What is the name of the keyword used to declare functions and procedures imported from a DLL?

8. How do you add resources to a DLL?

9. Does a resource DLL need to contain code as well as the resources?

10. Can a DLL containing resources be loaded statically (when the program loads)?

Exercises

1. Create a DLL that contains a procedure that displays a message box when called.

2. Create a calling application that will call the DLL in exercise 1.

3. Create a DLL containing a form and a calling application that will display the form.

4. Create a DLL that has two bitmap resources.

5. Create a program that will display on demand either bitmap resource in your new DLL. (Hint: Use a TImage component and the LoadFromResourceId method.)

6. **Extra Credit:** Write five DLLs, each of which contains the same strings but in different languages.

7. **Extra Credit:** Write a calling application that displays the strings you created in exercise 6. Enable the user to choose the language to be used in the application. Display the strings in the language chosen.

19

WEEK 3

DAY 20

Creating Components

Delphi provides a wide assortment of components to use in your applications. These components cover the basic Windows controls as well as provide some specialty components not inherent in Windows itself. Still, you might need to create a component of your own to perform a task not provided by the pre-installed components. Writing a component requires these steps:

1. Use the New Component dialog box to begin the creation process.
2. Add properties, methods, and events to the component's class.
3. Test the component.
4. Add the component to the Component palette.

Today you learn how to create components. As with most of the more difficult concepts in Delphi, it's not so bad after you've done it once or twice. You will learn this technique by building a component called TFlashingLabel. TFlashingLabel is a regular Label component that flashes its text. By the time the day is done, you will know what you need in order to create basic components.

Creating a New Component

Writing components requires a higher level of programming expertise than you have used up to this point. First, you have to create a class for your new component. The class needs to be designed so that some of its properties show up in the Object Inspector, whereas others will be used only at runtime. In addition, you will almost certainly have to write methods for your component. Some will be private to the component; others will be made public so that users of the component can access them. Finally, you might have to write events for the component. Obviously, there is some work involved. As great as Delphi's visual programming environment is, it won't help you here. Writing components is pure programming.

The New Component Dialog Box

The New Component dialog box gives you a head start on writing a component. To access the New Component dialog box, choose File | New to display the Object Repository and then double-click the Component icon. Figure 20.1 shows the New Component dialog box you see when creating a new component.

FIGURE 20.1.

The New Component dialog box.

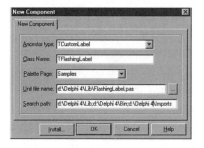

The Ancestor type field is used to specify an ancestor class for the new component. The classes of all installed components are listed in the Ancestor type combo box. When you create a new component, you should choose a base class that most closely matches the type of component you want to create.

For example, the FlashingLabel component is just a label that flashes. In that case, the standard Label component has everything you need to get started, so you could use a TCustomLabel for the ancestor class. If, on the other hand, you want to create a component that creates Windows shortcuts, you would probably derive the component from TComponent (the base class for all components) because there is no other VCL component that gives you a better base from which to work.

Note

> Delphi provides several classes that you can use as base classes for new components. The names of these classes all start with TCustom. For example, the base class for a TLabel is TCustomLabel. You can derive from one of these classes whenever you create a new component. The custom classes already provide the properties you are most likely to need for that component type, but the properties are not published (*published properties* are the properties shown in the Object Inspector at design time). All you have to do to make the properties published is re-declare the base class's properties in the published section of your component's class declaration. This is important because after a property is published, it can't be unpublished. Starting with a custom class enables you to choose exactly the properties you want published.

When you derive a new component from an existing component, you are using the Object Pascal feature called *inheritance*. It's been a while since I talked about inheritance, so refer to Day 3, "Classes and Object-Oriented Programming," if you need a refresher course. Inheriting from a component is, in effect, taking everything that component has and adding some functionality of your own. The class you are inheriting from is the base class, and the new class is the derived class. In the previous example, TCustomLabel would be the base class and TFlashingLabel would be the derived class.

After you select an ancestor class, type the name of your new component's class in the Class Name field. The classname should begin with a *T* and should describe the function the class performs. The component you build today will have the name TFlashingLabel (you'll begin creating the component soon). If you choose a classname that already exists in the component library, the New Component dialog box will tell you so when you click the OK button. You will have to choose a unique classname before you can continue.

Note

> There's no reason that you have to begin the classname with *T*; it just happens to be customary for Borland classes. (The use of *T* in Borland classes is a Borland tradition that goes back to the early days of Turbo Pascal. It was used in Turbo Vision, OWL, and now in VCL.) Some people use *T* when deriving from a Borland class but not when creating their own classes. It's entirely up to you.

20

Note

Professional component writers learned long ago to be sure that their component classes have unique names. Imagine the problems if two component vendors both name a component TFancyLabel. At TurboPower where I work, our Async Professional components start with TApd, our Orpheus components start with TOr, Abbrevia components start with TAb, and so on. Although this doesn't guarantee that these component names won't clash with those of other vendors, it certainly goes a long way to prevent that from happening.

The Palette Page field enables you to specify the page on the Component palette where you want the component's icon to appear. (The component's icon won't actually appear on the Component palette until you install the design package containing the component.) You can choose an existing tab on the Component palette, or you can type the name of a new tab you want Delphi to create for this component.

The Unit file name field is used to specify the name of the file that will contain the component's source. Delphi automatically creates a unit filename based on the component's name, but you can change the supplied filename if you want. The Search path field is used to specify the search path that Delphi should use when looking for component packages. You won't usually need to modify this field.

The Install button is used to install the new component directly into a package. You need not worry about that now, though, because you will use the default package that Delphi provides for miscellaneous components.

Creating the FlashingLabel Component

You are now ready to perform the first steps in creating the TFlashingLabel component. As I said earlier, this component is a regular Label component that flashes its text on the screen. With that in mind, let's get started creating the component:

1. Choose File | New to invoke the Object Repository.
2. Double-click the Component icon in the Object Repository. The New Component dialog box is displayed.
3. From the Ancestor type combo box, choose the TCustomLabel class as the base class.
4. Type TFlashingLabel in the Class Name field.
5. The Palette Page field contains Samples. Leave this field as is. The new component will be added to the Samples page of the Component palette when you install the component.

6. Click OK to close the New Component dialog box. The Code Editor appears and displays a new source code unit.

7. Save the unit as `FlashingLabel.pas`.

Listing 20.1 shows the source unit as it appears now.

LISTING 20.1. FlashingLabel.pas.

```pascal
unit FlashingLabel;

interface

uses
  Windows, Messages, SysUtils, Classes, Graphics,
  Controls, Forms, Dialogs, StdCtrls;

type
  TFlashingLabel = class(TCustomLabel)
  private
    { Private declarations }
  protected
    { Protected declarations }
  public
    { Public declarations }
  published
    { Published declarations }
  end;

procedure Register;

implementation

procedure Register;
begin
  RegisterComponents('Samples', [TFlashingLabel]);
end;

end.
```

20

As you can see, the `TFlashingLabel` class is derived from `TCustomLabel`. The class declaration is empty except for the access keywords (`private`, `public`, `protected`, and `published`). You can fill in the blanks later after I've had a chance to go over what comprises a component.

As you can see, the New Component dialog box gives you a head start by filling out some of the basic parts of the component's unit for you. You still have to do the hard stuff, but at least the Register procedure is written and the class declaration is started. Let me sidetrack here and talk about the Register procedure.

The Register Procedure

Registering the component is necessary so that Delphi knows what components are in the component library and on what tab they should appear. A typical Register procedure looks like this:

```
procedure Register;
begin
  RegisterComponents('Samples', [TMyComponent]);
end;
```

The Register procedure calls RegisterComponents to register the component. RegisterComponents takes two parameters. The first parameter is the name of the Component palette page on which the component will appear after it is installed; the second parameter is an array of components to be registered. If you were creating an entire library of components, you could register them all at one time by placing each component's classname in the array. For example:

```
procedure Register;
begin
  RegisterComponents('Essentials 1',
    [TEsLabel, TEsScrollingMarquee, TEsCalendar,
     TEsCalculator, TEsDateEdit, TEsNumberEdit, TEsMenuButton,
     TEsColorComboBox, TEsTile, TEsGradient, TEsRollUp]);
end;
```

This Register procedure registers 11 components and places them on the Component palette tab called "Essentials 1." Most of the time you will be dealing with one component at a time, but you can certainly register more than one component if you need to.

 Note

> The Register procedure is also used to register component editors and property editors. Component and property editors are special editors, usually dialog boxes, that aid in modifying a component or a component's property at design time. I won't discuss component and property editors in this book because they are beyond the book's scope.

At this point the component doesn't do anything special, but before you go on with the component's creation, I need to explain what makes up a component. After that, you'll write the rest of the TFlashingLabel component. Keep the component that you just created (such as it is) open in the IDE because you'll need it a little later.

Component Properties and Methods

A big part of writing components is writing the component's properties and methods. Events are also a big part of writing components, but let's talk first about properties and methods, and then I'll discuss events.

Properties

You have been using properties a lot in your journey thus far; from a user's perspective you know what properties are. Now you need to understand properties from a component writer's perspective. Before you write components, you need to understand what properties are—and what they are not.

Specifically, properties are not class data fields. It is natural to think of properties as data fields of the class to which they belong. After all, you treat properties just like class data fields when you perform actions like this:

```
var
  W : Integer;
begin
  W := Width;
  Height := W * 2;
```

But properties are not class data fields, and you must keep that in mind when writing components. Properties differ from class data fields in many ways but have at least one feature in common with data fields: They have a specific data type. A property's type can be one of the integral data types (Integer, Word, Double, string, and so on), a class (TCanvas, TFont, and so on), or a record (TRect, for example).

What properties are, then, is a special type of object that meets the following criteria:

- Properties have an underlying data field that is used to store the property's value.
- Properties can implement a write method.
- Properties can implement a read method.
- Properties can use direct access instead of read and write methods.
- Properties can be read-only or write-only.
- Properties can have a default value.
- Properties can be published or non-published.

For this to make more sense, let's take a look at these features of properties one at a time.

20

Properties Have Underlying Class Data Fields

Each property has an underlying class data field associated with it. It is this data field that holds the actual value associated with a property. Take a simple assignment, for example:

```
Label.Caption := 'Pat McGarry';
```

This statement assigns a string to the Caption property of a Label component. What happens behind the scenes is more than just a simple assignment, though. Because a Caption property is of the string type, it has a string object as its underlying data field. When an assignment is made like this one, the underlying data field is given the value of the assigned string. Using an underlying data field is necessary because a property does not have the capability to store data on its own.

You can name the underlying data field anything you want, but tradition dictates that the data field associated with a property have the same name as the property, with the addition of a leading *F*. For example, the data field associated with the Caption property is named FCaption.

Note

> This association between the property and its underlying data field can be the source of much confusion when you start writing components. It's not that it's difficult to understand; it's just that you might mix up the two when writing code for the component. For example, you might accidentally write
>
> ```
> Left := 20;
> ```
>
> when you mean to write
>
> ```
> FLeft := 20;
> ```
>
> This results in all sorts of interesting behavior in your component. You'll see why when I discuss write methods in the next section.

The underlying data field is almost always declared as private. This is because you want your users to modify the data field through the property or by calling a method, but never directly. This way you are in control of the data field as much as possible, which leads you to the next feature of properties.

Properties Can Have Write Methods

When you make an assignment to a property, many things can happen behind the scenes. Exactly what happens depends on the specific property. For example, this code looks simple:

```
Left := 20;
```

But several things happen when this line is executed. First, the underlying data field, FLeft, is changed to the new value. Next, the form (assuming this code was executed from a form) is moved to the new left position using the Windows API function MoveWindow. Finally, the form is repainted by calling Invalidate for the form.

How does all that happen? It happens through the Left property's write method. The write method is a method that is called any time the property is assigned a value. You can use the write method to do validation of the assigned value or to perform special processing.

You declare a property's write method when you declare the property. Here's an example of a typical property declaration:

```
property FlashRate : Integer
  read FFlashRate write SetFlashRate;
```

This declaration contains syntax that you haven't seen before because it is syntax specific to properties. First of all, notice that the property is declared with the property keyword and that the property type follows the property name. The second line of code tells the compiler that the property is read directly from the FFlashRate data field (I'll talk more about read methods in just a bit), and that the property uses a write method called SetFlashRate. You can name the write method anything you want, but traditionally the write method has the same name as the property prepended with the word *Set*.

When the property is written to (assigned a value), the write method associated with the property will be called automatically. The write method must be a procedure and must have one parameter. That parameter must be of the same type as the property itself. For example, the write method's declaration for the FlashRate property would be

```
procedure SetFlashRate(AFlashRate : Integer);
```

The value passed to the write method is the value that was assigned to the property. So, given this line:

```
FlashingLabel.FlashRate := 1000;
```

You end up with the value of 1000 passed to the SetFlashRate function. What you do with the value within the write method depends on a wide variety of factors. At a minimum, you assign the value to the associated data field. In other words, the write method would look like this:

```
procedure TFlashingLabel.SetFlashRate(AFlashRate : Integer);
begin
  FFlashRate := AFlashRate;
  { Do some other stuff. }
end;
```

20

Note | The use of the leading *A* for the parameter name in a write method is another Delphi tradition.

You will nearly always do something more than assign the value to the underlying data field. If you are only assigning the value to the data field associated with the property, you don't need a write method for the property. I'll explain that in just a moment. First, let's look at read methods.

Properties Can Have Read Methods

The read method works exactly like the write method (aside from the obvious difference). When a property's value is read, the read method is executed and the value of the underlying data field is returned.

The name of the read method is the property name preceded by *Get*. The read method takes no parameters and returns the property type. For example, if you were to use a read method for the FlashRate property, it would be declared like this:

```
function GetFlashRate : Integer;
```

The read method might perform some processing and then return the value of the underlying data field, FFlashRate in this case. The reading of a property happens in many different ways. Sometimes it's the result of an assignment to a variable:

```
Rate := FlashingLabel.FlashRate;
```

At other times it is used within a statement:

```
case FlashingLabel.FlashRate of
  1000 : SpeedUp;
  { etc. }
end;
```

Regardless of how the property is read, the read method is called each time a read takes place.

Notice that a couple of paragraphs ago I said *if* you are using a read method. Frequently you won't use a read method but instead will use direct access to retrieve the value of the data field associated with a property. Let's take a look at direct access right now.

Properties Can Use Direct Access

You don't have to use read and write methods for your properties. If you are assigning a value to the underlying data field or reading the value of the underlying data field, you can use direct access. The declaration for a property using direct access looks like this:

```
property FlashRate : Integer
  read FFlashRate write FFlashRate;
```

This snippet tells the compiler that the data field itself (`FFlashRate`) is used for both the `read` and the `write` specifiers rather than a `read` method or a `write` method. When the property is written to, the data field is changed and nothing more takes place. When the property is read, the value of the underlying data field is returned. It's as simple as that.

> **Note**
>
> It is common to use direct access when reading the property and to use a `write` method for writing to the property. Take a look at this earlier example of a property declaration:
>
> ```
> property FlashRate : Integer
>   read FFlashRate write SetFlashRate;
> ```
>
> The property uses direct access for reading, but it uses a `write` method for writing. Writing to a property often produces side effects, as I explained in the previous section. In fact, the capability to spawn side effects is one of the big strengths of properties. To cause side effects when your property is written to, you use a `write` method. Reading a property, on the other hand, is usually just a matter of returning the value of the underlying data field. In that case, direct access makes the most sense.

Properties Can Be Read-Only or Write-Only

You can specify a property to be read-only or write-only. Making a property read-only is a useful feature (VCL has many read-only properties). For example, you might have a property that you want the user to be able to read but not modify. It could be that modifying the property directly would have adverse effects on the component, so you need to protect against that.

Making a property read-only is easy, you simply omit the `write` specifier in the property's declaration:

```
property FlashRate : Integer
  read FFlashRate;
```

If the user attempts to write to a property that is declared as read-only, he or she will get a compiler error that says "`Cannot assign to a read-only property`". As you can see, making a property read-only is very simple.

You can make a property write-only by omitting the `read` specifier from the property's declaration. It's difficult to imagine a use for a property that can be written to but not read, but you certainly can write such a property, if necessary.

20

Properties Can Have Default Values

A *default value* is another useful feature of properties. You will notice that when you place a component on a form, many properties that are displayed in the Object Inspector already contain values. These are the default values as defined by the component writer. Assigning default values makes life easier for the component user. All properties should have a default value, if possible. This enables the user to change only specific properties and leave the rest alone. Certain types of properties (such as string properties) do not lend themselves to default values, but most do.

> **Note**
>
> String properties cannot have a default value.

Like the `read` and `write` methods, the default value is set when the property is declared. Let's go back to the component's `FlashRate` property. Declaring the `FlashRate` property with a default value would look like this:

```
property FlashRate : Integer
  read FFlashRate write SetFlashRate default 800;
```

Now, when the `FlashingLabel` component is displayed in the Object Inspector, the value of `800` (milliseconds in this case) will already be displayed for the `FlashRate` property.

> **Note**
>
> Setting a default value for the property displays only the default value in the Object Inspector. It does *not* set the value of the underlying data field for the property. You must still assign the default value to the data field in the component's constructor. For example, the constructor for the `FlashingLabel` component would look like this:
>
> ```
> constructor TFlashingLabel.Create(AOwner : TComponent);
> begin
>   inherited;
>   FFlashRate := 800;
>   { Other things here. }
> end;
> ```
>
> Be sure to set the appropriate values for all class data fields that correspond to properties with default values.

If you don't want to use a default value for a property, omit the `default` specifier in the property's declaration.

Properties Can Be Published, Public, or Private

Some properties are available at design time. These properties can be modified at design time through the Object Inspector and can also be modified or read at runtime. These properties are said to be *published*. Simply put, a published property is one that shows up in the Object Inspector at design time. Any properties located in the published section of the component's class declaration will be displayed in the Object Inspector at design time.

Other properties, called *public properties*, are runtime-only. These properties can't be accessed at design time (they don't show up in the Object Inspector). Properties of this type are declared in the public section of the component's class declaration.

Private properties are properties that are used internally by the component and are not available to the component users. Private properties are declared in the protected or private sections in the component's class declaration.

Writing Methods for Components

Writing methods for components is no different than writing methods for any Object Pascal class. Your component's methods can be private, protected, or public. It pays to keep in mind access levels as you write components.

Determining what methods to make public is easy. A *public method* is one that users of your component can call to cause the component to perform a specific action. The use of private versus protected methods is more difficult to decide. After programming for a while, you will be better able to recognize the situations when protected access should be used instead of private access.

Generally speaking, though, use private methods for tasks that are internal to the component and should not be accessible to derived classes. Use protected methods for tasks that are internal to the component, but are tasks that derived classes might want to alter to provide additional functionality to the component.

20

> **Note**
>
> Read and write methods for properties are usually made protected. Thus, you enable classes derived from your component to modify the behavior of the read and write methods by overriding the method.

As I said earlier, methods of components are just methods and, for the most part, can be treated as regular class member functions.

Adding Functionality to `TFlashingLabel`

A little later today I'll talk about events and how to write them, but for now you have enough information to write your first component. The FlashingLabel component has the following features:

- A property called FlashRate that controls the blink rate
- A property called FlashEnabled that turns the flashing on or off
- Write methods for the FlashRate and FlashEnabled properties
- Default values for the FlashRate and FlashEnabled properties
- A private class member (a TTimer class instance) to control the timing of the flash
- All the characteristics of a regular Label component

First, I'll show you the complete FlashingLabel unit. After that, I'll go over what is happening with the code. Listing 20.2 shows the FlashingLabel unit.

LISTING 20.2. FlashingLabel.pas.

```
unit FlashingLabel;

interface

uses
  Windows, Messages, SysUtils, Classes, Graphics, Controls,
  Forms, Dialogs, StdCtrls, ExtCtrls;

type
  TFlashingLabel = class(TCustomLabel)
  private
    { Private declarations }
    FFlashEnabled : Boolean;
    FFlashRate    : Integer;
    Timer         : TTimer;
  protected
    { Protected declarations }

    { Protected write methods for the properties. }
    procedure SetFlashEnabled(AFlashEnabled : Boolean);
    procedure SetFlashRate(AFlashRate : Integer);

    { OnTimer event handler. }
    procedure OnTimer(Sender : TObject); virtual;
  public
    { Public declarations }
    constructor Create(AOwner : TComponent); override;
  published
    { Published declarations }
```

```
      { The component's properties. }
      property FlashEnabled : Boolean
        read FFlashEnabled write SetFlashEnabled default True;
      property FlashRate : Integer
        read FFlashRate write SetFlashRate default 800;

      { All the properties of TCustomLabel redeclared. }
      property Align;
      property Alignment;
      property AutoSize;
      property BiDiMode;
      property Caption;
      property Color;
      property Constraints;
      property DragCursor;
      property DragKind;
      property DragMode;
      property Enabled;
      property FocusControl;
      property Font;
      property ParentBiDiMode;
      property ParentColor;
      property ParentFont;
      property ParentShowHint;
      property PopupMenu;
      property ShowAccelChar;
      property ShowHint;
      property Transparent;
      property Layout;
      property Visible;
      property WordWrap;
      property OnClick;
      property OnDblClick;
      property OnDragDrop;
      property OnDragOver;
      property OnEndDock;
      property OnEndDrag;
      property OnMouseDown;
      property OnMouseMove;
      property OnMouseUp;
      property OnStartDock;
      property OnStartDrag;
  end;

procedure Register;

implementation
```

20

continues

LISTING 20.2. CONTINUED

```
constructor TFlashingLabel.Create(AOwner : TComponent);
begin
  inherited;

  { Set the data fields to their default values. }
  FFlashEnabled := True;
  FFlashRate    := 800;

  { Initialize the timer object. }
  Timer := TTimer.Create(Self);

  { Set the timer interval using the flash rate. }
  Timer.Interval := FFlashRate;

  { Assign our own OnTimer event handler to the
  { TTimer OnTimer event. }
  Timer.OnTimer := OnTimer;
end;

procedure TFlashingLabel.SetFlashEnabled(AFlashEnabled : Boolean);
begin
  { Set FFlashEnabled data field. }
  FFlashEnabled := AFlashEnabled;

  { Don't start the timer if the component is on a form
  { in design mode. Instead, just return. }

  if csDesigning in ComponentState then
    Exit;

  { Start the timer. }
  Timer.Enabled := FFlashEnabled;

  { If flashing was turned off, be sure that the label
  { is visible. }
  if not FFlashEnabled then
    Visible := True;
end;

procedure TFlashingLabel.SetFlashRate(AFlashRate : Integer);
begin
  { Set the FFlashRate data field and the timer interval. }
  FFlashRate := AFlashRate;
  Timer.Interval := AFlashRate;
end;
```

```
procedure TFlashingLabel.OnTimer(Sender : TObject);
begin
  { If the component is on a form in design mode,
  { stop the timer and return. }
  if csDesigning in ComponentState then begin
    Timer.Enabled := False;
    Exit;
  end;

  { Toggle the Visible property each time the timer
  { event occurs. }
  Visible := not Visible;
end;

procedure Register;
begin
  RegisterComponents('Samples', [TFlashingLabel]);
end;

end.
```

The Class Declaration

First, let's take a look at the class declaration. Notice that the `private` section declares three class data fields. The first two, `FFlashEnabled` and `FFlashRate`, are the data fields associated with the `FlashEnabled` and `FlashRate` properties. The third declaration looks like this:

```
Timer : TTimer;
```

This declares a pointer to a `TTimer` object. The `TTimer` object is used to regulate the flash rate.

> **Note**
>
> I haven't discussed timers yet. A *timer* is set up to fire at a specified interval (in milliseconds). When a timer fires, a `WM_TIMER` message is sent to the window that owns the timer and, as a result, the `OnTimer` event is triggered. For example, if you set the timer interval to 1,000 milliseconds, your `OnTimer` event will be called nearly every second. I should point out that the `WM_TIMER` message is a low-priority message and can be preempted if the system is busy. For this reason, you can't use a regular timer for mission-critical operations. Still, for non-critical timings, the `TTimer` does a good job. (For more information on timers, refer to the Delphi help under `TTimer` or the `WM_TIMER` message.)

20

The protected section of the class declaration contains declarations for the write methods for the FlashRate and FlashEnabled properties. The protected section also declares the OnTimer function. This function is called each time a timer event occurs. It is protected and declared as virtual, so derived classes can override it to provide other special handling when a timer event occurs. For example, a derived class might want to change the color of the text each time the label flashes. Making this method virtual enables overriding of the function to add additional behavior.

The Published Section

Finally, notice the published section. This section contains declarations for the FlashEnabled and FlashRate properties. In the case of the FlashEnabled property, the read specifier uses direct access, the write specifier is set to the SetFlashEnabled method, and the default value is set to True. The FlashRate property uses a similar construct.

Notice that following the two property declarations, I have declared all the properties of TCustomLabel that I want republished. If you don't perform this step, the usual properties of a label component won't be available to the class at runtime nor later at design time (after you install the component to the Component palette).

The Implementation Section

Now turn your attention to the implementation section. First you see the TFlashingLabel Create constructor. Here you see that the default values for the class data fields representing the FlashEnabled and FlashRate properties are assigned. Remember that you declared default values for these properties, but that affects only the way the property is displayed in the Object Inspector. So you must assign the actual values in the constructor.

Notice these three lines (comments removed):

```
Timer := TTimer.Create(Self);
Timer.Interval := FFlashRate;
Timer.OnTimer := OnTimer;
```

The first line creates an instance of the TTimer object. The second line assigns the value of the FFlashRate data field to the Interval property of the Timer component, which sets the timer interval that will be used to flash the text on the label. Finally, the last line assigns the OnTimer function to the OnTimer event of the Timer object. This ensures that when a timer event occurs, the component will receive notification.

The SetFlashEnabled procedure is the write method for the FlashEnabled property. This procedure first assigns the FFlashEnabled data field to the value of AFlashEnabled.

Next, the Enabled property of the Timer object is set according to the value of AFlashEnabled. By writing to the FlashEnabled property, the user of the component can turn the flashing on or off. This function also contains a code line that sets the Visible property to True when flashing is disabled. This eliminates the situation in which the flashing could be turned off in mid-flash and, as a result, keep the text hidden.

The SetFlashRate Procedure

Now turn your attention to the SetFlashRate procedure. This is the write method for the FlashRate property. The user can assign a value to the FlashRate property to control how fast the component flashes. (A rate of 1200 is slow, and a rate of 150 is very fast.) This function contains these lines:

```
FFlashRate := AFlashRate;
Timer.Interval := AFlashRate;
```

This procedure simply assigns the value of AFlashRate first to the FFlashRate data field and then to the Interval property of the Timer object. This ensures that if the user changes the flash rate at runtime, the flash rate will change accordingly.

The OnTimer method doesn't require much explanation. This method is called in response to an OnTimer event. All you do is toggle the component's visible state each time a timer event occurs. In other words, if the FlashRate were set to 1000, the timer events would occur nearly every second. When the first timer event occurs, the component is hidden. A second later, the next timer event occurs and the component is shown. This continues until the FlashEnabled property is set to False or until the application closes. Finally, at the end of the unit you see the component registration.

Enter the code from Listing 20.2 into the FlashingLabel.pas file that Delphi created for you earlier (when you used the New Component dialog box). Don't worry about typing the comment lines if you don't want to. A bit later I'll show you how to test the component to see whether it works.

20

Tip

Delphi's class completion makes declaring read and write methods for properties easy. Let's say, for example, that you typed this property declaration:

```
property FlashRate : Integer
  read FFlashRate write SetFlashRate;
```

The next step would probably be to declare and define the SetFlashRate method. Guess what? Delphi will do it for you! Just press Ctrl+Shift+C and Delphi will create any read or write methods you haven't yet defined, and it will even add a declaration for the data field (FFlashRate in this example).

Tip

If you have Delphi Professional or Client/Server, you can copy the property redeclarations directly from the VCL source. Just open \Delphi 4\Source\Vcl\ StdCtrls.pas, copy the properties list from the TLabel class declaration, and paste it into your class declaration.

The ComponentState Property

I'm getting a little ahead of myself here, but I want to point out some code that I didn't discuss in the analysis of Listing 20.2. There is one important line in the SetFlashEnabled function that requires explanation. Here's that line, and the one that follows:

```
if csDesigning in ComponentState then
  Exit;
```

This code checks whether the component is being used on a form at design time. If the form is being used at design time, you need to prevent the timer from starting. When a component is placed on a form in the Form Designer, it does not necessarily have full functionality—the Form Designer can't fully approximate a running program. In this case, you don't want the timer to run while the component is being used in design mode.

Note

You could write the TFlashingLabel component so that the label flashes at design time as well as runtime. It is easier not to deal with that now, plus it gives me a chance to talk about the ComponentState property.

All components have a property called ComponentState. The ComponentState property is a set that indicates, among other things, whether the component is being used at design time. If the set includes csDesigning, you know that the component is being used on a form in the Form Designer. In this case, when you determine that the component is being used at design time, you can return from the OnTimer function without starting the timer.

This code, then, checks whether the component is being used on a form in the Form Designer. If the component is being used in the Form Designer, the timer is turned off, and the method exits without performing the remaining code in the method. The timer, by default, will be started in the TFlashingLabel constructor, so it needs to be immediately turned off if the component is being used at design time.

Testing the Component

Ultimately, you will add your newly created component to the Component palette. First, though, you must test your component to be sure that it compiles and that it functions as you intended. This is a vital step in component development, and one that many component writers overlook. There's no point in being in a hurry to add a new component to the Component palette. First be sure that the component works as expected and then worry about adding the component to the Component palette.

To test your component, write an application that will serve as a testing ground. Because you can't drop the component on a form from the Component palette, you have to create the component manually. In this case, because your FlashingLabel component has two properties, you want to make sure that each property works.

For that reason, your test program will need to turn the flashing mode on and off. In addition, the test program should enable you to set several flashing rates to see whether the FlashRate property performs as designed. Figure 20.2 shows the test program running. This will give you an idea of what you'll be trying to accomplish.

FIGURE 20.2.

The test program running.

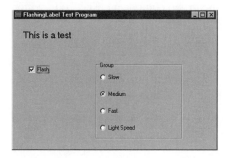

Now that you've had a peek at the test program, let's create it. As always, start with a blank form. First, add the check box and radio group components as you see them in Figure 20.2:

1. Change the form's Name property to MainForm and the Caption property to FlashingLabel Test Program.

2. Using Figure 20.2 as a pattern, add a CheckBox component to the form. Change its Name property to FlashBox, its Caption property to Flash, and its Checked property to True.

20

3. Double-click the check box to create an event handler for the OnClick event. When the Code Editor displays the OnClick handler, type this code at the cursor (the name of the FlashingLabel component will be Flasher):

```
Flasher.FlashEnabled := FlashBox.Checked;
```

This will enable or disable flashing depending on the state of the check box.

4. Place a RadioGroup component on the form. Change its Name property to Group and its Caption property to Flash Speed.

5. Double-click on the Value column next to the Items property. When the String Editor is displayed, type these lines:

```
Slow
Medium
Fast
Light Speed
```

Click OK to close the String Editor. The strings you typed will be displayed as radio buttons in the group box.

6. Set the ItemIndex property to 1. The Medium radio button will be selected.

7. Double-click the radio group component. The Code Editor will display the OnClick event handler for the group box. Type the following code at the cursor:

```
case Group.ItemIndex of
  0 :   Flasher.FlashRate := 1200;
  1 :   Flasher.FlashRate := 800;
  2 :   Flasher.FlashRate := 400;
  3 :   Flasher.FlashRate := 150;
end;
```

This will set the FlashRate value of the FlashingLabel component based on the radio button selected.

8. Save the project in the same directory where your TFlashingLabel component resides. Save the main form's unit as FlshTstU and the project as FlashTst (remember, I use short filenames for the book's code, but you can use long filenames if you want).

Okay, now you add the component itself. Because this component isn't yet visual (you can't add it from the Component palette), you will have to add it manually.

1. Click the Add to Project button (from the toolbar, from the main menu, or from the Project Manager context menu). When the Add to Project dialog box is displayed, choose the FlashingLabel.pas file and click OK.

2. Navigate to the top of the unit and add FlashingLabel to the unit's uses list.

3. Add this declaration in the private section of the TMainForm class:

```
Flasher : TFlashingLabel;
```

4. Double-click the form's background to create an OnCreate event handler for the
   form. Type the following code in the event handler:

```
Flasher := TFlashingLabel.Create(Self);
Flasher.Parent := Self;
Flasher.SetBounds(20, 20, 200, 20);
Flasher.Font.Size := 16;
Flasher.Caption := 'This is a test';
Flasher.FlashRate := 800;
```

Now you are ready to test the component. Click the Run button to compile and run the
test program. If you encounter any compiler errors, carefully check your code and fix
any errors the compiler points out.

When the program runs, click the Flash check box to turn the flashing on or off. Change
the flash rate by choosing one of the radio buttons in the group box. Hey, it works!
Congratulations, you've written your first component.

Adding the Component to the Component Palette

After the component is working properly and you are satisfied with it, you can add it to
the Component palette. To add the FlashingLabel component to the Component palette,
choose Component | Install Component. The Install Component dialog box will appear.
This dialog box enables you to add a component to a package. Figure 20.3 shows the
Install Component dialog box.

FIGURE 20.3.

*The Install Component
dialog box.*

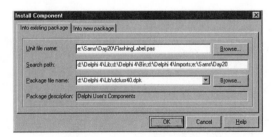

20

Okay, you're ready to add the FlashingLabel component to the Component palette.
Perform the following steps:

1. Choose Component | Install Component from the main menu. The Install
   Component dialog box is displayed.

2. Click the Browse button to the right of the Unit file name field. When the Unit
   file name dialog box comes up, locate the FlashingLabel.pas file and click Open.

3. Now look at the `Package file name` field. It should contain the file `DCLUSR40.DPK`. If not, click the drop-down button and select `DCLUSR40.DPK` from the list. If you don't see this package listed, click the Browse button and find the file (it is in the `\Delphi 4\Lib` directory).

4. Click OK to close the Install Component dialog box. Delphi displays a message telling you that it is about to build and install the package. Click Yes to continue.

5. Delphi builds and installs the package. When the process is complete, Delphi displays a message box telling you that the `TFlashingLabel` component has been registered.

Your component will now appear on the Samples page of the Component palette. Check the Samples page on the Component palette and you will see a button that has the Delphi default component icon. If you pause over the button, the tooltip says `FlashingLabel`.

Start a new project and test the `FlashingLabel` component by dropping it on the form. Note that all the usual properties of a `Label` component are present in the Object Inspector, as well as the `FlashRate` and `FlashEnabled` properties. Note also that the default values you specified for these properties are displayed in the Object Inspector.

I want to explain what you did in step 3. Delphi has a default package called `DCLUSR40` that can be used to install individual components. I had you install the `FlashingLabel` component in this package primarily because `TFlashingLabel` is a single component (not part of an overall component library), and that's what this package is for. You could have created a new package rather than use the `DCLUSR40` package, but it is easier to use the package provided.

Adding a Custom Bitmap to the Component's Button

You might have noticed a problem with your newly installed component: The button for the `FlashingLabel` component on the Component palette has the default Delphi bitmap. You can't have that! Fortunately, you can specify a bitmap for your new component. You have to create a bitmap and place it in a compiled resource file (a `.dcr` file).

> **Tip**
>
> Sometimes you might want to take the button for the base class and modify it slightly to represent your new component. In that case, start the Image Editor and open one of the `.dcr` files in the `\Delphi 4\Lib\Obj` directory. You'll have to hunt to find the exact bitmap. For example, the bitmap for the `Label` component is in the file called `Stdreg.dcr`. Open that file, copy the `TLABEL` bitmap to the Clipboard, begin a new resource file, and paste the bitmap from the Clipboard into a new bitmap resource called `TFLASH-INGLABEL`. Modify the bitmap as desired and then save the resource project.

The bitmap for the component's button must be 24×24 pixels. Most of the time a 16-color bitmap is sufficient. Delphi uses the lower-left pixel in the bitmap for the transparent color, so keep that in mind when designing your component's bitmap. (Delphi bitmaps use the dark yellow color as the transparent color, so you can follow that convention if you want.)

> **Note**
>
> Be sure you create a bitmap resource and not an icon resource. The Component palette buttons are often called icons, but their images are bitmaps and not icons.

After you create the resource file, Delphi automatically adds the component's bitmap to the Component palette when you install the component's package. For this to happen, you must follow a specific naming convention for the bitmap.

Specifically, the resource file must have a bitmap resource that exactly matches the class-name of the component. For example, to create a bitmap for the FlashingLabel component's button, you use Image Editor to create a resource file that contains a bitmap resource called TFLASHINGLABEL. You can name the resource file anything you want.

Now that you have created a resource file, you must tell Delphi to link the resource file with the component's code. To do that, add a line like this to your component's source code:

```
{$R Flashing.res}
```

The $R compiler directive tells the compiler to include the contents of a resource file with the unit's compiled code. Now rebuild the package. If you've done everything correctly, the bitmap you created for the button will show up in the Component palette.

> **Note**
>
> Notice that the filename extension of the resource file in the preceding code snippet is .res. The .res extension is used interchangeably with the .dcr extension. Some component vendors use a unique naming convention for their compiled resources and don't use either .res or .dcr. The filename extension is not important when using the $R compiler directive. What is important, however, is that the file contains valid resources.
>
> As an alternative, you can also add the $R directive directly to the package source. Most of the time this is not necessary, though.

20

Caution

You can add compiled resources only in one place. Place the $R compiler directive in either the package source or in the component's unit, but not both. If you add the same resources more than once, you will get a compiler error and the package will not install.

Tip

If you have a library of several components, you can use one resource file for all of the component's bitmaps. You don't need to have a separate resource file for each component in your library.

Writing Events for Components

Writing events requires some planning. When I speak of events, I am talking about two possibilities. Sometimes an event occurs as the result of a Windows message, and sometimes an event occurs as a result of a change in the component. An event triggered by a Windows message is more or less out of your control. You can respond to this type of event, but you generally don't initiate the event. The second type of event is triggered by the component itself. In other words, as the component writer, you are in control of when this type of event occurs.

Working with events at this level can be confusing. I'll try to get past that confusion and show you how events can be used on a practical level. To do this, let's add an event to the TFlashingLabel class. First, however, let's cover a few of the event basics.

Events Overview

To begin with, you should understand that events are properties, and, as such, they have all the features that a regular property has. Events use a private data field to store their values, as do other properties. In the case of an event, the underlying data field contains the address of a function that will be called when the specified event occurs. Like properties, events can be published or non-published. Published events show up in the Object Inspector just as published properties do.

Second, events are *method pointers*. Method pointers are like function super-pointers: They can point not only to a function in a class instance, but they can also point to a function in an instance of an unrelated class. As long as the function declarations match (the same return type and the same function parameters), the method pointer happily calls the function regardless of where it's located. For example, the OnClick event of a

TLabel object can point to an event-handling function in a TEdit object, a TForm object, a TListBox object, and so on. Method pointers are more complicated than that, but I won't go into the gory details.

Note

Event handlers must always be procedures. An event might pass one or more parameters depending on the type of the event, but it can't return a value. You can get information back from the event handler, though, by using one or more var parameters and enabling the user to change those parameters to achieve a particular behavior.

You might deal with events on any one of several levels. For example, you might want to override the base class event handler for a particular event to add some functionality. Let's say you want something special to happen when the user clicks on your component with the mouse. There's no use going to all the trouble of creating a new event for a mouse click because the event already exists in the form of the base class's OnClick event. You just tag onto that event rather than create a new event to catch the mouse click.

Another way you might deal with events is by creating an event that you trigger from within the component. I will describe this type of event first. As I said, you're going to add an event to the TFlashingLabel component that you created earlier. Adding this event requires that you also add a new property. The event will be called OnLimitReached, and the new property will be called FlashLimit. This event will be fired after the component flashes the number of times specified by FlashLimit. If FlashLimit is 0 (the default), the OnLimitReached event will never be fired.

Writing a user-defined event for a component can be divided into five basic tasks:

1. Determine the event type.
2. Declare the underlying data field.
3. Declare the event.
4. Create a virtual method that is called when the event is to be triggered.
5. Write code to trigger the event.

Let's walk through these steps so that you better understand what is involved.

Determining the Event Type

Earlier, when I discussed properties, I said that a property is of a specific type. The same is true of events. In the case of events, though, the type is a method pointer that includes

20

a description of the event handler's parameters. Yesterday, Day 19, "Creating and Using DLLs," I talked a little about function pointers when I discussed DLLs.

As I have said several times, there are two basic types of events. One is the *notification event*. This event tells you that something happened, but it doesn't give you any other details. The function declaration of the event handler for a notification event looks like this:

```
procedure Clicked(Sender : TObject);
```

The only information you get in a notification event is the sender of the event. Delphi provides the TNotifyEvent type for notification events. Any events you create that are notification events should be of the TNotifyEvent type.

The other type of event is an event that has more than one parameter and actually passes information to the event handler. If you want to, you can create this type of event for your components. Let's say you want to use an event handler that is prototyped like this:

```
procedure LimitReached(Sender : TObject; var Stop : Boolean);
```

Using this type of event handler enables the user to modify the Stop parameter, thereby sending information back to the component. If you are going to create events that have parameters, you need to declare your own method type.

Let's say you want to write an event type for the preceding method declaration and that the event type will be named TLimitReachedEvent. It would look like this:

```
TLimitReachedEvent =
  procedure(Sender : TObject; var Stop : Boolean) of object;
```

Although that's kind of confusing, all you have to do is copy this pattern and then add or remove parameters as needed. After you have the event type defined, you can declare an event to be of the type TLimitReachedEvent. (This won't make a lot of sense until you work through the whole process, so bear with me.)

Note

Place the declaration for a new event type in the type section of the unit just above the class declaration. For example:

```
unit FlashingLabel;

interface

uses
  Windows, Messages, SysUtils, Classes, Graphics, Controls,
  Forms, Dialogs, StdCtrls, ExtCtrls;
```

```
type

  TLimitReachedEvent =
    procedure(Sender : TObject; var Stop : Boolean) of object;

  TFlashingLabel = class(TCustomLabel)
  private
{ Rest of unit follows. }
```

Try to determine to the best of your ability what type of events (if any) you need for your component. If you need only notification events, you will create your events to be of the TNotifyEvent type. If your events will pass parameters to the event handler, you need to define your own event type.

Declaring the Underlying Data Field

Declaring the underlying data field is the simple part. All you have to do is declare a private data field with the same type as your event. It looks like this:

```
FOnLimitReached : TLimitReachedEvent;
```

As with properties, the data field's name is the same as the event name with the *F* on the front.

Declaring the Event

Now that you have determined the event type, you can declare the event for the component. The declaration for an event looks almost identical to the declaration for any other property. Here's a typical declaration for an event:

```
property OnSomeEvent : TNotifyEvent
  read FOnSomeEvent write FOnSomeEvent;
```

For the most part, this looks like the property declarations that you dealt with earlier. Notice that there is no default specifier. Notice also that the read and write specifiers both point to the FOnSomeEvent data field. This illustrates that events use direct access and do not use read and write methods. Finally, notice that in this example the event's type is TNotifyEvent.

The OnLimitReached event will pass parameters, so you must define a special type and apply it to the event. Given that, your declaration for the OnLimitReached event looks like this:

```
property OnLimitReached : TLimitReachedEvent
  read FOnLimitReached write FOnLimitReached;
```

20

Soon I'll show you the entire unit so that you can see it in perspective. (If you want to look ahead, check out Listing 20.3.)

Creating a Virtual Method to Trigger the Event

Creating a virtual method to trigger the event requires explanation. You will trigger the event as a result of some change within the component. In this case, you are going to trigger the event when the number of times the component has flashed reaches the value of the FlashLimit property. You trigger an event by calling the event:

```
var
  Stop : Boolean;
begin
  Stop := False;
  FOnLimitReached(Self, Stop);
```

You trigger the event from one of several places in the component based on different factors. To centralize this trigger, you create a virtual method that triggers the event. The virtual method will have the same name as the event, minus the *On* part and prepended with *Do*.

 Note

There are two popular naming conventions for naming methods that generate events. The first naming convention removes the *On* prefix and replaces it with *Do*. In the case of the OnLimitReached event, the virtual method that generates the event would be called DoLimitReached. The second naming convention drops the *On* prefix and leaves it at that. I've used both naming conventions, but I have a slight preference for the former.

First, declare the method in the class declaration:

```
procedure DoLimitReached; virtual;
```

Then, write the method that actually triggers the event. That method will look like this:

```
procedure TFlashingLabel.DoLimitReached;
var
  Stop : Boolean;
begin
  Stop := False;
  if Assigned(FOnLimitReached) then
    FOnLimitReached(Self, Stop);
  FlashEnabled := not Stop;
end;
```

There are several issues to note here. First, notice that you set up the default value of the Stop parameter. If the user doesn't modify the parameter, the value of Stop will be

False. The Stop parameter is used to determine whether the flashing should stop when the FlashLimit value is reached. In the event handler for the event (in the application that uses the component), the user can set Stop to True to cause the flashing to stop or can leave the Stop parameter as is to enable the flashing to continue. Notice that Self is passed in the first parameter, setting the Sender parameter to the component's pointer.

Now, notice the statement that triggers the event:

```
if Assigned(FOnLimitReached) then
    FOnLimitReached(Self, Stop);
```

If the component user has attached an event handler to the event, you call the event handler. If no event handler has been attached, you do the default handling for the event. (In this case, there is no default handling.) It is important to enable the user to ignore the event if he or she so chooses. This code enables that choice.

> **Note**
>
> One concept that is difficult to grasp when writing events is that the component itself does not provide the event handler. The application using the component provides the event handler; you merely provide the mechanism by which the event handler can be called when the event occurs.

> **Caution**
>
> If the user hasn't defined an event handler for your event, the event will be nil (no value assigned). Never call an event handler without first ensuring that the event has been assigned. Attempting to call an event that has not been assigned will result in an Access Violation in your component.

As I mentioned earlier, DoLimitReached is a virtual method. It is a virtual method because derived classes might want to redefine the event's default behavior. Because you were kind enough to make the method virtual, any components derived from your component only have to override the DoLimitReached function to change the default event-handling behavior. This makes it easy to change the behavior of the event without having to hunt through the code and locate every place the event is triggered. The event is triggered only here in the DoLimitReached method.

Writing Code That Triggers the Event

Somewhere in the component there must be code to call the DoLimitReached method (which, in turn, triggers the event). In the case of the TFlashingLabel component, you

20

call DoLimitReached from the OnTimer procedure. Here's how the function looks after being modified to trigger the event:

```
procedure TFlashingLabel.OnTimer(Sender : TObject);
begin
  { If the component is on a form in design mode, }
  { stop the timer and return. }
  if csDesigning in ComponentState then begin
    Timer.Enabled := False;
    Exit;
  end;

  { Toggle the Visible property each time }
  { the timer event occurs. }
  Visible := not Visible;

  { Trigger the event if needed. Only increment }
  { the counter when the label is visible. }
  if (FFlashLimit <> 0) and Visible then begin

    { Increment the FlashCount data field. }
    Inc(FlashCount);

    { If the FlashCount is greater than or equal to   }
    { the value of the FlashLimit property, reset the }
    { FlashCount value to 0 and trigger the event.    }
    if FlashCount >= FFlashLimit then begin
      FlashCount := 0;
      DoLimitReached;
    end;
  end;
end;
```

As you can see, when the FlashLimit is reached, the DoLimitReached method is called and the event is triggered. By the way, you count only every other OnTimer event. If you incremented the counter every time the OnTimer function was called, you would get an inaccurate count because the OnTimer event is fired twice for every flash (on and off). The Count variable is a class data field and FlashLimit is a property.

Overriding Base Class Events

The preceding discussion ties in with something else I want to mention briefly. If you want to override the default behavior of one of the events defined in the base class, all you have to do is override its event-triggering function as I've described. Let's say you want to override the default OnClick event to make the speaker beep when the component is clicked. All you do is override the Click function of the base class like this:

```
procedure TFlashingLabel.Click;
begin
  { Beep the speaker and then call the base class }
  { Click method for the default handling. }
  MessageBeep(-1);
  inherited;
end;
```

Because this function is declared as dynamic in the base class, it will be called automatically any time the component is clicked with the mouse. It will work only when the component is visible, so keep that in mind if you try to click the component while it is flashing. The call to MessageBeep is there just to prove that it works.

Putting It All Together

You took a peek at most of the new and improved TFlashingLabel component in the preceding pages, but let's look at the entire component to put it all in perspective. Listing 20.3 shows the source file for the finished TFlashingLabel component. Study the implementation of the OnLimitReached event to gain an understanding of how events should be implemented in your components. Listing 20.4 contains the main unit of the modified test program. The MainFormLimitReached method shows use of the OnLimitReached event.

LISTING 20.3. FlashingLabel.pas (NEW AND IMPROVED).

```
unit FlashingLabel;

interface

uses
  Windows, Messages, SysUtils, Classes, Graphics, Controls,
  Forms, Dialogs, StdCtrls, ExtCtrls;

type

  TLimitReachedEvent =
    procedure(Sender : TObject; var Stop : Boolean) of object;
```

continues

20

LISTING 20.3. CONTINUED

```pascal
TFlashingLabel = class(TCustomLabel)
private
  { Private declarations }
  FFlashEnabled    : Boolean;
  FFlashLimit      : Integer;
  FFlashRate       : Integer;
  FOnLimitReached : TLimitReachedEvent;

  FlashCount       : Integer;
  Timer            : TTimer;
protected
  { Protected declarations }

  { Protected write methods for the properties. }
  procedure SetFlashEnabled(AFlashEnabled : Boolean);
  procedure SetFlashRate(AFlashRate : Integer);
  procedure DoLimitReached; virtual;
  procedure Click; override;

  { OnTimer event handler. }
  procedure OnTimer(Sender : TObject); virtual;
public
  { Public declarations }
  constructor Create(AOwner : TComponent); override;
published
  { Published declarations }

  { The component's properties. }
  property FlashEnabled : Boolean
    read FFlashEnabled write SetFlashEnabled default True;
  property FlashRate : Integer
    read FFlashRate write SetFlashRate default 800;
  property FlashLimit : Integer
    read FFlashLimit write FFlashLimit default 0;

  property OnLimitReached : TLimitReachedEvent
    read FOnLimitReached write FOnLimitReached;

  { All the properties of TCustomLabel redeclared. }
  property Align;
  property Alignment;
  property AutoSize;
  property BiDiMode;
  property Caption;
  property Color;
  property Constraints;
  property DragCursor;
  property DragKind;
```

```pascal
    property DragMode;
    property Enabled;
    property FocusControl;
    property Font;
    property ParentBiDiMode;
    property ParentColor;
    property ParentFont;
    property ParentShowHint;
    property PopupMenu;
    property ShowAccelChar;
    property ShowHint;
    property Transparent;
    property Layout;
    property Visible;
    property WordWrap;
    property OnClick;
    property OnDblClick;
    property OnDragDrop;
    property OnDragOver;
    property OnEndDock;
    property OnEndDrag;
    property OnMouseDown;
    property OnMouseMove;
    property OnMouseUp;
    property OnStartDock;
    property OnStartDrag;
  end;

procedure Register;

implementation

constructor TFlashingLabel.Create(AOwner : TComponent);
begin
  inherited;

  { Set the data fields to their default values. }
  FFlashEnabled := True;
  FFlashRate    := 800;
  FFlashLimit   := 0;
  FlashCount    := 0;

  { Initialize the timer object. }
  Timer := TTimer.Create(Self);

  { Set the timer interval using the flash rate. }
  Timer.Interval := FFlashRate;
```

continues

20

LISTING 20.3. CONTINUED

```
      { Assign our own OnTimer event handler to the
      { TTimer OnTimer event. }
      Timer.OnTimer := OnTimer;
  end;

procedure TFlashingLabel.SetFlashEnabled(AFlashEnabled : Boolean);
begin
  { Set FFlashEnabled data field. }
  FFlashEnabled := AFlashEnabled;

  { Don't start the timer if the component is on a form
  { in design mode. Instead, just return. }

  if csDesigning in ComponentState then
    Exit;

  { Start the timer. }
  Timer.Enabled := FFlashEnabled;

  { If flashing was turned off, be sure that the label
  { is visible. }
  if not FFlashEnabled then
    Visible := True;
end;

procedure TFlashingLabel.SetFlashRate(AFlashRate : Integer);
begin
  { Set the FFlashRate data field and the timer interval. }
  FFlashRate := AFlashRate;
  Timer.Interval := AFlashRate;
end;

procedure TFlashingLabel.OnTimer(Sender : TObject);
begin
  { If the component is on a form in design mode,
  { stop the timer and return. }
  if csDesigning in ComponentState then begin
    Timer.Enabled := False;
    Exit;
  end;

  { Toggle the Visible property each time }
  { the timer event occurs. }
  Visible := not Visible;

  { Trigger the event if needed. Only increment }
  { the counter when the label is visible. }
  if (FFlashLimit <> 0) and Visible then begin
```

```
    { Increment the FlashCount data field. }
    Inc(FlashCount);

    { If the FlashCount is greater than or equal to   }
    { the value of the FlashLimit property, reset the }
    { FlashCount value to 0 and trigger the event.    }
    if FlashCount >= FFlashLimit then begin
      FlashCount := 0;
      DoLimitReached;
    end;
  end;
end;

procedure TFlashingLabel.DoLimitReached;
var
  Stop : Boolean;
begin
  Stop := False;
  if Assigned(FOnLimitReached) then
    FOnLimitReached(Self, Stop);
  FlashEnabled := not Stop;
end;

procedure TFlashingLabel.Click;
begin
  { Beep the speaker and then call the base class }
  { Click method for the default handling. }
  MessageBeep(-1);
  inherited;
end;

procedure Register;
begin
  RegisterComponents('Samples', [TFlashingLabel]);
end;
end.
```

LISTING 20.4. FlshTstU.pas.

```
unit FlshTstU;

interface

uses
  Windows, Messages, SysUtils, Classes, Graphics, Controls, Forms,
Dialogs,
  StdCtrls, ExtCtrls, Flashing;
```

continues

LISTING 20.4. CONTINUED

```
type
  TMainForm = class(TForm)
    FlashBox: TCheckBox;
    Group: TRadioGroup;
    procedure FormCreate(Sender: TObject);
    procedure GroupClick(Sender: TObject);
    procedure FlashBoxClick(Sender: TObject);
  private
    { Private declarations }
    Flasher : TFlashingLabel;
    procedure OnLimitReached(Sender : TObject; var Stop : Boolean);
public
    { Public declarations }
  end;

var
  MainForm: TMainForm;

implementation

{$R *.DFM}

procedure TMainForm.FormCreate(Sender: TObject);
begin
  Flasher := TFlashingLabel.Create(Self);
  Flasher.Parent := Self;
  Flasher.SetBounds(20, 20, 200, 20);
  Flasher.Font.Size := 16;
  Flasher.Caption := 'This is a test';
  Flasher.FlashRate := 800;
  Flasher.FlashLimit := 5;
  Flasher.OnLimitReached := OnLimitReached;
end;

procedure TMainForm.OnLimitReached(Sender : TObject; var Stop : Boolean);
begin
  { The OnLimitReached event handler. Set Stop to }
  { true to stop flashing or leave as-is to }
  { continue flashing.}
  Stop := True;
end;

procedure TMainForm.GroupClick(Sender: TObject);
begin
  case Group.ItemIndex of
    0 :  Flasher.FlashRate := 1200;
    1 :  Flasher.FlashRate := 800;
```

```
    2 :   Flasher.FlashRate := 400;
    3 :   Flasher.FlashRate := 150;
  end;
end;

procedure TMainForm.FlashBoxClick(Sender: TObject);
begin
  Flasher.FlashEnabled := FlashBox.Checked;
end;

end.
```

This component and the FlashTst test program are included with the book's code. However, the component's source unit is called Flashing.pas.

Run the test program to see whether the event works as advertised. Experiment with the test program to get a better feeling for how the event and the event handler work. Notice that the speaker beeps when you click on the label (as long is it is visible). This is because of the overridden dynamic method called Click. I added this function to illustrate how to override a base class event.

 Note

> If you want to install the new and improved FlashingLabel component on the Component palette, open the DCLUSR40 package and click on the Compile Package button. The old version of FlashingLabel will be updated to the new version.

Writing events takes time to master. You have to kiss a lot of frogs before being rewarded with the prince (or princess). In other words, there's no substitute for experience when it comes to writing events. You just have to get in there and do it. You'll probably hit a few bumps along the way, but it will be good experience, and you'll find yourself a better programmer for it.

20

Summary

Well, you're in the big league now. Writing components isn't necessarily easy, but when you have a basic understanding of writing components, the world is at your fingertips. If you are anything like me, you will learn to enjoy your nonvisual programming time as much as you enjoy the visual programming you do. If this chapter seems overwhelming, don't feel bad. You might have to let it soak in for a few days and then come back to it. You might have to read several different documents on writing components before it all comes together. Keep at it and it will eventually make sense.

Workshop

The Workshop contains quiz questions to help you solidify your understanding of the material covered and exercises to provide you with experience in using what you have learned. You can find answers to the quiz questions in Appendix A, "Answers to the Quiz Questions."

Q&A

Q Is there any reason I must know how to write components?

A No. You can use the basic components that Delphi gives you in your applications. You might never need to write components.

Q Can I buy components?

A Yes. A wide variety of sources exist for third-party component libraries. These libraries are sold by companies that specialize in VCL components. In addition, many freeware or shareware components are available from various online sources. Be sure to search the Internet for sources of VCL components.

Q Can I use my Delphi components with C++Builder?

A Yes. C++Builder has the capability to compile and install Delphi components.

Q Do I have to use `read` and `write` methods to store my property's value?

A No. You can use direct access and store the property's value directly in the underlying data field associated with the property.

Q What's the advantage of using a `write` method for my properties?

A Using a `write` method enables you to perform other operations when a property is written to. Writing to a property often causes the component to perform specific tasks. Using a `write` method enables you to carry out those tasks.

Q Why would I want a property to be public but not published?

A A published property is displayed in the Object Inspector at design time. Some properties don't have a design-time interface. Those properties should be made public so that the user can modify or read them at runtime but not at design time.

Q How do I test my component to be sure it works correctly before I install it?

A Write a test program and add the component's source file to your project. In the constructor of the main form, create an instance of your component. Set any properties that you need to set prior to the component being made visible. In the test program, manipulate your component's public properties to see whether everything works properly.

Q Do I have to write events for my components?

A Not necessarily. Some components make use of events; others do not. Don't go out of your way to write events for your components, but by the same token don't shy away from writing events when you need them.

Quiz

1. Must a property use a `write` method? Why or why not?
2. Must a property have an underlying data field? Why or why not?
3. Can you create a component by extending an existing component?
4. What happens if you don't specify a `write` specifier (either a `write` method or direct access) in a property's declaration?
5. What does direct access mean?
6. Must your properties have a default value? Why or why not?
7. Does the default value of the property set the underlying data field's value automatically?
8. How do you install a component on the Component palette?
9. How do you specify the button bitmap that your component will use on the Component palette?
10. How do you trigger a user-defined event?

Exercises

1. Review the `FlashingLabel` component source in Listing 20.3. Study it to learn what is happening in the code.
2. Remove the `FlashingLabel` component from the component library. Reinstall the `FlashingLabel` component.
3. Write a test program that uses three `FlashingLabel` components, all with different flash rates.
4. Change the bitmap for the `FlashingLabel` button on the Component palette to one of your own design.
5. Write a `write` method for the `FlashLimit` property of the `FlashingLabel` component so that the user can't enter a number greater than 100.
6. Change the `OnLimitReached` event for the `FlashingLabel` component to a regular notification event (Hint: Use `TNotifyEvent`).
7. **Extra Credit**: Write a component of your own design.
8. **Extra Credit**: Test your new component and install it on the Component palette.

20

DAY 21

Delphi and C++Builder

When Borland released Delphi 1 a few years ago, it was a huge success. Now on version 4, Delphi continues to be a huge success today. Sometime after Delphi 2, Borland decided to leverage the success of Delphi by creating a RAD development environment for C++. Borland leveraged that success in more ways than one. One way was by reusing parts of Delphi in C++Builder. In this chapter you learn about how Delphi and C++Builder are similar and how they are different. You also learn how to exchange code between Delphi and C++Builder and how to convert code from C++Builder to Delphi.

Similarities Between Delphi and C++Builder

Delphi and C++Builder are more similar than they are different. Let's look at those similarities in the following sections.

The IDE

If you have used both Delphi and C++Builder, you might have been struck by how similar their Integrated Development Environments (IDEs) are. Those of you who haven't used both Delphi and C++Builder (and even those who have), take a look at Figures 21.1 and 21.2. One of these figures is a screen shot of Delphi 3 and the other is a screen shot of C++Builder 3. I have removed the icons and program name from the title bars so that it isn't immediately apparent which is which. Can you tell the difference?

FIGURE 21.1.

Delphi or C++Builder?

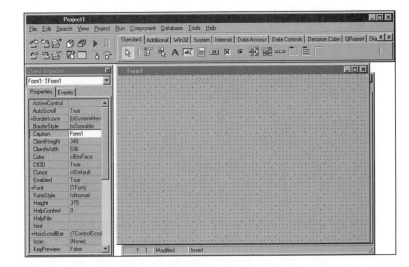

FIGURE 21.2.

Delphi or C++Builder?

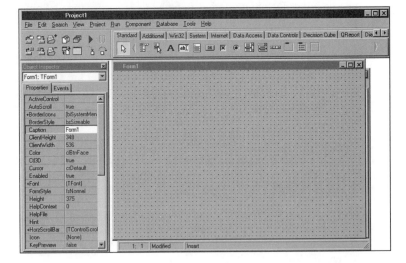

Do you give up? Figure 21.1 shows the Delphi IDE and Figure 21.2 shows the C++Builder IDE. If you have used both Delphi and C++Builder, you might have recognized from the Object Inspector which figure shows the Delphi IDE and which shows the C++Builder IDE. The Delphi Object Inspector shows properties with values of `True` and `False`, whereas the C++Builder Object Inspector shows `true` and `false`.

The point of this exercise is that the IDEs of C++Builder 3 and Delphi 3 are nearly identical. (You might have noticed I used Delphi 3 for this illustration rather than Delphi 4. I used Delphi 3 because I wanted to compare it with C++Builder 3, the latest version of C++Builder at the time of this writing, and the version that corresponds to Delphi 3.)

When you start examining the menus, you will see some differences, naturally, but for the most part the IDEs are so similar that if you know how to use one of these development environments, you know how to use the other. This has obvious benefits. For example, let's say your company has been using Delphi and now wants to add C++ to its toolset. Using C++Builder as your C++ development tool saves you time and money because your programmers don't have to learn a new development environment. That leads to another similarity between Delphi and C++Builder: the Visual Component Library.

The Visual Component Library

Not only are the IDEs of Delphi and C++Builder nearly identical, but they also share the exact same component library in the VCL. The VCL is written in Object Pascal, but both Delphi and C++Builder share the same VCL (with some minor differences that I address later in the section, "VCL Enhancements").

Note

There has been a fair amount of discussion on the Borland newsgroups among C++ programmers on the subject of a Pascal component library in a C++ development environment. Some C++ programmers can't get over the fact that the VCL is written in Object Pascal. Most programmers, though, take the sensible approach of not caring what language the VCL is written in. They just want to get their work done on time and within budget. For these programmers, the added productivity of C++Builder far outweighs the language issue.

21

The fact that both Delphi and C++Builder use the same framework is again a huge benefit if you use both Delphi and C++Builder. Other than the syntactical differences between Object Pascal and C++, the VCL components are used identically in the two IDEs. Take the following Delphi code:

```
if OpenDialog1.Execute then
  Memo1.Lines.LoadFromFile(OpenDialog1.FileName);
```

Now look at the C++Builder equivalent:

```
if (OpenDialog1->Execute())
  Memo1->Lines->LoadFromFile(OpenDialog1->FileName);
```

As you can see, there is no difference in the use of VCL. The only differences are the differences between C++ syntax and Object Pascal syntax. This means that you don't have to learn a new framework if you want to switch between Delphi and C++Builder, or vice versa. For a company with a large number of programmers, this means that you can leverage your programmers' knowledge to the maximum. Even if you are a single programmer, knowing both Delphi and C++Builder is very valuable.

Form Files

The form files used in Delphi and C++Builder are also identical. You can create a form in Delphi and reuse that form in C++Builder. Later I will explain exactly how to do that in the section "Reusing Forms." Although creating forms in Delphi and C++Builder is easy, it still takes time to design and create complex forms. By reusing your forms, you don't have to repeat work that has already been done.

Packages

Both Delphi and C++Builder use packages. In almost all cases, packages created for Delphi can be used in C++Builder. They will probably have to be recompiled in C++Builder, but that is a trivial task. The capability of C++Builder to use Delphi packages means that you have a wealth of commercial, shareware, and freeware VCL components available to you. These components are almost always written with Delphi, so they can be used in both Delphi and C++Builder. At this time you cannot use packages written for C++Builder in Delphi, but that might change with the later versions of these two products.

Differences Between Delphi and C++Builder

Although Delphi and C++Builder have many similarities, they also have many differences. Most of the differences are a result of the variations in the Object Pascal and C++ languages.

Other differences are due to what I like to call the "leapfrog effect." In the beginning there was Delphi 1. After that, naturally, came Delphi 2. After Delphi 2 was released, Borland began working on C++Builder. C++Builder 1 was patterned after Delphi 2 (which was released about a year before C++Builder 1). As such, C++Builder 1 acquired most of its features from Delphi 2. C++Builder 1 didn't add anything significant to what Delphi 2 offered—it was primarily a copycat. Shortly after C++Builder 1 was released, Borland released Delphi 3.

C++Builder 3 followed (Borland skipped version 2 of C++Builder to match Delphi's version number). C++Builder 3 is patterned after Delphi 3, just as C++Builder 1 was patterned after Delphi 2. However, C++Builder 3 added several features not found in Delphi 3 (the Project Manager, for example). Delphi 4 inherited the features introduced in C++Builder 3 and, of course, added a number of new features. C++Builder 4 will likely contain the new features of Delphi 4, will add more new features, and so on. This leapfrogging will likely continue for some time, with each release (whether it be Delphi or C++Builder) gaining the benefit of the previous release and adding new features of its own.

Now let's look at the differences between Delphi and C++Builder.

Language

The most obvious difference between Delphi and C++Builder is that C++Builder generates C++ code and Delphi generates Object Pascal code, which leads to variations in the IDEs of the two products. For example, Delphi has a menu item under the File menu called Use Unit. C++ uses header files (.H or .HPP files) for each unit, so that menu item in C++Builder is called Include Unit Hdr. These types of differences abound throughout the two IDEs for obvious reasons.

Filename Extensions

Delphi and C++Builder use different filename extensions for project and support files. This is partly a result of the language differences between the two products. The contrasting filename extensions enable you to easily distinguish a Delphi file from a C++Builder file. Table 21.1 lists the various project elements and their respective file extensions for both Delphi and C++Builder.

21

TABLE 21.1. DELPHI AND C++BUILDER FILE EXTENSIONS.

Element	Delphi	C++Builder
Project file	.DPR	.BPR
Project group file	.BPG	.BPG
Source file	.PAS	.CPP
Header file	None	.H or .HPP
Form file	.DFM	.DFM
Compiled binary file	.DCU	.OBJ
Compiled resources	.RES or .DCR	.RES
Saved desktop settings	.DSK	.DSK
Project options	.DOF	None
Package source files	.DPK	.BPK
Compiled package	.BPL	.BPL

Notice that in some cases the filename extensions used by Delphi and C++Builder are the same.

IDE

The Delphi 4 IDE is brand new. In particular, the following features are new to the Delphi 4 IDE and are not found in the current version of C++Builder:

- Dockable menu, toolbars, and Component palette
- New button bitmaps for the IDE toolbar buttons
- Bitmaps for key menu items
- Dockable tool windows

Some of the IDE enhancements listed here are cosmetic (hey, it doesn't hurt to give an application a facelift every once in awhile!). Other enhancements, such as the dockable toolbars, menus, and tool windows, are productivity boosters.

Code Editor

The Delphi 4 Code Editor has many features not found in C++Builder. In particular, the following features are found in Delphi 4:

- Module navigation
- Code completion

- Class completion
- Code parameters

Module navigation is a feature specific to the Object Pascal language, so it's no surprise that C++Builder doesn't have module navigation—but why doesn't C++Builder have code completion and code parameters? Delphi compiles the current unit each time the code completion or code parameters features are invoked. This is possible due to the incredible speed of the Object Pascal compiler. C++ code takes much longer to compile, so it is not feasible to implement code completion and code parameters in C++Builder using this same design. There are alternative means of implementing these features, so future versions of C++Builder might very well have code completion and code parameters.

C++Builder does not have class completion because it is a feature new to Delphi 4. The next version of C++Builder will likely have class completion.

Code Explorer

The Code Explorer is also new to Delphi 4, so it is not found in any version of C++Builder. This is also a feature I expect to see in future versions of C++Builder.

VCL Enhancements

The Delphi 4 VCL includes a few enhancements to VCL not yet found in C++Builder. In particular, these classes are new to VCL in Delphi 4:

- TActionList
- TControlBar
- TDateTimePicker
- TPageScroller
- TSimpleMail
- Additional QuickReports components: TQRTextFilter, TQRCSVFilter, TQRHTMLFilter
- Additional client/server MIDAS components for DCOM connections, CORBA connections, OLE Enterprise connections, and others

As with many of the additions to Delphi 4, these new VCL components will almost certainly be added to the next version of C++Builder.

21

C++Builder Can Compile Pascal Units

C++Builder can compile Pascal units just as easily as it can compile C++ units. This means that you can add a Pascal source file directly to a C++Builder project and C++Builder will compile the unit and link that unit's code into the project's EXE. You can add a Delphi form and unit to a C++Builder project and that form will be called just like a native C++Builder form. C++Builder has the capability to compile Pascal units, but Delphi can't compile C++Builder source files. Delphi 4 can, however, create C++ object files (.obj) from Object Pascal source.

ActiveX Support

Support for creating ActiveX controls is slightly different in C++Builder than in Delphi. Primarily, C++Builder ActiveX controls make use of the ActiveX Template Library (ATL), a C++ framework for ActiveX creation.

Delphi Compiles Faster and Produces Smaller EXEs

Delphi programs will always compile faster than C++Builder programs. Pascal compiles much faster than C++ because it isn't as complex. C++Builder's use of pre-compiled headers and the incremental linker helps reduce the effects by speeding up compile and link times, but Delphi programs still compile much faster than C++Builder programs.

Along the same lines, Delphi programs are always smaller than C++Builder programs. This is because of a number of factors, but primarily because the VCL is written in Object Pascal. Because the VCL is written in Object Pascal, a C++Builder program has to include both the C++ Runtime Library and the Object Pascal Runtime Library. Both C++ and Pascal use different exception handling and runtime type information code, which results in extra code in a C++Builder application.

Converting from Delphi to C++Builder

At some point you might need to convert an application from Delphi to C++Builder or from C++Builder to Delphi. I have done dozens of such conversions and, although time-consuming, they are not difficult. (By the way, when converting a project, I run Delphi and C++Builder simultaneously.) In the following section I discuss converting only from Delphi to C++Builder. Converting the other way is simply a variation of the same concepts.

> Why discuss converting a Delphi application to C++Builder and not the other way around? Primarily because Delphi has a larger installed base (it's been on the market longer) and the most likely conversion is from Delphi to C++Builder. That does not necessarily mean that developers are switching to C++Builder from Delphi. I have done nearly 200 such conversions for TurboPower Software (my employer). In that case, I was converting our products' example programs, which were written in Delphi, to C++Builder. This was necessary when we began supporting our components for use in C++Builder.

Converting a project from Delphi to C++Builder involves two basic steps. The first step is to copy the Delphi application's forms to the C++Builder project. The second step is to modify the Delphi code. Let's look at these two steps in more detail.

Copying the Delphi Forms

The first thing you need to do is copy the Delphi forms to the C++Builder application. A C++Builder form and a Delphi form use the same basic format, but there is at least one significant difference that you should be aware of.

It is obvious that a form file contains the size and position of the form itself and of every component on the form. What might not be obvious, however, is that the form file also contains information about events and event handlers. Specifically, the form file includes a description of any event handlers that have been created for the form and for any components on the form. In a Delphi form file, the events contain references to event handlers in Pascal.

In a C++Builder form file, the events point to C++ event handlers. Naturally, you will have to remove the Pascal references in order to use the form in C++Builder. It isn't important that you understand this in detail, but it is a factor you will have to deal with when converting a Delphi form to C++Builder.

Here are the steps required to copy a Delphi main form:

1. Open the project in Delphi and make note of the main form's filename and its Name property.

2. Switch to C++Builder and select the main form. Change the Name property to the same name as the Delphi project's main form.

3. Save the C++Builder project. Save the main form's unit with the same filename the form had in Delphi (minus the .PAS extension, of course). Save the project with the same project name as the Delphi project.

21

4. Switch to Windows Explorer. Copy the main form's form file (the .DFM file) from the Delphi project's directory to the C++Builder project's directory. Make sure that you copy the file, not move it. Explorer will warn you that a file with the same filename exists in the destination directory. Click Yes to overwrite the form file in the C++Builder directory. If you don't get this warning, you have done something wrong in saving the C++Builder unit.

5. Switch back to C++Builder. A dialog box will be displayed that says Module XXX.CPP's time/date has changed. Reload?. Click Yes to reload the form. When the form reloads, it will contain the components found on the Delphi form.

6. Make sure that the form is selected and then choose Edit | Select All from the C++Builder main menu to select all the form's components. Now choose Edit | Cut from the main menu, immediately followed by Edit | Paste. This step ensures that all the declarations for the individual components are placed in the main form's header file.

At this point you need to be certain that all references to the Delphi event handlers are removed from the C++Builder form file. Doing this is simple, as follows:

1. Choose File | Save from the C++Builder main menu or click the Save File button on the toolbar.

2. C++Builder will display a message box for each event handler associated with the form, as shown in Figure 21.3. Click Yes each time the dialog box is displayed to remove all event handlers. Be aware that you might have to click Yes dozens of times to remove all the event handlers. (I've had to remove as many as 100 event handlers for a single form!)

FIGURE 21.3.

Removing event handlers from the form.

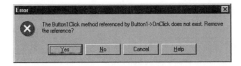

At this point, you are done copying the form itself. Now you can move on to converting the code.

Note

You need to repeat this form-copying process for every form in the Delphi application.

Converting the Code

Converting the code from Delphi to C++Builder is much more difficult than copying the form. There are many ways to proceed, but I'll explain the method that I use. First, look for any variables and methods that were created by the programmer and not by Delphi, as follows:

1. Locate the main form's class declaration in the Delphi unit.

2. Make note of any variables or methods declared in the private or public sections.

3. Copy any such declarations to the Clipboard. For example, part of the Delphi class declaration might look like this:

```
private
  { Private declarations }
  DrawColor : TColor;
  procedure DoDrawing;
  function  SetDrawColor : Integer;
```

   In this case you would copy the declarations for DrawColor, DoDrawing, and SetDrawColor.

4. Switch back to C++Builder. Display the main form's header in the Code Editor. Locate the private section and paste the code from the Clipboard.

5. Convert the declarations you pasted to C++ syntax. For example, the declarations in the example in step 3 would look like this after being converted:

```
private:  // User declarations
  TColor DrawColor;
  void DoDrawing();
  int SetDrawColor();
```

6. Switch back to Delphi. In the implementation section of the Delphi unit, locate any methods declared in the class declaration (DoDrawing and SetDrawColor in this example). Copy the methods in the Delphi unit to the Clipboard.

7. Switch to C++Builder. Paste the methods copied in step 6 from the Clipboard to the form's source unit. Convert the first line of the methods (the method header) from Pascal syntax to C++ syntax. Don't worry about the function bodies or the begin and end statements. You'll fix that later.

Copying the Event Handlers

The next step is to copy the code for the event handlers in the Delphi unit to the C++Builder unit. The best way I have found to do this is to start at the top of the `implementation` section in the Delphi unit and work down. Here are the steps to take when you encounter an event handler in the Delphi code:

1. Make note of the event handler's name. If the name is `Button1Click`, you know that the event handler is for the `OnClick` event of the component named `Button1`.
2. Copy the code inside the event handler to the Clipboard.
3. Switch to C++Builder. Generate an event handler that matches the event handler from which you copied the code.
4. Paste the Delphi code from the Clipboard into the event handler.

Repeat steps 1 through 4 for every event handler in the Delphi unit. When you are done, you will have several event handlers in your C++Builder project.

Using the Replace Text Dialog Box

The event handlers in the Delphi form file contain Pascal code, so you need to convert that code to C++. Fortunately, you can do a lot of the conversion with C++Builder's Replace Text dialog box. Table 21.2 lists the Pascal syntax you are searching for and the C++ syntax that is the replacement text. Spaces in the search or replace text are denoted by a small dot. In most cases, you will want to perform the Find and Replace operations in the order listed in Table 21.2.

TABLE 21.2. FIND AND REPLACE TEXT WHEN CONVERTING FROM DELPHI TO C++BUILDER.

Description	Find Text	Replace Text
Equality operator	·=·	·==·
Assignment operator	:=	=
Inequality operator	<>	!=
Membership operator	.	->
String quote	'	"
Begin comment	{	//
End comment	}	(Nothing)
Pascal `True` keyword	True	true
Pascal `False` keyword	False	false
`if` statement	if·	if·(
Start of block	begin	{
End of block	end;	}
End of block (form 2)	end	}

Description	Find Text	Replace Text
Pascal then statement	then	)·
Pascal do statement	·do·	(Nothing)
Pascal not statement	not·	!
Pascal nil keyword	nil	NULL
Pascal case statement	case·	switch·(
Pascal case statement	·of·	)·{
Pascal Self keyword	Self	this

When performing the Find and Replace, you should use the Replace All option, but you need to take care when doing so. For example, you don't want to replace all occurrences of a period with -> starting at the top of the file because the first several lines of every C++Builder source unit contain include statements with filenames.

Make sure that if you replace Pascal comments (which begin with { and end with }) with C++ comments, you do so *before* replacing the begin and end statements. Also, when replacing words such as end, you should turn on the Whole Words Only option in the Replace Text dialog box. This ensures that you don't accidentally replace individual characters within longer words. Be aware that some of your Find and Replace operations could have undesirable side effects (such as replacing the period that separates a filename and its extension with ->).

Tip

Consider writing a Microsoft Word macro that performs the Find and Replace operations shown in Table 21.2. It can save you a great deal of time if you have a lot of units to convert.

After you have performed the Find and Replace operations, you will have a file that is a mixture of Pascal and C++. The easy part is finished, and now you must go to work converting the rest of the file by hand. You have to know enough about each language to know how to convert Pascal syntax to C++ syntax. You're on your own from this point on, but I can point out a few issues to be aware of as you convert the rest of the file.

21

The Pascal `with` Statement

First, there is no C++ equivalent to the Pascal `with` statement. Take this code, for example:

```
with MyForm do begin
  Width   := 200;
  Height  := 500;
  Caption := 'Hello there';
end;
```

When you convert this code to C++Builder, you have to specifically reference each property:

```
MyForm->Width = 200;
MyForm->Height = 500;
MyForm->Caption = "Hello there";
```

The Pascal `as` Statement

Another Pascal statement that requires some work to convert is the as statement. You frequently see code like this in Delphi programs:

```
with Sender as TButton do
  Click;
```

In C++Builder, this code is translated as follows:

```
TButton* button = dynamic_cast<TButton*>(Sender);
if (button)
  button->Click();
```

Dealing with Strings

Another area that requires special attention is string handling. Pascal has string manipulation functions that operate on the `string` data type. C++Builder, on the other hand, has the `AnsiString` class, which has its own string manipulation functions. Take, for example, this Pascal code:

```
X := StrToInt(Edit.Text);
```

This code is translated to C++Builder code like this:

```
X = Edit->Text.ToInt();
```

Converting Sets

As with strings, the C++Builder equivalent to Pascal sets is a C++ class. In the case of sets, the C++ class is called `Set`. The following code examples illustrate conversion of Pascal set syntax to C++Builder's Set class. I used the Font property's Style member to illustrate. First look at the Pascal code:

```
{Clear the set.}
Font.Style := [];
{ Add the bold and italics styles. }
Font.Style := Font.Style + [fsBold, fsItalic];
{ Remove the italics style. }
Font.Style := Font.Style - [fsItalic];
{ See if the set contains the fsBold style. }
if fsBold in Font.Style then
  { Code here if the font is bold. }
```

Here's the C++Builder equivalent to this code:

```
// Clear the set.
Font->Style.Clear();
// Add the bold and italics styles.
Font->Style = Font->Style << fsBold << fsItalic;
// Remove the italics style.
Font->Style = Font->Style >> fsItalic;
// See if the set contains the fsBold style.
if (Font->Style.Contains(fsBold))
  // Code here if the font is bold.
```

I can't explain every difference between Object Pascal and C++ in this chapter, but these few examples should be enough to get you started. If you are using C++Builder, you should check out my C++Builder book, *Sams Teach Yourself Borland C++Builder 3 in 21 Days* (ISBN 0-672-31266-2). That book explains some of the differences between Object Pascal and C++ in detail.

Reusing Forms

You don't have to convert Delphi forms to C++ at all if you don't want to. You can use Delphi forms in C++Builder just as they are. Simply add the .PAS file for the form directly to your C++Builder project. C++Builder will create a header for the Delphi unit that you can use in any C++Builder units that reference the Delphi form.

Note

Although you can add a Delphi form to a C++Builder project, you cannot edit the form with the C++Builder Form Designer. Any modifications that you want to make to the form visually must be made from the Delphi IDE. You can, however, edit the form as text from within the C++Builder IDE. Choose the View As Text option from the C++Builder Form Designer's context menu to edit the form in text format.

21

Summary

Delphi and C++Builder are not so much competing products as they are complementary products. If you know how to program with C++Builder, learning Delphi is relatively easy. Moving from Delphi to C++Builder isn't quite as easy because of the complexity of the C++ language, but if you decide to move from Delphi to C++Builder, you can at least be assured that you won't have to learn a new framework. Without question, being proficient in both Delphi and C++Builder makes you a more valuable programmer.

Workshop

The Workshop contains quiz questions to help you solidify your understanding of the material covered and exercises to provide you with experience using what you have learned. You can find the answers in Appendix A, "Answers to the Quiz Questions."

Q&A

Q Can I use Pascal units in a C++Builder project?

A Yes. Add the Pascal unit to your project just as you would add a C++ unit. Be sure to put the Pascal units above any C++ units that reference code in the Pascal units in the Project Manager.

Q Can I use C++ units in my Delphi projects?

A No. You can use Pascal units in C++Builder but not the other way around.

Q As a programmer, I'm curious about something: Are the Delphi and C++Builder IDEs built from the same code base?

A Yes. Although Delphi and C++Builder have obvious differences, they have many similarities, so Borland uses a single code base for both IDEs.

Q Why do my Delphi projects compile so much faster than my C++Builder projects?

A Because Object Pascal is less complex than C++ and thus compiles faster.

Q I have heard that if I know C++Builder, learning Delphi is simple. Is that true?

A Not exactly, no. Despite stereotypes regarding Pascal, Delphi's Object Pascal is relatively complex. Although going from C++Builder to Delphi is easier than the reverse, it is still not something that should be approached lightly.

Quiz

1. Do Delphi and C++Builder project files have the same filename extension?

2. Do Delphi and C++Builder form files have the same filename extension?

3. Can you use packages from third-party component vendors in both Delphi and C++Builder?

4. Can you open a Delphi form file in C++Builder?

5. Can you edit a Delphi form file using the C++Builder Form Designer?

6. Can you use a C++Builder source unit in Delphi?

7. Which is better, Delphi or C++Builder?

Exercises

1. If you have C++Builder, take an example from the Delphi Demos directory and convert it to C++Builder.

2. Take an example in the C++Builder Examples directory and convert it to Delphi.

3. Take a break, you've finished your 21st day!

21

WEEK 3

In Review

This was a pretty productive week, wasn't it? Unlike Visual Component Library (VCL) components, COM and ActiveX controls can be used by a wide variety of programming environments. The good news is that Delphi gives you the fastest route to ActiveX creation of any programming environment available today.

You probably had no idea that database operations could be so easy. Easy is a relative thing. I wouldn't go so far as to say that database programming is ever simple, but Delphi certainly makes it easier than it would be in other programming environments.

On Day 19, you learned about dynamic link libraries (DLLs). Regardless of whether you decide to use DLLs right away, you can at least see their benefits and can make an informed decision regarding their use in your programs. If you plan on calling Delphi forms from programs not written in Delphi, you will have to use DLLs. DLLs are not difficult, but here again, a little experience goes a long way.

On Day 20, you learned about creating your own components. You either loved it or you were left scratching your head. If the latter is the case, don't worry about it. You might never have to write your own components. There are plenty of sources for good, commercial-quality components. (See Appendix B, "Delphi Internet Resources," for a few.) Plus, you can always go back and tackle Day 20 again after you've accumulated some time in your Delphi log book. If you enjoyed learning about writing components, it was probably difficult for you to read the last chapter! I'd be willing to bet that at some time during Day 20 you could have been overheard saying, "Wow!" Writing your own components is rewarding—no question. I had time only to scratch the surface of covering how to write components. There is a lot more to learn, and much of that can be learned by experience only. This chapter gives you enough to get you started.

Finally, you learned about Delphi and C++Builder and how they can work together. Delphi and C++Builder are two great products. If you know how to use one of these programming environments, learning the other is very easy. The more you know, the more valuable you are as a programmer.

BONUS DAY

Building Internet Applications

Are you one of those people who think the Internet is just a fad, something that will never last? If so, let me tell you something…you're wrong! The Internet is huge and it's getting bigger every day. In part, the Internet is about the Web and about people spending hour after hour browsing the Web. But the Internet is also about file transfers, email, and electronic commerce. The Internet is big business. It isn't going away anytime soon, so you might want to polish your Internet programming skills. Thankfully, Delphi makes it easy to experiment with Internet programming and to do serious Internet programming as well.

Today, you look at some aspects of Internet programming with Delphi. There's a whole world waiting out there on the Internet, so let's get to it.

Internet Components Available in Delphi

The Internet components in Delphi are located on the Internet page of the Component palette and come in two categories. The first category is a group of components provided by NetMasters. With one exception, these are native VCL components. The exception is the THTML control, which is an ActiveX control. Table BD.1 lists the NetMasters controls and provides a description of each control. The controls are listed in the order in which they appear on the Component palette.

TABLE BD.1. NETMASTERS ACTIVEX INTERNET CONTROLS.

Control	Description
TNMDayTime	Obtains the date and time from Internet daytime servers.
TNMEcho	Sends text to and receives text from Internet echo servers.
TNMFinger	Obtains information about a user from an Internet finger server.
TNMFTP	Performs file transfers between networked machines using FTP (File Transfer Protocol).
TNMHTTP	Performs file transfers using HTTP (Hypertext Transport Protocol). Hypertext documents are normally viewed in a Web browser. You use THTTP to retrieve Web documents that don't need to be displayed in a Web browser.
TNMMsg	Sends simple ASCII text messages using TCP/IP.
TNMMSGServ	Receives messages sent with the TNMMsg control.
TNMNNTP	Sends messages to and receives messages from Internet news servers using NNTP (Networking News Transfer Protocol).
TNMPOP3	Retrieves email messages from mail servers using POP3 (Post Office Protocol).
TNMUUProcessor	Encodes or decodes MIME or uuencoded files.
TNMSMTP	Sends email through SMTP (Simple Mail Transfer Protocol) mail servers.
TNMStrm	Sends data streams to a network or Internet stream server.
TNMStrmServ	Receives streams sent by the TNMStrm control.
TNMTime	Obtains the date and time from Internet time servers.
TNMUDP	Transfers data across networks using UDP (User Datagram Protocol).
TPowersock	Encapsulates the Winsock API.
TNMGeneralServer	Used for general TCP/IP servers.
THTML	Displays HTML (Hypertext Markup Language) files. This is a Web browser component.
TNMURL	Converts URL data to a readable string and string data to URL format.

The second category of controls includes native VCL components provided by Borland. The TClientSocket and TServerSocket components come with both the Professional and Client/Server versions of Delphi. The Web Broker components (TWebDispatcher, TPageProducer, TQueryTableProducer, and TDataSetTableProducer) come with only the Client/Server version. The VCL Internet components are listed in Table BD.2.

TABLE BD.2. NATIVE VCL INTERNET COMPONENTS.

Component	Description
TClientSocket	Manages a TCP/IP client socket connection.
TServerSocket	Manages a TCP/IP server socket connection.
TWebDispatcher	Converts an ordinary data module to a Web module.
TPageProducer	Enables building of dynamic HTML pages.
TQueryTableProducer	Takes TQuery results and generates an HTML document from them.
TDataSetTableProducer	Takes TDataSet records and generates an HTML document from them.

These two groups of controls give you all the power you need to build high-quality Internet applications.

Building a Web Browser

One of the most visible Internet programming tasks is building a Web browser. Certainly it's the most glamorous. The good news is that it can also be the easiest.

Who Needs Yet Another Browser?

You might be wondering why anyone would want to build a Web browser. After all, the world already has Netscape Navigator and Internet Explorer, so who needs another browser? True enough, you probably aren't going to try to build a Web browser that competes with Netscape or Microsoft. On the other hand, consider a company that has hundreds or even thousands of employees who need access to the Web. It can be very costly to license thousands of copies of a commercial Web browser. On the other hand, you can write a quality Web application with Delphi in just a few hours, thereby saving the company a lot of money.

Another reason a company might want a custom Web browser is to restrict access to the Web. For example, there might be sites on the Internet that employees have to visit from time to time. A custom Web browser enables access to authorized sites on the Web but not to any other (unauthorized) sites. In fact, a custom browser is perfect for your kids!

Finally, one of the most compelling reasons for a custom Web browser is an *intranet*. An intranet is a Web site that is local to a particular network. An intranet can contain a variety of information for a company's internal use—information on company benefits, company policies, an employee address book, meeting schedules, or even information on the company bowling league. A custom Web application can provide access to an intranet and prevent access to the Internet.

So with that in mind, you'll build a simple Web browser. You'll probably be surprised how easy it is.

First Steps in Building Your Browser

The THTML control is a ready-to-use Web browser. All you have to do is place one of these controls on a form and call the RequestDoc method. Well, that might be a little oversimplified, but you can display a Web document from anywhere on the Internet as easily as that. With that in mind, let me show you how quickly you can write a Web browser application. Here are the first steps:

1. Start with a new application. Change the form's Name property to WebMain and the Caption property to EZ Web Browser.

2. Place a Panel component on the form and change its Align property to alTop and its Height property to 60. Clear the Caption property.

3. Place a ComboBox component on the panel. Move it near the top of the panel and make it as wide as the panel itself. Change the Name property to URLComboBox. Change the Text property to an URL of your choice (try http://www.turbopower.com). Double-click the Constraints property and change the AnchorHorz constraint to akStretch.

4. Place a StatusBar component on the form. It will automatically position itself at the bottom of the form. Change its Name property to StatusBar and its SimplePanel property to True.

5. Place an HTML control in the middle of the form. Change its Align property to alClient. The HTML control fills the screen. Change the Name property to HTML.

   Now your form should look similar to the one shown in Figure BD.1. If your application doesn't look exactly like Figure BD.1, adjust as necessary or just leave it. (A little individuality isn't a bad thing, after all.)

   At this point, you should save the project. Save the form as WebBrwsU.pas and the project as WebBrows.dpr. Now you'll add just enough functionality to make the browser do something useful.

FIGURE BD.1.

Your new Web browser after the first steps.

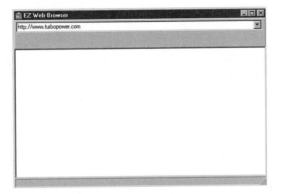

6. Click on the URL combo box. Generate an event handler for the OnClick event. Type the following code in the event handler:

```
if URLComboBox.Text <> '' then
  HTML.RequestDoc(URLComboBox.Text);
```

The RequestDoc method loads the requested document after first checking that the combo box contains text.

7. Now generate an event handler for the OnKeyPress event. Type the following code in the event handler:

```
if Key = Char(VK_RETURN) then begin
  Key := #0;
  if URLComboBox.Text = '' then
    Exit;
  URLComboBoxClick(Sender);
end;
```

This code first checks the Key parameter to see whether the Enter key was pressed. If so, it sets Key to 0 and calls the URLComboBoxTest method (created in step 6). Setting Key to 0 prevents the speaker from beeping when the Enter key is pressed. The call to the URLComboBoxClick method loads the URL into the Web browser.

8. Now compile and run the program. Type an URL in the combo box and press Enter. If you typed in a valid URL, the page will load in the HTML control.

Wow! A Web browser in 15 minutes! Notice that the browser acts like any other Web browser...well, sort of. You need to add a lot of functionality, but it's a start.

Note

> If you are fortunate enough to have a full-time Internet connection, your new browser will work immediately. If you are using dial-up networking with auto dial enabled, the dialer will start automatically and connect to your Internet service provider (ISP). If you don't have dial-up networking installed, you have to connect to the Internet manually before running the program.

Adding a Progress Indicator

You now have a good start on your Web browser. One of the features you are missing is some status information on each page as it loads. What you'll do is add a routine that updates the status bar as a page loads. You make use of the THTML control's OnUpdateRetrieval and OnEndRetrieval events to obtain periodic status updates. You will use the GetBytesTotal and GetBytesDone methods to calculate a percentage and then display the percentage loaded in the status bar. Ready?

1. Click on the HTML control on your form. Generate an event handler for the OnUpdateRetrieval event. Add code to the event handler so that it looks like this:

```
procedure TWebMain.HTMLUpdateRetrieval(Sender: TObject);
var
  Total   : Integer;
  Done    : Integer;
  Percent : Integer;
begin
  Total := HTML.RetrieveBytesTotal;
  Done  := HTML.RetrieveBytesDone;
  if (Total = 0) or (Done = 0) then
    Percent := 0
  else
    Percent := ((Done * 100) div Total);
  StatusBar.SimpleText := Format(
    'Getting Document: %d%% of %dK', [Percent, Total div 1024]);
end;
```

2. Now generate an event handler for the OnEndRetrieval event. Type this code in the event handler:

```
StatusBar.SimpleText := 'Done';
```

Take a closer look at the code in step 1. There isn't very much to it. The GetBytesTotal method tells you how many bytes are in the document or the embedded object currently being loaded (objects include images). The GetBytesDone method gives the number of bytes that have been retrieved for the page or object up to this point. From there it's a simple matter to calculate the percentage of the object that has been retrieved. Finally,

BD

you format a string with the information obtained from the HTML control and send it to the status bar. The code in step 2 simply updates the status bar after the entire document has been loaded.

Run the program again and watch what happens when you load a page. The status bar shows the percentage loaded for the page and for any embedded objects.

Some Finishing Touches

Now for some finishing touches. First, you'll add some buttons beneath the URL combo box. (For a peek at the finished product, see Figure BD.2.) Here goes:

1. Place a button on the panel beneath the URL combo box. Make its Name property GoBtn and change its Caption to Go!.

2. Generate an event handler for the OnClick event for the new button. Enter the following code in the event handler:
   ```
   URLComboBoxClick(Self);
   ```

3. Place another button on the panel, just to the right of the first button. Change the Name to StopBtn and the Caption to Stop.

4. Generate an event handler for the OnClick event for this button and type the following code in the event handler:
   ```
   HTML.Cancel(0);
   StatusBar.SimpleText := 'Done';
   ```

5. Place a third button on the panel to the right of the other two buttons. Change the Name property to ReloadBtn. Change the Caption property to Reload.

6. Create an event handler for the OnClick event for this button and enter the same code as in step 2:
   ```
   URLComboBoxClick(Self);
   ```

7. Place a fourth (and final) button on the panel. Change the Name to SourceBtn and change the Caption to View Source.

8. Create an event handler for the OnClick event and enter this code:
   ```
   HTML.ViewSource := not HTML.ViewSource;
   if HTML.ViewSource then
     SourceBtn.Caption := 'View Document'
   else
     SourceBtn.Caption := 'View Source';
   ```

Your form should now look like the one shown in Figure BD.2.

FIGURE BD.2.

The EZ Web Browser with buttons in place.

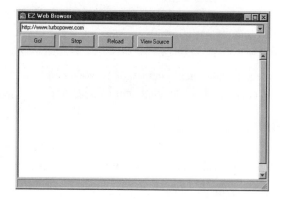

These steps introduce a couple of new THTML elements. The Cancel method stops the process of loading a document. The ViewSource property is used to toggle between viewing the document as HTML source or as a regular HTML document.

Now run the program again. Check out the new buttons and see what they do. In particular, give the View Source button a try.

Okay, you're almost done with your Web browser. Let's add a couple of more features. You are going to respond to two more events of the THTML control in order to provide more status information.

1. Generate an event handler for THTML's OnDoRequestDoc event. Type this code in the event handler:

   ```
   StatusBar.SimpleText := 'Connecting to ' + URL + '...';
   ```

2. Now create an event handler for the OnBeginRetrieval event. When the event handler appears, type this code:

   ```
   StatusBar.SimpleText := 'Connected...';
   URLComboBox.Items.Insert(0, URLComboBox.Text);
   ```

In this sequence, step 1 makes use of the OnDoRequestDoc event, which is generated when a document is requested. The URL parameter of the DoRequestDoc event handler is the URL of the site to which you are connected. As long as the URL is provided, you can use it to build a string to display in the status bar. Step 2 adds a little more status information when the document actually starts to load. It also takes the URL and adds it to the URL combo box's list. You need to make sure that you have connected to a site before adding the URL to the list of visited sites.

Congratulations, you have finished (or nearly finished) your first Internet application. Figure BD.3 shows the EZ Web Browser in operation.

FIGURE BD.3.

The finished EZ Web Browser displaying a page.

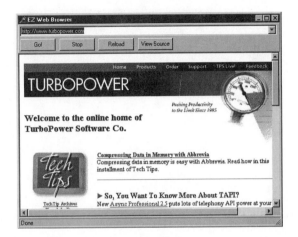

Hey, that's good work! There are some things that your Web browser doesn't do, but it does a lot, so you can be proud. Stand back and admire your work. You can take your new creation and add some new features of your own. One feature you might want to add is a list of URLs that can be used to implement browse buttons (back and next). You could also replace the standard buttons with a toolbar and add glyphs to the toolbar's buttons. If you really want to add the ultimate touch, provide an animation while the document is loading so that your users can tell when your browser is doing something. You can do that most easily with a TImageList component, although the TAnimate component would work, too.

The THTML control has several properties that I didn't cover. Most of these properties have to do with user preferences such as background color, the color of links, the color of visited links, the various fonts used for each heading size, and so on. I'm not going to explain those properties because they are easy to figure out. For the most part you can just accept the default values for these properties. If you want to customize your browser further, though, you can certainly spend some time reviewing the properties list for the THTML control.

Listing BD.1 lists the browser program's main unit.

LISTING BD.1. WebBrwsU.pas.

```
unit WebBrwsU;

interface
```

continues

```
uses
  Windows, Messages, SysUtils, Classes, Graphics, Controls, Forms,
Dialogs,
  StdCtrls, ExtCtrls, OleCtrls, NMHTML, ComCtrls;

type
  TWebMain = class(TForm)
    Panel1: TPanel;
    URLComboBox: TComboBox;
    StatusBar: TStatusBar;
    HTML: THTML;
    GoBtn: TButton;
    StopBtn: TButton;
    ReloadBtn: TButton;
    SourceBtn: TButton;
    procedure URLComboBoxClick(Sender: TObject);
    procedure URLComboBoxKeyPress(Sender: TObject; var Key: Char);
    procedure HTMLUpdateRetrieval(Sender: TObject);
    procedure HTMLEndRetrieval(Sender: TObject);
    procedure GoBtnClick(Sender: TObject);
    procedure StopBtnClick(Sender: TObject);
    procedure ReloadBtnClick(Sender: TObject);
    procedure SourceBtnClick(Sender: TObject);
    procedure HTMLDoRequestDoc(Sender: TObject; const URL: WideString;
      Element: HTMLElement; DocInput: DocInput;
      var EnableDefault: WordBool);
    procedure HTMLBeginRetrieval(Sender: TObject);
  private
    { Private declarations }
  public
    { Public declarations }
  end;

var
  WebMain: TWebMain;

implementation

{$R *.DFM}

procedure TWebMain.URLComboBoxClick(Sender: TObject);
begin
  if URLComboBox.Text <> '' then
    HTML.RequestDoc(URLComboBox.Text);
end;

procedure TWebMain.URLComboBoxKeyPress(Sender: TObject; var Key: Char);
begin
  if Key = Char(VK_RETURN) then begin
```

```
      Key := #0;
      if URLComboBox.Text = '' then
        Exit;
      URLComboBoxClick(Sender);
    end;
end;

procedure TWebMain.HTMLUpdateRetrieval(Sender: TObject);
var
  Total   : Integer;
  Done    : Integer;
  Percent : Integer;
begin
  Total := HTML.RetrieveBytesTotal;
  Done  := HTML.RetrieveBytesDone;
  if (Total = 0) or (Done = 0) then
    Percent := 0
  else
    Percent := ((Done * 100) div Total);
  StatusBar.SimpleText := Format(
    'Getting Document: %d%% of %dK', [Percent, Total div 1024]);
end;

procedure TWebMain.HTMLEndRetrieval(Sender: TObject);
begin
  StatusBar.SimpleText := 'Done';
end;

procedure TWebMain.GoBtnClick(Sender: TObject);
begin
  URLComboBoxClick(Self);
end;

procedure TWebMain.StopBtnClick(Sender: TObject);
begin
  HTML.Cancel(0);
  StatusBar.SimpleText := 'Done';
end;

procedure TWebMain.ReloadBtnClick(Sender: TObject);
begin
  URLComboBoxClick(Self);
end;

procedure TWebMain.SourceBtnClick(Sender: TObject);
begin
  HTML.ViewSource := not HTML.ViewSource;
  if HTML.ViewSource then
    SourceBtn.Caption := 'View Document'
```

continues

```
    else
      SourceBtn.Caption := 'View Source';
  end;

procedure TWebMain.HTMLDoRequestDoc(Sender: TObject; const URL:
WideString;
  Element: HTMLElement; DocInput: DocInput; var EnableDefault: WordBool);
begin
  StatusBar.SimpleText := 'Connecting to ' + URL + '...';
end;

procedure TWebMain.HTMLBeginRetrieval(Sender: TObject);
begin
  StatusBar.SimpleText := 'Connected...';
  URLComboBox.Items.Insert(0, URLComboBox.Text);
end;

end.
```

Using Internet Explorer as an ActiveX Control

If you have Microsoft Internet Explorer installed on your system, you can use it as an ActiveX control. The first thing you need to do is import the control into Delphi's Component palette. After that, you can place it on a form just as you would any control. First, let me show you how to import Internet Explorer. (I showed you how to import ActiveX controls on Day 15, "COM and ActiveX," but it doesn't hurt to review.) Here are the steps:

1. Choose Component | Import ActiveX Control from the main menu. The Import ActiveX dialog box is displayed.

2. Locate Microsoft Internet Controls (Version 1.x) in the list of ActiveX controls (see Figure BD.4). If you have Internet Explorer 3 installed, the version number will be 1.0. If you have Internet Explorer 4 installed, the control will be listed as version 1.1. Notice that the Class names field shows TWebBrowser as the control contained in this file. If you have Internet Explorer 4, the Class names field will also show TWebBrowser_V1 (the original WebBrowser control) and TShellFolderViewOC.

FIGURE BD.4.

The Import ActiveX dialog box.

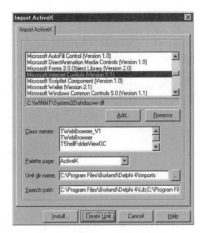

3. Click Install to install the control (the rest of the fields on this dialog box can be left on their default values).

4. The Install dialog box appears asking for a package name. Click on the Into new package tab at the top of the dialog and type IE in the File name field. (You can type a description if you want, but it's not necessary.) Click OK to create the package.

5. A confirmation dialog box appears asking whether you want to build and install the package. Click Yes to create the package.

Delphi builds the package and then displays a dialog box saying that the TWebBrowser control has been installed. Now you can try out the control:

1. First, choose File | Close All to close all windows, and then create a new application.

2. Click the ActiveX tab on the Component palette. Choose the WebBrowser control and drop it on your main form. Size the control as desired, but leave room on the form for a button.

3. Drop a Button component on the form. Double-click the button to generate an OnClick event handler. Type the following code in the event handler (use any URL you want):

```
WebBrowser1.Navigate('http:\\www.turbopower.com',
  EmptyParam, EmptyParam, EmptyParam, EmptyParam););
```

As you might surmise, the Navigate method loads the document in the Web browser.

4. Click the Run button to run the program.

When the program runs, click the form's button. The Web page will load and be displayed in the WebBrowser control.

When you install this control, Delphi creates a unit called SHDocVw_TLB.pas. You can look at this unit to see what properties and methods are available for TWebBrowser.

> You can find documentation for the WebBrowser control on Microsoft's Web site. Search the Microsoft site for the text Reusing the WebBrowser Control.

Notice that you can't redistribute the TWebBrowser control itself without obtaining a license from Microsoft. However, if you know your users have Internet Explorer installed on their systems, your application will work because the control is already installed. You still have to register the control on your user's machine for your application to run. See "Deploying Internet Applications" later in this chapter for more information on registering ActiveX controls.

Sending Mail

There are many reasons you might want to send mail from one of your applications. The good news is that sending email isn't difficult at all. Maybe you want your program users to be able to email you with any problems they encounter. In that case, your application could pop up a form containing a Memo component and a Send button. Your users can type text in the Memo component, press the Send button, and the message is emailed to you. You can even go so far as to attach a log file from your application to diagnose any problems the user is having.

The TNMSMTP control is used for sending mail through an SMTP server. SMTP is an odd protocol in that it doesn't require authenticated logon to the server (at least on most SMTP servers). You can simply connect to any mail server, send the email message, and disconnect. The Host property is used to specify the host name of the mail server to which you want to connect. Most of the time, you can just use mail as the host name. Specifying mail tells the TNMSMTP control to connect to your local mail server, whether it's your ISP's mail server or your company's mail server.

If you want, you can specifically set the mail server name (such as mail.mycompany.com), but it isn't usually necessary. If you specify an incorrect mail server, you get an ESockError exception. The Port property is used to specify the port on which to connect. The default SMTP port is port 25. The `Port` property defaults to a value of 25, so you shouldn't have to change this property.

All the pertinent information for the mail message itself is contained in the `PostMessage` property. This property is a class that contains properties such as `ToAddress`, `FromAddress`, `Subject`, `Body`, and so on. You fill in the appropriate fields of the `PostMessage` property and then send the message.

Before you can send a mail message, you need to connect to the SMTP server. This is done with the `Connect` method:

```
SMTP.Host := 'mail';
SMTP.Connect;
```

After you're connected, you can send the email. The `OnConnect` event handler is a good place for this code because you know that you are connected to an SMTP server. For example:

```
procedure TMainForm.SMTPConnect(Sender: TObject);
begin
  with SMTP.PostMessage do begin
    FromAddress := 'bilbo@baggins.com';
    ToAddress.Add('gandolf@baggins.com');
    Subject := 'Test';
    Body.Add('This is a test');
  end;
  SMTP.SendMail;
end;
```

This code sets up the `FromAddress`, `ToAddress`, `Subject`, and `Body` parameters of the `PostMessage` property and then sends the message with the `SendMail` method. It's as simple as that. Notice that the `ToAddress` and `Body` properties of `PostMessage` are `TStringLists`. The mail message body can contain several lines of text, so it's not surprising that the `Body` property is a `TStringList`. The `ToAddress` property is also a `TStringList`, so you can specify several recipients for the message.

 Note

> The `FromAddress` and `ToAddress` fields are required fields. All other fields (even the message body) are optional.

After you know the message has been sent successfully, you can disconnect from the SMTP server. The `OnSuccess` event is generated when the mail has been sent. Your `OnSuccess` event handler might be as simple as the following:

```
void __fastcall TForm1.SMTPSuccess(TObject *Sender then
begin
  SMTP.Disconnect;
end;
```

You can send several messages per connection, of course. If you have several messages to send, you don't have to disconnect from the server and reconnect for each message. Just connect once, send all your messages, and then disconnect from the server.

Your mail message might go through without incident, or it might fail in one way or another. In either case, you must be prepared to disconnect from the server. The OnFailure event is generated if the mail message fails to go through, so you can use that event to disconnect from the server as well as the OnSuccess event. The book's code, found at http://www.mcp.com/info, contains a simple mail program that illustrates how to send mail with TNMSMTP.

Deploying Internet Applications

If your Internet application uses only the VCL Internet components, there is nothing special to do when you deploy your application unless you are using runtime packages. If you are using runtime packages, you need to ship INET40.BPL, and if you are using the page producer components, ship INETDB40.BPL as well.

Deploying an application that uses ActiveX controls, however, requires more work. ActiveX controls must be registered on the machine on which your application will run. The easiest way to register ActiveX controls is with a good installation program. InstallShield Express comes with Delphi Professional and Client/Server versions, so you should try that program. Another good installation program is Wise Install from Great Lakes Business Solutions. The better installation programs register, as part of the installation process, the ActiveX controls that your application uses.

If you don't use a commercial installation program, you have to manually register any ActiveX controls your application uses. The TREGSVR.EXE utility is used to register and unregister ActiveX and OCX controls. This utility is in your Delphi 4\Bin directory. For example, to install the EZ Web Browser application you created earlier today, you ship the following files:

```
HTML.OCX
NMOCOD.DLL
NMSCKN.DLL
NWM3VWN.DLL
NMORENU.DLL
WEBBROWS.EXE
```

After you install all these files, you have to run TREGSVR.EXE on the HTML.OCX and NMOCOD.DLL files to register them. From the command line, you type

```
TREGSVR HTML.OCX
```

Do the same for NMOCOD.DLL. The THTML control is now registered on your user's machine and your program will run as intended.

> **Note**
>
> If you don't register your ActiveX controls properly, your users will see a message box that says, "Class not registered." when they attempt to run your program. Your application will then terminate, leaving your users wondering what went wrong.

To unregister a control, use the /u switch as follows:

```
TREGSVR /u HTML.OCX
```

Here again, a good installation program will have an uninstall option that takes care of this for you.

As you can see, ActiveX controls require a bit of work to install after your application is built. If you aren't aware of the fact that you need to register the ActiveX controls, it can lead to confusion for both you and your users. By the way, the files needed to deploy an application using the THTML control total about 900KB, so using ActiveX controls can be expensive in terms of disk space. I prefer to use native VCL controls whenever possible for exactly this reason.

Summary

Today you learned about the Internet components provided in Delphi. You built a simple but usable Web browser with the THTML control, and you learned how to send mail using the TNMSMTP control. Internet programming is big business right now. It certainly can't hurt to have some Internet programming experience.

Workshop

The Workshop contains quiz questions to help you solidify your understanding of the material covered and exercises to provide you with experience in using what you have learned. You can find the answers to the quiz questions in Appendix A, "Answers to the Quiz Questions."

Q&A

Q What components or controls should I use to create a TCP/IP client/server application?

A Use the `TClientSocket` and `TServerSocket` components.

Q Can I create Web pages from my database tables?

A Yes. The `TQueryTableProducer` and `TDataSetTableProducer` components create an HTML document from a database table. You can learn more about these components by examining the sample projects in the `Delphi 4\Demos\Webserv` directory.

Q The `TNMSMTP` control is for receiving mail and the `TNMPOP3` control is for retrieving mail. Why are there two controls for email operations?

A There are two controls because there are two separate mail protocols: one for sending mail (SMTP) and one for retrieving mail (POP3).

Q When were most of the Internet protocols (SMTP, POP3, FTP, UDP, and so on) defined?

A You might be surprised to learn that many protocols used in Internet programming have been around for 20 years or more even though the Internet is much younger than that. The Internet protocols were originally designed for the UNIX platform.

Quiz

1. What control do you use to display Web pages?
2. What control do you use to connect to newsgroups?
3. What is the name of the method used to display an HTML document with the `THTML` control?
4. What event is generated when an HTML document has completed loading?
5. What control do you use to send email messages?
6. What control do you use to retrieve email messages?
7. What is the name of the method used to send mail with the `TNMSMTP` control?
8. Can you freely distribute the Internet Explorer ActiveX control?
9. What is the name of the utility used to register ActiveX controls?
10. What company provides the bulk of the Internet controls that come with Delphi?

Exercises

1. Write an application for sending email. The application's main form should have fields for the *from* address, the *to* address, the mail subject, and the message text.

2. Add Forward and Back buttons to the EZ Web Browser application and make them operational.

3. **Extra Credit:** Add animation to the EZ Web Browser application so that the user can tell when the browser is loading a document.

BD

APPENDIX A

Answers to the Quiz Questions

This appendix provides the answers to the quiz sections at the end of each chapter.

Day 1

1. What is the filename extension of a Pascal unit?

   `.pas`

2. What is the name of the keyword that marks the section in which variables are declared?

   `var`

3. What does the `IntToStr` function do?

   The `IntToStr` function converts an integer value into a Pascal string.

4. What is the purpose of the uses list in a Pascal unit?

   The uses list in a Pascal unit lists the units that this unit is dependent on. The compiler needs to be able to see those units in order to compile the current unit.

5. Are the following two declarations different? Why or why not?

   ```
   var
     top : Integer;
     Top : Integer;
   ```

   The declarations are identical because the Pascal language is not case sensitive.

6. How do you concatenate Pascal strings?

   By using the + operator. (You can also use the StrCat function for null-terminated strings.)

7. How can you embed a control character in a string?

   By using the # symbol followed by the ASCII value of the character you want to embed.

8. What is the maximum length of a short string?

   255 characters.

9. Look at this line of code:

   ```
   MyArray : array [0..10] of Byte;
   ```

   How many bytes can this array hold?

   11 bytes (0 through 10).

10. What is the index number of the first element of an array, 0 or 1?

    That depends on how the array is declared. This array has a base index of 0:

    ```
    Array1 : array [0..9] of Integer;
    ```

    This array, however, has a base index of 1:

    ```
    Array2 : array [1..10] of Integer;
    ```

Day 2

1. What statements are executed in the event an if expression evaluates to True?

   The statement immediately following the if statement. If a code block follows an if statement, the entire code block will be executed.

2. How many return values can a function return?

   One. On the other hand, if you implement variable parameters, a function can effectively return more than one value.

3. Besides syntax, what is the difference between a `while` loop and a `repeat` loop?

   A `while` loop checks the conditional expression at the beginning of the loop. A `repeat` loop checks the conditional expression at the end of the loop.

4. What do the `Break` and `Continue` procedures do?

   The `Break` procedure is used to break out of a loop. The statement following the body of the loop will be executed after a call to `Break`. The `Continue` procedure forces program execution back to the top of the loop.

5. What is a global variable?

   A variable that is in scope anywhere in the program. It can be accessed by any function in the program.

6. Can a record contain a mixture of data types (`Char`, `Integer`, `Word`, and so on)?

   Yes, a structure can contain any number and type of data members.

7. How do you access the members of a record?

   With the dot operator (`.`). Here's an example:

   ```
   record.LastName = "Noble";
   ```

8. How many functions or procedures can a program have?

   There is no practical limit to the number of functions or procedures a program can have.

9. Can a function call another function or procedure?

   Yes, functions and procedures can, and often do, call other functions or procedures.

10. Is it legal to have arrays of records?

    Yes, you can have arrays of records just as easily as you can have arrays of integers, bytes, or strings.

Day 3

1. How do you clear a set of all values?

   By assigning an empty set constructor to the set—like this:

   ```
   Font.Style := [];
   ```

2. What is the purpose of having private fields and methods?

   Private data members protect data from being modified directly by users of the class. Private data members can be modified through public member functions or properties, but not directly.

3. How can you keep fields private and yet enable users to read and set their values?

   By using methods or properties.

4. When is a class's destructor called?

   The destructor is called when the object is destroyed.

5. What does it mean to override a method of the base class?

   To override a method means to replace a method in the base class with a method in your derived class. The new method must have the exact same name, parameters, and return type to override the base class method.

6. How can you override a base class method and still get the benefit of the operation the base class method performs?

   Call the base class function from within the overridden function:

   ```
   procedure MyClass.DoIt;
   begin
     Inherited DoIt;
     { do some other stuff }
   end;
   ```

7. What operator is used to dereference a pointer?

   The pointer operator (^).

8. Can a class contain other class instances as fields?

   Yes. It's very common.

9. What keyword is used to specify a pointer that has no value?

   The nil keyword.

10. What is the as keyword used for?

    To cast a pointer from a derived type to an ancestor type, or vice versa.

Day 4

1. How do you invoke the main window's Customize dialog box?

   Right-click any toolbar and choose Customize from the context menu.

2. When you have the Customize dialog box open, how do you add buttons to a toolbar?

   Simply drag an item from the Commands page to a toolbar and drop it where you want the item to appear on the toolbar.

3. How do you remove buttons from a toolbar?

   Drag unwanted buttons off the bottom of the toolbar and drop them.

4. What's the easiest way to place multiple components of the same type on a form?

Hold the Shift key when you click the component in the Component palette. Each time you click on the form, a new component will be placed.

5. What's the easiest way to place a component in the center of the form?

Double-click the component's button in the Component palette.

6. List the file types needed to build an application in Delphi.

The `.dpr`, `.pas`, and `.dfm` files.

7. What VCL method do you use to display a form modelessly?

The `Show` method.

8. What VCL method do you use to display a form modally?

The `ShowModal` method.

9. How can you attach an event to an event handler that has been previously defined?

In the Object Inspector, switch to the Events page. In the value column next to the event, click the drop-down arrow button. A list of compatible event handlers is displayed. Choose one.

10. When using the Object Inspector, how can you enumerate the choices for a particular property?

Double-click the value column next to the property name in the Object Inspector. Each time you double-click, the value changes to the next item in the list.

Day 5

1. Are all components visible at design time?

No. Only visual components can be seen at design time.

2. Is the `OpenDialog` component a visual component or a nonvisual component?

It's a nonvisual component. Although it is displayed at runtime, it is considered nonvisual because it is not visible at design time.

3. What is the name of the VCL class that represents a Delphi form?

`TForm`.

4. Do all versions of Delphi ship with the same set of components?

No. The Professional version comes with more components than the Standard version. Likewise, the Client/Server version comes with more components than does the Professional version.

A

5. Are all VCL classes ultimately derived from `TObject`?

   Yes.

6. Name one nonvisual VCL component.

   `TOpenDialog`, `TSaveDialog`, `TRegistry`, `TColorDialog`, `TTimer`, `TImageList`, `TFontDialog`, and many more, are all nonvisual VCL components.

7. Do all components share certain common properties?

   Yes. All components are ultimately derived from `TComponent`, so they all have the properties found in `TComponent`, such as `Name` and `Owner`.

8. Name two common properties that all visual components share.

   Common properties that all visual components share include `Top`, `Left`, `Owner`, `Parent`, `Width`, `Height`, and so on.

9. Can two or more components share the same event handler?

   Yes.

10. What is the VCL terminology for a Windows device context? What is the name of the VCL class that encapsulates device contexts?

    A canvas is a Windows device context. VCL encapsulates device contexts through the `TCanvas` class.

Day 6

1. When do you use Ctrl+drag in selecting components?

   When selecting components that are children of another component (components on a panel, for example).

2. What significance does the first component selected have when aligning a group of components?

   It is the anchor component. It retains its position, and all other components are aligned to it.

3. What is the quickest method to select a group of components?

   Drag a bounding rectangle around (or just touching) them.

4. How can you make a group of components all have the width of the group's widest component?

   Select all the components you want to modify. Then choose Edit | Size from the main menu and choose the Grow to Largest radio button.

5. What happens when you double-click a component on a form?

The default event handler for that component is displayed in the Code Editor. In the case of many components, the OnClick event handler will be displayed. In some special cases (such as the Image component), a dialog box is displayed.

6. What does the Align property's alClient option do?

   It forces the component to fill the entire client area of its parent, regardless of how the parent (usually a form) is sized.

7. What does the ellipsis following a menu item mean?

   Traditionally, it means that choosing that menu item will result in a dialog being displayed.

8. What two ways can you move a menu item?

   In the Menu Designer, you can drag the menu to a new location or you can use cut and paste.

9. How do you add menu accelerators to menu items?

   When typing the caption for the menu item, add the ampersand (&) before the shortcut key you choose as the shortcut for that menu item. For example, the Caption for the File | Exit menu item would read E&xit.

10. How do you initially disable a menu item?

    Set its Enabled property to False.

Day 7

1. Can you change the Name property of a component at runtime?
   Yes, but it's a very bad idea.

2. What property is used to enable and disable controls?
   The Enabled property.

3. How can you tell at runtime that a button is disabled?
   Its text is grayed out.

4. What is the difference between the long hint and the short hint?
   The long hint is used for the status bar text, and the short hint is used for the tooltip text.

5. Name three of the four methods that can be used to tell a control to repaint itself.
   Invalidate, Repaint, Refresh, and Update.

6. How many types of combo boxes are there?
   Three: simple, drop-down, and drop-down list.

7. How is the `ModalResult` property used for button components?

   When a button with a `ModalResult` property set to a whole number is clicked, the form will close. The value of the `ModalResult` property for the button clicked will be the return value from the `ShowModal` method.

8. What component is often used as a container for other components?

   The `Panel` component. Several others qualify, too.

9. What is the return value from the `Execute` method for an `OpenDialog` component if the user clicks OK to close the dialog box?

   `true`.

10. How do you make the `SaveDialog` component into a Save As dialog box?

    Just change its `Title` property to `Save As`.

Day 8

1. When do you use the Inherit option when selecting an object in the Object Repository?

   Use the Inherit option when you want all the features of the base object and you want the inherited object to change if the base object changes.

2. What is the procedure for saving a project to the Object Repository?

   To save a project to the Object Repository, choose Project | Add to Repository from the main menu.

3. What happens to inherited forms when you change the base form?

   When you change the base form, all the inherited forms change to reflect the change made to the base form.

4. Where in the form's class declaration do you place user method declarations?

   You place user method declarations in the `private` or `public` sections of the class declaration. Never place user declarations in the Delphi-managed section of the class declaration (unless you know what you are doing).

5. Where do you place the method definition (the method itself) when you add your own methods to Delphi code?

   In the `implementation` section of the unit.

6. How can you determine who wrote a particular object in the Object Repository?

   You can tell who wrote an object in the Object Repository by switching to the Details view. The object's author is listed there.

7. Where do you add and delete pages in the Object Repository?

You add or delete pages in the Object Repository from the Object Repository configuration dialog box (which you get by selecting Tools | Repository from the main menu).

8. Is it easier to create a basic application from scratch or by using the Application Wizard?

It is easier to create a new application by using the Application Wizard in almost all cases.

A

9. Which is better for small applications: static linking or dynamic linking using packages?

For small applications, static linking is usually better than dynamic linking (no runtime packages).

10. Can you create a resource script file containing a string table with a text editor?

Yes, you can easily create a string table with a text editor. You only need to understand the basic layout of a string table.

Day 9

1. How can you quickly switch between a unit's form and source code when working with Delphi?

Use the F12 key to quickly switch between the Form Designer and the Code Editor.

2. If you remove a file from your project via the Project Manager, is the file removed from your hard drive?

No, it is only removed from the project.

3. How do you set the main form for an application?

Go to the Forms page of the Project Options dialog box and select the form you want to be the main form in the Main form combo box.

4. What does it mean if you do not have Delphi Auto-create forms?

You will have to take the responsibility of creating the forms before using them.

5. How do you add new items to your unit using the Code Explorer?

Right-click and choose New from the Code Explorer context menu. Type in the declaration for the new item and hit Enter.

6. What is the significance of generating debug information for your application?

When debug information is generated, you will be able to step through your code during debugging sessions.

7. What is the Find in Files option used for?

Find in Files is used to find text in files.

8. What is the keyboard shortcut for saving a file in the Code Editor?

Ctrl+S (assuming that you're using the default keymapping).

9. How do you set a bookmark in an editor window? How many bookmarks are available?

Set a bookmark with Ctrl+K+0 through Ctrl+K+9. There are 10 bookmarks available.

10. How do you set a file to read-only in the Code Editor?

Choose Read Only from the Code Editor context menu.

Day 10

1. How do you set a breakpoint on a particular code line?

Click in the gutter (the left margin) on that code line. You can also press F5 or choose Toggle Breakpoint from the Code Editor context menu.

2. What is an invalid breakpoint?

A breakpoint that is inadvertently set on a source code line that generates no compiled code.

3. How do you set a conditional breakpoint?

Set the breakpoint, choose View | Debug Windows | Breakpoints from the main menu, click the breakpoint in the Breakpoint List window, and then choose Properties from the Breakpoint List context menu. Set the condition in the Condition field of the Edit Breakpoint dialog box.

4. How can you change the properties of an item in the Watch List?

Double-click the item in the Watch List window. The Watch Properties dialog box is displayed. Modify the properties as needed.

5. What's the quickest way to add a variable to the Watch List?

Click the variable and press Ctrl+F5 (or choose Add Watch at Cursor from the Code Editor context menu).

6. What tool do you use to view the data fields and methods of a class?

The Debug Inspector is used to view classes and records.

7. How do you trace into a method when stepping with the debugger?

Use F7 or Run | Trace Into to step into a method.

8. How can you change the value of a variable at runtime?

Click the variable and then choose Evaluate/Modify from the Code Editor context menu (or choose Run | Evaluate/Modify from the main menu). Change the value in the Evaluate/Modify dialog box.

9. How can you send your own messages to the Event Log?

You can send your own messages to the Event Log by calling the Windows API function, `OutputDebugString`.

10. What does the Integrated debugging option on the Debugger Options dialog box do?

When this option is on and the program is run from the IDE, the program runs under control of the debugger. When this option is off, the program runs without using the debugger.

Day 11

1. How is the transparent color used for icons and cursors?

The background shows through wherever the transparent color is used on the icon or cursor.

2. How do you choose a color in the Image Editor?

Click a color in the color palette.

3. How do you select an area on a bitmap to cut or copy?

Choose the Marquee tool and then drag a rectangle with the mouse. You could also use Edit | Select All to select the entire image or the Lasso tool.

4. What is the maximum number of colors allowed in an Image Editor bitmap?

256.

5. What is a cursor's hot spot?

The exact pixel in the cursor that is used to report the screen coordinates to Windows when the mouse is clicked.

6. Can WinSight spy on hidden windows?

Yes. WinSight shows hidden windows as well as visible windows.

7. What's the fastest way to locate a window in the WinSight Window Tree?

Choose Window | Follow to Focus from the main menu and then click on the window you want to spy on.

8. How can you have your editor files automatically saved each time your program runs through the debugger?

   Turn on the Editor files option on the Preferences page (Autosave options section) of the Environment Options dialog box.

9. Where do you go to rearrange the contents of the Component Palette?

   Use the Palette page of the Environment Options dialog box.

Day 12

1. What component can you use to draw graphics on a form?

   Although you can draw directly on the form's canvas, the PaintBox component enables you to draw in a predefined area of a form (the area the PaintBox occupies).

2. Which TCanvas property controls the fill color of the canvas?

   The Brush property.

3. What does a clipping region do?

   The clipping region defines a canvas area within which drawing can take place, but outside which no drawing takes place. Any drawing outside the clipping region won't be displayed.

4. What function do you use to draw multiple lines of text on a canvas?

   The DrawText function with the DT_WORDBREAK flag.

5. What TCanvas method can be used to draw a bitmap with a transparent background?

   The BrushCopy method.

6. Which TCanvas method do you use to copy an entire bitmap to a canvas?

   You can use several, but the easiest and fastest is the Draw method. Others include BrushCopy, StretchDraw, and CopyRect.

7. How do you save a memory bitmap to a file?

   With the SaveToFile method.

8. What component do you use to play a wave file?

   The TMediaPlayer component. To play a wave file using the Windows API, use the PlaySound function.

9. What is the TimeFormat property of TMediaPlayer used for?

The `TimeFormat` property is used to set the time format based on the media type being played. Some media types can use several time formats (CD audio, for example).

10. Can you record wave audio with the `MediaPlayer` component?

    Yes, but you have to jump through some hoops.

Day 13

1. How do you attach an event handler to a toolbar button's `OnClick` event?

   In the Object Inspector, click the Event tab. Click the drop-down arrow next to the `OnClick` event. Choose an event handler from the list.

2. Can you put controls other than buttons on toolbars?

   Yes. You can put virtually any type of component on a toolbar. Combo boxes are commonly found on toolbars.

3. What is the name of the `TActionList` event you respond to when doing command enabling?

   The `OnUpdate` event.

4. What does the `SimplePanel` property of the `StatusBar` component do?

   It forces the status bar to have a single panel.

5. How do you change the status bar text manually?

   For a simple status bar, use the following:

   `StatusBar.SimpleText := 'Text';`

6. How do you enable and disable menu items and buttons?

   For individual components, set the component's `Enabled` property to `True` to enable the component or `False` to disable it. For several components that have a common task, create an `Action` for that task and set the `Action`'s `Enabled` property accordingly.

7. How do you access the printer in a Delphi application?

   Through the `Printer` function.

8. What method do you call to begin printing with the `TPrinter` class?

   The `BeginDoc` method.

9. What method of `TPrinter` do you call when you want to start a new page when printing?

   The `NewPage` method.

10. How do you change the cursor for a component at runtime?

Modify the component's Cursor property.

Day 14

1. How do you set the help file that your application will use?

Use the Project Options dialog (Application page) or set the HelpFile property of the Application object at runtime.

2. How do you implement F1 key support for a particular form or dialog box?

Just assign a nonzero value to the HelpContext property. Make sure that there is a corresponding help context ID in the help file and that the help file has been set for the application.

3. What method do you call to display the index for your help file?

The HelpCommand method.

4. What types of objects can an exception raise?

Any class derived from Exception.

5. Is it legal to have more than one except statement following a try statement?

No, there can only be one except statement.

6. How do you raise an exception?

With the raise keyword—for example,

```
raise EMyException.Create('An error occurred.');
```

7. What is the default value of the TRegistry class RootKey property?

```
\HKEY_CURRENT_USER
```

8. Must you call CloseKey when you are done with a key?

No. The TRegistry destructor will close the key for you. You shouldn't leave a key open indefinitely, though.

9. What is the difference between SendMessage and PostMessage?

PostMessage posts the message to the Windows message queue and returns immediately. SendMessage sends the message and doesn't return until the message has been handled.

10. What is the name of the VCL method that is used to send a message directly to a component?

The Perform method.

Day 15

1. What is the base (or parent) interface for all COM interfaces?

   The base interface from which all other interfaces are derived is IUnknown.

2. What is a GUID?

   A GUID is a 128-bit integer that uniquely identifies a COM object (interface, class, or type library).

3. What happens when a COM object's reference count reaches 0?

   When a COM object's reference count reaches 0, the COM object is unloaded from memory by Windows.

4. What is the name of the Delphi utility used when working with type libraries?

   The utility used to modify type libraries is the Type Library Editor.

5. How do you create GUIDs when writing COM objects in Delphi?

   You don't have to specifically create GUIDs when creating COM objects in Delphi. Delphi creates the GUIDs for you automatically (trick question, I know). If you want to specifically create a GUID in your code, you can press Ctrl+Shift+G in the Code Editor. Delphi will generate and insert a GUID in your code.

6. What do you choose from the Object Repository when creating an ActiveX from a VCL component?

   To create an ActiveX control from an existing VCL component, choose the ActiveX Control item in the Object Repository.

7. Can you use Delphi-created ActiveX controls in Visual Basic?

   Yes, you can use Delphi ActiveX controls in VB. You must be sure that the ActiveX contains version information, but otherwise a Delphi ActiveX should work in VB with no trouble.

8. After your ActiveX control is built and registered, how do you install it to the Delphi Component palette?

   To install an ActiveX control to the Delphi Component palette, choose Component | Import ActiveX Control from the Delphi main menu.

9. How do you unregister an ActiveX that you have created?

   To unregister an ActiveX control, you can either choose Run | Unregister ActiveX Server from the main menu or you can run the TREGSVR utility on the ActiveX with the -u switch. You can also uninstall an ActiveX control from the Import ActiveX dialog box.

10. Can you use the ActiveX controls created in Delphi on a Web page?

    Yes. Delphi ActiveX controls are designed to be deployed on a Web page.

A

Day 16

1. What is a local database?

   A database that resides on the user's machine rather than on a database server. This term usually refers to Paradox or dBASE tables.

2. What is the purpose of the BDE?

   The BDE provides your Delphi application access to databases.

3. Are a dataset and a table the same thing? If not, explain the difference.

   No, they are not the same thing. A dataset might include an entire table's contents, or it might contain only a small subset of the table.

4. Name one advantage of cached updates.

   Cached updates reduce network traffic, enable you to modify a read-only dataset, and enable you to make several changes and then either commit or roll back all changes at once.

5. What is a stored procedure?

   An application that acts on a database and resides on a database server.

6. What is the purpose of the SQL property of the TQuery component?

   The SQL property contains the SQL statements to execute when the Open or Execute methods are called.

7. Name one reason you might want to use your own TDatabase object instead of the default.

   To allow automatic login to a database.

8. Why would you want to keep a connection to a remote database open even when you are not currently using the connection?

   To reduce the time required to log in to the database each time a connection is requested.

9. What does the TBatchMove component do?

   TBatchMove enables you to create or modify one dataset with the contents of another dataset.

10. What is a BDE alias?

    A set of parameters that describes a database connection.

Day 17

1. What's the fastest and easiest way to create a database form?

   With the Database Form Wizard.

2. How do you control the order and number of columns that appear in a DBGrid component?

   With the Columns Editor. (Right-click a DBGrid component and choose Columns Editor from the context menu.)

3. What component enables you to display a dataset in table format?

   The DBGrid component.

4. How can you add or remove buttons from a DBNavigator?

   By modifying the VisibleButtons property.

5. What component do you use to display BLOB image data?

   The DBImage component.

6. What property is common to all data-aware components?

   The DataSource property (among others).

7. What property is used to select the field that a data component is linked to?

   The DataField property.

8. Can you rearrange the columns in a DBGrid component?

   Yes. Use the Columns Editor at design time or drag and drop them at runtime.

9. Which component is used to edit and display text fields in a database?

   The DBEdit component.

10. What does BLOB stand for?

    Binary large object.

Day 18

1. What method do you call to create a database table at runtime?

   CreateTable.

2. What does the Edit method of TTable do?

   The Edit method puts the dataset in edit mode so that records can be modified.

3. What method do you call when you want to apply the changes made to a record?

   The Post method.

4. How do you create a new data module?

   Through the Object Repository.

5. Is a data module a regular form?

   A data module is very similar to a regular form but not the same.

6. What method do you call to print a QuickReport?

   The `Print` method.

7. What type of QuickReport band displays the dataset's data?

   A detail band.

8. What component is used to display the page number on a report?

   The `QRSysData` component can display page numbers, the current date, the current time, and more.

9. How can you preview a report at design time?

   Right-click the report and choose Preview from the context menu.

10. What is the `QRExpr` component used for?

    The `QRExpr` component is used to display the results of an expression (usually a calculated result).

Day 19

1. How do you load a DLL using static loading?

   In your calling application declare any functions or procedures contained in the DLL using the `extern` keyword. The DLL will automatically load when the application starts.

2. How do you load a DLL using dynamic loading?

   Use the Windows API function `LoadLibrary`.

3. How do you call a function or procedure from a DLL that has been loaded statically?

   Call the function or procedure just as you would call a regular function or procedure.

4. What steps do you have to take to ensure that a function or procedure in your DLL can be called from outside the DLL?

   The function or procedure must be exported from the DLL. Place the function or procedure name in the `exports` section of the DLL.

5. In the case of a DLL that has been dynamically loaded, can you unload the DLL at any time or only when the program closes?

   You can unload the DLL any time you want (using the `FreeLibrary` function).

6. What must you do to display a Delphi form contained in a DLL from a non-Delphi program?

   Create an exported function that the calling application can call. In this function, create the form and display it. Be sure the function is declared with the `stdcall` keyword.

7. What is the name of the keyword used to declare functions and procedures imported from a DLL?

   The `external` keyword.

8. How do you add resources to a DLL?

   Link a compiled resource file (`.res` or `.dcr`) to the DLL with the `$R` compiler directive—for example,

   ```
   {$R Resources.res}
   ```

A

9. Does a resource DLL need to contain code as well as the resources?

   No. A resource DLL doesn't need any code.

10. Can a DLL containing resources be loaded statically (when the program loads)?

   It's possible, but there's rarely any reason to load a resource DLL statically. You need the return value from `LoadLibrary` to access resources in the DLL, so you might as well use dynamic loading for resource DLLs.

Day 20

1. Must a property use a `write` method? Why or why not?

   No. You can use direct access instead.

2. Must a property have an underlying data field? Why or why not?

   No, a property doesn't have to have an underlying data field, but most properties usually do. A property that doesn't store a value is unusual.

3. Can you create a component by extending an existing component?

   Absolutely. That's the easiest way to create a new component.

4. What happens if you don't specify a `write` specifier (either a `write` method or direct access) in a property's declaration?

   The property becomes read-only.

5. What does direct access mean?

   The underlying data member for the property is modified and/or read directly (no `read` method and no `write` method).

6. Must your properties have a default value? Why or why not?

   No, default values for properties are optional. Published properties should have a default value, though. Properties that are `string` properties cannot have a default value (and some other types of properties as well).

7. Does the default value of the property set the underlying data field's value automatically?

No, the default value only displays a value in the Object Inspector at design time. You must set the underlying data member to the default value in the component's constructor.

8. How do you install a component on the Component Palette?

Choose Component | Install from the main menu.

9. How do you specify the button bitmap that your component will use on the Component Palette?

Create a .dcr file with the same name as the component's source. The .dcr should contain a 24×24 bitmap with the same name as the component's classname. Be sure that the .dcr is in the same directory as the .pas file for the component.

10. How do you trigger a user-defined event?

Just call the event after checking whether an event handler exists for the event:

```
if Assigned(FOnMyEvent) then
  FOnMyEvent(Self);
```

Day 21

1. Do Delphi and C++Builder project files have the same filename extension?

No, Delphi and C++Builder project files do not have the same filename extension. Delphi projects have a .dpr extension and C++Builder projects have a .bpr extension.

2. Do Delphi and C++Builder form files have the same filename extension?

Yes. Both Delphi and C++Builder have .dfm filename extensions.

3. Can you use packages from third-party component vendors in both Delphi and C++Builder?

In most cases, you can use packages from third-party component vendors in both Delphi and C++Builder. In some cases, the packages will have to be rebuilt with C++Builder. Ask the component vendor for packages compatible with C++Builder.

4. Can you open a Delphi form file in C++Builder?

Yes. You cannot edit the form (add or remove components), but you can view the form.

5. Can you edit a Delphi form file using the C++Builder Form Designer?

No, you cannot edit a Delphi form file using the C++Builder Form Designer. However, you can edit the Delphi form as text by choosing View As Text from the C++Builder context menu.

6. Can you use a C++Builder source unit in Delphi?

   With the current version of Delphi, you cannot use a C++Builder source unit in Delphi.

7. Which is better, Delphi or C++Builder?

   Neither Delphi or C++Builder is better. Both have their strengths. It depends largely on whether you prefer Pascal or C++.

A

Bonus Day

1. What control do you use to display Web pages?

   The THMTL control.

2. What control do you use to connect to newsgroups?

   The TNMNNTP control.

3. What is the name of the method used to display an HTML document with the THTML control?

   RequestDoc.

4. What event is generated when an HTML document has completed loading?

   The OnEndRetrieval event.

5. What control do you use to send email messages?

   The TNMSMTP control.

6. What control do you use to retrieve email messages?

   The TNMPOP3 control.

7. What is the name of the method used to send mail with the TNMSMTP control?

   SendMail.

8. Can you freely distribute the Internet Explorer ActiveX control?

   No, you must obtain a license from Microsoft to distribute the Internet Explorer ActiveX control.

9. What is the name of the utility used to register ActiveX controls?

   TREGSVR.EXE.

10. What company provides the bulk of the Internet controls that come with Delphi?

    NetMasters.

APPENDIX **B**

Delphi Internet Resources

Delphi has been around for several years now, so there are some very good
sources of information about it available on the Internet. These resources fall
into four basic categories: commercial Web sites (including Borland's own Web
site), user Web sites, newsgroups, and publications. What follows is a brief
description of some of these categories.

Be sure to check out my errata page for the book at `www.home.turbopower.com/`
`~kentr/delphi`, as well as the book's Web site for examples and sample code
(`www.mcp/com/info`).

INPRISE Corporation

INPRISE Corporation (formerly Borland International) is the best source of
information on Borland products. The INPRISE Web site (`www.inprise.com`)
has the latest news on Delphi, any patches that are available, FAQ pages, and
listings of vendors that sell Delphi components or supporting utilities. Be sure
to check this site from time to time to see whether there is any new news on
Delphi.

Commercial Web Sites

Commercial Web sites are sites that belong to companies that sell Delphi components commercially. Table B.1 contains a partial list of sites (in no particular order) that you might want to check out.

TABLE B.1. COMMERCIAL WEB SITES.

Company Name (Web Address)	Description/Features
TurboPower Software (www.turbopower.com)	With more than 10 years in the business, TurboPower is the oldest vendor of tools for Borland products. TurboPower specializes in Delphi and C++Builder components and utilities. Its AsyncProfessional is the premier serial communications component package.
Raize Software Solutions (www.raize.com)	General-purpose VCL components.
DevSoft (www.dev-soft.com)	Home of IP*Works, Internet components for C++Builder and Delphi.
Out and About Productions (www.o2a.com)	DTalk speech enabling components.
Skyline Tools (www.imagelib.com)	Home of ImageLib, an image manipulation component library.
QuSoft AS (www.qusoft.com)	Makers of QuickReport.
TeeChart Pro (www.teemach.com)	Home of the TeeChart component.
SCT Associates, Inc. (www.sct-associates.com)	Home of the Ace Reporter.
Engineering Objects International (www.inconresearch.com/eoi)	Engineering and Scientific components.
Luxent Development Corp. (www.luxent.com)	Success Ware, Light Lib, and AS/400 Middleware.

This is by no means a complete list of commercial sites. For a more complete list, refer to the INPRISE Delphi Tools Page at www.inprise.com/delphi/deltools.html.

User Web Sites

The following are Delphi user sites set up by Delphi users and for Delphi users. The sites are listed in no particular order. These pages contain links to other pages, so when you get started, you can enjoy many hours of browsing. In particular, the Delphi Deli has a huge list of links.

Delphi32.com
www.delphi32.com

Dr. Bob's JBuilder, C++Builder, and Delphi Clinic
www.drbob42.com

The Delphi Deli
www.delphideli.com

The Delphi Super Page
sunsite.icm.edu.pl/delphi

Torry's Delphi Pages
www.torry.ru

The Delphi Games Creator
www.users.dircon.co.uk/~zeus

B

Newsgroups

INPRISE sponsors newsgroups so that Borland users can help one another with questions about using Borland products. These are private newsgroups that INPRISE has set up for its users. All you have to do is point your newsreader to forums.inprise.com, and you will find thousands of messages in dozens of newsgroups. For complete information, see the Newsgroups page on the INPRISE Web page (www.inprise.com/ newsgroups).

Publications

There are several Delphi periodical publications. Some of the major publications are listed here. Most of these sites offer a free trial issue:

Delphi Developer's Journal (The Cobb Group)
www.cobb.com/ddj

Visual Developer (Coriolis Group)
www.coriolis.com

Delphi Developer (Pinnacle Publishing)
www.pinpub.com/delphi

Delphi Informant (Informant Communications Group)
www.informant.com/delphi

Delphi Magazine
www.itecuk.com/delmag

INDEX

A

Delphi 4 Developer's Guide

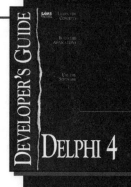

—*Xavier Pacheco, Steve Teixeira, et al.*

Delphi 4 Developer's Guide is an advanced-level reference showing developers what they need to know most about Delphi 4. The authors deal with developers every day and offer sound skills, advice, and technical knowledge on the most advanced features of Delphi 4. The covered topics include advanced-level components such as embedded links, special features and DLLs, creating your own Visual Component Libraries, advanced OOP, and Object Pascal. The authors discuss issues about application design and framework concepts for client/server, enterprise, and desktop-level database applications, along with Delphi's Multitier Distributed Applications Services Suite (MIDAS) and how it works with Delphi.

This is the most advanced developers' technical reference on Delphi 4. Xavier Pacheco and Steve Teixeira are the award-winning authors of *Delphi 2 Developer's Guide* and are key members of Borland's Delphi development team. This book contains the latest information on the best ways to build efficient, usable applications with Delphi 4, including Borland's new enterprise features, cross-component compatibility, and Internet-enabling capabilities.

Price: $59.99 USA/$85.95 CAN	*Advanced*
ISBN: 0-672-31284-0	*1,200 pages*

Charlie Calvert's C++Builder 3 Unleashed

—*Charlie Calvert*

Charlie Calvert's C++Builder 3 Unleashed teaches you how to use object-oriented programming to maximize your code reusability, develop Web applications by incorporating ActiveX and Internet functions into your programs, employ property editors to check your documents, and create updated, dynamic links between documents with OLE. You will also learn about implementing the new multimedia features to program 2D and 3D graphics, writing multimedia instructions for Windows with DirectX, connecting to your corporate data with scalable database tools, and developing C++ programs visually with drag-and-drop methods. Finally, this book covers how to Internet-enable client/server applications for your entire network.

Price: $59.99 USA/$85.95 CAN	*Intermediate–Advanced*
ISBN: 0-672-31265-4	*1,200 pages*

Sams Teach Yourself JBuilder 2 in 21 Days

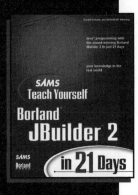

—Don Doherty

Sams Teach Yourself JBuilder 2 in 21 Days is in the format of the other best-selling *Sams Teach Yourself* books. This book presents information on JBuilder 2 and teaches you how to use it to develop. JBuilder 2 is Borland International's updated graphical development environment that uses the Java programming language and is compatible with Sun's JDK 1.2. Because JBuilder's programming language is Java, this book also teaches you how to program with Java within the JBuilder development environment, touching on Java fundamentals and the object-oriented approach. It doesn't assume that you already know Java.

JBuilder has built an excellent reputation in the Java development market in the tradition of Delphi and C++Builder. With its updated capabilities and release timed with Sun's JDK 1.2, it should gain even more ground in version 2.

Price: $39.99 USA/$57.95 CAN   *Beginning–Intermediate*
ISBN: 0-672-31318-9   *700 pages*

Sams Teach Yourself Borland C++Builder 3 in 21 Days

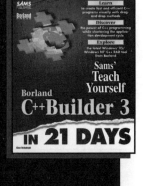

—Kent Reisdorph

The drag-and-drop power of Borland C++Builder 3 is yours to command with *Sams Teach Yourself Borland C++Builder 3 in 21 Days*. In no time, you'll be able to rapidly build programs from reusable ActiveX controls, Java Beans, and Delphi components. Using the methods taught in this book, you can increase your productivity and leverage your knowledge of C++ 3 and Delphi to develop mainstream applications. The proven, step-by-step techniques of the *Sams Teach Yourself* series show you how to accomplish specific tasks with this powerful new programming interface. This is a key revision to an already-successful Borland Press book, with 30 percent new and updated content by a well-known author in the Borland development community.

Stop programming C++ the old-fashioned way and start tapping into the visual programming power of Borland C++Builder 3! It has a large potential customer base, and most developers are predicted to upgrade within 6 months of the product release.

Price: $39.99 USA/$57.95 CAN   *Beginning–Intermediate*
ISBN: 0-672-31266-2   *832 pages*

Add to Your Sams Library Today with the Best Books for Programming, Operating Systems, and New Technologies

The easiest way to order is to pick up the phone and call

1-800-428-5331

between 9:00 a.m. and 5:00 p.m. EST.

For faster service please have your credit card available.

ISBN	Quantity	Description of Item	Unit Cost	Total Cost
0-672-31284-0		Delphi 4 Developer's Guide	$59.99	
0-672-31265-4		Charlie Calvert's C++Builder 3 Unleashed	$59.99	
0-672-31318-9		Sams Teach Yourself JBuilder2 in 21 Days	$39.99	
0-672-31266-2		Sams Teach Yourself Borland C++Builder 3 in 21 Days	$39.99	
		Shipping and Handling: See information below.		
		TOTAL		

Shipping and Handling: $4.00 for the first book, and $1.75 for each additional book. If you need to have it NOW, we can ship the product to you in 24 hours for an additional charge of approximately $18.00, and you will receive your item overnight or in two days. Overseas shipping and handling adds $2.00 per book. Prices subject to change. Call for availability and pricing information on latest editions.

201 W. 103rd Street, Indianapolis, Indiana 46290

1-800-428-5331 — Orders   1-800-835-3202 — Fax   1-800-858-7674 — Customer Service

Book ISBN 0-672-31286-7